21世纪英语专业系列教材·新世纪翻译系列教程
西安外国语大学立项资助教材

C-E Translation
of Diplomatic News

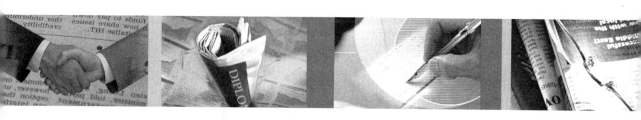

外交新闻汉英翻译

主编 李琴
编者 曹怀军 祖赟 孙晓娅 张旭

北京大学出版社
PEKING UNIVERSITY PRESS

图书在版编目(CIP)数据

外交新闻汉英翻译 / 李琴主编. —北京：北京大学出版社，2018.5
（21世纪英语专业系列教材·新世纪翻译系列教程）
ISBN 978-7-301-28340-0

Ⅰ. ①外…　Ⅱ. ①李…　Ⅲ. ①新闻—英语—翻译—教材　Ⅳ. ①G210

中国版本图书馆 CIP 数据核字(2017) 第 114793 号

书　　　名	外交新闻汉英翻译 WAIJIAO XINWEN HANYING FANYI
著作责任者	李　琴　主编
责任编辑	郝妮娜
标准书号	ISBN 978-7-301-28340-0
出版发行	北京大学出版社
地　　　址	北京市海淀区成府路 205 号　100871
网　　　址	http://www.pup.cn　　新浪微博：@北京大学出版社
电子信箱	bdhnn2011@126.com
电　　　话	邮购部 010-62752015　发行部 010-62750672　编辑部 010-62759634
印　刷　者	北京溢漾印刷有限公司
经　销　者	新华书店
	787 毫米 ×1092 毫米　16 开本　26.75 印张　690 千字 2018 年 5 月第 1 版　2018 年 5 月第 1 次印刷
定　　　价	68.00 元

未经许可，不得以任何方式复制或抄袭本书之部分或全部内容。
版权所有，侵权必究
举报电话：010-62752024　电子信箱：fd@pup.pku.edu.cn
图书如有印装质量问题，请与出版部联系，电话：010-62756370

序 一

几个月前，我参加一次中欧研讨会，主题是台湾海峡两岸关系。中方的几位学者深入透彻地分析了两岸关系的形势，重申了中国的立场。遗憾的是现场两位翻译都把"中国大陆"翻译成 mainland China。显然他们不知道对于面前的西方学者而言，mainland China 正代表了西方话语体系中"两个中国"的观点。我很纳闷，为什么放着中国官方使用的 mainland of China, Chinese mainland, China's mainland 等多种表述不用，两位译员偏偏使用对中方不利的表述呢？想来想去，是译员们的知识结构有问题，他们的中译英能力也不够扎实。至于一些外语院校的研究生不知道和平共处五项原则是什么，打造人类命运共同体如何用外文表述，中国到底有多少邻国，中国人大、全国政协的英文是什么不会翻译的现象相当普遍。这不，近日期末老师们判卷子时遇到的一些问题很令人吃惊。一位老师告诉我，他看了近20份卷子，对于中共十八大这个词汇的中译英，居然没有一个是准确的。

问题出在哪里？我想答案并不复杂。长期以来，我们在教学中注重了学生外译中的培养，对中译外训练不够恐怕是主要原因之一。尤其是翻译专业的学生，可能对西方的外国翻译理论有着扎实的了解，对外国文学也颇为熟悉，做起翻译实践相当一部分训练都侧重了外国文学的中译。如果他们很少翻译介绍中国的各类文本，突然让他们从事中译外，必然会十分吃力。

然而，根据中国翻译协会的调查，中国经济的快速发展，中国文化的对外介绍力度加大，特别是中国近年来逐渐被推到世界舞台中央，以前所未有的程度参与全球治理催生了中译外事业的快速发展，目前中译外已经占据翻译市场工作量的60%。处在新时代，翻译的新任务就是更加准确地对外介绍中国。在这个背景下，翻译教材必须更加突出培养学生的中译外能力。

可喜的是，近日我看到西安外国语大学几位中青年教师编写的《外交新闻汉英翻译》教材，眼前为之一亮。概括说，这部教材从实际需求出发，目的是培养学生翻译

外交新闻汉英翻译
C-E TRANSLATION OF DIPLOMATIC NEWS

实践能力，提高学生讲述中国故事的水平，增强学生阐述中国立场的功底，锤炼学生展示中国文化魅力的本领。

这部教材共有十五个单元，前两个单元是对外交新闻的概述和外交理念翻译的总论，其余十三个单元分门别类按照场景和形式各有侧重。

具体说，这本教材具有三个突出特点，这些也正是这本教材的价值所在。

第一个亮点是门类齐全。一般人谈到外交翻译，恐怕就想到外事接待、迎来送往、宾主寒暄、酒会祝词等等。然而，编者把各类外交翻译分成了十三个场景和形式，清晰专注，多而不乱，有利于学生逐一掌握各类文本和场合的翻译技巧。虽然场合和文本不同，但是各个单元的核心内容又显示出高度的一致。阅读这本教材，让人甚至可以在脑海里看到教师们带领着学生从一个外事场合走到另一个场合，从一场历练到下一场历练。不难想象，如果学生们都比较扎实地掌握了这些知识和本领，就完全能够胜任各种场合的外事翻译。此外，作为一本教材，有十五个单元也便于纳入年度教学计划。从内容的划分可以看出编者作为教师的专业思考和职业匠心。

第二个亮点是内容实用。每一个单元都包括两个范例，然后是文本解读、翻译解析。解析部分除涉及翻译技能，还有一个部分专门提供历史上的翻译和相关题目的翻译，由此拓展学生的翻译知识。随后的学生译作讲评则针对初学翻译人员遇到的难点和容易犯的错误一一予以剖析。每一个单元最后都有充足的实战练习题以及参考译文。的确，翻译需要反复实践。光靠看书听讲座是培养不出高级译者的。读着这本教材，我还想到一位翻译教育家有一次告诉我，能让学生记住的往往不是你如何正确地翻译，而是那些出现的错误。

说到实用，最为可贵的还是这本书所囊括的各种知识点。外交翻译，尤其在中国开展特色大国外交的新时代，已经成为中国对外翻译最具代表性的形式，其涉及面之广，知识点之多，几乎到了包罗万象的程度。今天的外交翻译绝不局限于外事领域，而是涉及中国政治、经济、教育、科技、军事、文化、历史、法律、生态环境、健康卫生等等。其实，只要读一读中国党和国家领导人在重要的外事场合发表的演讲，就必然发现外交翻译的内容之浩瀚。经常每一句讲话就包含了一个知识点。所以，阅读这本教材，不仅是学习翻译，同时也是扩大视野、丰富知识的过程。从这个角度看，这本书几乎成为讲述中国故事的一本小百科，也自然构成学生们提高和拓展自己的一个知识宝库。

需要特别强调的是，今天中国人学习外语，当然要研究外国语言和文学，研究别人才能提高自己。但是，国际形势变了，中国的国际地位提升了，仅仅满足于外译中或者局限在文学翻译领域，已经远远不能满足社会的现实需求。今天的时代，是对外大力讲好中国故事的时代，是积极构建中国国际话语体系的时代，是利用中国智慧参与全球治理的时代。中译外，译好中国的话语和故事比历史上任何时候都更加急迫和重要。对于培养时代需求的翻译专业人员，这本书的确编写的非常及时。

第三个亮点就是其内容的权威性。外交翻译特别要求翻译人员具备高度的政治性、政策敏感性和用语的精准性。比如，20世纪90年代邓小平提出当时中国外交的24字方针里有"韬光养晦"四个字。是照历史书上翻译成隐藏实力、以图未来，还是突出邓小平关于"不扛旗、不当头"的思想，翻译成不高调行事，译者们有所争论，这种争论至今也还在中外学者之间经常发生。凭着对邓小平外交思想的深入理解，外交部的翻译们提出了 keep a low profile 的译法，这才是利用英文对当时24字方针中这四个字最精准的诠释。再有，2013年习近平主席提出建设"一带一路"后，国内学者经常使用的中文提法是"一带一路战略"，敏感的外事翻译们使用的译文不是 strategy，而是 initiative。今天，越来越多的国人都意识到这个译法的高妙。由此可以看出，外交翻译需要的不仅是高超的外语能力，还需要深厚的国际知识积累和敏锐的政策水平。

因此，选择合适、权威的素材至关重要。这本书的编者很好地把握了这点，所遴选的案例都是最权威的官方译文。

有人说，译文没有最好，只有更好。的确，随着不断收到国际受众的反馈，翻译们修改自己过去的译法是常见的事。如果今后某个词汇、某句话的翻译与这本教材不同，纯属正常。

当然，既然选择的是官方发表过的文本，就不可能包括一些外事场合不被记录在案或者不被公开的内容，包括中外双方私下的玩笑、惊心动魄的谈判、机智说理的交谈等。任何一本教材的承载是有限的。目前这本教材所包含的智慧足以让广大学生受益。

衷心祝贺西外的教师们及时推出的这部翻译教育力作！

黄友义
中国翻译协会常务副会长
2018年1月

序 二

基于与中国外交部、环球网长期稳定的新闻翻译项目合作，西安外国语大学高级翻译学院开发了创新型课程"外交新闻翻译工作坊"，围绕外交新闻翻译实践，拓展学生的国际视野，激发对外交问题的主动思考，促进对外交概念、原则的精准把握，建构外交新闻翻译实践能力。课程取得了良好的教学效果，不少学生在全国新闻翻译大赛中获奖，跨专业考入清华大学、中国人民大学等高校的国际新闻专业，进入中国外交部、中联部等国家部委，环球网、中国日报等新闻媒体从事相关工作。基于对课程实践效果的检验，结合我校"翻译教学与研究中心"在翻译课程与教学领域的理论研究成果，李琴教授率领团队对课程进行多轮修改，为《外交新闻汉英翻译》一书顺利付梓出版奠定了扎实的理论与实践基础。

较之以往同类教材，该教材的主要特点是：情境化，围绕外交新闻的时空情境组织学习单元；整合化，围绕真实翻译问题求解组织从事外交新闻翻译所需的跨学科知识体系；思维显化，围绕职业译者和学习者翻译的真实译文分析翻译思维过程，解构常见误区，启发反思，激发学习者翻译图示重构。

一、**情境化**：后现代主义的知识观认为，知识受到时空限制，受到理论范型、价值观等文化因素的影响，其意义具有情境性。纽伯特提出"翻译情境限制目的语文本再造，即使熟练的翻译人员已经内化了各种类型的情境，但是仍须不断应对新情境的挑战"。可见情境在翻译实践和学习中的重要意义。然而，囿于教育理念与教学条件的制约，传统翻译教学中，教师选择翻译任务往往是从可及性出发，要么取材自身翻译经历，要么取材网络，材料往往具有以下缺陷：（1）具有随机性，不能完全代表社会需求的发展方向；（2）缺乏社会情境，不能提供翻译决策的必要情境条件，无法充分体现翻译问题的结构特征，无法结合社会需求分析，引导学生进行价值判断，实施翻译决策。该教材取材外交部网站新闻翻译项目，遴选出"驻外报道""外交访问报道""国际会议报道""外交会晤报道""外交演讲报道""吹风会报道""记者招待会报道"等十三个具体情境，具有常见性、代表性。基于这些情境的功能特征识别核心翻译问题、探究解决方案，有利于避免大而化之地讨论外交新闻翻译。教材对范例情境进行细致分析，在理论与实践之间搭建起一道桥梁，有利于帮助学习者归纳提炼出具有高度可迁移性的微观操作范式，从而可以对未来同类翻译实践产生指导。

二、整合化：外交新闻翻译的学习过程，是一个问题解决过程，是一个将认识系统、价值系统、方法系统在实践关系中进行统一的过程，需要整合翻译、新闻、外交等多领域知识，综合决策。然而分别对各个知识体系进行教学，在面对实际翻译问题的时候，学习者依然会感到束手无策，无法实现知识的有机融合和有效迁移。如何整合不同知识体系一直是困扰翻译教师的问题。为解决以上问题，该教材采取了与以往不同的编写体例，以外交新闻翻译范例为中心形成组织架构，旨在通过真实翻译问题求解统合多元知识系统，解决跨专业课程讲授过程中知识庞杂、无法形成合力的问题，对于提高教学绩效，实现译者个人发展、终身教育具有重要意义。

三、思维显化：该教材的另一特点是围绕真实案例实现对职业翻译思维和学习者翻译思维的外显分析。在传统的翻译教学中，翻译策略性知识长期得不到关注，处于背景化状态。教学中要么强调有关语言文化的陈述性知识，要么强调有关语言转换技巧的程序性知识，在理论讲授和实践操作中以产品为关注点，而偏偏将思维过程这一片灰色区域留给学生自己感悟，由于课程未能将"自我知识"囊括在内，个体对自身作为学习者、思考者、问题解决者的角色缺乏认识，在大量的试误后所习得的翻译能力与专家知识存在较大偏差。而该教材的设计，使得翻译学习者得以积极体验、自主探究，通过阅读翻译过程描述，观察职业翻译与翻译学习者的思维差异，从而有意识地反思自身实践，主动建构外交新闻翻译所需的认识系统、价值系统、方法系统，实现翻译思维方式的转变和品质的升华。

从以上意义上来说，该书是一部注重实践、关注知识整体性、注重翻译思维培养的教材，有助于达成"翻译项目工作坊"的学习效果。学习本书的过程，相信会成为学习者依托实践提升自身外交新闻翻译能力的愉悦旅程。

西安外国语大学高级翻译学院院长
贺莺
2018年7月于西安

前　言

我国外交新闻翻译实践已经有60余年的发展历史。但是迄今为止，国内外出版的实用翻译类教材中，还鲜有以"外交新闻翻译"为独立主题的教材。党的十八大以来，我国的外交事业迎来了发展的新机遇，公共外交作为外交工作的重要组成部分，被提升到国家发展的战略高度，国内各大外交新闻相关网站成为发布外交外事活动信息、阐述中国对外政策、讲述中国故事的重要平台，外交新闻翻译也成为对外宣介中国的重要渠道。外交新闻翻译涉及外交翻译与新闻翻译两大领域，兼具外交翻译的严肃性和新闻翻译的时效性，对译者的翻译能力和职业素养要求很高，特别是外交新闻汉英翻译，对于全世界关注和了解中国外交动态发挥着重要的窗口作用。《外交新闻汉英翻译》一书就是在新的时代背景下，为总结我国外交新闻翻译实践、探索我国外交新闻翻译原则、策略与方法，增强我国对外宣传能力及效果，助推"中国文化走出去"发展战略的实施编写而成的。

本教材的编写基于西安外国语大学高级翻译学院国家级翻译实践教育基地外交新闻翻译项目，以及依托该项目开发的"外交新闻翻译工作坊"课程。外交新闻翻译项目为外交部新闻司公共外交办公室英文网站翻译招标项目。项目在运营之初，通过层层考试选拔几十名优秀学生译者进入项目组，同时组织若干具有丰富翻译实践经验的优秀教师承担项目审校工作，将师生分为译审组、管理组、语料组、资料组、译员组，并制定各组工作手册；通过学生分组合作、中外教师指导、前后五重审校确保译文质量，为项目顺利、高效运行奠定坚实的基础。为了解决新老译员更替时新译员的培训问题，高级翻译学院以该项目为依托开发了"外交新闻翻译工作坊"课程，将项目实践过程中遇到的问题、得到的反馈和总结的经验在课堂上进行分享。课堂内容基于外交新闻翻译项目，但又不限于项目，而是拓展到外交新闻翻译乃至外交翻译的普遍规律上，既有针对性，又有普适性。本教材的编写不仅是对外交新闻翻译项目实践经验的总结，也是对"外交新闻翻译工作坊"课程的提炼和建设。

外交新闻汉英翻译
C-E TRANSLATION OF DIPLOMATIC NEWS

  本教材以高等院校翻译专业本科高年级学生及翻译专业硕士（MTI）为使用对象，兼及英语语言文学专业本科高年级学生、非英语专业研究生、外交新闻翻译从业者和爱好者，以及外事、外交或新闻翻译领域的教学工作者等，为他们提供一本外交新闻翻译领域的实用教科书和翻译实践指导用书。

  本教材的基本编写理念为"实用为主、篇章入手、讲练结合"。

  "实用为主"是指该教材的编写紧紧围绕"实用"二字，依托西安外国语大学高级翻译学院国家级翻译实践教育基地外交新闻翻译项目，具备充足的原生态翻译文本资料、翻译记忆库、语料库等，教材中所涉外交新闻翻译范例、译例解析、学生习作评析等，均源自外交新闻翻译项目的每日翻译实践，且经外交新闻翻译专家审定，主编与编者均为该项目经验丰富的一审、二审和总审教师，保证了翻译取材、译例解析、译法总结等的实践性、权威性、时代性和原生态。该教材将用于外交新闻翻译课程的教学实践和外交新闻翻译项目组的每日翻译实践中去，真正实现源于实践并指导实践。

  "篇章入手"是指本教材摆脱了翻译教材编写的传统做法，即"词汇—单句—篇章"逐级推进的编写体例，从外交新闻篇章入手，总结不同外交新闻篇章的文本类型、结构特点、翻译方法等，自上而下逐级解析，形成一个科学、系统的编写体例规范。

  "讲练结合"是指该教材的编写将理论讲解与实战练习有机结合起来，在练习安排上与理论讲解实现最优化的对接，有针对性地讲什么就练什么，并辅以练习答案，使得该教材的使用者能够通过日常练习与答案比照，对自身学习效果进行检测和判断，从而有针对性地查漏补缺，进一步优化学习效果。

  本教材共计十五章，内容涵盖了外交新闻翻译常见题材和文本类型，包括外交访问、外交会晤、驻外报道、外交访谈、例行记者会、吹风会、外交函电、国际会议等的报道，以及领导人发表演讲与致辞、签署外交公报、声明、备忘录等重要外交文书的报道，并辅以外交新闻翻译常用外交机构、外交职衔、外交术语、外交新闻传播媒介的英译和网址链接等附录。每一单元的编写内容由以下几部分组成：1. 单元简介：本单元外交新闻文本类型和概念简介；2. 翻译范例：以外交新闻篇章为单位，将翻译范例以汉英文本对照的形式呈现，附相关注解，分析翻译范例的文本结构特点，并对相关翻译策略和技巧进行提炼和总结；3. 学生译作讲评：选择与单元主题相关的学生翻译习作一篇，对习作中出现的问题要点进行校改和解析；4. 实战练习：搭配与本单元外交新闻文本类型翻译相关的实战练习题；5. 参考译文：提供相应的参考译文供教师和学生参考，利于学生对学习效果进行反思和评价；6. 单元小结：总结本单元主要内容要点及相关翻译策略和技巧；7. 延伸阅读：有些章节后还附有延伸阅读材料，包括资深外交翻译家经验谈、外交相关知识简介等。

本教材是集体智慧的结晶，主编和编写人员均为西安外国语大学高级翻译学院教师，从事外交新闻翻译实践教学多年，担任西安外国语大学高级翻译学院国家级翻译实践教育基地外交新闻翻译项目一审、二审和总审等，具有丰富的外交新闻翻译项目审稿经验和学生外交新闻翻译实践原生态文本积累，为本教材编写的顺利进行提供了保障。教材编写人员简介如下：

李琴：西安外国语大学教授、博士；英国剑桥大学英语学院访问学者；陕西省"百人计划"入选人；西安外国语大学国家级翻译实践教育基地外交新闻翻译项目总审；主讲课程包括英美文学、文学翻译、外交翻译、新闻编译等；发表学术论文二十余篇，出版专著两部，编著一部，主编教材一部，参编教材一部，主持国家社科基金项目、教育部人文社会科学研究项目、教育部留学回国人员科研启动金项目、全国基础教育外语教学研究资助金项目等国家级、省部级科研项目十余项；作为第一或第二参研人参与国家社科基金项目、教育部人文社会科学研究项目、国家社科基金重大特别委托项目招标课题、国家社科基金教育学项目等国家级和省部级科研项目9项。

曹怀军：西安外国语大学高级翻译学院讲师，外国语言学与应用语言学硕士；英国谢菲尔德大学访问学者；研究方向为外交翻译、专利翻译、专门用途外语；西安外国语大学"优秀教师"；中国翻译协会语言服务能力培训与评估（LSCAT）首批认证培训师；西安外国语大学国家级翻译实践教育基地外交新闻翻译项目总审。

祖赟：西安外国语大学高级翻译学院讲师，外国语言学与应用语言学硕士；中美富布莱特项目访问学者；研究方向为翻译教学、文化翻译、新闻翻译。主持和参与陕西省教育科学"十二五"规划课题、陕西省社会科学基金项目等多项科研项目，曾荣获西安外国语大学校级教学成果特等奖和二等奖；西安外国语大学国家级翻译实践教育基地外交新闻翻译项目一线审校。

孙晓娅：西安外国语大学高级翻译学院讲师，上海外国语大学翻译学硕士，新加坡南洋理工大学应用语言学硕士；研究方向为翻译理论与实践、英语学术写作；主讲课程包括文化翻译、平行文本阅读等；2006年获第三届"新纪元全球华文青年文学奖"文学翻译组一等奖；笔译实践经验丰富，曾先后服务于IBM、上海市虹口区政府、上海亚士帝信息工程公司、联合国环境署等公司或机构；西安外国语大学国家级翻译实践教育基地外交新闻翻译项目一线审校。

张旭：西安外国语大学高级翻译学院助教，外国语言学与应用语言学硕士；研究方向为新闻翻译、文化翻译、翻译技术；主讲课程包括网络新闻编译、外交新闻翻译、计算机辅助翻译、文化人类学；中国社会科学院重大课题"中华文明探源的神话学研究"核心成员；国家出版基金项目、"十二五"国家重点图书出版规划项目"神话学文库"翻译项目主持人；曾荣获陕西省普通高等学校教学成果二等奖、西安外国语大学"优秀教师"；西安外国语大学国家级翻译实践教育基地外交新闻翻译项目总审。

本教材的编写分工如下：李琴撰写第一单元，并负责全书的内容编排、体例设计、通稿和审定工作；曹怀军撰写第二、五、九、十、十一、十二、十三单元和附录Ⅱ；祖赟撰写第三、四、六、七、十四单元和附录Ⅰ；孙晓娅撰写第八、十五单元；张旭撰写附录Ⅲ，并负责全书的文字校对工作。

本教材在编写过程中受到了西安外国语大学高级翻译学院国家级翻译实践教育基地外交新闻翻译项目组的大力支持；北京大学出版社郝妮娜编辑对书稿进行了悉心细致的校审，西安外国语大学高级翻译学院王维刚老师在编写素材的收集和整理方面也给予了大量帮助，在此一并表示衷心的感谢。由于编写时间紧，编者水平有限，错漏之处在所难免，恳请专家学者和广大读者不吝指正。

主编　李琴
2016 年 7 月于陕西西安

目 录

第一单元　外交新闻翻译概述···1
Unit One　　A General Introduction to Diplomatic News Translation

第二单元　新闻报道中外交理念的翻译···18
Unit Two　　Translation for Diplomatic Concepts in News Coverage

第三单元　驻外报道的翻译··42
Unit Three　Translation for News from Mission Overseas

第四单元　外交访问报道的翻译···72
Unit Four　　Translation for Coverage of Diplomatic Visits

第五单元　国际会议报道的翻译··101
Unit Five　　Translation for Coverage of International Conferences

第六单元　外交会晤新闻报道的翻译··124
Unit Six　　Translation for Coverage of Diplomatic Meetings

第七单元　发表外交演讲报道的翻译··151
Unit Seven　Translation for Coverage of Diplomatic Speeches

第八单元　吹风会报道的翻译···182
Unit Eight　Translation for Coverage of Press Briefings

第九单元　记者招待会报道的翻译···209
Unit Nine　　Translation for Coverage of Press Conferences

第十单元　立场表态类报道的翻译···234
Unit Ten　　Translation for Coverage of Positions and Attitudes

第十一单元　外交访谈报道的翻译···259
Unit Eleven　Translation for Coverage of Diplomatic Interviews

第十二单元	发表外交公报报道的翻译	282
Unit Twelve	Translation for Coverage of Issuing Diplomatic Communiqués	
第十三单元	发表外交声明报道的翻译	306
Unit Thirteen	Translation for Coverage of Issuing Diplomatic Statements	
第十四单元	签署外交备忘录报道的翻译	331
Unit Fourteen	Translation for Coverage of Signing Diplomatic Memorandum	
第十五单元	外交函电报道的翻译	362
Unit Fifteen	Translation for Coverage of Diplomatic Correspondence	
附 录 I	世界主要国家外交机构及外交职衔	388
Appendix I	Diplomatic Organs and Diplomatic Titles in Major Countries	
附 录 II	国内外主要外交新闻网站	401
Appendix II	Major Diplomatic News Websites Home and Abroad	
附 录 III	中国外交术语英译	408
Appendix III	English for Chinese Diplomatic Terms	

UNIT 1

外交新闻翻译概述
A General Introduction to Diplomatic News Translation

单元简介 Introduction

外交新闻翻译是新闻翻译的一种,又具有外交翻译的特点,在翻译的内容、结构、原则、策略、方法、功能、目的、传播方式等方面都具有鲜明的特点,受社会文化、意识形态、诗学语境等的影响也更为深刻。

我国外交新闻翻译的主要内容包括重大国际事件报道,驻外机构活动报道,国家领导人外交访问、外交会晤、发表演讲与致辞、签署重要文件的报道,大型国际会议报道,外交吹风会报道,例行记者会报道,外交发言人表态,外交访谈和外交函电的报道,等等。我国外交新闻翻译是国家外交思想和外交实践的再现,具有高度的政策性和政治敏感性,对传播中国声音、塑造国家良好形象起到重要作用,因此在翻译原则上,强调严肃、严谨、准确;翻译策略上,以异化为主,归化为辅;翻译方法上,多采用全译。

外交新闻翻译的严肃性、政策性和准确性要求译者具有较高的语言素养、政治素养、信息素养以及跨文化知识积累,才能严谨精准、优质高效地应对外交新闻中出现的种种语言和文化现象。

本章将从我国外交新闻翻译的特点、内容、原则、策略和方法,以及对译者素养的要求等方面一一进行详述。

C-E TRANSLATION OF DIPLOMATIC NEWS

一、外交新闻翻译：概念与范畴

外交新闻翻译的内涵较为复杂。首先，它是一种翻译活动或翻译行为。翻译是人类历史上一项悠久而丰富的实践活动，从古至今，人们对翻译进行了传统语文学视角、语言学视角、文化视角以及其他跨学科视角的多样阐释。翻译包括语内翻译、语际翻译和符际翻译三种基本类型。在当代社会，随着学科发展的日渐成熟与完善，人们对翻译的认识也不断深化，对翻译进行界定变得越来越困难，但是翻译的基本属性并未动摇：翻译是一项语言或符号转换活动；语符的转换过程会受到来自社会、文化、思维、语言等各个层面的影响，因此被赋予不同学科和领域的特色；翻译行为所属领域和学科不同，翻译的原则、策略和方法也会有所不同，呈现出不同的特点。据此，对于翻译的研究要将其置于具体的学科范围之内，有针对性地，因地、因时制宜地对相关翻译原则、策略、方法等进行分析、归纳和总结。同理，对外交新闻翻译的研究，也应将翻译行为置于"新闻"和"外交"的范畴之内进行详细解读。

其次，外交新闻翻译属于新闻翻译的范畴。新版《辞海》将"新闻"界定为"报社、通讯社、广播电台、电视台等新闻机构对当前政治事件或社会事件所作的报道。要求迅速及时、真实、言简意明，以事实说话。形式有消息、通讯、特写、记者通信、调查报告、图片新闻、电视新闻等"。这一界定言简意赅，道出了新闻的内容、特点、形式等。事实上，随着社会生活的丰富和发展，新闻的内涵已经得到很大拓展，例如，就反映社会生活的内容而言，新闻包括政治新闻、经济新闻、法律新闻、军事新闻、科技新闻、文教新闻、体育新闻、社会新闻等；就结构而言，新闻包括标题、导语、主体、背景和结语等部分；就载体而言，新闻可通过电视、广播、报纸、杂志、互联网广告媒体、移动互联网媒体等媒介进行传播；就报道形式而言，新闻有倒金字塔式、正金字塔式、折衷式、平铺直叙式四类写作形式[①]；就新闻与读者的关系而言，可分为硬新闻和软新闻，等等。新闻具有如此丰富的内涵，无疑对新闻的翻译形成了严峻的挑战。所谓新闻翻译，是把用一种文字写成的新闻（原语新闻，News in Language A）用另一种语言（译语语言，Language B）表达出来，经过再次传播，使译语读者（Language B readers）不仅能获得原语新闻记者所报道的信息，而且还能得到与原语新闻读者（Language A readers）大致相同的教育或启迪，获得与原语读者大致相同的信息和/或文学享受。（刘其中，2009：2）但是，由于"新闻"本身的复杂性，使得新闻翻译不仅仅是一种语言转换活动，更是与国家的意识形态、社会生活、文化思维、诗学语境等因素紧密相关并受其影响，随着国家和地区的不同而呈现出不同的形态和特点，具有不同的功能，实现不同的目的和宗旨，采取不同的翻译原则、策略与方法。

最后，外交新闻翻译不仅具有一般新闻翻译的特点，还具有外交翻译的特点。按照翻译方向，我国的外交新闻翻译可以分为汉译外和外译汉两种类型，其中汉译英和英译汉所占比重最大，受众最为广泛。本书重在探讨汉英外交新闻的翻译，因此，如非特别

---

① http://baike.baidu.com/view/14325.htm

说明，本书以下所指外交新闻翻译，均特指汉英外交新闻翻译。众所周知，外交活动是国家以和平手段对外行使主权的活动，如参加国际组织和会议，与其他国家互派使节、进行谈判、签订条约和协定等。外交新闻也是新闻中内容最为严肃、要求最为严格、政治敏感度最高的类型。外交新闻翻译不仅具有新闻翻译的一般特点，而且还被赋予了外交活动的性质，具有外交活动的基本内涵，在翻译的内容、结构、形式等各层面，翻译的理解、转换、接受、传播等各环节，以及翻译原则、策略和方法等各方面具有鲜明的特点，不同于一般意义上的新闻翻译。外交新闻翻译还属于外宣翻译的范畴，具有外宣翻译的特点。所谓外宣翻译"是翻译的一种特殊形式，指在全球化背景下，以让世界了解中国为目的、以汉语为信息源、以英语等外国语为信息载体、以各种媒体为渠道、以外国民众（包括境内的各类外籍人士）为主要传播对象的交际活动。"（张健，2013：22）一般来说，我国外宣翻译要达到宣传效果的最大化，需要遵循"外宣三贴近"原则，即贴近中国发展的实际，贴近国外受众对中国信息的需求，贴近国外受众的思维习惯。（黄友义，2004：27）但是，我国外交新闻翻译是外宣翻译中非常特殊的一种，特殊在政治性强、措辞严谨、政治敏感度高，它宣传的是我国的外交思想理念、大政方针、政策法规等，遵循的是传播中国声音、树立中国形象的基本宗旨，恪守的是严肃、谨慎、客观、准确的宣传标准，因此外交新闻翻译要将"信"置于首位，在确保字斟句酌、准确传递中国政治与外交话语的前提下，以外国受众易于理解的方式将新闻的内容和信息传递出去，达到宣传、沟通和交流的目的。

综上所述，外交新闻翻译是对外交领域新闻文本的翻译活动，它具有新闻翻译的一般特点，又兼具外交翻译的性质和内涵，其"外交性"和"政策性"远远大于一般新闻翻译，要求准确、严谨地传递信息，表达主张，以实现与国外受众的有效沟通与交流。

二、中国外交新闻的内容

中国外交新闻的内容与我国外宣政策、方针与宗旨息息相关。2014年9月14日，中共中央政治局委员、中央书记处书记、中宣部部长刘奇葆在全国外宣工作会议上强调，对外宣传是一项全局性战略性的工作，要认真学习贯彻习近平总书记系列重要讲话精神，围绕党和国家工作大局，以塑造国家良好形象、维护国家根本利益、传播中华优秀文化、服务党和国家对外战略为基本任务，讲好中国故事、传播好中国声音、阐释好中国特色，营造于我有利的国际舆论环境。[①] 刘奇葆部长的讲话阐明了当前我国外宣工作的主要宗旨，即"传播好中国声音，塑造国家良好形象"。新闻传播作为国家对外宣传的重要路径，对我国外宣目标和效果的实现无疑具有重要意义。在这一宗旨的指引下，中共中央宣传部、文化部、广电总局、新闻出版总署、国务院新闻办公室、外交部新闻司等我国重要宣传和新闻机构，以及其他相关重要国家部委和地方机构本着及时、准确、公开、透明的原则，通过互联网等传播方式，持续不断地推出介绍我国政治、经济、文

---

① 《刘奇葆：传播好中国声音 塑造国家良好形象》，http://news.xinhuanet.com/politics/2014-09/14/c_1112473487.htm

化、社会发展情况的新闻报道，阐述我国的外交政策、大政方针、法制法规等，向世界展现一个新兴大国的良好形象。

目前我国外交新闻的主要传播载体包括纸媒、电视、互联网等，其中互联网作为最为迅捷的信息传播途径，在我国外交新闻发布和传播载体中扮演着越来越重要的角色。外交新闻大致可分为四大类，即国家领导人或外交部官员的外交活动、国家领导人进行外事活动之前外交部所作的简报、大使的外交活动和大使的著述。要了解中国外交新闻的主要内容，中华人民共和国外交部网站可谓最全面、最权威的外交新闻发布平台。如果对中国外交部网页上的"外交新闻"栏目做一个概览，可发现我国外交新闻（主要采取新闻报道的形式）的内容囊括了以下几大版块：重大国际事件的报道、驻外机构活动的报道、国家领导人外交访问的报道、大型国际会议的报道、国家领导人外交会晤的报道、国家领导人发表外交演讲或致辞的报道、外交吹风会的报道、例行记者会的报道、外交发言人表态、外交访谈的报道、国家领导人签署重要外交文书的报道、外交函电的报道等。这些新闻报道，对全方位、立体化地展示我国外交理念、外交活动和外交风采，以及"传播好中国声音、塑造国家良好形象"起到了积极的作用，是我国外交新闻的重要内容，也是我国外交新闻翻译的重要内容。有鉴于此，本书将主要围绕上述几大版块的内容探讨汉英外交新闻的翻译。

三、中国外交新闻的语言特点

中国外交新闻的语言不仅具有一般新闻语言的特点，诸如具体、准确、简练、通俗，更重要的是，它还具有外交语言的特点。中国外交新闻作为对国家外交政策、立场的表达，以及对各种外交活动的描述，不可避免地会大量引用、转述或重述中外高层领导人的讲话内容和精神、中外高层领导人互致函电的内容、外交发言人的表态、中外领导人签署的重要纲领性文件或外交文书的内容概要，以及中外领导人对具体国际事件、外交事件或外交活动发表的看法和观点，表达的态度和立场等。上述这些内容无不是国家外交政策、大政方针、法制法规等的再现。因此，外交新闻的语言不仅是新闻语言，更是外交语言，那么它就不可避免地带有外交语言的特点。我国外交语言的基本特点，可简要归纳如下：

（一）严肃性与文学性的结合

外交语言是在外交实践的各种场合中使用的语言，是对我国外交政策、原则、立场等政治话语的表达。我国的外交语言在阐述外交思想、表达外交立场、化解外交冲突、解决外交问题中起到不可估量的作用，其严肃性是不言而喻的。无论是在外交文件的签署、外交文书的撰写，还是外交表态和发言中，我国高层领导人、政府发言人或外交外事工作者在使用外交话语时都恪守严谨准确的原则，审慎思考、字斟句酌，反复思量后，才予以表达，每个词、每个字都极尽准确，经得起推敲，对表达我国外交思想、树立我国外交形象、维护我国与其他国家之间良好的外交关系，维护我国政治、经济、文化、军事利益，乃至维护世界和平与稳定都起到重要的作用。

我国外交语言除了严肃准确之外，还具有鲜明的中国特色，具体表现为对中国传统俗语谚语、比喻修辞，以及诗词歌赋等的使用。例如在李克强总理治国理政的重要表述中，就多次使用了中国人民喜闻乐见、口口相传的俗语和谚语，举例如下：

改革贵在行动，<u>喊破嗓子不如甩开膀子</u>①。中国的改革进入了深水区，也可以说是攻坚期，的确是因为它要触动原有的利益格局。

不论国际风云如何变幻，我们<u>咬定青山不放松</u>，做一些有利于当前、更有利于长远的事情，保证中国今后十年、二十年乃至更长时期的持续健康发展。我们在工作中，一定要考虑更好地让机制来发挥作用，不能"<u>头痛医头、脚痛医脚</u>"。要做对当前有用、对长远有利的事。

援引中国古诗词也是我国国家领导人在外交话语中频繁使用的措辞之道。例如习近平主席在博鳌亚洲论坛2013年年会上的主旨演讲中，就多次引用了中国古诗词，以便更为形象、简练地表达思想。试举几例如下：

"<u>一花独放不是春，百花齐放春满园</u>。"世界各国联系紧密、利益交融，要互通有无、优势互补，在追求本国利益时兼顾他国合理关切，在谋求自身发展中促进各国共同发展，不断扩大共同利益汇合点。

"<u>海纳百川，有容乃大</u>。"我们应该尊重各国自主选择社会制度和发展道路的权利，消除疑虑和隔阂，把世界多样性和各国的差异性转化为发展活力和动力。

我国领导人还常常使用比喻等修辞手法来使语言更为形象生动。李克强总理在2015年3月15日召开的十二届全国人大三次会议闭幕后的中外记者招待会上，就多次使用了比喻的修辞手法来表达中国在改革关键之年的施政思路，被新闻媒体誉为"巧喻妙答"②，试举几例如下：

我想起中国人发明的围棋，既要谋势，又要做活，<u>做活有两只眼。形象地讲，稳增长和调结构就是两只眼</u>，做活了就可以谋大势，当然这需要眼光、耐力和勇气。

环保等执法部门也要敢于担当，承担责任。对工作不到位、工作不力的也要问责，渎职失职的要依法追究，<u>环保法的执行不是棉花棒，是杀手锏</u>。

对推动两岸经济合作来说，<u>需要两个轮子一起转</u>，一个轮子就是要加强两岸经

---

① 画线部分为笔者所加，以示强调。
② 《李克强记者会"语录"：巧喻妙答透视施政思路》，http://lianghui.people.com.cn/2015npc/n/2015/0315/c3936802669 5618.html

贸合作的制度化建设，比如说像ECFA后续协商。另一个轮子就是扩大相互开放。对大陆来说，尤其是要重视在大陆投资的台湾企业。

在我国领导人的外交话语中，俚语、俗语、谚语、诗词曲赋，以及比喻修辞等文学性语言的使用可谓无处不在，包括一些政府和外交工作人员在外交场合也不时地引经据典，或采用通俗易懂的语言表情达意。文学性语言的使用，能使言语表达更为形象、生动、凝练和通俗，不仅有助于外籍人士理解，加强沟通效果，而且为严肃的外交语言平添了许多生动的色彩，使我国外交语言在严谨审慎的同时，生动形象、喜闻乐见。

（二）模式化与个性化的结合

所谓外交语言的模式化，是指我国外交语言中常常使用一些高度概括性的表达方式来表述我国的施政纲领、政策方针等，例如"中国梦""互利共赢""互联互通""新型大国关系""命运共同体""依法治国""精准扶贫"等，其中相当一部分还与数字紧紧相连，可以模式化为"N个X"（严文斌，2015：8），例如"一国两制""一带一路""两个一百年""双目标""三个代表""三严三实""四个全面""五位一体""八项纪律""八荣八耻"，等等。这些高度概括性的、模式化的政治话语表达方式简洁凝练、形象生动、朗朗上口、易于记忆和传播，因此在我国政治文献和表述中频频出现，对我国大政方针的内宣和外宣起到了积极的促进作用，甚至逐渐为外媒所接纳和引用。

我国外交话语中还有一个重要组成部分，就是国家领导人针对我国内政外交的个性化表述。这些个性化表述不仅充分彰显了领导人的身心修养与个人魅力，而且生活化、接地气、质朴实在、通俗易懂、与时俱进，因而深得民心。例如2008年胡锦涛主席在纪念改革开放30周年大会上的报告中说："只要我们不动摇、不懈怠、不折腾，坚定不移地推进改革开放，坚定不移地走中国特色社会主义道路，就一定能够胜利实现这一宏伟蓝图和奋斗目标。""不折腾"这一我国北方民众常用俗语因其通俗形象而引起了网络热议，迅速走红。再如李克强总理在2015年政府工作报告中谈到简政放权的问题时说"大道至简，有权不可任性。""任性"一词瞬间传遍网络媒体，被广为引用，总理也因此被称赞为"很潮""萌萌哒"。习近平主席在长期的治国理政实践中，也形成了一套颇具个人魅力的语言风格，正如《平易近人——习近平的语言力量》一书的编者所说，"习近平总书记在他的系列重要讲话中，常用打比方、讲故事的方式阐述深刻的道理，用大白话、大实话等俗文俚语来释疑解惑，用中国优秀传统文化元素来提纲挈领、纵横捭阖。总之，习近平总书记的语言，平实中蕴含着大智慧，更有一种透彻、直指人心的力量。"（陈锡喜，2014：001）例如，习主席曾用"打'老虎'，拍'苍蝇'"来比喻坚决查处不正之风与腐败问题；将群众路线教育实践活动的总要求归结为"照镜子、正衣冠、洗洗澡、治治病"十二字；用"打铁还需自身硬"说明要不断加强党的自身建设；用"小康不小康、关键看老乡"来强调大力促进农民增加收入；引用中国古诗

外交新闻翻译概述
A General Introduction to Diplomatic News Translation

文"苟日新、日日新、又日新"来阐述中华民族的创新精神,等等。俗文俚语、形象比喻、古代诗词的综合运用形成了习近平主席鲜明的语言风格,备受国内民众的褒扬,也为外国媒体和民众所称道。

(三)原则性与分寸感的结合

外交语言是一个国家外交思想、外交风格、国际地位、对外关系等的体现,强权政治必然采用强权话语,弱势国家话语难免低调含蓄。我国在长期的外交活动中,形成了"不畏强暴、主持公道、坚持原则、求同存异、实事求是、说话算数"的外交风格和特点(何群、李春怡,2011:39)。在外交语言的使用上,则形成了原则性与分寸感结合、义正词严与委婉含蓄并举的语言特点。在事关和平稳定、国家主权、领土完整等中华民族核心利益的问题上,我国外交话语往往义正词严、不容异议,例如我国对台湾问题的重要表态:

> 我们对台大政方针是<u>明确的</u>、<u>一贯的</u>,不会因台湾政局变化而改变。我们将坚持"九二共识"政治基础,<u>继续推进</u>两岸关系和平发展。我们将坚决遏制任何形式的"台独"分裂行径,维护国家主权和领土完整,<u>绝不让</u>国家分裂的历史悲剧重演。①

但是在涉及双边或多边关系,以及处理国际问题和地区冲突时,我国则一贯奉行独立自主的和平外交政策,恪守维护世界和平、促进共同发展的外交宗旨,中共十八大更是提出了"和平、发展、合作、共赢"的外交新理念,因此在外交措辞上常常显得委婉含蓄,有理、有利、有节,严谨克制,把握分寸。例如我国在朝鲜半岛问题上的表态:

> 中方在朝鲜半岛问题上的立场是<u>一贯</u>、<u>明确的</u>。我们<u>一贯主张</u>朝鲜半岛应实现无核化,各方应共同努力维护朝鲜半岛和平稳定。中方认为,六方会谈是推动实现有关目标的有效机制。我们<u>希望</u>各方都能着眼长远,推动重启六方会谈,各方应在六方会谈框架下加强接触、增进互信、改善关系、化解矛盾,全面均衡解决各方关切,切实落实"9·19"共同声明确定的各项目标,推进朝鲜半岛无核化进程,共同维护朝鲜半岛的和平稳定。中方<u>愿</u>与国际社会一道,为实现这一目标作出不懈努力。②

在我国的外交语言中,表示分寸感的词汇还有很多,根据外交关系的不同,外交事件的性质等,分为不同的层级,例如表达肯定的有"理解""支持""欣赏""欢

---

① 《习近平:对台方针不会因台政局变化而变》,http://china.caixin.com/2016-03-06/100916777.html
② 《外交部:当前朝鲜半岛局势复杂敏感 望各方保持冷静》,http://gb.cri.cn/27824/2013/01/24/6651s4002016.htm

迎""乐见""感谢"等,表达否定的有"遗憾""关注""严重关注""敦促""强烈敦促""反对""坚决反对""强烈反对""谴责""强烈谴责",等等。我国外交语言的分寸感,充分体现了一个负责任大国协调国际与地区矛盾、维护世界和平和谐的外交形象。

上述外交语言的特点在我国外交新闻中得到了充分的再现。如何在外交新闻汉译中体现我国新闻语言和外交语言的双重特点,准确传递外交新闻措辞中蕴含着的我国外交政策、原则和立场,是外交新闻译者面临的重大挑战。

四、外交新闻汉英翻译的原则

外交新闻属于"硬新闻"的范畴。所谓硬新闻,是指关系到国计民生以及人们切身利益的新闻,包括党和国家的重大方针政策的制定和改变、时局变化、市场行情、股市涨落、疾病流行、天气变化、重大灾难事故,等等。① 相对于向受众提供娱乐、使其开阔眼界、增长见识、陶冶情操的软新闻而言,硬新闻的信息性较强,更为严肃,在翻译时需以原文为中心,以准确传递信息为宗旨。外交新闻除了具有硬新闻的性质,还具有外交性质,是国家外交思想和外交实践的再现,具有高度的政策性和政治敏感性,因此,外交新闻的翻译首先是外交翻译,然后才是新闻翻译,换句话说,外交新闻翻译的首要原则就是外交翻译的原则。以我国目前外交新闻发布和翻译的最权威平台,即中华人民共和国外交部网站为例,该网站英文网页上发布的新闻均采取了异化的翻译策略,严格忠实于原文,甚至在确保文法和意义传递正确的前提下,做到了字字对应的翻译,充分体现了外交翻译的基本原则,即"准确至上""抠字眼""不擅自随意解读",可以说,这也是我国外交新闻汉英翻译的基本原则。我国著名外交翻译家、外交部英文专家施燕华女士曾用"外交翻译,一字千金"来形容外交翻译中的政治敏感性,例如对"坦诚"这个词的翻译,它由两个字组成,一个是坦率,一个是真诚,"到底把它落脚在坦率还是真诚?这里面又有学问了。如果两国谈得是比较好的,而且分歧不是很大,但是还是把大家的意见全都说出来了,那就可以用坦率。而有的时候,两国谈得也挺好,但是大家还是有很多分歧的,那还要有一个真诚。翻译坦诚的时候,就要知道两国关系的程度。"② 看似简单的两个字,背后蕴含着如此丰富的外交关系内涵,可见外交翻译真可谓是字斟句酌,一字千金。

外交新闻汉英翻译的基本原则是与我国外交事业的发展并行不悖的。党的十八大以来,我国领导人的一系列外交活动和在不同外交场合的重要表述,都标志着中国外交进入了一个新的阶段。中国新外交的最主要特征是连续性,即继承中国宝贵外交遗产,延续已经建立起来的中国外交原则、框架、机制、安排等。③ 同时,我国外交的风格也

---

① http://baike.baidu.com/view/936389.htm
② 《施燕华:外交翻译 一字千金》,http://www.china.com.cn/zhuanti/zyw/2007-04/06/content_8077481.htm
③ 《庞中英:习近平新外交思想解读》,http://cpc.people.com.cn/pinglun/n/2013/0418/c78779-21180569.html

在逐步转变，由被动到主动，从防御到进取，从面子到里子，从中庸和重商，到"有原则、讲情谊、讲道义"的转变，也就是从"韬光养晦"转向"奋发有为"。① 近年来，我国外交不断推出新理念，积极探索走出一条中国特色的大国外交之路，在对外翻译中，也更加强调中国话语权的建立，彰显中国特色，越来越多地使用直译的翻译方法，尽管有时不可避免地会显露出"中式英语"的痕迹，但是这一点已经为外媒所逐渐接受，因为"随着中国国家实力逐步增强，国际地位逐步提高，国际上聆听中国的'欲望'也在增强，这种情况下，'中国表达'便具备了被国际接受乃至再传播的可能性。"（严文斌，2015：10）有研究者研读了近年来美国《时代周刊》和《新闻周刊》两大主流媒体对中国的报道文章后指出，美国期刊对中国报道中的汉语文化词汇很少采用意译的翻译方法，而是倾向于异化的翻译策略，使用完全音译、音译加解释、完全按汉语形式直译以及直译加解释的翻译方法。（朱天文，2003：34）当然，异化策略的使用也与新闻本身强调使用直接引述来增强真实性与客观性有直接的关系，但主要是我国外交翻译的性质、特点和一贯原则，以及我国国家实力的增强、国际地位的不断提高使然。

近年来，有学者以我国若干外交新词的翻译为例，提出了外交翻译"政治等效"的原则。（杨明星，2008，2012，2014，2015；Yang，2012）"政治等效"的具体内涵是：外交翻译一方面要准确、忠实地反映原语和说话者的政治思想和政治语境，另一方面要用接受方能够理解的译入语来表达，使双方得到的政治含义信息等值，同时使译文起到与原文相同的交际功能。虽然这一原则的提出也受到了其他学者的质疑（王平兴，2016），但是在新的时代背景和我国外交风格渐渐转型的历史语境下，"政治等效"的外交翻译原则对我国外交理念的高效传播，以及建构和谐健康的外交关系具有积极的意义，对我国外交新闻翻译也具有重要指导意义，因为外交新闻翻译不仅是外交翻译，还具有新闻翻译的特点，强调译文的传播效果和交际功能。

五、外交新闻汉英翻译的策略与方法

大体而言，新闻翻译的方法可依据原语新闻价值的不同、译文形式的不同，以及二次传播的需要分为全译、摘译和编译三种。（刘其中，2009：8）

全译（Full Translation）是将原语语言写成的新闻稿全部转化为译入语新闻的翻译方法。这样的新闻一般都十分重要，二次传播的价值较高，翻译时必须逐段甚至逐句进行，既要译出原语新闻的深层含义，又要保留它的基本结构和风格。对其内容，翻译人员不能随意增减。

摘译（Summary Translation）是译者根据"本媒体"的编辑方针只将原语新闻中值得进行二次传播的部分转化为译语新闻的翻译方法。

编译（Trans-editing）是通过翻译和编辑的手段，将以原语语言写成的新闻进行翻译、综合、加工，使之成为用译语语言表达出来的新闻的翻译方法。

---

① 《那些改变我们的外交新理念》，http://news.sina.com.cn/o/2013-12-28/132029106447.shtml

外交新闻汉英翻译
C-E TRANSLATION OF DIPLOMATIC NEWS

编译是目前新闻翻译领域使用最为频繁的一种翻译方法。英国华威大学翻译与比较文化研究中心教授苏珊·巴斯奈特和英国莱斯特大学社会学讲师贝尔萨博士在合著的 Translation in Global News 一书中，援引弗米尔的"目的论"、勒菲弗尔的"改写"理论，以及埃文—佐哈尔的"多元系统理论"等来强调新闻翻译适应目的语文化和受众的必要性和重要性，认为"新闻翻译的过程其实就是新闻编辑的过程，在这个过程中，译者要不断地对所译编的新闻稿进行查对、修正、修改、润色，最后是发表。"（Bielsa Esperanca & Susan Bassnett, 2009: 63）并因此而提出了新闻翻译"绝对归化"（absolute domestication）的策略。然而，外交新闻翻译是新闻翻译中非常特殊的一种翻译类型，它是一个主权国家外交政策与思想的体现和传播，在中国的社会文化语境下，更是与国家的大政方针息息相关，具有高度的政治敏感性，要求忠实准确地向世界发出中国声音，传递中国信息，塑造中国形象，不容随意阐释和修改，因此，我国的外交新闻汉英翻译主要采用异化的翻译策略，采取全译的翻译方法，要求忠实于原文，字斟句酌，准确至上。

异化策略的本质属性是"以原作者为中心"，要求译者在翻译的过程中努力再现原作的语言、结构、意义以及原作者的意旨。异化策略的优势是可以在目的语中引入原语的语言结构、表达方式、诗学特征和文化要素，促进不同民族间的文化交流；从弱小民族的语言向强势民族语言翻译中如果采用异化策略，可能会成为一种抵抗强势民族的文化殖民和文化霸权、彰显弱小民族文化身份的手段。异化策略框架下的翻译方法可包括零翻译（zero translation）、音译（transliteration）、逐词翻译（word-for-word translation）和直译（literal translation）（熊兵，2014: 84—85）。在外交新闻汉英翻译中，主要采用直译法，间或也会使用音译法，例如将"不折腾"翻译为"buzheteng"[①]，以及逐字翻译的方法，特别是针对那些政治意义较强，政治敏感度很高的语汇，甚至需要一一对应原文词句和语序进行翻译。

近年来，我国外交风格逐步转变，不断推出新理念、新术语、新概念、新名词，成为我国外交新词（diplomatic neologism）的一部分，这是我国提升外交话语权、建构特色鲜明的外交话语体系、塑造外交新形象的重要举措。一般来说，外交新词包括全新词、新义旧词和外来词（杨明星，2014: 103），中国外交新词则以全新词居多。外交新闻作为我国外交话语的主要载体之一，也越来越多地涌现出这些外交新词。外交新词在汉译英时常常采用忠实基础上的创新译法，以新词译新词，例如对"中国梦"（the Chinese Dream）、"新型大国关系"（a new model of major-country relationship）、"一带一路"（the Belt and Road）等新兴词汇的翻译，这种创新译法也属直译，但是并不依据或套用西方的话语逻辑，而是完全采用中国特色话语模式传播中国外交理念，具有鲜明的时代特色和外交内涵。但是，新理念、新术语等的翻译，正是因为其"新"，所以目前译法众多，译名不够统一，给我国外交新闻翻译带来一定困扰。这些概念和术语的译法还有

[①] *People's Daily Online*, Jan.8, 2009

外交新闻翻译概述
A General Introduction to Diplomatic News Translation

待时日进一步检验和确定,也有待相关权威部门对不同的译法加以统一和规范。

异化的翻译策略虽然有助于准确传达我国的外交政策和理念,但是也有其弊端,例如有时译文不符合译入语的语言习惯,生硬拗口、可读性差。有学者指出,目前我国外宣翻译中存在内宣和外宣不分、缺少外宣研究、文风不平和、特色词汇翻译难懂等问题(徐明强,2014:11—12),外交新闻翻译作为外宣翻译的一个重要组成部分,也或多或少地存在上述问题。坦率来讲,有一部分原因恐怕还得归咎于异化策略和直译法的使用。在这种情况下,外宣"三贴近"原则和上述"政治等效"原则可以给我们带来一些启发。所幸这些问题已经在慢慢改观,"近年来,外交翻译工作的一个努力方向,就是结合中央领导及我部(外交部,笔者注)领导对外讲话的场合及听众特点,尽量用外国人听得懂、易理解的语言进行翻译,在确保忠实原文的基础上,使译文更加生动顺畅。实践证明,这样做效果很好,受到了普遍的好评。"(施燕华,2009:12)可见,我国的外交翻译正在改变以往完全异化的翻译策略,逐步尝试向异化为主、归化为辅转型,这对我国外交理念更为有效地对外传播显然大有裨益,外交新闻翻译亦然。

外交新闻的翻译除了在内容上要高度关注外交语汇的翻译外,还要在形式上遵循新闻的结构特点。一般来说,不同的新闻机构有不同的写作指南(stylebook),规定了不同的体例规范,"新闻机构在新闻翻译中就像是一个大的超文本,其审查制度、格式惯例、运作流程、任务分配、译员守则及翻译指引等都是超文本因素;这些因素在新闻机构的运作、原文报道、译者及译文读者之间起着协调的作用。"(张美芳,2011:51)新闻由标题、导语、主体、背景和结语等部分组成。标题一般包括引标题、正标题和副标题;导语是新闻开头的第一段话,是新闻的引子,概括新闻的主要内容;主体是新闻的主干,用充足的事实材料对导语进行进一步的扩展和阐述;背景是新闻的辅助部分,对新闻的社会或自然语境进行解释;结语是对新闻的最后概括和总结,有时在结语中也会引发新的话题。这些新闻结构要素中,以前三个为主,后两个为辅。本书对外交新闻翻译策略和方法的阐述,也依照新闻标题、导语、主体、背景和结语的特点依次展开。新闻机构作为超文本因素,贯穿于新闻写作的各个组成部分,特别是在新闻的电头部分,一般都会有播发新闻的机构的名称,在翻译时要严格按照该新闻机构的体例要求。以我国的国家级通讯社新华社为例,其电头体例一般为通讯社、地点、日期,有时还会加上记者名字,如新华社北京5月5日电(记者:张三),译为英文,即BEIJING, May 5 (Xinhua)。译例如下:

China underscores equal implementation of UN resolution on DPRK

Source: Xinhua | 2016-03-07 17:59:06 | Editor: huaxia

BEIJING, March 7 (Xinhua) — China on Monday called for a fair and balanced execution of the UN resolution against Pyongyang, adding that the responsibility to do so does not stop with China.

图片说明是新闻的一个组成部分，因而也是新闻翻译的一部分。新闻图片说明一般包括小题和正文两个部分。小题是用极其精练的字词高度概括图片信息的说明性文字，一般只用在非常重要的新闻图片中。正文是图片说明的主要部分，一般将新闻中的若干主要要素，即几个"W"交代清楚，例如人物（who）、时间（when）、地点（where）、事件（what）等。图片说明正文的翻译原则与其他新闻文字一致，需要注意的是应注明新闻人物的姓名、身份、头衔，以及在图片中所在的位置等。此外，新闻图片说明的翻译常用现在式，强调图片为读者带来的"即视感"。新闻图片说明的翻译还要求文字精练，避免与新闻导语中使用过的词汇重复（刘其中，2009：268）。

六、外交新闻翻译对译者的要求

外交新闻翻译的严肃性、政策性要求译者具有良好的语言素养、政治素养、信息素养，以及跨文化知识积累，才能准确、高效地应对外交新闻中出现的种种语言现象和新闻事实的翻译。

（一）语言和知识素养

语言和知识素养是翻译工作者必备的基本素养，就外交新闻译者而言，对语言和知识素养的要求更高、更严格，这是由外交新闻翻译的政治性和严肃性决定的。正所谓"外事无小事"，外交则更无小事，要求译者字字小心，处处留意。对于外交新闻译者而言，语言能力涵盖了理解能力、转换能力和表达能力，特别是对语境的理解和把握能力，直接影响到后续转换和表达的准确性。以外交新闻翻译中常常遇到的一词多义现象为例，同样的词语在不同的语境中往往具有不同的含义，"同样的一些话，在正常情况下是一种含义，但在外交文件中却是另一种含义"（金桂华，2003：78）。这样的例子比比皆是，如我国政治话语中经常出现的"关注"一词，在不同的话语表述中表达的含义并不一致（何群、李春怡，2011：179—180）。

中国政府将密切关注事态的进展。
The Chinese government will follow closely the latest development.

国际社会应切实关注发展中国家，特别是最不发达国家面临的严重困难和危机。
The international community should pay real attention to the enormous difficulties and crises facing developing countries, the least developed countries in particular.

中央十分关注港澳地区在这场金融危机中所遇到的困难。
The Central Government is very much concerned about the difficulties of Hong Kong and Macao in the financial crisis.

我们关注人的价值、权益和自由，关注人的生活质量、发展潜能和幸福指数。

We <u>care about</u> people's value, rights and interests and freedom, the quality of their life, and their development potential and happiness index.

从上述译例中可见，外交新闻译员只有准确理解了同一词汇在不同语境中的确切内涵，才能在译语中根据不同上下文进行准确表达。

外交新闻中常常援引的国家领导人的演讲或发言中，常出现中国诗词曲赋和谚语俗语等，也要求译者具有较强的语言能力才能应付自如。中国翻译协会在其网站上或在其与中国外文局对外传播研究中心主办的学术期刊《中国翻译》的"词语选译"等栏目中会不时地选登一批国家领导人重要讲话中经常使用的古诗词、俗语谚语等的译文，以及我国重要施政纲领和政治术语的译文以供参考，外交新闻译员对这些语言知识的日积月累对提高翻译质量大有裨益。

外交新闻译者还需具备较高的知识素养，在日常翻译工作中注意跨文化和百科知识的积累，熟谙中外政治体制、职衔称谓、组织机构、民族构成、宗教信仰、媒体运作等方面的异同，了解世界政治、经济、文化、外交、军事、科技、医学等专业领域的基本知识，才能在外交新闻翻译工作中做到游刃有余。

（二）政治素养

外交新闻的翻译属于政治翻译。政治翻译就要讲政治，需要译者具有良好的政治素养，例如准确的政治政策理解力、时事政治新闻的追踪和把握能力、新闻背景知识的积累和总结能力、国际关系的领悟能力以及对政治话语和用词的敏感性。我国老一辈外交翻译家在这方面可谓经验丰富，语重心长，例如"外事翻译工作必须注意掌握用词的政治含义和政治分寸"（过家鼎，2002：59），"政治翻译不能任意删字，当然也不能任意加字，或者离开原文自由发挥"，"要仔细衡量用词的政治含义与影响"，"要注意掌握分寸，用词轻重要恰如其分"，要求译者"有政策头脑和政治敏感"。（程镇球，2003：18—22）作为我国外交话语重要载体的外交新闻，自然要求译者具备相当的政治素养，才能在对外宣传国家外交政策、树立我国外交形象、建构和谐外交关系方面起到积极的作用。这里着重探讨一下外交用词翻译的政治敏感性，试举我国对台湾问题的一贯用词和表态的翻译为例：

"中国台湾"——台湾是中华人民共和国不可分割的一部分，这是我国对台湾问题的一贯立场，对"台湾"一词的翻译要求准确表达我国政府的严正立场，针对宣扬"台独"的少数分裂势力，我国对"台湾"的翻译要求非常谨慎，无论在任何场合都不允许发生误译。目前我国常见的对"中国台湾"的译法有"Taiwan, China"，"Chinese Taiwan"，"Chinese Taipei"。与"中国台湾"相对应的"中国大陆"，应译为the mainland of China, China's mainland。

"台湾问题"——对于"台湾问题"的翻译，我国曾将其译为Taiwan issue，后改译为Taiwan question，原因在于issue一词有dispute（争议）之涵义，暗含台湾是我国与他国的领土纠纷，这有悖于我国一再严正声明的"台湾是中华人民共和国不可分割的一部分"的事实立场，改译后避免了issue一词带来的不恰当内涵。同理，"涉藏问题"也不能译为Tibet Issue或Tibet-related Issue，而应译为Tibet question或Tibet-related question。

近来，关于我国与邻国存在领土争议的诸如"钓鱼岛""南沙群岛""西沙群岛""黄岩岛"等岛屿问题的新闻报道频频见诸报端。对于这些岛屿的翻译，外交新闻译者一定要明确我国政府维护国家主权的立场，在翻译中使用我国对这些岛屿的称谓。例如上述岛屿应依次译为the Diaoyu Islands，the Nansha Islands，the Xisha Islands，the Huangyan Island，而不是西方或他国使用的the Senkaku Islands，the Spratly Islands，the Parasol Islands，the Panatag Shoal等。

对国际双边或多边关系的表述也是我国外交新闻报道中常见的政治话语。外交新闻译者一定要对不同国家之间的关系有充分的了解和把握，才能避免错译或漏译。例如我国国家主席习近平与美国总统奥巴马在2013年"庄园会晤"、2014年"瀛台夜话"和2015年"白宫秋叙"三次长谈后，将中美关系定位为"相互尊重、合作共赢的中美新型大国关系"，开创了中美关系的新局面。对于"新型大国关系"的翻译，现译为 a new model of major-country relationship，而非 a new model of major power relationship，是因为power有"强权"意味，不符合我国不强权、不称霸，建立和谐外交关系的原则立场，如若译为major power relationship，难免会沦为少数"中国威胁论"鼓吹者的口实。此类的例子并不鲜见。2009年12月，时任中国驻英国大使傅莹应英语联盟之约，做了"更好地了解中国"的演讲，演讲中就提到邓小平阐述我国外交原则的"韬光养晦"（原意为不要试图做超出自己能力的事）一词被西方误译为"咬紧牙关、等待时机"，从而为"中国威胁论"推波助澜的事实。[①]可见，外交新闻译者对我国外交关系、政策和立场的把握，对于在新的时代语境下准确传递中国外交之声、塑造中国外交形象起着关键性的作用。

除了外交用词的准确性之外，外交新闻译者还需掌握外交表态的分寸感。我国国家领导人或外交发言人的表态是外交新闻话语的重要组成部分，在用词上非常讲究轻重缓急，要求译者具有高度的政治敏感性和分寸感，在译语中选择合适的词汇，准确表达原语的感情色彩和程度，如下例所示：

实现核能完全和平利用是全人类的共同愿望。中国<u>一贯主张</u>全面禁止和彻底销毁核武器，<u>坚定奉行</u>自卫防御的核战略，<u>始终恪守</u>在任何时候和任何情况下不首先使用核武器的政策，<u>明确承诺</u>无条件不对无核武器国家和无核武器区使用或威胁使用核武器。中国<u>坚决反对</u>核武器扩散，<u>积极支持</u>加强国际核安全努力，<u>坚定支持</u>各国平等享有和平利用核能权利。（http://paper.people.com.cn/rmrbhwb/html/2010-04/14/content_487638.htm）

[①] 傅莹：《更好地了解中国——在英语联盟的演讲（2009-12-10）》，http://www.fmprc.gov.cn/ce/ceuk/chn/dsjh/t633252.htm

It is the shared aspiration of mankind to see nuclear energy used solely for peaceful purposes. China <u>has consistently stood for</u> the complete prohibition and thorough destruction of nuclear weapons and <u>stayed firmly committed to</u> a nuclear strategy of self-defense. We <u>have adhered to</u> the policy of no-first-use of nuclear weapons at any time and under any circumstance, and <u>made the unequivocal commitment</u> that we will unconditionally not use or threaten to use nuclear weapons against non-nuclear-weapon states or nuclear-weapon-free zones. We <u>firmly oppose</u> nuclear weapons proliferation, and <u>strongly support</u> efforts to enhance international nuclear security and the equal right of all countries to the peaceful use of nuclear energy.

外交新闻译者的政治素养还应当包括与时俱进的"动态忠实观"的建立。所谓"动态忠实观",是指外交新闻译者要时时把握我国外交动态和国际关系的发展变化,以及相应的外交用词的更新变化,在把握外交翻译以"忠实"为最高原则的基础上,做到与时俱进,避免延用时过境迁的政治语汇而造成的不必要的误解,甚至矛盾冲突。例如我国近年来不断推出的外交新词"一带一路""互联互通""中国梦""中华民族伟大复兴"等的英文表达,随着我国外交思想的不断对外宣传,其内涵也在不断丰富和成熟,由最初的多种译法并举发展到后来的统一规范化,如"一带一路"的翻译,就曾经有过"One Belt, One Road"、"One Belt & One Road"、"Belt and Road"等多种表达,2015年,国家发改委会同外交部和商务部等相关部门,将"一带一路"译法统一为the Belt and Road,英文缩写为B&R(金勇、崔玉娇,2015:53)。我国曾提出"和平崛起"的理念,译为peaceful rise,后调整为"和平发展",译为peaceful development,原因在于peaceful rise一词容易被一些"中国威胁论"者曲解和借题发挥。由此可见,译者一定要不断跟进国内外相关表述的变化,与时俱进地采用最为恰切的表达进行翻译,才能准确传递信息,同时影响和引导外媒的相关表述,避免被曲解,甚至恶意利用。再例如现有一些国名、地名、机构和组织名,随着这些国家政治的变迁或组织机构的发展而发生变化,在翻译时也要谨而慎之。我国以往将"缅甸"译为Burma,现译为Myanmar,因为Burma是英国对缅甸实行殖民统治时的旧称,1989年缅甸政府开始启用Myanmar一词对外宣示主权,以示与英国殖民统治的决裂;乌克兰在苏联解体前译为the Ukraine,苏联解体后成为独立国家,译为Ukraine,虽然看似只有一个定冠词之差,但事关一个国家的主权问题,即使一个定冠词也不可轻视;"金砖四国"旧译为BRICs,现译为BRICS,原因是南非共和国的加入使"金砖四国"变成了"金砖五国",旧译中小写的s变为新译中大写的S,是南非共和国英译名的首字母。这样的例子还有很多,足以表明外交新闻译员树立与时俱进的"动态忠实观"的重要性。

(三)信息素养

据美国图书馆协会的定义,信息素养"是人能够判断确定何时需要信息,并且能够对信息进行检索、评价和有效利用的能力"。随着翻译所涉领域的日渐广泛，信息素养已经成为翻译工作者必备的一项基本素养和能力，特别是在信息化程度高度发展的当今社会，翻译工作者在不同专业领域的翻译活动中，时刻需要检索、加工和利用相关信息以确保翻译质量，对于外交新闻译者而言，同样需要具备一定的信息素养，才能高效应对外交新闻翻译过程中随处可见的人名、地名、组织机构名、报纸杂志媒体名、法律法规文件名以及各类外交术语和专有名词。这类词一般来说都具有约定俗成或已被规范化的译名，不需要也不能够随便翻译，而是有待查询其官方的、权威的专业译名，才能避免出现谬误。《中国译典》总编奚德通认为，"好翻译是查出来的，而不是翻出来的。要成为翻译高手，你得首先成为一个查询高手。"[①]这句话对于一般翻译而言可能有些言过其实，但是对于需要应对各类专业名词和术语的外交新闻译者而言，绝非夸张。

目前我国已经编纂出版了一批专业用语词典和工具书，其中收集了大量已经被官方统一规范化了的固定译法，例如新华社译名室编的《世界人名翻译大辞典》、中国地名委员会编的《外国地名译名手册》、外交部组织编写的《汉英外交政治词汇》、中国对外翻译出版公司出版的《各国国家机构手册》、商务印书馆出版的《世界报刊、通讯社、电台译名手册》、外语教学与研究出版社出版的《英汉美英报刊词典》等，还有《中国新闻年鉴》《世界知识年鉴》等各类年鉴，以及《中国大百科全书（新闻出版卷）》《不列颠百科全书》《中国军事百科全书》《汉英外事实用词典》《辞海》等各类辞典。这类工具书虽然极大地方便了外交新闻译者的日常查询工作，提高了译文的准确度，但同时也具有纸媒载体的弊端，即信息更新慢，知识易过时。国际外交风云变幻莫测，外交新闻中几乎每天都会涌现出一批新名词、新表达，纸媒工具书对于以动态性和时效性著称的新闻翻译而言，显然有力不从心之处。因此，外交新闻译者更多地需要借助网络进行查询和翻译，这就需要外交新闻译者具有良好的信息素养，能够通过网络技术准确、高效地搜索、筛选、确定、检验相关表达的译法并加以利用。百度、必应、维基百科等都可以成为外交新闻译者的常用网络检索平台。然而，网络媒介虽然信息发布迅捷、集中、更新快，但是译名较为混乱，缺乏规范，需要译者将若干条译名进行反复检验和确认后才能启用，这无疑增加了译者的负担，对于准确性要求极高的外交新闻译者而言，更是苦不堪言。借助各种网络信息技术，自信应对网络时代信息爆炸带来的困扰，取其利而避其害，准确高效地完成翻译工作，是外交新闻译者必备的信息素养。

参考文献：

Bielsa, Esperanca & Susan Bassnett. *Translation in Global News*. London and New York: Routledge, 2009.

Yang Mingxing. The Principles and Tactics on Diplomatic Translation: A Chinese Perspective. *Babel, International Journal of Translation*, 2012(1).

---

① 奚德通：《好翻译是"查"出来的》，http://www.chinafanyi.com/bbsv1/read.asp?id=1306

陈锡喜:《平易近人——习近平的语言力量》,上海:上海交通大学出版社,2014年。
程镇球:《政治文章的翻译要讲政治》,《中国翻译》2003年第3期。
过家鼎:《注意外交用词的政治含义》,《中国翻译》2002年第6期。
何群、李春怡:《外交口译》,北京:外语教学与研究出版社,2011年。
黄友义:《坚持"外宣三贴近"原则,处理好外宣翻译中的难点问题》,《中国翻译》2004年第6期。
金桂华:《杂谈外交语言》,《外交学院学报》2003年第1期。
金勇、崔玉娇:《国际新闻翻译中的译名偏误现象及对策》,《现代传播》2015年第12期。
刘其中:《英汉新闻翻译》,北京:清华大学出版社,2009年。
施燕华:《外交翻译60年》,《中国翻译》2009年第5期。
王平兴:《"政治等效"翻译:臆想还是现实?》,《中国翻译》2016年第1期。
徐明强:《外宣翻译的苦恼》,《中国翻译》2014年第3期。
徐亚男:《外交翻译的特点以及对外交翻译的要求》,《中国翻译》2000年第3期。
熊兵:《翻译研究中的概念混淆——以"翻译策略"、"翻译方法"和"翻译技巧"为例》,《中国翻译》2014年第3期。
严文斌:《"趣"说政治话语对外传播》,《中国翻译》2015年第5期。
杨明星:《论外交语言翻译的"政治等效"——以邓小平外交理念"韬光养晦"的译法为例》,《解放军外国语学院学报》2008年第5期。
杨明星、闫达:《"政治等效"理论框架下外交语言的翻译策略——以"不折腾"的译法为例》,《解放军外国语学院学报》2012年第3期。
杨明星:《中国外交新词对外翻译的原则与策略》,《中国翻译》2014年第3期。
杨明星、李志丹:《"政治等效"视野下"窜访"译法探究》,《中国翻译》2015年第5期。
张健:《外宣翻译导论》,北京:国防工业出版社,2013年。
张美芳:《翻译中的超文本成分:以新闻翻译为例》,《中国翻译》2011年第2期。
朱天文:《美国新闻期刊中汉英翻译采用的策略和方法》,《上海科技翻译》2003年第3期。

新闻报道中外交理念的翻译
Translation for Diplomatic Concepts in News Coverage

单元简介 Introduction

外交理念是指有关一国外交的基本观念和指导思想。党的十八大以来，党中央大力推进外交理论实践创新，相继提出中国梦、坚持贯彻正确义利观、构建中美新型大国关系、"亲诚惠容"周边外交、"一带一路"、亚投行、亚洲新安全观等新的外交理念。合作共赢、打造"命运共同体"成为外交主旋律。中国外交已经显示出在全球进行战略布局和运筹的意识和能力，外交布局更加自主、更加灵活、也更加稳健。

外交理念贯穿于外交会晤、国际会议、外交访谈、记者发布会、外交声明等各种相关新闻报道中。只有透彻理解这些外交理念，才能对这些不断出现的新术语做出正确的翻译与阐释。本章重点聚焦这些外交理念的意义、内涵及其翻译。

新闻报道中外交理念翻译范例分析
Sample of Translation for Diplomatic Concepts in News Coverage

范例一（Sample I）

2015，中国特色大国外交的全面推进之年（节本）
2015/12/12

2015: A Year of Flying Colors for Pursuing Major-Country Diplomacy with Distinctive Chinese Features (Abbreviated Version)
2015/12/12

2015年，我们在以习近平同志为总书记的党中央坚强领导下大力推进"四个全面"的战略部署，顺利通过"十三五"规划建议，奏响了到2020年全面建成小康社会、实现第一个百年奋斗目标的嘹亮号角。

In 2015, under the leadership of the CPC Central Committee with Comrade Xi Jinping as the General Secretary, we worked hard to implement the Four-Pronged Comprehensive Strategy and adopted a proposal on China's 13th Five-Year development plan; and we are endeavoring to achieve the first centenary goal, i.e. to finish the building of a moderately prosperous society in China by 2020.

***

飞速发展的外交实践不断刷新着中国外交的思路和理念。继去年中央外事工作会议提出构建以合作共赢为核心的新型国际关系这一中国外交的努力目标之后，中国又推出了打造"人类命运共同体"的重大理念。从亚洲博鳌论坛到联合国系列峰会，习近平主席以人类命运共同体为主题发表重要演讲，全面系统阐述这一重大主张，倡导建立平等相待、互商互谅的伙伴关系；营造公道正义、共建共享的安全格局；谋求开放创新、包容互惠的发展前景；促进和而不同、兼收并蓄的文明交流；构筑尊崇自然、绿色发展的生态体系，形成了打造人类命运共同体"五位一体"的总路径和总布局。

China's fast-paced diplomatic practices have created a new vision for China's diplomacy. At last year's Central Conference on Work Relating to Foreign Affairs, the building of a new type of international relations featuring win-win cooperation was set as the goal of China's diplomacy. This year, China put forward a new vision of building a community of shared future for mankind. In his important addresses made at the annual meeting of Boao Forum for Asia and the summits at the United Nations, President Xi Jinping elaborated on what this vision is about. The following is what President Xi envisions: partnerships based on equality, consultation, mutual understanding and accommodation; a security architecture featuring fairness, justice, joint contribution and shared benefits; open, innovative and inclusive development that benefits all; inter-civilization exchanges that promote harmony and inclusiveness and respect differences; and an ecosystem that puts Mother Nature and green development first. Together, these five elements constitute a broad vision for building a community of shared future for mankind.

***

我们将以推进"一带一路"建设为主线，突出互联互通与产能合作两大重点，推动中国与世界各国发展战略继续深入对接。我们将与沿线各国加强探讨与协作，实现"一带一路"建设更多早期收获，打造亚投行、丝路基金和产能合作标志性项目，推动达成新的自贸协定和现有自贸协定升级，在互利共赢基础上为国内经济发展拓宽国际市场，增添外部动力。

We will give priority to pursuing the Belt and Road Initiative, focus on connectivity and production capacity cooperation, and achieve synergy between the development strategies of China and other countries concerned. We will strengthen discussion and coordination with countries along the Belt and Road and make the Belt and Road Initiative deliver more early outcomes. Flagship projects will be launched by the AIIB and the Silk Road Fund in production capacity cooperation. We will work to conclude new free trade agreements and upgrade the existing ones, and on the basis of achieving win-win outcomes, expand the international market and increase external driving force for promoting economic growth at home.

新闻背景：2015年12月12日，由中国国际问题研究院和中国国际问题研究基金会联合主办的"2015年国际形势与中国外交研讨会"在北京开幕。近200名与会者来自全国各地和各有关部委的35个学术研究机构、20多家中央及地方媒体等单位。研讨会的主题为"国际秩序演变与中国特色大国外交"，围绕七个议题展开讨论：国际格局与大国关系；国际安全与地区热点；世界经济格局演变；中国周边形势发展变化；中国对发展中国家外交；中国外交年度回顾及展望；"一带一路"倡议的进展及问题等。外交部长王毅出席开幕式并发表了题为《2015年，中国特色大国外交的全面推进之年》的重要演讲。

原文链接：http://www.fmprc.gov.cn/web/wjbz_673089/zyjh_673099/t1323795.shtml

译文链接：http://www.fmprc.gov.cn/mfa_eng/zxxx_662805/t1329609.shtml

新闻报道中外交理念的翻译
Translation for Diplomatic Concepts in News Coverage

一、范例一文本结构分析（Text Structure Analysis of Sample I）

范例一节选自一篇有关王毅部长发表演讲的新闻稿。原新闻稿的第一自然段为导语，介绍了时间（2015年12月12日）、人物（外交部长王毅）、事件（出席国际形势与中国外交研讨会开幕式并发表演讲）以及相关背景（研讨会由中国国际问题研究院、中国国际问题研究基金会主办）。从第二自然段开始为正文，即演讲全文，王毅总结了中国2015年在外交方面取得的重大成果和进展，并表示2016年是"十三五"规划的开局之年，中国外交将认真践行中国特色大国外交理念，积极承担中国应当肩负的国际责任，为全面建成小康社会营造更良好的外部环境，为世界和平与发展事业续写新的篇章。

二、范例一翻译解析（Translation Analysis of Sample I）

由于是年度盘点，王毅部长在演讲中提纲挈领，高度概括，总结了2015年中国外交的丰硕成果，并阐明了2016年中国特色大国外交的新理念。有关中国特色大国外交的相关概念及其翻译的讨论汇编整理如下：

（一）新型大国关系（A New Model of Major-country Relationship）

"新型大国关系"是近年来在新的形势下中国提出的一个概念。2013年6月7日，国家主席习近平在美国加利福尼亚州安纳伯格庄园同美国总统奥巴马举行中美元首会晤。在"庄园会晤"中双方确认共同构建新型大国关系，并明晰了其内涵，勾画了其路径。习近平对中美新型大国关系的内涵做了精辟概括：不冲突、不对抗（no conflict or confrontation）；相互尊重（mutual respect）；合作共赢（win-win cooperation）。①

对于新型大国关系，西方媒体比较常见的译法是a new type of major power relationship，而我国外交部则使用了创新的译法a new model of major-country relationship，准确地传递了中国特色大国关系理念的内涵。（杨明星、李志丹，2015：91）按照《美国传统词典（第4版）》，power是指a person, group, or nation having great influence or control over others，带有明显的霸权概念，而我们所说的"大国"只是从人口或面积方面来说规模较大。中国一贯主张国家不分大小、强弱、贫富，一律平等，反对各种形式的霸权主义和强权政治。（王平兴，2014：100）中国追求和平共处、合作共赢，major power的概念不符合中国的发展理念，所以中国在相关语境中都坚持使用country这个中性词，如：传统大国（traditional major country）、贸易大国（major trade country）、负责任的发展中大国（responsible major developing country）等。（杨明星，2015：101—105）这一译法逐渐得到西方媒体的认可，并于2013年12月5日正式出现在美国政府官方文件*US Fact Sheet on Strengthening US-China Economic Relations*（《美国关于加强美中经济关系的简报》）中。以下实例摘自外交部相关报道：

---

① 《中美元首明晰新型大国关系内涵及构建路径》，http://news.xinhuanet.com/2013-06/09/c_116107044.htm

在中国特色大国外交的指引下，中国将构建长期健康稳定发展的新型大国关系，推进周边命运共同体建设，加强同发展中国家团结合作，推动国际体系和国际秩序向着更加公正、合理的方向发展。

(http://www.fmprc.gov.cn/ce/cebe/chn/stxw/t1251302.htm)

Guided by the concept of major-country diplomacy with Chinese characteristics, we will work to build a sound and stable framework for major-country relations, create a community of common future with our neighbors, strengthen unity and cooperation with other developing countries, and strive to make both the international system and the international order more just and equitable.

(http://www.fmprc.gov.cn/mfa_eng/wjb_663304/zwjg_665342/zwbd_665378/t1251298.shtml)

落实两国元首会晤成果、推进中美新型大国关系建设，对两国乃至世界都至关重要。双方同意深化务实合作，妥善管控分歧，将不冲突不对抗、相互尊重、合作共赢的精神体现到各自的政策和行动中。

(http://www.fmprc.gov.cn/ce/cohk/chn/xwdt/wsyw/t1058688.htm)

Implementing the outcomes of the Presidents' meeting and promoting the building of a new model of major-country relationship between China and the United States are critically important for both countries and the world as a whole. The two sides agreed to deepen practical cooperation, to well manage differences, to embody the spirit of non-conflict, non-confrontation, mutual respect, and win-win cooperation in their policies and actions.

(http://www.fmprc.gov.cn/mfa_eng/zxxx_662805/t1061828.shtml)

（二）"一带一路"倡议（The Belt and Road Initiative）

"一带一路"分别是指"丝绸之路经济带"（the Silk Road Economic Belt）和"21世纪海上丝绸之路"（the 21st-Century Maritime Silk Road）。2013年9月和10月，国家主席习近平在出访中亚和东南亚国家期间，先后提出了共建"丝绸之路经济带"和"21世纪海上丝绸之路"的重大倡议，得到国际社会的高度关注。[①]

"一带一路"被提出时，各英文媒体的译法基本都是"One Belt, One Road"（缩写为OBOR），或者在中间加上and一词。比如"一带一路"门户网的首页标识语为："一带一路"对时代负责 One Belt and One Road, Responsible for Times。[②]2015年5月19日，全国人大外事委员会主任委员傅莹应邀出席美国芝加哥大学首届美中关系论坛框架下的学生公开论坛并发表演讲时，将"一带一路"的英文处理为the land and maritime Silk Road

---

[①]《授权发布：推动共建丝绸之路经济带和21世纪海上丝绸之路的愿景与行动》，http://news.xinhuanet.com/2015-03/28/c_1114793986.htm

[②] http://www.edailu.cn

programs,① 用"丝绸之路"这一具象化了的文化交流符号帮助外国人理解"一带一路"的核心概念,得到了译界赞赏,并引发了翻译"写实"与"写意"的学术探讨。②

2015年9月23日,国家发改委会同外交部、商务部等部门对"一带一路"英文译法进行了规范,要求在对外公文中统一将"一带一路"的简称译为the Belt and Road,英文缩写用B&R。"倡议"一词译为initiative,且使用单数,不使用strategy, project, program, agenda等措辞。③下面即是一则规范的翻译实例:

>"一带一路"是促进共同发展、实现共同繁荣的合作共赢之路,是增进理解信任、加强全方位交流的和平友谊之路。中国政府倡议,秉持和平合作、开放包容、互学互鉴、互利共赢的理念,全方位推进务实合作,打造政治互信、经济融合、文化包容的利益共同体、命运共同体和责任共同体。
>
> (http://news.xinhuanet.com/2015-03-28/c_1114793986.htm)
>
> The Belt and Road Initiative is a way for win-win cooperation that promotes common development and prosperity as well as a road towards peace and friendship by enhancing mutual understanding and trust and strengthening all-round exchanges. The Chinese government advocates peace and cooperation, openness and inclusiveness, mutual learning and mutual benefit. It promotes practical cooperation in all fields, and works to build a community of shared interests, future and responsibility featuring mutual political trust, economic integration and cultural inclusiveness.
>
> (http://en.ndrc.gov.cn/newsrelease/201503/t20150330_669367.html)

上面的实例中已经提到了与"一带一路"紧密关联的另一个概念,即"互联互通"(connectivity)。关于"互联互通"的内涵和意义,习近平主席在2014年11月8日"加强互联互通伙伴关系"东道主伙伴对话会的讲话中做了明确阐释:

> 今天,我们要建设的互联互通,不仅是修路架桥,不光是平面化和单线条的联通,而更应该是基础设施、制度规章、人员交流三位一体,应该是政策沟通、设施联通、贸易畅通、资金融通、民心相通五大领域齐头并进。这是全方位、立体化、网络状的大联通,是生机勃勃、群策群力的开放系统。
>
> (http://news.xinhuanet.com/2014-11/08/c_127192119.htm)
>
> The connectivity we talk about today is not merely about building roads and

---

① 傅莹芝加哥大学演讲全文:《中国的成长与"秩序之争论"》,http://www.guancha.cn/fuying/2015_05_21_320437_3.shtml
② 【双语趣】《"一带一路"翻译:写实党VS写意党》,http://mp.weixin.qq.com/s?__biz=MjM5ODYzNzAyMQ==&mid=206561784&idx=1&sn=13957f2d955f7ebad22f1c1326c0512b&scene=2&from=timeline&isappinstalled=0#rd
③ 《我委等有关部门规范"一带一路"倡议英文译法》,http://www.sdpc.gov.cn/gzdt/201509/t20150921_751695.html

bridges or making linear connection of different places on surface. More importantly, it should be a three-way combination of infrastructure, institutions and people-to-people exchanges and a five-way progress in policy communication, infrastructure connectivity, trade link, capital flow, and understanding among peoples. It is a wide-ranging, multi-dimensional, vibrant and open connectivity network that pools talent and resources from all stakeholders.

(http://www.fmprc.gov.cn/mfa_eng/topics_665678/ytjhzzdrsrcldrfzshyjxghd/t1210466.shtml)

"一带一路"和互联互通是相融相近、相辅相成的。如果将"一带一路"比喻为亚洲腾飞的两只翅膀，那么互联互通就是两只翅膀的血脉经络。

(http://news.xinhuanet.com/2014-11/08/c_127192119.htm)

The Belt and Road Initiative and the connectivity endeavor are compatible and mutually reinforcing. If the Belt and Road are likened to the two wings of a soaring Asia, then connectivity is like their arteries and veins.

(http://www.fmprc.gov.cn/mfa_eng/topics_665678/ytjhzzdrsrcldrfzshyjxghd/t1210466.shtml)

（三）命运共同体（The Community of Shared Future）

习近平就任总书记后首次会见外国人士就表示，国际社会日益成为一个你中有我、我中有你的"命运共同体"，面对世界经济的复杂形势和全球性问题，任何国家都不可能独善其身。（王伟光，2015：20—23）2012年中共十八大明确提出，"要倡导人类命运共同体意识"。[①]"命运共同体"的理念，系统阐释了中国坚持和平发展的决心，明确了中国的作用、角色和道路，有助于实现亚洲乃至世界的和平发展、合作共赢。[②]"命运共同体"的译文常见的有community of shared future，community of common future等。

习近平在2015年博鳌论坛开幕式上发表主旨演讲时提出了迈向命运共同体的"四个坚持"：坚持各国相互尊重、平等相待，坚持合作共赢、共同发展，坚持实现共同、综合、合作、可持续的安全，坚持不同文明兼容并蓄、交流互鉴。（All countries should steadfastly respect one another and treat each other as equals, pursue win-win cooperation and common development, achieve common, comprehensive, cooperative, and sustainable security, and interact with and learn from each other in a spirit of inclusiveness.）尤其是谈到"合作共赢、共同发展"时还引用了世界其他地方的谚语，来阐释合作的必要性。原文及译文如下：

---

① 《中共首提"人类命运共同体"倡导和平发展共同发展》，http://cpc.people.com.cn/18/n/2012/1111/c350825-19539441.html
② 《学习习近平外交理念 理解十大"关键词"》，http://news.xinhuanet.com/politics/2015-08/12/c_128119843.htm

东南亚朋友讲"水涨荷花高",非洲朋友讲"独行快,众行远",欧洲朋友讲"一棵树挡不住寒风",中国人讲"大河有水小河满,小河有水大河满"。这些说的都是一个道理,只有合作共赢才能办大事、办好事、办长久之事。

(http://news.xinhuanet.com/politics/2015-03-29/c_127632707.htm)

Our friends in Southeast Asia say that the lotus flowers grow taller as the water rises. Our friends in Africa say that if you want to go fast, walk alone; and if you want to go far, walk together. Our friends in Europe say that a single tree cannot block the chilly wind. And Chinese people say that when big rivers have water, the small ones are filled; and when small rivers have water, the big ones are filled. All these sayings speak to one same truth, that is, only through win-win cooperation can we make big and sustainable achievements that are beneficial to all.

(http://english.boaoforum.org/hynew/19353.jhtml)

(四)"四个全面"战略布局(The "Four Comprehensives")

"四个全面"战略布局是党中央治国理政的总方略,并非外交理念,但在外交新闻报道中也会频繁提及,因而在此一并讨论。它与全方位大外交之间,是国内工作大局与国际工作大局的关系,二者密切互动、相互作用、相互促进,必须统筹兼顾、协调推进。它是实现"两个一百年"奋斗目标、走向中华民族伟大复兴中国梦的"路线图"。①

关于"四个全面"的翻译,主流媒体和各方专家都在进行热烈的讨论。2015年2月25日,新华社将其直译为Four Comprehensives,②西方媒体包括BBC、路透社、华尔街日报、法新社等均采纳了这一译文。但是形容词comprehensive本身应该是不具有复数形式的,而且这个词本身并没有明确所指,容易让西方读者不知所云。所以BBC的报道通过增加上下文的办法做了弥补:Mr. Xi's strategic blueprint, launched on Wednesday, was distilled into slogans known as the "four comprehensives".③

2015年两会之后出版的《政府工作报告》官方英文版则提出一个新的译法:Four-Pronged Comprehensive Strategy。④该译文的亮点主要在于prong一词的引入。查《柯林斯高阶英语词典》可知,prong的一个解释为The prongs of something such as a policy or plan are the separate parts of it。显然,这正是"四个全面"需要表达的含义。但是,由于"全面"一词位置的移动,使得译文回译后就成了"一项包含四个方面的全面战略",这与原文"'四个全面'战略布局"之间存在明显差异,违背了"以源语文本为准绳"的外

---

① 《全面建成小康社会是实现中国梦的关键一步——论学习贯彻习近平总书记关于"四个全面"的战略布局》,http://www.qstheory.cn/dukan/qs/2015-04/30/c_1115099493.htm

② *China Voice: Xi's "Four Comprehensives" a strategic blueprint for China*, http://news.xinhuanet.com/english/china/2015-02/25/c_127517905.htm

③ *China media back Xi's 'prosperous society' dream*, http://www.bbc.com/news/world-asia-china-31636045

④ *Full Text: Report on the Work of the Government*, http://news.xinhuanet.com/english/china/2015-03/16/c_134071473_2.htm

宣翻译原则。（李奉栖，2016：83）

　　黄长奇则根据英语提取首字母构成缩略语的组词规律，提出了她个人尝试性的译法：the 4Cs Strategic Blueprint。该译法的亮点在于添加Strategic Blueprint，清楚地表明了核心概念内涵，克服了中国特色时政词汇译文中容易出现的概念含糊、逻辑缺失的问题，传播效果有所提升。（黄长奇，2015：110）但是，英语中类似的构词法多见于不同单词并列的情况，如"4P营销理论"指的是product, price, promotion, place四个单词，而本例中四个C指的都是同一个单词comprehensive，缩写为4Cs是否符合英语惯例有待考证。

　　至于"四个全面"的具体内容，也就是"全面建成小康社会、全面深化改革、全面依法治国、全面从严治党"，翻译时根据上下文的不同，可以有语法上的变通，采用谓语动词、动词不定式、动名词、名词词组等不同形式。如新华社的译法为：comprehensively build a moderately prosperous society, comprehensively deepen reform, comprehensively implement the rule of law, and comprehensively strengthen Party discipline.① 中国日报网的译法为：comprehensively building a moderately prosperous society, comprehensively driving reform to a deeper level, comprehensively governing the country in accordance with the law, and comprehensively enforcing strict Party discipline.② 黄长奇建议的译法为：comprehensive development of a moderately prosperous society, comprehensive deepening of reforms, comprehensive implementation of the rule of law, and comprehensive enforcement of Party discipline.（黄长奇，2015：111）

范例二（Sample II）

积极树立亚洲安全观　共创安全合作新局面（节本）
New Asian Security Concept for New Progress in Security Cooperation (Abbreviated Version)

　　我们认为，应该积极倡导共同、综合、合作、可持续的亚洲安全观，创新安全理念，搭建地区安全和合作新架构，努力走出一条共建、共享、共赢的亚洲安全之路。

We believe that it is necessary to advocate common, comprehensive, cooperative and sustainable security in Asia. We need to innovate our security concept, establish a new regional security cooperation architecture, and jointly build a road for security of Asia that is shared by and win-win to all.

***

---

① *China Voice: Xi's "Four Comprehensives" a strategic blueprint for China*, http://news.xinhuanet.com/english/china/2015-02/25/c_127517905.htm

② *Dictionary of Xi Jinping's new terms*, http://usa.chinadaily.com.cn/china/2015-12/30/content_22867432.htm

中国始终是维护地区和世界和平、促进共同发展的坚定力量。中国同印度、缅甸共同倡导的和平共处五项原则，日益成为指导国家间关系的基本准则。中国一贯致力于通过和平方式处理同有关国家的领土主权和海洋权益争端，已经通过友好协商同14个邻国中的12个国家彻底解决了陆地边界问题。中国积极参与地区安全合作，同有关国家发起成立上海合作组织，倡导互信、互利、平等、协作的新安全观，支持东盟、南盟、阿盟等在地区事务中发挥积极作用。

China is a staunch force in upholding peace in the region and the world at large, and for promoting common development. The Five Principles of Peaceful Co-existence, which China initiated together with India and Myanmar, have become a basic norm governing state-to-state relations. China stays committed to seeking peaceful settlement of disputes with other countries over territorial sovereignty and maritime rights and interests. China has completely resolved, through friendly consultation, issues of land boundary with 12 out of its 14 neighboring countries. Being an active participant in regional security cooperation, China initiated, jointly with other relevant countries, the Shanghai Cooperation Organization. China advocates a new security concept featuring mutual trust, mutual benefit, equality and coordination. China supports the Association of Southeast Asian Nations (ASEAN), the South Asian Association for Regional Cooperation (SAARC), and the League of Arab States (LAS) in playing a positive role in regional affairs.

***

"亲望亲好，邻望邻好。"中国坚持与邻为善、以邻为伴，坚持睦邻、安邻、富邻，践行亲、诚、惠、容理念，努力使自身发展更好惠及亚洲国家。中国将同各国一道，加快推进丝绸之路经济带和21世纪海上丝绸之路建设，尽早启动亚洲基础设施投资银行，更加深入参与区域合作进程，推动亚洲发展和安全相互促进、相得益彰。

"Neighbors wish each other well, just like family members do to each other." China always pursues friendship and partnership with its neighbors, and seeks to bring amity, security and common prosperity to its neighborhood. It practices the principles of amity, sincerity, mutual benefit and inclusiveness and works hard to make its development bring more benefits to countries in Asia. China will work with other countries to speed up the development of the Silk Road Economic Belt and the 21st-Century Maritime Silk Road, and hopes that the Asian Infrastructure Investment Bank could be launched at an early date. China will get more deeply involved in the regional cooperation process, and play its due part to ensure that development and security in Asia facilitate each other and are mutually reinforcing.

***

中国人民正在努力实现中华民族伟大复兴的中国梦，同时愿意支持和帮助亚洲各国人民实现各自的美好梦想，同各方一道努力实现持久和平、共同发展的亚洲梦，为促进人类和平与发展的崇高事业作出新的更大的贡献！

The Chinese people, in their pursuit of the Chinese Dream of great national renewal, stand ready to support and help other peoples in Asia to realize their own great dreams. Let us work together for realizing the Asian dream of lasting peace and common development, and make greater contributions to advancing the noble cause of peace and development of mankind.

> 新闻背景：亚洲相互协作与信任措施会议（简称亚信会议）是一个有关安全问题的多边论坛，其宗旨在于通过制定多边信任措施，加强对话与合作，促进亚洲和平、安全与稳定。第四次峰会于2014年5月20日至21日在上海世博中心举行，国家主席习近平主持并作主旨讲话。在该讲话中，习近平主席明确提出了"共同、综合、合作、可持续"的新亚洲安全观。
> 原文链接：http://www.cica-china.org/chn/zyhyhwj/yxhy/t1158413.htm
> 译文链接：http://www.fmprc.gov.cn/mfa_eng/zxxx_662805/t1159951.shtml

一、范例二文本结构分析（Text Structure Analysis of Sample II）

范例二节选自有关习近平主席在亚信会议第四次峰会上发表主旨演讲的新闻报道。报道首先用了一句话作为导语，介绍了时间（2014年5月21日下午）、地点（上海）和事件（习近平主席在亚信峰会第一阶段会议上作主旨讲话）。然后全文转发了习近平主席的讲话。首先，习近平指出亚洲和平发展同人类前途命运息息相关，和平、发展、合作、共赢始终是亚洲地区形势主流，并明确提出建立"共同、综合、合作、可持续"的亚洲新安全观。然后，习近平代表中方提出建议，加强亚信能力和机制建设，深化各领域交流合作，增强亚信的包容性和开放性，推动亚信成为覆盖全亚洲的安全对话合作平台，并在此基础上探讨建立地区安全合作新架构。最后，习近平强调了中国坚定不移地走和平发展道路，始终维护地区与世界和平的立场。

二、范例二翻译解析（Translation Analysis of Sample II）

本节将继续聚焦外交理念的翻译。范例二的主题是亚洲新安全观，强调亚洲地区和平与发展，所以本节主要探讨亚洲新安全观以及中国周边外交方面的理念的翻译。

（一）亚洲新安全观（New Asian Security Concept）

近年来亚洲安全不断面临新挑战，中国作为亚洲唯一的联合国安理会常任理事国，有责任就维护亚洲局势发表见解。习近平主席在2014年3月海牙核安全峰会上首次提出"亚洲新安全观"（new Asian security concept），[①]并在同年5月亚信会议第四次峰会的

[①]《亚信峰会推动"亚洲新安全观"》，http://news.xinhuanet.com/comments/2014-05/19/c_1110742904.htm

主旨讲话中，正式将这一理念明确为"共同、综合、合作、可持续"的亚洲安全观。共同，就是要尊重和保障每一个国家的安全（respecting and ensuring the security of each and every country）；综合，就是要统筹维护传统领域和非传统领域安全（upholding security in both traditional and non-traditional fields）；合作，就是要通过对话合作，促进各国和本地区安全（promoting the security of both individual countries and the region as a whole through dialogue and cooperation）；可持续，就是要发展和安全并重以实现持久安全（focusing on both development and security so that security would be durable）。①

习近平指出，要建立亚洲新安全观，应当聚焦发展主题（focus on development），积极改善民生（actively improve people's lives），缩小贫富差距（narrow down the wealth gap），不断夯实安全的根基（cement the foundation of security）。要推动共同发展和区域一体化进程（advance the process of common development and regional integration），努力形成区域经济合作和安全合作良性互动、齐头并进的大好局面（foster sound interactions and synchronized progress of regional economic cooperation and security cooperation）。②

"亚洲新安全观"的英文用词基本已被普遍肯定，但在实际使用中，各个成分之间的顺序可以进行微调。以下实例是在不同场合谈到"亚洲新安全观"时的一些较为规范的表达形式：

中国倡导共同、综合、合作、可持续发展的亚洲安全观，倡导协商对话，而不是武力威胁；开放包容，而不是相互排斥；合作共赢而不是零和博弈，为地区安全合作开辟了广阔前景。

(http://www.fmprc.gov.cn/web/wjbxw_673019/t1379368.shtml)

China calls for an Asian security concept featuring common, comprehensive, cooperative, and sustainable security. It stands for consultation and dialogue, not threat of force; openness and inclusiveness, not mutual exclusion; and win-win cooperation, not zero-sum game. Such a concept opens up broad prospects for regional security cooperation.

(http://www.fmprc.gov.cn/mfa_eng/wjdt_665385/zyjh_665391/t1379376.shtml)

我们积极践行共同、综合、合作、可持续的亚洲安全观，结合地区现实促进非传统安全领域务实合作，推动探讨构建新的地区安全架构。

(http://www.fmprc.gov.cn/web/wjbxw_673019/t1429256.shtml)

We actively practiced the common, comprehensive, cooperative and sustainable security concept for Asia and promoted practical cooperation in non-traditional security fields and discussions on constructing a new regional security framework based on

---

① 《习近平在亚信第四次峰会上主旨讲话（全文）》，http://www.chinanews.com/gn/2014/05-21/6196012.shtml
② 同上。

regional realities.

(http://www.fmprc.gov.cn/mfa_eng/wjdt_665385/zyjh_665391/t1429989.shtml)

（二）"亲、诚、惠、容"周边外交（Neighborhood Diplomacy Featuring Amity, Sincerity, Mutual Benefit and Inclusiveness）

中国海陆总面积达1260多万平方公里，是世界上邻国最多的国家。而周边国家在社会制度、发展程度、宗教、民族、文化等方面存在巨大的差异性和多样性。① 面对这样的周边环境，中国周边外交一直以来的基本方针为"与邻为善，以邻为伴"（pursue friendship and partnership with neighboring countries），"睦邻、安邻、富邻"（foster a harmonious, secure and prosperous neighborhood），突出体现"亲、诚、惠、容"（follow the principles of amity, sincerity, mutual benefit and inclusiveness）。②

"亲、诚、惠、容"虽然形式上只有区区四个字，但恰恰是因为它过于简短，含义高度凝练，在翻译时反而容易出现理解和表达上的差错。中国对非洲的外交政策秉承的也是四字理念——"真、实、亲、诚"（sincerity, real results, affinity and good faith）。③ 其中也有"亲"和"诚"两个字，但官方给出的译文却并不相同。前者用的是amity和sincerity，④ 后者用的却是affinity和good faith。⑤ 反倒是周边外交理念中所提到的"诚"和中非外交理念中所提到的"真"用了同一个英文单词sincerity。可见，内涵意义的准确理解对于翻译至关重要。

下面，我们就"亲、诚、惠、容"的实际内涵进行逐字分析。所谓"亲"，就是坚持睦邻友好，守望相助；讲平等、重感情；常见面、多走动；多做得人心、暖人心的事，增强亲和力、感召力、影响力。Amity一词的英文解释正是peaceful, friendly relations between people or countries。根据语境需要，具体用法可以是amity between the two countries, in amity with等。所谓"诚"，就是要诚心诚意对待周边国家，争取更多朋友和伙伴。此处强调的是sincere的概念，即being genuine, without hypocrisy or pretense，其名词形式用sincerity。所谓"惠"，就是要本着互惠互利的原则同周边国家开展合作，编织更加紧密的共同利益网络。其思想根源发自于"和平共处五项基本原则"，因而继续沿用"和平共处五项基本原则"中的既定译法mutual benefit。根据语法句式的不同，可使用变体mutually beneficial。所谓"容"，就是要倡导包容的思想，强调亚太之大容得下大家共同发展，以更加开放的胸襟和更加积极的态度促进地区合作。Inclusive用来修饰团体或

---

① 《中国周边外交的新局面》，http://policy.csu.edu.cn/NewsDetail.aspx?ID=687"

② 《中国特色周边外交的四字箴言：亲、诚、惠、容》，http://news.xinhuanet.com/world/2013-11/08/c_118063342.htm

③ 《习近平"真、实、亲、诚"四字概括中国对非关系》，http://www.chinanews.com/gn/2013/03-25/4674313.shtml

④ *Toward Win-win Cooperation Through Amity, Sincerity, Mutual Benefit and Inclusiveness*, http://www.fmprc.gov.cn/mfa_eng/zxxx_662805/t1274296.shtml

⑤ *Trustworthy Friends and Sincere Partners Forever*, http://www.fmprc.gov.cn/mfa_eng/wjdt_665385/zyjh_665391/t1027951.shtml

新闻报道中外交理念的翻译
Translation for Diplomatic Concepts in News Coverage

组织时，意为allowing all kinds of people to belong to it, rather than just one kind of person，表达的正是"容"的概念。

以下是有关周边外交理念的一则翻译实例：

习近平强调，中国始终将周边置于外交全局的首要位置，视促进周边和平、稳定、发展为己任。中国坚持与邻为善、以邻为伴，坚持奉行睦邻、安邻、富邻的周边外交政策。

(http://www.xinhuanet.com/politics/2015-11/07/c_1117071632.htm)

Xi Jinping emphasized that China always gives top priority to its relations with the neighboring countries in overall diplomacy and regards the promotion of peace, stability and development of neighboring areas as its own duty. China persists in building a good-neighborly relationship and partnership with its neighbors and adheres to the foreign policy of bringing harmony, security and prosperity to neighbors.

(http://www.fmprc.gov.cn/mfa_eng/topics_665678/xjpdynxjpjxgsfw/t1313709.shtml)

（三）中国梦（Chinese Dream）

"中国梦"是党的十八大召开后习近平总书记提出的重要指导思想和重要执政理念，于2012年11月29日参观"复兴之路"展览时首次提出。[①] 所谓"中国梦"，就是要实现中华民族的伟大复兴，其核心目标可以概括为"两个一百年"的目标，也就是：到2021年中国共产党成立100周年时全面建成小康社会，到2049年中华人民共和国成立100周年时全面实现中华民族的伟大复兴，具体表现是国家富强、民族振兴、人民幸福。[②]

"中国梦"的概念刚刚被提出时，英文究竟该译为China Dream还是Chinese Dream，各大主流媒体的态度并不完全一致。就以2013年为例，采用China Dream的有6月6日BBC网站的文章What does Xi Jinping's China Dream mean?[③] 6月27日中国日报网的文章China Dream concerns the happiness of all Chinese[④]等；采用Chinese Dream的有7月16日CNN网站的文章On China, Episode 10 transcript: The Chinese Dream[⑤]，9月6日中国网的文章What is the Chinese dream?[⑥]等。

学界也对"中国梦"的译文进行了激烈的探讨。（刘润泽、魏向清，2015：99—106；张顺生、葛陈蓉，2015：51—53；邵斌，2014：131）支持译为Chinese Dream的学者认为，按照习近平主席在十二届全国人大一次会议闭幕会上的讲话，"中国梦是民

---

① 《习近平总书记阐释"中国梦"》，http://news.xinhuanet.com/ziliao/2013-05/08/c_124669102.htm
② http://baike.baidu.com/subview/1817221/9342599.htm
③ http://www.bbc.com/news/world-asia-china-22726375
④ http://www.chinadaily.com.cn/opinion/2013-06/27/content_16675573.htm
⑤ http://www.cnn.com/2013/07/16/world/asia/on-china-transcript-chinese-dream/index.html
⑥ http://www.china.org.cn/china/2013-09/06/content_30056525.htm

族的梦，也是每个中国人的梦。""中国梦归根到底是人民的梦，必须紧紧依靠人民来实现，必须不断为人民造福。"①显然，"民族""人民"的概念得到了充分的强调。另外，从语言生成的系统性来看，"美国梦"American Dream早已有之，再加上"英国梦"British Dream、"欧洲梦"European Dream作为参照，那么"中国梦"的英文说法自然应该同样采用形容词作为定语，译为Chinese Dream。（杨全红，2015：92）但是也有学者提出反对意见，认为American Dream译为"美国梦"是长期以来的误译，其正确意思应该是"美国人的梦"，因而不能作为参照。而"中国梦"的内涵是"国家富强、民族振兴、人民幸福"，其中的"国家""民族""人民"都指的是集体，这也符合社会主义制度下个人服从集体的价值观，因而"中国梦"的准确译法只能是China Dream。（李田心，2015：83—85）

目前，外交部采用的译法为the Chinese Dream，前面加定冠词the表示特定概念。例如：

> 我们的奋斗目标是，到2020年国内生产总值和城乡居民人均收入在2010年的基础上翻一番，全面建成小康社会；到本世纪中叶建成富强民主文明和谐的社会主义现代化国家，实现中华民族伟大复兴的中国梦。

(http://news.xinhuanet.com/politics/2013-04/07/c_115296408.htm)

The main goals we set for China are as follows: by 2020, China's GDP and per capita incomes for urban and rural residents will double the 2010 figures, and the building of a moderately prosperous society will be completed in all respects. By the mid-21st century, China will turn into a modern socialist country that is prosperous, strong, democratic, culturally advanced and harmonious; and the Chinese Dream, namely, the great renewal of the Chinese nation, will be realized.

(http://english.boaoforum.org/mtzxxwzxen/7379.jhtml)

在"中国梦"的基础上，习近平主席进一步提出了"亚太梦"的概念并解释了其内涵。其英文表达为the Asia-Pacific dream，注意其中使用名词Asia而非形容词Asian。示例如下：

> 在亚太经合组织领导人非正式会议上，习近平主席首次提出构建亚太梦并系统深入阐述其内涵，指出亚太梦的精神内核是亚太大家庭精神和命运共同体意识，根本目的是实现亚太地区的繁荣发展，引领世界发展的时代潮流，为人类社会的福祉与进步作出更大贡献。

(http://news.xinhuanet.com/politics/2015-01/01/c_1113849784.htm)

---

① 《在第十二届全国人民代表大会第一次会议上的讲话》，http://cpc.people.com.cn/xuexi/n/2015/0717/c397563-27322349.html

新闻报道中外交理念的翻译
Translation for Diplomatic Concepts in News Coverage

President Xi Jinping first called for pursuing the Asia-Pacific dream and elaborated on it during the APEC Economic Leaders' Meeting. He stressed that this dream is about fostering a sense of the Asia-Pacific community and shared future, jointly working for the prosperity and progress of the region, and driving global development and making greater contributions to the well-being of mankind.

(http://news.xinhuanet.com/english/china/2014-12/26/c_133879194_2.htm)

学生译作讲评
Analysis of Students' Translation Practice

原文链接：http://www.fmprc.gov.cn/chn/gxh/tyb///zyxw/t1191912.htm

新闻原文：习近平强调，中国坚持走和平发展道路，奉行亲、诚、惠、容的周边外交理念，与周边国家以心相交、以诚取信，睦邻友好、共同发展。中斯两国是相互信任、相互依靠的朋友和伙伴。两国关系经受住时间和国际风云变幻考验，是大小国家友好相处、互利合作的典范。我们坚定支持斯里兰卡维护独立、主权、领土完整，支持斯里兰卡人民选择适合本国国情的发展道路。

学生译文：Xi Jinping stressed China would stick to the path of peaceful development, uphold the concept of neighborhood diplomacy of "amity, sincerity, mutual benefit and inclusiveness", and communicate and win trust through sincerity with neighboring countries so as to develop good neighborly and friendly relations and promote common development. China and Sri Lanka are friends and partners of mutual trust and interdependence. The bilateral relations, having withstood the test of time and the changing international situation, have become a model of friendly coexistence and mutually beneficial cooperation among all countries, big or small. We firmly support Sri Lanka's efforts to safeguard its independence, sovereignty and territorial integrity and the Sri Lankan people's choice of development path conforming to its national conditions.

翻译评析：学生按照时态配合的原则，在宾语从句中采用了would stick的表达。但是"中国坚持走和平发展道路"的方针并不因为时间的推移而改变，其时态不应受到主句动词stressed时态的影响，这一点在政治文本中尤为重要。紧接着的"以心相交、以诚取信，睦邻友好、共同发展"看似完全并列，实则前两条表示行为，后两条表示目的或结果，学生准确地把握住了这一逻辑关系，在中间添加了so as to。问题出在前两条，汉语的四字并列结构非常具有迷惑性，似乎是完全对仗的，但仔细分析就会发现，"相交"是双向互动的，英语中后面搭配的介词应该是with，而"取信"是单向的，后面搭配的介词应该是from。译文中的win trust与with短语显然是无法搭配的，可将with短语提前，译文调整为communicate with neighboring countries and win trust through sincerity。倒数第二句的"大小国家"学生理解有误，按照现在的译文among all countries, big or small，其意

外交新闻汉英翻译
C-E TRANSLATION OF DIPLOMATIC NEWS

为"中国与斯里兰卡之间的关系成了世界各国关系的典范,无论国家大小",这显然不是原文的本意。原文是说大国与小国之间的相处之道可以借鉴中斯关系,译文可以调整为between large and small countries。

新闻原文:习近平强调,当前,中国人民正在努力实现中华民族伟大复兴的中国梦,斯里兰卡提出了国家振兴发展的"马欣达愿景",双方奋斗目标相互契合。中方愿同斯方一道,抓住机遇,规划合作,推动中斯战略合作伙伴关系走实走深,更好惠及两国人民。双方要保持高层互访,为两国关系发挥引领作用。[1]

学生译文:Xi Jinping stressed that currently the Chinese people are striving to realize the "Chinese Dream" of achieving the great rejuvenation of the Chinese nation, Sri Lanka puts forward the "Mahinda Vision" of national rejuvenation and development, and their objectives are integrated with each other. China is willing to work with Sri Lanka to seize the opportunity, plan the cooperation, and promote the development of the China-Sri Lanka strategic cooperative partnership to be practical and deepened, so as to better benefit the two peoples. Both sides should maintain the high-level exchanges and make it play a leading role in the bilateral relations.

翻译评析:第一句话中有一个时态问题。斯里兰卡提出"马欣达愿景"是已经发生的事情,谓语动词应改为has put forward。"双方奋斗目标相互契合"中的"契合"并不是"融合",而且their一词也欠妥当,写新闻稿的人应该也是"中国人民"的一员才对。该句译文可调整为and the objectives of the two sides correspond with each other。"走实走深"不能翻译为promote ... to be practical and deepened,那样给读者的暗示是以前并不practical,此处应调整为promote the China-Sri Lanka strategic cooperative partnership for solid and in-depth development。最后的"互访"在语义理解上有偏差,应译为mutual visits。

新闻原文:中方愿以建设21世纪海上丝绸之路为契机,同斯方加强在港口建设运营、临港工业园开发建设、海洋经济、海上安全等领域合作,探讨并确定先行先试项目,实现早期收获。希望双方加快推进自由贸易谈判,争取早日建成中斯自由贸易区。

学生译文:China is willing to take the construction of the 21st Century Maritime Silk Road as an opportunity to strengthen cooperation with Sri Lanka in such fields as the port construction and operation, the development and construction of industrial parks near the ports, maritime economy, and maritime security, as well as discuss and decide development-first and pilot-first projects so as to achieve early results. He hoped that both sides will accelerate the free trade talks and strive to get the early completion of the China-Sri Lanka free trade zone.

翻译评析:最后一句"希望"的主语没有明确提出,但此段话整体跟在"习近平强调"的内容后面,所以暗含主语应该是"习近平"。按照外交部的惯例,若汉语原文中

---

[1] 为了便于讨论,收入本书时对原稿中的长段落做了更细的切分。

新闻报道中外交理念的翻译
Translation for Diplomatic Concepts in News Coverage

引用了领导人以第一人称所作的讲话，英译时遵循的原则是：对于中方领导人用I，不做人称转述，对于外方领导人则用he或she。所以此处的正确译文应该是I hope that …。结尾处的get the early completion不够正式，可以调整为complete the construction of … at an early date。

新闻原文：中方鼓励更多中国企业积极参与斯里兰卡工业园、经济特区、基础设施项目建设，欢迎斯方作为创始成员国参与亚洲基础设施投资银行。双方要拓展旅游、文化、教育、宗教等领域交流合作，支持在斯里兰卡开展汉语教学。中方愿同斯方继续加强在联合国等多边框架内沟通协调，共同促进地区和平与发展。

学生译文：China encourages more Chinese enterprises to actively participate in the construction of industrial parks, special economic zones and infrastructure projects of Sri Lanka. China welcomes Sri Lanka to join the Asian Infrastructure Investment Bank as a founding member. The two sides should expand exchanges and cooperation in fields such as tourism, culture, education and religion. China supports to carry out Chinese teaching in Sri Lanka. China is willing to continue to enhance communication and coordination with Sri Lanka within the multilateral framework including the UN so as to jointly promote regional peace and development.

翻译评析：译文倒数第二句存在语法错误，英语中没有support to do的用法，另外，carry out Chinese teaching会有歧义，因为宗教中的教义常常使用teachings一词。该句可调整为China is in support of carrying out the teaching of Chinese in Sri Lanka. 下一句中的"框架"framework为可数名词，应加上s并去掉前面的the。"联合国"最好先写出全称the United Nations，再将简写UN标注在括号内才符合正式文体的要求。因此，最后一句中的相关部分可调整为within multilateral frameworks such as the United Nations (UN)。

新闻原文：拉贾帕克萨表示，斯中友好源远流长，两国关系在相互尊重、相互信任的基础上不断向前发展。斯方感谢中方长期给予的宝贵支持，中国的援助使斯里兰卡人民实实在在受益。斯方高度赞赏中方奉行和平共处五项原则和睦邻友好方针，愿意在此基础上同中方不断发展战略合作伙伴关系，将继续在涉及中国核心利益和重大关切问题上坚定支持中方。

学生译文：Mahinda Rajapaksa said that Sri Lanka and China enjoy a time-honored friendship, and the bilateral relations have developed constantly on the basis of mutual respect and mutual trust. Sri Lanka appreciates China's long-term and precious support, which has given Sri Lankan people tangible benefits. Sri Lanka highly appreciates China's adherence to the Five Principles of Peaceful Coexistence and good-neighborliness policy, based on which Sri Lanka is willing to continually develop the strategic cooperative partnership with China, and will firmly support China on issues concerning China's core interests and major concerns.

翻译评析：最后一句中的"睦邻友好"在译文中，漏掉了"友好"的概念，应当补充friendship，与good-neighborliness通过and并列，将原译文中的and调整为as well as，以使逻辑关系更为清楚，调整后的译文为appreciates China's adherence to the Five Principles of Peaceful Coexistence as well as the good-neighborliness and friendship policy。

新闻原文：习近平主席提出建设21世纪海上丝绸之路的倡议与斯方打造印度洋海上航运中心的设想不谋而合，斯方愿意同中方共同建设和经营好汉班托塔港和科伦坡港口城等重点合作项目，加速双边自由贸易谈判，加强经贸、能源、农业、基础设施建设、卫生医疗等领域合作。

学生译文：President Xi Jinping's initiative of building the 21st Century Maritime Silk Road coincides with Sri Lanka's assumption of building offshore shipping center in the Indian Ocean. Sri Lanka is ready to work together with China in the construction and operation of major cooperation projects such as the Hambantota Port and the Colombo Port City, accelerate bilateral free trade negotiations, and strengthen cooperation in fields including economy and trade, energy, agriculture, infrastructure construction, and health care.

翻译评析："设想"译为assumption并不准确。"设想"在这里是指"斯里兰卡打造海上航运中心的计划和愿景"，应采用vision一词。下一句的结构出了问题，原文中的"与中方共同"应当是统领整个句子的，"加速谈判""加强经贸等领域合作"也都是由双方共同努力的，可是译文中却成了work together与accelerate及strengthen并列，出现了逻辑上的错误。将译文句子的起首部分修改为Sri Lanka is willing to work with China to jointly well construct and operate such major cooperation projects，使得动词不定式to well construct and operate与后文并列即可。

实战练习
Translation Practice

一、请翻译下列句子，注意其中有关外交理念的表达（Translate the following sentences, paying attention to expressions of diplomatic concepts）。

1. 我们要进一步完善全球治理体系，推动建立以合作共赢为核心的新型国际关系，坚持共同、综合、合作、可持续的安全观。

（http://www.fmprc.gov.cn/ce/cehu/chn/zgyw/t1267222.htm）

2. 中国坚持走和平发展道路，始终奉行防御性的国防政策，坚持与邻为善、以邻为伴的周边外交政策，是维护地区和平稳定的坚定力量。

（http://www.fmprc.gov.cn/ce/cehu/chn/zgyw/t1267263.htm）

3. 我们坚持以和平方式通过友好协商解决矛盾分歧，坚持发展和安全并重，共谋互尊互信、聚同化异、开放包容、合作共赢的邻国相处之道。

（http://www.fmprc.gov.cn/ce/cgngy/chn/zgyw/t1312922.htm）

4. 中国倡导"一带一路"建设，坚持共商、共建、共享，将优先推进包括南亚在内的沿线互联互通。中国出资400亿美元成立丝路基金，倡导成立亚洲基础设施投资银行,将为本地区互联互通提供重要助力。

(http://www.fmprc.gov.cn/ce/cemx/chn/xw/t1272748.htm)

5. 中国始终将周边置于外交全局的首要位置,视促进周边和平、稳定、发展为己任。中国推动全球治理体系朝着更加公正合理的方向发展,推动国际关系民主化,推动建立以合作共赢为核心的新型国际关系,推动建设人类命运共同体,都是从周边先行起步。

(http://www.fmprc.gov.cn/ce/cgngy/chn/zgyw/t1312922.htm)

6. 当前,中国人民正按照中国共产党提出的"四个全面"战略布局,齐心协力为实现"两个一百年"奋斗目标和中华民族伟大复兴的中国梦而努力奋斗。

(http://www.fmprc.gov.cn/web/dszlsjt_673036/t1297682.shtml)

二、请翻译下列有关外交理念的新闻段落(Translate the following news excerpt on diplomatic concepts)。

王毅表示,2016年中国外交将在以习近平同志为总书记的党中央领导下,认真践行中国特色大国外交理念,积极承担中国应当肩负的国际责任,为全面建成小康社会营造更良好外部环境,为世界和平与发展事业续写新的篇章。一要全力为国内建设服务。以推进"一带一路"建设为主线,突出互联互通与产能合作两大重点,推动中国与世界各国发展战略继续深入对接。二要力争为全球经济引航。全力办好二十国集团杭州峰会,为构建创新、活力、联动、包容的世界经济作出新贡献。三要尽力为世界和平担当。致力于构建良性互动、合作共赢的大国关系框架,积极参与各类热点问题的政治解决和国际反恐合作,维护国际核不扩散体系,并就构建和平、安全、开放、合作的国际网络空间与各国加强对话与合作。四要积极为地区发展出力。推进亚洲命运共同体建设,维护地区稳定,促进经济发展。五要竭诚为同胞福祉尽责。以对人民群众的高度责任感和对国家民族的强烈使命感,进一步加快推进海外民生工程建设,全力为中国公民及企业在海外的合法利益与生命财产安全保驾护航。

(http://www.fmprc.gov.cn/web/zyxw/t1323794.shtml)

参考译文
Versions for Reference

一、请翻译下列句子,注意其中有关外交理念的表达(Translate the following sentences, paying attention to expressions of diplomatic concepts)。

1. We should further improve the global governance system, promote for establishment of the new type of international relations with cooperation for win-win results at the core, and stick to a common, comprehensive, cooperative and sustainable security concept.

2. China is committed to a path of peaceful development, a defense policy that is defensive in nature and a foreign policy of building friendship and partnership with its neighbors. China is a staunch force for peace and stability in the region.

3. We should stay committed to peaceful settlement of differences and disputes through friendly consultation, and we should give equal emphasis to both development and security. Together, we can achieve open, inclusive and win-win cooperation among neighbors on the basis of mutual respect and mutual trust by expanding common ground and narrowing differences.

4. The Belt and Road Initiative proposed by China will be implemented on the basis of wide consultation, joint contribution and shared benefits. Priority will be given to advancing connectivity along the routes in South Asia and other regions. By establishing a USD 40 billion Silk Road Fund and initiating the Asian Infrastructure Investment Bank, China hopes to generate strong impetus for connectivity in the region.

5. China's neighborhood occupies a top priority on its diplomatic agenda, and China has the unshakable responsibility to ensure peace, stability and development in its neighborhood. China is dedicated to promoting a more just and equitable global governance system, enhancing democracy in international relations as well as the building of a new type of international relations based on win-win cooperation and a community with a shared future for mankind. Efforts to reach this goal should naturally start in its neighborhood.

6. At present, in accordance with the Four Comprehensives put forward by the Communist Party of China, the Chinese people are making concerted efforts to strive for the realization of the Chinese Dream of great rejuvenation of the Chinese nation.

二、请翻译下列有关外交理念的新闻段落（Translate the following news excerpt on diplomatic concepts）。

Wang Yi noted that in 2016, China's diplomacy will, under the leadership of the CPC Central Committee with Comrade Xi Jinping as the General Secretary, earnestly implement the major-country diplomacy with Chinese characteristics and actively shoulder China's due international responsibilities so as to create a better external environment for comprehensively establishing a well-off society and write a new chapter for the peace and development cause of the world. First, spare no effort to serve the domestic construction. We will continuously promote the in-depth docking of the development strategies between China and other countries by focusing on the construction of the Belt and Road and highlighting the two priorities of connectivity and production capacity cooperation. Second, strive to lead the development of global economy. We will make every effort to ensure the success of the G20 Summit in Hangzhou so as to make new contributions to an innovative, energetic, coordinative and inclusive world economy. Third, spare no effort to shoulder the responsibility of safeguarding world peace. We will dedicate to forging a framework of major-country relations featuring sound interaction and win-win cooperation, actively participate in political solution of various hotspot issues and international counter-terrorism cooperation, safeguard the international nuclear non-proliferation system and enhance dialogue and cooperation with all other countries in establishing a peaceful, secure, open and cooperative international network space. Fourth, play an active role in regional development. We will push the construction of the Asian community of shared future, safeguard regional stability and promote economic development. Fifth, take responsibilities sincerely to serve the welfare of the compatriots. We will, with a high sense of duty and a strong sense of mission for the country and people, further accelerate the construction of overseas livelihood projects and do our best to protect the legitimate rights and interests, safety and property of overseas Chinese citizens and enterprises.

单元小结
Summary

本单元主要介绍了近年来我国新闻报道中高频出现的外交理念及其翻译。外交理念是所有外交活动的指导思想和根本原则，贯穿于高层互访、发言人表态、外交文件发布等各类外交活动的新闻报道中。翻译时应当首先检索既有的官方文件，来源渠道包括政府部门官网、官方媒体网站、翻译领域的权威学术期刊等，从汉英两种语言的相关文件阅读中充分理解外交理念的内涵，有既定官方译文的严格遵照既定译文，由于上下文语境的原因需要变通时尽量维持核心词根不变，只调整屈折变化。没有官方译文的要在充分理解原文的基础上仔细斟酌，确保译文不发生歧义，更不能传递出错误的信息。很多外交理念应当视为专有名词，译文中要注意首字母大写。对于新出现的外交理念，不仅要注意学习其相应的英译名，还要注意积累与其相关的背景知识，如此才能在翻译这些外交理念时做到得心应手。

参考文献：

黄长奇：《"四个全面"英译调研及翻译建议》，《中国翻译》2015 年第 3 期。
李奉栖：《"四个全面"的英译探析》，《上海翻译》2016 年第 1 期。

李田心:《论"中国梦"的英译和American Dream的汉译》,《安徽理工大学学报(社会科学版)》2015年第4期。

刘润泽、魏向清:《"中国梦"英译研究再思考——兼论政治术语翻译的概念史研究方法》,《中国外语》2015年第6期。

邵斌:《基于语料库的"中国梦"翻译的实证研究》,《中国英汉语比较研究会第11次全国学术研讨会暨2014年英汉语比较与翻译研究国际研讨会摘要集》2014年第1期。

王平兴:《汉英翻译中的政治考量》,《中国翻译》2014年第5期。

王伟光:《大国思维与大国战略　中国已成长为全球关键性大国》,《人民论坛》2015年第34期。

杨明星:《"新型大国关系"的创新译法及其现实意义》,《中国翻译》2015年第1期。

杨明星、李志丹:《"政治等效"视野下"窜访"译法探究》,《中国翻译》2015年第5期。

杨全红:《"中国梦"英译辨析》,《中国翻译》2013年第5期。

张顺生、葛陈蓉:《"中国梦"的诠释与英译——从"China Dream"到"Chinese Dream"》,《中国科技翻译》2015年第2期。

延伸阅读

外交翻译　一字千金

施燕华

施燕华,外交部英文专家、原翻译室主任,中国翻译协会常务副会长。曾担任邓小平、李先念等中央领导的翻译。参加了中美建交谈判、中美关于美国售台武器问题联合公报的谈判以及其他国家与我国的建交谈判。

外交翻译必须具有政治敏感性,因为涉及国家主权和国家利益方面的问题。比如在亚太经合组织当中,中国一共有三个成员,大陆、香港、台湾。那两个就不能叫做"成员国",他们不是国家。涉及领土争议地区的时候,要搞清楚各自不同的叫法。比如日本将钓鱼岛叫做尖阁诸岛。要吃透我方领导的意图,领会精神后再翻译。比如日本首相参拜靖国神社,他们辩解说是去参拜日本为国捐躯的军人,所以李肇星部长讲的时候,干脆就不说靖国神社了,直截了当地说日本首相去参拜二战时期的甲级战犯,让对方没有什么好辩论的,这个时候翻译就得跟上去,不能习惯性地说成参拜靖国神社。

对相关国家的地理、经济等背景情况及与中国的双边关系要有充分了解。那时候非洲有个国家的领导人跟我们说他们有个cassava,淀粉很多,希望我们帮助他们充分利用

新闻报道中外交理念的翻译
Translation for Diplomatic Concepts in News Coverage

起来。翻译不知道是什么东西，下面就全都翻译不下去了，后来我们大使馆的领导人知道是木薯，就可以翻译了。再比如说中马（马其顿）关系走过了不平凡的十年，不平凡怎么理解？可以是不同寻常，也可以是特别、非凡、出色、了不起的，存在多种选择。只有了解了中马关系的历史，才会知道这个不平凡的意思是有曲折，有一段不好的时光，这样翻译出来的意思才会准确。

在词语的选择上需要咬文嚼字，准确达意。比如在描述两国领导人会谈的时候，我们经常讲坦诚的交谈。"诚"包含了坦率和真诚两个意思，到底落脚在哪个意思上面？这里面又有学问了。如果两国谈得是比较好的，而且分歧不是很大，但是还是把大家的意见全都说出来了，那就可以用坦率。而有的时候，两国谈得也挺好，但是大家还是有很多分歧，那还要有一个真诚。

对经常涉及的关键文件、关键词要很清楚其具体内容，必要时加以解释。我们在谈到中美关系的时候，经常说要以三个公报为基础，对美国人来说一点问题都没有，对其他国家来说，特别是有些发展中国家不知道这三个文件是什么，翻译时就要酌情增加解释，说清楚三个公报分别是哪一年签署的，干什么用的。

翻译时还要考虑相关表达的地域特色和时代特色。中国人的政治术语很多，比如说实用主义，在中文中不是好词，表示为自己的利益服务，而字典上对这个词的翻译却是好词，翻译这类词时要注意不同语言中不同的联想意义。再比如，中文讲"血肉关系"一点不觉得难受，血肉凝成的友谊，两岸同胞的感情血浓于水。但如果翻译成"血"，人家就会感觉很难受、恶心，所以我们就要变一变再翻译。随着时代的变迁，很多表达方法还会出现不同的理解，比如说人权是一个基本生存权利，过去我们确实翻译成the right to life，但后来不行了，美国反堕胎以来，这个表达法变成了一种反堕胎的口号，所以我们就改了。

总的来说，外交翻译非常重要，即使用"一字千金"也不足以说明问题，因为根本无法用金钱去衡量。

（节录并编辑整理自施燕华在"中译外——中国走向世界之路高层论坛"的主题发言，中国网2007年4月6日发布）

驻外报道的翻译
Translation for News from Mission Overseas

单元简介
Introduction

驻外报道是指关于我国驻外使馆、总领馆、驻国际组织代表团和使团等驻外外交机构活动的新闻报道,是在新闻和媒体报道中宣传我国大政方针的一种重要方式。

驻外报道主要包括我驻外工作人员在所驻国的外事活动,例如会见、拜会、访问、考察、调研、交流、出席活动、发表文章、接受采访等;我国机构在外的活动报道,例如"中国第七批援厄瓜多尔军医组荣获勋章";还有驻在国政府官员和我驻外机构的活动报道,例如"马里总理做客中国大使官邸"。

驻外报道发挥着我国驻外外交机构的窗口桥梁作用,读者不仅可以获取我国驻外机构重要外交活动信息,还能了解我国政府的对外方针政策,以及对国内外重大事件的观点和立场。

驻外报道的翻译
Translation for News from Mission Overseas

UNIT 3

驻外报道翻译范例分析
Sample of Translation for News from Mission Overseas

范例一（Sample I）

驻日本大使程永华就靖国神社等问题与上智大学师生对谈交流（节本）
2014/01/21

Ambassador to Japan Cheng Yonghua Talks and Exchanges with Teachers and Students of Sophia University on Yasukuni Shrine and Other Issues (Abbreviated Version)
2014/01/21

2014年1月20日，驻日本大使程永华应邀赴上智大学与日本前驻美大使、该校特聘教授藤崎一郎进行对谈，该校师生100余人参加。

On January 20, 2014, H.E. Cheng Yonghua, Chinese Ambassador to Japan went to the Sophia University upon invitation and had a dialogue with former Japanese Ambassador to the United States and Distinguished Visiting Professor of the Sophia University Ichiro Fujisaki. More than 100 teachers and students of the University were present.

***

关于中日关系和靖国神社问题，程大使表示，当前中日关系同时面临领土、历史等如此之多的突出问题，局面前所未有的严峻。安倍首相不顾中方事先反复规劝和强烈反对，执意参拜供奉二战甲级战犯的靖国神社，给中日关系带来了致命打击。

Concerning the issues of the China-Japan relations and the Yasukuni Shrine, Ambassador Cheng said that, facing with so many prominent issues such as territory and history, the China-Japan relations are now in an unprecedentedly severe situation. Japanese Prime Minister Shinzo Abe, in total disregard of China's repeated exhortation and strong opposition beforehand, obdurately paid homage to the Yasukuni Shrine where Class-A war criminals of World War II are consecrated, bringing fatal blow to the China-Japan relations.

***

程大使详细阐述了中方为何强烈反对日本领导人参拜靖国神社，指出靖国神社战前是日本军国主义对外侵略的精神工具和象征，现在不仅供奉着二战甲级战犯，还极力美化歪曲侵略历史，宣扬与当今国际公论格格不入的错误史观。日本领导人参拜这个地方，事实上就是在直接或间接肯定"靖国史观"。程大使强调，历史就是历史，它是客观存在的事实，不容篡改，不容歪曲。历史潮流滚滚向前，谁开历史倒车、逆潮流而动，就会被历史无情地抛弃。

Ambassador Cheng elaborated on the reasons why China is strongly against Japanese leaders' worshiping of the Yasukuni Shrine, and pointed out that the Yasukuni Shrine was a spiritual tool and symbol of aggression of the Japanese militarism before the WWII, now it not only consecrates Class-A war criminals of the WWII but also vigorously whitewashes and distorts the history of aggression, advocating wrong historical views which are incompatible with the current international public opinion. Japanese leaders' visits to the place are in fact directly or indirectly affirming "the historical view of the Yasukuni Shrine". Ambassador Cheng stressed that history is history, which is an objective existence of facts, and no fabrication or distortion is ever allowed. The tide of history always flows forward, and people who turn the clock back to the backtrack of history and behave against the trend will be mercilessly abandoned by history.

***

关于如何打开严峻的中日关系，程大使表示，日本领导人参拜靖国神社，给本已困难的两国关系制造了新的重大政治障碍。现在日本领导人要做的是正确认识和反省历史，与侵略历史划清界限，为消除中日间的政治障碍做出努力。两国领导人会晤必须建立在诚意和善意的基础上，必须要有合适的气氛和环境，事实上日本领导人已经亲手关闭了与中方对话的大门。

As to how to thaw the severe China-Japan relations, Ambassador Cheng said that the Japanese leaders paying homage to the Yasukuni Shrine has created new and formidable political barriers to the already strained bilateral relations. Now the Japanese leaders should correctly look at and repent its history, make a clean break from its past of aggression and strive to remove the political barriers between China and Japan. Meetings of the leaders of the two countries must be conducted on the basis of sincerity and good will within proper atmosphere and environment. As a matter of fact, however, the Japanese leaders have closed the door of dialogues with China with their own hands.

***

关于钓鱼岛问题，程大使列举大量史实，强调是中国最先发现、命名和利用钓鱼岛，中国对钓鱼岛实行了长期管辖。日本政府强行推进"国有化"，损害了中国主权，背离了双方达成的有关谅解和共识。中方没有别的选择，不得不采取相应措施维护中国主权。

For the Diaoyu Islands issue, Ambassador Cheng listed a large number of historical facts to stress that it was China that first discovered, named and exploited the Diaoyu Islands, and the Diaoyu Islands had been under China's jurisdiction for a long time. The Japanese government forcibly promoted the "nationalization", which has harmed China's territorial sovereignty, and deviated from the related understanding and consensus reached between the two sides. China has no other choice but to take corresponding measures to safeguard China's sovereignty.

***

在场学生就靖国神社问题、中日关系、中美关系、东亚共同体等踊跃提问，程大使予以逐一解答，现场气氛十分热烈。之后，程大使还与中国留学生们进行交流，并合影留念。

Students at present actively raised questions on issues such as the Yasukuni Shrine, China-Japan relations, China-US relations and East Asian Community, and Ambassador Cheng answered the questions one by one, creating a warm atmosphere. Later, Ambassador Cheng had exchanges with overseas Chinese students and took a group photo to mark the occasion.

> 新闻背景：2013年12月26日，日本首相安倍晋三无视国际社会、亚洲邻国和日本民众的反对，悍然参拜了供奉有二战甲级战犯的靖国神社。这是安倍自就任首相以来的首次参拜。在此之前，安倍曾三次向靖国神社供奉祭品。靖国神社位于东京千代田区，供奉有包括东条英机在内的14名第二次世界大战甲级战犯。长期以来，日本部分政客、国会议员参拜靖国神社，导致日本与中国、韩国等亚洲国家关系恶化。中国政府针对日本领导人粗暴践踏中国和其他亚洲战争受害国人民感情、公然挑战历史正义和人类良知的行径表示强烈愤慨，向日方提出强烈抗议和严厉谴责。
>
> 原文链接：http://www.china-embassy.or.jp/chn/dszl/dszyhd/t1121438.htm
> 译文链接：http://www.fmprc.gov.cn/mfa_chn/zwbd_602255/t1121439.shtml

一、范例一文本结构分析（Text Structure Analysis of Sample I）

范例一是一则有关我国驻外工作人员在所驻国的外事活动的报道，主要内容为驻日大使程永华应邀赴上智大学与日本前驻美大使、该校特聘教授藤崎一郎进行对谈，针对中日关系、靖国神社问题、钓鱼岛问题等阐述中方立场。

该报道由三部分构成。第一段为导语，介绍对谈交流的时间（2014年1月20日）、人物和职衔（驻日本大使程永华、日本前驻美大使、特聘教授藤崎一郎）、地点（上智大学）、与会人员及人数（该校师生100余人）等。第二至五段是报道的主体部分，涵盖对谈交流的三个主要问题：靖国神社问题、中日关系问题、钓鱼岛问题。报道中以"关于……问题"开头，分别引出大使针对以上三个问题的观点和立场（注意程大使"表示""详细阐述""指出""强调""列举大量史实"等引出观点的表述）。最后一段作为结尾部分，就交流会现场互动及气氛做了简要报道。因篇幅所限，原文有所删节。

二、范例一翻译解析（Translation Analysis of Sample I）

（一）驻外人员活动报道标题的翻译（Translation of Headlines for Coverage of Diplomatic Personnel Activities Overseas）

关于我国驻外工作人员在所驻国外事活动的驻外报道，主要包括会见、拜会、访问、考察、调研、交流、出席活动、发表文章、接受采访等内容。例如驻外大使或总领事参加或出席当地活动、座谈、交流，驻外大使或总领事会见或拜会驻在国官员，驻外大使在驻在国报刊媒体发表文章、接受采访，等等。这一类驻外报道常见的标题形式有"驻德国大使史明德出席德国中国商会成立庆典"，"驻赞比亚大使李杰拜会前总统班达"，"驻葡萄牙大使黄松甫会见葡中青年企业家协会主席"，"驻英国大使刘晓明就中英关系、安倍参拜靖国神社等问题接受中国驻英媒体联合采访"等。下面就以上述驻外报道标题为例，探讨不同形式的驻外报道标题的翻译方法。

驻德国大使史明德出席德国中国商会成立庆典
(http://www.fmprc.gov.cn/mfa_chn/zwbd_602255/t1120668.shtml)
Ambassador to Germany Shi Mingde Attends Establishment Celebration of Chinese Chamber of Commerce in Germany
(http://www.fmprc.gov.cn/mfa_eng/wjb_663304/zwjg_665342/zwbd_665378/t1124624.shtml)

驻坦桑尼亚大使吕友清考察坦西部两省
(http://www.fmprc.gov.cn/mfa_chn/zwbd_602255/t1111985.shtml)
Ambassador to Tanzania Lv Youqing Inspects Two Western Tanzanian Regions
(http://www.fmprc.gov.cn/mfa_eng/wjb_663304/zwjg_665342/zwbd_665378/t1114067.shtml)

驻葡萄牙大使黄松甫会见葡中青年企业家协会主席
(http://www.fmprc.gov.cn/mfa_chn/zwbd_602255/gzhd_602266/t1114567.shtml)
Ambassador to Portugal Huang Songfu Meets with President of Portugal and China Young Entrepreneurs Association
(http://www.fmprc.gov.cn/mfa_eng/wjb_663304/zwjg_665342/zwbd_665378/t1117946.shtml)

驻赞比亚大使李杰拜会前总统班达
(http://www.fmprc.gov.cn/web/zwbd_673032/wshd_673034/t1574206.shtml)
Ambassador Li Jie Calls on Former President of Zambia Rupia Banda
(http://www.fmprc.gov.cn/mfa_eng/wjb_663304/zwjg_665342/zwbd_665378/t1574813.shtml)

驻英国大使刘晓明就中英关系、安倍参拜靖国神社等问题接受中国驻英媒体联

合采访

(http://www.fmprc.gov.cn/mfa_chn/dszlsjt_602260/ds_602262/t1116231.shtml)

Ambassador to UK Liu Xiaoming Gives Joint Interview to Chinese Media in UK on China-UK Relations, Shinzo Abe's Visit to Yasukuni Shrine and Other Issues

(http://english.cntv.cn/program/newsupdate/20140104/100721.shtml)

新任驻克罗地亚大使邓英接受《晨报》专访

(http://www.fmprc.gov.cn/mfa_chn/zwbd_602255/gzhd_602266/t1114168.shtml)

Newly-appointed Ambassador to Croatia Deng Ying Gives Exclusive Interview to *Jutarnji List*

(http://www.fmprc.gov.cn/mfa_eng/wjb_663304/zwjg_665342/)

驻英国大使刘晓明在英国《星期日电讯报》发表署名文章：《贸易战反映出中美"三观之争"》

(http://www.fmprc.gov.cn/ce/ceuk/chn/tpxw/t1574992.htm)

The Sunday Telegraph Publishes a Signed Article by Ambassador Liu Xiaoming Entitled The trade war reveals three conflicts of views

(http://www.fmprc.gov.cn/mfa_eng/wjb_663304/zwjg_665342/zwbd_665378/t1574996.shtml)

如上述标题翻译所示，驻某国大使在标题中表述为Ambassador to+国名；驻某地总领事译为Consul General in+地名。标题中常出现的动词有会见（meet with）、拜会（call on或pay a call on）、访问（visit）、交流（exchange with）、出席（attend）、发表文章（publish article）、接受采访（give interview to)等。时态均为一般现在时。大使或总领事"接受……专访"可以译为give exclusive interview to，"接受……联合采访"可以译为give joint interview to，"在……发表署名文章"可以译为publishes signed article in，报刊名称需用斜体。

（二）驻外人员活动报道导语的翻译（Translation of News Lead in Coverage of Diplomatic Personnel Activities Overseas）

关于驻外官员出席活动的报道，一般在导语部分介绍人物、时间、地点、活动名称、出席人员等。大使姓名在导语中首次出现时一般加敬称H.E.（即His Excellency），例如H.E. Cheng Yonghua, Chinese Ambassador to Japan。需要注意的是，英译时头衔前面不加任何冠词，首字母需大写。汉语报道中介绍与会外国官员时一般不出现人物全名，只出现姓氏，例如"肯尼亚国防部长奥马莫"，但翻译成英文时需要补充官员全名，如Secretary of Defense Raychelle Omamo of Kenya。此外，关于人名翻译，有些外国官员姓名在中文中有约定俗成的译名，例如意大利驻华使馆临时代办"孟昊天"、德国工商大会主席"施伟策"、德国亚太经济委员会中国事务发言人"薄睦乐"等，虽看似汉语姓名，如果翻译的时候不查阅资料文献，则会想当然地错译成中文姓名的拼音，使这些外国官员一下成了"中国人"，实际上上述姓名的正确译法为Augusto Massari, Eric Schweitzer和Martin Brudermuller。一些国际上惯用的人名，如国务院参事林毅夫教授翻译时，需要遵循惯例，翻译成Justin Yifu Lin。总而言之，在翻译时务必仔细查阅原文中人物的身份背景，以确认其相应的英译名。请看下面具体翻译实例：

2016年4月8日，外交部部长助理刘海星会见意大利驻华使馆临时代办孟昊天，就中意双边关系和共同关心的问题交换了意见。

(http://www.fmprc.gov.cn/web/wjbxw_673019/t1354243.shtml)

On April 8, 2016, Assistant Foreign Minister Liu Haixing met with Charge d'Affaires ad interim Augusto Massari of the Italian Embassy in China, exchanging views on China-Italy relations and issues of common concern.

(http://www.fmprc.gov.cn/mfa_eng/wjb_663304/zygy_663314/gyhd_663338/)

2014年1月16日，驻德国大使史明德出席德国中国商会成立庆典暨剪彩仪式，与德国联邦副总理兼经济和能源部长加布里尔、德国工商大会主席施伟策、德国亚太经济委员会中国事务发言人薄睦乐、柏林市政府经济部长宇泽和德国中国商会主席陈飞共同为中国商会剪彩。

(http://www.fmprc.gov.cn/ce/cede/chn/dszl/dshd/t1120667.htm)

On January 16, 2014, H.E. Shi Mingde, Chinese Ambassador to Germany attended the establishment celebration and ribbon-cutting ceremony of the Chinese Chamber of Commerce in Germany (CHKD), and cut ribbons along with Vice Chancellor and Minister of Economics and Energy of the Federal Republic of Germany Sigmar Gabriel, President of the Association of German Chambers of Industry and Commerce Eric Schweitzer, Spokesperson for China Affairs of the Asia-Pacific Committee of German Business Martin Brudermuller, Berlin's Senator for Economic Affairs Cornelia Yzer, and CHKD Chairman Chen Fei.

(http://www.fmprc.gov.cn/mfa_eng/wjb_663304/zwjg_665342/zwbd_665378/t1124624.shtml)

关于会晤的报道，一般在导语部分介绍会晤官员、时间、地点、主要内容等。通常"会见"译为meet with。身份高者会见身份低者，或主人会见客人，一般称接见或召见；身份低者会见身份高者，或客人会见主人，一般称拜会或拜见。"拜会"指拜访会见，多用于外交上的正式访问，可以译为pay a courtesy call on sb. 或pay a call on sb.。

不同国家中具有类似行政职责的政府部门名称和政府官员职衔，在中文中有时可能名称叫法相同，但在英文中却依各自国家而定，不可以一概而论。如就美国而言，"国务部"是Department of State，"国务部长"即指"国务卿"，英文是Secretary of

State。但"塞总统府国务部长"应该翻译成Senegalese Minister of State of the Presidential Palace,"格林纳达总理府新闻国务部长"的英文则是Director of the Government Information Service of the Office of the Grenadian Prime Minister。请看下面具体翻译实例:

2014年1月13日,国务院参事林毅夫教授拜会塞内加尔总统萨勒,就塞如何借鉴中国经验,探索符合自身国情的发展道路深入交换意见。驻塞大使夏煌、塞总统府国务部长姆巴耶·恩迪亚耶、总统外事顾问丹巴·巴及达喀尔大学经济学院院长阿里·姆巴耶在座。

(http://www.counsellor.gov.cn/gjhz/2014-01-17/51695.shtml)

On January 13, 2014, Professor Justin Yifu Lin, Counsellor of the State Council, paid a call on Senegalese President Macky Sall, exchanging in-depth views on how Senegal may draw on China's experience to explore a development road which conforms to its own national conditions. Ambassador to Senegal Xia Huang, Senegalese Minister of State of the Presidential Palace Mbaye Ndiaye, Diplomatic Adviser to the President Oumar Demba Ba and Dean of Faculty Economics and Management of the Cheikh Anta Diop University Aly Mbaye were present.

(http://www.fmprc.gov.cn/mfa_eng/wjb_663304/zwjg_665342/zwbd_665378/)

2013年11月6日,应驻格林纳达大使欧渤芊邀请,格林纳达总理府新闻国务部长加罗韦夫妇来大使官邸做客。格国家电视台主任泰特斯、新闻主管柯沃等在座。

(http://wcm.fmprc.gov.cn/pub/chn/gxh/tyb/zwbd/t1097467.htm)

On November 6, 2013, at the invitation of Chinese Ambassador to Grenada H.E. Mdm. Ou Boqian, Director of the Government Information Service of the Office of the Prime Minister Garowe and his wife paid a visit to the Ambassador's mansion house. Director of Grenada Broadcasting Network TV Titus, and News Director Kewo were present.

(http://www.fmprc.gov.cn/mfa_eng/wjb_663304/zwjg_665342/zwbd_665378/)

关于驻外官员接受采访、发表署名文章的新闻报道,在导语中会介绍有哪些媒体、针对什么问题进行采访、发表的文章名称是什么。媒体名称书写规范需要格外注意,英语和汉语在标点符号的使用上略有不同,报刊媒体的名称在汉语文本中需要用书名号标记,但在英译时需用斜体,例如《人民日报》译为*People's Daily*,《科技日报》译为*Science and Technology Daily*,《新闻报》译为*La Presse*。英语文本中,通讯社、电视台等媒体机构需将其首字母大写,并加上媒体缩写,如美国联合通讯社,译为The Associated Press (AP),中国国际广播电台译为China Radio International (CRI)。发表的文章名称在汉语文本中加书名号标记,在英文文本中加双引号标记,例如大使文章《让历史不再重演》译为"Let History not Repeat Itself"。请看下面具体翻译实例:

2014年1月8日，驻英国大使刘晓明接受《人民日报》、新华社、中央电视台、中新社、《中国日报》、中国国际广播电台及《科技日报》等中国驻英媒体的联合采访，就中英关系、安倍参拜靖国神社等回答了记者提问。

(http://www.fmprc.gov.cn/ce/ceuk/chn/dsxx/dashijianghua/t1116230.htm)

On January 8, 2014, H.E. Liu Xiaoming, Chinese Ambassador to the UK gave a joint interview to Chinese media in the UK, including *People's Daily*, Xinhua News Agency, China Central Television (CCTV), China News Service, *China Daily*, China Radio International (CRI) and *Science and Technology Daily*, and responded to the questions raised by the journalists on China-UK relations, Shinzo Abe's visit to the Yasukuni Shrine and other issues.

(http://www.fmprc.gov.cn/ce/ceuk/eng/HotTopics/davidcameron/t1105356.htm)

2014年1月13日出版的加拿大《新闻报》（*La Presse*）刊登驻蒙特利尔总领事赵江平的署名文章——《让历史不再重演》。全文如下：

(http://wcm.fmprc.gov.cn/pub/chn/gxh/mtb/zwbd/dszlsjt/t1118565.htm)

On January 13, 2014, Canadian *La Presse* published a signed article by Consul General of China in Montreal Zhao Jiangping, entitled "Let History not Repeat Itself". The full text is as follows:

(http://www.fmprc.gov.cn/mfa_eng/wjb_663304/zwjg_665342/zwbd_665378/)

（三）驻外报道中靖国神社问题的翻译（Translation of Yasukuni Shrine Issue）

近年来日本政要频频参拜靖国神社，为中日关系的发展投下阴影，成为始终制约中日关系的瓶颈。外交新闻报道中常出现关于日本政要参拜靖国神社，以及我国对这一问题所持立场和态度的相关表述，下文着重探讨驻外报道中对这些常见表述的翻译。

1. 关于日本政要参拜靖国神社行径的翻译

驻外报道中，描述日本政要参拜靖国神社的常见措辞包括"不顾……反对""公然参拜""鼓吹""一意孤行""拜鬼""执意参拜""冒天下之大不韪""顶礼膜拜"等，我国外交人员通过谴责性的强硬措辞来表明我国政府的反对立场。请看下面实例中关于这些表述的翻译：

日前，日本首相安倍晋三不顾亚洲各国的强烈反对，公然参拜靖国神社并签下总理内阁大臣的名号。安倍还鼓吹"侵略未定论"，质疑东京审判合法性，推动修改和平宪法，增加国防预算和军备。

(http://wcm.fmprc.gov.cn/pub/chn/gxh/mtb/zwbd/dszlsjt/t1118565.htm)

Days ago, Japanese Prime Minister Shinzo Abe, in total disregard of the strong opposition of all the Asian countries, paid a blatant homage to the Yasukuni Shrine and signed the courtesy name of Prime Minister. Abe also preached that "the definition of what constitutes aggression has yet to be established", questioned the legitimacy of Tokyo Trial, promoted the amendment of Peace Constitution, and increased defense budget and military preparedness.

(http://ae.china-embassy.org/eng/wjbfyrth/t1112096.htm)

日前，日本首相安倍晋三不顾中国等各方坚决反对，一意孤行到供奉着甲级战犯的靖国神社"拜鬼"。此举遭到亚太邻国和国际社会的强烈谴责。

(http://opinion.people.com.cn/n/2014/0113/c368020-24105820.html)

A few days ago, in disregard of the firm opposition of China and other parties, Japanese Prime Minister Shinzo Abe acted arbitrarily to visit the Yasukuni Shrine where the Japanese Class-A war criminals are consecrated to worship the "evil spirits", incurring strong condemnation from its neighboring countries in Asia-Pacific region and the international community as a whole.

(http://www.fmprc.gov.cn/mfa_eng/wjb_663304/zwjg_665342/zwbd_665378/)

但就在几天后，安倍首相不顾中方事先反复规劝和强烈反对，执意参拜供奉二战甲级战犯的靖国神社，给中日关系带来了致命打击。

(http://www.china-embassy.or.jp/chn/dszl/dszyhd/t1121438.htm)

However, several days after the meeting, Japanese Prime Minister Shinzo Abe, in total disregard of China's repeated exhortation and strong opposition beforehand, obdurately paid homage to the Yasukuni Shrine where Class-A war criminals of World War II are consecrated, bringing fatal blow to the China-Japan relations.

(http://www.fmprc.gov.cn/mfa_chn/zwbd_602255/t1121439.shtml)

在拥护和平、反对战争的呼声高涨之际，安倍却冒天下之大不韪，对昔日战犯顶礼膜拜，鼓吹日本军国主义历史观，试图将日本引向十分危险的方向。

(http://www.china-embassy.or.jp/chn/dszl/dszyhd/t1121438.htm)

At a time when calls for upholding peace and objecting wars are ever-growing, Abe, in total disregard of international opposition, paid homage to the former war criminals and advocated the historical view of Japanese militarism, which is an attempt to lead Japan toward a very dangerous direction.

(http://www.fmprc.gov.cn/mfa_chn/zwbd_602255/t1121439.shtml)

2. 关于参拜靖国神社本质的翻译

对于日本政要参拜靖国神社这一行为的本质，我国驻外报道常用表述包括"军国主义的精神象征""供奉甲级战犯""极右翼势力""美化侵略历史""颠覆国际社会的正义审判""公开挑战二战结果和战后国际秩序""倒行逆施，为侵略翻案、开历史倒车""公然挑衅""无耻行径"等，从而剖析和揭露日本参拜靖国神社的实质。请看下面实例中关于这些表述的翻译：

靖国神社不是普通的寺庙，而是日本军国主义的精神象征，里面供奉着二战中策划和发动日本对外侵略的14名甲级战犯及上千名其它各级战犯，是日本极右翼势力顶礼膜拜的地方。日本领导人的所作所为，目的是美化日本军国主义对外侵略历史，企图颠覆国际社会对"亚洲纳粹"的正义审判，公开挑战二战结果和战后国际秩序。

(http://wcm.fmprc.gov.cn/pub/chn/gxh/mtb/zwbd/dszlsjt/t1118565.htm)

The Yasukuni Shrine is not an ordinary shrine, but the spiritual symbol of Japanese militarism. Enshrining14 Class-A and over 1,000 other Japanese war criminals who planned and launched Japan's aggression against other countries during World War II, it is the place where the ultra-right-wing forces in Japan pay homage to. The words and deeds of the Japanese leaders are attempts to whitewash the history of aggression by militarist Japan, overturn the just trial the international community had made to "Asian Nazi", and blatantly challenge the results of World War II and post-war international order.

(http://ae.china-embassy.org/eng/wjbfyrth/t1112096.htm)

日本领导人参拜靖国神社是在历史问题上的倒行逆施，是企图为侵略翻案、开历史倒车。靖国神社战前就是日本军国主义对外侵略的精神支柱，现在仍供奉有14名二战甲级战犯，时至今日仍顽固坚持和宣扬"侵略有理"的军国主义历史观。

(http://www.fmprc.gov.cn/ce/cejp/chn/zrgx/rbsg/t1118281.htm)

The Japanese leaders' visit to the Yasukuni Shrine is a perverse act on historical issues which attempts to vindicate its aggression and turn back the wheels of the history. The Yasukuni Shrine has been a spiritual pillar of Japanese militarism towards foreign aggression before its war. To date, 14 Class-A war criminals remain consecrated there in order to stubbornly uphold and promote the militarism historical view of "rational aggression".

(http://www.fmprc.gov.cn/mfa_eng/wjb_663304/zwjg_665342/zwbd_665378/)

安倍此举，就是要为过去的侵略战争翻案，是对世界反法西斯战争的胜利成果和战后国际秩序的公然挑衅，严重伤害了曾遭受过日本侵略和殖民统治的各国人民感情。也正是此类否认侵略历史、不肯接受战后国际秩序的无耻行径，成为日本与亚洲邻国长期不睦的重要根源。

(http://opinion.people.com.cn/n/2014/0113/c368020-24105820.html)

Abe's act is to reverse the verdict of the past war of aggression, and is flagrant provocation to the success of the world anti-fascist war and the post-war international order, and has seriously affronted the feelings of the people of all countries that once suffered from Japanese militarist aggression and colonial rule. It is such infamous act of denying the history of aggression and refusing to accept the post-war international order that has become a major source of the long-term unneighborly relationship between Japan and its Asian neighboring countries.

(http://www.fmprc.gov.cn/mfa_eng/wjb_663304/zwjg_665342/zwbd_665378/)

3. 在靖国神社问题上我国所持立场和态度的翻译

驻外报道中，我国在靖国神社问题上所持立场和态度的常见表述包括"强烈反对和严厉谴责""不可接受，也不可原谅""强烈抗议"等，表明我方立场坚定、态度明确。以范例一为例，驻日大使程永华代表中国政府立场，态度坚定，义正词严。翻译这篇驻外报道时，英文措辞也需力求还原原文风格，体现我国立场和态度的不容模糊。请看下列具体翻译实例：

安倍的行为正把日本带向十分危险的方向，对地区和世界和平稳定带来严重损害，理所当然受到亚洲邻国和国际社会的<u>强烈反对和严厉谴责</u>。

(http://wcm.fmprc.gov.cn/pub/chn/gxh/tyb/zwbd/dszlsjt/t1118828.htm)

Abe's act is bringing Japan to a very dangerous direction and severely destroying peace and stability of the region and the world at large, which, as it should, has <u>aroused firm opposition and strong condemnation</u> of its Asian neighbors and the international community.

(http://www.fmprc.gov.cn/mfa_eng/wjb_663304/zwjg_665342/zwbd_665378/)

安倍参拜靖国神社对饱受日本侵略苦难的有关亚洲国家人民而言，就如同有人在希特勒墓前献花，当然<u>绝对不可接受，也不可原谅</u>。

For people of the relevant Asian countries who suffered the Japanese aggression, Shinzo Abe's visit to the Yasukuni Shrine is just as someone presents a bouquet before the tomb of Adolf Hitler, which <u>absolutely cannot be accepted and forgiven</u>.

(http://www.china-embassy.or.jp/chn/dszl/dszyhd/t1121438.htm)

我们对普通民众祭奠自己的亲属不持异议，但日本领导人参拜包括二战甲级战犯在内的"英灵"，意味着要颠覆对侵略战争性质和责任的认识，中方绝<u>不能接受</u>。

We have no objections to common people mourning their families. But China <u>can never accept</u> the Japanese leaders paying homage to the "kami" including Class-A war criminals of the WWII which means that Japan wants to overturn its understanding of the nature of the aggression war and its responsibility.

(http://www.fmprc.gov.cn/mfa_chn/zwbd_602255/t1121439.shtml)

上世纪80年代中期以来，每当日本领导人参拜靖国神社，都给中日关系带来严重干扰和伤害，中方也无一例外提出了<u>严正交涉和强烈抗议</u>。安倍首相对该问题的轻重及后果是完全清楚的，但他最终还是迈出了这一步，明知不可为而为之，性质十分恶劣。

(http://wcm.fmprc.gov.cn/pub/chn/gxh/mtb/zwbd/dszlsjt/t1118565.htm)

Since the mid-term of the 1980s, every visit to the Yasukuni Shrine by the Japanese leaders has resulted in severe disturbance and hurt to the China-Japan relations, and China <u>has lodged solemn negotiations and strong protest</u> in response each time. Prime Minister Shinzo Abe is totally clear about the seriousness and consequences caused by the issue, but he eventually went ahead with it anyway. The nature of the event is of great abomination since he did it although he knows very well that he should not.

(http://www.fmprc.gov.cn/mfa_eng/wjb_663304/zwjg_665342/)

中国政府对日美上述做法从上世纪50年代起就多次表示<u>坚决反对，不予承认</u>。

(http://www.china-embassy.or.jp/chn/dszl/dszyhd/t1121438.htm)

Since the 1950s, the Chinese government <u>has firmly opposed and never acknowledged</u> the above deals between Japan and the United States.

(http://www.fmprc.gov.cn/mfa_chn/zwbd_602255/t1121439.shtml)

范例二（Sample II）

驻泰国使馆举办中泰媒体新春联谊会（节本）
2014/01/13

Chinese Embassy in Thailand Holds Chinese–Thai Media New Year Gathering (Abbreviated Version)
2014/01/13

2014年1月10日，驻泰国使馆举办中泰媒体新春联谊会，来自《泰叻报》《民意报》《每日邮报》《每日新闻报》《经理人报》《经济基础报》、民族集团、电视3台、5台、9台等27家泰国主流媒体及泰国记者协会、泰国报业协会、泰国广播记者协会等机构代表，以及泰国华文媒体和我驻泰媒体代表共约100人出席。

On January 10, 2014, the Chinese Embassy in Thailand held a Chinese-Thai media New Year gathering. About 100 people attended the gathering, including representatives from 27 Thai mainstream media, such as *Thai Rath, Matichon, Post Today, Daily News, Manager Daily, Thansettakij,* Nation Multimedia Group, Channel 3, Channel 5 and Channel 9, and representatives from the Thai Journalists Association, the Press Association of Thailand and the Thai Broadcast Journalist Association, as well as Thai Chinese language media and Chinese media in Thailand.

***

宁赋魁大使出席。宁大使在致辞中表示，过去一年中泰关系发生了不少大事、喜事，特别是李克强总理作为中国新一届政府领导人首次访问泰国，推动中泰友好关系进入了新的历史时期。各位中泰媒体朋友们不仅充分报道了这一重要访问，还积极关注、报道两国在各领域的务实合作，包括中泰高铁合作、大熊猫合作等，感谢大家为弘扬中泰友好、促进两国各界交流合作做出的可贵贡献。

Chinese Ambassador to Thailand H. E. Ning Fukui was present. Ambassador Ning said in his speech that quite a few great and joyful events happened in China-Thailand relations in the past year. Particularly, Premier Li Keqiang paid his first visit to Thailand as a member of the new generation of the leadership of the Chinese government, which has pushed China-Thailand friendly relations to a new historical period. The Chinese and Thai media not only fully covered the important visit, but actively paid attention to and covered China-Thailand pragmatic cooperation in various fields, such as cooperation in China-Thailand high speed railway project and giant panda breeding. I would like to thank you for the valuable contribution you have made in carrying forward China-Thailand friendship and boosting bilateral exchanges and cooperation in every sector.

***

宁大使表示，虽然目前泰国政局出现了一些动荡，但中泰友谊已渗透进两国人民的血脉，基础牢固。中泰睦邻友好、互利合作将会不断谱写新的历史篇章。作为友好邻邦，我们衷心希望泰国早日恢复政治稳定、经济发展、人民安居乐业。我们也相信泰国人民有能力、有智慧，通过对话协商早日解决政治分歧，维护国家的长治久安。

Ambassador Ning said that despite some turbulence in the current political situation of Thailand, China-Thailand friendship has blended into the blood of the two peoples with a firm foundation. New historical chapters of China-Thailand good neighborly and friendly relations and mutually beneficial cooperation will continue to be composed. As friendly neighbors, we sincerely hope that Thailand restore political stability and economic development with its people residing and working in peace and contentment at an early date. We believe that the Thai people have the abilities and wisdom to resolve political differences through dialogue and consultation at an early date to maintain lasting peace and stability.

***

席间，宁大使与中泰媒体人亲切交谈。宁大使表示，驻泰国使馆愿意与各位媒体界人士保持密切联系，帮助中国人民更好地了解泰国，同时也帮助泰国人民更好地了解中国，共同为中泰友好、为地区和平、稳定与发展贡献绵薄力量。过去一年大家辛苦了，马年新春即将到来，祝大家马年快乐，身体健康。

At the dinner, Ambassador Ning had cordial talks with Chinese and Thai journalists. Ambassador Ning said that the Chinese Embassy in Thailand will maintain close contacts with all friends from the press, and help Chinese and Thai people to understand each other better, working together to make humble efforts to promote China-Thailand friendship, regional peace, stability and development. He appreciated the journalists for their hard work and dedication over the past year. With the Spring Festival of the Year of Horse around the corner, he expressed his New Year messages, wishing them a happy new year and good health.

***

泰国记者协会主席巴蒂等各媒体代表均感谢宁大使和使馆为此次活动所做精心准备和周到安排，表示联谊活动为中泰媒体以及和使馆间的交流创造了一个良好平台，期待今后进一步加强联系，共同为促进泰中友好作出努力。

President of the Thai Journalists Association Pradit Ruangdit and other media representatives all expressed gratitude to Ambassador Ning and the Embassy for their meticulous preparations and considerate arrangement for this activity. They said that the gathering creates a good platform for exchanges among Chinese media, Thai media and the Embassy. They looked forward to strengthening contacts in the future and jointly promoting Thailand-China friendship.

新闻背景：春节是中国最隆重的传统节日，每逢农历新年，我驻外使馆都要举行新春招待会等庆祝活动。2014年马年新春到来之际，我驻泰使馆举办中泰媒体新春联谊会，宁赋魁大使在新春会上致辞。2013年8月泰国陷入政治危机，12月泰国总理英拉解散国会下议院。2013年10月，李克强总理作为中国新一届政府领导人首次访问泰国。宁大使在新春会上谈及过去的一年泰国政局动荡、中泰两国的友好往来、日首相参拜靖国神社等问题，展望即将到来的农历新年中泰关系的发展。

原文链接：http://www.fmprc.gov.cn/mfa_chn/zwbd_602255/t1118385.shtml

译文链接：http://www.fmprc.gov.cn/mfa_eng/wjb_663304/zwjg_665342/zwbd_665378/

一、范例二文本结构分析（Text Structure Analysis of Sample II）

范例二是一篇关于我国驻外机构的活动报道，主要内容为驻泰使馆举办中泰媒体新春联谊会，宁赋魁大使在新春会上致辞。第一段为新闻导语，介绍驻外使馆（驻泰国使馆）举办的活动（中泰媒体新春联谊会）、参加人员（27家泰国主流媒体及泰国记者协会、泰国报业协会、泰国广播记者协会等机构代表）、人数（共约100人出席）；第二、三段介绍大使的致辞内容，主要针对中泰关系进行总结和展望，致辞中提到泰国"政局动荡"，"李克强总理作为中国新一届政府领导人首次访问泰国"，"中泰高铁合作"，"大熊猫合作"等重大外交事件；第四、五两段介绍新春会席间大使与中泰媒体人亲切交谈，媒体代表就新春联谊会向大使馆表示感激。因篇幅所限，原文有所删节。

驻外报道的翻译
Translation for News from Mission Overseas — UNIT 3

二、范例二翻译解析（Translation Analysis of Sample II）

（一）驻外机构活动报道标题的翻译（Translation of Coverage Headlines for Activities of Mission Overseas）

关于我国驻外机构以及驻在国政府官员的活动报道，主要包括以下几类：驻××使馆或驻××总领事馆举办××活动、记者会等，例如"中国驻俄罗斯大使馆为俄汉学家举行2014年新春招待会"；驻在国××官员出席××活动，发表××声明等，如"塞尔维亚总统出席中塞友谊大桥合龙仪式"及"埃及外交部发表声明谴责昆明'3·01'暴恐事件"；以及我国驻外机构的其他一系列活动，如"'多彩中华'中国少数民族文艺演出在金边举行"。

下面就以上述驻外报道标题为例，探讨不同形式的驻外报道标题的翻译方法。

"多彩中华"中国少数民族文艺演出在金边举行
(http://www.fmprc.gov.cn/mfa_chn/zwbd_602255/t1114274.shtml)
Art Performance of Chinese Ethnic Minorities "Colorful China" Held in Phnom Penh
(http://www.fmprc.gov.cn/mfa_eng/wjb_663304/zwjg_665342/zwbd_665378/)

驻埃及使馆就日本首相参拜靖国神社举办专题记者会
(http://www.fmprc.gov.cn/mfa_chn/zwbd_602255/t1114520.shtml)
Chinese Embassy in Egypt Holds Special Press Conference on Japanese Prime Minister's Visit to Yasukuni Shrine
(http://www.fmprc.gov.cn/mfa_eng/wjb_663304/zwjg_665342/zwbd_665378/)

中国驻俄罗斯大使馆为俄汉学家举行2014年新春招待会
(http://www.fmprc.gov.cn/mfa_chn/zwbd_602255/t1120925.shtml)
Chinese Embassy in Russia Holds New Year Reception of 2014 for Russian Sinologists
(http://www.fmprc.gov.cn/mfa_eng/wjb_663304/zwjg_665342/zwbd_665378/t1124617.shtml)

埃及外交部发表声明谴责昆明"3·01"暴恐事件
(http://www.fmprc.gov.cn/mfa_chn/zwbd_602255/t1134397.shtml)
Egyptian Foreign Ministry Issues Statement Condemning "March 1" Violent Terrorist Attack in Kunming
(http://www.fmprc.gov.cn/mfa_eng/wjb_663304/zwjg_665342/zwbd_665378/)

中国第七批援厄瓜多尔军医组荣获勋章
(http://china.huanqiu.com/News/fmprc/2013-11/4536897.html)
The Seventh Group of Medical Aid Team of PLA to Ecuador Awarded Medals
(http://www.fmprc.gov.cn/mfa_eng/wjb_663304/zwjg_665342/zwbd_665378/)

外交新闻汉英翻译
C-E TRANSLATION OF DIPLOMATIC NEWS

塞尔维亚总统出席中塞友谊大桥合龙仪式

(http://rs.chineseembassy.org/chn/sgxx/sghd/t1122257.htm)

Serbian President Attends Closure Ceremony of Bridge of China-Serbia Friendship

(http://www.fmprc.gov.cn/mfa_eng/wjb_663304/zwjg_665342/zwbd_665378/t1124583.shtml)

如上述标题翻译所示，我国驻××使馆举办××活动可以译为Chinese Embassy in ×× holds …；各种活动包括记者会（Press Conference）、新年招待会（New Year Reception）、新春招待会（Chinese Spring Festival Reception）、欢迎招待会（Welcome Reception）、新春联谊会（New Year Gathering）等。在我国驻外机构活动的新闻报道中，如"'多彩中华'中国少数民族文艺演出在金边举行"，"中国第七批援厄瓜多尔军医组荣获勋章"，翻译时如果使用被动语态，比如…is held, …is awarded, 则在标题中省略be动词，可以译为Art Performance Held in Phnom Penh, Medical Aid Team Awarded Medals。

（二）驻外机构活动报道导语的翻译（Translation of News Lead in Coverage of Activities of Mission Overseas）

以范例二为代表的我国驻外机构的活动报道，在导语中主要概括驻外机构名称、活动名称、主题、时间、地点以及参加官员等。我国驻外机构包括我国驻外使馆、领馆以及常驻联合国等政府间国际组织的代表团等代表机构。驻外大使馆具有外交官身份的人员，包括大使（ambassador）、公使（counselor）、公使衔参赞（minister counselor）、参赞（counselor）、一等秘书（first secretary）、二等秘书（second secretary）、三等秘书（third secretary）、随员（attaché），一些国家的attaché也有专员的意思，其身份属于秘书级别。领馆分为总领事馆（consulate-general）、领事馆（consulate）、副领事馆（vice-consulate）和领事代理处（consular agency）四级，其馆长或负责人分别为总领事（consul-general）、领事（consul）、副领事（vice consul）和领事代理（consular agent）。请看上述驻外机构以及外交人员职衔在新闻中的翻译实例：

2014年1月2日，中国驻埃及大使宋爱国在使馆举办专题记者会，向埃及新闻界深刻揭批日本领导人悍然参拜靖国神社的实质和目的，着重阐述中国政府和人民在这一问题上的严正立场。使馆冯飚公参等出席了活动。

(http://www.fmprc.gov.cn/zflt/chn/zxxx/t1114667.htm)

On January 2, 2014, H. E. Song Aiguo, Chinese Ambassador to Egypt held a special press conference in the Embassy to deeply expose and criticize the nature and purpose of Japanese leaders' blatant visits to the Yasukuni Shrine to the Egyptian press circle, particularly expounding the solemn position of the Chinese government and Chinese people on this issue. Minister Counselor Feng Biao and others were present at the activity.

(http://www.fmprc.gov.cn/mfa_eng/wjb_663304/zwjg_665342/zwbd_665378/)

2014年1月2日，由中国民族事务委员会、中国—东盟中心、中国驻柬埔寨使馆、柬埔寨中华文化发展基金会联合主办的"多彩中华"文艺演出在金边举行。驻柬埔寨使馆临时代办李志工、柬中友协主席艾桑奥、中华文化发展基金会理事长杨启秋、国家民委国际交流司副司长吴金光及中国—东盟中心秘书长马明强出席。

(http://www.fmprc.gov.cn/mfa_chn/zwbd_602255/t1114274.shtml)

On January 2, 2014, an art performance named "Colorful China" was held in Phnom Penh. The performance was co-sponsored by China's State Ethnic Affairs Commission (SEAC), ASEAN-China Center (ACC), Chinese Embassy in Cambodia and the Foundation of Promoting Chinese Culture in Cambodia. Charge d'Affaires ad Interim of the Chinese Embassy in Cambodia Li Zhigong, President of the Cambodia-China Friendship Association Ek Sam Ol, Director of the Foundation of Promoting Chinese Culture Yang Qiqiu, Deputy Director-General of the Department of International Exchanges of the SEAC Wu Jinguang and ACC Secretary-General Ma Mingqiang were present.

(http://www.fmprc.gov.cn/mfa_eng/wjb_663304/zwjg_665342/zwbd_665378/)

关于官员头衔的翻译，例1中"公参"是"公使衔参赞"的简称，是使馆参赞，译为Minister Counselor。例2中"临时代办"是指在外交代表大使或公使缺位或因故不能执行职务时，被委派代理其职务的外交人员，以临时代办的名义行使使馆首长的职权，译为Charge d'Affaires ad Interim[①]。

政府间国际组织（Inter-government Organization）常见的包括联合国（UN）、世界贸易组织（WTO）、东盟（ASEAN）、欧盟（EU）、八国集团（G8）、上海合作组织（Shanghai Cooperation Organization, SCO）、亚洲开发银行（Asia Development Bank, ADB）、国际结算银行（Bank for International Settlements, BIS）、国际原子能机构（International Atomic Energy Agency, IAEA）等。例2中中国—东盟中心的全称为ASEAN-China Center，缩写为ACC。一般来说，这些组织名称在新闻中首次出现的时候，英译时需要在全称后面括号加上缩写，再次出现时，则可以直接以缩写形式译出。

（三）驻外报道常用表达的翻译（Translation of Frequently Used Expressions in News from Mission Overseas）

1. 关于活动致辞的翻译

关于驻外机构活动的新闻报道中，常涉及感谢及祝贺之类的致辞，如"大家辛苦

---

① 临时代办，http://baike.baidu.com/link?url=Kh_soIW_iw_nHWVz78d2s5wyembgs3hdmLzcIJCfLlhZT6mjQ_Itnd4ldlnao6Pm63qeJY2VTBQ8_urw50oO4_

了""祝大家新年快乐、身体健康""预祝新的一年里马到成功"等。请看下面实例中这些表述的相应译文。

宁大使表示，驻泰国使馆愿意与各位媒体界人士保持密切联系，帮助中国人民更好地了解泰国，同时也帮助泰国人民更好地了解中国，共同为中泰友好、为地区和平、稳定与发展贡献绵薄力量。<u>过去一年大家辛苦了，马年新春即将到来，祝大家马年快乐，身体健康</u>。

(http://www.fmprc.gov.cn/ce/ceth/chn/xwdt/t1118384.htm)

Ambassador Ning said that the Chinese Embassy in Thailand will maintain close contacts with all friends from the press, and help Chinese and Thai people to understand each other better, working together to make humble efforts to promote China-Thailand friendship, regional peace, stability and development. He appreciated the journalists for their hard work and dedication over the past year. <u>With the Spring Festival of the Year of Horse around the corner, he expressed his New Year messages, wishing them a happy new year and good health.</u>

(http://www.fmprc.gov.cn/mfa_eng/wjb_663304/zwjg_665342/zwbd_665378/)

叶皓大使在致辞中感谢尼沙尼总统举办春节招待会。他表示2014年是中国农历的马年，马在中国文化中是活力、成功的象征。<u>预祝新的一年里，中阿关系继续绽放活力，万马奔腾，马到成功！</u>

(http://cs.mfa.gov.cn/gyls/lsgz/lqbb/t1122846.shtml)

In his speech, Ambassador Ye thanked President Nishani for holding the Chinese Spring Festival reception. He said that 2014 is the Chinese Year of the Horse, and horses symbolize vitality and success in the Chinese culture. <u>He wished the China-Albania relations lasting vitality, galloping development and all success in the new year.</u>

(http://www.fmprc.gov.cn/mfa_eng/wjb_663304/zwjg_665342/zwbd_665378/)

2. 表述活动现场的翻译

汉语四字格言简意赅，读起来铿锵有力。在外交新闻文体中，常用形象生动的四字词来凸显句式结构紧凑，音韵整齐，例如下面各例中的"天寒地冻、春意盎然""张灯结彩""异彩纷呈、高潮迭起"等。对于驻外报道中四字词的翻译，为了尽可能贴近原文的语义和句法结构，在再现原文语言意象美的同时，又使得英译文语言结构缜密，表述简练，可以运用介词结构、名词性短语、形容词短语等使得译文达到简洁凝练的表达效果。请看下面具体翻译实例：

窗外<u>天寒地冻</u>，驻俄使馆接待大厅内<u>春意盎然</u>。新春招待会自始至终洋溢着热

驻外报道的翻译
Translation for News from Mission Overseas
UNIT 3

烈、快乐、友好的节日气氛。宾主们畅叙友谊，相互祝福。

(http://china.huanqiu.com/News/fmprc/2014-01/4776678.html)

Freezing cold as it was outside, the reception hall of the Chinese Embassy in Russia was as warm as spring. A warm, joyful and friendly festival atmosphere permeated throughout the New Year reception. The hosts and guests recalled their friendship and exchanged their best wishes.

(http://www.fmprc.gov.cn/mfa_eng/wjb_663304/zwjg_665342/zwbd_665378/)

总统府内张灯结彩，悬挂了六盏象征喜庆的中国大红灯笼，来宾们品尝着中国饺子和各式阿式餐点，提前共庆中国传统新春佳节。

(http://china.huanqiu.com/News/fmprc/2014-01/4776678.html)

The Presidential Palace was decorated with colorful streamers and six big red Chinese lanterns which symbolize festivity. The guests tasted Chinese dumplings and a variety of Albanian cuisines to celebrate the traditional Chinese New Year in advance.

(http://www.fmprc.gov.cn/mfa_eng/wjb_663304/zwjg_665342/zwbd_665378/)

当晚，"文化中国·四海同春"艺术团的艺术家们为侨胞们献上了一台异彩纷呈、高潮迭起的演出，受到3000多名侨胞的热烈欢迎。

(http://cs.mfa.gov.cn/gyls/lsgz/lqbb/t1127550.shtml)

In that evening, artists from the Chinese art troupe "Cultures of China, Festival of Spring" staged a wonderful performance with one climax after another and received warm applause from over 3,000 overseas Chinese in France.

(http://www.fmprc.gov.cn/mfa_eng/wjb_663304/zwjg_665342/zwbd_665378/)

3. 表述活动性质和意义的翻译

在驻外机构的活动报道中，有时会描述某活动或事件的意义，常见表述有"载入史册""促进……迈上新台阶""为……注入新的活力""意义重大，影响深远"等。请看下面实例中这些表述的相应译文。

今天驻琅勃拉邦总领馆正式开馆，将作为老中友好的重要事件载入史册。中国在琅勃拉邦设领，将有力促进老挝北部地区同中国的传统友好交流与合作迈上新台阶，为中老关系发展注入新的活力。

(http://www.gov.cn/gzdt/2013-12/27/content_2555900.htm)

Today, the official opening of the Chinese Consulate-General in Luang Prabang will be written into the annals of history as a significant event of the Laos-China friendship. The establishment of the Chinese Consulate-General in Luang Prabang will greatly push the traditional friendly exchanges and cooperation between the northern area of Laos and China to a new high, and inject new vitality into the development of the China-Laos relations.

(http://www.fmprc.gov.cn/mfa_eng/wjb_663304/zwjg_665342/zwbd_665378/)

纪念是为了更好的传承，今天俄中双方代表共同纪念和缅怀那些为保卫年轻的苏维埃政权和赢得反法西斯战争而捐躯的俄中两国军人，<u>意义重大，影响深远</u>。

(http://ru.china-embassy.org/chn/sghd/t1130617.htm)

Today, <u>it is of great significance and far-reaching impact for</u> both Russian and Chinese representatives to jointly commemorate and honor the Russian and Chinese soldiers who sacrificed their lives to defend the newborn Soviet administration and to win the Anti-Fascist War.

(http://www.fmprc.gov.cn/mfa_eng/wjb_663304/zwjg_665342/zwbd_665378/)

学生译作讲评
Analysis of Students' Translation Practice

原文链接：http://www.fmprc.gov.cn/mfa_chn/zwbd_602255/t1101912.shtml

新闻原文：驻俄罗斯大使李辉出席"俄罗斯儒学研究"国际研讨会开幕式

学生译文：Ambassador Li Hui Attends the Opening Ceremony of the International Seminar on Confucian Studies in Russia

翻译评析：驻外新闻报道的标题应当信息准确，一目了然。学生将"驻俄罗斯大使李辉"译成Ambassador Li Hui，漏译"驻俄罗斯"这一重要界定成分，应补充为Ambassador to Russia Li Hui。标题中"俄罗斯儒学研究"是国际研讨会的会议名称，属于专有名称，学生译为Confucian Studies in Russia，将俄罗斯处理为介词短语，仿佛成为句子的地点状语，这样不仅会产生歧义，而且在形式上看起来也不像一个国际会议的名称。因此，标题可以改译为：Ambassador to Russia Li Hui Attends the Opening Ceremony of the International Seminar on Russian Confucianism Studies

新闻原文：2013年11月28日，俄罗斯科学院远东研究所与莫斯科大学孔子学院联合举办的"俄罗斯儒学研究"国际研讨会在远东所俄中友谊厅开幕。中国驻俄大使李辉，远东研究所所长、俄中友协主席季塔连科院士，莫斯科大学孔子学院中方院长任光宣，俄科学院哲学研究所所长布罗夫出席开幕式并分别致辞。中、俄、欧等各国汉学家、外交官和驻俄媒体代表约60人出席。

学生译文：On November 28, 2013, the international symposium with the theme of "Confucianism Study in Russia", jointly held by Institute of Oriental Studies of the Russian Academy of Sciences (RAS) and Confucius Institute of the Moscow State University, opened in Russia-China Friendship Hall in the Institute of Oriental Studies. Chinese Ambassador to Russia Li Hui, Director of Institute of Oriental Studies and Chairman of the Russia-China Friendship Association Academician Mikhail Titarenko, Chinese dean of Confucius Institute of the Moscow State University Ren Guangxuan, and Director of Institute of Philosophy of RAS Burov Vladilen addressed respectively at the opening ceremony. About 60 persons including Sinologists and diplomats of China, Russia and European countries and representatives of the media to Russia also attended.

翻译评析：学生译文中错译了"俄罗斯科学院远东研究所"这一机构名称。这属于特定机构，因此英文译名有相应的规范，"远东研究所"应译为Institute of Far Eastern Studies。国际研讨会在其友谊厅开幕，这个地点名词属于小地点，用介词at比in更恰当。"国际研讨会"的表述应当与标题一致，改为the international seminar。因此这段话中第一句的译文应当调整为On November 28, 2013, the international seminar with the theme of "Russian Confucianism Studies", jointly held by Institute of Far Eastern Studies of the Russian Academy of Sciences and Confucius Institute of the Moscow State University, opened at Russia-China Friendship Hall of the Institute of Far Eastern Studies.

第二句，在官员职衔的翻译上，学生译文将"俄中友协主席"处理为Chairman of the Russia-China Friendship Association，"孔子学院中方院长"译为Chinese dean of Confucius Institute，都是不规范的。"友协主席"通常译为President，而"中方院长"应当译为Chinese Director。学生译文在"……出席开幕式并分别致辞"这一句中漏译了were present at the opening ceremony。"汉学家"不是术语，英文中不需要大写首字母，译为sinologists即可。60人应改译为60 people。学生在"驻俄媒体"的翻译上照搬了"驻……大使"的译法，直接译为media to Russia是错误的，建议改为the media stationed in Russia。attend一词是及物动词，"60人出席"学生译为also attended，及物动词后面缺失名词宾语，应改译为About 60 people attended the event。综上所述，第二句译文可以调整为Chinese Ambassador to Russia H.E. Li Hui, Academician Mikhail Titarenko, Director of the Far East Institute and President of Russia-China Friendship Association, Chinese Director of Confucius Institute at the Moscow State University Ren Guangxuan, and Director of Institute of Philosophy of RAS Burov Vladilen were present at the opening ceremony and delivered speeches respectively. About 60 people including sinologists and diplomats of China, Russia and European countries and representatives of the media stationed in Russia attended the event.

新闻原文：李大使首先祝贺研讨会成功举办，并阐述了儒学思想的核心理念及对中国历史文化、社会生活和独立自主和平外交政策的深刻影响。李大使指出，面对今日新月异的科学技术发展和纷繁复杂的国际政治经济形势，儒家思想愈发显示出其超凡的智慧，不仅是中华民族的精神瑰宝，更在世界各地落地生根、开花散叶，影响一代又一代人，值得我们深入研究、学习和思考。

学生译文：Ambassador Li first congratulated the successful hosting of the seminar, and expounded the core idea of Confucian thought and its profound influence on China's history, culture, social life, and the independent and peaceful foreign policy. Ambassador Li pointed out that confronted with the currently rapid development of science and technology and the complex international political and economic situation, Confucian thought has more displayed its transcendental wisdom than ever before. Confucianism is not only the spiritual treasure of the Chinese nation, but also strikes roots and spreads out all around the world, affecting generation after generation which is worthy of our further research, study and thinking.

翻译评析：这一段的学生译文除了个别选词有待商榷，整体上质量不错。第一句中"祝贺……成功举办"，译为congratulated the successful hosting of…。"阐述"一词后跟两个名词短语"核心理念"和"深刻影响"，学生将其处理为expounded the core idea of … and its profound influence on，译文中巧妙地用了代词its指代"儒学思想"，只是"儒学思想"的表述可以调整为Confucianism，和标题中"儒学研究"（Confucianism Studies）一致。

这段译文的第二句中，有两个选词值得商榷：confronted with和complex。confront更多地运用于面对一些危险和挑战的语境中，而原文中面对日新月异的科学技术，选用faced with就可以了。complex一般指something has many different parts, and is therefore often difficult to understand。"纷繁复杂的国际形势"调整为complicated更为恰当。学生译文将"儒家思想愈发显示出其超凡的智慧"译为Confucian thought has more displayed its…，是受到汉语语序的影响，改译为Confucianism has displayed more of its transcendental wisdom会显得更为地道和自然。

新闻原文：李大使强调，俄罗斯儒学研究有着悠久的历史和坚实的基础，并随着中俄全面战略协作伙伴关系的深入发展日益焕发出新的生命力。我们高度评价远东研究所和莫斯科大学孔子学院为传播中华文化和发展两国人文交流与合作做出的积极贡献，希望大家在新的一年中携手并进，集成儒学精华，发扬儒学精神，共同为中俄全面战略协作伙伴关系健康深入发展而不懈努力。

学生译文：Ambassador Li stressed Confucian Studies in Russia enjoys a long history and a solid foundation, and shows its increasingly new vitality accompanied with the in-depth development of the China-Russia comprehensive strategic partnership. We speak highly of the positive contributions to spread the Chinese culture as well as develop the cultural exchanges and cooperation between the two countries made by Institute of Oriental Studies and the Confucius Institute at Moscow University. We hope that in the coming year we could go hand in hand, collect the essence of Confucianism, develop the spirit of Confucianism and jointly make unremitting efforts to the sound and in-depth development of the China-Russia comprehensive strategic partnership.

翻译评析：原文第一句中，"中俄全面战略协作伙伴关系"学生译文有明显的漏译，comprehensive strategic partnership的意思是全面战略关系，应根据原文补充完整为Comprehensive Strategic Partnership of Coordination。原文中"日益焕发出"决定了译文中应当使用现在进行时态，所以译文调整为is demonstrating…。

这段译文的第二句将made by Institute of Oriental Studies and the Confucius Institute at

Moscow University放置句末，离中心词the positive contributions过远，指代不清，会给读者造成阅读困难。因此，可以调整为the positive contributions made by Institute of Far Eastern Studies and the Confucius Institute at Moscow University to spreading the Chinese culture as well as developing the people-to-people and cultural exchanges and cooperation between China and Russia。此外，这句原文中"人文交流"除了文化交流之外还有人才交流的意思，所以学生译文应补充完整为people-to-people and cultural exchanges。

译文第三句中对原文两个动词"集成"和"发扬"的翻译，考虑到和宾语the essence以及the spirit的搭配，调整为extract the essence of Confucianism, carry forward the spirit of Confucianism更为地道。最后，"同为中俄全面战略协作伙伴关系健康深入发展而不懈努力"，学生译文中的make efforts to development应当加上动词promote。因此，最后一句可以调整为jointly make unremitting efforts to promote the healthy and in-depth development。

新闻原文：季塔连科院士、任光宣院长、布罗夫所长分别致辞，对中国大使馆长期以来为促进俄中文化和学术交流提供的大力支持表示衷心感谢，并详细介绍了儒学思想的历史发展和在俄罗斯及世界各国的传播历程，以及对人类道德建设和树立和平包容、相互尊重、互利共赢理念所具有的重要现实意义。……

学生译文：Academician Titarenko, Dean Ren Guangxuan and Director Burov delivered a speech respectively to express the heartfelt thanks to Chinese Embassy for its strong and long-term support for the cultural and academic exchanges between Russia and China, and gave a detailed introduction on the historical development of Confucian thought, its history of spreading to Russia and other countries of the world and its important practical implications for human moral construction and the establishment of the concept of peace and inclusiveness, mutual respect and mutual benefit and win-win result.

翻译评析：学生译文delivered a speech出现了名词单复数错误。"季塔连科院士、任光宣院长、布罗夫所长分别致辞"，多人致辞应当是复数形式，所以改为delivered speeches respectively。"为促进俄中文化和学术交流提供的大力支持"学生漏译了"促进"，译文可以增补为support for the promotion of。"人类道德建设"学生译为human moral construction，属中式英语，如果改为moral construction of mankind则表述更清晰，更地道。学生译文中将"重要现实意义"译为important practical implications，但implication这个词更多情况下有"后果"和"含意"的意思，故改为significance更贴近原文。

新闻原文：……他们指出，举行此次研讨会旨在深入探讨恢复儒家思想的原本魅力，更好地发挥其对当今世界各领域生活的重要指导作用。希望此次研讨会能够为发展俄中人文交流和俄中友好事业做出自己的贡献。

学生译文：They pointed out that the purpose of holding this seminar is to conduct in-depth discussion on the restoration of original charm of Confucian thought, and better play its important role in guiding the life in each area in today's world. It is expected that this seminar could contribute its share to developing Russia-China cultural and people-to-people exchanges and friendship.

翻译评析：对于原文"举行此次研讨会旨在深入探讨恢复儒家思想的原本魅力，更好地发挥其对当今世界各领域生活的重要指导作用"的语义和句法进行仔细分析，不难发现研讨会是为了探讨儒家思想的原本魅力，从而更好地发挥儒家思想的重要指导作用。那么学生译文中this seminar is to conduct discussion ... and better play...，将"探讨"和"发挥"处理为并列结构，就混淆了原句的句法结构，产生了歧义。为了明晰句子逻辑，可以将play一句处理为分词状语表递进关系。这部分可以改译为：They pointed out that the purpose of holding this seminar is to conduct in-depth discussion on the restoration of original charm of Confucianism, and better playing of its important role in guiding the life in each area in today's world.

学生译文最后一句将原文无主句"希望……"处理为it is expected，结构本是不错，但考虑到本段都在讲述与会人的致辞，而"希望"也是致辞人的希望，所以直接以they expect则更加明确。此外，"俄中友好事业"的"事业"一词不可随意删减，应补充the cause of bilateral friendship。因此，最后一句可以改译为They expected that this seminar could contribute its share to developing Russia-China people-to-people and cultural exchanges and the cause of bilateral friendship.

实战练习
Translation Practice

一、请翻译下列驻外报道的标题（Translate the following headlines of news from mission overseas）

1. 驻中非大使孙海潮会见中非红十字会会长
   (http://www.fmprc.gov.cn/web/wjdt_674879/zwbd_674895/)
2. 驻葡萄牙大使黄松甫访问圣若奥·德马德拉市
   (http://www.fmprc.gov.cn/ce/cept/chn/sghd/t1098654.htm)
3. 驻柬埔寨大使布建国拜会柬政府副首相盖金延
   (http://www.fmprc.gov.cn/web/wjdt_674879/zwbd_674895/)
4. 驻沙特大使李成文在《中东报》发文介绍"一带一路"
   (http://wcm.fmprc.gov.cn/pub/chn/gxh/mtb/zwbd/dszlsjt/t1146954.htm)
5. 阿尔巴尼亚总统首次为华人举办中国春节招待会
   (http://china.huanqiu.com/News/fmprc/2014-01/4792712.html)
6. 斯里兰卡总统、总理出席中国驻斯使馆组织的"欢乐春节—中斯大联欢"活动
   (http://www.fmprc.gov.cn/ce/celk/chn/xwdt/t1120416.htm)

驻外报道的翻译
Translation for News from Mission Overseas — UNIT 3

7. 智利代外长里韦罗斯为驻智大使杨万明送行

   (http://www.fmprc.gov.cn/ce/cechile/chn/sgxw/t1181509.htm)

8. 中国海军170编队访问阿根廷取得圆满成功

   (http://www.fmprc.gov.cn/web/wjdt_674879/zwbd_674895/)

9. 中国驻埃塞俄比亚使馆向亚的斯亚贝巴市社区小学校捐赠教学设备

   (http://et.china-embassy.org/chn/zagx/t1097879.htm)

10. 中华人民共和国驻登巴萨总领事馆正式开馆

    (http://www.fmprc.gov.cn/ce/cgmb/chn/wjbxw/t1217542.htm)

二、请翻译下面驻外报道中的句子（Translate the following sentences of news from mission overseas）

1. 2018年7月14日，驻冰岛大使金智健参加在冰岛都皮沃古尔市举办的"滚动的雪球"艺术展开幕式，冰岛总统约翰内松夫妇、都市市长约翰内松及各界人士约200余人出席。

   （http://www.fmprc.gov.cn/web/zwbd_673032/gzhd_673042/t1578394.shtml）

2. 金智健大使在致辞中对艺术展在促进东西方文化交流方面所发挥的重要作用予以积极评价，并强调指出，中国国家主席习近平倡导构建人类命运共同体，中国愿与冰岛在内的国家共同努力，共建人类美好未来。

   （http://www.fmprc.gov.cn/web/zwbd_673032/gzhd_673042/t1578394.shtml）

3. 2018年7月10日，驻克罗地亚大使胡兆明召开新闻发布会，重点就中国—中东欧国家（以下简称16+1）索非亚领导人会晤宣布克将主办下一次领导人会晤介绍相关情况。来自克国家电视台、NOVA电视台、《晨报》《晚报》等主流媒体、各大网络平台以及新华社驻克记者站等10多名记者出席。

   （http://www.fmprc.gov.cn/web/wjdt_674879/zwbd_674895/t1575875.shtml）

4. 2018年6月28日，驻马来西亚大使白天拜会马来西亚新任经济事务部长阿兹敏。双方就中马关系发展和两国经济合作深入交换意见。

   （http://www.fmprc.gov.cn/web/wjdt_674879/zwbd_674895/t1572905.shtml）

5. 白天大使向阿兹敏介绍了中马关系现状和中国对外经济合作概况，表示中马合作基础扎实，潜力巨大，前景广阔。中国政府愿同马新政府密切合作，推动中马合作再上新台阶。期待与阿精诚合作，挖掘两国经济合作更多潜力，使中马在产业转型升级、经济建设方面实现优势互补和共同发展。欢迎阿适时访华。

   (http://www.fmprc.gov.cn/web/wjdt_674879/zwbd_674895/t1572905.shtml)

三、请翻译下面一则驻外报道（Translate the following news from mission overseas）

驻赞比亚大使李杰向赞比亚总统伦古递交国书

2018年6月29日，驻赞比亚大使李杰在赞总统府向伦古总统递交国书，双方进行了亲切友好交谈。

李杰大使首先转达了习近平主席对伦古总统的亲切问候和良好祝愿。他表示，很高兴看到在伦古总统领导下，赞比亚经济社会事业持续发展，民众生活水平不断提高，国际和地区影响力日益提升。两国老一辈领导人缔造的中赞传统友谊历久弥坚，各领域务实合作取得丰硕成果，两国已成为风雨同舟、患难与共的好朋友、好伙伴、好兄弟。中方愿同赞方一道，用好中非合作论坛和共建"一带一路"平台，进一步拓展两国友好互利合作，不断提升中赞关系水平，更好造福两国和两国人民。

伦古总统请李大使转达对习近平主席的诚挚问候，对李大使履新致以热烈欢迎，并表示将大力支持李大使的工作。伦古总统高度评价赞中关系发展及两国各领域合作取得的丰硕成果，表示两国老一辈领导人为赞中全天候友好关系打下了坚实基础，两国各领域务实合作为双边关系发展提供了强有力支撑。伦古总统进一步表示，中非合作论坛是赞中两国加强合作的重要平台，他期待着出席2018年9月将在北京举行的中非合作论坛峰会。

（http://www.fmprc.gov.cn/web/zwbd_673032/wshd_673034/t1573140.shtml）

参考译文
Versions for Reference

一、请翻译下列驻外报道的标题 (Translate the following headlines of news from mission overseas)

1. Ambassador to Central Africa Sun Haichao Meets With President of the Central African Red Cross Society
2. Ambassador to Portugal Huang Songfu Visits São João da Madeira
3. Ambassador to Cambodia Bu Jianguo Calls on Cambodian Deputy Prime Minister Ke Kim Yan
4. Ambassador to Saudi Arabia Li Chengwen Publishes Article on *Asharq Al-Awsat* Introducing "Belt and Road"
5. Albanian President Holds First Chinese Spring Festival Reception for Chinese in Albania

6. Sri Lankan President and Prime Minister Attend "Happy Spring Festival—China-Sri Lanka Gala" Organized by Chinese Embassy in Sri Lanka
7. Acting Foreign Minister Edgardo Riveros of Chile Sees off Ambassador to Chile Yang Wanming
8. The PLA Navy Fleet No.170 Pays Successful Visit to Argentina
9. Chinese Embassy to Ethiopia Donates Teaching Facilities to Community Primary School in Addis Ababa
10. Consulate-General of the People's Republic of China in Denpasar Inaugurated

二、请翻译下面驻外报道中的句子（Translate the following sentences of news from mission overseas）

1. On 14th July 2018, Chinese Ambassador to Iceland Jin Zhijian attended the opening ceremony of Rolling Snowball Exhibition in Djúpivogur of Iceland. Among over 200 guests were President Guðni Jóhannesson and First Lady Eliza Reid of Iceland, Mayor Gauti Jóhannesson of Djúpivogur and guests from all sectors of Iceland.

2. In his remarks, Ambassador Jin Zhijian positively reviewed the important role played by Rolling Snowball Exhibition in promoting cultural exchanges between the East and the West. He stressed that Chinese President Xi Jinping put forward the vision to create a community of shared future for mankind. China is willing to work together with Iceland and other countries for a bright future for mankind.

3. On July 10th, Ambassador of the People's Republic of China to the Republic of Croatia H.E. Mr. Hu Zhaoming held a press-conference on which the relevant information about the Meeting of Heads of Government of China and Central and European Countries (abbreviation "16+1" Summit) in Sofia and the next one that would be hosted in Croatia were introduced. Croatian television, NOVA TV, *Morning Post*, *Evening Post* and other mainstream media and all big internet platforms, as well as Xinhua news agency in Croatia, in total more than 10 journalists, attended the conference.

4. On June 28, H.E. Bai Tian, the Chinese ambassador to Malaysia, called on Dato' Seri Azmin Ali, Minister of Economic Affairs of Malaysia. They exchanged views on development of China-Malaysia relations and economic cooperation between the two countries.

5. Ambassador Bai briefed the latter on the status quo of China-Malaysia relations and general picture of China's overseas economic cooperation. Bai said that China-Malaysia cooperation enjoys solid foundation, great potential and broad prospects. The Chinese government is willing to work closely with Malaysia's new government to push the bilateral cooperation to a new level. The Chinese side looks forward to cooperating with

Minister Azmin Ali to fully tap the potential of the bilateral economic cooperation to achieve common development. He invited the Minister to pay a visit to China at mutual convenience.

三、请翻译下面一则驻外报道（Translate the following news from mission overseas）

H.E. Mr. Li Jie, Chinese Ambassador to Zambia Presents Letter of Credence to H.E. President Edgar Lungu

On June 29th, 2018, H.E. Mr. Li Jie, Ambassador Extraordinary and Plenipotentiary of the People's Republic of China to the Republic of Zambia presented Letter of Credence to H.E. President Edgar Lungu at State House, during which they held friendly and cordial talks.

Ambassador Li conveyed cordial greetings and best wishes from H.E. Chinese President Xi Jinping to H.E. President Edgar Lungu. Ambassador Li said, under the leadership of H.E. President Lungu, Zambia has enjoyed continued economic and social progress, elevated living standards of the people and rising regional and global influence. The traditional China-Zambia friendship forged by the older generation of leaders of both countries has stood the test of time. The pragmatic cooperation in various fields has yielded fruitful achievements. The two countries have become good friends, good partners and good brothers who stand together rain or shine. The Chinese side is willing to work together with the Zambian side to make the best use of the platforms of Forum on China-Africa Cooperation (FOCAC) and the Belt and Road Initiative to expand mutually beneficial cooperation, enhance bilateral ties and deliver greater benefits to both countries and peoples.

H.E. President Edgar Lungu asked Ambassador Li to convey his sincere greetings to H.E. President Xi Jinping. He warmly welcomed Ambassador Li and expressed his strong support to Ambassador Li's work. President Lungu spoke highly of the development of Zambia-China relations and the fruitful achievements of bilateral cooperation in various fields. He expressed that the older generation of leaders of both countries have laid a solid foundation for the all-weather friendship and the pragmatic cooperation in various fields has provided strong support for the development of bilateral relations. President Lungu further stated that FOCAC is an important platform for Zambia and China to strengthen bilateral cooperation, and he is looking forward to attending the FOCAC Beijing Summit in September 2018.

驻外报道的翻译 3
Translation for News from Mission Overseas UNIT

单元小结
Summary

　　本单元主要介绍了各类驻外报道的翻译。驻外报道涵盖的内容丰富、类型多样。范例一介绍了驻外人员活动报道标题及导语的翻译,归纳了人名、职衔、媒体名称的翻译方法和规范。此外还总结了有关日本首相参拜靖国神社等敏感时政问题的常见英译表达。在翻译此类报道时,不仅要在语义上与原文对等,在语气、文风上也要尽量再现原文。范例二着重介绍了驻外机构活动报道的标题及导语的翻译,驻外人员职务的知识及其翻译。此外,还总结了有关我驻外机构活动报道的常见表述,如活动致辞、活动现场以及活动意义等。通过对驻外报道的翻译,可以了解到我国驻外机构重要外交活动信息,我国政府的对外方针政策、对国内外重大事件的观点和立场,以及相关常见表述的翻译方法和技巧。优秀的驻外报道新闻翻译能够发挥我国驻外外交机构的窗口桥梁作用,是外宣力度的重要体现。

外交访问报道的翻译
Translation for Coverage of Diplomatic Visits

单元简介 Introduction

外交访问一般包括国事访问、正式访问和非正式访问。国事访问指国家元首应他国元首邀请进行的访问,在所有访问类型中访问者享有的礼宾接待规格是最高的;正式访问是一国领导人应另一国领导人的正式邀请,对邀请国进行的访问,也可称为友好访问或正式友好访问,规格低于国事访问;非正式访问的礼仪活动一般从简,国家领导人以私人身份进行的访问称为私人访问,途经某国所进行的访问可称为过境访问,不便公开报道的访问则称为秘密访问。

外交访问的新闻报道常涉及以下内容:迎宾仪式、宴会活动、会晤会谈、参观游览、发表演讲、送宾道别,外交日程以及外交部谈领导人访问某国等。翻译外交访问新闻报道也要熟悉外交礼仪,如礼宾接待程序,各国不同民族习惯等。

Translation for Coverage of Diplomatic Visits

外交访问新闻翻译范例分析
Sample of Translation for Coverage of Diplomatic Visits

范例一（Sample I）

李克强抵达巴西利亚对巴西进行正式访问（节本）
2015/05/19
Li Keqiang Arrives in Brasília to Pay an Official Visit to Brazil (Abbreviated Version)
2015/05/19

应巴西联邦共和国总统罗塞夫邀请，国务院总理李克强于当地时间18日下午乘专机抵达巴西利亚空军基地，开始对巴西进行正式访问。李克强总理夫人程虹同机抵达。

On the afternoon of May 18 local time, at the invitation of President Dilma Rousseff of the Federative Republic of Brazil, Premier Li Keqiang arrived at the Brasilia Air Base by special plane, starting his official visit to Brazil. Premier Li Keqiang's wife Mme. Cheng Hong arrived by the same plane.

***

巴方礼兵分列红地毯两侧，吹起嘹亮的军号向远道而来的贵宾致敬。李克强夫妇同前来迎接的巴西政府高级官员、巴西利亚空军基地司令等亲切握手。中国驻巴西大使李金章也前来迎接。

The Brazilian guard of honor, lining up on either side of the red carpet, saluted the distinguished guests from afar with resonant bugle. Premier Li Keqiang and his wife warmly shook hands with the senior officials of the Brazilian government, Commander of the Brasilia Air Base who were greeting them. Li Jinzhang, Chinese Ambassador to Brazil, also greeted them at the airport.

***

李克强指出，拉美地区为人类文明和进步作出了重要贡献，对当今世界发展走向发挥着重要影响。近年来，中拉关系实现跨越式发展，建立了平等互利、共同发展的全面合作伙伴关系。我期待通过此次拉美之行，进一步密切中拉交流，巩固传统友谊，推动产能合作，促进双向贸易投资，打造中拉全方位互利合作升级版。

Li Keqiang pointed out that Latin America has made great contribution to human civilization and progress of human society and is playing a significant role in the current development of the world. In recent years, China and Latin America have made leap-frog development in bilateral relations, establishing a comprehensive cooperative partnership featuring equality, mutual benefit and common development. He hopes that this visit could help to enhance China-Latin America exchanges, consolidate traditional friendship, push forward cooperation in production capacity, promote two-way trade and investment, and build an upgraded version of China-Latin America comprehensive and mutually beneficial cooperation.

***

访问巴西期间，李克强将同罗塞夫总统举行会谈并共见记者，共同出席美丽山水电站特高压直流输电项目视频奠基仪式、中巴工商界峰会，分别会见巴参、众议长。除首都巴西利亚以外，李克强还将访问里约热内卢，考察中巴装备合作成果，参观中国装备制造业展览等。

During his visit to Brazil, Li Keqiang will hold talks and meet the press with President Dilma Rousseff, attend a video ground-breaking ceremony for the ultra-high voltage electricity transmission project in the Belo Monte hydroelectric dam and China-Brazil Business Summit, have separate meetings with presidents of Brazil's Federal Senate and Chamber of Deputies. Besides Brazilian capital of Brasília, Li Keqiang will also pay a visit to Rio De Janeiro to inspect the achievements made in bilateral cooperation in equipment and visit the Chinese Equipment Manufacturing Industry Exposition.

***

李克强和夫人程虹是在圆满结束对爱尔兰的过境访问后抵达巴西利亚的。离开香农机场时，爱尔兰政府代表、财政部长等高级官员和中国驻爱尔兰大使徐建国到机场送行。

Li Keqiang and his wife Mme. Cheng Hong arrived in Brasília after successfully concluding their transit visit to Ireland. Upon their departure from Shannon Airport, representatives of the government, Finance Minister and other senior officials of Ireland as well as Xu Jianguo, Chinese Ambassador to Ireland, bade them farewell at the airport.

新闻背景：应巴西联邦共和国总统罗塞夫、哥伦比亚共和国总统桑托斯、秘鲁共和国总统乌马拉、智利共和国总统巴切莱特邀请，国务院总理李克强于2015年5月18日至26日对拉美四国巴西、哥伦比亚、秘鲁、智利进行正式访问，并过境爱尔兰和西班牙。这是继2014年国家主席习近平成功访问拉美后，中国对拉美的又一次重大外交行动。当地时间5月18日18时许，总理专机抵达巴西利亚空军基地，李克强走出专机舱门，踏上巴西首都巴西利亚的红地毯，正式开始拉美四国首访。

原文链接：http://news.xinhuanet.com/world/2015-05/19/c_1115326957.htm

译文链接：http://www.fmprc.gov.cn/mfa_eng/topics_665678/lkqdbxglbyblzljxzsfw/t1265427.shtml

外交访问报道的翻译
Translation for Coverage of Diplomatic Visits

一、范例一文本结构分析（Text Structure Analysis of Sample I）

范例一是一则关于领导人抵达访问国目的地机场的新闻报道，主要内容包括我国出访领导人、当地时间、地点、欢迎仪式、我国领导人观点、访问日程等。

第一段为新闻导语，介绍我国出访领导人及配偶（李克强总理及夫人程虹）、出访国（巴西）、目的地（巴西利亚空军基地）、当地时间（18日下午）、邀请方领导人（巴西联邦共和国总统罗塞夫）等内容。

第二段主要内容为欢迎仪式，介绍欢迎仪式场景（巴方礼兵分列红地毯两侧，吹起嘹亮的军号向远道而来的贵宾致敬）以及出席官员（巴西政府高级官员、巴西利亚空军基地司令、中国驻巴西大使李金章）。

第三段介绍李克强总理的主要观点，期待通过此次访问，中巴全面战略伙伴关系，乃至中拉关系都能取得新的、更大的发展。

第四、五段介绍李克强总理此次访问期间的日程安排，并简要总结此次访问之前对爱尔兰的过境访问。

二、范例一翻译解析（Translation Analysis of Sample I）

（一）外交访问报道标题的翻译（Translation of Headlines Covering Diplomatic Visits）

有关外交访问的新闻报道常涉及迎宾仪式、宴会活动、会晤会谈、参观游览、发表演讲、送宾道别等内容。一般来说，国事访问指一国国家元首应另一国国家元首的邀请，对该国进行的正式外交访问，是两个国家间最高规格的外交交流，如"习近平抵达阿布扎比开始对阿拉伯联合酋长国进行国事访问"。一国领导人应另一国领导人的正式邀请，对邀请国进行的访问称为"正式访问"，如"李克强将对澳大利亚、新西兰进行正式访问"，有时也可称为友好访问或正式友好访问，如"汪洋对肯尼亚进行正式友好访问"。非正式外交访问中，领导人途经某国所进行的访问称为过境访问，如"李克强前往巴西途中在爱尔兰过境访问"。

外交访问新闻还包括对于外交日程的报道，如"李克强结束出访回京"及"英国外交大臣哈蒙德将访华"等。

下面就以上述外交访问报道标题为例，探讨不同形式的访问报道标题的翻译方法。

李克强将对澳大利亚、新西兰进行正式访问
(http://www.gov.cn/premier/2017-03/17/content_5178377.htm)
Li Keqiang to Pay Official Visits to Australia and New Zealand
(http://www.fmprc.gov.cn/mfa_eng/wjdt_665385/wsrc_665395/t1446687.shtml)
汪洋对肯尼亚进行正式友好访问
(http://www.fmprc.gov.cn/web/zyxw/t1570380.shtml)

Wang Yang Pays an Official Goodwill Visit to Kenya

(http://www.fmprc.gov.cn/mfa_eng/zxxx_662805/t1571315.shtml)

习近平将对阿联酋、塞内加尔、卢旺达和南非进行国事访问，出席金砖国家领导人第十次会晤，过境毛里求斯并进行友好访问

(http://www.xinhuanet.com/politics/leaders/2018-07/12/c_1123117264.htm)

Xi Jinping to Pay State Visits to the United Arab Emirates, Senegal, Rwanda and South Africa, Attend the 10th BRICS Summit and Make a Stopover in Mauritius for a Friendly Visit

(http://www.fmprc.gov.cn/mfa_eng/wjdt_665385/wsrc_665395/t1576860.shtml)

习近平抵达阿布扎比开始对阿拉伯联合酋长国进行国事访问

(http://www.fmprc.gov.cn/web/wjdt_674879/gjldrhd_674881/t1578848.shtml)

Chinese President Arrives in Abu Dhabi for State Visit to UAE

(http://www.fmprc.gov.cn/mfa_eng/wjdt_665385/wshd_665389/t1578887.shtml)

李克强结束出访回京

(http://www.gov.cn/guowuyuan/2018-01/11/content_5255788.htm)

Li Keqiang Returns to Beijing after Concluding His Visit

(http://www.mfa.gov.cn/ce/ceun/eng/zgyw/t1525736.htm)

英国外交大臣哈蒙德将访华

(http://www.fmprc.gov.cn/web/wjdt_674879/wsrc_674883/t1329029.shtml)

UK Foreign Secretary Hammond to Visit China

(http://www.chinadailyasia.com/nation/2015-12-31/content_15366360.html)

李克强前往巴西途中在爱尔兰过境访问

(http://news.xinhuanet.com/politics/2015-05/17/c_1115310554.htm)

Li Keqiang Pays a Transit Visit to Ireland on His Way to Brazil

(http://www.fmprc.gov.cn/mfa_eng/zxxx_662805/t1265034.shtml)

如上述新闻标题翻译所示，最高规格的国家元首国事访问译为State Visit，对某国进行国事访问，译为Pay State Visit to；正式访问招待规格较国事访问稍低，通常译为Official Visit，其中正式友好访问译为Official Goodwill Visit，友好访问译为Goodwill Visit或Friendly Visit；过境访问属于非正式访问（Unofficial Visit）的一种，可以译为Pay a Transit Visit to或者Make Stopover Visit to。一般介绍外交访问活动日程安排的标题有"……将访问……"，可以译为... to Visit ...，to do结构表示将来发生，在标题中不出现助词will；介绍领导人抵达某地开始正式访问的标题如"××抵达……开始对……进行正式访问"，可以译为×× Arrives in ... to Pay an Official Visit to ...，或者×× Arrives in ... Starting ... Official Visit to ...；关于结束访问的标题有"××结束对……的访问回到北京"，通常可以使用动词"conclude"，译为×× Concludes His Visit to ... and Returns to

外交访问报道的翻译
Translation for Coverage of Diplomatic Visits **UNIT 4**

Beijing，或××Returns to Beijing after Concluding His Visits to …，时态均采用一般现在时。

（二）外交访问报道导语的翻译（Translation of News Lead in Coverage of Diplomatic Visits）

外交访问报道的新闻导语，通常涵盖我国出访领导人、到访时间、到访国、到访国领导人和官员等信息。按照国际惯例，外交访问一般是一国领导人应邀对另一国进行访问。在新闻导语中，常出现××领导人应××领导人的邀请，对该国进行访问等表述。"应……的邀请"可以译为at the invitation of或upon invitation。

外交访问报道中的时间，通常介绍的是当地时间某月某日或当地时间某日上午（下午），即使原文中不出现表示月份的时间，在译文中也要具体到月和日，例如范例一中"当地时间18日下午"，则根据这则新闻报道的具体月份，译为On the afternoon of May 18 local time。

"外交访问中领导人乘专机抵达……"的英文表述可以译为arrive at … by special plane。"技术经停"是指本国航机因技术需要（如添加燃料、飞机故障或气象原因备降）在协议国降落、经停。① 在外交访问中，"技术经停"是非正式外交访问中"过境访问"的一种具体表述形式，一般发生在飞行时间较长的访问途中。例如××领导人在前往某地访问途中，在某地技术经停，对该国进行过境访问，可以译为×× took a technical stopover in …或×× made a technical stop at …。请看下面具体翻译实例：

应巴西联邦共和国总统罗塞夫邀请，国务院总理李克强于当地时间18日下午乘专机抵达巴西利亚空军基地，开始对巴西进行正式访问。李克强总理夫人程虹同机抵达。

(http://news.xinhuanet.com/world/2015-05/19/c_1115326957.htm)

On the afternoon of May 18 local time, at the invitation of President Dilma Rousseff of the Federative Republic of Brazil, Premier Li Keqiang arrived at the Brasilia Air Base by special plane, starting his official visit to Brazil. Premier Li Keqiang's wife Mme. Cheng Hong arrived by the same plane.

(http://www.fmprc.gov.cn/mfa_eng/topics_665678/lkqdbxglbyblzljxzsfw/t1265427.shtml)

当地时间9月26日，应邀访问白俄罗斯的国务院副总理张高丽在明斯克会见了白俄罗斯总统卢卡申科，27日同白俄罗斯总理米亚斯尼科维奇举行会谈。

(http://cpc.people.com.cn/n/2014/0928/c64094-25748930.html?ol4f)

On September 26 local time, Vice Premier Zhang Gaoli, when visiting Belarus upon invitation, met with President Alexander Lukashenko of Belarus in Minsk, and held talks

---

① 技术经停权，http://baike.baidu.com/link?url=0vBHfyD1u4UZX73EP59CfMyZ5rcFl07GVgbTGAjR9NVsQ1Bty7daA6mFaNn9z2VoB70LSBrEW20c-pfOK-lOXK

with Prime Minister Mikhail Myasnikovich of Belarus on September 27.

(http://www.fmprc.gov.cn/mfa_eng/zxxx_662805/t1196782.shtml)

当地时间7月13日，国家主席习近平抵达希腊罗德岛，在前往巴西出席金砖国家领导人第六次会晤并对拉美四国进行国事访问途中进行技术经停，会见希腊领导人，就两国关系发展交换意见。

(http://news.xinhuanet.com/2014-07/13/c_1111588889.htm)

On July 13 local time, President Xi Jinping made a technical stop at the island of Rhodes, Greece, on his way to Brazil to attend the sixth BRICS Summit and pay state visits to four Latin American countries. He met with the Greek leaders and exchanged views on the development of the bilateral relations with them.

(http://www.fmprc.gov.cn/mfa_eng/topics_665678/xjpzxcxjzgjldrdlchwdbxagtwnrlgbjxgsfwbcxzlldrhw/t1174660.shtml)

（三）外交访问报道常用表达的翻译（Translation of Frequently Used Expressions in Coverage of Diplomatic Visits）

1. 有关机场迎宾的翻译

从程序上说，接待国事访问的第一步，首先是接机。礼宾安排在很多国家有严格固定的程序要求，一般来说是依照惯例甚至法律而行的。大多数国家派正部级代表去机场迎接外国领导人、元首或者政府首脑，随后再举行正式的欢迎仪式。当然，为了表示重视，外国领导人亲赴机场迎送他国领导人的场面也不在少数。①

国事或正式访问中，受访国一般在机场铺红地毯，设礼兵列队迎接贵宾，在新闻报道中常表述为"礼兵分列红地毯两侧，向××行注目礼或致敬"，可以译为the guard of honor (the guard of courtesy) lined up on both sides along the red carpet and saluted ××。

隆重的欢迎设有献花仪式，献花者往往是儿童或女青年，在新闻报道中常表述为"当地儿童向××献上鲜花"，可以译为local children presented a bunch of flowers to ××。

领导人下飞机后会同迎候官员依次握手问候，在新闻报道中常表述为"同××亲切握手""互致问候"等，可以分别译为warmly shook hands with ×× 和exchanged greetings with ××。

关于飞机"舷梯"的描述，通常使用ramp, the accommodation ladder或the gangway ladder等词，走出机舱译为walked out of the cabin。请看下面具体翻译实例：

巴方礼兵分列红地毯两侧，吹起嘹亮的军号向远道而来的贵宾致敬。李克强夫妇同前来迎接的巴西政府高级官员、巴西利亚空军基地司令等亲切握手。中国驻巴

---

① 解析：领导人访问有哪些迎宾礼仪程序要求，http://china.huanqiu.com/hot/2015-04/6244606.html

西大使李金章也前来迎接。

(http://news.xinhuanet.com/world/2015-05/19/c_1115326957.htm)

  The Brazilian guard of honor, lining up on either side of the red carpet, saluted the distinguished guests from afar with resonant bugle. Premier Li Keqiang and his wife warmly shook hands with the senior officials of the Brazilian government, Commander of the Brasilia Air Base who were greeting them. Li Jinzhang, Chinese Ambassador to Brazil, also greeted them at the airport.

(http://www.fmprc.gov.cn/mfa_eng/topics_665678/lkqdbxglbyblzljxzsfw/t1265427.shtml)

  习近平抵达罗德岛迪亚哥拉斯机场时,希腊总理萨马拉斯专程从首都雅典前来,并率多名内阁部长和罗德市市长到机场欢迎。习近平在舷梯旁同萨马拉斯握手,互致问候。身着当地传统服装的希腊青年向习近平献花。希腊礼兵沿红地毯两侧列队,向习近平致敬。

(http://news.xinhuanet.com/2014-07/13/c_1111588889.htm)

  Upon arrival at the Rhodes Diagoras International Airport, Xi Jinping received a warm welcome from Prime Minister Antonis Samaras of Greece, who came all the way from the capital city of Athens and led many cabinet ministers and the mayor of the city of Rhodes. Xi Jinping shook hands with Samaras beside the ramp and exchanged greetings with him. The local youth, dressed in traditional costumes, presented a bouquet to Xi Jinping, and the honor guards lined up on both sides along the red carpet and saluted Xi Jinping.

(http://www.fmprc.gov.cn/mfa_eng/topics_665678/xjpzxcxjzgjldrdlchwdbxagtwnrlgbjxgsfwbcxzlldrhw/t1174660.shtml)

  李克强总理走出机舱时,礼兵分列红地毯两侧行注目礼。韩国政府高级官员在机场迎候。中国驻韩国大使邱国洪也到机场迎接。

(http://cpc.people.com.cn/n/2015/1031/c64094-27761091.html)

  As Premier Li Keqiang walked out of the cabin, the honor guard lined up on both sides of the red carpet and saluted him with eyes. High-level officials from the ROK government awaited at the airport, and H.E. Qiu Guohong, Chinese Ambassador to the ROK, also welcomed him at the airport.

(http://www.fmprc.gov.cn/mfa_eng/zxxx_662805/t1311440.shtml)

  当地时间上午9时30分许,习近平乘坐的专机抵达西雅图佩因国际机场。习近平和夫人彭丽媛步出舱门。美国总统奥巴马代表、华盛顿州州长英斯利和夫人,联邦政府高级官员和西雅图市市长默里偕当地政要和各界友好人士来到舷梯前,热烈欢迎近平夫妇到访。当地儿童向习近平夫妇献上鲜花。

(http://paper.people.com.cn/rmrbhwb/html/2015-09/23/content_1615552.htm)

  At about 9:30 a.m. local time, President Xi Jinping arrived at the Paine Field Airport in Seattle by special plane. Xi Jinping and his wife Mme. Peng Liyuan walked out of the cabin door. Jay Inslee, Representative of President Barack Obama of the US and Governor of Washington State, and his wife, Ed Murray, senior official of the US Federal Government and Mayor of Seattle, as well as local political heavyweights and friendly personages of various circles came to the accommodation ladder to warmly welcome Xi Jinping and Mme. Peng Liyuan. Local children presented a bunch of flowers to them.

(http://www.fmprc.gov.cn/mfa_eng/zxxx_662805/t1300290.shtml)

2. 有关欢迎仪式的翻译

虽然各国可以按照自己的习俗来安排欢迎方式，但自从联合国成立以来，国家主权平等成为共识，外交礼仪上讲究"平等"与"对等"，也因此形成了一套通用的礼仪。例如，为进行国事访问的国家元首所举行的欢迎仪式往往包括鸣放礼炮21响、军乐团奏两国国歌、检阅陆海空三军仪仗队、检阅分列式等。为进行正式访问的政府首脑举行的欢迎仪式同元首的国事访问大体相同，主要区别是礼炮鸣放为19响。①

在外交访问新闻报道中，描述隆重的欢迎仪式（a grand welcome ceremony）常见的表述包括"鸣放……响礼炮"（… rounds of gun salute were fired, … a 21-gun salute was presented …, twenty-one gun salutes were fired …）、"登上检阅台"（ascended to/ stepped onto the reviewing stand）、"军乐队高奏……国歌"（the military band played … national anthem）、"检阅三军仪仗队"（inspected /reviewed the honor guard of the three services, inspected/ reviewed the three-service honor guard）、观看分列式（watched the march-past）等。请看以下具体翻译实例：

12时10分许，习近平夫妇在查尔斯王储夫妇陪同下抵达骑兵检阅场皇家检阅台。按英国皇家最高规仪，伦敦塔桥和格林公园分别鸣放62响和41响礼炮。习近平夫妇登上皇家检阅台，伊丽莎白二世女王和丈夫菲利普亲王迎接。仪仗队敬礼，军乐队高奏中国国歌。在菲利普亲王陪同下，习近平检阅了仪仗队。

(http://news.xinhuanet.com/mrdx/2015-10/21/c_134734807.htm)

At around 12:10 p.m., accompanied by Prince Charles and his wife Camilla, President Xi Jinping and Mme. Peng Liyuan arrived at the Royal Pavilion on House Guards Parade. In accordance with the highest standard of royal etiquette of the UK, 62 rounds of gun salute from the Tower of London and 41 from the Green Park were fired respectively. After ascending to the Royal Pavilion, President Xi Jinping and Mme. Peng Liyuan were greeted personally by Queen Elizabeth Ⅱ and her husband Prince Philip. The guard of honor saluted and the military band played China's national anthem. Accompanied by

---

① 领导人访问有哪些迎宾礼仪程序要求，http://china.huanqiu.com/hot/2015-04/6244606.html

Prince Philip, Xi Jinping inspected the guard of honor.

(http://www.fmprc.gov.cn/mfa_eng/zxxx_662805/t1308109.shtml)

迈特帕里总督夫妇在草坪中央迎接习近平和彭丽媛，习近平登上检阅台，军乐队奏中国国歌，鸣礼炮21响。习近平检阅仪仗队。习近平回到检阅台，军乐队再奏中国国歌。草坪另一侧，一群当地学生挥舞中国国旗欢迎习近平和彭丽媛。

(http://news.xinhuanet.com/politics/2014-11/20/c_1113332954.htm)

Governor-General Mateparae and his wife greeted Xi Jinping and Mme. Peng Liyuan at the center of the lawn. Xi Jinping stepped onto the reviewing stand. The military band played the national anthem of China, and a 21-gun salute was presented. Xi Jinping reviewed the guard of honor. Then Xi Jinping went back to the reviewing stand, and the military band played the national anthem of China again. On the other side of the lawn, a group of local students waved the national flags of China to welcome Xi Jinping and Mme. Peng Liyuan.

(http://www.fmprc.gov.cn/mfa_eng/zxxx_662805/t1213875.shtml)

侯赛因和谢里夫在机场举行隆重欢迎仪式。中巴两国国旗迎风飘扬。礼兵在红地毯两侧列队行注目礼。在侯赛因和谢里夫共同陪同下，习近平登上检阅台，军乐队奏响中巴两国国歌。习近平检阅了三军仪仗队。

(http://news.xinhuanet.com/world/2015-04/20/c_1115030709.htm)

Mamnoon Hussain and Nawaz Sharif held a grand welcome ceremony at the airport. The national flags of China and Pakistan waved in the wind. The guard of courtesy, lining up on both sides of the red carpet, saluted them with eyes. Xi Jinping, accompanied by Mamnoon Hussain and Nawaz Sharif, stepped onto the reviewing stand, and the military band played the national anthems of China and Pakistan. Xi Jinping then reviewed the honor guard of the three services.

(http://www.fmprc.gov.cn/mfa_eng/wjdt_665385/wshd_665389/t1256847.shtml)

俄罗斯政府在机场举行了欢迎仪式，习近平检阅了俄罗斯三军仪仗队，并观看了分列式。

(http://cpc.people.com.cn/n/2015/0509/c64094-26973452.html)

The Russian government held a welcome ceremony at the airport. Xi Jinping inspected the three-service honor guard of Russia and watched the march-past.

(http://www.fmprc.gov.cn/mfa_eng/topics_665678/xjpcf1_665694/t1025226.shtml)

3. 有关转达问候的翻译

在非元首级别政府官员访问时，出于外交礼仪需要，通常会向对方转达该国政府首脑或国家元首的亲切问候，或转达口信。"转达××对××的亲切问候"可以译为conveyed kind greetings from ×× to ××。"亲切问候"有时也译为cordial greetings，但其措辞略显客气，亲切感不够强，故而多见kind greetings。"转达口信"可以译为××conveyed sb.'s oral message to ××。请看以下具体翻译实例：

> 汪洋首先转达了习近平主席致朴槿惠总统的口信。习近平在口信中积极评价中韩关系发展，强调愿同朴槿惠总统保持密切沟通，就共同关心的问题及时交换意见，深化中韩战略合作伙伴关系。
>
> (http://cpc.people.com.cn/n/2015/0124/c64094-26442566.html)

Wang Yang firstly conveyed President Xi Jinping's oral message to President Park Geun-hye, in which Xi Jinping spoke positively of the development of China-ROK relations, and stressed his willingness to keep close communication with President Park Geun-hye and exchange views timely on issues of common concern so as to deepen the China-ROK strategic cooperative partnership.

(http://www.fmprc.gov.cn/mfa_eng/zxxx_662805/t1231747.shtml)

> 俞正声转达了习近平主席、李克强总理和张德江委员长对普密蓬国王、诗琳通公主和泰国政府领导人的亲切问候。
>
> (http://www.fmprc.gov.cn/mfa_chn/zyxw_602251/t1284025.shtml)

Yu Zhengsheng conveyed kind greetings from President Xi Jinping, Premier Li Keqiang, and Chairman of the Standing Committee of the National People's Congress (NPC) Zhang Dejiang to King Bhumibol Adulyadej, Princess Maha Chakri Sirindhorn and government leaders of Thailand.

(http://www.fmprc.gov.cn/mfa_eng/zxxx_662805/t1285033.shtml)

4. 有关结束访问道别的翻译

机场送宾同样也是外事礼仪中重要的部分，在关于结束访问的新闻报道中，常涉及对机场送行以及欢送仪式的描述。例如："到机场为××送行"可以译为see sb. off at the airport或bid him/her farewell at the airport；"同××亲切握手话别"可以译为warmly shook hands with ×× to bid farewell。

关于对领导人结束访问回京的报道，例如在圆满结束对某国的正式访问后，××乘专机回到北京，可以译为×× returned to Beijing by special plane after successful conclusion of his official visits to ...；通常，领导人结束访问后，随行人员也"同机抵京"，可以译为arrived in Beijing by the same plane；敬称"夫人彭丽媛""夫人程虹"等，翻译时可以使用"Mme.，这是法语词Madame（夫人）的缩写。例如Xi Jinping and his wife Mme. Peng Liyuan。请看以下具体翻译实例：

> 当晚，习近平结束对古巴的访问，离开圣地亚哥，启程回国。劳尔率古巴国务委员会第一副主席兼部长会议第一副主席迪亚斯-卡内尔、外长罗德里格斯等古方高

级官员到机场送行。劳尔同习近平亲切握手话别。

(http://news.xinhuanet.com/mrdx/2014-07/25/c_133509158.htm)

In the evening, Xi Jinping concluded his visit to Cuba, left Santiago de Cuba and set out for China. Raúl led Miguel Díaz-Canel, First Vice President of the Council of State and First Vice President of the Council of Ministers of Cuba, Foreign Minister Bruno Rodriguez and other Cuban senior officials to see Xi Jinping off at the airport. Raúl warmly shook hands with Xi Jinping to bid farewell.

(http://www.fmprc.gov.cn/mfa_eng/zxxx_662805/t1178228.shtml)

当地时间晚11时25分许，习近平和夫人彭丽媛在出席了美国总统举行的隆重国宴之后，乘车抵达安德鲁斯空军基地。礼兵在红地毯两侧列队，军乐队奏乐，美方高级官员到机场送行。

(http://news.sina.com.cn/o/2015-09-27/doc-ifxiehns3399589.shtml)

At around 11:25 p.m. local time, Xi Jinping and his wife Mme. Peng Liyuan arrived at the Andrews Air Force Base by car after attending the grand state banquet held by the US President. High-level US officials saw them off at the airport with the honor guard lining up on both sides of the red carpet and the military band playing music.

(http://www.fmprc.gov.cn/ce/ceth/eng/zgyw/t1302675.htm)

在圆满结束对巴西、哥伦比亚、秘鲁、智利的正式访问后，国务院总理李克强于5月29日上午乘专机回到北京。李克强总理夫人程虹同机抵京。回国途中，李克强和夫人程虹过境西班牙马略卡进行技术经停。离开马略卡时，西班牙政府高级官员和中国驻西班牙大使吕凡到机场送行。

(http://www.xinhuanet.com/world/cnleaders/lkqcf1505/)

On the morning of May 29, 2015, Premier Li Keqiang returned to Beijing by special plane after successful conclusion of his official visits to Brazil, Colombia, Peru and Chile. Mme. Cheng Hong, wife of Premier Li Keqiang, arrived in Beijing by the same plane. On their way home, Li Keqiang and his wife, Mme. Cheng Hong, made a technical stop at Majorca, Spain. When they left Majorca, senior officials from the Spanish government and H.E. Lv Fan, Chinese Ambassador to Spain, saw them off at the airport.

(http://www.fmprc.gov.cn/mfa_eng/topics_665678/lkqdbxglbyblzljxzsfw/)

范例二 (Sample II)

开启面向全球的中英全面战略伙伴关系黄金时代
——外交部长王毅谈习近平主席对英国进行国事访问（节本）
2015/10/23

Opening up a Golden Era for Globally-Oriented China-UK Comprehensive Strategic Partnership
——Foreign Minister Wang Yi's Comments on President Xi Jinping's State Visit to the UK (Abbreviated Version)
2015/10/23

2015年10月19日至23日，国家主席习近平对英国进行国事访问。行程结束之际，外交部长王毅向记者介绍此访情况。

From October 19 to 23, 2015, President Xi Jinping paid a state visit to the UK. At the end of the visit, Foreign Minister Wang Yi briefed journalists on the visit.

***

王毅说，继习近平主席9月成功对美国进行国事访问并出席联合国成立70周年系列峰会后，中国外交在金秋10月再次开启新的航程。在中英全面战略伙伴关系步入第二个十年、中欧建交40周年之际，习近平主席首次对英国进行国事访问，全面推动中英关系发展，开启中英全面战略伙伴关系黄金时代，为中欧合作注入了新动力，为中西交流互鉴谱写了新篇章。

Wang Yi said that China charted a new diplomatic course again in October after President Xi Jinping's successful state visit to the US and attendance at the summits marking the 70th anniversary of the United Nations (UN) in September. This year unfolds the second decade of China-UK comprehensive strategic partnership and marks the 40th anniversary of the establishment of the diplomatic relations between China and the European Union (EU). President Xi Jinping made his first state visit to the UK to comprehensively promote the development of China-UK relations and open up a golden era for China-UK comprehensive strategic partnership, injecting new energy to China-Europe cooperation and adding a new chapter in exchanges and mutual learning between China and the West.

***

"志合者，不以山海为远。"5天时间里，习近平主席横跨亚欧大陆，行程近2万公里，出席30多场活动，既访首都，也赴外地；既看城市，也进乡村；既有严肃的政治日程，也有轻松的亲民互动；既有传统的隆重仪式，也有现代的创意展示，在金秋时节奏响友谊与合作的新乐章，展示中国特色大国外交的新实践。英方高度重视习近平主席

外交访问报道的翻译
Translation for Coverage of Diplomatic Visits
UNIT 4

此访,给予超高规格礼遇。伊丽莎白二世女王今年5月在新一届英国议会开幕式上亲自宣布习近平主席访英消息,此访期间,以年近九旬的高龄为习近平主席举行隆重欢迎仪式,两次设宴款待习近平主席夫妇,王室三代众多成员参加接待,查尔斯王储夫妇为习近平主席此访特地调整日程,还亲自前往下榻饭店迎请,成为此访与习近平主席会面最多的王室成员;卡梅伦首相访前两次就此访有关安排专门致函习近平主席,邀请习近平主席夫妇赴乡间别墅做客,并亲自陪同出席伦敦多场活动和访问曼彻斯特,同习近平主席进行长时间深入会谈。伦敦塔桥和格林公园根据英国王室最高规仪共鸣放103响礼炮。国际舆论高度关注习近平主席此访,进行了许多重量级报道,积极评价此访是英多年来最重要来访,向世人展示了中英关系的重要性,是开辟中英关系广阔前景的"超级国事访问"。

"Friends with shared interests can cooperate regardless of distance." During the five days, President Xi Jinping traveled nearly 20,000 km across the Eurasian continent to attend over 30 activities both in the capital and other parts of the country, in cities and the countryside. There are both serious political agenda and relaxed interactions with the common people; both grand traditional ceremonies and modern innovation shows. The visit starts a new chapter of friendship and cooperation in the golden autumn and represents the new practice of major-country diplomacy with Chinese characteristics. The UK attached great importance to President Xi Jinping's visit and gave a super-high standard of protocol. Queen Elizabeth II announced personally about President Xi Jinping's state visit at the opening ceremony of the new UK Parliament this May. During the visit, the Queen, who is nearly 90 years old, held a grand welcoming ceremony and hosted two banquets for President Xi Jinping and his wife. Three generations of the royal family attended the reception. Prince Charles and his wife adjusted their schedule specially for the state visit, went to the hotel to welcome them in person and were the royal members who met Xi Jinping most. Prime Minister David Cameron sent letters to President Xi Jinping twice for the arrangements related to the visit before they came, invited President Xi Jinping and his wife to his country retreat, accompanied them in person to attend many events in London and the visit to Manchester, and had in-depth talks with President Xi Jinping for a long time. In accordance with the highest etiquette of the UK royal family, the London Tower Bridge and Green Park fired 103-gun salute in total. Paying high attention to President Xi Jinping's visit, international media made many heavyweight reports, speaking positively of the visit as the most important to the UK for many years, which shows the importance of China-UK relations to the world and becomes a "super state visit" of opening up broad prospects of China-UK relations.

***

王毅最后说,习近平主席此访立足英国,面向欧洲,辐射全球,是我国运筹大国关系和外交全局的重大行动,取得了丰硕成果,获得了圆满成功。

At last, Wang Yi said that focusing on the UK with a reach to Europe and the world, President Xi Jinping's visit is China's significant action in planning relations between major countries and overall diplomacy, and has achieved fruitful results and a complete success.

> 新闻背景：应大不列颠及北爱尔兰联合王国女王伊丽莎白二世邀请，国家主席习近平于2015年10月19日至23日对英国进行国事访问。此访是十年来中国国家主席首次对英国进行国事访问，具有里程碑式的历史意义。此访不仅得到了英方的高度重视和超高规格礼遇，访问期间，中英双方还就经贸、人文交流等达成59项协议和共识，并决定共同构建面向21世纪全球全面战略伙伴关系。舆论认为习主席的成功访问为中英关系的"黄金时代"拉开序幕。
>
> 原文链接：http://politics.people.com.cn/n/2015/1023/c1001-27734312.html
>
> 译文链接：http://www.fmprc.gov.cn/mfa_eng/zxxx_662805/t1309370.shtml

一、范例二文本结构分析（Text Structure Analysis of Sample II）

范例二是外交部长王毅在国家主席习近平对英国进行国事访问结束之际，向记者介绍访问情况的新闻报道。一般国家元首出访后，外交部会召开记者招待会，对访问进行总结概括。此类新闻报道的主要内容概括出访期间的活动、成绩和重要意义。

第一段为导语，说明国家领导人（国家主席习近平）、访问时间（2015年10月19日至23日）、地点（英国），并说明介绍访问情况的人（外交部部长王毅）。

第二、三段中，王毅总结习近平主席访英期间的活动内容，以及受到的高规格礼遇。

第四段作为新闻的结尾部分，王毅总结习近平主席访英的重要意义。因篇幅所限，原文有所删节。

二、范例二翻译解析（Translation Analysis of Sample II）

（一）外交访问报道标题的翻译（Translation of Headlines Covering Diplomatic Visits）

此类新闻报道通常由主标题和副标题构成，副标题位于主标题之后，起补充和解释主标题的作用。通常情况下，主标题不能完全包括或表述的重要内容，往往由副标题来承担。主标题高度概括国家领导人出访的意义，汉语原文采取短小精炼、对仗工整、提纲挈领的语言，汉译英时，不但要保证忠实和准确，还要符合原文的措辞风格；副标题一般为××谈××访问某国，常见的表达为"××谈××访问某国"，或"××谈××出席某会晤"，译为×× Talks About ×× 's Visits to ...或×× Talks About ×× 's Attendance at ...。请看下面具体翻译实例：

把握新机遇　开启新里程　谱写新篇章
——外交部长王毅谈习近平主席出席金砖国家领导人会晤、访问拉美四国并出席中拉领导人会晤

(http://news.xinhuanet.com/world/2014-07/26/c_126799675.htm)

Seize New Opportunities, Embark on New Path and Write New Chapter
—— Foreign Minister Wang Yi Talks about President Xi Jinping's Attendance at BRICS Summit and China-Latin America and the Caribbean Summit, and Visits to Four Latin American Countries

(http://www.fmprc.gov.cn/mfa_eng/wjdt_665385/zyjh_665391/t1178527.shtml)

铺设友谊、理解、合作的桥梁
——外交部长王毅谈习近平主席出席荷兰核安全峰会并访问欧洲四国和联合国教科文组织总部、欧盟总部

(http://news.xinhuanet.com/world/2014-04/02/c_1110067100.htm)

Building a Bridge of Friendship, Understanding and Cooperation
—— Foreign Minister Wang Yi Talks About President Xi Jinping's Attendance at Nuclear Security Summit in the Netherlands and Visits to Four European Countries, UNESCO Headquarters and EU Headquarters

(http://www.fmprc.gov.cn/mfa_eng/wjdt_665385/zyjh_665391/)

（二）范例二文本英译解析（Translation Analysis on the Text of Sample II）

1. 巧用动词

汉语外交新闻文本中，句式常见动宾结构，在一个句子中甚至会出现多个并列的动宾结构。英译时首先要注意动宾搭配是否合理；其次，并非所有的汉语动词在英文中都要一一对应翻译为动词，英语可以采取分词、动名词、不定式等非谓语形式来体现动词的意思。

下面，请看范例二中具体翻译实例：

王毅最后说，习近平主席此访<u>立足英国，面向欧洲，辐射全球</u>，是我国运筹大国关系和外交全局的重大行动，取得了丰硕成果，获得了圆满成功。

At last, Wang Yi said that <u>focusing on the UK with a reach to Europe and the world</u>, President Xi Jinping's visit is China's significant action in planning relations between major countries and overall diplomacy, and has achieved fruitful results and a complete success.

中国将继续推进稳增长、促改革、调结构、惠民生、防风险，促进经济持续健康发展；继续坚持互利共赢的开放战略，寓中国发展于世界繁荣发展之中。

China will continue to <u>ensure growth, promote reform, make structural adjustment,</u>

improve people's well-being and forestall risks to promote a sound and sustained economic development. China will continuously stick to the open strategy of mutual benefit and win-win results and put China's development in world prosperity and development.

上述第1例中,"立足英国,面向欧洲,辐射全球"这三个动宾短语,在译文中并没有一一译为英文的动宾短语,而是首先将其处理为分词状语结构focusing on the UK,修饰President Xi Jinping's visit。通过对"面向"和"辐射"这两个动词的深层语义进行剖析,不难看出原文指的是访问的影响遍及欧洲乃至全球,因此译文中巧妙地采取介词结构with a reach to Europe and the world,从而使得英文句式更加紧凑,富有逻辑。

第2例中,"稳增长、促改革、调结构、惠民生、防风险"构成并列动宾结构,译文中针对各个名词宾语搭配合适的动词非常关键,译文中采用动词ensure, promote, make, improve 和forestall,既保留了原文的动宾结构,又能兼顾搭配的合理性和语义的完整。

此外,外交新闻英译文本中,谓语动词的选择往往也是译文的亮点所在。汉语原文中,冗长的时间状语从句,在翻译时会为译文构句造成困难;汉语原文中常见一个句子中包含多个主谓结构短语同时出现的情况,在翻译时会出现主语随意变换而与话题不一致的情况,造成衔接不当或缺乏连贯性等问题。因此,结合原文文本的话题,选取适当的谓语动词,将其处理为主谓结构的句子,从而确保译文句式结构清晰,句法简练。请看下面具体翻译实例:

在中英全面战略伙伴关系步入第二个十年、中欧建交40周年之际,习近平主席首次对英国进行国事访问,全面推动中英关系发展,开启中英全面战略伙伴关系黄金时代,为中欧合作注入了新动力,为中西交流互鉴谱写了新篇章。

This year unfolds the second decade of China-UK comprehensive strategic partnership and marks the 40th anniversary of the establishment of the diplomatic relations between China and the European Union (EU). President Xi Jinping made his first state visit to the UK to comprehensively promote the development of China-UK relations and open up a golden era for China-UK comprehensive strategic partnership, injecting new energy to China-Europe cooperation and adding a new chapter in exchanges and mutual learning between China and the West.

习近平主席指出,惟以心相交,方成其久远。中英关系发展的源泉来自两国人民的相互理解、支持、友谊。中英分别是东西方文明有代表性的国家,人文交流合作潜力巨大。

President Xi Jinping pointed out that only the two peoples treat each other earnestly can the friendship last long. The development of China-UK relations comes from the mutual understanding, support and friendship between the two peoples. Being respectively the representative countries in eastern and western civilizations, China and the UK enjoy

外交访问报道的翻译
Translation for Coverage of Diplomatic Visits 4 UNIT

great potential in people-to-people and cultural exchanges and cooperation.

上述第1例中，"在中英全面战略伙伴关系步入第二个十年、中欧建交40周年之际"本是原文中的时间状语，英语译文将其处理为主谓结构的句子，通过unfolds和marks两个动词，巧妙地解决了由原文状语冗长而引起的译文构句困难的问题。

第2例中，"人文交流合作潜力巨大"这一主谓结构短语，实际上也是围绕"中英"两国这一话题展开的，在翻译时，为了避免出现多个主语替换而破坏译文的连贯性，译文确定主语为China and the UK，谓语动词选用enjoy同宾语great potential搭配，从而更符合英文的表达习惯。

2. 排比和比喻的翻译

排比是一种将内容相关、结构类似、语气一致的词组或句子排列成串的修辞形式，用来表示强调和层层深入。这一修辞反映了中国文化注重对称的思维特点，语言结构讲究平衡对应，用词倾向于重复。使用排比修辞，能够使得文章读起来朗朗上口，气势磅礴，格外醒目。

汉语外交新闻中频繁使用排比修辞，而英语常忌讳重复，不像汉语一样大量使用排比结构。将汉语排比修辞翻译成英语时，通常使用融合技巧将多个排比结构融合起来，或根据搭配意义选用不同的词组或句式结构，从而避免重复，再现汉语句意，表述准确地道。请看范例二中具体翻译实例：

> 5天时间里，习近平主席横跨亚欧大陆，行程近2万公里，出席30多场活动，既访首都，也赴外地；既看城市，也进乡村；既有严肃的政治日程，也有轻松的亲民互动；既有传统的隆重仪式，也有现代的创意展示，在金秋时节奏响友谊与合作的新乐章，展示中国特色大国外交的新实践。
>
> During the five days, President Xi Jinping traveled nearly 20,000 km across the Eurasian continent to attend over 30 activities both in the capital and other parts of the country, in cities and the countryside. There are both serious political agenda and relaxed interactions with the common people; both grand traditional ceremonies and modern innovation shows. The visit starts a new chapter of friendship and cooperation in the golden autumn and represents the new practice of major-country diplomacy with Chinese characteristics.

汉语原文中"既……也……"四个分句形成排比句式，在翻译的时候采取融合技巧，将分句两两融合：涉及习近平主席到访之处的两个分句"既访首都，也赴外地；既看城市，也进乡村"融为一句，采用both ... and ...句型，译为both in the capital and other parts of the country, in cities and the countryside；涉及访问内容活动的两个分句"既有严肃的政治日程，也有轻松的亲民互动；既有传统的隆重仪式，也有现代的创意展示"融为

89

一句，译为There are both serious political agenda and relaxed interactions with the common people; both grand traditional ceremonies and modern innovation shows，避免多次重复There be结构。

合作共赢才能办大事、办长久事。发展中英关系已成为两国各界广泛共识，<u>符合两国人民根本利益，符合时代发展进步潮流，符合国际社会殷切期待</u>，有利于促进世界繁荣和发展。

Win-win cooperation can guarantee the success of major tasks and tasks with long-term interests. Developing China-UK relations has become consensus commonly held by various circles of both countries. It <u>conforms to the fundamental interests of both peoples, complies with the trend of development and progress of the times, accords with the ardent expectations of the international community</u>, and conduces to the promotion of world prosperity and development.

原文中"符合……根本利益，符合……进步潮流，符合……殷切期待"构成排比句型，行文流畅，气势磅礴，着重强调中英关系的重要意义；英文却应避免重复，在选词时要格外注意动宾搭配。因此，根据宾语"根本利益""进步潮流""殷切期待"，分别选取不同动词conform to, comply with, accord with进行搭配。

习近平主席同英方达成上述重要合作共识和成果，<u>丰富了中英关系的内涵</u>，<u>凸显了中英两个大国的战略眼光</u>，<u>展现了</u>以合作共赢为核心的新型国际关系理念给全球发展带来的<u>光明前景</u>。

President Xi Jinping and the UK reached the above-mentioned important cooperation consensus and results, which <u>enriches the connotation</u> of China-UK relations, <u>highlights the strategic visions</u> of China and the UK as major countries and <u>showcases the bright prospect</u> brought by the concept of new type of international relations with win-win cooperation as its core.

汉语中修辞排比也可以是句子成分排比，即一个句子中把结构相同或相似、意思密切相关、语气一致的词语或句子成串地排列。在本例中，"丰富了……凸显了……展现了……"构成该句的成分排比。在英译时，需要根据原文动宾结构中的宾语，选择不同动词进行搭配。译文分别根据"内涵""战略眼光""光明前景"这三个名词宾语，选用动词enrich，highlight以及showcase与其搭配。

比喻是一种常见的修辞手法，人们时常把某些品质、特征与某些事物联系起来进行联想，语言上就形成了比喻修辞。英汉语言在比喻手法上虽然有着许多相似之处，但有时由于英汉文化差异，英语文化的人难以产生同汉语文化的人相同的联想，这就构成了

外交访问报道的翻译
Translation for Coverage of Diplomatic Visits

翻译的困难。由于外交新闻文本的特殊性，文体的正式性和权威性等特点，在翻译这一修辞手法时需要酌情考虑。请看下面具体翻译实例：

针对国际社会对中国经济形势的担忧，习近平主席强调，中国经济运行总体平稳，主要指标处于合理区间和预期目标之内，中国经济不会<u>硬着陆</u>。

In view of the concerns from the international community towards China's economic situation, President Xi Jinping emphasized that China's economy is stable on the whole, with major indicators in reasonable ranges and at expected goals. China's economy will not <u>experience a hard landing</u>.

习近平主席此访受到英国各界人士热烈欢迎，习近平主席所到之处，五星红旗和欢迎标语汇成<u>红色的海洋</u>。可以说，习近平主席走到哪里，媒体的聚光灯就投射到哪里，民众的目光就汇聚到哪里，极大激发了英国民众了解中国、认识中国的热情，<u>播下了长久友谊的种子</u>，为中英合作奠定了更加坚实的民意基础。

In the visit, President Xi Jinping enjoyed a warm welcome by people from all circles of the UK. Wherever President Xi Jinping went, the five-starred red flags and welcome slogans <u>merged into a sea of red</u>. The media's spotlight would cast and people's eyes would follow wherever President Xi Jinping went, which highly stimulated the British people's enthusiasm to know about China and to learn about China, <u>sowed the seeds of long-term friendship</u> and laid a more solid public opinion basis for China-UK cooperation.

习近平主席在短短一个月内接连访问美、英这两个西方<u>政治重镇</u>，有力促进了大国之间的良性互动，展现了中国外交的生机活力。

During the short period of only one month, President Xi Jinping's successive visits to the US and the UK, two western <u>political heavyweights</u>, have strongly promoted positive interactions among major countries and displayed the vitality of China's diplomacy.

上述第1例中，"硬着陆"是一种比喻，指国民经济经过一段过度扩张之后的急剧回落。经济硬着陆指的是采用强力的财政货币政策，一次性在较短的时间内，通过牺牲较多的国民收入将通胀率降到正常水平。[1]这里采用隐喻修辞，将经济变化比喻为飞机着陆，对于中西文化的人来说都不陌生，因此英译时采取直译，译为experience a hard landing；第2例中，原文采取暗喻的修辞，将五星红旗和红色标语汇成的到处是红色的景象，比喻成"红色的海洋"，将中英长久友谊比作"种子"，把习近平主席访问英国比作"播种"，译文中也分别采取直译的方法，译为merged into a sea of red和sowed the seeds of long-term friendship。第3例中，"重镇"一词原意是军事要地，指军事上占重

---

[1] 硬着陆，http://baike.baidu.com/link?url=NKkBVvD4kO_bJbEUfly4iSuOWXF-2oS68pH-9wobY301CSTFOXCdDfOjv_RdSs98fKOaGrYdMaLcqEjeOB4tAw-VXgscgIAZQ5tKDMBcJkO

要战略位置的城镇,也泛指在其他某方面占重要地位的城镇。这里采用换喻修辞,用"镇"这一地域指称来指代国家,强调美、英两国在政治上地位非常重要。因此,显然不可按照字面意思直译为towns(城镇),故而译为two western political heavyweights,意指"极具影响力的事物"。

学生译作讲评
Analysis of Students' Translation Practice

原文链接:http://www.fmprc.gov.cn/mfa_chn/zyxw_602251/t1171730.shtml#userconsent#

新闻原文:聚天时地利人和,谋和平发展合作
——外交部长王毅谈习近平主席对韩国进行国事访问

学生译文:Combining Good Opportunity, Favorable Geographic Conditions and People's Support, Promoting Peace, Development and Cooperation
——Foreign Minister Wang Yi Talks About President Xi Jinping's State Visit to ROK

翻译评析:针对主标题"聚天时地利人和,谋和平发展合作",要想翻译出"聚"和"谋"的深层含义,首先要考量这两个动词所连接的宾语是什么意思。"天时地利人和"在汉语文化中,意指古时作战时的自然气候条件,地理环境和人心向背。学生译文的理解是正确的。但考虑到本篇新闻谈的是中韩关系,people's support指代不清,此外,Good Opportunity, Favorable Geographic Conditions等遣词也不够简练,对仗性不强,在此基础上,建议改为Good Timing, Geographical Convenience and Harmonious Human Relations;"聚"意指"聚集",而不是"结合",译为gather更加准确,"谋"应当理解为"寻求"而不是"推动",译为seek更加准确。综上,主标题可以改译为Gathering Good Timing, Geographical Convenience and Harmonious Human Relations, Seeking Peace, Development and Cooperation。

新闻原文:2014年7月3日至4日,国家主席习近平对韩国进行国事访问。访问结束之际,外交部长王毅向随行记者介绍了此访有关情况。

学生译文:From July 3 to July 4, 2014, President Xi Jinping paid a state visit to Republic of Korea (ROK). Upon the conclusion of the visit, Foreign Minister Wang Yi introduced relevant information about this visit to accompanying journalists.

翻译评析:本段主要针对定冠词讨论其用法。一般情况下,定冠词用以指代上文提过的人或事物:第一次提到用a或an,以后再次提到用the,例如上文提到Xi Jinping paid a state visit,下文中"访问结束之际",则是upon the conclusion of the visit;在国家名称、机关团体、组织等专有名词前,需要定冠词the,如中华人民共和国是the People's Republic of China,美国是the United States,韩国则是the Republic of Korea;此外,定冠词the用以特指某(些)人或某(些)事物,如"此访有关情况"和"随行记者"都是有所特指,因此都需要加上定冠词,译为the relevant information和the accompanying journalists，包括下文中不止一次提到的"中韩关系"，都需要加上定冠词译为the China-ROK relations。

新闻原文：王毅介绍说，习近平主席这次访问韩国是一次走亲戚、串门式的访问，目的是增进两国人民友好感情，推动中韩关系再上新台阶。

学生译文：Wang Yi said that President Xi Jinping's present visit to South Korea is just like a call on relatives or neighbors, aiming to strengthen the friendship between the two peoples and promote China-ROK relations to a new height.

翻译评析：学生译文将"习近平主席这次访问韩国"译为President Xi Jinping's present visit to South Korea。"这次访问"没有必要逐字直译为present visit，译为President Xi Jinping's visit就足以表达清楚原文所指；关于国名和组织机构等表述，在全文首次出现时用全称，之后再次提到则用简称，本句中"韩国"应简称为the ROK；"走亲戚、串门式的"这一表述中包含两层含义：拜访亲戚以及做客邻居，针对"做客邻居"，英文中很少采用call on neighbors这样的搭配，译为"a call on relatives or a drop in neighbors"则更加地道。综上，这一句可以改为Wang Yi said in his introduction that President Xi Jinping's visit to the ROK is like a call on relatives or a drop in neighbors, aiming to strengthen the friendship between the two peoples and promote the China-ROK relations to a new high once again.

新闻原文：王毅说，此访还拓展了中韩合作的空间和舞台，赋予中韩关系更大责任。习近平主席强调，中方主张通过对话解决半岛核问题，各方应该保持耐心定力，积极对话接触，相互释放善意，照顾各方关切。

学生译文：Wang Yi said that this visit also expands the scope and stage for cooperation between China and the ROK and gives a greater responsibility to the China-ROK relations. President Xi Jinping stressed that China stands for the settlement of the nuclear issue on the Korean Peninsula through dialogue; both sides should maintain patience and determination, actively hold talks and keep contact, mutually show goodwill to each other and take care of all parties concerned.

翻译评析：原文第一句，学生将"赋予中韩关系更大责任"译为gives a greater responsibility to the China-ROK relations是中式英语，give一词体现了译者非常明显的中式思维。可以改为endows the China-ROK relations with greater responsibility.

原文第二句，"保持耐心定力"学生译为maintain patience and determination，这样的搭配不够地道，结合常见短语keep patient，建议改为keep patience and determination更为地道；两国间的"对话接触"显然不可能只有一次，所以"接触"不应翻译为单数形式，建议改为keep contacts；"照顾各方关切"的意思是说能够照顾到各方所关切的事，学生译为take care of all parties concerned产生了歧义，成为"相关各方"的意思，应改为take care of the concerns from all parties。"中方主张……"和"各方应该……"这两个句子之间，不一定要用分号隔开，也可以单独成句。

新闻原文：习近平主席重申中方支持半岛南北方改善关系，最终实现自主和平统一。习近平主席的主张标本兼治、兼顾各方，既着眼当前，又放眼长远，体现了中方一贯秉持的客观公正立场。韩方高度赞赏中方劝和促谈，愿同中方加强沟通协调。

学生译文：President Xi Jinping reiterated that China supports the southern and northern sides of the Korean Peninsula to improve relations so as to eventually achieve independence, peace and reunification. President Xi Jinping's proposal tackles both the cause and effect of the issue and balances all sides, not only focusing on the current but also looking to the long term. It reflects the objective and impartial position that China always upholds. The ROK side highly appreciates China's prompting peace talks and advocating the spirit of solidarity, and is willing to strengthen communication and coordination with China.

翻译评析：原文第一句，"最终实现自主和平统一"的意思是朝鲜半岛以自主的、和平的方式实现统一，而不是achieve independence, peace and reunification所表达出的"实现自主、和平和统一"的意思，所以建议改为achieve independent and peaceful reunification。

原文第二句，"兼顾各方"的意思是考虑到各方面因素，可以译为takes all sides into consideration；"着眼当前，放眼长远"意指不但要注重目前形势，还有看到未来发展，在中文中，"当前"和"长远"是两个时间概念，英译时应当化虚为实，可以译为not only focusing on the current but also looking to the long term。

原文第三句，"赞赏中方劝和促谈"，学生译为appreciates China's prompting peace talks and advocating the spirit of solidarity，可以补充为"appreciates China's efforts in prompting peace talks"使得语义更清晰完整，而"劝和促谈"本就是促进和谈之意，再补充advocating the spirit of solidarity反而画蛇添足。

实战练习
Translation Practice

一、请翻译下列外交访问报道的标题(Translate the following headlines of the coverage of diplomatic visits）

    1. 习近平出席塔吉克斯坦总统拉赫蒙家宴

              (http://news.xinhuanet.com/mrdx/2014-06/13/c_133404402.htm)

    2. 习近平在劳尔·卡斯特罗全程陪同下访问古巴圣地亚哥

              (http://news.xinhuanet.com/mrdx/2015-10/24/c_134745434.htm)

    3. 习近平抵达利雅得开始对沙特阿拉伯进行国事访问

              (http://www.fmprc.gov.cn/web/zyxw/t1333115.shtml)

    4. 李克强抵达首尔开始对韩国进行正式访问

              (http://cpc.people.com.cn/n/2015/1031/c64094-27671091.html)

5. 习近平参观阿根廷共和国庄园

    (http://news.xinhuanet.com/world/2014-07/20/c_1111699307.htm)

6. 汪洋将对刚果（布）、乌干达和肯尼亚进行正式友好访问

    (http://www.xinhuanet.com/2018-06/06/c_1122946268.htm)

7. 走亲访友话合作　携手发展创未来

    ——外交部长王毅谈习近平主席对蒙古国进行国事访问

    (http://news.xinhuanet.com/mrdx/2014-08/23/c_133577659.htm)

8. 习近平结束对越南和新加坡的国事访问后回到北京

    (http://www.fmprc.gov.cn/mfa_eng/topics_665678/xjpdynxjpjxgsfw/t1313670.shtml)

9. 复兴丝绸之路共建和谐周边

    ——外交部长王毅谈习近平主席出席上海合作组织杜尚别峰会并访问塔吉克斯坦、马尔代夫、斯里兰卡、印度

    (http://politics.people.com.cn/n/2014/0920/c1001-25698241.html)

10. 王毅谈访问肯尼亚成果

    (http://news.xinhuanet.com/world/2015-01/11/c_1113951618.htm)

二、请翻译下列外交访问报道中的段落（Translate the following paragraphs from the coverage of diplomatic visits）

1. 当地时间5月17日下午，国务院总理李克强在前往巴西进行正式访问途中，在爱尔兰香农技术经停，并对爱尔兰进行过境访问。

    (http://news.xinhuanet.com/politics/2015-05/17/c_1115310554.htm)

2. 当习近平乘坐的专机进入巴基斯坦领空时，巴基斯坦8架"枭龙"战机起飞全程护航。当地时间20日10时50分许，专机抵达努尔·汗空军机场。习近平和彭丽媛步出舱门时，机场响起21响礼炮，向中国贵宾致敬。巴基斯坦总统侯赛因夫妇、总理谢里夫夫妇来到舷梯前，同习近平和彭丽媛热情握手，热烈欢迎习近平对巴基斯坦进行国事访问。

    (http://news.sina.com.cn/c/2015-04-21/071931741391.shtml)

3. 当李克强步出舱门时，号手吹号致敬，礼兵沿红地毯两侧列队欢迎。欧盟高级官员和中国驻欧盟使团团长杨燕怡、中国驻比利时大使曲星等在舷梯旁迎接。

    (http://www.xinhuanet.com/world/2017-06/02/c_1121072436.htm)

三、请翻译下面一则外交访问报道（Translate the following coverage of diplomatic visit）

习近平抵达开罗开始对埃及进行国事访问

当地时间1月20日，国家主席习近平抵达埃及首都开罗，开始对埃及进行国事访问。

当习近平乘坐的专机进入埃及领空时，埃及空军8架战机升空护航。当地时间下午5时35分许，专机抵达开罗国际机场。习近平步出舱门，埃及总统塞西率政府高级官员在舷梯旁热情迎接，礼兵分列红地毯两侧。

习近平向埃及人民致以诚挚问候和良好祝愿。习近平指出，中埃同为世界文明古国，两国人民友好交往源远流长。埃及是最早同新中国建交的阿拉伯国家和非洲国家。建交以来，两国始终相互理解和尊重、相互信任和支持，双边关系保持健康稳定发展。塞西总统2014年12月访华期间，双方将两国关系提升为全面战略伙伴关系，为两国各领域合作开辟了更加广阔的空间。中埃关系正处在承前启后、继往开来的重要阶段。我期待着同塞西总统等埃及领导人就双边关系和共同关心的问题深入交换意见，对两国关系发展作出长远规划，共同开创中埃全面战略伙伴关系新局面。

王沪宁、栗战书、杨洁篪等陪同人员同机抵达。

中国驻埃及大使宋爱国也到机场迎接。

习近平是在结束对沙特阿拉伯国事访问后抵达埃及的。离开沙特时，沙特王储继承人穆罕默德、国务大臣艾班等到机场送行。习近平专机离开沙特前，沙特战机全程护航。

埃及是习近平此次中东之行的第二站。习近平还将对伊朗进行国事访问。

(http://www.fmprc.gov.cn/web/zyxw/t1333523.shtml)

参考译文
Versions for Reference

一、请翻译下列外交访问报道的标题(Translate the following headlines of coverage of diplomatic visits）

1. Xi Jinping Attends Family Banquet Held by President Emomali Rahmon of Tajikistan
2. Xi Jinping Visits Santiago de Cuba in the Company of Raúl Castro at All Times
3. President Xi Jinping Arrives in Riyadh for State Visit to Saudi Arabia
4. Li Keqiang Arrives in Seoul and Starts Official Visit to ROK

Translation for Coverage of Diplomatic Visits

5. Xi Jinping Visits Argentine Republic Farm
6. Wang Yang to Pay Official Goodwill Visits to Republic of Congo, Uganda and Kenya
7. Visiting Relatives and Friends to Discuss Cooperation Joining Hands to Develop a Better Future
   —Foreign Minister Wang Yi Talks about President Xi Jinping's State Visit to Mongolia
8. Xi Jinping Returns to Beijing after Concluding State Visits to Viet Nam and Singapore
9. Revive the Silk Road and Jointly Build a Harmonious Neighborhood
   —Foreign Minister Wang Yi Talks About President Xi Jinping's Attendance at the SCO Summit in Dushanbe and Visits to Tajikistan, Maldives, Sri Lanka and India
10. Wang Yi Talks about Achievements of His Visit to Kenya

二、请翻译下列外交访问报道中的段落（Translate the following paragraphs from the coverage of diplomatic visits）

1. On the afternoon of May 17 local time, on his way for an official visit to Brazil, Premier Li Keqiang took a technical stopover in Shannon of Ireland to pay a transit visit to the country.

2. When Xi Jinping's special plane entered Pakistani territorial airspace, eight Pakistani Air Force JF-17 Thunder fighter jets took off to escort it. At around 10:50 a.m. local time, the special plane arrived at the Nur Khan Air Force Airport. As Xi Jinping and his wife Mme. Peng Liyuan stepped out of the cabin door, twenty-one gun salutes were fired to show respect to the distinguished Chinese guests. Pakistani President Mamnoon Hussain and Prime Minister Nawaz Sharif as well as their wives went to the gangway ladder to warmly shake hands with Xi Jinping and Mme. Peng Liyuan and extend warm welcome for Xi Jinping's state visit to Pakistan.

3. When Li Keqiang stepped out the cabin door, trumpeters blew the horns and saluted to him, and the guard of honor lined up on both sides of the red carpet to welcome Premier Li Keqiang. Senior officials of the EU, H.E. Yang Yanyi, Head of the Chinese Mission to the EU and H.E. Qu Xing, Chinese Ambassador to Belgium as well as others greeted Li Keqiang beside the gangway.

三、请翻译下面一则外交访问报道（Translate the following coverage of diplomatic visit）

Xi Jinping Arrives in Cairo, Starting His State Visit to Egypt

On January 20, 2016 local time, President Xi Jinping arrived in the capital of Egypt Cairo and started his state visit to Egypt.

Upon entering Egypt's airspace, Xi Jinping's special plane was escorted by 8 fighter jets of the Egyptian Air Force. At about 5:35 p.m. local time, the special plane arrived at the Cairo International Airport. When Xi Jinping stepped out of the cabin door, senior governmental officials of Egypt including President Abdel Fattah al-Sisi warmly welcomed him by the accommodation ladder, and guards of courtesy lined up on both sides of the red carpet.

Xi Jinping extended sincere greetings and best wishes to the Egyptian people. He pointed out that both China and Egypt are countries with ancient civilizations and the two peoples enjoy time-honored friendly exchanges. Egypt was the first Arab and African country that established diplomatic relations with the People's Republic of China. Since the establishment of the diplomatic relations, the two countries have treated each other with mutual understanding, respect, trust and support, and bilateral relations have been maintaining a healthy and stable development. During President Abdel Fattah al-Sisi's visit to China in December 2014, the two sides elevated bilateral relations to a comprehensive strategic partnership, opening up broader space for bilateral cooperation in all sectors. Currently China-Egypt relations are at the important stage of inheriting the past and opening up the future. He looked forward to exchanging in-depth views with President Abdel Fattah al-Sisi and other Egyptian leaders on bilateral relations and other topics of common interest so as to make long-term planning for the development of bilateral relations and jointly open up a new situation of China-Egypt comprehensive strategic partnership.

Wang Huning, Li Zhanshu, Yang Jiechi and other delegation members arrived by the same plane.

H.E. Song Aiguo, Chinese Ambassador to Egypt, also welcomed them at the airport.

Xi Jinping arrived in Egypt after wrapping up his state visit to Saudi Arabia. When he left Saudi Arabia, Deputy Crown Prince Mohammed bin Salman, Minister of State Musaed bin Mohammed Al-Aiban and other Saudi Arabian officials saw him off at the airport. The fighter jets of Saudi Arabia escorted Xi Jinping's special plane all the way before it left the country.

Egypt is the second stop of Xi Jinping's Middle East visit. He will also pay a state visit to Iran.

单元小结
Summary

本单元针对外交访问的类型以及外交访问新闻报道的翻译进行归类和探讨,总结了新闻标题、导语、常见表达方式的翻译。以范例一为例,介绍外交访问类型和外事礼仪程序,针对机场迎宾、欢迎仪式、领导人转达问候和祝愿、结束访问道别等常见内容,总结惯用句型,探讨翻译方法;以范例二为例,总结外交部长谈领导人出访事宜一类新闻主标题、副标题的翻译,新闻架构的内容,并就此类新闻进行文本分析,从原文的分析、译文的表达、修辞等层面探讨翻译方法,归纳动词巧用和巧译的方法,探讨修辞手法在英汉语言应用和翻译上的异同。外交访问报道涉及内容庞杂,翻译此类新闻不但要谙熟外事礼仪,民族文化习俗,更要从语言角度把握原文正式性、权威性等特点,准确传达原文信息和风格。

延伸阅读

"外交访问"有多少种?

根据国际上通行的做法,外国国家元首、政府首脑和其他领导人出访他国时,依其不同性质,主要分为以下几类:

国事访问(state visit),指一国国家元首应另一国国家元首的邀请,对该国进行的正式外交访问,是两个国家间最高规格的外交交流。正式访问的礼宾规格与国事访问大体相同,主要的区别是在欢迎仪式上的礼炮鸣放为19响(国事访问21响)。

工作访问(working visit)的规格低于国事访问。通常这类访问仅限于国家间内阁部长以下,其特点是时间短,不需要繁琐的仪式,领导人为磋商重大问题举行的会晤往往采用这种形式。

"正式访问"的英文表达是official visit,指一国领导人应另一国领导人的正式邀请,对邀请国进行的访问,有时也可称为友好访问(goodwill visit)或正式友好访问(official goodwill visit)。

非正式访问(unofficial visit)中,国家领导人以私人身份进行的访问称为私人访问(private visit),途经某国所进行的访问可称为"顺道访问"(stopover visit),不便公开报道的访问则称为秘密访问(highly confidential visit)。过境访问(transit visit)一般发生在飞行时间较长的访问途中。

此外，国家之间还会进行礼节性访问（courtesy/ceremonial visit），并会对他国的访问进行回访（return visit），如果时间紧促则会开展短暂访问、闪电式访问（brief visit/flying visit）。

来源：中国日报网站

(http://language.chinadaily.com.cn/2015-05/20/content_20769981.htm)

解析：领导人访问有哪些迎宾礼仪程序要求

礼宾安排在很多国家有严格固定的程序要求，一般来说是依照惯例甚至法律而行的。大多数国家派正部级代表去机场迎接外国领导人，元首或者政府首脑随后再举行正式的欢迎仪式。

虽然各国都会按照自己过往的习俗来确定欢迎方式，但自从联合国成立以来，国家主权平等成为共识，外交礼仪上对于"平等"与"对等"的讲究更为重要了，也因此形成了一套通用的礼仪。例如，为进行国事访问的国家元首所举行的欢迎仪式往往包括鸣放礼炮21响、军乐团奏两国国歌、检阅陆海空三军仪仗队、检阅分列式。为进行正式访问的政府首脑举行的欢迎仪式同元首的国事访问大体相同，主要区别是礼炮鸣放为19响。

至于礼炮鸣放为何要21响，据外交部礼宾司介绍，"21"响是国际传统，来历也颇为有趣。早在400多年以前，英国战舰上只能放21门炮，行驶在公海上，如果遇到友好国家的船只，为了表示敬意和解除武装，全部放炮。如果到一个国家加水加油，也要先将炮全部鸣放。此后逐渐演变为国家元首访问的鸣炮传统。因为单数象征吉祥，所以迎接外国政府首脑到访时就改为鸣放19响。

除此之外，最有趣的大概是各国欢迎仪式中不同的民族习惯了。俄罗斯喜欢用面包和盐招待客人，新西兰毛利族人要和来访的领导人碰鼻，摩洛哥会端上一盘蜜枣请客人享用。在英国，一般欢迎仪式的焦点是从英国皇家骑兵卫队阅兵场到白金汉宫1.6公里的王室马车队伍，外国领导人会与女王夫妇坐上由黄金装饰的王室马车。（根据人民网记者赵明昊报道进行整理）

来源：人民网

(http://www.chinanews.com/gn/2015/04-21/7221858.shtml)

UNIT 5

国际会议报道的翻译
Translation for Coverage of International Conferences

单元简介 Introduction

国际会议是指数个国家或地区的代表为解决共同关心的重大问题，协调彼此利益，在共同讨论的基础上寻求或采取共同行动而举行的大型集会。议题通常涉及政治、经济、能源、环境、军事等方面。按照参加国家的数量可以分为双边会议和多边会议；按照与会代表的性质可以分为政府间会议和民间会议；按照与会代表的级别可以分为领导人峰会、部长级会议、大使级会议、工商界论坛等。

会议报道涵盖会议的策划筹备、宗旨主题、时间地点、与会代表、会议成果等内容。若国家领导人参会，还会有其发言及主张的相关报道。读者能够从国际会议报道中了解国际社会的主流思想动向以及与会各国的立场态度，并得以观察国际秩序的发展趋势和各个国家的话语权情况。

外交新闻汉英翻译
C-E TRANSLATION OF DIPLOMATIC NEWS

国际会议类报道翻译范例分析
Sample of Translation for Coverage of International Conferences

范例一（Sample I）

亚太经合组织第二十二次领导人非正式会议在北京举行
习近平主持会议并发表讲话
倡导推进区域经济一体化共建互信、包容、合作、共赢的亚太伙伴关系（节本）
2014/11/11

The 22nd Asia-Pacific Economic Cooperation (APEC) Economic Leaders' Meeting Held in Beijing
Xi Jinping Presides over the Meeting and Delivers a Speech, Advocating Promotion of Regional Economic Integration and Joint Building of the Asia-Pacific Partnership Featuring Mutual Trust, Inclusiveness, Cooperation and Win-win Results (Abbreviated Version)
2014/11/11

2014年11月11日，亚太经合组织第二十二次领导人非正式会议在北京怀柔雁栖湖国际会议中心举行。各成员领导人围绕"共建面向未来的亚太伙伴关系"主题深入交换意见，共商区域经济合作大计，达成广泛共识。中国国家主席习近平主持会议。习近平在讲话中强调，面对新形势，亚太经济体应深入推进区域经济一体化，打造发展创新、增长联动、利益融合的开放型亚太经济格局，共建互信、包容、合作、共赢的亚太伙伴关系，为亚太和世界经济发展增添动力。

On November 11, 2014, the 22nd APEC Economic Leaders' Meeting was held at the Yanqi Lake International Convention Center in Huairou District, Beijing. Leaders of APEC members exchanged in-depth views on the topic of "Co-building the Future-oriented Asia-Pacific Partnership", jointly discussed major plans on regional economic cooperation and reached broad consensus. President Xi Jinping presided over the meeting. Xi Jinping stressed in his speech that in face of the new situation, the Asia-Pacific economies should further promote regional economic integration, create an open Asia-Pacific economic pattern driven by development and innovation and featuring interlinked growth and interests integration, and co-build the Asia-Pacific partnership featuring mutual trust, inclusiveness, cooperation and win-win results so as to add impetus to economic development of the Asia-Pacific region and the world at large.

***

习近平强调，开展互联互通合作是中方"一带一路"倡议的核心。中方欢迎志同道合的朋友积极参与有关合作，共同将"一带一路"建设成为大家的合作之路、友好之路、共赢之路。

Xi Jinping stressed that it is the core of the Belt and Road Initiative to carry out cooperation for connectivity. The Chinese side welcomes friends of common aspirations to actively participate in relevant cooperation and jointly build the Belt and Road into a path of cooperation, friendship and win-win results for all parties.

各经济体领导人一致认为，在当前全球经济形势下，要加快亚太自由贸易区建设，积极推进区域经济一体化，加强基础设施建设，促进互联互通。各方赞同习近平主席提出的有关倡议和主张，高度评价中国为促进亚洲和世界经济繁荣、推动亚太经合组织发展发挥的重要作用，感谢中方为举办本次会议所做的出色工作。

All economic leaders unanimously hold that in the current global economic situation, it is important to accelerate the construction of the FTAAP, actively advance regional economic integration, promote infrastructure construction and enhance connectivity. All parties agreed to relevant initiatives and propositions raised by President Xi Jinping, spoke highly of the important role of China in promoting economic prosperity in Asia and the world at large and in pushing forward the development of APEC, and appreciated the excellent work of the Chinese side in hosting this meeting.

***

会议发表了《北京纲领：构建融合、创新、互联的亚太——亚太经合组织领导人宣言》和《共建面向未来的亚太伙伴关系——亚太经合组织成立25周年声明》。

The meeting issued *The 22nd APEC Economic Leaders' Declaration: Beijing Agenda for an Integrated, Innovative and Interconnected Asia-Pacific* and the *Statement on the 25th Anniversary of APEC: Shaping the Future through Asia-Pacific Partnership*.

新闻背景：亚太经合组织领导人非正式会议是亚太经合组织最高级别的会议。1993年美国提议在亚太经合组织第五届部长级会议之后召开一次首脑会议。由于没有得到全体成员的赞同，该首脑会议被定名为"领导人非正式会议"。与会领导人统一着休闲装，以营造一种较为轻松的气氛。此后该会议成为常态，每年举行一次。会议就有关经济问题发表见解，交换看法，会议形成的领导人宣言是指导亚太经合组织各项工作的重要纲领性文件。亚太经合组织第二十二次领导人非正式会议于2014年秋天在北京雁栖湖举行。这是该会议第二次在中国举行。范例一节选自外交部对本次会议的报道。

原文链接：http://www.fmprc.gov.cn/ce/cohk/chn/xwdt/zt/ydyl/t1209650.htm

译文链接：http://www.fmprc.gov.cn/ce/cohk/eng/xwdt/zt/apec/t1210349.htm

一、范例一文本结构分析（Text Structure Analysis of Sample I）

范例一节选自一则大型国际会议新闻报道，主要内容包括会议的举行时间和地点、会议主题、与会各方主要观点、会议成果、会后活动等。会议新闻报道通常由三部分构成：第一部分为导语，说明会议的举行时间与地点、与会人员和主持人、会议的主要思想等。该部分简明扼要，通常能够独立构成一篇完整的简明新闻。例如在本条报道中，第一段囊括了会议的名称（亚太经合组织第二十二次领导人非正式会议）、时间（2014年11月11日）、地点（北京怀柔雁栖湖国际会议中心）、主题（共建面向未来的亚太伙伴关系）、主持人（习近平主席）以及主要观点（推进区域经济一体化，打造开放型亚太经济格局，共建亚太伙伴关系）。第二部分为正文，通常按照时间顺序或者会议流程详细报道会议的召开情况。在本例中，首先介绍了会议地点的自然环境（风光旖旎，草木青翠）和会议开始的具体景象（20位领导人抵达，习近平迎候并与他们一一握手），然后用较大的篇幅详细介绍了与会各方的主要观点，其中又以本国领导人的主张为重点（习近平强调……，各经济体领导人一致认为……），最后写明会议落幕，并介绍会议成果（发表了一个纲领和一则声明）。第三部分为结尾，介绍相关背景并说明举办该会议的重要意义，或补充介绍会后活动等其他信息，例如实地参观、小规模会谈、接受专访、召开记者会、举行宴会、观看演出等等（如本例中的种植亚太伙伴林）。该部分为可选内容，不是每条会议报道中都会出现。

二、范例一翻译解析（Translation Analysis of Sample I）

（一）会议报道超长标题的翻译（Translation of Long Headlines of Coverage of International Conferences）

新闻标题是以大于正文的字号，用精警的词语，对新闻内容和中心思想富有特色的浓缩和概括。（彭朝丞，1996：9）标题的作用就在于帮助读者选择新闻、阅读新闻和理解新闻。（刘其中，2004：124）外交新闻标题翻译时为了保证忠实性，基本采用直译的方法，译文在意义和结构上与原文保持一致。会议报道比较简单的标题形式为"某会议在某地举行"（例如"上合组织成员国政府首脑理事会第十三次会议在阿斯塔纳举行"），或是"某领导人主持/出席某会议"（例如"李克强主持上海合作组织成员国总理第十四次会议"）。此时需注意，为了凸显新闻的时效性，应当使用一般现在时态来表示过去发生的事情。（廖志勤，2006：45）但是在外交新闻中，大型国际会议报道的标题并非总是这样简单，而是常常力图在标题中传递出更多的信息，尤其是领导人在会议上的主要讲话精神，这就会使得标题大幅度增容，在文字长度上远远超过常规新闻标题。比如范例一的原文标题多达67个字，共包含了3个小分句。对于如此长的标题，汉语原文的处理方式一般是用断行或空格进行间隔，以尽量避免使用标点符号。范例一的原文标题在原始网页中的排版如截图所示：

国际会议报道的翻译
Translation for Coverage of International Conferences
UNIT 5

习近平主持亚太经合组织第二十二次领导人非正式会议
2014/11/11

亚太经合组织第二十二次领导人非正式会议在北京举行

习近平主持会议并发表讲话

倡导推进区域经济一体化共建互信、包容、合作、共赢的亚太伙伴关系

但是英语中的空格已经被用作了切分单词的标识符,无法再被用来代替标点符号,而且英语重形合,通常不接受多个分句的直接堆砌,这就要求翻译时对标题中的信息进行分析,按照适当的逻辑重新组句,以产出符合英语语法规则的译文。经过简单的逻辑分析,即可发现"倡导"后面引导了"推进"和"共建"两个宾语,并且整体用来表明"讲话"的主要内容,英语中可以采用–ing形式来表达。但"习近平主持会议"与"会议在北京举行"是主谓均不相同、各自完全独立的两句话,无法合并,所以译文最终采用了将第一句话升格,替换掉原始大标题的办法。译文网页版面截图如下:

The 22nd Asia-Pacific Economic Cooperation (APEC) Economic Leaders' Meeting Held in Beijing
2014/11/11

Xi Jinping Presides over the Meeting and Delivers a Speech, Advocating Promotion of Regional Economic Integration and Joint Building of the Asia-Pacific Partnership Featuring Mutual Trust, Inclusiveness, Cooperation and Win-win Results

会议报道中这样的超长标题不在少数。下面这个实例的原文标题达到了74个汉字,网页采用了断行排版的方式进行表达,如下所示:

> 习近平出席中非合作论坛约翰内斯堡峰会开幕式并发表致辞
> 提出把中非关系提升为全面战略合作伙伴关系
> 全面阐述中国发展对非关系政策理念
> 宣布深化中非合作重要举措
>
> (http://www.fmprc.gov.cn/web/zyxw/t1321408.shtml)
>
> Xi Jinping Attends the Opening Ceremony of the Johannesburg Summit of the Forum on China-Africa Cooperation and Delivers a Speech, Proposing to Upgrade China-Africa Relations to Comprehensive Strategic and Cooperative Partnership, Comprehensively Expounding China's African Policy and Announcing Major Measures to Deepen China-Africa Cooperation
>
> (http://www.fmprc.gov.cn/mfa_eng/topics_665678/xjpffgcxqhbhbldhdjbbwnfjxgsfwb fnfyhnsbzczfhzltfh/t1322278.shtml)

C-E TRANSLATION OF DIPLOMATIC NEWS

这个标题虽然长，但逻辑层级其实没有多复杂，很显然，"提出""阐述""宣布"为三个并列成分，共同描述"致辞"的主要内容，英语中可以使用三个-ing形式并列起来，作为前面"发表致辞"的伴随状语，注意最后一个并列成分前面需要添加and。重新组织后的译文为完整的一句话，各个成分之间紧密衔接，不需要再借助排版的手段。

再看下面这个实例。标题原文中使用了空格进行分隔，但是不能想当然地认为两个空格隔开的三个部分之间是完全并列的。实际上，"强调"一词统领了这三个部分，而且从逻辑上看，"凝心聚力"和"精诚协作"都是手段，而"推动上海合作组织再上新台阶"是目的。理顺逻辑关系后译文表达如下：

习近平出席上海合作组织杜尚别峰会并发表重要讲话
强调凝心聚力 精诚协作 推动上海合作组织再上新台阶
(http://www.fmprc.gov.cn/ce/cgkhb/chn/zgyw/t1190759.htm)
Xi Jinping Attends SCO Summit in Dushanbe and Delivers Important Speech, Stressing Cohering People's Will and Power and Coordinating Sincerely to Push SCO to a New Level
(http://www.fmprc.gov.cn/mfa_eng/topics_665678/zjpcxshzzcygyslshdsschybdtjkstmedfsllkydjxgsfw/t1191482.shtml)

下面这个标题原文中通过"时"字表明了两个分句之间的逻辑关系，但是因为"强调"后面的内容又是一个完整的句子，而非像前述实例中那样仅为短语，原文使用空格作了分隔。译文为了维持原文的信息呈现顺序，将"……时"这个状语成分调整成了主句，如下所示：

习近平出席中英工商峰会时强调 中国将继续坚持互利共赢的对外开放战略
(http://news.xinhuanet.com/politics/2015-10/22/c_128343783.htm)
Xi Jinping Attends China-UK Business Summit, Stressing that China Will Continue Sticking to Its Opening-Up Strategy Featuring Mutual Benefit and Win-Win Results
(http://www.fmprc.gov.cn/mfa_eng/zxxx_662805/t1308473.shtml)

标题较长时，句子结构可能比较复杂，对于主语的选择需要多加注意。比如下面的例子中就要注意不能将两位领导人并列做主语，因为后面的谓语动词"表示"是由"李克强"一人做出。另外，"增进青年和媒体友好"原文中并未明确"增进"的动作发出者是谁，不宜妄作猜测，解决办法是将译文调整为被动语态：

李克强与俄罗斯总理梅德韦杰夫共同出席中俄青年友好交流年
闭幕式暨中俄媒体交流年开幕式时表示

国际会议报道的翻译
Translation for Coverage of International Conferences — UNIT 5

增进青年和媒体友好交流 让中俄友谊薪火相传

(http://www.fmprc.gov.cn/web/zyxw/t1325536.shtml)

Li Keqiang Attends Closing Ceremony of China-Russia Youth Friendly Exchange Year and Opening Ceremony of China-Russia Media Exchange Year with Prime Minister Dmitry Medevedev of Russia, Expressing That Youth and Media Friendly Exchanges Should Be Enhanced to Pass Down China-Russia Friendship from Generation to Generation

(http://www.fmprc.gov.cn/mfa_eng/zxxx_662805/t1326356.shtml)

最后再看一个综合性的实例，原文及其译文如下：

中国–拉共体论坛首届部长级会议在北京隆重开幕
习近平出席开幕式并发表重要讲话
强调牢牢抓住中拉整体合作新机遇
共同谱写中拉全面合作伙伴关系新篇章

(http://www.fmprc.gov.cn/web/gjhdq_676201/gjhdqzz_681964/lmhjlbgjgtt_683624/xgxw_683630/t1226550.shtml)

First Ministerial Meeting of China-CELAC Forum Grandly Opens in Beijing
Xi Jinping Attends Opening Ceremony and Delivers Important Speech, Stressing Firm Grasp of New Opportunities in China-CELAC Overall Cooperation to Jointly Write New Chapter of China-CELAC Comprehensive Cooperative Partnership

(http://www.fmprc.gov.cn/mfa_eng/zxxx_662805/t1227318.shtml)

这个例子中，原文每一行与其他行的衔接关系都不同。前两行是完全独立的两个句子，英语译文最终也只得沿用了断行排版的形式来表达。第二、三行之间是伴随的关系，"强调"即为"讲话"的内容，宜采用-ing形式表达。末两行之间是手段与结果的关系，译文通过动词不定式to来表示。总之，碰到这种情况，需要沉着冷静，仔细分析其中的逻辑关系，借助不同的语言手段将各个部分衔接起来。对于完全独立的句子，则可以通过断行排版进行划分。

（二）近期重大会议及其主题和成果（Latest Major Conferences with Their Themes and Outcomes）

重大国际会议通常定期召开，并且经常会回顾往届会议中的议题及成果，需要不断学习积累有关这些会议的既定表达，才能在以后的外交新闻翻译中提高效率。下面就以2015年为例，介绍中方参与了的主要国际会议及其主题等相关内容的双语表达。

1. 中国——拉美和加勒比国家共同体论坛首届部长级会议（the first ministerial meeting

of the Forum of China and the Community of Latin American and Caribbean States (CELAC)）于1月8日至9日在北京举行。会议的主题是"新平台、新起点、新机遇——共同努力推进中拉全面合作伙伴关系"（A new platform, a new starting point and new opportunities——work together to promote the China-Latin America comprehensive cooperative partnership）。①会议通过了关于中拉合作的北京宣言（the Beijing Declaration）、五年合作规划（the five-year cooperation plan）、论坛运行规则（the operation rules for the Forum）等三个重要文件，构成了中拉论坛的政策依据、行动纲领和机制保障。②

2. 亚非领导人会议（the Asian-African Summit）于4月22日至23日在印度尼西亚首都雅加达举行，会议主题为"加强南南合作，促进世界和平繁荣"（Strengthening South-South Cooperation to Promote World Peace and Prosperity），来自约100个国家和国际组织的领导人或代表出席会议。中国国家主席习近平发表题为《弘扬万隆精神 推进合作共赢》（Carry Forward the Bandung Spirit for Win-win Cooperation）的重要讲话。24日，参加会议的各国领导人来到万隆，纪念万隆会议召开60周年（commemorate the 60th anniversary of the Bandung Conference）。③

3. 第十七次中欧领导人会晤（the 17th China-EU Summit）于6月29日在布鲁塞尔举行，国务院总理李克强和欧洲理事会主席图斯克（President Donald Tusk of the European Council）、欧盟委员会主席容克（President Jean-Claude Juncker of the European Commission）共同主持。双方发表了《第十七次中国欧盟领导人会晤联合声明》（Joint Statement of the 17th China-EU Summit）、《中欧气候变化问题联合声明》（China-EU Joint Statement on Climate Change），并发布《中欧区域政策合作报告（2006—2015）》（Report on China-EU Regional Policy Cooperation (2006—2015)）。④

4. 金砖国家领导人第七次会晤（the 7th BRICS Summit）于7月9日在俄罗斯南部城市乌法举行，主题为"金砖国家伙伴关系——全球发展的强有力因素"（BRICS Partnership—A Powerful Factor of Global Development）。习近平主席发表题为《共建伙伴关系 共创美好未来》（Jointly Build Partnership for Bright Future）的主旨讲话。紧接着，上海合作组织成员国元首理事会第十五次会议（the 15th Shanghai Cooperation Organization (SCO) Summit）于7月10日也在乌法举行，习近平主席发表题为《团结互助 共迎挑战 推动上海合作组织实现新跨越》（Unite and Help Each Other and Address Challenges Together to Promote the SCO for New Leapfrog Progress）的重要讲话。"双峰会"分别通过《乌法宣言》（Ufa Declaration）、《金砖国家经济伙伴战略》（the Strategy for BRICS Economic Partnership），并批准《上海合作组织至2025年发展战略》

---

① http://www.chinacelacforum.org/chn/zyxw/t1226550.htm
② http://www.chinatoday.com.cn/ctchinese/chinaworld/article/2015-02/04/content_667192.htm
③ http://www.xinhuanet.com/world/cnleaders/xijinping/xjpcf1504/yfhy.htm
④ http://news.xinhuanet.com/world/2015-06/30/c_1115773722.htm

（the SCO Development Strategy Toward 2025）等纲领性文件，为金砖和上合的未来发展描绘了蓝图。①

5. 联合国发展峰会（the UN Sustainable Development Summit）于9月25日至27日在纽约联合国总部举行，习近平主席出席并发表题为《谋共同永续发展 做合作共赢伙伴》（Seek Common and Sustainable Development and Forge a Partnership of Win-win Cooperation）的重要讲话。峰会正式通过了2030年可持续发展议程（the 2030 sustainable development agenda）。②次日，习近平主席在联合国大会一般性辩论（the General Debate of the 70th Session of the UN General Assembly）中发表了题为《携手构建合作共赢新伙伴 同心打造人类命运共同体》（Working Together to Forge a New Partnership of Win-win Cooperation and Create a Community of Shared Future for Mankind）的重要讲话。③

6. 上海合作组织成员国政府首脑理事会第14次会议（the 14th meeting of the Council of Heads of Government (Prime Ministers) of the Shanghai Cooperation Organization (SCO) member states）于12月14日至15日在河南郑州举行。总理们强调，应切实落实《上合组织至2025年发展战略》（the SCO Development Strategy Toward 2025）、《上合组织成员国多边经贸合作纲要》（the Program for Multilateral Cooperation in Trade and Economy of the SCO Member States）及其落实措施计划（the Action Plan for its implementation）、《2012—2016年上合组织进一步推动项目合作的措施清单》（the List of Events for Further Development of Project Activities in the Framework of the SCO for 2012—2016），进一步扩大在经贸、金融、投资、交通、电信、海关、农业、能源领域的合作。④

范例二（Sample II）

李克强出席第三届"开放式创新"莫斯科国际创新发展论坛开幕式并发表演讲（节本）
2014/10/15

Li Keqiang Attends and Addresses the Opening Ceremony of the Third Moscow International Forum for Innovative Development "Open Innovations" (Abbreviated Version)
2014/10/15

当地时间10月14日，国务院总理李克强于上午在莫斯科与俄罗斯总理梅德韦杰夫共同出席第三届"开放式创新"莫斯科国际创新发展论坛开幕式，并发表题为《以创新实

---

① http://www.xinhuanet.com/world/cnleaders/xijinping/xjpcf201507/index.htm
② http://cn.chinagate.cn/news/node_7229776.htm
③ http://politics.people.com.cn/n/2015/0929/c1024-27644905.html
④ http://news.sina.com.cn/c/sz/2015-12-15/doc-ifxmpnuk1564932.shtml

C-E TRANSLATION OF DIPLOMATIC NEWS

现共同发展包容发展》的演讲。

On the morning of October 14 local time, Premier Li Keqiang attended the opening ceremony of the third Moscow International Forum for Innovative Development "Open Innovations" along with Prime Minister Dmitry Medvedev of Russia in Moscow, and delivered a speech entitled "Achieving Common and Inclusive Development Through Innovation".

***

李克强强调，中国的改革开放是世界上最大规模的创新活动，取得了巨大成就。但中国仍是最大的发展中国家，要实现更大更好发展，关键是进一步解放思想，坚持走改革创新之路。我们要破除束缚创新的壁垒，建设"创新型政府"，通过简政放权，给市场让出空间，降低市场准入门槛。我们要构建激励创新的机制，深化科技体制改革，给创新者更大自主支配权，让创造发明者获得应有回报。我们要营造保护创新的环境，不断完善法制，规范市场环境，维护市场秩序。我们要打造创新驱动型经济，支持企业创新，用创新的办法挖掘巨大的内需潜力，推进结构优化升级。

Li Keqiang stressed that China's opening-up is the innovation of the largest scale in the world and has scored tremendous achievements. But China is still the largest developing country. In order to achieve greater and better development, the key is to further emancipate our mind and stick to the path of reform and innovation. We should eliminate the barriers constraining innovation, build the "innovative government", and through streamlining administration and delegating power to the lower levels, make room for the market and lower the threshold of market access. We should construct a mechanism stimulating and encouraging innovation and deepen the reform of the scientific and technological system, so as to provide innovators with greater autonomy and reward innovators and inventors for what they deserve. We should create an innovation-protecting environment, continuously perfect the legal system, standardize the market environment and maintain the market order. We should forge an innovation-driven economy, support enterprise innovation, tap tremendous potential of domestic demand through innovative methods, and promote the structural optimization and upgrading.

***

梅德韦杰夫在演讲中表示，创新合作是俄中合作的优先方向，俄方将加大投入，推进两国高科技、信息、工业等领域合作项目，支持两国中小企业、科研机构、高校加强交流合作，与中方合作建设经济特区，促进两国的共同发展。

Dmitry Medvedev said in his speech that innovative cooperation is the priority of Russia-China cooperation. Russia will increase inputs to promote the cooperation projects between the two countries in such fields as high-tech, information and industry, support small- and medium-sized enterprises, science and research institutions as well as institutions of higher learning from the two countries in strengthening exchanges and cooperation, and work with China to build a special economic zone, so as to promote the common development of the two countries.

两国总理还现场回答了提问。
Premier Li Keqiang and Prime Minister Medvedev also answered questions on the spot.

第三届莫斯科国际创新发展论坛由俄罗斯联邦政府主办，中方应俄方邀请作为唯一"伙伴国"参加。来自世界各国的科技、投资、经贸、教育界人士共约800人出席开幕式。
The third Moscow International Forum for Innovative Development was sponsored by the government of the Russian Federation. China attended as the only "partner country" upon Russia's invitation. Attending the opening ceremony were about 800 people from the communities of science and technology, investment, economic and trade, and education of various countries around the world.

> 新闻背景：莫斯科国际创新发展论坛是一个致力于新科技和国际创新领域合作前景的讨论平台，从2012年开始已连续举办三届。2014年"开放式创新"国际论坛于10月14日至16日在莫斯科科技城举行，来自全球70个国家的15 000多名与会者齐聚莫斯科，了解前沿技术成果，为在21世纪取得领先地位寻找具有前途的模式。李克强总理出席开幕式并发表演讲。
> 原文链接：http://www.fmprc.gov.cn/ce/ceuk/chn/zgyw/t1200642.htm
> 译文链接：http://www.fmprc.gov.cn/mfa_eng/zxxx_662805/t1201071.shtml

一、范例二文本结构分析（Text Structure Analysis of Sample II）

会议报道除了像范例一那样，以会议本身为关注重点，采用"某会议在某地举行"的形式外，还可能以领导人为关注重点，采用"某领导人出席某会议"的形式进行报道，如范例二所示。此时，因为关注重点转移，会议仅仅是该领导人工作所涉及的一个场景，所以新闻报道的结构会有所不同。在新闻导语中，表现形式为"某年某月某日，某领导人在某城市出席了某会议，并发表了具有某题目的演讲"。此时所谈到的日期仅仅是该领导人出席会议的日期，未必代表会议的起止时间，所以常常会见到"出席某会议开幕式""出席某会议闭幕式"的表述。在新闻正文部分，则以该领导人的讲话内容为主，而不会详细介绍会议流程。如果该领导人是与其他国家的领导人共同出席该会议，则可能会附带介绍其他国家领导人的主要讲话内容，但篇幅上只占较少比例。第三部分为结尾，是对会前会后相关活动的报道，例如该领导人在会议前后的相关访问、会见、记者会、陪同人员等。第四部分为背景，介绍会议的主办方、与会国家和人数、会议的宗旨与意义等。最后两个部分为可选部分，不是每条报道都会出现。

二、范例二翻译解析（Translation Analysis of Sample II）

（一）会议名称的翻译（Translation of Conference Titles）

会议的名称是对整个会议的综合表述，浓缩其中的信息通常涉及参会范围、会议级别、主要议题、会议地点、会议序次等，例如"伊朗核问题六国与伊朗外长会"就反映了参会范围（六国与伊朗）、会议级别（外长）及主要议题（伊朗核问题）。"第51届慕尼黑安全会议"则包括了会议地点（慕尼黑）、会议序次（第51届）以及主要议题（安全问题）。国际会议的命名很多情况下都是多语种同时发布的，外界很难确定哪个语种的名称为原文，哪个语种的名称为译文。在翻译中涉及会议名称时，首先要做的肯定是检索其官方网站或其他权威媒体，以既定名称为准。此处我们无意探讨会议名称如何翻译方为"正途"，而是以对照列举的方式来观察学习国内外一些重要会议的中英文名称。请看以下实例：

金砖国家领导人非正式会晤
the Informal Meeting of BRICS Leaders
(http://www.fmprc.gov.cn/mfa_eng/zxxx_662805/t1212222.shtml)

大湄公河次区域经济合作第五次领导人会议
the fifth Summit of the Greater Mekong Sub-region (GMS) Economic Cooperation Program
(http://www.fmprc.gov.cn/mfa_eng/zxxx_662805/t1221882.shtml)

第51届慕尼黑安全会议
the 51st Munich Security Conference
(http://usa.chinadaily.com.cn/china/2015-02/07/content_19517526.htm)

伊朗核问题六国与伊朗外长会
the Meeting of Foreign Ministers of the Six Countries and Iran on the Iranian Nuclear Issue
(http://www.fmprc.gov.cn/mfa_eng/zxxx_662805/t1214923.shtml)

上海合作组织成员国政府首脑（总理）理事会第十四次会议
the 14th meeting of the Council of Heads of Government (Prime Ministers) of the Shanghai Cooperation Organization (SCO) member states
(http://www.fmprc.gov.cn/mfa_eng/wjdt_665385/wsrc_665395/t1322086.shtml)

阿富汗问题2+2四方会晤
2+2 Quartet Meeting on the Afghan Issue
(http://www.fmprc.gov.cn/mfa_eng/zxxx_662805/t1323369.shtml)

"基础四国"第十三次气候变化部长级会议

the 13th BASIC Ministerial Meeting on Climate Change
　　　　　(http://en.ccchina.gov.cn/Detail.aspx?newsId=38550&TId=98)

亚欧互联互通产业对话会
the ASEM Industry Dialogue on Connectivity
　　　　　(http://www.fmprc.gov.cn/mfa_eng/wjdt_665385/wsrc_665395/t1265880.shtml)

　　从上文列举的前两个例子可以看出，"领导人会议"并不必然译为Leaders' Meeting，还有可能使用Summit（峰会）一词。另外，翻译"金砖国家"时要注意语境，BRICS这个名称中的五个字母分别代表着巴西（Brazil）、俄罗斯（Russia）、印度（India）、中国（China）和南非（South Africa）。而2010年12月之前的"金砖国家"中并没有南非South Africa，所以要译为BRIC或BRICs（词尾的s小写）。①如果是国际性的大型会议，如第三例中的"慕尼黑安全会议"有五十多个国家的数百名代表出席，则选用conference一词。第四例有关"伊朗核问题"的外长会中"六国"是特指中、美、俄、英、法、德这六国，所以Six Countries前面要加上定冠词the。紧接着的例子的对比可以看出，meeting一词如果只表示某个组织的一次常规会议，则不需要大写首字母，但是成为会议名称的一部分时，却需要大写，如"2+2四方会晤"译为2+2 Quartet Meeting。最后两个例子表明，当会议名称太长时，可将其中的专有名词简化为首字母缩略形式，如用BASIC指代巴西（Brazil）、南非（South Africa）、印度（India）和中国（China）这"基础四国"，②用ASEM代表Asia-Europe Meeting（亚欧会议）。

　　有些会议的名称略有特殊之处，比如范例二的会议名称中还包括了会议主题"开放式创新"。注意该会议的中文名称中，"开放式创新"是同"第三届"一起作为修饰成分放在"莫斯科国际创新发展论坛"前面，而英语中将其理解为"第三届莫斯科国际创新发展论坛"的同位成分，放在后面核心词的位置上。范例一中的"亚太经合组织领导人非正式会议"英文名称并非APEC Leaders' Informal Meeting，而是APEC Economic Leaders' Meeting。还有UN Sustainable Development Summit，中文一般称为"联合国发展峰会"，省去了sustainable（可持续）一词。③再比如"2016年二十国集团峰会第一次协调人会议"的英文为2016 First G20 Sherpa Meeting，④其中的Sherpa显然不是普通字典中解释的"夏尔巴人"的意思。根据维基百科，A sherpa is the personal representative of a head of state or government who prepares an international summit，也就是所谓"协调人"的概念。总之，遇到这样的会议名称，还是应当尽力查证并遵照官方既定的译法。

---

① http://www.suduxx.com/dili/95267.html
② http://baike.baidu.com/view/3036600.htm
③ http://news.xinhuanet.com/world/2015-09/18/c_128241578.htm
④ http://www.fmprc.gov.cn/mfa_eng/zxxx_662805/t1331720.shtml

（二）会议报道导语的翻译（Translation of News Leads in Coverage of International Conferences）

新闻导语一般指新闻报道的第一段或开头几段，通常由最新鲜、最重要、最吸引人的事实构成。它或概括全篇，或提纲挈领，或提示要点，起着开门见山的作用，以吸引读者进一步读完全文。（陈明瑶，2001：12）中文导语中，主题往往位于相关信息之后，遵从次要到主要，由背景到任务，从辅助要素到主题信息的叙事模式。（朱献珑，2008：35）外交部的新闻稿件在翻译时通常维持中文的信息推进顺序，并不按照英文的导语风格进行调整，这一点需要加以注意。如会议报道导语的基本模式为"某月某日，某会议在某地举行，某领导人出席某会议并发表讲话"，或者附有该领导人离开某地或抵达某地的表述。翻译时基本用词为attend，"出席会议并致辞/讲话"可直接译为attend and address the meeting，但是如果添加了修饰成分（如"发表主旨讲话"）或者后面跟有讲话的主要内容，则要调整为attend the meeting and deliver a (keynote) speech, (stressing …)，如下例所示：

2014年11月26日，第18届南亚区域合作联盟峰会在尼泊尔加德满都市举行。南盟8个成员国领导人及9个观察员国高级别代表出席。中国作为观察员国与会，中方代表团团长、外交部副部长刘振民出席开幕式并发表题为"深化互利合作，携手共同发展"的讲话。

(http://news.163.com/14/1126/16/AC09BDFA00014SEH.html)

On November 26, 2014, the 18th South Asian Association for Regional Cooperation (SAARC) Summit was held in Kathmandu of Nepal. Attending the Summit were the heads of the eight member states as well as high-level representatives of the nine Observers of the SAARC. China was present as one of the Observers. Head of the Chinese delegation and Vice Foreign Minister Liu Zhenmin attended the opening ceremony and delivered a speech entitled "Enhancing Mutually Beneficial Cooperation and Seeking Common Development Hand in Hand".

(http://www.fmprc.gov.cn/mfa_eng/wjbxw/t1215247.shtml)

会议报道的导语中往往会提及会议由某领导主持，有哪些领导或国家出席了会议。一般"主持"用preside over，chair或host，"与会"用attend或were present。对于"共同出席"的翻译要特别注意。如范例二中的"李克强与梅德韦杰夫共同出席开幕式"，译为Li Keqiang and Dmitry Medvedev attended the opening ceremony together也没有错，但是并列主语的使用会使人误以为"李克强"和"梅德韦杰夫"共同作为这个句子的话题（topic），而这则新闻报道是以本国领导人为话题的，"梅德韦杰夫"只是在对李克强总理进行报道时提及的附带信息，所以这样的译文就造成信息重点发生了变化。而且该句后面还有"并发表演讲"的表述，显然"发表演讲"的主语并不包括"梅德韦杰夫"，所以译为Li Keqiang attended the opening ceremony along with Dmitry Medvedev才更为准确。另外,"与会成员"若为多个项目并列,为了避免句子头重脚轻,可以使用倒装语序,如上例中的Attending the Summit were ...。若考虑到行文的流畅性,也可统一调整为被动语态,如下面的实例所示:

当地时间12月20日上午,国务院总理李克强在曼谷出席大湄公河次区域经济合作第五次领导人会议开幕式。泰国总理巴育主持会议,缅甸总统吴登盛、柬埔寨首相洪森、老挝总理通邢、越南总理阮晋勇和亚洲开发银行行长中尾武彦与会。

(http://news.xinhuanet.com/world/2014-12/20/c_1113717344.htm)

On the morning of December 20 local time, Premier Li Keqiang attended the opening ceremony of the fifth Summit of the Greater Mekong Sub-region (GMS) Economic Cooperation Program in Bangkok, which was chaired by Prime Minister Prayuth Chan-ocha of Thailand, and attended by President U Thein Sein of Myanmar, Prime Minister Hun Sen of Cambodia, Prime Minister Thongsing Thammavong of Laos, Prime Minister Nguyen Tan Dung of Viet Nam and President of the Asian Development Bank (ADB) Takehiko Nakao.

(http://www.fmprc.gov.cn/mfa_eng/zxxx_662805/t1221882.shtml)

会议报道的导语中往往还会介绍该会议的主题/议题。英语译文中可以根据上下文选用focusing on,centering on,with the theme of等表达,或者使用介词on或动词discuss,cover等,也可根据具体情况灵活变通,如下面的实例所示(第一例摘自范例一):

各成员领导人围绕"共建面向未来的亚太伙伴关系"主题深入交换意见,共商区域经济合作大计,达成广泛共识。

Leaders of APEC members exchanged in-depth views on the topic of "Co-building the Future-oriented Asia-Pacific Partnership", jointly discussed major plans on regional economic cooperation and reached broad consensus.

杨洁篪强调,杭州峰会主题是"构建创新、活力、联动、包容的世界经济",全年工作将围绕"创新增长方式"、"更高效的全球经济金融治理"、"强劲的国际贸易和投资"、"包容和联动式发展"4项重点议题展开。

(http://www.chinadaily.com.cn/hqgj/jryw/2016-01-15/content_14487208.html)

Yang Jiechi emphasized that the Hangzhou Summit is themed on "Towards an Innovative, Invigorated, Interconnected and Inclusive World Economy". Bearing that in mind, the G20 will have four priorities this year: "breaking a new path for growth", "more effective and efficient global economic and financial governance", "robust international trade and investment" and "inclusive and interconnected development".

(http://www.g20.org/English/Dynamic/201601/t20160114_2106.html)

学生译作讲评
Analysis of Students' Translation Practice

原文链接：http://www.gov.cn/guowuyuan/2014-10/11/content_2762672.htm

新闻原文：李克强出席第七届中德经济技术合作论坛并发表演讲

学生译文：Premier Li Keqiang Attends 7th Germany-China Forum for Economic and Technological Cooperation and Delivers Speech

翻译评析：标题中的"发表演讲"被翻译为"delivers speech"表面上看似乎忠实于原文，并且与原文的语序也保持了高度对应。但是and前后显然不太平衡，有些头重脚轻，可以改译为addresses，与attends并列起来共同引导the forum作为宾语。关于论坛的名称，学生应该是通过网络搜索，查阅到了外媒中的相关报道，所以译为Germany-China。但在外交新闻翻译中有一个潜在的规则，即报道方前置，针对哪一方进行报道，就把哪一方放在前面。此处的文本背景是在报道李克强的活动，所以应该把中方放在前面，改为China-Germany。"技术"一词此处表示具体的生产技术，而不是技术科学，应该使用technical。故标题应修改为Premier Li Keqiang Attends and Addresses Seventh China-Germany Economic and Technical Cooperation Forum。

新闻原文：当地时间10月10日下午，国务院总理李克强在柏林与德国总理默克尔共同出席第七届中德经济技术合作论坛并发表题为《在开放中再续合作黄金季》的演讲。

学生译文：On the afternoon of October 10 local time, Premier Li Keqiang of the State Council and Chancellor Merkel of Germany jointly attended the 7th Germany-China Forum for Economic and Technological Cooperation in Berlin and delivered a speech entitled "Renew Cooperation Golden Season in the Open Atmosphere".

翻译评析：汉语中对外国元首的称呼通常为头衔加姓，所以学生非常忠实地对应了原文，但是要注意，英语中首次提及重要人物时，应当使用全名，所以应当修改为Chancellor Angela Merkel of Germany。

新闻原文：李克强表示，今年3月习近平主席访德期间，中德建立全方位战略伙伴关系。中德关系日趋成熟，经济深度融合，形成了"你中有我、我中有你"的利益共同体。

学生译文：Li Keqiang said that when Chinese President Xi Jinping visited Germany in March this year, China and Germany set up the comprehensive strategic partnership. The China-Germany relations become increasingly mature and share a deep fusion of economy, forming a highly interdependent interest community.

翻译评析：学生把"习近平主席访德期间"翻译为时间状语从句，从意思上来讲当然是正确的，但是不符合新闻语言的简练原则，而且in March this year也显得啰唆和累赘。可以把when引导的状语从句修改为介词短语during President Xi Jinping's visit to Germany this March。"全方位"的翻译选词不准，应该是all-round，学生用的

comprehensive通常翻译为"全面"。后一句话使用一般现在时态是个明显的语法错误，原文是在讲述自从3月中德建立全方位战略伙伴关系以来，中德关系如何发展，并形成了某种利益共同体，属于现在完成时的用法，故应将become修改为have become。"经济深度融合"是伴随"关系日趋成熟"而出现的一种状态，而不是"关系"的另外一个谓语，可调整为with the economies deeply integrated。"'你中有我，我中有你'的利益共同体"利用了汉语中对仗的修辞手法，英语中找不到对应的表达，但也不能直接省译，可以修改为forming a community of common interests featuring mutual inclusiveness。

新闻原文： 李克强强调，对外开放是中国的基本国策，关系国家发展和民族命运，我们对此坚定不移。中国的对外开放是更加积极主动、更深层次、更高水平的开放，在区域上由东部沿海向内陆、沿边拓展，在产业上不仅高水平开放制造业，而且加快开放服务业，在途径上注重引进来与走出去并行。中国的对外开放是营商环境更加规范、公平、透明的开放，外资企业和内资企业都是中国经济的组成部分，我们在市场准入、政策支持、合法权益保障上对内外资企业一视同仁。中国的对外开放是互利互惠、双赢多赢的开放，既造福本国也惠及世界。中国将继续奉行互利共赢的对外开放战略，与各国一道建设开放公平的全球大市场。

学生译文： Li Keqiang stressed that China will unswervingly carry out the basic state policy of opening-up, which concerns the development of the country and the future of the nation. China's opening-up is characterized by more proactivity, deeper layer and higher level, with expansion from the eastern coastal areas to the inland and border areas in terms of areas. As for the industry, China not only opens the manufacturing industry to a high level, but also accelerates the openness of the service industry. With respect to the approach, China attaches importance to both bringing in and going out. China's opening-up is characterized by a more standard, fairer and more transparent business environment. Both foreign-funded and domestic-funded enterprises are parts of China's economy, thus we treat them equally without discriminations in market access, policy support and legitimate rights and interests protection. China's opening-up is mutually beneficial and reciprocal, win-win and multi-win, not only benefiting its own but also the whole world. China will continue to pursue a mutually beneficial and win-win strategy of opening-up, and build an open and fair global market along with other countries.

翻译评析： 学生译文中的第一句话意思不够准确，"对外开放是中国的基本国策"这样一个判断性陈述被淡化为of短语，失去了原来的强调意味，可重新翻译为opening-up to the outside world is a fundamental state policy of China, concerning the development of the country and the future of the nation, and we will stick to it unswervingly。"更深层次"用greater depth较好。"在区域上"不能直译为in terms of areas（在面积上），应当修改为in terms of geographical coverage才是原文的真正含义。"在产业上"和"在途径上"都是和"在区域上"并列的，共同用来解释中国对外开放的特色，而学生

的译文则显得结构上有些松散，不能很好地反映这种并列关系，可改译为with expansion from the eastern coastal areas to the inland and border areas in terms of geographical coverage, opening-up of the manufacturing industry at a high level as well as acceleration of the opening-up of the service industry in terms of lines of industry, and focused attention on the parallel development of bringing in and going out in terms of development approach。"合法权益保障"的译文处前后都有and，各个词语之间的逻辑关系不清，可以调整为policy support as well as protection of legitimate rights and interests。下一句的"既造福本国也惠及世界"存在逻辑问题，世界当然是包括这个"本国"的，所以不能直接并列起来，可以添加at large，调整为benefiting both the country itself and the whole world at large。

新闻原文：李克强说，中国有条件、有能力实现今年经济增长7.5%左右的目标，将经济增长保持在合理区间。只要实现比较充分的就业，居民收入继续增长，质量效益不断提高，经济增长比7.5%高一点、低一点都是可以的。

学生译文：Li Keqiang said that China has conditions and abilities to realize the goal of economic growth at 7.5% this year and keep it in a reasonable range. As long as China achieves relatively full employment, resident income continues to increase and quality and benefit constantly improve, economic growth either higher or lower than 7.5% is tolerable.

翻译评析：学生译文的第二句话中将"China achieves relatively full employment"，"resident income continues to increase"和"quality and benefit constantly improve"处理为三个互相并列的成分，属于逻辑理解有误。"resident income"怎么可能和"China"并列起来？原文的意思应当是"就业比较充分、居民收入增长、质量效益提高"并列起来，作为中国"实现"的宾语。另外，"可以的"译为tolerable（可以容忍的）显然不太恰当，感情色彩完全不对。该句可重新译为As long as China achieves relatively full employment, continued increase in resident income, and constant improvement of quality and benefit, it is acceptable that economic growth is a bit higher or lower than 7.5 percent。

新闻原文：李克强表示，中德合作只有升级版，没有终极版。双方加强创新合作，可以为两国经济发展和繁荣创造更好条件，通过互学互鉴，用智慧拆解难题，开启未来。

学生译文：Li Keqiang said that cooperation between China and Germany only has updated edition, but no ultimate edition. Strengthening innovative cooperation between two countries will create better conditions for their economic development and prosperity. They can learn from each other and use wisdom to analyze and solve problems to open the future.

翻译评析："只有升级版，没有终极版"在英语中有非常贴切的对应强调句式no...but，所以应该调换语序，译为has no ultimate but only upgraded edition。下一句中的"双方加强合作"是双方主动发出了加强合作的动作，而不是其他主体做出了加强双方合作的行为，所以译文应当把the two countries处理为动名词短语的逻辑主语，即The two countries strengthening innovative cooperation will …。"通过互学互鉴"是方式状语，而不是谓语动作,"用智慧拆解难题"的重点在于"拆解难题"而不在于"用智慧",本句可重新译为Through learning from each other, the two countries can analyze and solve problems with wisdom and initiate a better future。

新闻原文:默克尔在演讲中表示,德中合作既是立足当前,更是放眼长远。德中建立和发展创新伙伴关系,将给两国合作和各自发展注入新的动力。德国是中国企业值得信赖的投资目的地,德方将为中国企业提供良好的投资环境,希望两国企业进一步加强互利合作,为两国关系发展作出积极贡献。

学生译文:Merkel said in her speech that the cooperation between Germany and China stands not only from the present, but also from the long run. The establishment and development of an innovation partnership between Germany and China would inject fresh impetus into bilateral cooperation and their respective development. Germany is a trustworthy investment destination for Chinese enterprises, and it will provide a favorable investment environment for Chinese enterprises. She hoped that businesses in Germany and China could further strengthen mutually beneficial cooperation, and make active contributions to the development of the bilateral relations.

翻译评析:译文末句中的She hoped时态不对,德国总理对中德合作的期待并非是发生在过去的一次性动作,而是一直持续到新闻报道的同时和之后。译文可以调整为She expressed her hope that ....。

新闻原文:第七届中德经济技术合作论坛由中国国家发展和改革委员会与德意志联邦经济和能源部共同举办,中德政府高级官员和两国经济界人士共约600人出席。

学生译文:The seventh Chinese-German Forum for Economic and Technological Cooperation is co-sponsored by the National Development and Reform Commission of China and Federal Ministry for Economic Affairs and Energy of Germany. It is attended by about 600 senior government officials and businessmen from China and Germany.

翻译评析:本段译文时态不对,应当全部改为过去时态,即was co-sponsored和was attended。另外,原文说得是所有与会人士共约600人,而译文中的600有可能被理解为仅指government officials。"经济界人士"的概念较大,businessmen一词不足以表达。所以末句译文考虑调整为Present were about 600 people including senior officials from the Chinese and German governments as well as people from economic communities of the two countries。

外交新闻汉英翻译
C-E TRANSLATION OF DIPLOMATIC NEWS

实战练习
Translation Practice

一、请翻译下列国际会议报道的标题（Translate the following headlines of coverage of international conferences）

1. 李克强出席中日省长知事论坛开幕式并致辞
   (http://www.fmprc.gov.cn/web/zyxw/t1558713.shtml)
2. 气候变化巴黎大会开始举行 国家主席习近平出席开幕活动
   (http://www.fmprc.gov.cn/web/zyxw/t1319770.shtml)
3. 外交部副部长张明出席环印度洋联盟第十四届部长理事会会议
   (http://www.fmprc.gov.cn/ce/cgmb/chn/wjbxw/t1199018.htm)
4. 习近平出席联合国发展峰会并发表重要讲话
   强调以2015年后发展议程为新起点 努力实现各国共同发展
   (http://www.fmprc.gov.cn/ce/ceie/chn/zgyw/t1300883.htm)
5. 习近平出席二十国集团领导人第九次峰会第二阶段会议
   会议宣布中国主办2016年二十国集团领导人峰会
   (http://csnew.fmprc.gov.cn/web/ziliao_674904/zt_674979/ywzt_675099/2014zt_675101/xjpzxcfjtdg_675215/zxxx_675217/t1211481.shtml)
6. 杨洁篪出席第八次金砖国家安全事务高级代表会议
   (http://www.fmprc.gov.cn/web/zyxw/t1573003.shtml)
7. 李克强抵达金边出席澜沧江—湄公河合作第二次领导人会议并对柬埔寨进行正式访问
   (http://www.fmprc.gov.cn/web/zyxw/t1524704.shtml)
8. 王毅主持安理会维护国际和平与安全公开辩论会
   (http://news.xinhuanet.com/2015-02/24/c_127512872.htm)

二、请翻译下面一则国际会议报道（Translate the following coverage of international conference）

习近平出席第二届世界互联网大会开幕式并发表主旨演讲
强调加强沟通，扩大共识，深化合作
共同构建网络空间命运共同体
刘云山主持开幕式并致辞

2015年12月16日上午，第二届世界互联网大会在浙江省乌镇开幕。国家主席习近平出席开幕式并发表主旨演讲，强调互联网是人类的共同家园，各国应该共同构建网络空间命运共同体，推动网络空间互联互通、共享共治，为开创人类发展更加美好的未来助力。

刘云山在主持开幕式时说，习近平主席出席大会并发表主旨演讲，充分体现了中国政府对这次大会的高度重视。构建网络空间命运共同体，是国际社会的共同责任。希望各位嘉宾深入研讨、加强互鉴、凝聚共识，为共同构建和平、安全、开放、合作的网络空间，建立多边、民主、透明的全球互联网治理体系，贡献智慧和力量。

开幕式前，习近平同与会嘉宾集体合影。

王沪宁、栗战书、杨洁篪、王钦敏等参加上述活动。

第二届世界互联网大会12月16日至18日举行，主题为"互联互通·共享共治——构建网络空间命运共同体"。来自五大洲120多个国家和地区的政府代表、国际组织负责人、互联网企业领军人物、著名企业家、专家学者、大学生代表等共2000多名嘉宾参加。

(http://www.fmprc.gov.cn/web/zyxw/t1324884.shtml)

参考译文
Versions for Reference

一、请翻译下列国际会议报道的标题（Translate the following headlines of coverage of international conferences）

1. Li Keqiang Attends and Addresses the Opening Ceremony of China-Japan Governor Forum
2. UN Climate Change Conference in Paris Starts
   President Xi Jinping Attends Opening Events
3. Vice Foreign Minister Zhang Ming Attends the 14th Meeting of the Council of Ministers of the Indian Ocean Rim Association
4. Xi Jinping Delivers Important Speech at UN Sustainable Development Summit, Stressing Realization of Common Development of All Countries from New Starting Point of Post-2015 Development Agenda
5. Xi Jinping Attends the Second Phase of 9th G20 Leaders' Summit, During Which China Was Announced to Host the G20 Leaders' Summit in 2016
6. Yang Jiechi Attends the 8th Meeting of the BRICS High Representatives for Security Issues
7. Li Keqiang Arrives in Phnom Penh to Attend the 2nd LMC Leaders' Meeting and Pay Official Visit to Cambodia

8. Wang Yi Presides over Security Council Open Debate on Maintaining International Peace and Security

二、请翻译下面一则国际会议报道（Translate the following coverage of international conference）

Xi Jinping Attends Opening Ceremony of the Second World Internet Conference and Delivers Keynote Speech, Emphasizing Stepping up Communication, Broadening Consensus and Deepening Cooperation to Jointly Build a Community of Shared Future in Cyberspace
Liu Yunshan Chairs and Addresses the Opening Ceremony

On the morning of December 16, 2015, the second World Internet Conference was convened in Wuzhen, Zhejiang Province. President Xi Jinping attended the opening ceremony and delivered a keynote speech, emphasizing that the Internet is a common space for mankind, and all countries should jointly build a community of shared future in cyberspace and promote connectivity, sharing and co-governance of cyberspace so as to help create a better future for the development of mankind.

While chairing the opening ceremony, Liu Yunshan said that President Xi Jinping's attendance at the conference and delivery of a keynote speech fully demonstrate the high attention that the Chinese government pays to the conference. Building a community of shared future in cyberspace is a common responsibility of the international community. It is hoped that guests present will conduct in-depth discussions, strengthen mutual learning and pool consensus, so as to contribute wisdom and strength to jointly building a peaceful, secure, open and cooperative cyberspace and establishing a multilateral, democratic and transparent global Internet governance system.

Prior to the opening ceremony, Xi Jinping took group photos with attending guests.

Wang Huning, Li Zhanshu, Yang Jiechi, Wang Qinmin and others attended the above-mentioned activities.

The second World Internet Conference was held from December 16 to 18, with the theme of "An Interconnected World Shared and Governed by All—Building a Community of Common Future in Cyberspace". Over 2,000 guests including government representatives, principals of international organizations, leading figures of Internet enterprises, famous entrepreneurs, experts and scholars, and representatives of college students from over 120 countries and regions of the five continents attended the conference.

单元小结
Summary

本单元主要介绍了国际会议报道的翻译。国际会议报道一般有两种角度,要么以会议本身为关注点,要么以领导人参会为关注点,在翻译时要注意根据不同的报道角度凸显信息重点。会议名称的翻译需要考虑的政治因素较多,要不断提高网络搜索技能,遵照沿用官方既定的名称,或参照以往及外媒中的平行文本。会议报道的标题往往较长,可以通过非谓语动词、从句、连接词、断行排版等手段,解决标题中出现多个独立语句的问题。关于会议宗旨、会议表态、会议成果的表述要注意积累常用句型和表达。会议主题和重要观点往往还会在以后的新闻报道中重复提及,所以对于重大会议的相关内容及其英文表述要注意学习积累,才能提高翻译效率。

参考文献:

陈明瑶:《论等值标准与新闻导语翻译》,《上海科技翻译》2001年第2期。
廖志勤:《英文新闻标题及其翻译策略》,《中国科技翻译》2006年第2期。
刘其中:《新闻翻译教程》,北京:中国人民大学出版社,2004年。
彭朝丞:《新闻标题学》,北京:人民日报出版社,1996年。
朱献珑:《英语对外报道导语的语篇分析及译写策略》,《上海翻译》2008年第4期。

外交会晤新闻报道的翻译
Translation for Coverage of Diplomatic Meetings

单元简介
Introduction

两国元首外交的主要内容包括正式会议、会晤、非正式会晤、国事访问、友好访问等。外交会晤是高层领导之间的见面，分为正式会晤和非正式会晤。会晤主要针对双方关切的重大问题进行面对面、高效务实的沟通，双方领导人阐述各自的观点，以及代表各自政府的官方观点。会晤的另一种创新形式是"集体会晤"，通常是一国领导人出访时，在时间非常紧、会晤对象又比较多的情况下，在某一出访地邀请周边国家领导人一同会晤。这也是中国外交上的创新，增加了中国外交的立体性。会晤新闻报道主要涵盖会晤领导人、时间、地点、背景、主要议题、各方观点、出席人员等。读者通过会晤报道可以了解双方所达成的共识、建立的关系、双方的立场态度等。

Translation for Coverage of Diplomatic Meetings

外交会晤新闻报道翻译范例分析
Sample of Translation for Coverage of Diplomatic Meetings

范例一（Sample I）

习近平同美国总统奥巴马在中南海会晤
强调要以积水成渊、积土成山的精神推进中美新型大国关系建设（节本）
2014/11/12

Xi Jinping Holds Meeting with President Barack Obama of the US at Zhongnanhai, Stressing Promoting Construction of New Model of Major-Country Relationship Between China and the US with Spirit of "Accumulating Droplets to Form a Pool and Heaping Earth to Put up a Mountain" (Abbreviated Version)
2014/11/12

2014年11月11日晚，国家主席习近平在中南海同美国总统奥巴马举行会晤。两国元首就中美关系及共同关心的重大国际和地区问题坦诚深入交换意见。

On the evening of November 11, 2014, President Xi Jinping held a meeting with President Barack Obama of the US at Zhongnanhai. The two heads of state made candid and in-depth exchanges of views on China-US relations and major international and regional issues of common concern.

晚上的中南海，水波荡漾，树影婆娑。习近平在瀛台前迎接奥巴马，两国元首亲切握手，互致问候。习近平欢迎奥巴马来华出席亚太经合组织领导人非正式会议并对中国进行国事访问。

Zhongnanhai in the evening saw rippling lake water and flickering tree shadows. Xi Jinping greeted Obama in front of Yingtai, and the two heads of state shook hands warmly and exchanged greetings. Xi Jinping welcomed Obama's attendance at the Asia-Pacific Economic Cooperation (APEC) Economic Leaders' Meeting in China and his state visit to China.

瀛台桥上，两国元首凭栏远眺。亭台楼阁，错落有致，华灯初上，熠熠生辉。古老的瀛台见证了几百年中国的变迁。习近平向奥巴马介绍瀛台历史。习近平表示，了解中国近代以来的历史对理解中国人民今天的理想和前进道路很重要。

On the Yingtai Bridge, the two heads of state leant on the railing overlooking the pavilions scattered around under glorious lights. Xi Jinping briefed Obama on the history of Yingtai, which has witnessed the vicissitudes of China for centuries. Xi Jinping said that knowing the modern history of China is of great importance to understanding Chinese people's ideal today and their development path.

两国元首拾阶而上，来到涵元殿举行会晤。

125

The two heads of state walked up the steps and held a meeting at the Hanyuan Hall.

***

习近平说，我高兴地看到，在双方共同努力下，在推进中美新型大国关系建设方面取得不少早期收获。

Xi Jinping said I delightedly see that with joint efforts of both sides, lots of early achievements have been made in promoting the construction of a new model of major-country relationship between China and the US.

奥巴马表示，我愿意同习近平主席就广泛的问题及时交换意见，推动美中新型大国关系建设不断迈上新台阶。

Obama said that he is willing to exchange views timely with President Xi Jinping on a wide range of issues, so as to promote the construction of a new model of major-country relationship between the US and China to a higher level continuously.

习近平邀请奥巴马共进晚宴。席间，两国元首就治国理政进行深入交流。习近平指出，要了解今天的中国、预测明天的中国，必须了解中国的过去，了解中国的文化。中美国情各异，历史文化、发展道路、发展阶段不同，应该相互理解，相互尊重，聚同化异，和而不同。

Xi Jinping invited Obama to dinner, at which the two heads of state exchanged in-depth views on governance and administration of state affairs. Xi Jinping pointed out that to understand today's China and predict tomorrow's China, one has to know China's past and culture. China and the US have different national conditions, history and culture, and development paths, and stand in different development phases. The two countries should understand and respect each other, and live in harmony by focusing on similarities and allowing divergences.

***

奥巴马表示，美方愿意同中方坦诚沟通对话，增进相互了解，相互借鉴经验，有效管控分歧，避免误解和误判。

Obama said that the US is willing to sincerely conduct communication and dialogues with China, enhance mutual understanding, learn from each other's experience, and effectively manage and control disparities so as to avoid misunderstanding and misjudgment.

夜色渐沉，两国元首聊兴不减，信步来到迎熏亭茶叙。

In the gathering darkness, the two heads of state strolled to the Yingxun Pavilion to enjoy tea while chatting with great interest.

***

习近平强调，我们要坚持从战略高度和长远角度出发，以积水成渊、积土成山的精神，不断推进中美新型大国关系建设。

Xi Jinping stressed that we should adhere to continuously pushing forward the construction of the new model of major-country relationship between China and the US from a strategic and long-term perspective, with the spirit of "accumulating droplets to form a pool and heaping earth to put up a mountain".

两国元首12日将继续举行会谈，进一步交换意见。

The two heads of state will continue to hold talks on November 12 to further exchange views.

杨洁篪等参加上述活动。

Yang Jiechi and others were present at the above activities.

新闻背景：2014年亚太经合组织（APEC）领导人会议周活动于11月5日至11日在北京举行，会议的主题为"共建面向未来的亚太伙伴关系"，议程包含领导人非正式会议、部长级会议、高官会等系列会议。美国总统奥巴马于11月10日至12日来华出席亚太经合组织领导人非正式会议并对中国进行国事访问。11月11日晚，国家主席习近平与奥巴马在中南海举行会晤，媒体称之为中南海的"瀛台夜话"。当晚，原定90分钟的宴会持续了近两个小时，原定30分钟的茶叙持续了近1个小时。直到夜里11点多，习奥二人才挥手告别。两国元首就中美关系及共同关心的重大国际和地区问题坦诚深入交换意见，提出以积水成渊、积土成山的精神，不断推进中美新型大国关系建设。奥巴马访华期间，习近平与奥巴马在北京进行了多场长时间的双边会谈，并取得多项共识和成果。舆论认为，在两国元首"马拉松式"的会谈后，两国关系有了大幅度进展。

原文链接：http://news.xinhuanet.com/world/2014-11/11/c_1113206517.htm

译文链接：http://www.fmprc.gov.cn/mfa_eng/zxxx_662805/t1210355.shtml

---

一、范例一文本结构分析（Text Structure Analysis of Sample I）

范例一是一则外交会晤新闻报道，主要内容包括会晤的时间、地点、场景、步骤、主题、双方主要观点等。

新闻标题介绍会晤双方领导人以及会晤主题。第一段为导语，介绍会晤双方人物、时间、地点和主要议题等，例如在本条报道的导语中就包括会晤双方（习近平、奥巴马）、时间（2014年11月11日晚）、地点（中南海）、主要议题（中美关系及共同关心的重大国际和地区问题）等信息。

新闻报道的主体部分以两国元首会晤场景变换为顺序，每一个场景都包括由双方主要观点构成的会谈内容：先介绍习近平主席瀛台前迎接美国总统奥巴马，说明此次会晤的背景（奥巴马来华出席亚太经合组织领导人非正式会议并对中国进行国事访问）；随即场景变换至瀛台桥上，习近平向奥巴马介绍瀛台历史，并称了解中国近代以来的历史对理解中国人民今天的理想和前进道路很重要；接着，两国元首前往涵元殿会晤，分别表达对构建新型大国关系的态度和立场（习近平说……、奥巴马表示……）；在晚宴上，两位领导人就治国理政进行深入交流，习近平指出中美应当聚同化异，和而不同。最后，两国领导人来到迎熏亭茶叙，习近平强调中美新型大国关系的战略意义，倡导从战略高度和长远角度出发，以积水成渊、积土成山的精神，不断推进中美新型大国关系建设。因篇幅所限，原文有所删节。

最后两段结尾部分主要介绍会谈后续安排以及其他参与会晤活动的人员。

二、范例一翻译解析（Translation Analysis of Sample I）

（一）外交会晤报道标题的翻译（Translation of Headlines for Coverage of Diplomatic Meetings）

外交会晤报道的标题最简单的表述方法为"领导人+会见+国家（机构）+头衔+人名"，例如"李克强会见埃塞俄比亚总理海尔马里亚姆"。另一种常见的外交会晤新闻标题形式为"××同××举行会晤+主旨观点"，例如范例一"习近平同美国总统奥巴马在中南海会晤 强调要以积水成渊、积土成山的精神推进中美新型大国关系建设"，"习近平与奥朗德举行会谈 两国元首一致同意 不断开创中法友好合作新局面"。下面就以上述外交会晤报道标题为例，探讨不同形式的会晤报道标题的翻译方法。

王毅会见联大主席吕克托夫特
(http://www.fmprc.gov.cn/mfa_eng/zxxx_662805/t1302355.shtml)
Wang Yi Meets with President Mogens Lykket of UN General Assembly
(http://www.fmprc.gov.cn/mfa_eng/zxxx_662805/t1302355.shtml)

李克强会见埃塞俄比亚总理海尔马里亚姆
(http://www.fmprc.gov.cn/mfa_chn/zyxw_602251/t1293738.shtml)
Li Keqiang Meets with Prime Minister Hailemariam Desalegn of Ethiopia
(http://www.fmprc.gov.cn/mfa_eng/zxxx_662805/t1294309.shtml)

习近平会见美国国会众参两院领导人
(http://www.fmprc.gov.cn/mfa_eng/zxxx_662805/t1302667.shtml)
Xi Jinping Meets with Leaders of Senate and House of Representatives of US Congress
(http://www.fmprc.gov.cn/ce/cggb/eng/xwdt/t1302667.htm)

习近平与奥朗德举行会谈 两国元首一致同意 不断开创中法友好合作新局面
(http://au.china-embassy.org/eng/xw/t1311758.htm)
Xi Jinping Holds Talks with François Hollande and Two Heads of State Agree to Constantly Open up New Situation of China-France Friendly Cooperation
(http://www.fmprc.gov.cn/mfa_eng/wjdt_665385/wshd_665389/t1311758.shtml)

外交会晤新闻报道的翻译
Translation for Coverage of Diplomatic Meetings

从以上实例可以看出，"××会见××"可以译为meets with，"××同××进行会晤"可以译为holds meeting with，"××与××举行会谈"可以译为holds talks with，时态采用一般现在时。一般情况下，如果中文标题中同时出现国家（机构）、头衔、人名时，译文多采用"头衔+人名+of+国家（机构）"的形式，例如President Mogens Lykket of the UN General Assembly。如果副标题中进一步说明领导人会晤的主旨观点，译文中可以采取分词结构，如范例一中"强调推进中美新型大国关系建设"可以译为Stressing Promoting Construction of New Model of Major-Country Relationship Between China and the US；有时译文可采取并列结构，如"习近平与奥朗德举行会谈 两国元首一致同意……"可以译为Xi Jinping Holds Talks with François Hollande and Two Heads of State Agree to …。

（二）外交会晤报道导语的翻译（Translation of News Lead in Coverage of Diplomatic Meetings）

外交会晤报道的导语通常涵盖会晤双方领导人、时间、地点、背景和主要议题等信息。如范例一，介绍人物、时间、地点的句式可翻译为 On a date, ×× held a meeting (met) with ×× at a place in a city，时态采用一般过去时；介绍主要议题的惯用表述"双方就……问题坦诚深入交换意见"可以译为… made candid and in-depth exchanges of views on …，"就……交换意见"可以译为exchange views on …；在一些新闻报道的导语中也介绍会晤背景，如"××会见来华出席……活动的××"，可以译为×× met with ××, who was in China to attend …；"××会见来华进行国事访问的××"，可以译为×× met with ××, who came to China to pay a state visit …。

请看下面翻译实例：

当地时间11月14日下午，中国外交部长王毅在土耳其安塔利亚会见阿根廷外长齐默尔曼，就中阿双边关系和二十国集团峰会交换意见。

(http://cpc.people.com.cn/n/2015/1115/c117005-27817061.html)

On the afternoon of November 14 local time, Foreign Minister Wang Yi met with Foreign Minister Héctor Timerman of Argentina in Antalya of Turkey, exchanging views on China-Argentina relations and the G20 Summit.

(http://www.mfa.gov.cn/web/wjbzhd/t1314925.shtml)

2015年9月4日上午，国务院总理李克强在人民大会堂会见来华出席中国人民抗日战争暨世界反法西斯战争胜利70周年纪念活动的埃塞俄比亚总理海尔马里亚姆。

(http://paper.people.com.cn/rmrbhwb/html/2015-09/04/content_1606300.htm)

On the morning of September 4, 2015, Premier Li Keqiang met at the Great Hall of the People with Prime Minister Hailemariam Desalegn of Ethiopia, who was in China to attend the commemorations marking the 70th anniversary of the victory of the Chinese

People's War of Resistance against Japanese Aggression and the World Anti-Fascist War.

(http://www.fmprc.gov.cn/mfa_eng/zxxx_662805/t1294309.shtml)

2015年3月26日下午,国务院总理李克强在人民大会堂会见来华进行国事访问并出席博鳌亚洲论坛2015年年会的亚美尼亚总统萨尔基相。

(http://paper.people.com.cn/rmrbhwb/html/2015-03/27/content_1547645.htm)

On the afternoon of March 26, 2015, Premier Li Keqiang met at the Great Hall of the People with President Serzh Sargsyan of Armenia, who came to China to pay a state visit and attend the Boao Forum for Asia (BFA) Annual Conference 2015.

(http://www.fmprc.gov.cn/mfa_eng/wjdt_665385/wshd_665389/t1249975.shtml)

(三)外交会晤报道常用表达的翻译(Translation of Frequently Used Expressions in Coverage of Diplomatic Meetings)

1. 有关两国关系表述的翻译

领导人在谈及两国关系时,中方领导人会将中国放在前面,如"中埃关系""中法关系"等,外方领导人会将本国放在首位,例如"美中关系""阿中关系"等。在翻译时也要遵循这一顺序,不可随意调整。

关于双边关系,中国常常用"伙伴关系"来定位双边关系。常见名称主要包括:伙伴关系(partnership)、全面伙伴关系(comprehensive partnership)、合作伙伴关系(cooperative partnership)、全面合作伙伴关系(comprehensive cooperative partnership)、战略伙伴关系(strategic partnership)、战略合作伙伴关系(strategic cooperative partnership)、全面战略伙伴关系(comprehensive strategic partnership)、新型战略伙伴关系(new type of strategic partnership)、全面战略合作伙伴关系(comprehensive strategic partnership of cooperation)、全天候战略合作伙伴关系(all-weather strategic partnership of cooperation)、全面战略协作伙伴关系(comprehensive strategic partnership of coordination)、建设性战略伙伴关系(constructive strategic partnership)、面向21世纪的战略伙伴关系(strategic partnership for the 21st century)、面向21世纪的全面合作伙伴关系(comprehensive partnership of cooperation for the 21st century)、面向21世纪全球全面战略伙伴关系(global comprehensive strategic partnership for the 21st century)等。请看下面翻译实例:

本·萨拉赫表示,中国是帮助阿尔及利亚发展的真诚可信伙伴。阿中全面战略伙伴关系发展蓝图已定,阿方对两国关系发展高度满意,愿继续坚定推进双边各领域的友好交往合作。

(http://www.fmprc.gov.cn/ce/cebel/chn/zgyw/t1293741.htm)

Abdelkader Bensalah said that China is a sincere and reliable partner who assists with Algeria's development. The blueprint of developing Algeria-China comprehensive strategic partnership has been laid out. Algeria is highly satisfied with the development of the bilateral relations and is willing to continue to firmly promote bilateral friendly exchanges and cooperation in various fields.

(http://www.fmprc.gov.cn/mfa_eng/zxxx_662805/t1294311.shtml)

尼方愿与中方继续坚定地相互支持，不断提升尼中全面合作伙伴关系。尼方再次对西藏灾区遭受的伤亡和损失表示慰问。

(http://news.china.com/zh_cn/domesticgd/10000159/20150625/19895734.html)

Nepal is willing to work with China to continue firmly supporting each other and constantly enhance Nepal-China comprehensive cooperative partnership. Nepal expresses condolences again over the casualties and losses caused by the earthquake in the Tibet Autonomous Region.

(http://www.fmprc.gov.cn/mfa_eng/wjdt_665385/wshd_665389/t1276306.shtml)

习近平主席这次访英十分成功，推动两国关系迈上新台阶。两国宣布共同构建英中面向21世纪全球全面战略伙伴关系，符合双方利益，是双赢的决定。

(http://paper.people.com.cn/rmrbhwb/html/2015-10/24/content_1625169.htm)

The successful visit of President Xi Jinping to the UK elevates bilateral relations to a new high. Both nations announced to jointly build the China-UK global comprehensive strategic partnership for the 21st century, which conforms to the interests of both sides and is a win-win decision.

(http://www.fmprc.gov.cn/mfa_eng/zxxx_662805/t1309372.shtml)

2. 有关双方合作、化解分歧表述的翻译

外交会晤中，双边合作几乎是会晤双方的必谈话题。针对会晤双方开展双边合作的常用表达包括：加快推进……等领域合作（accelerate cooperation with ... in ... and other fields），在……等领域加大合作力度（strengthen cooperation in areas such as ...），提升……等方面合作水平（promote the cooperation level in the aspects such as ... / uplift the level of bilateral cooperation in ...），在……等领域打造合作新亮点（create new cooperation highlights in the fields such as ...），积极落实……共识（actively implement the important consensuses reached by both sides ...），抓紧落实……合作倡议（swiftly implement ... cooperative initiatives ...）等等。请看下面具体翻译实例：

李克强指出，中方愿同缅方加快推进基础设施建设等领域合作；抓紧落实孟中印缅经济走廊等合作倡议，进一步便利区域互联互通；积极开展产能合作，提升农业、水利和灾后安置、重建等方面合作水平。

(http://paper.people.com.cn/rmrbhwb/html/2015-09/05/content_1606581.htm)

Li Keqiang pointed out that China is willing to accelerate cooperation with Myanmar in infrastructure construction and other fields, swiftly implement the Bangladesh-China-India-Myanmar Economic Corridor and other cooperative initiatives to further facilitate regional connectivity, and actively conduct production capacity cooperation to promote the cooperation level in the aspects such as agriculture, water conservancy, and post-disaster resettlement and reconstruction.

(http://www.fmprc.gov.cn/mfa_eng/zxxx_662805/t1294308.shtml)

李克强指出，中奥合作有基础和优势，更有机会和潜力。中方愿同奥方共同努力，在环保、新能源、可再生能源、农业、科技等领域打造合作新亮点，提升两国金融、民用航空合作水平。

(http://politics.people.com.cn/n/2015/0326/c70731-26756456.html)

Li Keqiang pointed out that the cooperation between China and Austria enjoys opportunities and potential as well as foundations and advantages. China is willing to make joint efforts with Austria to create new cooperation highlights in the fields such as environmental protection, new energy, renewable energy, agriculture, and science and technology, and uplift the level of bilateral cooperation in finance and civil aviation.

(http://www.fmprc.gov.cn/mfa_eng/topics_665678/xjpcxbayzlt2015nnh/t1250020.shtml)

世界有目共睹，中美双方就几乎所有重大国际和地区问题都保持着密切有效的沟通和协调。虽然在处理一些问题时思路和方法并不完全一致，但两国总是积极寻求解决问题的途径，从而消除猜疑，化解分歧，达成共识。请看下列有关化解分歧表述的翻译：

习近平指出中美国情各异，历史文化、发展道路、发展阶段不同，应该相互理解，相互尊重，聚同化异，和而不同。

(http://news.xinhuanet.com/world/2014-11/11/c_1113206517.htm)

China and the US have different national conditions, history and culture, and development paths, and stand in different development phases. The two countries should understand and respect each other, and live in harmony by focusing on similarities and allowing divergences.

(http://www.fmprc.gov.cn/mfa_eng/zxxx_662805/t1210355.shtml)

本例中谈及中美四点不同：国情、历史文化、发展道路、发展阶段。考虑到英语行文习惯，译文中采取两个不同谓语动词搭配名词，译为have different national conditions 和stand in different development phases。原文中有四个短语"相互理解，相互尊重，聚同化异，和而不同"，怎样明晰其内在逻辑结构非常关键。译文通过增译live in harmony将原文隐含意义明晰化，用by focusing on similarities and allowing divergences简洁直观地把"聚同化异，和而不同"表达出来，从而达到语义逻辑明晰，句法结构准确。

美国支持中国改革开放,无意遏制或围堵中国,因为这样做不符合美国的利益。美方愿意同中方坦诚沟通对话,增进相互了解,相互借鉴经验,有效管控分歧,避免误解和误判。

(http://news.xinhuanet.com/world/2014-11/11/c_1113206517.htm)

The US is supportive to China's reform and opening-up and has no intention of suppressing or containing China, for it is not in conformity with the US's interests. The US is willing to sincerely conduct communication and dialogues with China, enhance mutual understanding, learn from each other's experience, and effectively manage and control disparities so as to avoid misunderstanding and misjudgment.

(http://www.fmprc.gov.cn/mfa_eng/zxxx_662805/t1210355.shtml)

在国家间表示化解分歧意愿时,常采用"无意遏制或围堵""沟通对话""管控分歧""避免误解和误判"等表述来表达立场和做法。本例汉语原文由多个动词结构组成:"支持改革""无意遏制或围堵""沟通对话""增进了解""借鉴经验"等,译文则凸显了英语语言的静态特征,采用形容词短语is supportive to,动名词结构no intention of suppressing or containing,介词短语in conformity with,名词短语communication and dialogues等表达汉语的动态特征,这也符合外交新闻文本较为正式的语体特征。

3. 有关中国政策立场以及治国理政思想的翻译

2012年中国共产党十八大以来,习近平总书记就改革发展和治国理政提出了一系列新思想、新观点和新论断,提出了指导改革开放与中国特色社会主义建设的系列治国理政思想。总结其核心内容的英文表述包括:全面深化改革(comprehensively deepen the reform),推进依法治国(promote the management of state affairs in accordance with the law),加强执政党建设(strengthen the building of the ruling party),坚持和发展中国特色社会主义道路(unswervingly follow the path of socialism with Chinese characteristics),坚定维护国家主权、安全和领土完整(firmly safeguard national sovereignty, security and territorial integrity),维护民族团结和社会稳定(maintain ethnic solidarity and social stability),走和平发展道路(pursue the path of peaceful development),实现中华民族伟大复兴的中国梦(realize the Chinese Dream of the great rejuvenation of the Chinese nation),等等。

请看下列外交会晤新闻报道中,有关领导人介绍各自国情、政策方针,交流治国理政思想的翻译实例:

席间,两国元首就治国理政进行深入交流。习近平向奥巴马介绍了中国全面深化改革、推进依法治国、加强执政党建设等情况,强调我们已经找到一条符合国情的发展道路，这就是中国特色社会主义道路。

(http://news.xinhuanet.com/world/2014-11/11/c_1113206517.htm)

Xi Jinping invited Obama to dinner, at which the two heads of state exchanged in-depth views on governance and administration of state affairs. Xi Jinping introduced to Obama China's comprehensive deepening of reform, promoting the management of state affairs in accordance with the law, strengthening the building of the ruling party, and others. Xi Jinping stressed that China has found a development path conforming to its own national conditions, that is, the path of socialism with Chinese characteristics.

(http://www.fmprc.gov.cn/mfa_eng/zxxx_662805/t1210355.shtml)

中国政府必须顺乎民意，坚定维护国家主权、安全和领土完整，维护民族团结和社会稳定，坚定不移走和平发展道路。

(http://news.xinhuanet.com/world/2014-11/11/c_1113206517.htm)

The Chinese government must comply with the people's will, firmly safeguard national sovereignty, security and territorial integrity, maintain ethnic solidarity and social stability, and unswervingly pursue the path of peaceful development.

(http://www.fmprc.gov.cn/mfa_eng/zxxx_662805/t1210355.shtml)

王毅说，中国奉行独立自主的和平外交政策，坚持走和平发展道路，实施全方位对外开放战略。习近平主席提出，要推动建立以合作共赢为核心的新型国际关系，这是我们愿同世界各国长期践行和追求的方向。

(http://news.xinhuanet.com/2015-06/10/c_1115570279.htm)

Wang Yi said that China follows an independent foreign policy of peace, sticks to the path of peaceful development and implements a strategy of all-around opening-up. President Xi Jinping pointed out that we should promote the building of a new type of international relations featuring win-win cooperation, which we are willing to practice and pursue with other countries in the long term.

(http://www.fmprc.gov.cn/ce/ceuk/eng/zgyw/t1273412.htm)

4. 有关会晤后续活动的翻译

一些外交会晤新闻报道中会涉及会晤后续活动，例如"领导人会见后，共同发表……联合声明"，"见证……等领域合作协议签署"，一般可以译为jointly issued the Joint Statement of …以及jointly witnessed the signing of cooperative agreements in fields such as …。请看以下翻译实例：

会谈后，两国总理共同见证了双边经济技术、电力、金融、能源、航空等领域合作文件的签署。

(http://paper.ce.cn/jjrb/html/2015-09/05/content_255596.htm)

Translation for Coverage of Diplomatic Meetings

After the talks, both prime ministers witnessed the signing of the bilateral cooperative agreements in areas such as economy, technology, electricity, finance, energy and aviation.

(http://www.fmprc.gov.cn/mfa_eng/zxxx_662805/t1294309.shtml)

会谈后,两国元首共同发表了《中法元首气候变化联合声明》,共同见证了两国政府和企业间多项合作文件的签署,涉及经贸、金融、能源、环保、人文等多个领域。

(http://news.xinhuanet.com/politics/2015-11/02/c_1117017449.htm)

After the talks, the two heads of state jointly issued the Joint Statement of Heads of State of China and France on Climate Change, and jointly witnessed the signing of a number of cooperative documents between the governments and enterprises of the two countries, involving many fields such as economy, trade, finance, energy, environmental protection and people-to-people and cultural engagement.

(http://www.fmprc.gov.cn/mfa_eng/zxxx_662805/t1311758.shtml)

会晤结束后,习近平在卡梅伦陪同下乘车前往当地小镇体验酒吧文化。两国领导人边饮啤酒,边品尝英国特色小吃"炸鱼和薯条",并同当地民众交谈。

(http://paper.people.com.cn/rmrbhwb/html/2015-10/24/content_1625169.htm)

After the meeting, Xi Jinping, accompanied by Prime Minister David Cameron, went to local town by car to experience the pub culture. The two leaders had beers and the British specialty food fish and chips, and communicated with local residents.

(http://www.fmprc.gov.cn/mfa_eng/zxxx_662805/t1309372.shtml)

范例二(Sample II)

习近平会见俄罗斯总统普京
2015/09/03
Xi Jinping Meets with President Vladimir Putin of Russia
2015/09/03

2015年9月3日,国家主席习近平在人民大会堂会见俄罗斯总统普京。
On September 3, 2015, President Xi Jinping met with President Vladimir Putin of Russia at the Great Hall of the People.

习近平感谢俄罗斯对中国人民抗日战争暨世界反法西斯战争胜利70周年纪念活动给予积极支持,感谢俄罗斯派方队参加阅兵。习近平指出,中俄分别是第二次世界大战亚洲和欧洲主战场,为第二次世界大战最终胜利付出的牺牲最大,作出的贡献也很大。今年我们两国领导人相互出席彼此举办的纪念卫国战争胜利70周年庆典和中国人民抗日战争暨世界反法西斯战争胜利70周年纪念活动，就是为了促进地区及世界和平，为人类和平与进步事业注入正能量。

Xi Jinping thanked Russia for its active support in the commemorations of the 70th anniversary of the victory of the Chinese People's War of Resistance against Japanese Aggression and the World Anti-Fascist War and thanked Russia for sending a military group to participate in the military parade. Xi Jinping pointed out that as the main battlefields in the World War II in Asia and Europe respectively, China and Russia made the greatest sacrifice and contributed greatly to the final victory of the WWII. This year, leaders of the two countries attended each other's activities commemorating the 70th anniversary of the victory of the Great Patriotic War and commemorating the 70th anniversary of the victory of the Chinese People's War of Resistance against Japanese Aggression and the World Anti-Fascist War. This is to promote regional and world peace and inject positive energy into the cause of human peace and progress.

习近平强调，中方发展中俄全面战略协作伙伴关系和扩大全方位务实合作的方针是坚定不移的。双方要扩大金融、投资、能源、地方合作，要制定好丝绸之路经济带建设和欧亚经济联盟建设对接合作的长期规划纲要，落实好合作项目。中俄同为联合国创始成员国和安理会常任理事国，要继续加强协作，推动国际社会利用联合国成立70周年契机，回顾历史，开创未来，维护第二次世界大战胜利成果，坚持《联合国宪章》宗旨和原则，构建以合作共赢为核心的新型国际关系。

Xi Jinping stressed that China's policy to develop China-Russia comprehensive strategic partnership of coordination and expand all-round practical cooperation is unswerving. The two sides should expand cooperation in areas of finance, investment and energy and between local governments, formulate long-term outline plan of cooperation in docking the construction of the Silk Road Economic Belt and the construction of the Eurasian Economic Union and earnestly implement cooperative projects. As founding members of the United Nations and permanent members of its Security Council, China and Russia should continue to strengthen coordination, and promote the international community taking the 70th anniversary of the founding of the United Nations as an opportunity to look back into the past, create the future, maintain the victorious outcomes of the WWII, adhere to the purposes and principles of the "UN Charter" and build the new type of international relations with win-win cooperation as its core.

普京表示，很高兴来华参加纪念中国抗战胜利70周年盛典，中方的纪念大会和阅兵式令人印象深刻。今年中国人民解放军方队和俄罗斯军队方队分别首次参加了彼此纪念活动，具有重要意义。习近平主席今天上午在纪念大会上发出要致力于和平的明确有力信息，俄方对此高度赞赏。俄方坚定致力于深化俄中全面战略协作伙伴关系，愿继续推进两国能源、石化、金融、航天、科技、制造业等各领域务实合作，加强同中方在联合国等国际和地区组织中的协调配合。

Vladimir Putin said that he is glad to visit China and attend the commemorations marking the 70th anniversary of the victory of the War of Resistance against Japanese Aggression, and China's commemoration and military parade were impressive. This year, the square teams of the Chinese People's Liberation Army and the Russian army attended each other's commemorative activities for the first time, which was of great significance. Russia highly appreciates the clear and powerful message of commitment to peace that President Xi Jinping delivered at the commemoration this morning. Russia is committed to deepening Russia-China comprehensive strategic partnership of coordination, and is willing to continue to push forward practical cooperation in various areas such as energy, petrochemicals, finance, aerospace, science, technology and manufacturing and to strengthen coordination and cooperation with China in international and regional organizations such as the UN.

会见后，两国元首共同见证了外交、基础设施、地方、教育、科技、海关、经济、能源、投资、金融、贸易、电力、交通、网络、汽车等领域合作协议的签署。

After the meeting, the two heads of state jointly witnessed the signing of cooperative agreements in fields such as diplomacy, infrastructure, local government, education, science, technology, customs, economy, energy, investment, finance, trade, electricity, transportation, network and automobile.

王沪宁、栗战书、杨洁篪等参加会见。

Wang Huning, Li Zhanshu, Yang Jiechi and others attended the meeting.

新闻背景：2015年是世界反法西斯战争胜利70周年，也是中国人民抗日战争胜利70周年。9月3日，纪念中国人民抗日战争暨世界反法西斯战争胜利70周年阅兵在北京举行。共有49个国家应邀出席纪念活动，其中有30位国家元首、政府首脑等外国领导人，19位政府高级别代表，此外还有10位国际和地区组织负责人应邀出席。中国是抗击日本侵略的主战场，苏联是抗击德国法西斯的主战场，两国蒙受的劫难也是最为严重的。2014年2月6日，习近平主席和普京总统决定，2015年双方共同举办庆祝世界反法西斯战争胜利暨中国人民抗日战争胜利70周年活动。

原文链接：http://news.xinhuanet.com/mrdx/2015-09/04/c_134589591.htm

译文链接：http://www.fmprc.gov.cn/mfa_eng/zxxx_662805/t1294319.shtml

外交新闻汉英翻译
C-E TRANSLATION OF DIPLOMATIC NEWS

一、范例二文本结构分析（Text Structure Analysis of Sample II）

范例二也是一则外交会晤新闻报道，主要内容包括领导人会晤的时间、地点、背景、主题、双方主要观点等。

标题为"××会见××"，只包括会晤双方，不涉及会晤主题。这类标题不同于范例一的标题，其在副标题处涉及会晤主题。

第一段为导语，说明会晤双方人物（习近平、普京）、时间（2015年9月3日）、地点（人民大会堂）。第二、三、四段构成新闻的主体部分，由双方领导人各自的观点和立场构成。三段分别以"习近平感谢……"、"习近平强调……"、"普京表示……"起首。首先介绍习近平主席对俄罗斯总统普京来华参加中国人民抗日战争暨世界反法西斯战争胜利70周年纪念活动表示感谢和欢迎；其次介绍习近平主席主要观点，要坚定不移发展中俄全面战略协作伙伴关系并扩大全方位务实合作；最后介绍普京观点，普京赞赏纪念大会和阅兵式，赞扬习近平在阅兵活动中的讲话，表示愿意致力于深化俄中全面战略协作伙伴关系并加强合作。

最后两段是新闻的结尾部分，说明会晤后的相关活动以及其他参与会晤活动的人员。

二、范例二翻译解析（Translation Analysis of Sample II）

（一）有关表达感谢的翻译（Translation of Expressions of Appreciation）

会晤双方表达对对方的感谢，最为简单和常见的句式是"……感谢……的支持（帮助）"，常译为thank ... for ... support (help)，或appreciate sb.'s support (help)；感谢对方具体做了什么的时候，可以译为thank ... for sth./ doing sth.，例如范例一，thanked Russia for sending a military group to participate ...，以及下面第3个例句译文中thanked ... for their years of active maintenance。此外，表达感谢还常译为be truly grateful或express gratitude to。请看下列翻译实例：

习近平感谢俄罗斯对中国人民抗日战争暨世界反法西斯战争胜利70周年纪念活动给予积极支持，感谢俄罗斯派方队参加阅兵。

(http://news.xinhuanet.com/mrdx/2015-09/04/c_134589591.htm)

Xi Jinping thanked Russia for its active support in the commemorations of the 70th anniversary of the victory of the Chinese People's War of Resistance against Japanese Aggression and the World Anti-Fascist War and thanked Russia for sending a military group to participate in the military parade.

(http://www.fmprc.gov.cn/mfa_eng/zxxx_662805/t1294319.shtml)

亚达夫和柯伊拉腊表示，感谢中国政府在尼困难和危急时刻派外长专程来尼出席尼泊尔地震灾后重建国际会议。4·25特大地震后，中国领导人、政府、各地方省区和各界人士第一时间给予尼方慰问和救援，尼政府和人民发自内心地表示感谢，这再次证明中国是尼最可靠的朋友，最亲密的邻邦，最值得信赖的伙伴。

(http://news.xinhuanet.com/2015-06/25/c_1115713680.htm)

Ram Baran Yadav and Girija Prasad Koirala thanked Chinese government for sending the Foreign Minister to Nepal for the international conference on Nepal's reconstruction at the difficult and critical moment for Nepal. After the huge earthquake on April 25, China's leaders, government, local provinces and regions and people from all circles offered Nepal immediate condolences and rescue, for which the government and people of Nepal are truly grateful. It proves again that China is Nepal's most reliable friend, closest neighbor and most trustworthy partner.

(http://www.fmprc.gov.cn/mfa_eng/wjdt_665385/wshd_665389/t1276306.shtml)

习近平欢迎奥吉奥来华出席中国人民抗日战争暨世界反法西斯战争胜利70周年纪念活动，感谢巴布亚新几内亚政府和人民多年来对位于巴布亚新几内亚拉包尔市的中国抗战将士陵园予以积极维护。

(http://news.xinhuanet.com/politics/2015-09/03/c_1116458658.htm)

Xi Jinping welcomed Michael Ogio's visit to China to attend the commemorations marking the 70th anniversary of the victory of the Chinese People's War of Resistance against Japanese Aggression and the World Anti-Fascist War, and thanked the PNG government and people for their years of active maintenance of the cemetery of Chinese soldiers who died in the War of Resistance against Japanese Aggression in Rabaul, PNG.

(http://www.fmprc.gov.cn/mfa_eng/topics_665678/jnkzsl70zn/t1294138.shtml)

（二）有关历史回顾表述的翻译 (Translation of Expressions of Historical Review)

首先，双方回顾在历史上的作为时，译文时态一般采取过去式，例如China and Russia made the greatest sacrifice and contributed greatly to the final victory of the WWII。提及双方关系多年来的发展情况时，时态一般为完成时，例如Since the establishment of the diplomatic relations 45 years ago, the China-Ethiopia relations have always been one of the leading relations of China-Africa friendly cooperation。其次，在表达双方关系时，措辞准确非常关键，例如"好朋友"，"重要合作伙伴"，"好兄弟"，"长期战略伙伴"等，在译文选择上也需要忠实于原文，在下列第2和第3个例句中，分别译为good friend, important cooperative partner, good brothers 以及 long-term strategic partners。此外，在外交新闻翻译中，如果原文中使用修辞手法，译文多采取直译的方法，以突显原文的权威性。如范例一 "以积水成渊、积土成山的精神"，译为with the spirit of "accumulating droplets to form a pool and heaping earth to put up a mountain"。第4个例子中"两国关系虽经历风雨，但传统友谊的种子一直在两国人民心中传承并茁壮成长"译为Although China-Czech relations have undergone storms, the seeds of traditional friendship have always been inherited and thriving in the hearts of the two peoples。具体翻译实例如下：

习近平指出，中俄分别是第二次世界大战亚洲和欧洲主战场，为第二次世界大战最终胜利付出的牺牲最大，作出的贡献也很大。

(http://news.xinhuanet.com/mrdx/2015-09/04/c_134589591.htm)

Xi Jinping pointed out that as the main battlefields in the World War II in Asia and Europe respectively, China and Russia made the greatest sacrifice and contributed greatly to the final victory of the WWII.

(http://www.fmprc.gov.cn/mfa_eng/zxxx_662805/t1294319.shtml)

李克强表示，埃塞是中国在非洲的好朋友和重要合作伙伴。两国人民都曾经英勇抗击法西斯侵略，为世界反法西斯战争胜利作出历史贡献。建交45年来，中埃关系一直走在中非友好合作前列。

(http://news.xinhuanet.com/world/2015-09/04/c_1116461079.htm)

Li Keqiang said that Ethiopia is China's good friend and important cooperative partner in Africa. The two peoples conducted valiant struggles against fascist aggression and made historical contribution to the final victory of the World Anti-Fascist War. Since the establishment of the diplomatic relations 45 years ago, the China-Ethiopia relations have always been one of the leading relations of China-Africa friendly cooperation.

(http://www.fmprc.gov.cn/mfa_eng/wjdt_665385/wshd_665389/t1294309.shtml)

习近平指出，中国和安哥拉是好兄弟和长期战略伙伴。2010年我访问安哥拉期间，两国正式建立了战略伙伴关系。5年来，两国各领域友好合作取得显著成果，给两国人民带来实实在在的利益。相信总统先生此次访问将为中安战略伙伴关系注入新的动力。

(http://news.china.com.cn/2015-06/10/content_35781324.htm)

Xi Jinping pointed out that China and Angola are good brothers and long-term strategic partners. During my visit to Angola in 2010, the two countries formally established the strategic partnership. Over the past five years, bilateral friendly cooperation in all areas has scored remarkable achievements, bringing tangible benefits to the two peoples. I believe Mr. President's visit will inject new impetus to China-Angola strategic partnership.

(http://www.fmprc.gov.cn/mfa_eng/zxxx_662805/t1272383.shtml)

刘延东首先转达张德江委员长对哈马切克的问候，并表示，中捷两国关系虽经历风雨，但传统友谊的种子一直在两国人民心中传承并茁壮成长。

(http://news.xinhuanet.com/2015-06/16/c_1115637766.htm)

Liu Yandong firstly conveyed Chairman Zhang Dejiang's greetings to Jan Hamáček, and said that although China-Czech relations have undergone storms, the seeds of traditional friendship have always been inherited and thriving in the hearts of the two peoples.

(http://www.chinese-embassy.org.uk/eng/zgyw/t1274346.htm)

（三）有关双方相互支持表述的翻译 (Translation of Expressions of Mutual Support)

会晤双方谈及双方共同身份的表述，例如："……都是文明大国"，"……都是世界主要经济体"，"……同为联合国安理会常任理事国"，"……是唇齿相依、守望相助的亲密友好邻邦"等，可以译为both ... are major civilizations, as major world economies, as permanent members of the UN Security Council和as close and friendly neighbors, ... are mutually dependent like the lip and teeth。

双方表达相互支持时，常采用"支持……+ 动词"的表述形式，可以采用动词support或back，例如：supports the construction of the AIIB, backs China in playing a bigger role in international organizations。还常见be supportive to的形式，例如：The US is supportive to China's reform and opening-up。表达"愿意"合作或推动关系等想法时，可以翻译为stands ready to或is willing to等。请看下面具体翻译实例：

> 卡梅伦表示，英国和中国都是文明大国，两国应该通过更好了解并尊重彼此的看法，支持对方实现发展和稳定。两国经济互补性强，英方愿在扩大合作中同中方实现互利共赢。

(http://paper.people.com.cn/rmrbhwb/html/2015-10/24/content_1625169.htm)

David Cameron noted that both the UK and China are major civilizations. The two countries should support each other to realize development and stability through better mutual understanding and respect. The two economies are highly complementary, and the UK stands ready to achieve mutual benefits and win-win results by expanding cooperation with China.

(http://www.fmprc.gov.cn/mfa_eng/zxxx_662805/t1309372.shtml)

> 卡梅伦表示，英国和中国都是世界主要经济体，同为联合国安理会常任理事国，理应成为合作伙伴。英国支持中国在国际机构中发挥更为重要的作用，支持亚洲基础设施投资银行建设和国际货币基金组织改革，支持人民币国际化，愿在推动欧中关系发展方面发挥积极作用。

(http://paper.people.com.cn/rmrbhwb/html/2015-10/24/content_1625169.htm)

David Cameron noted that as major world economies and permanent members of the UN Security Council, the UK and China should be cooperative partners. The UK backs China in playing a bigger role in international organizations, supports the construction of the Asian Infrastructure Investment Bank (AIIB), the reform of the International Monetary

Fund (IMF) and the internationalization of RMB, and is willing to play a positive role in promoting EU-China relations.

(http://www.fmprc.gov.cn/mfa_eng/zxxx_662805/t1309372.shtml)

王毅说，中尼是唇齿相依、守望相助的亲密友好邻邦。4·25特大地震使中尼同时受灾，两国政府和人民相互支持，共克时艰。

(http://news.china.com/zh_cn/domesticgd/10000159/20150625/19895734.html)

Wang Yi said that as close and friendly neighbors, China and Nepal help each other and are mutually dependent like the lip and teeth. The huge earthquake on April 25 affected China and Nepal at the same time, and both governments and peoples supported each other and tackled the difficulties together.

(http://www.fmprc.gov.cn/mfa_eng/zxxx_662805/t1276306.shtml)

学生译作讲评
Analysis of Students' Translation Practice

原文链接：http://www.mfa.gov.cn/web/wjbxw_673019/t1314445.shtml

新闻原文：安哥拉总统会见中国政府非洲事务特别代表钟建华

学生译文：Angolan President Meets with Chinese Government's Special Representative on African Affairs Zhong Jianhua

翻译评析：标题翻译通常采用一般现在时，学生使用动词meets with。标题中一般避免使用's表所属关系，如 Chinese government's，所属关系可以用 of Chinese government 表达。因此，标题可以改译为President of Angola Meets with Special Representative of Chinese Government on African Affairs Zhong Jianhua。

新闻原文：2015年11月12日，安哥拉总统多斯桑托斯会见来安出席安独立40周年纪念活动的中国政府非洲事务特别代表钟建华。驻安大使崔爱民参加会见。

学生译文：On November 12, 2015, Angolan President Jose Eduardo dos Santos met with Chinese Government's Special Representative on African Affairs Zhong Jianhua, who was in Angola to attend celebrations of the 40th anniversary of independence of Angola. Ambassador to Angola Cui Aimin attended the meeting.

翻译评析：外交新闻正文部分，××会见××，采用一般过去时，译为met with。非英语人名出现拼写符号时，在英语译文中需要保留原语拼写符号，建议将Jose Eduardo dos Santos改为José Eduardo dos Santos。

针对"来安出席安独立40周年纪念活动的"，学生使用定语从句who was in Angola to attend celebrations of the 40th anniversary of independence of Angola，默认为"40周年"和"纪念活动"是所属关系，即"40周年的纪念活动"。如果改译为动词marking，会更加凸显原文逻辑，使语言增色。

外交会晤新闻报道的翻译
Translation for Coverage of Diplomatic Meetings UNIT 6

外交新闻中，中国驻某国大使××在文中首次出现通常表述为H.E. ××, Chinese Ambassador to …，H.E.是His Excellency的简写，是英语中对国家元首、政府首脑、主教、大使、法官等尊贵人物的尊称前缀。综上所述，第一段可以改译为：On November 12, 2015, President José Eduardo dos Santos of Angola met with Special Representative of the Chinese government on African Affairs Zhong Jianhua, who visited Angola to attend commemorations marking the 40th anniversary of Angola's independence. H.E. Cui Aimin, Chinese Ambassador to Angola, attended the meeting.

新闻原文：钟特代首先转达习近平主席对多斯桑托斯总统的亲切问候，多斯桑托斯总统表示感谢，并请钟大使转达他对习近平主席的良好祝愿。

学生译文：Special Representative Zhong firstly conveyed the cordial greetings of President Xi Jinping to President Jose Eduardo dos Santos. President Jose Eduardo dos Santos expressed his appreciation and asked Representative Zhong to give his best wishes to President Xi Jinping.

翻译评析：学生译文中将"钟特代"译为Special Representative Zhong。一般来说，姓名首次出现在新闻文本中时要翻译其全名，之后再次出现时，中文姓名还是需要翻译全名，外国姓名则可以只保留姓氏，所以补充Special Representative Zhong Jianhua是必要的。同样，后面一句里"钟大使"和"习近平主席"也要保留全名，分别译为Ambassador Zhong Jianhua和President Xi Jinping。"转达祝愿"这个动宾搭配学生翻译为give his best wishes to，将give一词改译为convey则显示措辞和语气的正式。这一段可以改译为：Special Representative Zhong Jianhua first conveyed President Xi Jinping's kind greetings to President José Eduardo dos Santos. President José Eduardo dos Santos expressed his gratitude and asked Ambassador Zhong Jianhua to convey his best wishes to President Xi Jinping.

新闻原文：钟特代祝贺安独立40周年取得的成就，表示中国政府高度重视发展对安关系，愿同安方一道努力，积极落实多斯桑托斯总统今年6月访华成果，不断推动中安战略伙伴关系迈上新台阶。

学生译文：Special Representative Zhong congratulated the Angolan president on the achievements Angola had made in the 40 years since independence, and said that the Chinese government attaches great importance to the development of Sino-Angolan ties, and is ready to implement, through joint efforts with the Angolan side, agreements reached during President Eduardo dos Santos' June visit to China and to push the strategic partnership between the two countries to new levels.

翻译评析：原文中"祝贺……取得的成就"可以简洁地译为"congratulated on the achievements Angola has made"，不需要重复congratulate somebody on sth.的常规译法；在外交部网站新闻稿件中，"中国和××国的关系"常译为relations between China and ××，一般不用ties和Sino等词，但不同机构有不同的规范和惯例，这里仅就外交部而言

143

如此。

　　学生译文中将"积极落实……访华成果"译为is ready to implement ... agreements，而一般会晤成果并非仅指agreements，所以可以改译为actively implement the outcomes of。"中安战略伙伴"处理为名词短语China-Angola strategic partnership更为简洁，同时，"不断推动"应该补充完整为constantly push。

　　因此，这一段可以改译为：Special Representative Zhong Jianhua congratulated on the achievements Angola has made over the 40 years since independence. He said that the Chinese government attaches great importance to developing its relations with Angola, and is willing to join efforts with Angola to actively implement the outcomes of President José Eduardo dos Santos' visit to China this June and constantly push China-Angola strategic partnership to new stages.

　　新闻原文：多斯桑托斯总统高度评价中国为促进安和平发展事业所作的贡献，表示安正处于新的发展阶段，对安中关系发展充满期待，愿进一步深化同中国全方位合作，特别是投融资领域合作，为中国企业在安发展创造条件，在中国支持和帮助下实现更好发展。

　　学生译文：President Jose Eduardo dos Santos spoke highly of China's contributions to the peaceful development of Angola, and said that his country is in the new stage of development, and he is full of expectation for the development of Angola-China relations. Angola is willing to deepen cooperation with China in all fields, particularly in the areas of investment and financing, create favorable conditions for the development of Chinese enterprises in Angola and to realize better development with China's support and assistance.

　　翻译评析："和平发展事业"学生译文中处理为peaceful development，这里漏译"事业"一词，应完整译为the cause of Angola's peaceful development；原文中出现国名简称"安"若干次，为遵循外交新闻文本的正式性和严谨性，尽量避免使用his country或者my country之类的说法；这一部分可以改译为President José Eduardo dos Santos spoke highly of China's contributions to the cause of Angola's peaceful development. He said that Angola is at a new stage of development, and is full of expectations for the development of Angola-China relations.

　　原文最后一句话的中文逻辑不甚明了，需要在译文中加以明晰化。"愿进一步深化合作"与"为中国企业在安发展创造条件"是并列关系，"在中国支持和帮助下实现更好发展"是进一步总结上文所说，这里隐含的意思是安哥拉能够实现更好发展。因此，译文可通过适当添加连接词的方式，将原文中暗含的语言逻辑体现出来，建议修改为：Angola is willing to further deepen cooperation with China in all fields, especially in investment and financing, and create favorable conditions for the development of Chinese enterprises in Angola, so as to realize better development with China's support and help.

实战练习
Translation Practice

一、请翻译下列外交会晤报道的标题（Translate the following headlines of coverage of diplomatic meetings）

1. 杨洁篪会见美军参联会主席邓福德

    (http://www.gov.cn/guowuyuan/2017-08/17/content_5218472.htm)

2. 李克强同德国总理默克尔举行会谈

    (http://www.xinhuanet.com/mrdx/2018-07/10/c_137313512.htm)

3. 杨洁篪会见美国宾夕法尼亚大学校长古特曼一行

    (http://news.xinhuanet.com/politics/2015-09/11/c_1116539744.htm)

4. 王毅外长会见越南驻华大使阮文师

    (http://www.fmprc.gov.cn/ce/celt/chn/xwdt/t1298642.htm)

5. 王毅与伊朗外长扎里夫举行会谈

    (http://www.fmprc.gov.cn/mfa_chn/zyxw_602251/t1238311.shtml)

6. 李克强会见国际货币基金组织总裁拉加德

    (http://www.fmprc.gov.cn/mfa_chn/zyxw_602251/t1247959.shtml)

7. 李克强会见出席中国发展高层论坛2015年年会境外代表并座谈

    (http://www.fmprc.gov.cn/mfa_chn/zyxw_602251/t1247961.shtml)

8. 张德江分别会见亚美尼亚总统萨尔基相、斯里兰卡总统西里塞纳

    (http://www.fmprc.gov.cn/mfa_chn/zyxw_602251/t1248910.shtml)

二、请翻译下列外交会晤报道中的句子（Translate the following sentences from coverage of diplomatic meetings）

1. 李克强表示，埃塞是中国在非洲的好朋友和重要合作伙伴。建交45年来，中埃关系一直走在中非友好合作前列。中方坚定支持埃方发展经济、改善民生的努力，愿为埃方提供力所能及的帮助。

    (http://www.gov.cn/guowuyuan/2015-09/04/content_2924951.htm)

2. 奥吉奥表示，很高兴来华同中国人民一道纪念抗战胜利70周年。建交30多年来，巴新同中国的关系得到长足发展。巴新感谢中国长期以来对巴布亚新几内亚的帮助和支持，愿深化同中方各领域合作，感谢中方支持巴新主办2018年亚太经合组织会议。

    (http://cpc.people.com.cn/n/2015/0901/c64094-27538112.html?ol4f)

3. 在第二次世界大战中，中国是东方主战场，缅甸也是亚洲重要战场。两国人民为世界反法西斯战争胜利作出了重大贡献。我们愿通过这次纪念活动，同各国一道

铭记历史，缅怀先烈，共同维护来之不易的和平。

(http://news.xinhuanet.com/politics/2015-09/04/c_1116460683.htm)

4. 习近平强调，中华民族注重"和"的理念，主张和平、和谐、和而不同。联合国193个会员国要相互尊重、团结和睦、同舟共济，携手努力构建以合作共赢为核心的新型国际关系。

(http://news.xinhuanet.com/2015-09/03/c_1116458440.htm)

5. 2015年11月2日，国家主席习近平在人民大会堂同法国总统奥朗德举行会谈。两国元首高度评价中法关系发展，同意继续合力前行，不断开创两国友好合作新局面。

(http://news.xinhuanet.com/politics/2015-11/02/c_1117017449.htm)

三、请翻译下面一则外交会晤报道（Translate the following coverage of diplomatic meeting）

习近平会见美国国务卿蓬佩奥

2018年6月14日，国家主席习近平在人民大会堂会见美国国务卿蓬佩奥。

习近平指出，中美两国在维护世界和平稳定、促进全球发展繁荣方面拥有广泛共同利益、肩负重要责任。中美合作可以办成有利于两国和世界的大事，希望双方团队按照我同特朗普总统北京会晤达成的共识，加强沟通，增进互信，管控分歧，扩大合作，推动中美关系沿着正确轨道向前发展，更好造福两国人民和世界各国人民。

习近平强调，中美建交近40年来两国关系发展历程给我们的重要启迪就是，要始终正确看待彼此战略意图，尊重和照顾彼此核心利益和重大关切。中方一直致力于同美国发展相互尊重、平等相待、互利共赢的合作关系。双方要加强高层交往及机制性对话，拓展各领域合作，扩大地方和人文交流，不断夯实两国关系基础。希望美方慎重妥善处理台湾、经贸摩擦等敏感问题，防止中美关系受到大的干扰。双方要就重大国际地区和全球性问题加强沟通和协调，共同做世界和平建设者、国际秩序维护者。

蓬佩奥首先转达特朗普总统对习近平主席的问候，特别是感谢习近平主席在朝鲜半岛问题上提供的重要意见和帮助。蓬佩奥表示，在两国元首共同引领下，美中关系不断发展。美方重视发展对华关系，愿与中方加强沟通，处理好突出问题，深化各领域务实合作，并协力应对国际和地区挑战。美方赞赏中方在政治解决朝鲜半岛核问题方面发挥的重要作用，愿同中方共同努力，推动实现朝鲜半岛无核化和持久和平。

习近平请蓬佩奥转达对特朗普总统的问候。习近平强调，此次特朗普总统同金正恩委员长实现历史性会晤并取得积极成果，这是半岛核问题政治解决进程的重要一步，中方向双方表示衷心祝贺。半岛问题错综复杂，解决起来必然是一个循序渐进的过程。希望美朝双方坚持相互尊重、相向而行，继续为政治解决半岛问题作出不懈努力。中方坚定致力于半岛无核化，坚持维护半岛和平稳定，坚持通过对话协商解决问题。中方愿继续发挥积极、建设性作用，同包括美方在内的有关各方一道，推进半岛问题政治解决进程。

杨洁篪、王毅等参加会见。

(http://www.mfa.gov.cn/mfa_chn/zyxw_602251/t1277464.shtml)

参考译文
Versions for Reference

一、请翻译下列外交会晤报道的标题（Translate the following headlines of coverage of diplomatic meetings）

1. Yang Jiechi Meets with Chairman of U.S. Joint Chiefs of Staff Joseph Dunford
2. Li Keqiang Holds Talks with German Chancellor Angela Merkel
3. Yang Jiechi Meets with President of University of Pennsylvania Amy Gutmann and Her Delegation
4. Foreign Minister Wang Yi Meets with Ambassador of Vietnam to China Nguyen Van Tho
5. Wang Yi Holds Talks with Foreign Minister Mohammad Javad Zarif of Iran
6. Li Keqiang Meets with Managing Director Christine Lagarde of IMF
7. Li Keqiang Meets and Holds Talks with Overseas Delegates Attending Annual Meeting of China Development Forum 2015
8. Zhang Dejiang Meets with President Serzh Sargsyan of Armenia and President Maithripala Sirisena of Sri Lanka Respectively

二、请翻译下列外交会晤报道中的句子（Translate the following sentences from coverage of diplomatic meetings）

1. Li Keqiang said that Ethiopia is China's good friend and important cooperative partner in Africa. Since the establishment of the diplomatic relations 45 years ago, the China-Ethiopia relations have always been one of the leading relations of China-Africa friendly cooperation. China firmly supports Ethiopia's efforts in developing economy and improving people's livelihood, and is willing to offer help within its ability.

2. Michael Ogio said that he is glad to visit China and commemorate with the Chinese people the 70th anniversary of the victory of the Chinese People's War of Resistance against Japanese Aggression. Since the establishment of the diplomatic relations over 30 years ago, the PNG-China relations have enjoyed substantial development. PNG appreciates China's long-term help and support to PNG, is willing to deepen cooperation with China in all fields, and thanks China for supporting PNG in hosting the APEC meeting in 2018.

3. During the World War II, China was the main battlefield in the East, while Myanmar was also an important battlefield in Asia. Both peoples made great contributions to the victory of the World Anti-Fascist War. By means of the commemorations, we are willing to join other countries to remember the history, honor the martyrs and jointly safeguard the hard-won peace.

4. Xi Jinping stressed that the Chinese nations attaches importance to the idea of "harmony" and advocates peace, harmony and harmony in diversity. The 193 member states of the UN should respect each other, unite in harmony, help each other and jointly strive to build a new type of international relations featuring win-win cooperation.

5. On November 2, 2015, President Xi Jinping held talks with President François Hollande of France at the Great Hall of the People. The two heads of state spoke highly of the development of China-France relations and agreed to continue joining efforts for progress and constantly open up new situation of bilateral friendly cooperation.

三、请翻译下面一则外交会晤报道（Translate the following coverage of diplomatic meeting）

Xi Jinping Meets with Secretary of State Mike Pompeo of the US

On June 14, 2018, President Xi Jinping met at the Great Hall of the People with Secretary of State Mike Pompeo of the United States (US).

Xi Jinping pointed out that both China and the US share extensive and common interests and shoulder important responsibilities in safeguarding world peace and stability and promoting global development and prosperity. The China-US cooperation can accomplish major achievements conducive to both countries and the world. It is hoped that teams of the two sides will reinforce communication, enhance mutual trust, manage and control differences, and expand cooperation according to the consensus reached by President Donald Trump and me during the meeting in Beijing, so as to promote the development of bilateral relations along the right track and better benefit the two peoples and the people of all countries in the world.

Xi Jinping stressed that it is an important enlightenment derived from the nearly 40 years of development process of bilateral relations after China and the US established diplomatic relations that the two countries should always view each other's strategic intentions in a correct way, and respect and take care of each other's core interests and major concerns. China is always committed to developing cooperative relations with the US featuring mutual respect, equal treatment, and mutual benefit and win-win results. The two sides should strengthen high-level exchanges and institutional dialogues, expand cooperation in various fields, and expand local and people-to-people and cultural exchanges, in a bid to continuously cement the foundation of bilateral relations. It is hoped that the US will prudently and properly handle sensitive issues including the Taiwan problem and economic and trade frictions to avoid major interferences in bilateral relations. China and the US should enhance communication and coordination in major international and regional and global issues, and work together as constructors of world peace and vindicators of international order.

Mike Pompeo first conveyed President Donald Trump's greetings to President Xi Jinping, especially Donald Trump's appreciation for President Xi Jinping's important advice and help over the Korean Peninsula issue. Mike Pompeo expressed that the US-China relations have enjoyed continuous development under the joint guidance of the two heads of state. The US attaches importance to developing relations with China, and is willing to, together with the Chinese side, enhance communication, well handle prominent issues, deepen practical cooperation in various fields, and meet international and regional challenges with joint efforts. The US appreciates China's vital role in the political settlement of the Korean Peninsula nuclear issue, and stands ready to make joint efforts with China to promote realization of the denuclearization and lasting peace on the Korean Peninsula.

Xi Jinping asked Mike Pompeo to convey his greetings to President Donald Trump. He stressed that President Donald Trump and Chairman Kim Jong-un realized a historic meeting this time and achieved positive outcomes, which was an important step in the process of the political settlement of the Korean Peninsula nuclear issue. China extends heartfelt congratulations to both sides. The Korean Peninsula issue is complex and its solution must be a gradual process. China hopes the US and the Democratic People's Republic of Korea will adhere to mutual respect and meet each other halfway, and continuously make unremitting efforts for the political settlement of the Korean Peninsula issue. China firmly adheres to the denuclearization of the Korean Peninsula, upholds peace and stability of the Korean Peninsula, and sticks to the settlement of issues through dialogue and negotiation. China is willing to continue to play an active and constructive role, and work with all parties concerned including the US to promote the process of the political settlement of the Korean Peninsula issue.

Yang Jiechi, Wang Yi and others attended the meeting.

(http://www.fmprc.gov.cn/mfa_eng/zxxx_662805/t1569844.shtml)

单元小结
Summary

外交会晤报道记录我国重大外交事件，是了解我国外交关系、外交战略的重要依据。本单元针对外交会晤新闻报道，总结了新闻标题、导语、常见表达方式的翻译。会晤一般在国家高层领导人之间举行，探讨国家重大关切问题，表明态度，增进彼此关系。会晤报道经常涉及以下话题：表示支持与感谢、重申双方关系、阐明国情与政策、表明态度和立场、强调合作共赢、回顾历史、展望未来等。本单元就上述话题的惯用表述及其翻译进行归纳和总结，从英汉语言对比的层面，分析句子的句法成分和内部逻辑，探讨相应的翻译方法。本单元还对"双边关系"这一重要外交概念做出了详细分类和解读，探讨双边关系常用表达的翻译。

UNIT 7

发表外交演讲报道的翻译
Translation for Coverage of Diplomatic Speeches

单元简介
Introduction

外交演讲是国家领导人和高级外交官代表国家在外交场合发表的演说，是针对国家事务和对外关系表明立场、阐明观点、宣传主张的一种演讲，是领导人参与国际公务活动的一种方式。外交演讲包括领导人出席国际会议发表演讲、为重大庆典或仪式致辞，以及访问知名学府发表演讲等，其目的主要在于阐明观点和主张，争取国际支持，传播民族文化。

外交演讲不仅是一门科学，更是一门艺术。领导人借助国际重大外交场合发表演讲，是表达态度、增进交流、促进友好的绝佳方式，也是领导人展现个人形象的舞台。因此，外交演讲的翻译应该尊重原文本"信息型"和"表达型"的类型特点，兼顾语义转换和交际功能的实现。译文要在最大限度地保留原文句法和语义结构，尽量做到"忠实"于原文信息的同时，采用地道的语言传递演讲者的精神风貌、睿智幽默以及语气情态，以更好地达到演讲的交际功能。

C-E TRANSLATION OF DIPLOMATIC NEWS

发表外交演讲报道翻译范例分析
Sample of Translation for Coverage of Diplomatic Speeches

范例一 (Sample I)

习近平出席中国—拉美和加勒比国家领导人会晤并发表主旨讲话
全面阐述中国对拉美政策主张 宣布建立平等互利、共同发展的中拉全面合作伙伴关系
成立中国—拉共体论坛（节本）
2014/07/18

Xi Jinping Attends China–Latin America and the Caribbean Summit and Delivers Keynote Speech, Comprehensively Expounding China's Policies and Propositions Toward Latin America, Announcing Establishment of China–Latin America Comprehensive Cooperative Partnership of Equality, Mutual Benefit and Common Development, and Establishment of China–CELAC Forum (Abbreviated Version)
2014/07/18

2014年7月17日下午，中国—拉美和加勒比国家领导人会晤在巴西利亚举行。本次会晤由中方倡议，中国国家主席习近平、巴西总统罗塞夫等出席。

On the afternoon of July 17, 2014, China-Latin America and the Caribbean Summit was held in Brasilia. The Summit was proposed by China. President Xi Jinping of China, President Dilma Rousseff of Brazil and others were present.

***

会晤开始前，习近平与罗塞夫共同迎接出席会晤的拉美和加勒比国家领导人和代表，同他们一一握手并集体合影。

Before the Summit, Xi Jinping and Rousseff jointly welcomed the leaders and representatives of the Latin American and Caribbean countries attending the Summit, shook hands one by one and posed for group photos with them.

***

习近平同与会各国领导人在亲切、友好、务实的气氛中，围绕"平等互利、合作共赢、共同发展"的主题，共叙友谊，共谋发展，共商合作，一致决定建立平等互利、共同发展的中拉全面合作伙伴关系，共同宣布成立中国—拉共体论坛。习近平发表了题为《努力构建携手共进的命运共同体》主旨讲话，宣布中方对促进中拉合作的倡议和举措，提出构建政治上真诚互信、经贸上合作共赢、人文上互学互鉴、国际事务中密切协作、整体合作和双边关系相互促进的中拉关系五位一体新格局，打造中拉携手共进的命运共同体。

Translation for Coverage of Diplomatic Speeches

Xi Jinping and the leaders of other countries renewed friendship, sought common development and discussed cooperation in a sincere, friendly and practical atmosphere around the theme of "equality, mutual benefit, win-win cooperation and common development", agreeing to establish the China-Latin America comprehensive cooperative partnership of equality, mutual benefit and common development, and jointly announced the establishment of the Forum of China and Community of Latin American and Caribbean States (CELAC). Xi Jinping delivered a keynote speech entitled "Striving to Build a Hand-in-Hand Community of Common Future", announcing China's proposals and measures on promoting China-Latin America cooperation, proposing to build up a Five-in-One new pattern of China-Latin America relations: sincerely trust each other in politics, cooperate with each other for a win-win outcome in economy and trade, learn from each other in people-to-people and cultural exchanges, closely cooperate with each other in international affairs, and promote each other in overall cooperation and bilateral relations, so as to forge a hand-in-hand community of common future.

***

习近平指出，当前，中国人民正在为实现中华民族伟大复兴的中国梦而奋斗，拉美和加勒比各国人民也在为实现团结协作、发展振兴的拉美梦而努力。共同的梦想和共同的追求，将中拉双方紧紧联系在一起。

Xi Jinping pointed out that currently the Chinese people are striving to achieve the "Chinese Dream" of great rejuvenation of the Chinese nation, while the peoples of Latin American and Caribbean countries are also struggling for the "Latin American Dream" of realizing solidarity, cooperation, development and revitalization. The common dreams and shared pursuit closely connect China and Latin America.

***

拉美和加勒比国家领导人纷纷表示，今天，我们本着团结合作的精神相聚在一起，共同规划合作未来，揭开拉中关系和南南合作新篇章。拉美和加勒比国家具有丰富自然和人力资源，都在推进改革发展，希望借鉴中国的成功经验，促进共同、可持续发展。双方要加强对话合作，携手促进国际关系民主化，推动建立更加公正合理的国际经济金融秩序。

Leaders of Latin American and Caribbean countries said that today, we gather together in the spirit of solidarity and cooperation and jointly charter the course for future cooperation, opening up a new chapter of Latin America-China relations and South-South cooperation. With abundant natural and human resources, Latin American and Caribbean countries are promoting reforms and development, hoping to learn from China's successful experience to promote common and sustainable development. The two sides should strengthen dialogues and cooperation, jointly promote democratization of international relations, and promote the establishment of a more just and reasonable international economic and financial order.

外交新闻汉英翻译
C-E TRANSLATION OF DIPLOMATIC NEWS

***

巴西总统罗塞夫主持会议。她最后表示,这次会晤取得成功,具有重要历史意义。感谢习近平主席提出的一系列重要倡议和举措,拉美和加勒比国家将同中方共同努力,落实好这些倡议,建设好中拉论坛,实现共同发展繁荣。

President Dilma Rousseff of Brazil chaired the Summit. She finally noted that the success of this Summit is of vital historic significance. She extended her thanks to President Xi Jinping for putting forward a series of important proposals and measures. Latin American and Caribbean countries will make joint efforts with China to well implement these proposals and effectively build the CELAC-China Forum to achieve common development and prosperity.

***

会后,中拉双方发表了《中国—拉美和加勒比国家领导人巴西利亚会晤联合声明》。

After the Summit, China and Latin America issued together the "Joint Statement on China-Latin America and the Caribbean Summit in Brasilia".

新闻背景:中国—拉美和加勒比国家领导人会晤于2014年11月17日在巴西利亚举行,来自中国、巴西、拉共体"四驾马车"及部分其他拉美国家的领导人出席会晤。本次会晤由中方倡议,是中拉领导人的第一次集体会晤。会晤期间,中拉领导人围绕"平等互利、合作共赢、共同发展"的主题,共叙友谊,共谋发展,共商合作,一致决定建立平等互利、共同发展的中拉全面合作伙伴关系,共同宣布成立中国—拉共体论坛。范例一节选自外交部对本次会议的报道。

原文链接:http://news.xinhuanet.com/world/2014-07/18/c_1111687937.htm

译文链接:http://www.fmprc.gov.cn/mfa_eng/wjb_663304/zzjg_663340/ldmzs_664952/xwlb_664954/t1176650.shtml

---

一、范例一文本结构分析(Text Structure Analysis of Sample I)

范例一是一则关于领导人出席国际会议并发表外交演讲的新闻报道,主要内容包括演讲的时间、地点、场合、与会各方人员以及领导人主要演讲内容。通常情况下,外交演讲新闻报道的导语部分包含演讲时间、地点、场合、演讲人等信息,有的新闻则在导语部分还会涉及与会人员、主持人以及演讲题目和主题思想等信息。在本条报道中,第一、二、三段囊括了演讲时间(2014年7月17日下午)、地点(巴西利亚)、场合(中国—拉美和加勒比国家领导人会晤)、演讲人(习近平)、与会人员(巴西总统罗塞夫等)、演讲题目(《努力构建携手共进的命运共同体》)以及主旨思想(宣布中方倡议和举措,提出构建中拉关系五位一体新格局,打造中拉携手共进的命运共同体);

发表外交演讲报道的翻译
Translation for Coverage of Diplomatic Speeches

接下来以领导人的讲话精神为主，介绍领导人演讲内容（常用表达有……指出，……强调，……最后强调等），概括领导人演讲的主要观点和主张（本文因篇幅所限，对演讲原文稍作删减）；最后三段总结其他国家出席领导人的观点（拉美和加勒比国家领导人纷纷表示……），以及大会成果（会后，中拉双方发表了《中国—拉美和加勒比国家领导人巴西利亚会晤联合声明》）。

二、范例一翻译解析（Translation Analysis of Sample I）

（一）外交演讲报道标题的翻译（Translation of Coverage Headlines for Diplomatic Speeches）

外交演讲新闻标题最常见的表述方法为"××出席××会议并发表××演讲"，如"习近平出席第二届世界互联网大会开幕式并发表主旨演讲"，或"××在××开幕式致辞"，如"李源潮在第三届中国—南亚博览会开幕式上致辞"；另一种针对领导人出访某地名校并发表演讲进行报道，如"驻卡塔尔大使高有祯在乔治敦大学多哈分校演讲"。外交演讲新闻报道标题的时态一般采用一般现在时。还有一种常见的外交演讲新闻报道标题由主标题和副标题构成，主标题一般是"××发表演讲"，副标题则涉及演讲题目或主题，如"习近平在阿拉伯国家联盟总部发表重要演讲 共同开创中阿关系发展美好未来 推动中阿民族复兴形成更多交汇"，这种形式多见于领导人出席重大国际会议并发表重要讲话，阐述中国立场态度以及主旨精神。下面就通过一些实例，探讨不同形式的外交演讲新闻报道标题的翻译。

习近平出席第二届世界互联网大会开幕式并发表主旨演讲
(http://cpc.people.com.cn/n1/2015/1217/c64094-27938940.html)
Xi Jinping Attends Opening Ceremony of Second World Internet Conference and Delivers Keynote Speech
(http://www.fmprc.gov.cn/mfa_eng/zxxx_662805/t1325603.shtml)
李源潮在第三届中国—南亚博览会开幕式上致辞
(http://www.fmprc.gov.cn/mfa_chn/zyxw_602251/t1272742.shtml)
Li Yuanchao Addresses Opening Ceremony of the 3rd China-South Asia Expo
(http://www.fmprc.gov.cn/mfa_eng/zxxx_662805/t1273543.shtml)
驻卡塔尔大使高有祯在乔治敦大学多哈分校演讲
(http://www.fmprc.gov.cn/mfa_chn/wjdt_611265/zwbd_611281/t1098836.shtml)
Ambassador to Qatar Gao Youzhen Delivers Speech at Georgetown University in Doha
(http://www.fmprc.gov.cn/mfa_eng/wjb_663304/zwjg_665342/zwbd_665378/)
驻约旦大使高育生在约旦国际事务协会就"中阿关系"发表演讲
(http://www.fmprc.gov.cn/ce/cejo/chn/gdxw/t1150501.html)

155

Ambassador to Jordan Gao Yusheng Delivers Speech on China-Arab Relations at Jordan's World Affairs Council

(http://www.fmprc.gov.cn/mfa_eng/wjb_663304/zwjg_665342/zwbd_665378/)

李克强向英国智库发表题为《共建包容发展的美好世界》的演讲

(http://news.xinhuanet.com/world/2014-06/19/c_126639354.html)

Li Keqiang Delivers Speech Entitled "Jointly Building a Better World for Inclusive Development" to UK's Think Tanks

(http://www.fmprc.gov.cn/mfa_eng/wjb_663304/zzjg_663340/xos_664404/xwlb_664406/t1167241.shtml)

习近平在阿拉伯国家联盟总部发表重要演讲 共同开创中阿关系发展美好未来 推动中阿民族复兴形成更多交汇

(http://www.xinhuanet.com/world/2016-01/22/c_1117855429.htm)

Xi Jinping Delivers Important Speech at Headquarters of the League of Arab States, Stressing to Jointly Create a Bright Future for Development of China-Arab Relations and Promote National Rejuvenation of China and Arab States to Form More Convergence

(http://www.fmprc.gov.cn/mfa_eng/topics_665678/xjpdstajyljxgsfw/t1334587.shtml)

习近平出席中非合作论坛约翰内斯堡峰会开幕式并发表致辞

提出把中非关系提升为全面战略合作伙伴关系 全面阐述中国发展对非关系政策理念 宣布深化中非合作重要举措

(http://www.fmprc.gov.cn/web/zyxw/t1321408.shtml)

Xi Jinping Attends the Opening Ceremony of the Johannesburg Summit of the Forum on China-Africa Cooperation and Delivers a Speech, Proposing to Upgrade China-Africa Relations to Comprehensive Strategic and Cooperative Partnership, Comprehensively Expounding China's African Policy and Announcing Major Measures to Deepen China-Africa Cooperation

(http://www.fmprc.gov.cn/mfa_eng/topics_665678/xjpffgcxqhbhbldhdjbbwnfjxgsfwbfnfyhnsbzczfhzltfh/t1322278.shtml)

从以上实例可以看出，"发表演讲"可以译为deliver speech，"为……致辞"可以译为address …，"就某话题发表演讲"可以译为deliver speech on …，"发表题为……的演讲"可以译为deliver speech entitled …，时态常采用一般现在时。对于标题中涉及演讲主题或主旨精神，多采用动名词形式，可以译为Stressing … 或 proposing …。演讲具有不同类别，可包括即席讲话（impromptu remarks）、开幕词（opening remarks）、闭幕词（closing remarks）、主旨演讲（keynote speech）等。

发表外交演讲报道的翻译 **7** UNIT

Translation for Coverage of Diplomatic Speeches

（二）外交演讲新闻报道常用表达的翻译（Translation of Frequently Used Expressions in Coverage of Diplomatic Speeches）

1. 关于演讲时间、场合、题目或主题的翻译

演讲主题的介绍中可能会明确出现"发表题为……的演讲"的字样，可以译为deliver a speech entitled …，有时候根据汉语原文可在speech前面添加important，special等修饰词，表达"重要讲话，特别致辞"等含义，演讲题目翻译时多采用动名词形式。有时新闻中或许不出现演讲题目，而直接介绍主题，采用"介绍了""详细介绍了""阐述了""深入阐述了"等表述，可以翻译为introduce …，give a detailed introduction to，expound one's view on …及elaborate in depth on …等。"应邀"出席或"应邀"发表演说可以译为 at invitation 或者 upon invitation。请看下面翻译实例：

2014年4月8日，驻日本大使程永华应邀赴日本言论NPO发表演讲，介绍了十二届全国人大二次会议和全国政协十二届二次会议有关情况和精神，并阐述了对当前中日关系的看法。

(http://www.fmprc.gov.cn/ce/cejp/chn/gdxw/t1147674.htm)

On April 8, 2014, H.E. Cheng Yonghua, Chinese Ambassador to Japan, delivered a speech at Japan's Genron NPO upon invitation, introducing the relevant information and the spirit of the second session of the 12th National People's Congress (NPC) and the second session of the 12th Chinese People's Political Consultative Conference (CPPCC), and expounding his views on the current China-Japan relations.

(http://www.fmprc.gov.cn/mfa_eng/wjb_663304/zwjg_665342/zwbd_665378/)

2016年6月21日，外交部副部长王超应邀出席在北京举办的"第三届中非媒体合作论坛"开幕式并致辞。

(http://www.fmprc.gov.cn/web/wjbxw_673019/t1373895.shtml)

On June 21, 2016, Vice Foreign Minister Wang Chao attended at invitation the opening ceremony of the 3rd Forum on China-Africa Media Cooperation in Beijing and delivered a speech.

(http://www.fmprc.gov.cn/mfa_eng/wjdt_665385/wshd_665389/t1374595.shtml)

21日，国家主席习近平在开罗阿拉伯国家联盟总部发表题为《共同开创中阿关系的美好未来》的重要演讲，强调中阿两个民族彼此真诚相待，这份信任牢不可破。我们要共建"一带一路"，确立和平、创新、引领、治理、交融的行动理念，推动中阿两大民族复兴形成更多交汇。

(http://www.xinhuanet.com/world/2016-01/22/c_1117855429.htm)

On January 21, 2016 local time, President Xi Jinping delivered an important speech entitled "Jointly Create a Brighter Future for China-Arab Relations" at the headquarters of the League of Arab States (LAS) in Cairo, stressing that the two nations treat each other with sincerity and such trust is unbreakable. Both sides should join hands to build the "Belt and Road", establish the action concepts of peace, innovation, guidance, governance and integration, and promote the national rejuvenation of China and the Arab states to form more convergence.

(http://www.fmprc.gov.cn/mfa_eng/topics_665678/xjpdstajyljxgsfw/t1334587.shtml)

2. 关于主持及到会情况的翻译

很多关于领导人出席会议发表演讲的新闻中会讲到会议由某某主持,有哪些国家领导人出席了会议。一般来说,"主持"译为 preside over, chair 或 host,"与会"译为 attend 或 be present,"陪同出席"可以译为 attend as company。请看下面翻译实例:

莫斯科大学校长萨多夫尼奇、亚非学院院长阿贝尔加季耶夫及200多名莫大师生出席。

(http://news.sina.com.cn/o/2014-04-30/085830038847.shtml)

Rector of the MSU Victor Antonovich Sadovnichy, Director of the IAAS Igor Ishenalievich Abylgaziyev, and over 200 teachers and students of the MSU were present.

(http://www.fmprc.gov.cn/mfa_eng/wjb_663304/zwjg_665342/zwbd_665378/)

当地时间11月17日,国家主席习近平在澳大利亚联邦议会发表题为《携手追寻中澳发展梦想 并肩实现地区繁荣稳定》的重要演讲。澳大利亚众议长毕晓普主持,澳大利亚总理阿博特、参议长帕里、工党领袖肖顿陪同出席。

(http://news.xinhuanet.com/world/2014-11/17/c_1113283064.htm)

On November 17 local time, President Xi Jinping delivered an important speech at the Federal Parliament of Australia entitled "Pursuing Chinese and Australian Development Dreams Hand in Hand and Achieving Regional Prosperity and Stability Shoulder to Shoulder". Speaker of the House of Representatives Bronwyn Bishop of Australia presided. Prime Minister Tony Abbott, President of the Senate Stephen Parry and Leader of the Labor Party Bill Shorten of Australia attended as company.

(http://www.fmprc.gov.cn/mfa_eng/topics_665678/xjpzxcxesgjtldrdjcfhdadlyxxlfjj xgsfwbttpyjjdgldrhw/t1212614.shtml)

3. 关于演讲现场气氛的翻译

针对演讲现场气氛,新闻中常用"座无虚席","经久不息的热烈掌声"等语汇来描述热烈的气氛,以表达演讲人受欢迎的程度。在新闻翻译中,翻译这类描述性语言,特别是形容词和副词,需要把握分寸,注意用词的准确度和忠实度。请看下面翻译实例:

演讲期间，莫斯科大学亚非学院会议大厅座无虚席，两旁过道都站满了老师和学生。现场气氛热烈、友好。整个活动持续了两个多小时。

(http://news.sina.com.cn/o/2014-04-30/085830038847.shtml)

During the speech, all seats were occupied in the conference hall of the MSU Institute of Asian and African Studies, and even the aisles on the sides of the hall were filled by teachers and students. It was in a warm and friendly atmosphere, and the whole activity lasted over two hours.

(http://www.fmprc.gov.cn/mfa_eng/wjb_663304/zwjg_665342/zwbd_665378/)

米诺斯市会议中心楼上楼下观众席爆满，许多听众站在走道上聆听讲座，杜大使的演讲引起听众的阵阵共鸣与经久不息的热烈掌声。

(http://www.fmprc.gov.cn/ce/cegr/chn/zxgx/t1098316.htm)

The Milos Conference Center was packed with audience upstairs and downstairs, and some of them even stood in the aisle to listen to the speech. Ambassador Du's speech aroused rounds of resonance and prolonged applause from the audience.

(http://www.fmprc.gov.cn/mfa_eng/wjb_663304/zwjg_665342/zwbd_665378/)

当习近平步入众议院会议厅时，全场起立欢迎。在热烈掌声中，习近平发表演讲。

(http://news.xinhuanet.com/world/2014-11/17/c_1113283064.htm)

When Xi Jinping stepped into the chamber of the House of Representatives, he received a standing ovation by the whole audience. In the warm applause, Xi Jinping delivered the speech.

(http://www.fmprc.gov.cn/mfa_eng/topics_665678/xjpzxcxesgjtldrdjcfhdadlyxxlfjjxgsfwbttpyjjdgldrhw/t1212614.shtml)

（三）范例一文本英译解析（Translation Analysis on the Text of Sample I）
1. 定语英译

汉语外交新闻文本中长句较多，"修饰语+中心词"是构成汉语长句的一个重要手段。汉语中名词修饰语通常前置，而英语中名词修饰语可出现在名词之前，也可以分词、介词结构或者定语从句的形式出现在名词之后。所以，在英译时，译者需结合两种语言的特点，选用准确而又地道的表达，将汉语名词修饰语灵活、恰当地处理为英语中的介词结构、分词短语、后置定语等。请看范例一中相关例句的翻译解析：

会晤开始前，习近平与罗塞夫共同迎接出席会晤的拉美和加勒比国家领导人和代表，同他们一一握手并集体合影。

Before the Summit, Xi Jinping and Rousseff jointly welcomed the leaders and representatives of the Latin American and Caribbean countries attending the Summit, shook hands one by one and posed for group photos with them.

汉语例句中有两个并列定语"出席会晤的"和"拉美加勒比国家"修饰中心语"领导人和代表",英译时分别采取of ...介词结构和attending ...现在分词结构,置于中心语the leaders and representatives之后,从而使得译文逻辑严密,句法结构平衡,符合英语表达习惯。

习近平同与会各国领导人在亲切、友好、务实的气氛中,围绕"平等互利、合作共赢、共同发展"的主题,共叙友谊,共谋发展,共商合作,一致决定建立平等互利、共同发展的中拉全面合作伙伴关系,共同宣布成立中国—拉共体论坛。

Xi Jinping and the leaders of other countries renewed friendship, sought common development and discussed cooperation in a <u>sincere, friendly and practical</u> atmosphere around the theme <u>of "equality, mutual benefit, win-win cooperation and common development"</u>, agreeing to establish the China-Latin America comprehensive cooperative partnership <u>of equality, mutual benefit and common development</u>, and jointly announced the establishment of the Forum of China and Community of Latin American and Caribbean States (CELAC).

汉语例句中定语"亲切、友好、务实的"修饰中心语"气氛",英译时采取形容词修饰名词的结构;而定语"平等互利、合作共赢、共同发展的"修饰中心语"主题","平等互利、共同发展的"修饰中心语"中拉全面合作伙伴关系",在英译时均采用of ...介词结构,分别置于中心词theme和the China-Latin America comprehensive cooperative partnership之后。

习近平发表了题为《努力构建携手共进的命运共同体》主旨讲话,宣布中方对促进中拉合作的倡议和举措,提出构建政治上真诚互信、经贸上合作共赢、人文上互学互鉴、国际事务中密切协作、整体合作和双边关系相互促进的中拉关系五位一体新格局,打造中拉携手共进的命运共同体。

Xi Jinping delivered a keynote speech <u>entitled</u> "Striving to Build a Hand-in-Hand Community of Common Future", announcing China's proposals and measures <u>on promoting China-Latin America cooperation</u>, proposing to build up a Five-in-One new pattern of China-Latin America relations: <u>sincerely trust each other in politics, cooperate with each other for a win-win outcome in economy and trade, learn from each other in people-to-people and cultural exchanges, closely cooperate with each other in international affairs, and promote each other in overall cooperation and bilateral relations</u>, so as to forge a <u>hand-in-hand</u> community of common future.

汉语例句中定语"题为《努力构建携手共进的命运共同体》",英译时采取过去分词结构entitled ...置于中心词之后;定语"中拉携手共进的",翻译时将其处理为一个形容词hand-in-hand;长定语是外交措辞中较为突出的语言特征,该句中"政治上真诚互信、经贸上合作共赢、人文上互学互鉴、国际事务中密切协作、整体合作和双边关系相互促进"作为定语修饰"中拉关系五位一体新格局",在英译时采取了用冒号解释说明的方法。也可以参考习近平演讲原文的翻译(详见范例二),其中将其翻译为a five-dimensional relationship characterized by ...分词结构,更显措辞巧妙之处。

综上所述,以上译例包含汉语定语的四类英译方法:形容词修饰中心语,多个形容词并列排序,置于中心语之前;将汉语定语转换为英语介词结构,置于中心语之后;利用现在分词或过去分词解决多个定语同时修饰一个中心语的问题;增译,加入表示定语与中心语之间逻辑关系的词(如上文characterized by)等,使得句式结构合理,逻辑清晰。

2. 名词化结构

英语中的名词化结构可以使语体获得正式、严肃、客观的效果。名词化结构使用越频繁,语体的正式程度则越高。以下译例中,大量的英语名词化结构再现了汉语原文正式、严肃的文体特征。请看范例一中相关例句的翻译解析:

双方要加强对话合作,携手促进国际关系民主化,<u>推动建立</u>更加公正合理的国际经济金融秩序。

The two sides should strengthen dialogues and cooperation, jointly promote democratization of international relations, and <u>promote the establishment of</u> a more just and reasonable international economic and financial order.

巴西总统罗塞夫主持会议。她最后表示,这次会晤取得成功,<u>具有重要历史意义</u>。

President Dilma Rousseff of Brazil chaired the Summit. She finally noted that the success of this Summit is <u>of vital historic significance</u>.

拉美和加勒比国家<u>具有丰富的自然和人力资源</u>,都在推进改革发展,希望借鉴中国的成功经验,促进共同、可持续发展。

<u>With abundant natural and human resources</u>, Latin American and Caribbean countries are promoting reforms and development, hoping to learn from China's successful experience to promote common and sustainable development.

以上译例中,例句1将"建立"处理为英文的名词化结构the establishment of ...;例句2将动宾结构"具有……意义"巧妙转换为介词结构of ... significance,将其处理为主语this Summit的表语成分;例句3中,"具有"这一动词在不同语境下可以有不同的翻

译方法,在译例原文中"具有""推进""希望借鉴"等动词结构貌似并列,实则呈现不同的逻辑关系,仔细推敲会发现"拉美和加勒比国家具有丰富的自然和人力资源"这一信息可以作为次要信息,起修饰作用,而"推进改革"等信息才是主要信息。因此,将"具有……"这一次要信息弱化,处理为介词结构with abundant natural and human resources,更加贴近于原文文本的信息层次,也使得英文句式更加紧凑、精练。

3. 逻辑关系:隐性到显性

英语中常用多种显性的衔接手段来显示句子与语篇的语义层次和逻辑关系。汉语在句法结构上缺乏表示语义层次的显著标记,行文多用并列结构,从字面上难以分辨语义重心和逻辑关系,读者需要根据语境做出判断。在汉译英过程中,应充分考虑两种语言的差异,挖掘出汉语文本中隐含的逻辑关系,通过添加连接词、使用动名词和分词结构等方式,在英文中将原语的语义层次和逻辑关系显性化。请看范例一中相关例句的翻译解析:

习近平发表了题为《努力构建携手共进的命运共同体》主旨讲话,<u>宣布</u>中方对促进中拉合作的倡议和举措,<u>提出</u>构建政治上真诚互信、经贸上合作共赢、人文上互学互鉴、国际事务中密切协作、整体合作和双边关系相互促进的中拉关系五位一体新格局,<u>打造</u>中拉携手共进的命运共同体。

Xi Jinping <u>delivered</u> a keynote speech entitled "Striving to Build a Hand-in-Hand Community of Common Future", <u>announcing</u> China's proposals and measures on promoting China-Latin America cooperation, <u>proposing to</u> build up a Five-in-One new pattern of China-Latin America relations: sincerely trust each other in politics, cooperate with each other for a win-win outcome in economy and trade, learn from each other in people-to-people and cultural exchanges, closely cooperate with each other in international affairs, and promote each other in overall cooperation and bilateral relations, <u>so as to forge</u> a hand-in-hand community of common future.

汉语文本中"发表""宣布""提出""打造"几个动词从形式上看似并列,实则有隐性逻辑关系,需要译者仔细分析语义和句法结构,通过增加逻辑连词,或者改变动词语法形式,将隐性逻辑关系显性化,从而使英文逻辑清晰,句式结构紧凑。该译例中,分词announcing和proposing分别作为delivered a keynote speech的伴随状语,通过增加so as to这一逻辑连词,强调"打造命运共同体"这一最终目标,从而和上文的衔接更加紧密。

习近平最后指出,当前,中国人民正在为实现中华民族伟大复兴的中国梦而奋斗,拉美和加勒比各国人民也在为实现团结协作、发展振兴的拉美梦而努力。共同的梦想和共同的追求，将中拉双方紧紧联系在一起。让我们抓住机遇，开拓进取，努力构建携手共进的命运共同体，共创中拉关系的美好未来。

Lastly, Xi Jinping pointed out that currently the Chinese people are striving to achieve the "Chinese Dream" of great rejuvenation of the Chinese nation, <u>while</u> the peoples of Latin American and Caribbean countries are also struggling for the "Latin American Dream" of realizing solidarity, cooperation, development and revitalization. The common dreams and shared pursuit closely connect China and Latin America. Let's <u>seize</u> the opportunity, <u>forge</u> ahead, and <u>try hard to build</u> a hand-in-hand community of common future, <u>so as to</u> create a splendid future for China-Latin America relations.

译例中第一句有两个并列句子："中国人民……奋斗"和"拉美和加勒比各国人民……努力"，在英译时增加逻辑连词while，以增强句子之间的衔接和连贯。第二句中几个并列动词"抓住""开拓""构建""共创"，在英译时，增加连词so as to，将整句处理为以"共创……未来"为目标的语义结构。

范例二（Sample II）

努力构建携手共进的命运共同体
——习近平在中国—拉美和加勒比国家领导人会晤上的主旨讲话（节本）
2014/07/17

Build a Community of Shared Future for Common Progress
Keynote Speech by H.E. Xi Jinping
President of the People's Republic of China
At China–Latin American and Caribbean Countries Leaders' Meeting
(Abbreviated Version)
2014/07/17

尊敬的罗塞夫总统，
尊敬的索利斯总统，
尊敬的各位同事：
President Dilma Rousseff,
President Luis Guillermo Solis,
Dear Colleagues,

大家好！很高兴同大家相聚一堂，共商中拉关系发展大计。感谢罗塞夫总统热情洋溢的致辞。见到这么多拉美和加勒比新老朋友，我感到十分愉快。今天下午是"中拉时间"。中拉这么多领导人能相聚在一起，本身就是个具有世界影响的历史事件。

Good afternoon. I am so pleased to meet you all here to discuss the development of China-Latin America and Caribbean relations. I want to thank President Rousseff for her warm remarks. It's really a great joy to see so many old and new friends in Latin America and the Caribbean. This afternoon belongs to China and Latin American and Caribbean relations. The fact that the leaders of China and so many Latin American and Caribbean countries are gathering here is in itself of historic and global significance.

***

借此机会，我谨代表中国政府和中国人民，并以我个人的名义，向你们并通过你们，向拉美和加勒比各国人民，致以诚挚的问候和良好的祝愿！

I wish to take this opportunity to express, on behalf of the Chinese government and people and in my own name, sincere greetings and best wishes to you and, through you, to the people of Latin American and Caribbean countries.

***

中方倡议举行这次会晤，目的是加强对话、凝聚共识，从最高层面推动中拉关系向更高水平发展。这既符合我们双方的现实利益和长远利益，也有利于促进南南合作。

China has proposed this meeting because we want to enhance dialogue, build consensus and boost the growth of China-Latin American and Caribbean relations from the top level. This not only serves our immediate and long-term interests but also contributes to South-South cooperation.

***

感谢罗塞夫总统女士和巴西政府，在主办世界杯足球赛和金砖国家领导人会晤的同时，高度重视并精心筹办这次重要会晤。拉共体"四驾马车"成员国之前做了大量协调工作，各位同事专程前来参加会晤，充分体现了对加强中拉关系、推进整体合作的支持，我对此深表赞赏和感谢。

I want to thank President Rousseff and the Brazilian government for attaching high importance to and making meticulous preparations for this important meeting while they played host to the FIFA World Cup and the BRICS Summit. I appreciate the coordination efforts made by the extended "Troika" of CELAC before this meeting, and I thank all of you for traveling here to attend the meeting. This fully reflects your support for strengthening China-Latin America and Caribbean relations and advancing our overall cooperation.

***

"志合者，不以山海为远。"中拉相距遥远，但双方人民有着天然的亲近感。1949年中华人民共和国成立至今，在几代人共同努力下，中拉关系一步一个脚印，走过了60多年的光辉历程。新世纪以来，中拉关系呈现全面快速发展的良好态势。特别是2008年国际金融危机爆发后，中拉发挥各自优势，同舟共济，共克时艰，双方关系实现跨越式发展。

As an old Chinese saying goes, "Nothing can separate people with common goals and ideals, not even mountains and seas." Although China and Latin America and the Caribbean are far apart geographically, there is a natural feeling of affinity between our peoples. The relationship between China and Latin America and the Caribbean has come a long way since the founding of the People's Republic of China in 1949. Thanks to generations of concerted efforts by both sides, it has made solid and steady progress for the last 60 years and more. In the new century, this relationship has shown a sound momentum of comprehensive and fast growth. Since the outbreak of the international financial crisis in 2008 in particular, China and Latin America and the Caribbean have, building on their respective strengths, forged close unity in overcoming the difficult period and achieved a quantum leap in their relations.

***

在此，我提议，通过这次会晤，共同宣布建立平等互利、共同发展的中拉全面合作伙伴关系，努力构建政治上真诚互信、经贸上合作共赢、人文上互学互鉴、国际事务中密切协作、整体合作和双边关系相互促进的中拉关系五位一体新格局。

Here, I wish to propose that we jointly announce at this meeting the establishment of a comprehensive and cooperative partnership featuring equality, mutual benefit and common development between China and Latin America and the Caribbean, and work together to build a five-dimensional relationship characterized by sincerity and mutual trust in the political field, win-win cooperation on the economic front, mutual learning and emulation in the cultural sphere, close coordination in international affairs, as well as synergy between China's cooperation with the region as a whole and its bilateral relations with individual regional countries.

***

当前，中国人民正在为实现中华民族伟大复兴的中国梦而奋斗，拉美和加勒比各国人民也在为实现团结协作、发展振兴的拉美梦而努力。共同的梦想和共同的追求，将中拉双方紧紧联系在一起。让我们抓住机遇，开拓进取，努力构建携手共进的命运共同体，共创中拉关系的美好未来！

The Chinese people are now striving to realize the Chinese dream of the great renewal of the Chinese nation. The people of Latin American and Caribbean countries are also working toward the Latin American dream of unity, coordination, development and rejuvenation. The shared dream and pursuit have brought us closely together. Let us seize the opportunities presented to us and work together to blaze new trails in building a community of shared future for common progress and usher in a bright future for the relations between China and Latin America and the Caribbean.

谢谢大家。
Thank you.

原文链接：http://news.xinhuanet.com/world/2014-07/18/c_1111688827.htm

译文链接：http://www.fmprc.gov.cn/mfa_eng/wjdt_665385/zyjh_665391/t1184869.shtml

一、范例二文本结构分析（Text Structure Analysis of Sample II）

外交演讲或致辞中，演讲者通常先是对在场人员表示感谢、致以敬意并表明此次演讲的目的和态度。例如在本例中，第一至四段，演讲人利用"很高兴……"，"感谢……"，"致以诚挚的问候和良好的祝愿……"，"深表赞赏和感谢……"等表述，向会议主办方、主持人表达谢意并致敬；并表明演讲目的是加强对话、凝聚共识，从最高层面推动中拉关系向更高水平发展。第五段，回顾历史，着眼现实，以情制胜，引起共鸣，拉近距离。在本例中，习近平主席回顾了60年来的中拉友好关系，以此作为双方深化全面互利合作的契机。习主席以一句谚语"志合者，不以山海为远"开头，拉近了与聆听者的距离。第六段，习主席针对双方平等互待、互利合作、交流互鉴等方面提出打造中拉关系五位一体新格局；最后一段为结束语，是演讲主旨和精神的升华。本例中习主席总结中国梦与拉美梦息息相关紧密相连。因篇幅所限，原文有所删节。

二、范例二翻译解析（Translation Analysis of Sample II）

（一）外交演讲常用表达的翻译（Translation of Frequently Used Expressions in Diplomatic Speeches）

1. 关于欢迎、感谢及致敬的翻译

外交演讲往往在开篇会表达欢迎、感谢以及致敬，常见表述为"代表××向××致以问候"，"对××表示热烈欢迎"，"向……致以崇高的敬意"，"向……表示衷心感谢"，请看下面翻译实例：

> 借此机会，我谨代表中国政府和中国人民，并以我个人的名义，向你们并通过你们，向拉美和加勒比各国人民，致以诚挚的问候和良好的祝愿！
>
> (http://news.xinhuanet.com/world/2014-07/18/c_1111688827.htm)
>
> I wish to take this opportunity to express, on behalf of the Chinese government and people and in my own name, sincere greetings and best wishes to you and, through you, to the people of Latin American and Caribbean countries
>
> (http://www.fmprc.gov.cn/mfa_eng/wjdt_665385/zyjh_665391/t1184869.shtml)
>
> 欢迎来北京出席亚太经合组织第26届部长级会议。出席今天会议的有各经济

体的部长或代表,亚太经合组织秘书处执行主任、亚太经合组织工商咨询理事会主席,观察员代表。我们对你们的到来表示热烈的欢迎!

(http://china.huanqiu.com/News/fmprc/2014-11/5195516.html)

Welcome to Beijing to attend the 26th APEC Ministerial Meeting. Attending today's meeting are ministers or ministers' representatives from APEC economies, executive director of the APEC Secretariat, president of the APEC Business Advisory Council and observers. We wish to extend a warm welcome to all of you.

(http://www.fmprc.gov.cn/ce/cohk/eng/xwdt/zt/apec/t1208615.htm)

在此,我谨向长期以来关心中国发展、为中墨友好事业做出贡献的各位朋友致以崇高的敬意,向本次研讨会的主办方UNAM大学中墨研究中心表示衷心感谢!

(http://wcm.fmprc.gov.cn/pub/chn/gxh/mtb/zwbd/dszlsjt/t1132592.htm)

Here, I would like to pay high tribute to all the friends who have long been caring about China's development and making contribution to the China-Mexico friendship, and to express my heartfelt appreciation to the organizer of this seminar, the China-Mexico Study Center (CECHIMEX) of the National Autonomous University of Mexico (UNAM)!

(http://www.fmprc.gov.cn/mfa_eng/wjb_663304/zwjg_665342/zwbd_665378/)

2. 关于演讲主旨、阐述主张的表述

外交演讲的主旨包括参与国际会议的主要议题,访问某国的目的和意义等。演讲人阐述主张常涉及演讲方的主要观点和立场、重大决定和举措等。请看下列翻译实例:

今天,亚非国家领导人汇聚在美丽的雅加达,共同纪念万隆会议召开60周年,共商亚非友好合作和发展振兴大计,具有十分重要的意义。

(http://news.xinhuanet.com/politics/2015-04/22/c_1115057390.htm)

Today, we, the leaders of Asian and African countries, are gathered here in this beautiful city of Jakarta to commemorate the 60th anniversary of the Bandung Conference, and to discuss important issues bearing on friendship and cooperation between Asia and Africa as well as development and rejuvenation in our respective countries. To me, this is a conference of far-reaching significance.

(http://www.fmprc.gov.cn/mfa_eng/wjdt_665385/zyjh_665391/t1259844.shtml)

我这次访问期间,双方决定把中澳关系提升为全面战略伙伴关系,并宣布实质性结束中澳自由贸易协定谈判。这两项重要成果将有助于我们推动中澳关系百尺竿头、更进一步。

(http://news.xinhuanet.com/world/2014-11/17/c_1113283064.htm)

During my visit, the two sides have decided to elevate our bilateral relations into a comprehensive strategic partnership and announced the substantial conclusion of the FTA negotiations. These two important outcomes will further boost China-Australia relations.

(http://www.fmprc.gov.cn/mfa_eng/topics_665678/xjpzxcxesgjtldrdjcfhdadlyxxlfjjxg sfwbttpyjjdgldrhw/t1212614.shtml)

我这次访欧，就是为了同欧盟新一届领导人进一步增进政治互信，与工商界共同探讨推动全球产能合作之道，加强双方人文交流，开创中欧关系发展新局面。

(http://news.xinhuanet.com/politics/2015-06/30/c_1115760599.htm)

I have now come to Europe to enhance political mutual trust with the new EU leadership. We will discuss with the business community ways to promote global cooperation on production capacity, and strengthen our people-to-people and cultural exchanges. This, I believe, will help China-EU relations make new progress.

(http://www.fmprc.gov.cn/mfa_eng/zxxx_662805/t1277193.shtml)

（二）外交新词的翻译 (Translation of Diplomatic Neologisms)

随着中国经济的快速崛起，中国国际地位大幅提升，中国外交日趋活跃，涌现了一大批新观点、新概念、新术语。这些外交新词特色鲜明、内涵丰富，是中华民族优秀文化的结晶和中国外交思想的重要载体，已成为现代汉语中最活跃、最重要的组成部分之一。它们在传播中国传统文化和外交理念、推行国家外交政策、提升对外形象和国际话语权等方面发挥了举足轻重的作用。（杨明星，2014：103）中国外交新词是外交新闻翻译工作中的重点和难点，在西方国家外交话语体系中很难找到恰当的对应词。在翻译实践中必须认真研究外交概念和术语的语言特征和文化意象，采用有效的翻译原则和策略，最大限度地传递原语的政治信息和情感意义。请看以下外交新词的翻译：

中国梦：the Chinese dream

中国民族伟大复兴：the great rejuvenation/revitalization/renewal of the Chinese nation

中拉关系五位一体新格局：a five-dimensional relationship

命运共同体：a community with a shared future

跨越式发展：achieve a quantum leap

新常态：the New Normal

"一带一路"倡议：the Belt and Road Initiative

丝绸之路经济带和21世纪海上丝绸之路：the Silk Road Economic Belt and the 21st-Century Maritime Silk Road

全球经济治理：global economic governance

互联互通：connectivity

发展战略对接：docking of development strategies

澜湄合作：Lancang-Mekong Cooperation (LMC)

发表外交演讲报道的翻译
Translation for Coverage of Diplomatic Speeches

（三）成语和谚语的翻译（Translation of Idioms and Proverbs）

我国领导人在外交演讲中常常引经据典，大量使用成语和谚语，以平衡句法结构，实现音韵之美、强化表达效果等修辞意义。英译这些成语和谚语时，修辞意义的准确传递是非常重要的。常用的翻译方法包括直译法、释义法、简化译法等。请看下列习近平主席在演讲中引用的成语和谚语的翻译：

直译法：

这是我担任中国国家主席一年多来，第二次到拉美和加勒比走亲访友……

(http://news.xinhuanet.com/world/2014-07/18/c_1111688827.htm)

I took office as the Chinese President over one year ago, this is the second time for me to visit relatives and friends in Latin America and the Caribbean...

(http://www.fmprc.gov.cn/mfa_eng/wjdt_665385/zyjh_665391/t1184869.shtml)

"志合者，不以山海为远。"中拉相距遥远，但双方人民有着天然的亲近感。

(http://news.xinhuanet.com/world/2014-07/18/c_1111688827.htm)

"Nothing can separate people with common goals and ideals, not even mountains and seas." Although China and Latin America and the Caribbean are far apart geographically, there is a natural feeling of affinity between our peoples.

(http://www.fmprc.gov.cn/mfa_eng/wjdt_665385/zyjh_665391/t1184869.shtml)

国之交在于民相亲

(http://news.xinhuanet.com/world/2014-07/18/c_1111688827.htm)

State-to-state relationship is underpinned by people-to-people amity.

(http://www.fmprc.gov.cn/mfa_eng/wjdt_665385/zyjh_665391/t1184869.shtml)

非洲有句谚语，"一根原木盖不起一幢房屋"。中国也有句古话，"孤举者难起，众行者易趋"。

(http://paper.people.com.cn/rmrbhwb/html/2015-04/23/content_1557235.htm)

As an African proverb goes, "One single pillar is not sufficient to build a house." In China, we have an old saying, which reads, "The going is difficult when doing it alone; the going is made easier when doing it with many others."

(http://www.fmprc.gov.cn/mfa_eng/wjdt_665385/zyjh_665391/t1259844.shtml)

简化译法：

特别是2008年国际金融危机爆发后，中拉发挥各自优势，同舟共济，共克时艰，双方关系实现跨越式发展。

(http://news.xinhuanet.com/world/2014-07/18/c_1111688827.htm)

Since the outbreak of the international financial crisis in 2008 in particular, China and Latin America and the Caribbean have, building on their respective strengths, forged close unity in overcoming the difficult period and achieved a quantum leap in their relations.

(http://www.fmprc.gov.cn/mfa_eng/wjdt_665385/zyjh_665391/t1184869.shtml)

"同心而共济，始终如一，此君子之朋也。"我相信，在中澳双方共同努力下，中澳两国人民友谊完全能够跨越高山和大海，如同耸立在澳大利亚中部的乌鲁鲁巨岩一样不畏风雨、屹立长存，如同横亘在中国北方的万里长城一样<u>绵延不断、世代相传</u>。

(http://news.xinhuanet.com/world/2014-11/17/c_1113283064.htm)

As a Chinese saying goes, "<u>True friendship exists only when there is an abiding commitment to pursue common goals</u>." I am confident that with our joint efforts, the friendship between Chinese and Australian people will span over mountains and oceans. Such friendship will withstand rain and storm and <u>be as strong and everlasting</u> as the majestic Uluru Rock in central Australia and the Great Wall in northern China.

(http://www.fmprc.gov.cn/mfa_eng/topics_665678/xjpzxcxesgjtldrdjcfhdadlyxxlfjjxgsfwbttpyjjdgldrhw/t1212614.shtml)

释义法：

1949年中华人民共和国成立至今，在几代人共同努力下，中拉关系<u>一步一个脚印</u>，走过了60多年的光辉历程。

(http://news.xinhuanet.com/world/2014-07/18/c_1111688827.htm)

The relationship between China and Latin America and the Caribbean <u>has come a long way</u> since the founding of the People's Republic of China in 1949. Thanks to generations of concerted efforts by both sides, it has made solid and steady progress for the last 60 years and more.

(http://www.fmprc.gov.cn/mfa_eng/wjdt_665385/zyjh_665391/t1184869.shtml)

亚非国家加强互利合作，能产生"<u>一加一大于二</u>"的积极效应。

(http://paper.people.com.cn/rmrbhwb/html/2015-04/23/content_1557235.htm)

By working closely together, Asian and African countries <u>will gain far more than what their combined strengths could produce</u>.

(http://www.fmprc.gov.cn/mfa_eng/wjdt_665385/zyjh_665391/t1259844.shtml)

学生译作讲评
Analysis of Students' Translation Practice

原文链接：http://www.fmprc.gov.cn/mfa_chn/zyxw_602251/t1096047.shtml
新闻原文：汪洋出席中国—太平洋岛国经济发展合作论坛并发表主旨演讲
学生译文：Wang Yang Attended the "China-Pacific Island Countries Economic

Development and Cooperation Forum" and Addressed a Keynote Speech

翻译评析：标题翻译中动词attend和address的时态应采用一般现在时。address一词使用错误，在表示某人在某会议致辞时，address后面直接跟会议或论坛名称。如：李源潮在第三届中国—南亚博览会开幕式上致辞，可以译为Li Yuanchao Addresses Opening Ceremony of the 3rd China-South Asia Expo。"中国—太平洋岛国经济发展合作论坛"属于专有名词，应大写首字母而不加双引号。因此，标题可以改译为：Wang Yang Attends and Delivers Keynote Speech at China-Pacific Island Countries Economic Development and Cooperation Forum。

新闻原文：2013年11月8日，国务院副总理汪洋在广州出席第二届中国—太平洋岛国经济发展合作论坛暨2013中国国际绿色创新技术产品展，并发表题为《让"中—太"友好合作之舟破浪前行》的主旨演讲。

学生译文：On November 8th, 2013, Chinese Vice Premier Wang Yang attended the "2013 China International Green Technology Innovation Products Exhibition of the 2nd China-Pacific Island Countries Economic Development and Cooperation Forum", and addressed a keynote speech entitled "Ride the Wave of Challenges for China-Pacific Friendly Cooperation".

翻译评析："第二届中国—太平洋岛国经济发展合作论坛暨2013中国国际绿色创新技术产品展"是会议名称，属于专有名称，翻译时大写首字母即可，不应加双引号。而对"暨"这个词的理解是准确翻译这一标题的前提，学生误将其理解为"……的"，翻译为… of。事实上，"暨"这个词经常出现在会议标题中，其意为"和"，译为and就可以了。因此，这个会议名称可以改译为the second China-Pacific Island Countries Economic Development and Cooperation Forum and the 2013 China International Green Innovative Products & Technologies Show。

演讲标题中将"中—太间的友好合作"比喻为"乘风破浪"前行的"舟"，"乘风破浪"这一成语的翻译便成为难点。学生将其翻译为ride the wave of challenges for，意思是为了"中—太友好合作"而迎接巨浪的挑战，语义信息与原文有所偏离，且略显啰嗦，可将其改译为 Let China-Pacific Friendly Cooperation Advance Against the Waves。

新闻原文：汪洋强调，与太平洋岛国发展友好合作关系，是中国外交工作的一项长期战略方针。中国与太平洋岛国的合作是平等的、真诚的、务实的。中方愿与各岛国同舟共济、精诚合作，共同缔造南南合作的典范。实践已经并将继续证明，中国是太平洋岛国可以信赖的真心朋友，可以倚重的合作伙伴。

学生译文：Vice Premier Wang Yang highlighted that the friendly cooperation with pacific island countries is a long-term strategy of China's diplomacy. The cooperation between China and pacific island countries is based on the principle of equality, sincerity and pragmatism. China stands ready to cooperate with each and every island country in good faith to cross river in the same boat to set up a role model for South-South cooperation. It has been proved and will be proved that China is a sincere, reliable friend and cooperative partner of Pacific island countries.

翻译评析：基于外交演讲新闻文本的正式性，翻译时确保信息准确无误非常关键。学生译文第一句漏译"发展"和"方针"，造成了原文重要信息的缺失。译文第二句中，学生又无端地增译on the principle of，将原文信息随意改为"在平等、真诚、务实的原则上的"。综上所述，以上两句可以改译为Wang Yang highlighted that developing friendly cooperation with the Pacific island countries is part of the long-term strategy guideline of China's diplomacy. The cooperation between China and the Pacific island countries is equal, sincere and pragmatic。

在原文最后一句的翻译上，学生译文将"可以信赖的真心朋友，可以倚重的合作伙伴"笼统译为a sincere, reliable friend and cooperative partner。实际上，这样会产生理解上的歧义，究竟sincere和reliable修饰的中心词是什么呢？为了明晰语义，可以改为a reliable and sincere friend and a dependable cooperative partner。

"同舟共济""精诚合作"这类四字格在领导人演讲中十分常见，也体现汉语语言讲求音韵对仗这一特点。学生逐字直译为in good faith to cross river in the same boat，表述冗长、缺乏美感，和China以及island countries搭配也略显生硬。这两个四字格可以采取释义方法，表达原文中相互合作和支持的意思即可。故改译为China is ready to firmly stand and closely cooperate with each and every island country。

新闻原文：汪洋宣布中方进一步支持太平洋岛国经济社会发展的一系列措施，主要包括：支持岛国重大项目建设，向建交的岛国提供共计10亿美元优惠性质的贷款；设立10亿美元专项贷款，用于岛国基础设施建设；支持岛国开发人力资源，今后4年为岛国提供2000个奖学金名额，帮助培训一批专业技术人员；……

学生译文：Wang Yang announced that China will give its further support to the measures taken by the Pacific island countries to promote its economic and social development. It mainly includes the support for major projects launched in those countries; providing one billion USD preferential loans to whom we have established diplomatic relations with, setting up a one billion USD special-purpose loan to facilitate the construction of infrastructure in the Pacific island countries; the support for the development of human resources in those countries by offering 2000 scholarships in the following four years and helping them to train a number of professionals; ...

翻译评析：译文中几个代词its，it，those，whom指代模糊。外交新闻文本中涉及阐述我国立场和主张的文字时应当力求语义明晰，避免模糊指代造成的误解。因此可以改译为：Wang Yang announced a series of measures China will take to further support the economic and social development of the Pacific island countries, which includes supporting the construction of major projects of the island countries and providing a total of one billion USD in preferential loans to the island countries China has established diplomatic relations with.

在"今后4年为岛国提供2000个奖学金名额"一句中，"提供奖学金名额"与

"帮助培训一批专业技术人员"是递进关系,而非并列关系。译文建议改为offering 2,000 scholarships over the next four years to help Pacific island countries train a batch of professionals。其中,"一批"专业人员翻译成a batch of更准确。

新闻原文:……支持岛国发展医疗卫生事业,继续为岛国援建医疗设施,派遣医疗队,提供医疗器械和药品;支持岛国发展农业生产,加强农林产品加工与贸易合作,办好示范农场等合作项目;支持岛国保护环境和防灾减灾,为岛国援建一批小水电、太阳能、沼气等绿色能源项目。

学生译文:…the support for the development of their medical and health services by continuing to provide assistance to the construction of their medical facilities, sending medical corps, and providing medical apparatus and instruments, and pharmaceuticals; the support for the island countries to develop agricultural production, strengthen cooperation in agricultural and forestry products processing and trade and well carry out cooperative projects such as demonstration farm and others; the support for the island countries to protect environment, prevent and reduce disasters and aid island countries in the construction of a good number of small hydropower stations, solar energy and biogas and other green energy projects.

翻译评析:在"支持岛国发展医疗卫生事业,继续为岛国援建医疗设施,派遣医疗队,提供医疗器械和药品"这句话里出现了几个动词,分析原文不难看出"继续为岛国"后面三个动词"援建""派遣""提供"是并列关系,在翻译的时候,学生没有分析清楚这几个动词之间的逻辑关系,把continuing,sending和providing处理为动名词并列结构,偏离了原文的语义结构。因此,可以改译为supporting the development of the medical and health services in the island countries, by continuing to provide assistance in the construction of the medical facilities, send medical corps and provide medical apparatus, instruments, and pharmaceuticals.

在"支持岛国发展农业生产,加强农林产品加工与贸易合作,办好示范农场等合作项目"一句中,学生按照中文语序把"农林产品加工与贸易合作"译成agricultural and forestry products processing and trade,而实际上原文的意思是农林产品的加工与贸易合作,因此语序应该调整成processing and trade of agricultural and forestry products。"办好……项目"可以译成well conducting …projects。

本段中学生把"支持……"几乎全部处理为the support for the island countries to do的名词结构,而原文中"支持岛国发展……","支持岛国保护……"等主要强调"支持"这一行为举措,译为supporting the island countries in sth.则更简洁明了。最后一句"为岛国援建……"可以处理为"支持岛国……"的并列结构,翻译为providing aid for island countries…。

译文最后当属粗心错误,分析原文"一批小水电、太阳能、沼气等绿色能源项目"不难看出,"一批"实际修饰"绿色能源项目",而不是"小水电",所以可以改译为a batch of small green energy projects such as hydropower stations, solar energy and methane。

C-E TRANSLATION OF DIPLOMATIC NEWS

新闻原文：汪洋强调，应对气候变化、拯救地球家园，是全人类的共同挑战，也是太平洋岛国的重大关切。中方理解各岛国的特殊处境和诉求，愿意与岛国全面加强绿色发展合作，共同提高应对和适应气候变化的能力。

学生译文：Wang Yang stressed that dealing with climate change and saving our home planet is the common challenge to all mankind as well as the major concern of Pacific island countries. China understands the special situation and demands of each island country and is willing to comprehensively strengthen cooperation in green development and improve the ability to deal with and adjust to climate change together with island countries.

翻译评析：译文最后一句介词短语with island countries出现在句尾，究竟是improve the ability的宾语补足语还是strengthen cooperation的宾语补足语，会引起歧义。分析原文不难看出，"和岛国加强合作"是途径，而"共同提高应对和适应气候变化的能力"是目标，因此可以改译为strengthen its cooperation in green development with the island countries in order to jointly improve the ability to deal with and adjust to climate change。

实战练习
Translation Practice

一、请翻译下列外交演讲报道的标题（Translate the following headlines of coverage of diplomatic speeches）

1. 外交部副部长李保东在2016年核安全峰会立陶宛筹备会上的发言
   (http://www.fmprc.gov.cn/mfa_chn/ziliao_611306/zyjh_611308/t1277987.shtml)
2. 李克强出席第八届夏季达沃斯论坛开幕式并发表致辞
   (http://www.fmprc.gov.cn/mfa_chn/zyxw_602251/t1190050.shtml)
3. 王勇国务委员在东盟地区论坛第四次救灾演习开幕式上的讲话
   (http://www.fmprc.gov.cn/mfa_chn/ziliao_611306/zyjh_611308/t1266967.shtml)
4. 外交部副部长李保东在联合国新版中文网站启动仪式上的致辞
   (http://www.fmprc.gov.cn/mfa_chn/ziliao_611306/zyjh_611308/t1253596.shtml)
5. 李克强在第三届中国—中东欧国家经贸论坛上的致辞
   (http://www.fmprc.gov.cn/mfa_chn/ziliao_611306/zyjh_611308/t1103315.shtml)
6. 王毅部长在博鳌亚洲论坛2015年年会"东盟共同体：一体化的新起点"分论坛上的讲话
   (http://www.fmprc.gov.cn/mfa_chn/ziliao_611306/zyjh_611308/t1249578.shtml)
7. 王毅部长在中巴友好交流年巴方启动仪式上的致辞
   (http://www.fmprc.gov.cn/mfa_chn/ziliao_611306/zyjh_611308/t1237475.shtml)
8. 王毅部长在中国—拉共体论坛首届部长级会议上的主旨发言
   (http://www.fmprc.gov.cn/mfa_chn/ziliao_611306/zyjh_611308/t1227808.shtml)

发表外交演讲报道的翻译
Translation for Coverage of Diplomatic Speeches

二、请翻译下列外交演讲报道中的句子（Translate the following sentences in coverage of diplomatic speeches）

1. 我们刚刚步入2015年。拉美和加勒比的朋友们为了推进中拉论坛建设、促进中拉全面合作伙伴关系发展，不远万里来到北京，同我们相聚一堂。我谨代表中拉论坛中方筹备委员会和中国外交部，再次对你们表示热烈欢迎。

    (http://www.fmprc.gov.cn/mfa_chn/ziliao_611306/zyjh_611308/t1227808.shtml)

2. 2008年，我担任国家副主席时首次出访就选择了蒙古国。踏上这块美丽的土地，我深深感到这里是物华天宝的好地方。时隔6年，我再次来到蒙古国，看到这里是一片欣欣向荣的景象，充满生机活力，感到由衷的高兴，我对勤劳勇敢的蒙古国人民取得的发展成就，表示衷心的祝贺！

    (http://www.fmprc.gov.cn/mfa_chn/ziliao_611306/zyjh_611308/t1184896.shtml)

3. 借此机会，我宣布，中国有关机构正式加入经合组织发展中心。明年，中国将举办二十国集团峰会，我们愿与各方共谋发展之策，也欢迎经合组织提供有力支持。中国人历来推崇"知行合一"。让我们携起手来，既做思想者也做行动者，想出更多好主意，拿出更多务实行动，推动共同发展，更好地增进全人类福祉。

    (http://www.fmprc.gov.cn/mfa_chn/ziliao_611306/zyjh_611308/t1278215.shtml)

4. "亲望亲好，邻望邻好。"中国坚持与邻为善、以邻为伴，坚持睦邻、安邻、富邻，践行亲、诚、惠、容理念，努力使自身发展更好惠及亚洲国家。中国将同各国一道，加快推进丝绸之路经济带和21世纪海上丝绸之路建设，尽早启动亚洲基础设施投资银行，更加深入参与区域合作进程，推动亚洲发展和安全相互促进、相得益彰。

    (http://www.fmprc.gov.cn/mfa_chn/ziliao_611306/zyjh_611308/t1158070.shtml)

三、请翻译下面一则外交演讲（Translate the following diplomatic speech）

携手追寻中澳发展梦想并肩实现地区繁荣稳定
——在澳大利亚联邦议会的演讲
中华人民共和国主席 习近平

女士们，先生们，朋友们：

大家好！在这南半球阳光明媚的日子里，有机会来到澳大利亚联邦议会同大家见面，我感到十分荣幸。首先，我谨代表中国政府和人民，并以我个人的名义，向在座各位朋友，并通过你们向全体澳大利亚人民，致以诚挚的问候和良好的祝愿！

我这次来澳大利亚，是应科斯格罗夫总督和阿博特总理的邀请，对澳大利亚进行国事访问，并出席在布里斯班举行的二十国集团领导人第九次峰会。澳大利亚作为东道主，主办了一届富有成果、令人难忘的二十国集团领导人峰会，体现了澳大利亚在国际和地区事务中的重要地位和影响。我对澳方成功办会表示祝贺！

这是我第五次踏上这片古老而又充满活力的澳洲大陆。1988年以来，我访问过除塔斯马尼亚州之外的五个州和两个地区，对澳大利亚有着美好的回忆。长相独特的袋鼠，憨态可掬的考拉，白云朵朵的羊群，独具匠心的悉尼歌剧院，辽阔无垠的旷野，给我留下了深刻印象。所到之处，我都看到了澳大利亚人民对中国人民的深厚情谊。

澳大利亚幅员辽阔，物产丰饶，经济发达，文化多元，风景独特。澳大利亚不仅是个"骑在羊背上的国家"和"坐在矿车上的国家"，更是一个富有活力、开拓创新的国家，产生了许多蜚声世界的科学家，为人类文明进步作出突出贡献。许多同人类生活息息相关的重要发明，比如无线网络、电冰箱、超声波扫描仪等都出自澳大利亚科学家之手。2008年北京奥运会主场馆之一"水立方"国家游泳中心，就是中澳建筑师合作智慧的结晶。

几天前，我们在"水立方"为参加亚太经合组织第二十二次领导人非正式会议的来宾举行了欢迎晚宴，"水立方"的匠心独具、巧妙构思依然让大家赞叹不已。

我对澳大利亚人民的创新精神表示钦佩，衷心祝愿澳大利亚的未来更加美好、人民更加幸福。

(http://www.fmprc.gov.cn/mfa_chn/ziliao_611306/zyjh_611308/t1211901.shtml)

参考译文
Versions for Reference

一、请翻译下列外交演讲报道的标题(Translate the following headlines of coverage of diplomatic speeches)

1. Statement by H.E. Li Baodong Vice Foreign Minister of China at Vilnius Sherpa Meeting of the Nuclear Security Summit 2016
2. Li Keqiang Attends and Addresses Opening Ceremony of the Eighth Summer Davos Forum
3. Remarks by Chinese State Councilor Wang Yong at Opening Ceremony of ARF Disaster Relief Exercise 2015
4. Remarks by Vice Minister of Foreign Affairs Li Baodong at the Joint Launch Event for New Chinese Website of the United Nations
5. Remarks by Premier Li Keqiang of China at Third China-Central and Eastern European Countries Economic and Trade Forum
6. Speech by Foreign Minister Wang Yi at the Session "ASEAN Community: A Major Milestone for Asian Integration" of the Boao Forum for Asia Annual Conference 2015

发表外交演讲报道的翻译
Translation for Coverage of Diplomatic Speeches UNIT 7

7. Remarks by Foreign Minister Wang Yi at the Inauguration of The Year of China-Pakistan Friendly Exchanges
8. Keynote Speech by Foreign Minister Wang Yi at the First Ministerial Meeting of the China-CELAC Forum

二、请翻译下列外交演讲报道中的句子(Translate the following sentences in coverage of diplomatic speeches)

1. A few days into 2015, we are gathering here with Latin American and Caribbean (LAC) friends who have traveled long distances to Beijing for the development of the China-CELAC Forum and the growth of China-LAC partnership of comprehensive cooperation. On behalf of the Forum's preparatory committee on the Chinese side and the Chinese Foreign Ministry, I would like to extend a warm welcome to you all.

2. Mongolia was the first country I visited as Vice President of China in 2008. As soon as I set foot on the beautiful land of Mongolia, I was deeply impressed by its naturally endowed abundance. Six years later, I am here again. What I see is a thriving country, dynamic and full of vitality. With heartfelt joy, I wish to extend our sincere congratulation to you, the brave and hardworking people of Mongolia, on your achievements.

3. Here I wish to announce the formal accession of a Chinese institution to the OECD Development Center. As China will play host to the G20 summit next year, we look forward to discussing with all parties ways to advance development, and the OECD's strong support is more than welcome in this connection. The Chinese culture emphasizes the need to match knowledge with action. Let us think and act together to come up with better ideas and more concrete actions to advance the common development and wellbeing of the entire human race.

4. "Neighbors wish each other well, just like family members do to each other." China always pursues friendship and partnership with its neighbors, and seeks to bring amity, security and common prosperity to its neighborhood. It practices the principles of amity, sincerity, mutual benefit and inclusiveness and works hard to make its development bring more benefits to countries in Asia. China will work with other countries to push forward the building of the Silk Road Economic Belt and 21st-Century Maritime Silk Road, and hopes that the Asian Infrastructure Investment Bank (AIIB) could be launched at an early date. China will get more deeply involved in the regional cooperation process, and play its due part to ensure that development and security in Asia facilitate each other and are mutually reinforcing.

C-E TRANSLATION OF DIPLOMATIC NEWS

三、请翻译下面一则外交演讲（Translate the following diplomatic speech）

Jointly Pursue Dream of Development for China and Australia and Realize Prosperity and Stability in Our Region

Address by H.E. Xi Jinping

President of the People's Republic of China

Ladies and Gentlemen,

Dear Friends,

Good afternoon! I am delighted to have this opportunity to meet you here at the Parliament of Australia on such a sunny day in the southern hemisphere. On behalf of the Chinese government and people and in my own name, I wish to extend warm greetings and best wishes to you and, through you, to all the Australian people.

I am paying a state visit to Australia at the invitation of Governor-General Sir Peter Cosgrove and Prime Minister Tony Abbott, and I have just attended the ninth G20 Summit in Brisbane. Australia has hosted a fruitful and memorable G20 summit, which demonstrates its important status and influence in international and regional affairs. I extend congratulations to Australia on the success of the summit!

This is the fifth time I set foot on this ancient and dynamic continent of Australia. Since 1988, I have visited five states and two territories of Australia except Tasmania. These visits have left a great impression on me, and I still cherish vivid memories of the strange-looking kangaroo, the cute koala bear, flocks of white sheep, the ingenious Sydney Opera House and boundless expanses of the Outback. Everywhere I went, I have personally experienced the goodwill of the Australian people towards the Chinese people.

Australia has a vast territory, rich resources and an advanced economy, and it is renowned for its diverse culture and unique landscape. It is not just a country "on the sheep's back" or a country "sitting on mine carts"; more importantly, Australia is a country of dynamism and innovation. It has produced many world-renowned scientists and made outstanding contribution to the progress of human civilization. Many inventions that are important to our life, such as WiFi technology, refrigerators and ultrasound scanners, were made by Australian scientists. China's National Aquatics Center, known as the "Water Cube" and used as one of the main venues during the 2008 Beijing Olympic Games, was jointly designed by Chinese and Australian architects.

Just several days ago, I hosted a welcoming banquet for the guests attending the 22nd APEC Economic Leaders' Meeting in the "Water Cube" and they were all impressed by its ingenious and creative architecture.

发表外交演讲报道的翻译
Translation for Coverage of Diplomatic Speeches

In this connection, let me express my admiration for the ingenuity of the Australian people and sincerely wish Australia an even better future and its people greater happiness.

单元小结
Summary

本单元主要介绍了外交演讲和外交演讲新闻报道的翻译。演讲新闻主要介绍了新闻标题、导语等翻译，涉及演讲题目、场合、现场气氛等内容；对演讲新闻中具有突出语言特征的长句，从英汉双语对比的层面进行了分析，探讨了翻译方法。外交演讲新闻文本有其固有的编写原则，即对于领导人讲话进行报道时，可以总结其主要观点和主张，但对于措辞本身不可以随意添加、删减或篡改。把握外交演讲新闻文本这一特征，在翻译时也应做到语义信息准确无误，句式结构逻辑清晰。演讲稿案例主要分析了演讲辞常常涉及的内容，如感谢、致敬、提出主张、引经据典等；特别介绍了演讲中外交新词以及成语、谚语的翻译策略。在翻译外交新词时要考虑的政治因素较多，其政治敏感性决定了政治等效是最为重要的翻译原则。译员要熟悉词汇背景和语境，忠实、准确地反映原文的政治思想和政治语境。对于成语、谚语的翻译，多采用直译、释义、简化等方法，演讲的宗旨是传达"中国声音"，拉近彼此距离，对于成语、谚语的翻译，忠实和达意最为关键，这样不仅能够让听众了解本国的经典文化，还能以此拉近与听众的距离，更能展现演讲者的睿智和风采。

参考文献：

杨明星：《中国外交新词对外翻译的原则与策略》，《中国翻译》2014 年第 3 期。

延伸阅读

习近平演讲为何"走心"3个特点打动人

演讲，不仅是一门科学，更是一种艺术。

在重大外交活动中，习近平都会以演讲的方式，传递中国声音，表达中国态度。其演讲特点可亲可敬又沉稳大气，善于打比喻、讲故事，内容"接地气"、风格真性情。

特点一：接地气

一位优秀的演讲者善于拉近与聆听者之间的距离。

习近平的演讲就具有这样的效果。他经常采用比喻和一些极具生活气息的表达，让人们能够听得懂，记得住。这些很"接地气"的大众语言轻松自然、令人耳目一新。

在今年3月27日举行的中法建交50周年纪念大会上，习近平引用拿破仑的话，巧妙地将中国比喻成一头睡醒的狮子。他说，"中国这头狮子已经醒了，但这是一只和平的、可亲的、文明的狮子"。

11月17日，在澳大利亚议会大厦的演讲一开始，习近平就微笑着说，"这是我第五次踏上这片古老而又充满活力的澳洲大陆。1988年以来，我访问过除塔斯马尼亚州之外的五个州和两个地区，对澳大利亚有着美好的回忆。"短短两句生活味十足的话，习近平就拉近了自己与澳洲人民的距离，难怪会被澳大利亚媒体誉为"最了解澳大利亚的中国领导人"。

"也有人说，现在北京的蓝天是APEC蓝，美好而短暂，过了这一阵就没了，我希望并相信通过不懈的努力，APEC蓝能够保持下去。"在前不久刚结束的APEC会议上，习近平的讲话质朴、充满了生活的气息，让人感觉到了另外一种力量。

特点二：讲故事

形成共鸣的故事，往往能够直达听众心灵。

2014年11月17日，在澳大利亚议会大厦的演讲中，习近平提到了一则澳大利亚孩子给他写信的故事。

"来之前不久，我和夫人收到了塔斯马尼亚州斯科奇—欧克伯恩学校16名可爱的小学生的来信，他们在信中描绘了那里的独特物产和美丽风光，特别提到了塔胡恩空中栈道、大峡谷，当然还有'塔斯马尼亚恶魔'，还说如果去大峡谷的话还有可能捡到美丽的孔雀羽毛。这让我充满了好奇。"

"我期待着明天的塔斯马尼亚州之行，期待着同这些孩子见面。"一段展现真情的话语，让人感受到了一个亲切的"习大大"。

特点三：充满自信

2013年3月22日至30日，习近平出访俄罗斯、坦桑尼亚、南非、刚果，并出席在南非德班举行的金砖国家领导人第五次会晤，这也是中共十八大和全国两会后，中国最高领导人首次出访。在莫斯科国际关系学院演讲和在刚果国会演讲时，习近平在媒体的聚光灯下显得温和、放松和自如，演讲中也加进了不少自己当场的思考和发挥，并与听众现场互动。自信从容，习近平展现的新风格，给国际社会留下了深刻的印象。

自信从容是一位出色的演讲者所必备的品质。

这种风格在之后的演讲中俯首可拾。2014年11月9日，习近平在出席APEC工商领导人峰会时表示，"大时代需要大格局，大格局需要大智慧。亚太发展前景取决于今天的决断和行动。我们有责任为本地区人民创造和实现亚太梦想。"

有评论说，习近平的发言自信沉稳，从中我们明显可以感觉到，中国的自信心增强了，在国际上发声的"底气"也更足了。

（根据人民网记者曾伟报道进行整理）

来源：人民网

(http://politics.people.com.cn/n/2014/1118/c1001-26048960.html)

吹风会报道的翻译
Translation for Coverage of Press Briefings

单元简介 Introduction

吹风会（briefing）是用来向记者发布新闻、介绍或解释国家政策、外交事件等重大问题的会议，又称媒体吹风会或新闻吹风会。

外交部门吹风会的具体内容是由外交部有关人士向媒体介绍国家领导人的外事活动，例如进行国事访问、访问国际组织、参加国际重大外事活动等，或者就外事领域的重大活动举行专题吹风会。通过吹风会，政府部门向外界阐述我国对外方针政策、通报我国领导人外事活动以及相关主题消息。读者可以获悉我国重要外交活动信息以及我国政府相关政策和立场。与新闻发布会和记者招待会相比，吹风会会场中采访的气氛比较轻松，答问比较详细。

Translation for Coverage of Press Briefings

吹风会报道翻译范例分析
Sample of Translation for Coverage of Press Briefings

范例一（Sample I）

外交部就习近平主席对巴基斯坦进行国事访问并赴印度尼西亚出席亚非领导人会议和万隆会议60周年纪念活动举行中外媒体吹风会（节本）

2015/04/17

Ministry of Foreign Affairs Holds Briefing for Chinese and Foreign Media on President Xi Jinping's State Visit to Pakistan and Attendance of the Asian-African Summit and Activities Commemorating the 60th Anniversary of the Bandung Conference in Indonesia (Abbreviated Version)

2015/04/17

外交部17日举行中外媒体吹风会，外交部副部长刘振民、部长助理刘建超介绍了习近平主席即将对巴基斯坦进行国事访问并赴印度尼西亚出席亚非领导人会议和万隆会议60周年纪念活动有关情况，并回答了记者提问。

On April 17, 2015, the Ministry of Foreign Affairs held a briefing for Chinese and foreign media, during which Vice Foreign Minister Liu Zhenmin and Assistant Foreign Minister Liu Jianchao briefed on President Xi Jinping's upcoming state visit to Pakistan and attendance of the Asian-African Summit and activities commemorating the 60th anniversary of the Bandung Conference in Indonesia, and answered questions from the journalists.

关于对巴基斯坦进行国事访问，刘建超表示，巴基斯坦是中国的重要邻国和全天候战略合作伙伴。当前，中巴关系保持良好发展势头。两国高层交往密切，各领域互利合作顺利推进，在国际和地区问题上保持密切协调与配合。

As for the state visit of President Xi Jinping to Pakistan, Liu Jianchao pointed out that Pakistan is an important neighbor and all-weather strategic cooperative partner of China. At present, China and Pakistan enjoy a sound development momentum in bilateral relations, close high-level exchanges, smooth advancement of mutually beneficial cooperation in all areas and frequent coordination and cooperation in international and regional affairs.

***

刘建超指出，巴基斯坦是习近平主席今年首次出访的第一站，此访也是中国国家主席9年来首次访巴，是中国最高领导人面向周边的又一重大外交行动，将推动中巴双边关系再上新台阶，具有重大而深远的意义。

Liu Jianchao pointed out that Pakistan is chosen as the first destination of President Xi Jinping's first overseas visit this year. This visit is also the first visit paid by a Chinese President to the country over the nine years and another major diplomatic action of the Chinese top leader toward the neighboring countries, which will promote bilateral relations to a new high and be of vital and far-reaching significance.

***

关于赴印度尼西亚出席亚非领导人会议和万隆会议60周年纪念活动，刘振民表示，为纪念1955年亚非会议（万隆会议）60周年及"亚非新型战略伙伴关系"10周年，印度尼西亚政府将于4月19日至24日在雅加达和万隆两地举办以"加强南南合作，促进世界和平繁荣"为主题的亚非领导人会议和万隆会议60周年纪念活动。

With regard to the attendance of the Asian-African Summit and activities commemorating the 60th anniversary of the Bandung Conference in Indonesia, Liu Zhenmin said that in order to commemorate the Asian-African Conference in 1955 (the Bandung Conference) as well as the 10th anniversary of the establishment of the new type of strategic partnership between Asia and Africa, the Indonesian government will hold the Asian-African Summit under the theme "Strengthening South-South Cooperation to Promote World Peace and Prosperity" and activities commemorating the 60th anniversary of the Bandung Conference in Jakarta and Bandung respectively from April 19 to 24.

***

刘振民指出，万隆会议是历史上首次由亚非国家自发举行的国际会议，具有划时代的意义。会议倡导"团结、友谊、合作"的万隆精神，揭开了发展中国家团结合作争取国家独立和主权、谋求经济发展和社会进步、维护世界和平、推动建立国际政治经济新秩序的历史新篇章。会议在中印缅倡导的和平共处五项原则基础上提出万隆会议十项原则，已成为国际关系中的基本原则。

Liu Zhenmin pointed out that the Bandung Conference, which was the first international conference initiated by Asian and African countries in history, is of epochal significance. The Conference, upholding the Bandung spirit of unity, friendship and cooperation, opened a new historical chapter for developing countries to strive for national independence and sovereignty, seek economic development and social progress, safeguard world peace and push for establishing a new global political and economic order through unity and cooperation. The ten principles proposed at the Conference on the basis of the Five Principle of Peaceful Co-existence jointly advocated by China, India and Myanmar have become basic principles governing international relations.

刘振民表示，当今世界，和平、发展、合作、共赢的时代潮流更加强劲。各国的相互联系、相互依存不断加深，越来越成为我中有你、你中有我的命运共同体。在此背景下，坚持和弘扬和平共处五项原则、万隆会议十项原则以及《联合国宪章》的宗旨和原则，仍然任重而道远。在万隆会议召开60周年之际，亚非国家领导人再次聚首，共同商讨如何更好地继承、弘扬和践行万隆精神具有重要的现实意义。

Liu Zhenmin noted that today's world is witnessing a more vigorous trend of times featuring peace, development, cooperation and win-win results. All countries are now more deeply integrated with and dependent on each other, increasingly becoming a common future community where all of them are interconnected. Against this background, we still have a long way to go in adhering to and carrying forward the Five Principles of Peaceful Co-existence, the ten principles of the Bandung Conference as well as the purposes and principles of the UN Charter. On the occasion of the 60th anniversary of the Bandung Conference, it is of important realistic significance for Asian and African state leaders to once again gather together and discuss how to better inherit, carry forward and practice the Bandung spirit.

刘振民强调，长期以来，中国始终是亚非合作的积极倡导者和推动者。习近平主席此次与会充分显示了中方推动亚非合作、促进亚非国家共同发展的坚定立场。与会期间，习主席将出席亚非领导人会议、万隆会议60周年纪念活动，并在亚非领导人会议上发表讲话，就新形势下弘扬万隆精神、加强亚非合作阐述中方主张和立场。与会期间，习近平主席还将与有关国家领导人举行双边会见，就更好地推动亚非合作等交换意见。

Liu Zhenmin stressed that China has long been an active promoter and advocate of Asia-Africa cooperation. President Xi Jinping's upcoming attendance of the Summit fully embodies China's firm stance in promoting Asia-Africa cooperation and common development of Asian and African countries. During this visit, President Xi Jinping will attend the Asian-African Summit and the commemorations for the 60th anniversary of the Bandung Conference, and deliver a speech at the Summit, expounding China's proposition and stance on carrying forward the Bandung spirit and enhancing Asia-Africa cooperation under the new circumstances. On the sidelines of the Summit, President Xi Jinping will also hold bilateral meetings with leaders of relevant countries to exchange views on better promoting Asia-Africa cooperation and other topics.

新闻背景：2015年4月20日至24日，国家主席习近平对巴基斯坦进行国事访问并赴印度尼西亚出席亚非领导人会议和万隆会议60周年纪念活动。2015年4月17日，外交部就习近平主席此次出访举行中外媒体吹风会，外交部副部长刘振民、部长助理刘建超介绍了有关情况，并阐述了习主席此行的重要意义。范例一为该吹风会报道，原文和译文均略有删节和修改。

原文链接：http://news.xinhuanet.com/2015-04/17/c_1115008632.htm

译文链接：http://au.china-embassy.org/eng/xw/t1256380.htm

外交新闻汉英翻译
C-E TRANSLATION OF DIPLOMATIC NEWS

一、范例一文本结构分析（Text Structure Analysis of Sample I）

范例一是典型的外交吹风会报道的文本形式。外交吹风会报道的标题全面介绍吹风会的主要信息点，包括组织方和具体事件等。如果涉及领导人参加的多场活动，则一一列明。在范例一的标题中，主要信息包括组织方（外交部）、具体事件（习近平主席对巴基斯坦进行国事访问、赴印度尼西亚出席亚非领导人会议和万隆会议60周年纪念活动）等。导语部分介绍了吹风会召开日期、组织方、出席人员、主要内容等信息。正文是外交吹风会报道最重要的部分，由相关人员介绍领导人的外事活动，或者外事领域的重大活动。范例一正文主要介绍习近平主席将对巴基斯坦进行国事访问、赴印度尼西亚出席亚非领导人会议和万隆会议60周年纪念活动的相关情况。外交部相关人士介绍领导人活动时，会简要补充相关背景信息，例如在领导人进行国事访问的吹风会上简要介绍该国与我国的关系（"巴基斯坦是中国的重要邻国和全天候战略合作伙伴"）、两国领导人的互访情况、两国近年来举办过的或者将要举办的活动、访问的意义以及访问预期取得的成果，等等。类似的，在领导人出席重大外事、外交活动时，也会简要介绍该活动的概况以及领导人出席的系列活动、意义，等等。此外，外交吹风会报道文本一般会配发会场照片，采用"图+文"的形式呈现。

二、范例一翻译解析（Translation Analysis of Sample I）

（一）吹风会新闻标题的翻译（Translation of Headlines of Coverage of Press Briefings）

吹风会报道的标题内容涉及吹风会的主办方、事由（或主题）及参与群体。常见结构有以下几种："××（就某事由）举行（中外媒体）吹风会"，"××邀请××举行吹风会"，"××在××举行吹风会"和"××举行（某主题）吹风会"等。如果需要说明吹风会举办的地点，则在标题最后用in引导出表示地点的名词。请看下列吹风会报道标题及其翻译：

外交部就习近平主席出席俄罗斯纪念卫国战争胜利70周年庆典并访问俄罗斯、哈萨克斯坦、白俄罗斯举行中外媒体吹风会

(http://news.xinhuanet.com/world/2015-05/04/c_1115174001.htm)

The Ministry of Foreign Affairs *Holds a Briefing for Chinese and Foreign Media on President Xi Jinping's Attendance of Celebrations Marking 70th Anniversary of Russia's Victory in Great Patriotic War and His Visit to Russia, Kazakhstan and Belarus*

(http://www.fmprc.gov.cn/mfa_eng/zxxx_662805/t1100420.shtml)

外国记者新闻中心邀请李稻葵教授举行中国经济专题吹风会

(http://www.fmprc.gov.cn/web/wjdt_674879/cfhsl_674891/t1269455.shtml)

International Press Center Invites Professor David Daokui Li to Hold a Briefing on

China's Economy

(http://ipc.fmprc.gov.cn/eng/events/t1233764.htm)

全国妇联国际部部长牟虹在2014年APEC领导人会议周新闻中心举行吹风会

(http://ipc.fmprc.gov.cn/chn/hdjc/t1211656.htm)

Director of International Department of All-China Women's Federation (ACWF) Mu Hong Held a Briefing in 2014 APEC Economic Leaders' Week Media Center

(http://ipc.fmprc.gov.cn/eng/events/t1211662.htm)

由以上例子可见，"外交部就……举行（中外媒体）吹风会"可以译为"Ministry of Foreign Affairs Holds Briefing (for Chinese and Foreign Media) on …"；其他外交机构或人士就某事举行媒体吹风会依例翻译为"(Title + Name) Holds Briefing on …"的结构；邀请某人举行吹风会可以译为"… invites/invited … to hold a briefing on/to brief on …"。需要注意的是，我国领导人出访一般会同时访问数个国家或者参加多个外事活动，需将出访的国家及出席的活动名称悉数译出，不可随意删改。

（二）吹风会新闻报道常用表达的翻译（Translation of Frequently Used Expressions in Coverage of Press Briefings）

一般来说，举行吹风会的事由包括介绍领导人出访、重大外事活动、政府政策变动等情况，或邀请专业人士就某个领域（如中国经济局势）进行讲解等。相关新闻报道内容会涉及吹风会举行的时间、地点、事由、举办方、参与者等信息。常用句式有On (date), ... held a briefing on ... for ... 或On (date), ... invited ... to brief on/give a briefing on ... for ...。若提到吹风会的具体内容，可用 ... shared (views on ...) with ... 等来表达。见下列例句所示：

1月21日，外交部外国记者新闻中心邀请经济学家樊纲教授为30余名中外记者进行专题吹风，深入解读2013年中国国民经济运行有关数据，介绍中国经济总体运行态势及发展前景，并就中国经济再平衡、城镇化建设、地方融资平台风险控制等回答记者提问。

(http://ipc.fmprc.gov.cn/chn/hdjc/t1121094.htm)

On January 21, the International Press Center of the Ministry of Foreign Affairs invited Professor Fan Gang *to give a briefing on* the overall development and prospects of Chinese economy *for* more than 30 foreign and domestic journalists. Professor Fan *shared with* the journalists his in-depth readings of China's economic growth data of 2013 released lately by the National Bureau of Statistics and his *view on* the overall economic situation of China and prospects of Chinese economy. He also took questions on rebalance of China's economy, construction of urbanization and risk control of local financing platform.

(http://ipc.fmprc.gov.cn/eng/events/t1124891.htm)

C-E TRANSLATION OF DIPLOMATIC NEWS

如果是有关国家领导人出访的吹风会报道，往往会由外交部相关人员介绍访问的议程和意义。这类吹风会一般较为正式，多由专人主持，可用chair等动词表示。如需提到参会人员，可以说"... attended the briefing"或"(the briefing) was attended by ..."。例如：

2012年3月20日，外交部举行中外媒体吹风会，外交部部长助理马朝旭、亚洲司司长罗照辉分别介绍了胡锦涛主席出席首尔核安全峰会和金砖国家领导人第四次会晤并对柬埔寨进行国事访问的背景情况、主要活动和重要意义，并回答记者提问。外交部新闻司司长秦刚主持吹风会，百余名中外记者出席。

(http://www.fmprc.gov.cn/ce/cggb/chn/xwdt/t915594.htm)

On March 20, 2012, the Ministry of Foreign Affairs held a briefing for Chinese and foreign media. Assistant Foreign Minister Ma Zhaoxu and Director General of the Department of Asian Affairs Luo Zhaohui *introduced the background, main activities and significance of* President Hu Jintao's attendance of the Seoul Nuclear Security Summit and the fourth meeting of BRICS leaders and state visit to Cambodia and took questions of journalists. Director General of the Information Department Qin Gang *chaired the briefing* which was *attended by* nearly 100 Chinese and foreign journalists.

(http://ipc.fmprc.gov.cn/eng/events/t916582.htm)

答记者问是吹风会常见的一个环节，有的吹风会报道会摘录有代表性的问答内容，大部分报道则只以一句话简要说明吹风会上进行了答问环节。常用表达有：

答记者问 take questions from journalists/the press

回答记者提问 answer questions from Chinese/domestic and foreign media

回答外国驻华记者的提问 take questions from foreign resident journalists in China

此外，本篇报道中多处出现了外交术语，其规范的英译文整理如下表：

亚非领导人会议	the Asian-African Summit
万隆会议	the Bandung Conference
全天候战略合作伙伴	all-weather strategic cooperative partner
和平共处五项原则	the Five Principles of Peaceful Co-existence
中巴经济走廊	China-Pakistan Economic Corridor
中巴友好交流年	China-Pakistan Friendly Exchange Year
南南合作	South-South Cooperation
求同存异、协商一致	seek common grounds while shelving differences as well as reach consensus through consultation
《联合国宪章》	the UN Charter

吹风会报道的翻译
Translation for Coverage of Press Briefings — UNIT 8

（三）具体翻译问题解析 (Major Tips on Translation)

1. 词性转换

翻译中经常会遇到需要转换词性的情况，有时是语言之间固有的差异使然，有时则是为了使译文表达更为流畅地道。范例一第一段后半句中，"介绍"一词的宾语很长（"外交部副部长刘振民、部长助理刘建超介绍了习近平主席即将对巴基斯坦进行国事访问并赴印度尼西亚出席亚非领导人会议和万隆会议60周年纪念活动有关情况"），包含完整的主谓结构，但宾语中心词是"有关情况"这一名词短语。根据这一特点，译文将宾语中的"进行国事访问"和"出席"均处理为相应的名词形式（… Vice Foreign Minister Liu Zhenmin and Assistant Foreign Minister Liu Jianchao briefed on President Xi Jinping's upcoming state visit to Pakistan and attendance of the Asian-African Summit and activities commemorating the 60th anniversary of the Bandung Conference in Indonesia …），较长的宾语从而转化为两个并列的名词短语，使句子更加简洁易懂。翻译中遇到类似情况，即句子的某一成分较长时，可以参照此处的方法，即先分析该成分的内在结构，确定核心内容，再做出相应的调整。

2. 逻辑与断句

外交新闻报道多用长句，句子信息量大，层次丰富。翻译时应注意逻辑层次的划分和语句的组织，不可盲目照搬原文断句。范例一中，第一段即导语部分单句成段，包括了两个可独立成句的主谓结构，即"外交部举行吹风会"和"刘振民、刘建超介绍有关情况并答记者问"。译文以非限定性定语从句结构（… during which …）连接这两部分，既体现了前后半句的相对独立性，又突出了两者之间的紧密联系。

第二、三段介绍本次吹风会的事由之一，即习近平主席对巴基斯坦进行国事访问。第二段的一个翻译重点是第四、五句逻辑关系的理解和处理：

当前，中巴关系保持良好发展势头。两国高层交往密切，各领域互利合作顺利推进，在国际和地区问题上保持密切协调与配合。

At present, China and Pakistan enjoy a sound development momentum in bilateral relations, close high-level exchanges, smooth advancement of mutually beneficial cooperation in all areas and frequent coordination and cooperation in international and regional affairs.

按照上述译文，句中的几点信息为并列关系，即"中巴关系保持了良好的发展势头、密切的高层交往、顺利推进的各领域互利合作，以及国际和地区问题上的密切协调与配合"。事实上，这两句还可以作总分关系理解，即"中巴关系保持良好发展势头"，具体表现为"两国高层交往密切，各领域互利合作顺利推进，在国际和地区问题上保持密切协调与配合"。通过简单地添加一个介词，即可实现这种从并列到总分

189

的关系的转换（At present, China and Pakistan enjoy a sound development momentum in bilateral relations, *with* close high-level exchanges, smooth advancement of mutually beneficial cooperation in all areas and frequent coordination and cooperation in international and regional affairs.）。

第三段中，刘振民指出了习近平主席此次出访巴基斯坦的重要意义。这一长句可划分为以下三层：1）此访是习主席2014年首次出访的第一站；2）此访是中国国家领导人维护中巴友好关系和积极进行周边外交的重要举动；3）此访的实际意义。根据这一理解，译文对原句进行了断句（"此访……"处重新起句）和使用定语从句（which will promote ...）的处理，准确呈现了句子的逻辑关系（Liu Jianchao pointed out that Pakistan is chosen as the first destination of President Xi Jinping's first overseas visit this year. This visit is also the first visit paid by a Chinese President to the country over the nine years and another major diplomatic action of the Chinese top leader toward the neighboring countries, which will promote bilateral relations to a new high and be of vital and far-reaching significance.）。

3. 其他翻译问题

第六段翻译的主要难点在于"我中有你、你中有我"这两个四字词和"任重而道远"这一表达。对于前者，译文抛开了词形的限制，将其意译为interconnected，体现出了"彼此紧密联系"这一内在含义。对于"任重而道远"的翻译，译文则选取了"道远"（have a long way to go）这一层意思。由此可见，对于外交新闻文本中出现的文化特色词，要适当脱离语言外壳的限制，确保达意。

第七段即最后一段中出现了两次"与会期间"，但译文的处理完全不同。第一处引导的是习主席此次赴印尼的主要行程，即"出席亚非领导人会议、万隆会议60周年纪念活动，并在亚非领导人会议上发表讲话"，译为during this visit。第二处引导的则是习主席在印尼期间"顺便"进行的其他活动，如双边会见等，由于不是此行的主要活动，译为on the sidelines of the Summit更为准确贴切。

此外，本篇报道中还有一处值得注意的细节。按照中文习惯，国名简称一般取其第一个字。但有时为了避免混淆，会做一些特殊处理，如印度尼西亚写为"印（尼）"，以区别于印度，刚果民主共和国和刚果共和国按照各自首都中译名的第一个字区分，分别写为"刚果（金）"和"刚果（布）"等。本篇第五段出现了"中印缅"这一缩写词。根据背景信息，可知此处的"印"指的是印度而非印尼，切不可想当然地因为万隆会议是在印尼举行而对此处简称的指代对象产生误解。

吹风会报道的翻译
Translation for Coverage of Press Briefings

UNIT 8

范例二（Sample II）

中国中东问题特使吴思科就巴以和伊拉克局势举行中外媒体吹风会
2014/07/28
China's Special Envoy on the Middle East Issue Wu Sike Holds Briefing for Chinese and Foreign Media on Situations in Palestine, Israel and Iraq
2014/07/28

2014年7月28日，中国中东问题特使吴思科在外交部就当前巴以和伊拉克局势举行中外媒体吹风会，近30家中外媒体出席。

On July 28, 2014, China's Special Envoy on the Middle East Issue Wu Sike held a briefing for Chinese and foreign media on the current situations in Palestine, Israel and Iraq at the Foreign Ministry. Nearly thirty Chinese and foreign media were present.

吴思科首先介绍了他近期连续两次出访以色列、巴勒斯坦、伊拉克等8个中东地区国家和阿盟总部情况，阐述了中方原则立场和所作努力。关于巴以冲突，吴思科强调，立即实现停火是当务之急，空袭、地面军事行动、发射火箭弹等都要停；形成斡旋合力是重要保障，敦促有关冲突方尽快积极响应埃及停火倡议和国际社会斡旋努力；恢复并推进和谈是根本出路，呼吁以巴双方克服困难，相向而行，为早日复谈创造有利条件。

Wu Sike first introduced his recent two successive visits to eight Middle East countries such as Israel, Palestine, and Iraq and the Arab League headquarters, and expounded China's principled position and efforts. On the Palestine-Israel conflict, Wu Sike stressed that it is imperative to immediately cease fire, including air strikes, ground military operations and rocket projectile launch. He noted that it is an important safeguard to form mediating forces and urged the parties involved in the conflict to positively respond to the Egyptian ceasefire proposal and the mediation efforts of the international community at an early date. He said that it is the basic way out to resume and promote peace talks, and called for Israel and Palestine to overcome difficulties and meet each other halfway to create favorable conditions for an early resumption of the talks.

关于伊拉克局势，吴思科强调，加快推进政治和解是解决问题的关键；国际社会要在反恐问题上形成共识与合力，摒弃双重标准，并加快推动地区热点问题的政治解决。

On the situation in Iraq, Wu Sike stressed that the key to solving the issue is to accelerate political reconciliation, and that the international community should reach consensus and synergy on the issue of counter-terrorism, abandon double standards, and speed up political settlements to the regional hotspot issues.

吴思科还就巴以最新形势发展、国际斡旋前景、中国调解努力、中伊（拉克）经贸合作等问题回答了中外媒体提问。

Wu Sike also answered questions from Chinese and foreign media on the latest development of the Palestine-Israel situation, prospects of international mediation, China's efforts on mediation, and China-Iraq economic and trade cooperation.

> 新闻背景：由于历史、文化、宗教、经济等各方面的原因，近年来，阿拉伯国家与以色列之间争端不停，冲突不断。中东问题是自第二次世界大战结束以后持续时间最长的一个地区热点问题。中东地区重要的战略地位和战略资源牵动着许多国家的利益。有关耶路撒冷地位、边界、犹太人定居点、难民回归、水资源分配等问题一直是中东问题的核心。我国政府一直愿与国际社会一道，为推动中东和平进程取得新的发展发挥积极、建设性作用。吴思科曾任我国驻沙特阿拉伯大使、驻埃及大使兼驻阿拉伯国家联盟全权代表。2009年3月起任中国中东问题特使后，多次访问中东地区有关国家。
>
> 原文链接：http://ipc.fmprc.gov.cn/chn/hdjc/t1179624.htm
> 译文链接：http://www.fmprc.gov.cn/mfa_eng/wjbxw/t1178877.shtml

一、范例二文本结构分析（Text Structure Analysis of Sample II）

范例二与范例一文本结构完全相同，即由标题、简要说明吹风会基本信息的导语部分和介绍吹风会主要内容的正文部分构成。本篇报道介绍了相关人员（"中国中东问题特使吴思科"）就重要外交事件（"巴以和伊拉克局势"）进行说明的吹风会。与范例一相比，涉及的事由较单一，篇幅也较短。

二、范例二翻译解析（Translation Analysis of Sample II）

1. 简称的翻译

报道标题中出现的"巴以和伊拉克局势"包括了两个"局势"，即"巴以局势"和"伊拉克局势"。其中，"伊拉克局势"指伊拉克国内局势，而"巴以局势"不是指巴勒斯坦和以色列两国各自分别存在的局势，而是双方之间矛盾冲突的紧张局势。因此，除了范例二标题中的译法（Situations in Palestine, Israel and Iraq），还可以译为the Palestine-Israel Situation and the Situation in Iraq。在外交新闻中常会出现类似的简称，如印巴战争（Indo-Pakistan Wars）、朝核问题（DPRK Nuclear Issue）、台海危机（Taiwan Strait Crisis）等，必须弄清楚简写部分所指的具体对象，才能给出准确规范的译文。该范例还出现了国家名的简称可能造成歧义的情况。最后一段中的"中伊经贸合作"之"伊"指的是与本次吹风会有密切关系的伊拉克，因而在括号中注明国名全称，以区别于"伊（朗）"。虽然在英译文中不存在这一问题，但其反映的外交新闻文本细节及其翻译的严谨性是值得译者注意和学习的。

2. 关于参会情况的表述

第一段导语部分用逗号连接了两层意思，分别介绍1）吹风会的时间、地点、事由和2）参会规模。第二层意思相对独立，因而译文在此处重新起句，没有照搬原文一"逗"到底的做法。吹风会报道的导语中，在提及参会人员时，常采用"... held a briefing for..."的句式。但有时需要强调参会规模和人员构成，则另起一句加以说明。常见句式有："... attended the briefing/were present"和"There were ... at the briefing/attending the briefing/participating in the briefing"。请参见下列例句：

10月24日下午，中国人民外交学会会长杨文昌就"中国和平发展与和谐世界"国际研讨会举行中外记者吹风会。来自中央电视台、新华社、人民日报、中央人民广播电台、中国国际广播电台、美国合众国际社、英国全球广播新闻社、日本NHK电视台等约30家中外媒体参加了吹风会。

(http://www.fmprc.gov.cn/web/wjdt_674879/cfhsl_674891/t375408.shtml)

In the afternoon of October 24, Mr. Yang Wenchang, President of the Chinese People's Institute of Foreign Affairs (CPIFA), held a briefing for the journalists from home and abroad, introducing the upcoming international seminar on "China's Peaceful Development and a Harmonious World". About 30 Chinese and foreign media, such as CCTV, Xinhua News Agency, People's Daily, CNR, CRI, UPI, NHK, and Global Radio News, attended the press briefing.

(http://ipc.fmprc.gov.cn/eng/events/t375406.htm)

2017年3月21日，外交部就李克强总理对澳大利亚进行正式访问并举行第五轮中澳总理年度会晤、对新西兰进行正式访问举行中外媒体吹风会，外交部副部长郑泽光介绍有关情况，并回答中外记者提问。郑泽光表示，应澳大利亚总理特恩布尔、新西兰总理英格利希邀请，李克强总理将于3月22日至29日对澳、新两国进行正式访问。这是中国国务院总理时隔11年后再度访问澳、新，具有重要意义。

(http://www.fmprc.gov.cn/web/zyxw/t1447459.shtml)

On March 21, 2017, the Ministry of Foreign Affairs held a briefing for Chinese and foreign media on Premier Li Keqiang's official visit to Australia and attendance at the fifth China-Australia Annual Prime Ministerial Meeting as well as the official visit to New Zealand. Vice Foreign Minister Zheng Zeguang introduced relevant situation and answered questions from Chinese and foreign journalists. Zheng Zeguang said that, at the invitation of Prime Minister Malcolm Turnbull of Australia and Prime Minister Bill English of New Zealand, Premier Li Keqiang will pay official visits to Australia and New Zealand from March 22 to 29. This is the second visit of the Chinese Premier to Australia and New Zealand after 11 years, which is of great significance.

(http://www.fmprc.gov.cn/mfa_eng/zxxx_662805/t1448056.shtml)

3. 汉语四字结构的表述

外交新闻报道中经常用到汉语四字结构，以使表达更简洁、更有文采。这些四字结构有的是对成语、四字格的活用，有的则是把原本不是固定搭配的词语组合在一起。对于第一种情况，要根据四字结构所使用的具体语境来确定语义，灵活处理。范例二第二段最后，吴思科呼吁两个存在冲突和争端的国家"相向而行"，即希望双方能够做出妥协，共同朝着解决争端的方向迈进。译文处理为meet each other half way，很好地传达了这一层意思。对于第二种情况，则要仔细分析词语的构成和修饰关系，不可想当然。比如，第二段中，吴思科介绍了他出访相关中东国家和组织的情况，并阐述了中方立场。要注意，第一句中的"原则立场"不是"原则"（principle）和"立场"（position）这两个名词的并列，而是指"原则性立场"（principled position）。请注意观察下例中的四字结构及其译文：

马朝旭强调，中国是金砖国家合作的积极参与者，始终把同其他金砖国家的合作作为外交政策的重点之一。2011年3月，中国在海南三亚成功举办金砖国家领导人第三次会晤，会议通过的《三亚宣言》为金砖国家进一步拓展和深化合作奠定了良好基础。此次会晤期间，中方愿同各成员国共同努力，本着<u>同舟共济</u>、<u>互利共赢</u>的精神，加强在国际经济、金融、贸易、发展等领域的对话与合作，以<u>循序渐进</u>、<u>积极务实</u>的方式推进各领域合作，就共同关心的全球性问题沟通协调，深化金砖国家共同发展的伙伴关系。

(http://politics.people.com.cn/GB/1027/17474411.html)

He emphasized that China is an active participant in the cooperation of BRICS countries and always takes the cooperation with other BRICS countries as one of its top priorities of diplomatic policy. In March 2011, China successfully held the third meeting of BRICS leaders in Sanya, Hainan. *The Sanya Declaration* adopted at the meeting laid a solid foundation for BRICS countries to further expand and deepen cooperation. During the fourth meeting, China will make joint efforts with other participating countries to strengthen dialogue and cooperation in the international economic, financial, trade and development areas in the spirit of mutual help and mutual benefit, push forward cooperation in all fields step by step and in a pragmatic manner, communicate and coordinate on the global issues of common concern and deepen the partnership among

吹风会报道的翻译
Translation for Coverage of Press Briefings

BRICS countries for common development.

(http://ipc.fmprc.gov.cn/eng/events/t916582.htm)

此外，范例二中出现的外交新闻常用表达及其翻译见下表总结：

阿盟（阿拉伯国家联盟）	the Arab League (the League of Arab States)
巴以冲突	the Palestine-Israel conflict
停火	cease fire
空袭	air strike
地面军事行动	ground military operations
发射火箭弹	rocket projectile launch
政治和解	political reconciliation

学生译作讲评
Analysis of Students' Translation Practice

原文链接：http://news.xinhuanet.com/politics/2014-08/18/c_1112126824.htm

新闻原文：外交部就习近平对蒙古国进行国事访问举行中外媒体吹风会

学生译文：Foreign Ministry Holds a Briefing for Chinese and Foreign Media on Xi Jinping's State Visit to Mongolia

翻译评析：学生译文基本符合吹风会报道标题的常见形式，包含吹风会的主办方、参加对象和事由等信息。有一处细节需要注意：在标题中，为表达简洁，briefing一词前面有时不加不定冠词，即Foreign Ministry Holds Briefing for … on …。

新闻原文：2014年8月18日，外交部举行中外媒体吹风会，外交部部长助理刘建超介绍了习近平主席对蒙古国进行国事访问有关情况。

学生译文：On August 18, 2014, on a Foreign Ministry briefing for Chinese and foreign media, Assistant Minister of Foreign Affairs Liu Jianchao gave an introduction to President Xi Jinping's state visit to Mongolia.

翻译评析：首先，学生译作的表达不符合惯例。一般来说，"某某就某事举行吹风会"多译为sb. holds a briefing for … on… 的结构，而不能将吹风会放在作状语的介词短语中。其次，鉴于外交翻译对忠实度的要求较高，"介绍…有关情况"（introduce relevant information）不可以简化为"介绍"（give an introduction to）。

新闻原文：刘建超说，中蒙互为陆地边界线最长的邻国。蒙古国是最早同新中国建交的国家之一。建交65周年来，友好与合作始终是两国关系的主流。特别是在过去20年来，在《中蒙友好合作关系条约》精神指引下，中蒙关系一步一个台阶，不断取得新进展。

学生译文：Liu Jianchao said that China and Mongolia are neighboring countries, sharing the longest land border line. Mongolia is among the first to establish diplomatic relations with China. In the 65 years since the establishment of diplomatic relations, friendliness and cooperation have remained the mainstream. Particularly in the past 20 years, guided by the Treaty on Friendship and Cooperation between China and Mongolia, China-Mongolia relations made progress constantly and solidly.

翻译评析：本段中，中蒙关系"一步一个台阶，不断取得新进展"一句透露了有关中蒙两国关系进展的两点重要信息：（1）循序渐进；（2）不断发展。翻译时不可遗漏其中任何一点。学生译文选用constantly和solidly两个词均为"连续地、不间断地"之意，即只取了上述第二点信息，而没有将第一点体现出来。可改译为：... the China-Mongolia relations have made steady and constant progress。此外，学生译文对"《中蒙友好合作关系条约》"（the Treaty on Friendship and Cooperation between China and Mongolia）的译法不准确，应译为China-Mongolia Friendship and Cooperation Treaty。

新闻原文：中国政府高度重视中蒙关系，将发展对蒙关系作为中国周边外交政策的优先方向。当前，中蒙关系发展顺利，两国高层往来频繁，政治互信不断加深，经贸务实合作稳步推进，人文等各领域交流持续扩大。中国连续多年保持蒙最大贸易伙伴和投资来源国地位。

学生译文：Chinese government highly values China-Mongolia relations and places the development of the relations with Mongolia at priority in its foreign policy with the neighboring countries. Currently, China-Mongolia relations have been developing smoothly. The two countries have enjoyed frequent high-level exchanges, constantly deepening political mutual trust, steady progress in pragmatic cooperation of economy and trade, and continuously expanding exchanges in fields such as people-to-people and cultural exchanges. China has been the biggest trading partner and investor for Mongolia for consecutive years.

翻译评析：本段翻译的一个重点是第二句的逻辑关系。本句采取总分结构，即"中蒙关系发展顺利"的具体表现是"两国高层往来频繁，政治互信不断加深，经贸务实合作稳步推进，人文等各领域交流持续扩大"。学生译文将"总"和"分"的部分拆分为两个呈现并列关系的句子，不利于体现两者之间的逻辑关系。可将总说的内容处理为主句，分说的四点内容译为名词短语，并通过with连接，更好地突出这一逻辑关系，即：Currently, the China-Mongolia relations have been developing smoothly with frequent high-level exchanges between the two countries, constantly deepening political mutual trust, steady progress in practical cooperation in economy and trade, and continuously expanding exchanges in fields such as people-to-people and cultural engagement。最后一句提到，中国是蒙古最大的"投资来源国"（investment source），简单处理为investor，意思就变成了"中国是蒙古最大的投资者/方"，与原意不符。另外，学生译文给出的"周边外交政策"（foreign policy with the neighboring countries）译法不准确，应为neighborhood diplomacy。

新闻原文：刘建超说，此访是习近平主席就任国家主席后首次访问蒙古国，也是中

吹风会报道的翻译
Translation for Coverage of Press Briefings

国国家主席时隔11年再次访蒙,对中蒙关系发展意义重大。双方高度重视此次访问,做了大量精心准备。访问期间,习近平主席将同额勒贝格道尔吉总统举行会谈,签署并发表中蒙重要政治文件,共同见证一系列双边合作文件的签署,涵盖政治、经贸、金融、人文等领域。

学生译文: Liu Jianchao said, it's the first time for President Xi Jinping to visit Mongolia after taking office, and also the second visit to Mongolia by Chinese president after 11 years, which is of great significance for the development of the China-Mongolia relations. Both sides attach great importance to this visit and have made careful preparations. During the visit, President Xi Jinping will hold talks with President Tsakhiagiin Elbegdorj of Mongolia, sign and publish major political documents between the two countries, and jointly witness the signature of a series of bilateral cooperation documents covering such fields as politics, economy and trade, finance and culture.

翻译评析: 本段提到,中蒙两国高度重视此次访问,并为此做了"大量精心准备"。加粗显示的两个修饰词缺一不可,不能随意删减。可将学生译文中的made careful preparations改译为made plenty of careful preparations。

新闻原文: 习近平主席还将会见蒙古国国家大呼拉尔主席恩赫包勒德、总理阿勒坦呼亚格,在蒙古国国家大呼拉尔发表演讲,并出席经贸活动等。习近平主席将同蒙古国领导人全面总结和梳理中蒙关系发展基本经验和重要成就,为两国关系未来发展作出战略规划,明确今后一个时期中蒙关系的发展方向,使中蒙成为可以相互信任和负责任的好邻居、好伙伴、好朋友。

学生译文: President Xi Jinping will also meet with Chairman of the State Great Hural of Mongolia Zandaakhuu Enkhbold and Prime Minister Norovyn Altankhuyag, address the State Great Hural of Mongolia, and attend some economic and trade activities. President Xi Jinping will, together with the leaders of Mongolia, sum up and tease out the basic experience and significant achievements in the development of China-Mongolia relations in a comprehensive way, make strategic arrangements for the future development of the two countries' relations, clarify the direction of development for China-Mongolia relations in the near future, so that China and Mongolia will become mutually trustful and responsible good neighbors, partners and friends.

翻译评析: 在描述对两国关系未来的期望时,报道一连用了三个"好"字("好邻居、好伙伴、好朋友"),体现了对两国关系的重视和高度评价。学生译文只保留了第一处,看似更加简洁,但出于外交翻译严谨性的考虑,这三个"好"字必须逐一译出,一个都不能少:... to make China and Mongolia mutually trustworthy and responsible good neighbors, good partners and good friends。

新闻原文: 双方将进一步明确矿产资源开发、基础设施建设、金融合作"三位一体,统筹推进"的经贸合作思路,以互联互通和矿能大项目合作为优先方向,推动两国

C-E TRANSLATION OF DIPLOMATIC NEWS

务实合作取得新突破。双方将启动一批大的人文交流计划，扩大两国人员往来，进一步增进彼此了解和友好感情。双方还将就加强在联合国、上海合作组织、亚洲相互协作与信任措施会议的合作，共同推进丝绸之路经济带和亚洲基础设施投资银行建设交换意见。

学生译文：The two sides will further clarify the approach of economic and trade cooperation, namely the "trinity" of cooperation covering exploitation of mineral resources, construction of infrastructure, and financial cooperation in a balanced manner, give priority to interconnection, interworking and cooperation in major projects of mineral energy, and thus facilitate the two countries to make new breakthroughs in practical cooperation. The two sides will launch a batch of major cultural and people-to-people exchange plans, and expand personnel exchanges between the countries to further enhance mutual understandings and friendly relationship. The two sides will also exchange views on strengthening cooperation in the United Nations, the Shanghai Cooperation Organization (SCO), and the Conference on Interaction and Confidence-Building Measures in Asia (CICA), and jointly advancing the Silk Road Economic Belt and the building of the Asian Infrastructure Investment Bank (AIIB).

翻译评析：学生译文中对四字格结构"三位一体，统筹推进"的理解和表达值得注意。所谓"三位一体"，是指双方在三大领域（"矿产资源开发、基础设施建设、金融"）的合作要共同发展；"统筹推进"则强调三者要协调、平衡地发展。此处学生译文做得较好，用trinity一词来表达"三位一体"，又由于这个词在英文中是有宗教含义的（指圣父、圣灵、圣子三位一体），给它加上双引号，表示此处用的是该词的引申义，而非本义。此外，段落最后出现了多个国际组织和国际合作项目的名称。译文均给出了准确的全译，还在括号里提供了缩写形式，方便下文再次出现时指称，是比较常见的规范做法。

新闻原文：刘建超表示，相信在双方共同努力下，习近平主席此访必将全面提升中蒙关系水平，有力推动两国互利合作和友好交流，为中蒙各自发展提供更大助力，为促进地区和平与繁荣作出更大贡献。

学生译文：Liu Jianchao said that, with joint efforts of both countries, President Xi Jinping's visit will certainly raise the level of China-Mongolia relations in an all-round manner, and vigorously push forward mutual beneficial cooperation and friendly exchanges so as to provide greater help to the respective development of China and Mongolia, and make greater contributions to promoting regional peace and prosperity.

翻译评析："互利合作"这一表述中，"互"（"互相地"）修饰"利"（"有好处的"），而不是两个字分别修饰"合作"（cooperation）。因此，应表达为mutually beneficial cooperation，而不是译文中的mutual beneficial cooperation。学生译文还存在对原文用词过于亦步亦趋、不够灵活的情况。如本段中，"为促进地区和平与繁荣作出更大贡献"译为make greater contributions to promoting regional peace and prosperity。事实上，动名词promoting（"促进"）可有可无，去掉后完全不影响原意的表达。

除上述问题外，学生译文有多处选词不够正式、表达不够准确的问题。下表列出了这些不规范的翻译，并提供了建议译文：

原文	原译文	建议译文
发表（政治文件）	publish	release
签署	signature	signing
基本（经验）	basic	fundamental
明确……基本方向	clarify the direction of ...	chart the course for ...
今后一个时期	In the near future	In the next period
互联互通	interconnection, interworking	connectivity

实战练习
Translation Practice

一、请翻译下列吹风会的标题（Translate the following headlines of coverage of press briefings）

1. 外交部就习近平主席出席第三次核安全峰会并访问荷兰、法国、德国、比利时和联合国教科文组织总部、欧盟总部举行中外媒体吹风会

   (http://news.xinhuanet.com/world/2014-03/17/c_119810118.htm)

2. 驻比利时大使廖力强就习近平主席访比举行中比媒体吹风会

   (http://www.fmprc.gov.cn/ce/cebel/chn/dsxx/jgsz/zzxwc/t1139912.htm)

3. 外交部就李克强总理赴英国举行中英总理年度会晤并访问英国、希腊举行中外媒体吹风会

   (http://news.xinhuanet.com/politics/2014-06/12/c_1111119863.htm)

4. 外交部就习近平主席出席金砖国家领导人第六次会晤，访问巴西、阿根廷、委内瑞拉、古巴并出席中拉领导人会晤举行中外媒体吹风会

   (http://news.xinhuanet.com/world/2014-07/07/c_1111497993.htm)

5. 外交部就习近平主席出席上海合作组织成员国元首理事会第十四次会议并对塔吉克斯坦、马尔代夫、斯里兰卡、印度进行国事访问举行中外媒体吹风会

   (http://www.fmprc.gov.cn/ce/cein/chn/ssygd/xjp/t1189417.htm)

6. 外交部举办第六届"大爱无国界"国际义卖活动吹风会

   (http://news.xinmin.cn/domestic/2014/10/10/25605938.html)

7. 外交部就李克强总理出席东亚合作领导人系列会议并访问缅甸举行中外媒体吹风会

   (http://news.xinhuanet.com/politics/2014-11/06/c_1113150156.htm)

8. 外交部就李克强总理访问哈萨克斯坦并举行中哈总理第二次定期会晤、出席上海合作组织成员国政府首脑理事会第十三次会议、出席第三次中国—中东欧国家领

导人会晤并访问塞尔维亚、出席大湄公河次区域经济合作第五次领导人会议举行中外媒体吹风会

(http://www.fmprc.gov.cn/ce/cgmu/chn/gnxw/t1218739.htm)

二、请翻译下列吹风会报道中的句子（Translate the following sentences in a report on a press briefing）

1. 2014年3月17日，外交部举行中外媒体吹风会，外交部副部长李保东、王超分别介绍了习近平主席即将出席第三次核安全峰会，对荷兰、法国、德国、比利时进行国事访问，并访问联合国教科文组织总部、欧盟总部有关情况，并回答了记者提问。

2. 李保东介绍说，核安全问题关系到核能的科学利用和发展，关系到各国经济社会可持续发展和公众安全，关系到国际和平与安宁。

3. 此次核安全峰会以"加强核安全、防范核恐怖主义"为主题，53国领导人或代表，以及国际组织负责人将应邀与会。峰会活动内容丰富，形式多样，包括开、闭幕式、四次全体会议、互动式专题讨论等，将发表公报作为会议成果。

4. 李保东强调，习近平主席出席核安全峰会是新形势下中国在国际安全领域采取的重要外交行动。

5. 习近平主席将提出中国的"核安全观"，介绍中国在加强核安全方面采取的措施和取得的成就，推动国际合作。

6. 中方对此次峰会有两大期待，一是希望此次峰会能够承前启后，巩固前两届峰会成果，凝聚新共识；二是希望进一步推进各国合作，提高全球核材料和核设施安全水平，推动核能合理开发利用。

7. 王超指出，中国和欧洲是维护世界和平的两大力量，促进共同发展的两大市场，推动人类进步的两大文明。

8. 当前，中欧关系整体势头良好，欧盟连续10年保持中国第一大贸易伙伴地位。中欧都处在改革和发展关键阶段，中欧关系面临新的历史机遇。

9. 习近平主席此访是中国国家元首首访欧盟总部，将为中欧关系"定方向"，推动中欧关系朝着成熟稳定、互利共赢、包容互鉴方向发展。

10. 王超强调，习近平主席此访必将全面提升中国同往访四国和中欧关系水平，全方位推进中欧合作，成为中欧关系史上新的重要里程碑。

(http://www.fmprc.gov.cn/ce/cedk/chn/zgwj/t1138088.htm)

三、请翻译下面一则吹风会报道（Translate the following report on a press briefing）

外交部就二十国集团杭州峰会举行中外媒体吹风会
2016/05/27

2016年5月26日，外交部举行中外媒体吹风会，外交部长王毅介绍二十国集团杭州峰会有关情况，并回答了记者提问。

王毅表示，明天是二十国集团杭州峰会倒计时100天。9月4日至5日，习近平主席将与二十国集团成员、嘉宾国领导人及国际组织负责人齐聚杭州，共商世界经济合作大计，共襄全球发展盛举。二十国集团峰会迄今已举行过十次。今年，主席国的接力棒传到了中国手中。当前，世界经济正处于重要的转换期，既有机遇，更有挑战。国际社会对今年的二十国集团充满期待，对杭州峰会取得成果，让世界经济重焕生机充满期待。作为主席国，我们深感重任在肩。我们希望通过主办杭州峰会，聚焦世界经济面临的核心挑战和突出问题，与各方一道，寻找共同方案，贡献中国智慧。治标以求眼下稳增长，治本以谋长远添动力，推动二十国集团从危机应对机制向长效治理机制转型，引领世界经济增长和国际经济合作方向。

王毅表示，去年安塔利亚峰会上，习近平主席介绍了杭州峰会的主题、重点议题和中方办会总体设想。中方把"构建创新、活力、联动、包容的世界经济"作为峰会主题，并在议题上设置了"创新增长方式"，"更高效全球经济金融治理"，"强劲的国际贸易和投资"，"包容和联动式发展"四大板块。中方设置的主题议题得到各成员高度认同与支持。大家普遍认为，中方设想体现了长期性和战略性，也展现了宽广视野和雄心水平。

王毅介绍说，二十国集团活动纵贯全年，杭州峰会集其大成。全年将在中国20个城市举办66场各类会议，参与人数将达数万人次。二十国集团不仅属于20国，还属于全世界；关注的不仅是自身福祉，更是全人类的共同发展。自接任主席国到今天，二十国集团中国年已经过半，进展显著。中国已经做好准备，杭州已经做好准备，期待着各国贵宾的到来。接下来的100天，峰会筹备将进入冲刺阶段。我们还将举行多次协调人会议、财金渠道会议、专业部长会和各类配套活动，扩大共识、固化成果。

王毅表示，中方在办会过程中，始终坚持问题导向。针对各国政策出现的分化，我们将推动加大宏观政策协调力度，避免负面外溢效应。针对新旧动力转换青黄不接，我们将推动从创新和改革中挖掘新动力，实现强劲、可持续、平衡增长。针对世界经济中的风险和不确定因素，我们将推动完善全球经济治理，维护国际金融稳定。针对贸易投资低迷和保护主义抬头，我们将推动重振两大引擎，构建开放型世界经济。针对发展鸿沟仍未消除，我们将推动二十国集团率先行动，引领全球可持续发展合作。

王毅指出，为了实现上述目标，我们正在同各方一道，力争打造杭州峰会十大成果。一是制定创新增长蓝图。二是制定落实2030年可持续发展议程行动计划。三是制定结构性改革优先领域、指导原则和指标体系。四是制定全球贸易增长战略。五是制定全球投资政策指导原则。六是深化国际金融架构改革。七是创立三位一体的反腐败合作。八是发起支持非洲和最不发达国家工业化合作倡议。九是制定创业行动计划。十是推动气候变化《巴黎协定》尽早生效。我们期待杭州峰会能够合力为世界经济构筑牢固防线，共同推动世界经济增长，促进国际经济合作，加强全球经济治理。

王毅指出，除了上述成果，杭州峰会还有两大看点。一是丰富多彩的特色活动。我们安排迄今规模最大的工商峰会与领导人峰会背靠背举行，届时习近平主席将出席并发表主旨演讲。二十国集团领导人峰会前，将举行金砖国家领导人非正式会晤。二十国集团领导人峰会将于4日下午开幕，5日下午结束。习近平主席将主持会议。峰会后，习近平主席还将举行中外记者会，介绍峰会成果。二是开放包容的办会风格。中方始终重视听取各方意见，尊重不同声音。中方同二十国集团成员、嘉宾国、国际组织保持着密切交流互动，中方还将通过主办大型配套活动，广泛听取社会各界声音，打造最广泛共识。中方主动积极地走出去，全方位、多层次地开展二十国集团外围对话。我们走进联合国大会，走进77国集团，走进非盟总部，走进最不发达国家，介绍峰会情况，倾听各方诉求。对话活动覆盖所有联合国成员，尤其是130多个发展中国家。

王毅表示，最后的筹备工作最为关键重要，更需严谨务实。峰会的成功离不开各方的大力支持与配合。我们将继续秉持开放、包容、透明风格，同各方加强沟通协调，确保峰会取得圆满成功，实现二十国集团成员共赢，推动世界经济向着强劲、可持续、平衡增长目标迈出新的步伐。我们对此充满信心。杭州峰会的画卷正徐徐展开，让我们相约九月，共同期待！

(http://www.g20.org/dtxw/201605/t20160527_2286.html)

参考译文
Versions for Reference

一、请翻译下列吹风会报道的标题（Translate the following headlines of reports on press briefings）

1. Ministry of Foreign Affairs Holds Briefing for Chinese and Foreign Media on President Xi Jinping's Attendance at the Third Nuclear Security Summit and Visits to the Netherlands, France, Germany, Belgium, UNESCO Headquarters and EU Headquarters

2. Ambassador to Belgium Liao Liqiang Holds Briefings for Chinese and Belgian Media on President Xi Jinping's Visit to Belgium

3. Ministry of Foreign Affairs Holds Briefing for Chinese and Foreign Media on Premier Li Keqiang's Attendance at Annual China-UK Prime Ministers' Meeting in UK and Visits to UK and Greece
4. Ministry of Foreign Affairs Holds Briefing for Chinese and Foreign Media on President Xi Jinping's Attendance at Sixth BRICS Summit, Visits to Brazil, Argentina, Venezuela and Cuba, and Attendance at China-Latin America and the Caribbean Summit
5. The Ministry of Foreign Affairs Holds Briefing for Chinese and Foreign Media on President Xi Jinping's Attendance of the 14th Meeting of the Council of Heads of State of the Shanghai Cooperation Organization and His State Visits to Tajikistan, Maldives, Sri Lanka and India
6. Foreign Ministry Holds Briefing on the Sixth International Charity Sale "Love Knows No Borders"
7. The Ministry of Foreign Affairs Holds Briefing for Chinese and Foreign Media on Premier Li Keqiang's Attendance of East Asian Leaders' Meetings on Cooperation and His Visit to Myanmar
8. Ministry of Foreign Affairs Holds Briefing for Chinese and Foreign Media on Premier Li Keqiang's Visit to Kazakhstan and Holding of Second Regular Meeting with Prime Minister of Kazakhstan, Attendance at 13th Meeting of the Council of Heads of Government of the SCO Member States, Attendance at Third Meeting of Heads of Government of China and CEEC and Visit to Serbia, and Attendance at Fifth Summit of the Greater Mekong Subregion Economic Cooperation Program

二、请翻译下列吹风会报道中的句子（Translate the following sentences in a report on a press briefing）

1. On March 17, 2014, the Ministry of Foreign Affairs held a briefing for Chinese and foreign media. Vice Foreign Ministers Li Baodong and Wang Chao respectively introduced relevant information on President Xi Jinping's upcoming attendance at the third Nuclear Security Summit, state visits to the Netherlands, France, Germany and Belgium, and visits to the UNESCO Headquarters and the EU Headquarters, and answered questions from the journalists.
2. Li Baodong noted that the nuclear security issue concerns the scientific utilization and development of the nuclear energy, the sustainable development of economy and society and public safety of all countries, and the international peace and tranquility.
3. This year's Nuclear Security Summit will be themed "strengthen nuclear security, prevent nuclear terrorism", and leaders or representatives from 53 countries and the heads of the international organizations will attend the Summit upon invitation.

The Summit will be rich in content and forms, including the opening and closing ceremonies, four plenary meetings, interactive themed discussions and others. A communiqué will be issued as the outcome of the Summit.

4. Li Baodong stressed that President Xi Jinping's attendance at the Nuclear Security Summit will be an important diplomatic action taken by China in the field of international security under new circumstances.

5. President Xi Jinping will put forward China's "Approach to Nuclear Security", and introduce measures taken and achievements made by China in promoting nuclear security, so as to promote international cooperation.

6. China has two expectations for this Summit. First, China hopes the Summit can inherit the past, break new ground for the future, consolidate the achievements made through the last two summits and pool new consensuses. Second, China hopes the Summit can further promote cooperation among all countries, improve the security level of nuclear materials and facilities around the world, and push forward the reasonable development and utilization of nuclear power.

7. Wang Chao pointed out that, China and Europe are two major forces safeguarding world peace, two major markets promoting common development and two great civilizations pushing forward progress of the mankind.

8. Currently, the China-EU relations enjoy a sound overall momentum, and the EU has maintained its position as China's largest trading partner for ten successive years. Both China and the EU are at a crucial stage of reform and development, which brings new historical opportunities to the China-EU relations.

9. President Xi Jinping's visit will be the first time for the Chinese head of state to visit the EU Headquarters, which will "chart the course" for the China-EU relations and promote the China-EU relations towards a direction that is mature, stable, mutually beneficial, win-win, inclusive and of mutual learning.

10. Wang Chao stressed that, President Xi Jinping's visits will comprehensively upgrade China's relations with the four destination countries and the China-EU relations, promote China-EU cooperation in all fields, and become a new important milestone in the history of the China-EU relations.

三、请翻译下面一则吹风会报道（Translate the following report on a press briefing）

Ministry of Foreign Affairs Holds Briefing for Chinese and Foreign Journalists on G20 Hangzhou Summit

On May 26, 2016, the Ministry of Foreign Affairs held a briefing for Chinese and foreign journalists. Foreign Minister Wang Yi introduced the situation about the G20 Hangzhou Summit and answered questions from journalists.

Wang Yi stated that tomorrow will be the 100-day countdown to the G20 Hangzhou Summit. From September 4 to September 5, President Xi Jinping will join leaders of G20 members and guest countries as well as heads of the international organizations in Hangzhou to discuss world economy cooperation and participate in this grand event of global development. The G20 Summit has been held ten times so far. This year, the baton of the host state has been passed to China. Currently, the world economy is in the midst of important transformation with both opportunities and challenges. The international community is looking forward to this year's G20 Summit, and expects the G20 Hangzhou Summit to deliver results and to bring the world economy to life. As the host state, we are keenly aware of great responsibilities on our shoulders. We hope that through hosting G20 Hangzhou Summit, we can focus on the core challenges and prominent problems encountered by the world economy, work with all parties to seek for common solutions and contribute China's wisdom to this cause. We expect that we can offer temporary solutions to stabilize the economic growth at present as well as fundamental solutions to inject new impetus into the economy in the long term, so as to push the G20 Summit to transfer from a crisis responding mechanism to a long-term governance mechanism, lead world economic growth and guide the direction of international economic cooperation.

Wang Yi expressed that at the Antalya Summit last year, President Xi Jinping introduced the theme, key topics and China's overall hosting plan of the G20 Hangzhou Summit. China adopts "Toward an Innovative, Invigorated, Interconnected and Inclusive World Economy" as the theme of the summit, and sets up four main modules, namely "breaking a new path for growth", "more effective and efficient global economic and financial governance", "robust international trade and investment", and "inclusive and interconnected development". The theme and topics proposed by China are highly recognized and supported by all members. It is widely considered that China's ideas not only show a long-term and strategic vision, but also demonstrate broad horizon and ambition level.

Wang Yi introduced that G20 events will continue throughout the whole year of 2016, with Hangzhou Summit being the most important one. 2016 will see 66 meetings of various kinds held in 20 cities of China, with the number of attendees up to tens of thousands. The G20 not only belongs to its member countries but also belongs to the world, and it focuses not only on the wellbeing of its own but also the common development of all human beings. So far, China is halfway through its term since assuming the presidency of the G20, and it has achieved remarkable achievements. China, as well as the city of Hangzhou, is ready for all distinguished guests from different countries to come. The following 100 days will witness the final spurt of the preparation of the Hangzhou Summit. China will also hold several Sherpa Meetings, meetings on financial track, ministerial meetings and various supporting activities, in a bid to expand consensus and consolidate achievements.

Wang Yi said that China will stick to the problem-oriented principle in the Summit. In dealing with the differentiation of policies of different countries, we will push the increase of macro policies coordination in order to avoid the negative spillover effects. As for the temporary shortage of impetus during the transition period, we will advocate exploring new driving forces from innovation and reforms in order to achieve a strong, sustainable and balanced growth. We will facilitate and improve global economic governance and maintain international financial stability to solve risks and uncertainties in the global economy. Facing the downturn of trade and investment and the rise of protectionism, we will advance the revival of the two major engines and build an open global economy. China will promote the G20 to take the lead in pursuing cooperation for sustainable development throughout the world in a bid to bridge the development gap.

Wang Yi pointed out that in order to achieve the above goals, we are working together with other parties to strive to deliver ten results from the Hangzhou Summit. The first is to develop a blueprint of innovative growth. The second is to formulate action plans for the implementation of the 2030 Agenda for Sustainable Development. The third is to identify priority areas, guiding principles and index system for the structural reform. The fourth is to draft strategies for global trade growth. The fifth is to set out guiding principles for global investment policy. The sixth is to deepen the reform of international financial architecture. The seventh is to establish the three-in-one anti-corruption cooperation. The eighth is to launch a cooperative initiative to support the industrialization of African countries and the least developed countries. The ninth is to draw up entrepreneurship action plans. The tenth is to promote the early entry into force of the Paris Agreement on climate change. We look forward that the Hangzhou Summit, with concerted efforts of all parties, can build a solid defense line for the world economy, jointly boost world economic growth, promote international economic cooperation and strengthen global economic governance.

Wang Yi pointed out that in addition to the results above, there are also two highlights can be expected in Hangzhou Summit. The first is the diverse and colorful special events. We have arranged the largest ever business summit to be simultaneously held with the leaders' summit. President Xi Jinping will attend the summit and deliver a keynote speech. Before the G20 Leaders' Summit, an informal meeting of BRICS leaders will be held. The G20 Leaders' Summit will kick off on the afternoon of September 4 and close on the afternoon of September 5. President Xi Jinping will preside over the meeting. After the summit, President Xi Jinping will also hold a press conference for Chinese and foreign journalists and introduce the results of the summit. The second is the open and inclusive atmosphere throughout the summit. The Chinese side always pays attention to opinions from all sides, and respects different voices. China maintains close communication and interaction with G20 member states, guest countries and international organizations. Through hosting large-scale side events, China will listen to extensive voices from the society and forge the consensus with the widest coverage. China has proactively pursued the principle of "going global", and launched comprehensive and multi-layered dialogues outside the G20 circle. We have walked into the UN General Assembly, the G77, the headquarters of the African Union and the least developed countries to introduce the summit situation and hear their appeals. The dialogue has covered all UN members, especially more than 130 developing countries.

Wang Yi expressed that final preparations are the most crucial part and thus demand rigorous and practical efforts. The summit can't be a success without the great support and cooperation of all parties. We will continue to uphold the open, inclusive and transparent style and strengthen communication and coordination with all parties to ensure the complete success of the summit, so as to achieve a win-win situation for the G20 members and promote the global economy to take a new step toward the target of strong, sustainable and balanced growth. To this end, we are full of confidence. The scroll of the G20 Hangzhou Summit is slowly unfolding. Let us look forward to it together. See you in September!

单元小结
Summary

　　本单元主要介绍了外交吹风会报道的翻译。外交吹风会报道文本结构相对固定，主要由新闻标题、配图、导语、报道主体和结语等几部分构成。吹风会报道涉及的事由主要包括领导人出访、重大内政和外交事务等，文中往往会出现大量外交术语及专有名词。译者必须经过仔细查证，给出规范准确的译法。此外，这类报道多使用长句，信息量大，结构复杂，翻译时不可一味盲从原文的断句，要认真分析逻辑关系，采取拆句、补充关联词等方法，避免给读者造成误解，同时提高译文的可读性。最后，吹风会报道文体比较正式，即便是不属于术语或专有名词之列的词语在选择时也要注意语域。同时，要慎用it's，doesn't等缩略形式。

记者招待会报道的翻译
Translation for Coverage of Press Conferences

单元简介
Introduction

　　记者招待会是指某些政府部门召开的，由发言人向新闻媒体发布信息，介绍相关领域重要活动，并回答记者提问的会议。定期召开记者招待会的部门主要有外交部、国防部、商务部、卫生部等。

　　自2011年9月起，外交部例行记者会由每周两次增加到每周五次，以提高新闻发布的时效性。具体时间为每周一至周五下午3点，不设时间限制，直到记者没有问题为止，具体工作由外交部新闻司承担。会上首先由发言人发布中国重要外交活动信息、阐述中国在国际问题上的立场，然后由与会记者针对近期热点问题逐一提问，发言人予以解答。会后，现场实录的文字稿经过进一步的翻译审校通过外交部官网对外发布。除了例行记者会，外交部常常还会针对某个具体问题电话答记者问。

外交新闻汉英翻译
C-E TRANSLATION OF DIPLOMATIC NEWS

记者招待会报道翻译范例分析
Sample of Translation for Coverage of Press Conferences

范例一（Sample I）

11日外交部发言人华春莹主持例行记者会（节本）
2015/02/11

Foreign Ministry Spokesperson Hua Chunying's Regular Press Conference on February 11 (Abbreviated Version)
2015/02/11

据外交部消息称，2月11日下午外交部发言人华春莹主持例行记者会，解答相关问题。

According to the Ministry of Foreign Affairs, Foreign Ministry Spokesperson Hua Chunying held a regular press conference and answered relevant questions on the afternoon of February 11.

华春莹称，习近平主席特使、工业和信息化部部长苗圩将于2月15日至16日应邀出席克罗地亚总统基塔罗维奇就职仪式。

Hua Chunying announced that upon invitation, Minister of Industry and Information Technology Miao Wei will attend the inauguration ceremony of Croatian President Kolinda Grabar-Kitarovic as the Special Envoy of President Xi Jinping from February 15 to 16.

***

问：据了解，中美官员上月在菲律宾就反腐败合作举行磋商，内容包括美方帮助中方在美境内追逃追赃。你能否介绍更多细节？下轮磋商将于何时举行？中美是否会正式签署引渡条约？

Q: Chinese and American officials met in the Philippines last month to discuss anti-corruption cooperation, specifically how the US can help China go after suspected corrupt Chinese officials in the US and their assets. Can you give us more details about the talks? When can the next round of talks be expected to happen? Are China and the US looking at signing a formal extradition treaty?

答：中美两国在亚太经合组织（APEC）框架下一直保持良好的交流与合作关系。2014年北京APEC会议通过了《北京反腐败宣言》，成立了APEC反腐败执法合作网络，美方都给予了支持，习近平主席与奥巴马总统在会议期间也就加强反腐败合作达成了共识。

A: China and the US maintain sound exchanges and cooperation under the APEC framework. At the 2014 APEC Economic Leaders' Meeting, the Beijing Declaration on

记者招待会报道的翻译
Translation for Coverage of Press Conferences

9 UNIT

Fighting Corruption was adopted and the APEC Network of Anti-Corruption Authorities and Law Enforcement Agencies (ACT-NET) was established, both of which were supported by the US. President Xi Jinping and President Barack Obama have also agreed upon enhancing cooperation against corruption during their meeting on the sidelines of APEC.

今年1月,中美参加了在菲律宾举行的APEC反腐败工作组会议。今年8月,工作组将在菲律宾举行另一次会议。中方将继续与美方保持沟通,落实两国元首达成的反腐败合作共识,推动APEC各经济体落实《北京反腐败宣言》,加强在腐败人员遣返、资产返还等领域的务实合作。中方愿与其他APEC各经济体加强反腐败和追逃追赃合作。

Both the Chinese and American delegations attended the meeting of the APEC anti-corruption working group held in the Philippines this January. There will be another meeting in the Philippines this August. The Chinese side will stay in communication with the American side to implement the consensus reached by the leaders of the two countries on anti-corruption cooperation, encourage all APEC economies to follow through on the Beijing Declaration on Fighting Corruption, enhance practical cooperation in the repatriation of corrupt officials, recovery and return of proceeds of corruption and other areas. The Chinese side is ready to step up cooperation with other APEC economies to fight against corruption and go after the corrupt and their ill-gotten assets.

中方认为,中美双方在现有追逃合作的基础上,进一步探讨开拓各种有效的新途径是十分必要的。为此,中方将继续与美方保持沟通。

The Chinese side regards it necessary for China and the US to explore effective and new means to carry forward the current cooperation. The Chinese side will keep in touch with the American side in this regard.

新闻背景:外交部例行记者会每个工作日举行,根据2017年3月外交部网站的消息,三位发言人分别是陆慷、华春莹和耿爽。范例一是对2015年2月11日华春莹主持的例行记者会的新闻报道,原文见于人民网,译文选自外交部网站并略做修改。

原文链接:http://world.people.com.cn/n/2015/0211/c1002-26549556.html

译文链接:http://www.fmprc.gov.cn/mfa_eng/xwfw_665399/s2510_665401/2511_665403/t1236663.shtml

外交新闻汉英翻译
C-E TRANSLATION OF DIPLOMATIC NEWS

一、范例一文本结构分析（Text Structure Analysis of Sample I）

范例一是一则典型的记者招待会报道，主体内容为2015年2月11日外交部例行记者招待会的文字实录。转写为新闻发布时，前面添加了介绍性文字作为新闻导语，其中包括消息来源（通常为相关政府部门，如本例中的"外交部"）、记者招待会的时间（2月11日下午）、发言人姓名（华春莹）以及事实简述（主持例行记者会，解答相关问题）。有的新闻报道中，尤其是非例行记者会的情况下，可能还会写明该次记者招待会的主题，如"外交部发言人华春莹就马来西亚宣布马航MH370客机失事发表谈话"。导语部分通常简明扼要，按照新闻六要素的原则报道相关事实。新闻正文部分按照记者招待会的流程分为消息发布环节和记者提问环节。发言人所发布的外交消息可能是一条（如本例中的"苗圩出席克罗地亚总统就职仪式"），也可能是多条。如果是多条，则需逐条分段陈述。当然也可能完全没有消息发布环节。记者提问环节通常采用一问一答的形式，就当前时事热点问题进行提问、发表评论。这种报道中，通常不出现提问者的具体姓名、国别、所供职的新闻机构名称等，而仅仅列举问题本身。

二、范例一翻译解析（Translation Analysis of Sample I）

（一）发布消息的翻译（Translation of Announcement at Press Conferences）

记者招待会是各类官方机构为了塑造自我形象、回答受众关心的问题、便于媒体进行报道而专门为新闻记者举行的会议。提供信息是记者招待会第一项主要功能（靖鸣、刘锐，2004：54—58）外交部举行的记者招待会所发布的消息主要涵盖领导人互访、重要会议的召开、对重大事件的表态等。关于领导人互访，消息发布的句式通常为"应某领导人或某国政府邀请，某某领导人将于某月某日至某月某日期间对某国进行访问"。有时消息中还会介绍该领导人将出席某些庆典仪式或举行某些会谈。必要时，还会有具体细节及相关背景的介绍。关于重大会议，常见句式为"某会议将于某月某日在某地举行，某领导人将出席"。必要时还会加上会议主要议题及其他活动的介绍。请看下面的两个翻译实例：

应国家主席习近平邀请，阿根廷共和国总统克里斯蒂娜·费尔南德斯·德基什内尔将于2月3日至5日对中国进行国事访问。

在克里斯蒂娜总统访华期间，习近平主席将为克里斯蒂娜总统举行欢迎仪式和欢迎宴会，同克里斯蒂娜总统会谈，并共同出席合作文件签字仪式。李克强总理、张德江委员长将分别予以会见。

(http://www.china-embassy.or.jp/chn/fyrth/t1233003.htm)

At the invitation of President Xi Jinping, President Cristina Fernández de Kirchner of the Republic of Argentina will pay a state visit to China from February 3 to 5.

During President Cristina's visit to China, President Xi Jinping will hold a welcome ceremony and banquet for her, and hold talks with her. They will bear witness to the signing of cooperation documents. Premier Li Keqiang and Chairman Zhang Dejiang will meet with her on separate occasions.

(http://www.fmprc.gov.cn/mfa_eng/xwfw_665399/s2510_665401/2511_665403/t1233088.shtml)

1月12日，外交部长王毅访问苏丹期间，将在苏丹首都喀土穆同南苏丹冲突双方和东非政府间发展组织（伊加特）有关各方共同举行"支持伊加特南苏丹和平进程专门磋商"，商讨如何配合、支持伊加特斡旋努力，加快推动南苏丹和解进程，早日实现南苏丹和平稳定。

(http://www.china-embassy.or.jp/chn/fyrth/t1227472.htm)

On January 12, Foreign Minister Wang Yi will join the conflicting parties of South Sudan and relevant parties of the Intergovernmental Authority on Development (IGAD) in Khartoum, the capital of Sudan, during his visit there to host the Special Consultation in Support of the IGAD-led South Sudan Peace Process. There will be discussions on how to cooperate with and support IGAD in its mediation efforts, speed up South Sudan reconciliation process and realize peace and stability in South Sudan at an early date.

(http://www.fmprc.gov.cn/mfa_eng/xwfw_665399/s2510_665401/2511_665403/t1227486.shtml)

如上面的翻译实例及范例一所示，因为是宣布还未发生的事情，所以主体时态应选用一般将来时，而事实陈述与背景介绍则根据实际情况选用恰当的时态。如果仅仅说"应邀"，可以译为 upon invitation，如果出现了具体的邀请者，则译为 at the invitation of。对于汉语中过长的句子，应注意适当采用拆译的技巧，以提升译文的可读性。如上面第二个翻译实例中汉语原文只有一句话，译为英语时拆成了 Foreign Minister Wang Yi will join … 和 There will be discussions on … 两句，将原本稍显臃肿的信息分两句呈现，更有利于读者理解。

（二）记者提问用语的翻译（Translation of Questions at Press Conferences）

在记者招待会上，大多数情况是提问者直接发问一到两个问题，有时也有一个问题经过解答后又发生追问的情况，此外，还有可能在记者会后问及某些问题。而提问用语则基本分为以下几种模式：（1）观点问句：援引陈述已经发生的外交事件，询问官方的回应或评论。（2）事实问句：对于已经开始或即将发生的外交事件，询问更多的信息。（3）祈使问句：对于某些外交事件请求确认。（胡庚申、王静，2001：83—84）请看下面的翻译实例：

印度航空公司决定将其官网对"台湾"称呼改为"中国台北"。中国民航总局

外交新闻汉英翻译
C-E TRANSLATION OF DIPLOMATIC NEWS

2个多月前向包括印度航空公司在内的多家航空公司发出了正式要求。中方对此有何评论？

(http://www.fmprc.gov.cn/web/fyrbt_673021/t1574188.shtml)

India's flag carrier airline Air India has decided to change the reference of "Taiwan" into "Chinese Taipei" on its website. Two months ago China's civil aviation authority sent a formal communication to several airlines, including the Indian one. What is your comment on this?

(http://www.fmprc.gov.cn/mfa_eng/xwfw_665399/s2510_665401/2511_665403/t1574293.shtml)

最新一轮的中美经贸磋商已于本周末结束。本轮磋商在中国举行，下一轮应当在美国举行。现在是否有时间表？能否透露下次磋商的具体时间？刘鹤副总理是否有计划赴美继续推进中美经贸磋商？

(http://www.fmprc.gov.cn/web/fyrbt_673021/jzhsl_673025/t1565483.shtml)

The latest China-US trade talks ended over the weekend. This time is China's turn to hold the trade talks. Presumably, the next round of trade talks, whenever they happen, will be in the United States. Can you give us a timeframe for when the next round of trade talks may happen? Have you nailed down when the next meeting will be held? Does Vice Premier Liu have any plans at the moment to visit the United States to continue these trade discussions?

(http://www.fmprc.gov.cn/mfa_eng/xwfw_665399/s2510_665401/2511_665403/t1565728.shtml)

据报道，伊朗外长扎里夫将于本周日抵京。你能否证实？如属实，你能否提供更多细节？

(http://www.fmprc.gov.cn/web/fyrbt_673021/jzhsl_673025/t1558642.shtml)

According to reports, Iranian Foreign Minister Mohammad Javad Zarif Khonsari will arrive in Beijing on Sunday. Can you confirm it? If yes, do you have more details?

(http://www.fmprc.gov.cn/mfa_eng/xwfw_665399/s2510_665401/2511_665403/t1558711.shtml)

追问：外交部对中国赴英游客有没有发布什么旅行建议？

(http://www.fmprc.gov.cn/web/wjdt_674879/fyrbt_674889/t1395888.shtml)

Follow-up: Does the Foreign Ministry have any travel tips for Chinese visitors to the UK?

(http://www.fmprc.gov.cn/mfa_eng/xwfw_665399/s2510_665401/2511_665403/t1395926.shtml)

会后，有记者问及：据报道，近日，南非多个城市发生针对外国人的暴力袭击事件，有中国侨民的商铺遭到哄抢。请问中方做了哪些工作？

(http://www.fmprc.gov.cn/web/fyrbt_673021/jzhsl_673025/t1255612.shtml)

记者招待会报道的翻译
Translation for Coverage of Press Conferences

After the press conference, the following question was raised: according to media reports, violent attacks against foreigners took place in a number of cities in South Africa, and some Chinese-owned shops were looted. Please brief us on what the Chinese side has done.

(http://www.fmprc.gov.cn/mfa_eng/xwfw_665399/s2510_665401/2511_665403/t1255348.shtml)

翻译时，对于媒体的援引，可译为According to ×× (media/news agency)或者×× media reported that或者×× told the press that。陈述完相关事实后，实质提问部分有三种句型可用。一是一般疑问句，如Does China have any response to that? Can you give us more details? Will the Chinese leader attend the anniversary? 二是特殊疑问句，如What is China's comment on that? What effects will the maritime crisis management mechanism talks between China and Japan bring to the settlement of the Diaoyu Islands dispute? When will they be deployed? 三是陈述句，如Please brief us on the latest development of search and rescue. Please update us on the outcomes of the talks and the work plan in the next step。译者可根据实际情况合理选择，无须与原文中的句型严格对应。

（三）发言人常用答复语的翻译（Translation of Frequently Used Replies at Press Conferences）

记者招待会的目的在于宣传本国政策和立场，介绍时事发展动向，澄清是非曲直。因为事关国家形象与国际安全，发言人的话语同时具备鲜明性、论辩性和模糊性的特点。所谓鲜明性是指在重大国际问题上态度鲜明，支持各国人民的正义事业，反对霸权主义、强权政治和国际恐怖主义，在涉及国家主权和领土完整等问题上立场坚定，不容置疑。（李琴，2006：164）相关语句翻译时多用陈述句式，读起来明确而响亮，同时要注意副词、形容词、动词等在选词上的准确性。例如：

中方坚决反对并打击任何形式的网络攻击，这一立场是一贯的、明确的。

(http://www.fmprc.gov.cn/web/fyrbt_673021/jzhsl_673025/t1251566.shtml)

China firmly opposes and combats any form of cyber attack, and this stance remains consistent and clear.

(http://www.fmprc.gov.cn/ce/cgkotakinabalu/eng/wjbfyrth_4/t1251578.htm)

中方对也门首都萨那恐怖爆炸袭击造成大量人员伤亡表示强烈谴责。

(http://www.fmprc.gov.cn/web/fyrbt_673021/jzhsl_673025/t1247716.shtml)

The Chinese side strongly condemns the terrorist bombing attacks in Yemen's capital Sanaa which caused heavy casualties.

(http://www.fmprc.gov.cn/ce/cggb/eng/fyrth/t1247750.htm)

外交新闻汉英翻译
C-E TRANSLATION OF DIPLOMATIC NEWS

论辩性是指对于某些记者的挑衅性提问给予有理有据的辩驳，维护国家形象和正当权益。外交部发言人的应答目的在于劝服国际受众接受中国政府在相关问题上的立场，发言人需要针对国际受众存在的质疑或反对意见进行反驳或澄清。因而，论辩性是发言人应答的重要属性。（吴鹏、朱密，2015：54）此时译文语言要简洁有力、紧扣原文中的逻辑，译出驳论的气势来。如下面例子中的"恐怕"，若译为I am afraid将会是多么大的一个败笔：

（问：美国总统奥巴马昨天表示，他对中国可能利用自身"块头和肌肉"在南海地区向小国施压表示关切。中方对此有何评论？）

说到"块头和肌肉"，恐怕大家都很清楚，谁在世界上拥有最大"块头和肌肉"？我们已经多次阐明了中方在南海问题上的有关立场。中国是南海和平稳定的坚定维护者和促进者。

(http://www.fmprc.gov.cn/web/fyrbt_673021/jzhsl_673025/t1253702.shtml)

Speaking of "size and muscle", I believe everyone knows well who has the largest "size and muscle" in the world. We have stated on many occasions the position of the Chinese side on the South China Sea issue. China firmly upholds and promotes peace and stability of the South China Sea.

(http://www.fmprc.gov.cn/mfa_eng/xwfw_665399/s2510_665401/t1253821.shtml)

模糊性是指运用不确定或者不精确的语言进行表达。当记者的提问涉及我方暂时还不确定或暂时还不打算公开的信息时，就需要做出模糊的回答。语用含糊是外交活动中不可替代的一种言语技巧，是保证外交活动成功的一种重要手段。（魏在江，2006：45）请看下面的实例：

（问：据近日在昆明举行的中国医院协会人体器官获取组织联盟（OPO联盟）研讨会的消息，从明年1月1日起，中国将全面停止使用死囚器官作为移植供体来源。中方能否证实？）

中国政府一贯遵循世界卫生组织关于人体器官移植的指导原则，近年来也进一步加强了对器官移植的管理。2007年3月21日，中国国务院颁布实施了《人体器官移植条例》，规定人体器官捐献应当遵循自愿、无偿的原则。具体问题请你向主管的卫生部门了解。

(http://www.fmprc.gov.cn/web/fyrbt_673021/jzhsl_673025/t1216969.shtml)

The Chinese government always follows the World Health Organization's guiding principles on human organ transplant, and has strengthened its management on organ transplant in recent years. On March 21, 2007, the Chinese State Council enacted the Regulations on Human Organ Transplant, providing that human organ donation must be

记者招待会报道的翻译
Translation for Coverage of Press Conferences
UNIT 9

done voluntarily and gratis. You can raise your question to the public health authority for specifics.

(http://www.fmprc.gov.cn/mfa_eng/xwfw_665399/s2510_665401/2511_665403/t1216978.shtml)

上面的例子中发言人并没有直接回答记者的提问,违背了语言交际中的合作原则。因为该记者在问题中做了前提预设,无论回答"是"与"否",都会间接承认中方以前使用了死囚器官作为移植供体。发言人在此处使用了转移焦点策略,以"顾左右而言他"的方式,(熊永红、彭小妹,2009:73)强调中方在加强管理方面所做的努力。其他的模糊性语言还有relevant departments, in due course等。

范例二(Sample II)

外交部发言人华春莹就中方将举行抗战胜利70周年纪念活动答记者问
2015/03/02
Foreign Ministry Spokesperson Hua Chunying's Remarks on Commemorative Activities for 70th Anniversary of Victory of Chinese People's War of Resistance Against Japanese Aggression
2015/03/02

问:今年是中国人民抗日战争暨世界反法西斯战争胜利70周年,中方将举行哪些纪念活动?

Q: This year marks the 70th anniversary of the victory of the Chinese People's War of Resistance Against Japanese Aggression as well as the World Anti-Fascist War. What commemorative activities will be held on this occasion?

答:今年是世界反法西斯战争胜利70周年,也是中国人民抗日战争胜利70周年。中国人民抗日战争是世界反法西斯战争的重要组成部分,作为世界反法西斯战争的东方主战场,中国战场爆发时间最早、历时最长。中国人民抗日战争坚定了盟国与法西斯作战的信心,推动了世界反法西斯统一战线的形成,中国人民也为此付出了巨大的民族牺牲。

A: This year marks the 70th anniversary of the victory of the World Anti-Fascist War, as well as the Chinese People's War of Resistance Against Japanese Aggression. The Chinese People's War of Resistance Against Japanese Aggression is an important part of the World Anti-Fascist War. China is a main theater of the World Anti-Fascist War in the east. The war in China broke out the earliest and lasted for the longest. The Chinese People's War of Resistance

Against Japanese Aggression consolidated the Allies' confidence in fighting against fascism and contributed to the formation of a united front against fascism, for which the Chinese nation had sacrificed enormously.

长期以来，中国政府每逢五、逢十周年，都举行相关纪念活动。今年，我们将根据惯例并参照各国作法，在北京隆重举行纪念活动，包括举行纪念大会、阅兵式、招待会和文艺晚会，习近平主席等中国领导人将出席。中方还将邀请第二次世界大战主要参战国、亚洲国家和其他地区国家领导人、联合国等国际组织负责人、为中国抗战胜利作出贡献的国际友人或其遗属出席。

The Chinese government has a tradition of commemorating each quinquennial and decennial anniversary. In accordance with the common practice and in reference to routines of other countries, we will hold grand commemorations in Beijing this year, which include a commemoration meeting, a military parade, receptions and artistic performances. President Xi Jinping and other Chinese leaders will attend these activities. The Chinese side will also invite leaders from major belligerent states in the Second World War, Asian countries as well as countries in other regions, international organizations such as the United Nations and foreign friends who contributed to the victory of China's War of Resistance or their family members to these events.

中国政府隆重举行中国人民抗日战争和世界反法西斯战争胜利70周年纪念活动，目的是为了铭记历史、缅怀先烈、珍视和平、开创未来。我们希望通过举办纪念活动，唤起每一个善良的人对和平的向往和坚守，避免历史悲剧重演，共同捍卫二战胜利果实，开创人类更加美好的未来。

The Chinese government holds the grand commemorations marking the 70th anniversary of the victory of the Chinese People's War of Resistance Against Japanese Aggression as well as the World Anti-Fascist War, in a bid to memorize the history, honor the martyrs, cherish peace and open up to the future. Through hosting such activities, we hope that every human being with a kind heart can awake to the aspiration and commitment of peace, prevent the historical tragedy from happening again, jointly defend the victory of the Second World War and explore better prospects for humankind.

记者招待会报道的翻译
Translation for Coverage of Press Conferences

> 新闻背景：中国人民经过十四年艰苦卓绝的抗日战争，于1945年取得最终胜利。9月2日9时许，日本投降仪式在东京湾"密苏里"号战列舰上举行。中国作为第二次世界大战胜利者，与所有同盟国一起，将邪恶势力终结，为人类赢得持久和平，为世界反法西斯战争的胜利做出了巨大贡献。2015年是世界反法西斯战争暨中国抗日战争胜利70周年，外交部3月份时针对相关纪念活动举行了一次答记者问。范例二选自外交部官网相关报道。
>
> 原文链接：http://www.fmprc.gov.cn/ce/ceindo/chn/fyrth/t1241918.htm
>
> 译文链接：http://www.fmprc.gov.cn/mfa_eng/xwfw_665399/s2510_665401/2535_665405/t1241925.shtml

一、范例二文本结构分析（Text Structure Analysis of Sample II）

外交部除了例行记者会外，还会在其他工作时间以发言人名义电话回答记者提问，相关消息也会发布在外交部官网上，如范例二所示。这种报道的标题基本已经形成固定格式，统一为"外交部发言人××就××答记者问"。大部分情况下文内只有一问一答。有时候外交部也可能针对某个话题主动发布相关消息、阐明中方观点。如："外交部发言人陆慷就美国拉森号军舰进入中国南沙群岛有关岛礁邻近海域答记者问"，"外交部发言人华春莹就确认寻获MH370客机残骸一事发表谈话"。至于提问和回答的基本范式与例行记者会相同，此处不再赘述。

二、范例二翻译解析（Translation Analysis of Sample II）

范例二的文本结构特点与例行记者会的文字实录基本类似。标题中"就……答记者问"在外交部官网上的译文格式统一为someone's remarks on something，例如Foreign Ministry Spokesperson Hong Lei's Remarks on China's Handover of the First Batch of Emergency Relief Supplies to Vanuatu。具体问答句式的相关翻译问题已在前文加以剖析。

范例二中所谈到的主题内容，即有关抗击日本侵略战争的话题，是在记者会上被频繁谈到的话题，值得译者关注。中方对于中日关系的原则立场非常明确，愿意在中日四个政治文件基础上，继续推进中日战略互惠关系。①举办抗战胜利70周年纪念活动的目的是为了铭记历史、缅怀先烈、珍视和平、开创未来。然而遗憾的是，日方却在历史和钓鱼岛等问题上一再采取挑衅行动，造成中日之间的困难局面。②矛盾和冲突主要涉及历史问题、领土争端问题、贸易摩擦问题等等。其中历史问题最为凸显，包括侵华战争、南京大屠杀、慰安妇、参拜靖国神社等。领土争端问题则集中表现为钓鱼岛的主权归属问

---

① 《习近平向安倍阐明中方对中日关系的原则立场》，http://cpc.people.com.cn/n/2013/0906/c64094-22826177.html
② 《外交部：中日关系困局是日方一再采取挑衅行动造成》，http://politics.people.com.cn/n/2014/0404/c70731-24831100.html

题和东海划界问题。外交部记者招待会上，只要谈到中日关系，就很有可能涉及上述某个话题，所以本节将专门聚焦有关这些话题的常用表达及其翻译。

（一）历史问题的翻译（Translation of Historical Issues Between China and Japan）

近代日本对中国的侵略史可以追溯到1894年甲午战争时期。通过侵略战争，日本强迫清政府签订了许多不平等条约，在中国很多城市建立了日租界。①1937年7月悍然炮攻宛平城并进攻城外的卢沟桥，继而在12月侵占南京，大肆烧杀抢掠，南京大屠杀的暴行举世震惊。直到1945年9月日本在投降书上签字的八年间，中国人民饱受战火的摧残，②这段历史不容忘却。但是日本对其所犯的罪行并没有正确的认识，屡次试图混淆视听，为己辩白。③

所以涉及中日历史问题的话语在翻译时都需要慎重推敲，不能给居心叵测之人以可乘之机。首先，"抗日战争"一词在中国耳熟能详，大家都明白该词的确切含义，不会有任何歧义。可是译为英语时，若用Anti-Japanese War恐怕就会被某些别有用心的人刻意曲解为"反对日本人的战争"，这显然与事实不符。④中华民族历来是非常友善的民族，愿意与其他民族和平共处。"抗日战争"的准确翻译应当是the Chinese People's War of Resistance Against Japanese Aggression（中国人民抵抗日本侵略之战），⑤如范例二所示。如果要缩略表达时，可以使用范例二中的China's War of Resistance，以强调"抵抗（侵略）"之意，而不能以其他形式随意缩略。那些直接使用英语提问的西方记者可能不太注意这些细节，但我方对发言人的回答进行翻译时必须注意用词的准确性。

南京大屠杀是中华民族的屈辱和血泪史，是日本军国主义对中国人民犯下的残酷暴行。而日方频繁地做出一些不恰当的言论，试图否认历史，抵赖罪责。对于这些言论，外交部发言人都会坚定地予以驳斥，相关语句在翻译时必须传递出原文的气势来。下面的翻译实例摘自2014年2月5日"外交部发言人洪磊就日本广播协会经营委员否认南京大屠杀言论答记者问"，从中我们可以略窥一斑：

> 南京大屠杀是日本军国主义在侵华战争中犯下的残暴罪行，铁证如山，国际社会对此早有定论。日本国内极少数人试图抹杀、掩盖、歪曲这段历史，是对国际正义和人类良知的公然挑战，与日本领导人开历史倒车的错误行径一脉相承，应引起国际社会高度警惕。
>
> （http://www.fmprc.gov.cn/ce/cebw/chn/fyrth/t1125813.htm）
>
> The Nanjing Massacre is an atrocious crime committed by the Japanese militarism

---

① 甲午战争，http://www.qulishi.com/huati/jiawuzz/
②《抗日战争大事记》，http://games.52pk.com/zhuanti/kangzhan/
③《日本必须正确反省历史问题》，http://www.qstheory.cn/dukan/qs/2015-05/15/c_1115245368.htm
④《关于"抗日"一词英文翻译的几点思考》，http://news.gmw.cn/2015-08/20/content_16739338.htm
⑤《中央文献重要术语译文发布（2015年第四期）》，http://www.cctb.net/bygz/zywxsy/201507/t20150720_325517.htm

during its war of aggression against China. The international community has already rendered a verdict based on <u>irrefutable evidences</u>. It is a <u>blatant</u> challenge to international justice and human conscience when a handful of people in Japan attempted to <u>blot out, cover up and distort</u> that history. Such erroneous behavior follows those of the Japanese leader who tries to <u>reverse the history</u>. The international community should be highly vigilant against this.

(http://www.fmprc.gov.cn/ce/cohk/eng/xwdt/wjbt/t1125950.htm)

首先,"南京大屠杀"的英文表述为<u>the Nanjing Massacre</u>,而不用其他表示"杀戮"的词。因为massacre一词的英文解释为the killing of a large number of people at the same time in a violent and cruel way,其中的violent and cruel真实地反映了日本军国主义的实际所为。侵华的历史应当被明确地定性为invasion或aggression,而不是日方所辩称的其他任何性质。atrocious, irrefutable, blatant等形容词的选用非常清楚地传达出了爱好和平的人们对于日方丑陋行径的愤慨,翻译得非常到位。

日本侵华战争中犯下的另一大罪行是慰安妇问题。二战期间,日本在占领区强征民间妇女充当性奴隶,为日军提供性服务,犯下了严重的反人类罪行。加拿大、欧盟、韩国等都曾通过议案,要求日本道歉。①以下的翻译实例选自"2014年6月20日外交部发言人华春莹主持例行记者会"的报道,可以从中了解相关的表达。

强征"慰安妇"是日本军国主义在二战期间对亚洲等受害国人民犯下的严重反人道罪行,铁证如山。任何企图为侵略历史翻案的行为都是不得人心的。我们敦促日方切实正视和深刻反省侵略历史,以负责任态度信守"河野谈话"等对国际社会作出的表态和承诺,以实际行动妥善处理包括"慰安妇"问题在内的有关历史遗留问题。

(http://www.fmprc.gov.cn/web/fyrbt_673021/jzhsl_673025/t1167405.shtml)

The forced recruitment of "comfort women" is a <u>serious</u> crime <u>against humanity</u> committed by the Japanese militarism during the Second World War on people of Asia and other victimized countries. The evidence for their crimes is <u>iron-clad</u>. Any attempt to overturn the verdict on Japan's <u>history of invasion</u> will be <u>spurned</u> by the public. We urge the Japanese side to honestly face up to and reflect upon its <u>history of aggression</u>, honor its statements and commitments made to the international community, including the "Kono Statement" with a responsible attitude, and properly handle issues left over from history,

---

① 《加拿大通过议案要求日本就"慰安妇"问题道歉》, http://zqb.cyol.com/content/2007-11/30/content_1976356.htm;《欧洲通过议案要求日就慰安妇问题道歉》, http://www.jsw.com.cn/news/2007-12/15/content_1596079.htm;《韩国议会敦促日本向慰安妇正式道歉及赔偿》, http://world.huanqiu.com/exclusive/2012-08/3078264.html

including the "comfort women" issue with concrete actions.

(http://www.fmprc.gov.cn/mfa_eng/xwfw_665399/s2510_665401/t1167492.shtml)

和上面关于南京大屠杀的例子一样,日本侵略历史的性质必须明确。试图篡改历史的行为只会为人所不齿,spurn一词的使用甚至比原文的"不得人心"更为传神。另外,"comfort women"必须加引号,因为这是日方所使用的称呼,表示women who provide comfort,但这显然不能反映其本质。日方常常辩称各国被蹂躏的妇女同日本的随军妓女一样是"自愿的"。①可事实上这些女性根本就是被关押和被强迫的,过着生不如死的生活。美国国务卿希拉里在听取美国国务院高层官员的汇报时,已经提出要把日军"慰安妇(comfort women)"改称为"被强迫的性奴(enforced sex slaves)"。②虽然这一提法尚需时日才能得到国际社会的响应,但译者至少应当认识到,"comfort women"这一提法是不太恰当的,是不尊重事实的。

对于靖国神社的参拜是频繁引发中日冲突的另一个历史遗留问题。靖国神社的建立最初是为了纪念在明治维新时期为恢复明治天皇权力而牺牲的3500多名反幕武士,后来开始供奉各种战争中为日本战死的军人及军属。但是自1978年10月靖国神社宫司(即庙祝)松平永芳把东条英机等14名甲级战犯的名字列入靖国神社合祭起,靖国神社的性质发生了重大变化,不断引起纠纷。③以下的翻译实例选自2013年12月26日"外交部发言人秦刚就日本首相安倍晋三参拜靖国神社发表谈话"的报道,清楚反映了中方对此类事件的态度和立场。

2013年12月26日,日本首相安倍晋三不顾中方坚决反对,悍然参拜供奉有二战甲级战犯的靖国神社。中国政府对日本领导人粗暴践踏中国和其他亚洲战争受害国人民感情、公然挑战历史正义和人类良知的行径表示强烈愤慨,向日方提出强烈抗议和严厉谴责。

(http://www.fmprc.gov.cn/web/fyrbt_673021/dhdw_673027/t1112088.shtml)

On December 26, Prime Minister Shinzo Abe of Japan, in total disregard of the <u>strong opposition</u> of the Chinese side, paid a <u>blatant</u> homage to the Yasukuni Shrine, where <u>Class-A war criminals</u> of World War II are honored. The Chinese government expresses its <u>strong indignation</u> over the behavior of the Japanese leader which <u>grossly tramples</u> on the sentiment of the Chinese people and other Asian peoples victimized in the war and <u>openly challenges</u> the historical justice and human conscience, and <u>lodges a strong protest and severe condemnation</u> against the Japanese side.

(http://qa.china-embassy.org/eng/fyrth/t1112096.htm)

---

① 《日本高官否认强征"慰安妇"韩国对此深感失望》,http://news.sohu.com/20120829/n351761222.shtml
② 《慰安妇改为"日军性奴"触动了日本的哪根神经?》,http://int.gmw.cn/2012-07/13/content_4542659.htm
③ 《人为破坏!日本靖国神社发生爆炸》,http://roll.sohu.com/20151124/n427868394.shtml

（二）领土争端的翻译（Translation of Territorial Disputes Between China and Japan）

中日之间的领土争端矛盾最激烈的是钓鱼岛及其附属岛屿的主权归属问题。钓鱼岛群岛历来为中国的固有领土。1895年由于甲午海战失败，中国被迫签订不平等的《马关条约》，并割让台湾及其附属岛屿给日本。[①]1945年日本战败，台湾岛重新回到祖国怀抱，各种国际文件均明确指出，台湾及其周围岛屿归中国所有。但日本政府将附属于台湾岛的钓鱼岛等岛屿以归冲绳县管辖为借口交由美军占领。1970年美国向日本移交钓鱼岛的行政管辖权，但同时宣布与主权无关。[②]请看下面表明我方立场的相关实例：

> 钓鱼岛及其附属岛屿是中国固有领土，中方已全部命名。中方坚决反对日方损害中国领土主权的行为，日方为此采取的任何单方面措施都是非法和无效的，改变不了钓鱼岛及其附属岛屿属于中国的事实。
>
> (http://news.china.com/dydzd/gdxw/11127676/20140801/18678644.html)

The Diaoyu Island and its affiliated islands are China's inherent territory, and China has named them all. China is firmly opposed to any act by the Japanese side that undermines China's territorial sovereignty. Whatever unilateral measure Japan takes for this end is illegal and invalid, and will not change the fact that the Diaoyu Island and its affiliated islands belong to China.

(http://ca.china-embassy.org/eng/fyrth/t1179697.htm)

关于命名问题，日本政府将钓鱼岛群岛称为"尖阁诸岛"（the Senkaku Islands）。但是按照翻译当中"名从主人"的原则，钓鱼岛的正确翻译应该是the Diaoyu Island或者直接使用汉语拼音Diaoyu Dao，（杨全红，2014：84）如果要表达"群岛"的概念，再加上and its affiliated islands即可。在记者会上，外国记者提问时有可能会使用the Senkaku Islands，但对我方发言人的回答在翻译时必须坚持正确的译名。对于附属岛屿的译名也是相同的道理，正如发言人所说，无论日方如何命名，都是非法和无效的。外交翻译中应当坚持使用中方称谓来表达政治诉求，增强话语权，切实维护国家主权与民族利益。（朱义华，2012：97）

近年来，日本持续挑起事端，导致钓鱼岛争端时有激化。2012年9月日本公然宣布"从私人手中购买钓鱼岛"，并将其"国有化"。[③]中国提出强烈抗议。同年12月，中国开始在钓鱼岛海空开展立体巡航，明确不退让态度。[④]2013年11月，中国宣布划设东海防

[①]《日本侵华战争遗留问题探析》，http://www.faobserver.com/NewsInfo.aspx?id=11760
[②]《钓鱼岛历史》，http://www.njliaohua.com/lhd_959ls16buh0vngk59epo_1.html
[③]《聚焦钓鱼岛》，http://world.huanqiu.com/special/dyd/
[④]《中国首次在钓鱼岛海空立体巡航 明确不退让态度》，http://www.chinanews.com/gn/2012/12-13/4406749.shtml

空识别区,更好地维护国家安全。①日方则时常对中国海军舰艇的正常航行训练进行跟踪监视。下面是几则相关报道实例:

日本对中国领土钓鱼岛非法实施所谓"国有化",严重侵犯中国领土主权,导致中日关系陷入严重困难。我们敦促日方正视历史和现实,以实际行动纠正错误,停止一切损害中国主权的挑衅行动,为消除改善两国关系的阻碍作出努力。

(http://www.fmprc.gov.cn/ce/cggb/chn/ztlm/wjbfyrth/t1075102.htm)

Japan's <u>illegal</u> implementation of the so-called "nationalization" of China's Diaoyu Islands has grossly infringed upon China's territorial sovereignty and caused great difficulties to China-Japan relations. We urge the Japanese side to face up to history and facts, correct mistakes with concrete actions, desist from provocative actions that are detrimental to China's territorial sovereignty and remove obstacles to the improvement of bilateral relations.

(http://www.fmprc.gov.cn/ce/cepl/pol/xnyfgk/t1076131.htm)

钓鱼岛及其附属岛屿自古以来就是中国的固有领土,中国东海防空识别区覆盖这一区域完全合理合法,日方无权对此说三道四。日方上世纪60年代末划设防空识别区,非法将中国钓鱼岛划入其中,中方对此一贯坚决反对。

(http://www.fmprc.gov.cn/ce/cein/chn/fyrth/t1104627.htm)

The Diaoyu Island and its affiliated islands have been integral parts of China's territory since ancient times. It is fully reasonable and justifiable for China's Air Defense Identification Zone (ADIZ) in the East China Sea to cover this area. The Japanese side has no right to make irresponsible remarks. The ADIZ set up by Japan in late 1960s <u>illegally</u> included China's Diaoyu islands and China has always been firmly opposed to that.

(http://www.fmprc.gov.cn/ce/cenp/eng/fyrth/t1104719.htm)

翻译时,对于援引的日方错误言行,可以有三种办法表明态度。一是加双引号表示否定,即说话人并不认可该表述;二是在前面加so-called(所谓的),也表明说话人的不认同;三是直接在相关表述中加入相应的形容词或副词,明示说话人的态度和观点。如上面两个实例中的illegal和illegally(已用下划线标出)。

学生译作讲评
Analysis of Students' Translation Practice

原文链接:http://www.fmprc.gov.cn/web/fyrbt_673021/jzhsl_673025/t1160781.shtml

---

① 《中华人民共和国政府关于划设东海防空识别区的声明》,http://news.xinhuanet.com/mil/2013-11/23/c_125750439.htm

记者招待会报道的翻译
Translation for Coverage of Press Conferences

UNIT 9

新闻原文： 2014年5月29日外交部发言人秦刚主持例行记者会

学生译文： Foreign Ministry Spokesman Qin Gang Chairs Regular Press Conference on May 29, 2014

翻译评析： 标题的翻译学生选用了完整的主谓宾结构，"主持"翻译为chair一词并不合适，因为chair是指在开会时确定发言顺序、总体把握会议进程的人，履行的更多是程序上的职责，本人的讲话内容可能并不多。而记者会上的发言人要回答众多记者的提问，并不是chair the conference的概念。"发言人"一词学生虽然用了spokesman也没错，但是外交部的发言人有男性也有女性，而且伴随着女性意识的崛起，现代语言的发展方向也在逐渐淡化性别概念，因此spokesperson更为恰当。此外，外交部官网例行记者会报道标题的翻译常采用someone's regular press conference这样的表述方式，因此该标题可改译为Foreign Ministry Spokesperson Qin Gang's Regular Press Conference on May 29, 2014。

新闻原文： 应中共中央政治局委员、中央政法委书记孟建柱和国务委员杨洁篪邀请，俄罗斯联邦安全会议秘书帕特鲁舍夫将于6月4日至6日来华举行中俄执法安全合作机制首次会议和中俄第十轮战略安全磋商。

学生译文： At the invitation of CPC Central Committee Political Bureau Member and CPC Central Politics and Law Commission Secretary Meng Jianzhu and State Councilor Yang Jiechi, Security Council Secretary of the Russian Federation Nikolai Patrushev will visit China from June 4 to 6 to attend the first meeting of China-Russia Law-enforcement and Security Cooperation Mechanism and the 10th round of China-Russia Strategic Security Consultation.

翻译评析： 学生显然是把"中共中央政治局委员"看成与"中央政法委书记"类似的一个头衔，所以用了大写的Member与后面的Secretary并列。实际上，"中共中央政治局"是个专有名词，表示特定机构，而"委员"只是个普通名词，并非像President或Chairman那样的头衔。而且大量名词短语的堆积导致修饰关系不清，形成理解上的困难，因此该句起首部分可改译为At the invitation of Meng Jianzhu, member of the Political Bureau of the CPC Central Committee and Secretary of the CPC Central Politics and Law Commission。

新闻原文： 明天上午10点外交部将在这里举行中外媒体吹风会，邀请外交部副部长张明介绍中阿合作论坛第六届部长级会议有关情况并回答记者提问。欢迎大家参加。

学生译文： At 10 o'clock tomorrow morning, the Ministry of Foreign Affairs will give a press briefing here to the Chinese and foreign media and invite Vice Foreign Minister Zhang Ming to introduce relevant situations and answer the journalists' questions on the 6th Ministerial Meeting of China-Arab States Cooperation Forum. Welcome to the briefing.

翻译评析： 学生的译文完全忠实于原文。但是原文比较具有汉语的行文特色，如果细想其中的逻辑，就会是"外交部邀请外交部副部长来介绍……"，似乎有些自己请自己的意味。另外，"相关情况"用relevant situations选词不当，situation指的是情形、局势。此处应改译为relevant information。理顺逻辑并简化后的译文为：Vice Foreign

225

Minister Zhang Ming will give a press briefing here and take questions from the Chinese and foreign media on the 6th Ministerial Meeting …

新闻原文：问：据了解，李克强总理将与印度新总理莫迪通话。你能否证实？

学生译文：Q: There are reports that Premier Li Keqiang will hold talks with India's new Prime Minister Narendra Modi. Can you confirm that?

翻译评析："通话"一词比较模糊，学生误以为是hold talks，而talks一般都指"会谈"。参阅相关网络信息就会知道，其实此处指的是"通电话"，应该译为have a phone conversation。

新闻原文：答：据我了解，中印双方有两国总理通话的安排。我相信你很快就会得知有关消息。

学生译文：A: As far as I know, there are arrangements for the talks between Premier Li and his Indian counterpart. I believe you will get relevant information very soon.

翻译评析：此处的"相信"并不是对某件事情真实性的判断，而是对未来事件的预判，用am sure更贴切一些。"你很快就会得到有关信息"的主观性较强，对于此事"我"其实无法确定，改译为被动语态较好。译文可调整为I am sure relevant information will be released very soon。

新闻原文：问：英国政府相关部门正在对葛兰素史克公司展开调查。中方是否会就此与英方展开合作？

学生译文：Q: Government departments of the UK are investigating GlaxoSmithKline (GSK). Will China cooperate with the British side during the inquiry?

翻译评析：Investigate的宾语通常是事件、情况、起因等，公司名称直接做宾语并不常用。译者还漏译了原文主语中的"相关"二字。译文可修改为Competent departments of the UK government are making investigations of GlaxoSmithKline (GSK)。

新闻原文：答：葛兰素史克公司在中国出现的违法行为，中国的司法部门已经立案进行侦查和处理。我们也注意到英方对此事非常重视。葛兰素史克公司总部在英国，所以在处理此案的过程中，希望双方能够进行沟通和配合。

学生译文：A: The judicial department in China has already started relevant investigation and is in the process of dealing with the law-breaking practices of GSK. We have also noticed that the British side attaches great importance to this case. GSK is headquartered in the UK, so in the process of dealing with this case, we hope that both sides can keep in contact and cooperate with each other.

翻译评析：该句起首部分The judicial department in China中的介词in应该改为of，表示所属关系，而不是地理位置关系。末句的实际意思是"希望双方在处理此案的过程中能够进行沟通和配合"，所以译文应该把in the process of dealing with this case挪到句末，作为宾语从句内的状语。为了表达得更为简洁和地道，还可以将其简化为in dealing with this case。调整后的译文为so we hope that both sides can keep in contact and cooperate with each other in dealing with this case.

新闻原文：问：美方宣布将会延长在阿富汗驻军时间，到2016年全部撤出。中方如何看待美方这一举动？

学生译文：Q: The US announced that it will prolong the garrison in Afghanistan and will not completely withdraw until 2016. What is China's view on this?

翻译评析："延长驻军时间"翻译错误，garrison指的是所驻扎的军队，是没有办法被"延长"的。此句可以调整简化为it will put off the complete withdrawal of US troops in Afghanistan to 2016。

新闻原文：答：我们注意到前几天奥巴马总统在突访阿富汗时做出这样表态。在阿富汗问题上，中方一贯主张尊重阿富汗的主权、安全和领土完整。美方在阿富汗驻军的问题，应该负责任、稳妥地予以处理，有利于阿富汗的和平重建和本地区的和平、稳定与安全。我们也希望在这方面，美方能够保持透明。

学生译文：A: We have noticed that President Obama talked about this when he made a surprise visit to Afghanistan. On the issue of Afghanistan, China always respects the sovereignty, security and territory integrity of Afghanistan. On the issue of the stationing of troops, the US should handle it in a responsible and careful manner, so that the peaceful reconstruction and regional peace, stability and security can be boosted. We also hope that the US can stay transparent on this issue.

翻译评析："我们注意到"的重点是相关态度和立场，而不是某人曾经谈论过这件事。宾语加以调整，才能突出重点。另外，"几天前"被漏译。译文可修改为We have noticed such an announcement made by President Obama during his surprise visit to Afghanistan several days ago。第二句中的"一贯主张尊重……"最好用现在完成时态，即has always respected。第三句的结构比较松散，需要理顺逻辑，译文可以修改为The US should handle the issue of itself stationing troops in Afghanistan in a responsible and proper manner so as to contribute to the peaceful reconstruction as well as regional peace, stability and security in the region.

实战练习
Translation Practice

一、请翻译下列记者招待会中的消息发布（Translate the following announcements at press conferences）

1. 应纳米比亚政府邀请，交通运输部部长杨传堂将作为国家主席习近平特使，赴纳米比亚出席于3月21日举行的纳新总统根哥布就职仪式和纳独立25周年庆典。

    (http://news.china.com.cn/world/2015-03/18/content_35092307.htm)

2. 应保加利亚总理博里索夫、德国总理默克尔邀请，国务院总理李克强将于7月5日至10日对保加利亚进行正式访问并出席在索非亚举行的第七次中国—中东欧国家领导人会晤、赴德国主持第五轮中德政府磋商并对德国进行正式访问。

明天上午10:00,外交部将在蓝厅举行中外媒体吹风会,介绍李克强总理出访相关情况,欢迎广大记者朋友踊跃参加。

(http://www.fmprc.gov.cn/web/fyrbt_673021/jzhsl_673025/t1572535.shtml)

3. 为进一步发展中国和索马里友好合作关系,中国政府已于10月12日正式恢复驻索马里使馆。目前,中国已任命新的驻索马里大使。

正在索马里进行友好访问的中国外交部副部长张明以及索总统马哈茂德、外长贝莱等出席复馆仪式。当天,马哈茂德总统、贝莱外长还分别会见张明副部长,双方就新形势下中索关系发展深入交换意见,并达成广泛共识。索各界对中国恢复驻索使馆表示高度赞赏和热烈欢迎。

(http://www.fmprc.gov.cn/ce/ceph/chn/fyrth/t1199879.htm)

4. 11月15日,中国人民解放军援助利比里亚医疗队163名医护人员乘专机抵达利首都蒙罗维亚。这离习近平主席在上个月24日宣布中国协助西非国家抗击埃博拉疫情的新一轮援助举措不到一个月时间。

此次抵利的中国人民解放军援利医疗队具有丰富的传染病防治经验,曾参加过抗击非典等多项重大任务。他们将在即将于25日启用、由中国援建的利比里亚埃博拉治疗中心开展工作,全力救治埃博拉患者,同时还将培训利医务工作者,传授中国防控疫情经验。该治疗中心做到了中国建设、中国配备医护人员、中国运营,这在目前国际援助西非抗击埃博拉疫情行动中是独一无二的。

(http://www.fmprc.gov.cn/ce/cecz/chn/xwyd/fyrth/t1211771.htm)

二、请翻译下列记者招待会中的问答(Translate the following questions and answers at press conferences)

1. 问:据报道,16日,澳大利亚警方确认,警方当日突击悉尼发生劫持人质事件的咖啡馆,劫持者及2名人质死亡,4人受伤。中方对该事件有何评论?

答:中方反对任何针对无辜平民的暴力行为,对悉尼人质劫持事件的无辜遇害者表示哀悼,向澳大利亚政府和人民以及死伤民众家属表示诚挚的慰问和深切的同情。

(http://www.fmprc.gov.cn/ce/cegr/chn/ztlm/lxjzzdh/t1219755.htm)

2. 问:据报道,马里总统表示在上周访华时与中方签署了包括铁路建设等合作协议。中方能否确认?

答:中方愿意与非洲国家加强经贸合作,促进共同发展。凯塔总统访华的情况,我们已经发布了有关消息,请你查阅。

(http://news.163.com/14/0916/18/A69K9AB000014JB6.html)

3. 追问:这700人是否是中方迄今为止派出的最大规模的维和力量?他们属于什么

兵种?

答：刚才我已讲了，作为安理会常任理事国，中国一贯积极致力于参加联合国维和行动。目前我们是安理会五个常任理事国中派出维和人员最多的国家，迄今已参与16项联合国在非洲的维和行动，目前在非洲共有1800余名维和人员。我们愿继续加强对联合国驻南苏丹特派团维和行动的支持，我们正同联合国秘书处保持密切沟通，如有进一步消息的话，会及时发布。

(http://military.cnr.cn/gz/201409/t20140911_516421397.html)

4. 问：今年9月3日是第一个中国人民抗日战争胜利纪念日，中方将举行哪些纪念活动？习近平主席是否将出席有关活动？

答：今年2月，中国全国人大常委会作出决定，将每年的9月3日确定为中国人民抗日战争胜利纪念日。今天是9月1日，今年的纪念日活动怎么搞，谁出席，请大家再耐心等两天。

(http://www.fmprc.gov.cn/ce/cgmb/chn/zt/wjbfywthmz/t1187211.htm)

5. 会后有记者问及：据报道，中方在海南岛三亚海域扣押了1艘越南渔船和6名船员。请证实并介绍有关情况。

洪磊表示，经向中国海警局了解，7月3日上午，中国海警依法扣押一艘在中国海南岛三亚以南7海里中国领海内非法作业的越南渔船及6名船员。中方有关部门正在依法查处此案。中方再次要求越方采取必要措施，加强对渔民的管束和教育，杜绝类似事件再次发生。

(http://www.fmprc.gov.cn/ce/celb/chn/fyrth/t1171610.htm)

6. 问：8月15日，日本部分内阁成员参拜了靖国神社。中方对此有何评论？

答：日本内阁成员参拜供奉有二战甲级战犯的靖国神社，是对历史正义和人类良知的公然挑战，严重伤害中国等亚洲受害国人民感情。中国外交部刘振民副部长今天上午已紧急召见日本驻华大使木寺昌人，向日方提出严正交涉，表示强烈抗议和严厉谴责。

我愿重申，日本只有正视历史，以史为鉴，才能面向未来。我们敦促日本切实恪守深刻反省侵略历史的表态和承诺，以实际行动取信于国际社会，否则日本同亚洲邻国的关系就没有未来。

(http://www.gov.cn/gzdt/2013-08/15/content_2467423.htm)

参考译文
Versions for Reference

一、请翻译下列记者招待会中的消息发布（Translate the following announcements at press conferences）

1. At the invitation of the Namibian government, Minister of Transport Yang Chuantang,

as the Special Envoy of President Xi Jinping, will attend the inauguration ceremony of Namibian new president Hage Geingob as well as celebrations marking the 25th anniversary of Namibia's independence on March 21.

2. At the invitation of Bulgarian Prime Minister Boyko Borissov and German Chancellor Angela Merkel, Premier of the State Council Li Keqiang will travel to Bulgaria for an official visit and the Seventh Summit of Heads of Government of China and Central and Eastern European Countries in Sofia and then travel to Germany for the fifth round of China-Germany inter-governmental consultation and an official visit from July 5 to 10.

At 10:00 a.m. tomorrow morning, the Foreign Ministry will hold a briefing here for Chinese and foreign press on Premier Li Keqiang's travel. We welcome your participation.

3. In order to further advance the friendly and cooperative relations between China and Somalia, the Chinese government has officially re-opened the Embassy in Somalia on October 12. China has nominated the new Chinese Ambassador to Somalia the other day.

Vice Chinese Foreign Minister Zhang Ming, who is in Somalia for a goodwill visit, Somali President Hassan Sheikh Mohamud, Somali Foreign Minister Abdirahman Duale Beyle and other officials attended the re-opening ceremony. On the same day, President Mohamud and Foreign Minister Beyle met with Vice Chinese Foreign Minister Zhang Ming on separate occasions. They had an in-depth exchange of views and reached broad consensus on the growth of bilateral relations under the new circumstances. People of all circles in Somalia highly appreciate and warmly welcome China's re-opening of the Embassy.

4. A team of 163 medical workers of the People's Liberation Army (PLA) of China arrived in Monrovia, the capital city of Liberia, on November 15, less than one month away from President Xi Jinping's announcement of China's new round of assistance to West African countries in their fight against the Ebola epidemic on October 24.

The PLA contingent is made up of medical workers highly experienced in the prevention and treatment of infectious diseases who have participated in several major tasks such as combating the severe acute respiratory syndrome (SARS). The medical team will work in the Ebola treatment center built by China for Liberia, which will be put into use on November 25. They will do all that they can to treat patients diagnosed with Ebola, train medical workers in Liberia and impart China's experience in preventing and controlling epidemics. The treatment center is built, staffed and operated all by China. No other country has done the same so far in the international

记者招待会报道的翻译
Translation for Coverage of Press Conferences   9 UNIT

assistance to West Africa to fight against the Ebola epidemic.

二、请翻译下列记者招待会中的问答（Translate the following questions and answers at press conferences）

1. Q: According to media reports, the Australian police said on December 16 that the police stormed on that day the Sydney cafe where hostages were taken. Two captives and the attacker were killed, while four others were injured. What is China's comment on that?

   A: The Chinese side opposes all violent acts targeting innocent civilians, mourns those falling victim to the hostage incident in Sydney, and conveys sincere condolences and profound sympathy to the Australian government and people as well as families of those killed and injured.

2. Q: The President of Mali reportedly said that he came away with cooperation deals, including those on railways after his visit to China last week. Can the Chinese side confirm that?

   A: China is ready to enhance economic cooperation and trade with African countries, so as to promote common development. We have already issued the news release about Malian President Ibrahim Keita's visit to China. You may refer to that.

3. Follow-up: Are these 700 people the largest peacekeeping forces China has ever deployed? What kind of soldiers are they?

   Answer: As I just mentioned, as a permanent member of the UN Security Council, China has been proactively participating in the UN peacekeeping missions. Up to now, China has sent the most peacekeepers among the five permanent members of the UN Security Council, participated in 16 UN peacekeeping missions in Africa and has a total number of over 1,800 peacekeepers in Africa. We are willing to step up support to the peacekeeping activities of the UNMISS and are in close communication with the UN Secretariat. Further information will be released if there is any.

4. Q: September 3 this year will be the 1st Victory Day of the Chinese People's War of Resistance Against Japanese Aggression. What kind of commemorative activities will China hold? Will President Xi Jinping attend relevant activities?

   A: Last February, the Standing Committee of the National People's Congress (NPC) of China designated September 3 as the Victory Day of the Chinese People's War of Resistance Against Japanese Aggression. Today is September 1. As to how this year's Victory Day will be celebrated and whom the attendees will be, we will find out two days later. I suggest we wait in patience.

5. After the press conference, a journalist asked: it is reported that the Chinese side

detained one Vietnamese fishing boat and six crew members on board in waters off Sanya, Hainan Island. Please confirm that and give us more details.

Hong Lei: Information from the China Coast Guard shows that on the morning of July 3, the Chinese coast guard detained in accordance with law one Vietnamese fishing boat and six crew members on board that were conducting illegal operation in the territorial waters of China seven nautical miles to the south of Sanya of China's Hainan Island. Competent authorities of China are looking into and handling the case according to law. The Chinese side requests once again the Vietnamese side to take necessary measures to tighten up education and management of fishermen and avoid the recurrence of similar incidents.

6. Q: Some Japanese cabinet members paid homage to the Yasukuni Shrine on August 15. What is China's comment?

A: Japanese cabinet members' visit to the Yasukuni Shrine, where Class-A Second World War criminals are enshrined, is a blatant challenge to historical justice and conscience of mankind and severely hurts the feelings of people in China and other victimized Asian countries. Vice Chinese Foreign Minister Liu Zhenmin urgently summoned Japanese Ambassador to China Masato Kitera this morning, lodging solemn representations and expressing strong protest and severe condemnation.

I would like to reiterate that only by facing up to history and taking it as a mirror, will Japan be able to face towards the future. We urge Japan to truly honor its statement and commitment of reflecting on its history of invasion and take concrete actions to win the trust of the international community. Otherwise, the relations between Japan and its Asian neighbors would have no future.

单元小结
Summary

本单元主要介绍了记者招待会相关报道的翻译。记者招待会一般分为信息发布和答记者问两大环节。信息发布最常见的内容是领导人互访和重大会议的召开，在翻译时要注意选用恰当的时态，过长的句子可酌情采用拆译的技巧。答记者问环节需要掌握记者提问的几种常用句型及其翻译，并在发言人答语的翻译中注意语言的鲜明性、辩论性和模糊性。对于译文要不断揣摩完善，翻译出原文所要表达的气势来。在记者招待会上频繁出现的一个话题是中日争端，包括对侵华战争的历史如何正确认识，以及对于钓鱼岛群岛的领土争议。在相关话题的翻译中需要注意遵循"名从主人"的原则，从语言使用上捍卫国家主权。在对南京大屠杀、慰安妇、参

记者招待会报道的翻译
Translation for Coverage of Press Conferences

> 拜靖国神社等问题的翻译中,要注意通过词汇、标点符号等多种语言手段表明我方发言人的正义立场。

参考文献:

胡庚申、王静:《中外记者招待会用语特征分析》,《清华大学学报》(哲学社会科学版)2001年第3期。

靖鸣、刘锐:《记者招待会的功能和作用》,《改革与战略》2004年第2期。

李琴:《中国外交语言的特点及翻译》,《甘肃科技纵横》2006年第1期。

魏在江:《从语言看语用含糊》,《外语学刊》2006年第2期。

吴鹏、朱密:《外交部发言人应答话语的语用论辩研究:以刘为民就中美稀土贸易摩擦答记者问为例》,《国际新闻界》2015年第9期。

熊永红、彭小妹:《外交语言的语用策略分析——以外交部发言人答记者问为例》,《湖南农业大学学报》(社会科学版)2009年第3期。

杨全红:《翻译与守土有责——从钓鱼岛争端中的翻译事例谈起》,《上海翻译》2014年第4期。

朱义华:《从"争议岛屿"来看外宣翻译工作中的政治意识》,《中国翻译》2012年第6期。

UNIT 10

立场表态类报道的翻译
Translation for Coverage of Positions and Attitudes

单元简介 Introduction

在国际舞台上，各国政府经常需要针对某些国际事件或冲突争端，以当事方或第三方的身份，表明自己的立场和态度。最正式的表态方式是发布立场文件，递交联合国大会或者通过其他正式渠道发表，告知世界各国己方的立场和态度。除此之外，领导人讲话、记者招待会、媒体吹风会、外交访谈等都可能作为外交表态的场合。

外交表态通常由国家领导人或外交部做出，所针对的话题通常包括人权问题、领土争端、海洋主权、气候问题、重大灾难、经济贸易、网络安全、军事反恐、核问题，等等。我国需要表明或者重申立场的话题常常还包括台湾事务、涉藏事务和涉疆事务。所表明的态度主要有反对、赞赏、交涉、呼吁、谴责、慰问等。

立场表态类报道的翻译
Translation for Coverage of Positions and Attitudes

立场表态类报道翻译范例分析
Sample of Translation for Coverage of Positions and Attitudes

范例一（Sample I）

外交部受权发表中国政府关于菲律宾所提南海仲裁案管辖权问题的立场文件（节本）
2014/12/07
Ministry of Foreign Affairs Authorized to Release the Position Paper of the Chinese Government on Matter of Jurisdiction in South China Sea Arbitration Initiated by the Philippines (Abbreviated Version)
2014/12/07

外交部7日受权发表《中华人民共和国政府关于菲律宾共和国所提南海仲裁案管辖权问题的立场文件》，重申中国不接受、不参与该仲裁的严正立场，并从法律角度全面阐述中国关于仲裁庭没有管辖权的立场和理据。

On 7 December, the Ministry of Foreign Affairs was authorized to release the Position Paper of the Government of the People's Republic of China on the Matter of Jurisdiction in the South China Sea Arbitration Initiated by the Republic of the Philippines. The Position Paper reiterates its firm standing that China will neither accept nor participate in the arbitration, and elaborates at length on the legal basis for its position that the Arbitral Tribunal does not have jurisdiction over this case.

***

立场文件指出，菲律宾提请仲裁事项的实质是南海部分岛礁的领土主权问题，超出《联合国海洋法公约》的调整范围，仲裁庭无权审理。

The Position Paper states that the essence of the subject-matter of the arbitration is the territorial sovereignty over several maritime features in the South China Sea, which is beyond the scope of the United Nations Convention on the Law of the Sea and the jurisdiction of the Arbitral Tribunal.

立场文件指出，以谈判方式解决在南海的争端是中菲两国通过双边文件和《南海各方行为宣言》所达成的协议，菲律宾单方面将有关争端提交强制仲裁违反国际法。

The Position Paper states that China and the Philippines have agreed, through bilateral instruments and the Declaration on the Conduct of Parties in the South China Sea, to settle their relevant disputes through negotiation and that by unilaterally initiating the present arbitration, the Philippines has violated international law.

***

立场文件强调，仲裁庭对于菲律宾提起的仲裁明显没有管辖权；各国有权自主选择争端解决方式，中国不接受、不参与菲律宾提起的仲裁具有充分的国际法依据。

The Position Paper emphasizes that the Arbitral Tribunal manifestly has no jurisdiction over the present arbitration and that, by virtue of the freedom of every State to choose the means of dispute settlement, China's rejection of and non-participation in the present arbitration stand on solid ground in international law.

***

立场文件最后指出，菲律宾单方面提起仲裁的做法，不会改变中国对南海诸岛及其附近海域拥有主权的历史和事实，不会动摇中国维护主权和海洋权益的决心和意志，不会影响中国通过直接谈判解决有关争议以及与本地区国家共同维护南海和平稳定的政策和立场。

The Position Paper concludes that the unilateral initiation of the present arbitration by the Philippines will not change the history and fact of China's sovereignty over the South China Sea Islands and the adjacent waters; nor will it shake China's resolve and determination to safeguard its sovereignty and relevant maritime rights and interests; nor will it affect China's policy and position of resolving the disputes in the South China Sea by direct negotiation and working together with other States in the region to maintain peace and stability in the South China Sea.

新闻背景：2013年1月22日，菲律宾就中菲南海争议提起强制仲裁，企图非法获得南沙部分岛礁和黄岩岛主权，妄想将菲群岛基线向海200海里海域划定为菲专属经济区和大陆架，以便攫取其中的海洋资源。中方基于菲方违反《南海各方行为宣言》共识、菲所提事项存在事实和法律上的错误以及对中方的不实指责等拒绝参与仲裁，并于2014年12月7日发布立场文件，表明中方不接受也不参与菲方提起的这场仲裁。范例一选自新华网对于该立场文件发布的双语报道，收录至本书时对译文略做了调整。

原文链接：http://news.xinhuanet.com/english/bilingual/2014-12/07/c_133837662.htm

---

一、范例一文本结构分析（Text Structure Analysis of Sample I）

范例一是一则有关发布立场文件的新闻报道，主要内容为2014年12月7日外交部受权发布立场文件，重申中国政府对于南海诸岛及附近海域的主权，驳斥菲方的错误言行，明确表示中方不接受也不参与菲方提起的强制仲裁。新闻报道的第一部分为导语，首先介绍立场文件的发布时间（2014年12月7日）、发布机关（外交部）、文件名称（《中华人民共和国政府关于菲律宾共和国所提南海仲裁案管辖权问题的立场文件》）以及主要立场和态度（不接受、不参与该仲裁）。通过导语段落就能够基本清楚新闻事件的主

立场表态类报道的翻译
Translation for Coverage of Positions and Attitudes

要内容。第二部分为背景,讲明事件起因(菲律宾单方面提起并强制推进仲裁程序)。如果新闻报道中的事件比较复杂,则还需要梳理事件发展的主要脉络。第三部分是正文,介绍立场文件中的主要观点,也是此类新闻报道的重点。常用句式为"立场文件指出……","立场文件强调……"等。以本篇报道为例,立场文件首先明确指出相关事项超出仲裁庭的调整权力范围,继而指出菲律宾的单方行为违背相关协议并违反国际法,最后表明了中国在此问题上的态度,即"坚决维护中国主权和海洋权益,通过协商和谈判妥善解决南海问题"。

二、范例一翻译解析(Translation Analysis of Sample I)

根据基本立场的不同,外交表态大体可以分为支持、反对和中立三种。(杨烨,2008:128)支持的立场包括赞同、感谢、支持、祝贺、理解、同情等。反对的立场包括担忧、谴责、反对、交涉、抗议等。中立的说法包括"这是某国内政,我们不予评论","希望冲突双方能够管控分歧,妥善处理……"等等。

(一)反对型表态的翻译(Translation of Negative Attitudes)

各个国家的历史文化背景不同,思维模式存在差异,出于己方利益的考虑,对于同一事件会表现出不同的立场和态度。根据分歧程度的不同和语言分寸的把握,反对型表态可能以多种形式呈现,如"关注","严重关注","反对","强烈反对","谴责","抗议"等等。范例一中的"不接受、不参与"就是一种反对型表态。下面我们就以中菲南海争端为主线,介绍反对型表态的各种表达方法及其翻译过程中要注意的某些细节问题。

中菲南海争端源于20世纪50年代,主要是围绕黄岩岛等岛礁主权归属及海域划界问题。①中国政府针对此类争端一贯的主张是追溯历史,用事实说话,驳斥对方的无理主张。比如下面的表述:

> 中国早在13世纪的元朝时期就对包括黄岩岛在内的南海海域进行了天文和地理方位测量。这说明,中国至少在元朝就已经发现并利用了黄岩岛。1935年,中国政府水陆地图审查委员会审定公布的南海诸岛132个岛礁沙滩,黄岩岛位列其中,作为中沙群岛的一部分列入中国版图。
>
> (http://www.china.com.cn/international/txt/2012-06/11/content_25618573.htm)
> China conducted astronomical and geographical surveys of the South China Sea, including Huangyan Island, in the 13th century during the Yuan Dynasty. It shows that China discovered and exploited Huangyan Island in the Yuan Dynasty, to say the least. In

---

① 《中菲南海争端主要是围绕岛礁主权归属及海域划界问题而引发的争议》, http://www.hkfe.hk/news/data/2014-2-14/76486.html

1935, the Lands and Waters Mapping Review Committee of the then Chinese government approved and publicized the geographical names of 132 islands, shoals, reefs and sand bars in the South China Sea, and Huangyan Island, with the name of Scarborough Shoal, was included in the list as part of the Zhongsha Islands of the Chinese territory.

(http://www.fmprc.gov.cn/ce/ceph/eng/zt/nhwt/t941672.htm)

首先,"南海"的翻译是the South China Sea①而不是the South Sea,这是原则性问题,事关国家主权。同理,"东海"的正确译文应该是the East China Sea。涉及历史纪年的表达时,汉语习惯使用朝代或年号来指代,如"北宋末年""康熙年间"等。这样的表达对于不熟悉中国历史的英语读者意义不大,所以无论汉语原文中是否有相应的公元纪年法,英语译文中都应该将其补出,以清晰地传达时间概念,如上面第一个例子中的in the 13th century during the Yuan Dynasty。翻译过程中涉及历史时,要注意历史变迁可能导致现实情况的改变。如原文谈到了1935年的"中国政府水陆地图审查委员会",那时候新中国还未成立,"中国政府"显然并不是现在的中国政府,所以译文中必须添加then加以区分,译为the then Chinese government。当年所公布的132个岛礁沙滩命名中并无"黄岩岛"的提法,是因为当时使用的是"斯卡伯勒礁"的名称。为了避免对方在这种字眼上做文章,译文必须解释清楚,with the name of Scarborough Shoal为原文中没有的成分,增补的意义在于说明黄岩岛就是当年的斯卡伯勒礁,1935年就已经在中国地图上明确标注。但黄岩岛正确的译名依然必须是Huangyan Island,译名权也是维护主权的一部分。(丁立福,2014:31—36)

本着维护主权的坚定立场,中国政府退回了菲律宾单方面提交的对南海争议进行仲裁的照会,②并发布立场文件,阐明事实,剖析本质,明确表示不接受、不参与该仲裁。③范例一中采用的对应表达有两种,分别是will neither accept nor participate in和rejection of and nonparticipation in,表面上看似不予理会,实为一种强有力的反击,是一种更高姿态的驳斥。下面的表态起到的也是类似的作用。

问:菲律宾方面近日称中方正加紧在南海填海造陆,中方对此有何回应?

答:中国对南沙群岛及其附近海域拥有无可争辩的主权,中国在任何岛礁上的行动,都是中国主权范围内的事情,与菲律宾无关。

(http://wcm.fmprc.gov.cn/pub/ce/cgsy/chn/fyrth/t1162952.htm)

Q: What is your reaction to the Philippines saying that China is expanding reclamation in the South China Sea?

---

① http://www.fmprc.gov.cn/mfa_eng/topics_665678/nhwt/

②《中方退回菲律宾提交的南海问题仲裁照会》,http://news.sina.com.cn/o/2013-03-27/095926655732.shtml

③《中方不接受不参与南海仲裁》,http://world.people.com.cn/n/2014/1208/c157278-26169335.html

立场表态类报道的翻译
Translation for Coverage of Positions and Attitudes

A: China exercises indisputable sovereignty on the Nansha Islands and the adjacent waters. Any action taken by China on any island falls within China's sovereignty and has nothing to do with the Philippines.

(http://www.chinaembassy.org.pl/pol/fyrth/t1163315.htm)

菲律宾的"马德雷山脉号"军舰于1999年以故障为由坐滩我国仁爱礁。①虽经中国政府多次交涉,始终未将其拖走。2014年,菲律宾外交部发表声明,公然宣称其15年前谎称的"坐滩"船只系对仁爱礁的占领,自己戳穿了15年前编制的谎言。②中方明确地表示坚定维护主权的立场。翻译实例如下所示:

菲方近日就仁爱礁大肆炒作,到处打悲情牌,并将之纳入所谓国际仲裁,骗取国际社会同情和支持,企图使其对仁爱礁的"占领"合法化。中方坚定维护领土主权和海洋权益,菲方的图谋注定不会得逞。

(http://www.fmprc.gov.cn/ce/ceph/chn/sgdt/t1143880.htm)

Recently, the Philippine side has been playing up the issue of Ren'ai Reef, playing cards of sympathy everywhere, and including the issue into the so-called international arbitration, with an aim to gather sympathy and trust of the international community and legalize its occupation of the Ren'ai Reef. The Chinese side is steadfast in defending its territorial sovereignty and maritime interests and rights. The Philippines' plot is doomed to failure.

(http://english.cri.cn/6909/2014/04/04/191s820667.htm)

和前述一样,首先要注意仁爱礁的译名,应当按照"名从主人"的原则,译为Ren'ai Reef,而不是西方所称的Second Thomas Shoal。需要表明所指关系时,可以将Second Thomas Shoal放在括号中作为注释。此段话语中着重强调"表态",所以"中方坚定维护领土主权和海洋权益"并不是按照汉语的表面结构译为resolutely defends,而是将"坚定"提升为句子的表语,凸显了信息重点。

菲律宾一方除了在国际社会混淆视听外,还在国内制造舆论,煽动反华情绪,制作了三集纪录片《自由》,在菲律宾国家电视台播放。③对此,中方表示强烈不满,实例如下:

中方对菲方纪录片罔顾事实、颠倒黑白对中方进行无理和无据的指责表示强烈

---

① 《菲律宾欲修复仁爱礁坐滩军舰》,http://news.xinhuanet.com/mil/2014-03/24/c_126305594.htm
② 《中国对中菲南海争议的立场》,http://www.fmprc.gov.cn/ce/ceph/chn/sgdt/t1143880.htm
③ 《菲律宾全国动员播放南海纪录片 煽动反华情绪》,http://world.people.com.cn/n/2015/0614/c157278-27151283.html

不满,并对菲现政府大肆炒作南海问题,煽动中菲人民对立的作法表示严重关切。

(http://wcm.fmprc.gov.cn/pub/ce/ceus/chn/fyrth/t1276711.htm)

The Chinese side is strongly dissatisfied with the groundless criticism by the Philippine documentary which ignores the facts and confuses right and wrong, and is deeply concerned about the sitting Philippine government's hyping up of the South China Sea issue and fueling of confrontation between the Chinese and Philippine peoples.

(http://wcm.fmprc.gov.cn/pub/ce/ceus/eng/fyrth/t1276947.htm)

外交表态中的用词尤为谨慎,拿"关切"来说,常见的有"关切""深表关切""重大关切""严重关切"等,所传递出的政治立场和态度不同,程度依次递增。翻译时必须保证用词准确,忠实地反映出原文所表达的关切程度。(高彬,2014:59)

菲律宾的各种宣传炒作得到了某些西方国家的响应,他们声称南海问题"引发国际社会的关切"。[①]对于这样不恰当的表态,中方进行了有理有据的反驳:

近期,有一些人不断对南海问题表示关切。世上本无事,庸人自扰之。我不知道这些人到底关切什么。是航行自由吗?但是,大家都看到了,每年10万多艘各国船只安全自由地通过南海地区,没有任何问题。

(http://www.fmprc.gov.cn/ce/cgosaka/chn/fyrth/t1311150.htm)

Some people keep expressing concern about the South China Sea issue. As a Chinese saying goes, there won't be any trouble in the world, unless people look for trouble themselves. I wonder what on earth these people are concerned about. Is it about navigation freedom? However, as we have all seen, there are over 100,000 ships from countries around the world sailing safely and freely through the South China Sea every year with no problem at all.

(http://www.fmprc.gov.cn/mfa_eng/xwfw_665399/s2510_665401/2511_665403/t1311236.shtml)

中方发言人引经据典,表示"世上本无事,庸人自扰之",这是我国进入新媒体时代后外交辞令出现的一种新的风格,借用古典名言、网络用语以及民族谚语来传情达意,称为"非典型"外交辞令。(李晓华,2015:35)翻译时应当保持政治内涵等效、政治语境等效及修辞表达等效。(胡健、范武邱,2016:75—79)译文unless people look for trouble themselves一语点破本质,明确提醒某些西方国家不该无端插手。另外,译文中添加了as a Chinese saying goes,以表明下文语句的出处,增强了其说服力。

---

① http://www.fmprc.gov.cn/ce/cgosaka/chn/fyrth/t1311150.htm

（二）支持型表态的翻译（Translation of Positive Attitudes）

支持型表态主要出现在领导人会谈、政治文件、外交函电和发言人表态中。翻译时可以根据上下文采用名词、动词或形容词等多种形式灵活处理。如感谢的表达可以是be grateful to sb. for doing sth.，也可以是thank sb. for sth.，还可以是express one's appreciation for。下面的表格列举了部分常见的支持型表态及可供选择的译文表达：

表态	可用的译文表达
支持	support sb. in sth. / render one's (full) support to sth.
鼓励	encourage sb. to do sth. / encourage sth.
相信	believe that / is confident that / trust that / have faith in sth.
赞赏	express one's appreciation for sth.
感谢	be grateful to sb. for doing sth. / thank sb. for sth. / express one's appreciation for
愿意	be willing to do / be ready to do
祝贺	congratulate sb. on sth. / send congratulations to
慰问	express sympathy to sb. / extend condolence to sb. on sth.
呼吁	call for sth. / call on sb. to do sth.

下面的翻译实例体现了相关表达法在具体语境中的运用。请注意画线部分的具体用法，尤其是名词单复数以及介词搭配的问题：

  2015年3月14日，外交部长王毅致电瓦努阿图外长萨托·基尔曼，就瓦努阿图遭受超强飓风袭击，造成严重财产损失和人员伤亡表示同情和慰问，并表示中国政府和人民愿向瓦努阿图政府和人民提供力所能及的救灾援助。

(http://www.gov.cn/xinwen/2015-03/16/content_2834699.htm)

  On March 14, 2015, Foreign Minister Wang Yi <u>sent a condolence message to</u> Minister for Foreign Affairs, International Cooperation and External Trade Sato Kilman of Vanuatu, <u>extending sympathy and condolence over</u> the heavy property loss and casualties left by the ferocious hurricane that hit Vanuatu. He also expressed that the Chinese government and people <u>are ready to</u> assist the government and people of Vanuatu in disaster relief within their capability.

(http://www.fmprc.gov.cn/mfa_eng/zxxx_662805/t1246176.shtml)

  中方感谢乌方在反恐问题上给予中方的坚定支持，愿同乌方加强反恐交流合作，共同造福两国人民。

(http://world.people.com.cn/n/2014/0912/c1002-25652972.html)

  The Chinese side <u>is grateful to</u> Uzbekistan for its firm support in the counter-terrorism issue and <u>is willing to</u> enhance exchanges and cooperation on counter-terrorism with Uzbekistan and join efforts to benefit the two peoples.

(http://www.fmprc.gov.cn/mfa_eng/wjbxw/t1191950.shtml)

中方积极评价朴槿惠总统提出的"半岛信任进程"等设想,支持半岛南北双方谋求改善关系。中方始终坚持半岛无核化目标,愿同韩方一道推动尽早重启六方会谈,把半岛核问题真正纳入可持续、不可逆、有实效的对话进程。

(http://news.xinhuanet.com/2014-05/27/c_1110867307.htm)

China <u>speaks positively of</u> the concepts of "Trust-Building Process on the Korean Peninsula" proposed by President Park Geun-hye and <u>supports</u> the two sides on the Korean Peninsula to seek for improvement of their relations. China has always <u>adhered to</u> the goal of denuclearization of the Korean Peninsula, and <u>is willing to</u> work together with the ROK to promote an early resumption of the Six-Party Talks and bring the Korean Peninsula nuclear issue into a sustainable, irreversible and effective process of dialogue.

(http://www.fmprc.gov.cn/mfa_eng/zxxx_662805/t1160027.shtml)

(三)中立型表态的翻译(Translation of Neutral Attitudes)

有的时候,外交表态也可能是中立的,不偏向冲突中的任何一方。此时表态动词一般是"希望""呼吁""指出"等,而从句内部通常会用到情态动词would, could, should等。例如:

作为印、巴共同的邻国和朋友,中方真诚希望印巴双方继续通过对话协商,冷静、妥善处理有关分歧,共同致力于维护南亚地区的和平与稳定。

(http://www.fmprc.gov.cn/ce/ceat/chn/wjbfyrth/t1004473.htm)

As their common neighbour and friend, China sincerely <u>hopes</u> that the two sides <u>would continue</u> to calmly and properly resolve their differences through dialogues and negotiations and jointly safeguard peace and stability in South Asia.

(http://www.fmprc.gov.cn/ce/cglagos/eng/xwfb/fyrth/t1004665.htm)

还有一种中立型表态是不予评论,它符合我国不干涉别国内政的一贯原则。示例如下:

问:据报道,美国密苏里州大陪审团24日作出决定,不起诉枪杀非洲裔青年的白人警察威尔逊。中方对此事有何评论?

答:我注意到该案件有关审理广受关注。这是美国内部事务,我不予置评。

(http://www.fmprc.gov.cn/ce/cejp/chn/fyrth/t1214439.htm)

Q: The state grand jury of Missouri of the US made a decision on November 24 of not indicting a white policeman named Darren Wilson, who shot dead an African-American teenager. Does China have any comment on that?

A: I have noted that the trial has garnered wide attention. It belongs to America's internal affairs. I have no comment on that.

(http://www.fmprc.gov.cn/ce/cgct/eng/fyrth/t1214543.htm)

范例二（Sample II）

第69届联合国大会中方立场文件（节本）
Position Paper of the People's Republic of China at the 69th Session of the United Nations General Assembly (Abbreviated Version)

恐怖主义是全球公敌，严重威胁国际安全与发展。国际社会应按照联合国宪章及其他公认的国际法和国际关系准则，开展广泛合作，共同打击恐怖主义，全面执行安理会相关决议及联合国《全球反恐战略》。联合国及其安理会应在国际反恐斗争中发挥领导和协调作用。反恐应坚持标本兼治，不能搞双重标准。中方主张对国际恐怖主义新动向保持高度警惕，坚决打击恐怖分子利用互联网等现代通讯技术传播、煽动、蛊惑恐怖思想，招募恐怖分子，资助和筹划恐怖行为。

Terrorism is the common enemy of the world which poses a serious threat to international security and development. The international community should carry out extensive cooperation to jointly combat terrorism in accordance with the Charter of the United Nations and other universally recognized international law and norms governing international relations, and fully implement relevant Security Council resolutions and the UN Global Counter-Terrorism Strategy. The UN and its Security Council should play a leading and coordinating role in the battle against terrorism. A holistic approach that addresses both the symptoms and root causes of terrorism should be adopted and the practice of double standards in fighting terrorism must be rejected. China maintains that countries should stay vigilant against the development of international terrorism and crack down on the attempts of terrorists to spread, instigate and sell terrorist ideas, recruit terrorists, and finance and plan terrorist attacks with the use of the Internet and other modern communications technologies.

***

中方坚持实现朝鲜半岛无核化，坚持维护半岛和平稳定，坚持通过对话协商解决问题。对话协商是解决半岛有关问题的唯一有效途径，六方会谈是平衡解决各方关切、实现半岛无核化的现实有效平台。希望有关各方避免采取可能导致局势紧张升温的行动，积极开展接触对话，继续致力于通过谈判解决分歧，争取早日重启六方会谈。

China is committed to a denuclearized, peaceful and stable Korean Peninsula and settlement of relevant issues through dialogue and consultation. Dialogue and consultation is the only effective way to resolve relevant issues, and the Six-Party Talks is a practical and effective platform for addressing the concerns of all parties in a balanced manner and achieving denuclearization on the Peninsula. China hopes that the parties concerned will refrain from any action that may raise tensions, engage in contact and dialogue, stay committed to resolving differences through negotiation and work for the early resumption of the Six-Party Talks.

***

中方坚决反对大规模杀伤性武器及其运载工具的扩散。为实现防扩散目标，各国应致力于营造互信、合作的国际和地区安全环境，消除大规模杀伤性武器扩散的动因；坚持通过政治外交手段解决防扩散问题；切实维护和加强国际防扩散机制；平衡处理防扩散与和平利用科学技术的关系，摒弃双重标准。中方愿同有关各方加强交流合作，共同推动国际防扩散进程。

China is firmly opposed to the proliferation of WMDs and their means of delivery. To achieve the goal of non-proliferation, all countries should help build a global and regional security environment of mutual trust and cooperation, reduce the motivation for the proliferation of WMDs; resolve proliferation issues by political and diplomatic means; uphold and strengthen the international non-proliferation regime; and handle the relationship between non-proliferation and peaceful use of science and technology in a balanced way and abandon double standards. China will step up exchanges and cooperation with all parties to move forward the international non-proliferation process.

新闻背景：联合国大会立场文件是各国政府向联合国提交的，阐述本国针对地区热点问题以及发展、军控、人权等问题所持立场的文件。每年提交一次。范例二选自外交部官网发布的2014年中方立场文件。

原文链接：http://www.fmprc.gov.cn/ce/ceun/chn/zgylhg/t1188820.htm

译文链接：http://www.fmprc.gov.cn/mfa_eng/zxxx_662805/t1188610.shtml

---

一、范例二文本结构分析（Text Structure Analysis of Sample II）

范例二为外交新闻报道中的一种特殊形式，即全文刊登立场文件。所节选的第一段来自原文第三节"反对恐怖主义"，其前面的两节分别是"联合国成立70周年"和"联合国改革"。显然，立场文件各部分的排列顺序是以重要性为依据的。第二段选自原文的第六节"地区热点问题"，逐条表明了中国对于朝鲜半岛局势、阿富汗、中东、伊拉克、伊核等问题的立场和主张。最后一个自然段选自原文的第八节"军控、裁军和防扩散"，阐明了中国倡导和平利用核能，反对核扩散的立场。对于某个具体问题的立场表述通常包括以下主要内容：本国针对该议题的基本立场和态度（如"中方坚决反对大规模杀伤性武器及其运载工具的扩散"），本国赞成及签署的相关国际协议（如"《全球反恐战略》"），本国愿意采取的行动（"愿同有关各方加强交流合作，共同推动国际防扩散进程"）等。

二、范例二翻译解析（Translation Analysis of Sample II）

范例二中呈现的是中国政府对于各种热点问题的原则性立场，并非针对某一特定事件。作为从事外交相关翻译的译者，应当每年仔细研读外交部发布的联合国大会中方立场文件中、英文版，把握中方在热点问题上的基本态度，这有助于译者在翻译领导人或发言人针对具体事件的表态时，准确理解深层含义，产出最为恰当的译文。本节就以各种热点问题为例，研究立场表述常用语句。

（一）恐怖主义问题（On Terrorism）

正如范例二中所述，恐怖主义是全球公敌，各个国家都在加大投入，展开合作，严厉打击恐怖主义。中国也是"东突"等恐怖势力的受害者，对于反恐的态度是坚定的和一贯的。[①]此时常用的表达包括对恐怖活动的谴责、对受到伤害的人民和国家的慰问，以及对反恐行动的支持等。例如：

> 中国反对一切形式的恐怖主义，反对在反恐问题上实行"双重标准"。我们支持联合国及其安理会在国际反恐合作中发挥主导作用，希望国际社会继续加强合作，共同防范和打击恐怖主义。
>
> (http://big5.fmprc.gov.cn/gate/big5/www.fmprc.gov.cn/ce/ceun/chn/zgylhg/jjalh/alhzh/fk/t1039468.htm)

> China rejects terrorism in all its forms and manifestations. China rejects any double standard in dealing with counter-terrorism. We support the United Nations and the Security Council in the international cooperative effort against terrorism. We hope that the international community will continue to cooperate in the common effort to prevent and combat terrorism.
>
> (http://big5.fmprc.gov.cn/gate/big5/www.fmprc.gov.cn/ce/ceun/eng/chinaandun/securitycouncil/thematicissues/counterterrorism/t1041318.htm)

2017年11月25日，国家主席习近平向埃及总统塞西致慰问电，就11月24日埃及北西奈省阿里什市一清真寺发生严重恐怖袭击向无辜遇难者表示沉痛哀悼，向塞西总统、遇难者家属和受伤人员致以诚挚的慰问。

(http://www.fmprc.gov.cn/web/zyxw/t1513938.shtml)

[①]《崔天凯：东突恐怖势力罪证确凿 威胁中国国家安全》，http://www.chinanews.com/gn/2013/01-16/4490980.shtml

On November 25, 2017, President Xi Jinping sent a message of condolences to President Abdel-Fattah al-Sisi of Egypt over the severe terrorist attack on a mosque in El Arish, North Sinai Province, Egypt on November 24. He <u>expressed profound condolences</u> to the innocent victims and <u>extended sincere sympathies</u> to President Abdel-Fattah al-Sisi, the bereaved families and the injured.

(http://www.fmprc.gov.cn/mfa_eng/zxxx_662805/t1514512.shtml)

王毅强烈谴责袭击中国驻吉尔吉斯斯坦使馆事件,要求吉方尽快查明真相,严惩元凶,杜绝此类事件再次发生。中方支持双方进一步深化反恐合作,维护共同安全利益。

(http://www.fmprc.gov.cn/web/zyxw/t1393144.shtml)

Wang Yi <u>strongly condemned</u> the attack against the Chinese Embassy in Kyrgyzstan, and asked the Kyrgyz side to find out the truth as soon as possible, <u>punish those responsible</u> and avoid a reoccurrence of such attacks. China supports both sides to further deepen anti-terrorism cooperation so as to safeguard common security interests.

(http://www.fmprc.gov.cn/mfa_eng/zxxx_662805/t1393590.shtml)

(二)领土争端问题(On Territorial Disputes)

领土完整和海洋主权属于国家的根本利益,我国政府对于任何此类问题的态度一直都是坚定的、不可动摇的。由于各种历史问题,我国与周边国家存在某些陆地边境或海洋主权方面的争议。对此,我国的原则立场是坚定维护国家主权和领土完整。针对其他国家之间的边境冲突,我国的表态通常包括对伤及无辜的行为予以谴责、对伤亡表示同情和慰问,规劝双方管控分歧,通过对话和谈判,以和平的方式解决争端。以下是中方领导人和发言人相关表态:

在日本政府非法"购岛"一周年之际,日方不认真反省自身错误行为,反而对中方正常的海空活动说三道四,中方对此表示强烈不满。中方将继续采取必要措施坚定维护钓鱼岛主权。我们要求日方纠正错误,停止一切损害中国领土主权的行动,为消除改善两国关系的障碍作出实实在在的努力。

(http://wcm.fmprc.gov.cn/pub/ce/cgsy/chn/fyrth/t1075559.htm)

One year after the Japanese government's illegal "purchase" of the Diaoyu Islands, Japan does not seriously reflect on its mistakes. Rather, it is making irresponsible remarks on China's normal air and sea operations. China is <u>strongly dissatisfied about that</u>. China will continue to take necessary measures to <u>firmly defend sovereignty</u> over the Diaoyu Islands. We <u>urge Japan to correct mistakes</u>, stop all activities detrimental to China's territorial sovereignty and make real efforts to remove obstacles in the improvement of bilateral relations.

(http://www.fmprc.gov.cn/ce/ceuk/eng/HotTopics/fyrth/t1075618.htm)

中方欢迎巴以双方延长临时停火。当前，巴以正在开罗举行间接谈判。中方呼吁双方在停火期间保持最大限度克制，并以理性、负责任的态度加紧谈判，尽快达成长期停火协议。

(http://www.fmprc.gov.cn/ce/cekor/chn/fyrth/t1182811.htm)

China <u>welcomes</u> the extension of the temporary ceasefire between Palestine and Israel. At present, Palestine and Israel are having indirect negotiations in Cairo. China <u>calls on both sides to show maximum restraint</u> during the ceasefire, step up negotiations in a reasonable and responsible manner, and reach a long-term ceasefire agreement as soon as possible.

(http://sk.china-embassy.org/slo/fyrth/t1182935.htm)

（三）伊核、朝核问题（On Nuclear Issues of Iran and DPRK）

伊朗从20世纪50年代开始核能源开发活动。2003年初，伊朗宣布发现并提炼出能为其核电站提供燃料的铀。① 后又不顾国际社会的反对，执意坚持铀转化实验，并于2012年初制造出首个国产核燃料棒。② 朝鲜于20世纪50年代末开始核技术研究，2002年宣布退出《核不扩散条约》。2006年10月9日，朝鲜成功进行首次地下核试验。③ 中国是核不扩散体系的坚定维护者，也是伊核问题六方谈判及朝核问题六方谈判的参与者，常见的表态有"支持通过对话解决伊核/朝核问题"，"反对诉诸武力的选项"，和"不赞成单边制裁的冲动"。请参看以下翻译实例：

维护伊核问题全面协议的完整性和严肃性，有助于维护国际核不扩散体系及中东和平稳定，对通过政治外交手段解决其他热点问题也有示范意义。中方一贯坚决反对单边制裁和"长臂管辖"。

(http://www.fmprc.gov.cn/web/wjbxw_673019/t1562745.shtml)

Safeguarding the integrity and seriousness of the <u>JCPOA on the Iranian nuclear issue</u> is not only conducive to <u>upholding the international nuclear non-proliferation regime</u> and maintaining peace and stability in the Middle East, but also serves as an exemplar for the settlement of other hotspot issues through political and diplomatic means. China consistently and firmly opposes unilateral sanctions and "long-arm jurisdiction".

(http://www.fmprc.gov.cn/mfa_eng/wjbxw/t1563397.shtml)

中方坚定致力于半岛无核化，坚持维护半岛和平稳定，坚持通过对话协商解决

---

① 《伊朗核问题风波再起》，http://www.people.com.cn/GB/paper81/16831/1478971.html
② 《伊朗宣称已生产并测试首枚自制核燃料棒》，http://www.chinadaily.com.cn/hqzx/2012-01/02/content_14369694.htm
③ 《朝鲜核爆早有迹象》，http://www.gxbyw.com/toutiao/guoji/201601/37297.shtml

问题。中方愿继续发挥积极、建设性作用,同包括美方在内的有关各方一道,推进半岛问题政治解决进程。

(http://un.fmprc.gov.cn/web/tpxw/t1569025.shtml)

China <u>firmly adheres to the denuclearization of the Korean Peninsula</u>, upholds peace and stability of the Korean Peninsula, and <u>sticks to the settlement of issues through dialogue and negotiation</u>. China is willing to continue to play an active and constructive role, and work with all parties concerned including the US to promote the process of the political settlement of the Korean Peninsula issue.

(http://www.fmprc.gov.cn/mfa_eng/zxxx_662805/t1569844.shtml)

(四)港澳台问题(On Questions Related to Hong Kong, Macao and Taiwan)

由于历史原因,我国香港和澳门曾分别被英国和葡萄牙占据很长时间,形成了与大陆不同的政治、经济、文化体制。在中国政府的不懈努力下,他们分别于1997年和1999年回归祖国,以特别行政区的形式实现"一国两制"。而台湾直到今天为止,仍未与大陆实现统一。但是台湾是中国的一部分,这是不能否认的事实。中国政府解决台湾问题的基本方针是"和平统一、一国两制"。

本着"一个中国"的根本原则,在译文涉及港澳台时需要注意以下几点:"香港"的全称是the Hong Kong Special Administrative Region (SAR) of the People's Republic of China,可以简写为the Hong Kong SAR。在一般行文中,可以将其直接简称为Hong Kong,但是在谈到香港政府或者香港的统治时,必须加有SAR字样。"香港人"则翻译为Hongkongers。"澳门"的翻译也是相同的道理,一般使用the Macao SAR的表达,注意不要拼写成Macau,这是葡萄牙语中的拼写法,带有挥之不去的殖民色彩。"澳门人"翻译为Macanese。"台湾"的英文名称为Taiwan,注意要连写,不能从中断开。在英语表述中,不能有任何言辞以任何方式暗示台湾可能是一个"独立的国家",或者造成"一中一台"的暗示。同理,以mainland China来翻译"中国大陆"也是不严谨的,正确的译文应该是the Chinese mainland。台湾只是中国的一部分,所以China和Taiwan两个词不能作为同级词并列使用,不能出现China and Taiwan的表达,而应该表述为the Chinese mainland and Taiwan。海峡两岸各有一个机构致力于发展两岸关系(cross-Straits relations),它们分别是the Beijing-based Association for Relations Across the Taiwan Straits (ARATS) 和 the Taipei-based Straits Exchange Foundation (SEF),前者称为海峡两岸关系协会(海协会),后者称为海峡交流基金会(海基会)。另外,港澳台的很多地名、人名并非汉语拼音,香港的人名还可能是英文与粤语拼音相混合,比如世界卫生组织总干事陈冯富珍女士的英文名为Margaret Chan Fung Fu-chun,翻译过程中涉及这些名称时务必进行网络检索查证。以下是几则翻译实例:

香港回归以来,"一国两制"的实践取得巨大成就,这是任何客观和不带偏见

立场表态类报道的翻译
Translation for Coverage of Positions and Attitudes

10
UNIT

的人都不能否认的事实。香港是中国的特别行政区，香港事务纯属中国内政，英方无权干预，英方对香港的所谓"责任"根本不存在。

(http://et.china-embassy.org/chn/fyrth/t1243347.htm)

The "One Country, Two Systems" policy has gained substantial achievements since the return of Hong Kong. This is a fact that any objective and unbiased person will agree to. Hong Kong is a special administrative region of China, and Hong Kong affairs are entirely China's domestic affairs, which the UK side has no right to interfere in. There is no such thing as "obligation" that UK claims over Hong Kong.

(http://www.fmprc.gov.cn/mfa_eng/xwfw_665399/s2510_665401/t1243377.shtml)

2012年3月8日，外交部部长杨洁篪在北京会见澳门特别行政区行政长官崔世安。杨洁篪对澳门回归12年多来各方面取得的巨大成就表示祝贺，感谢特区政府对外交部和驻澳门公署工作的支持。

(http://www.gov.cn/gzdt/////2012-03/09/content_2087234.htm)

On March 8, 2012, Foreign Minister Yang Jiechi met with Chief Executive of the Macao Special Administrative Region (SAR) Chui Sai On in Beijing. Yang congratulated on the enormous achievements Macao has made in all aspects since its return 12 years ago and thanked the government of the Macao SAR for its support to the work of the Foreign Ministry and the Commissioner's Office.

(http://www.fmprc.gov.cn/mfa_eng/wjbxw/t913024.shtml)

无论台湾岛内局势发生什么变化，中国政府坚持一个中国原则、反对"台独"、反对"两个中国"和"一中一台"的立场没有改变，也不会改变。在维护国家主权和领土完整的重大问题上，中国政府的意志坚如磐石，绝不容忍任何形式的"台独"分裂活动。

(http://www.fmprc.gov.cn/web/fyrbt_673021/t1332288.shtml)

The Chinese government sticks to the One-China principle and opposes "Taiwan independence", "two Chinas" and "one China, one Taiwan". This position remains unchanged and will not change regardless of what happens in Taiwan. On such a major issue as safeguarding state sovereignty and territorial integrity, the Chinese government has rock-solid determination and never tolerates any separatist activities aiming at "Taiwan independence".

(http://www.fmprc.gov.cn/mfa_eng/xwfw_665399/s2510_665401/t1332293.shtml)

（五）涉疆、涉藏问题（On Questions Related to Xinjiang and Tibet）

中国的行政区划中包括五个民族自治区，外交表态中经常提到的是新疆维吾尔自治区和西藏自治区。首先从名称上来讲，这两个自治区的标准英文分别为the Xinjiang Uyghur Autonomous Region和the Tibet Autonomous Region (TAR)，可以分别简称为

C-E TRANSLATION OF DIPLOMATIC NEWS

Xinjiang和Tibet。因为是民族自治地区，很多地名都是以民族语言发音为准，而不是使用拼音。比如他们的自治区首府分别拼写为Urumqi和Lhasa。新疆的主要困扰是"东突"势力的分裂活动。西藏的主要困扰是"藏独"和达赖喇嘛问题。达赖喇嘛是藏传佛教格鲁派两大活佛转世系统之一的称号，也是西藏政教最高首领。叛逃国外的是十四世达赖丹增嘉措，英文为the 14th Dalai Lama (Tenzin Gyatso)，可以简称为the Dalai Lama。下列实例当中可以看到涉疆涉藏问题表态时常用的表达：

近日中国新疆发生的暴力恐怖袭击案件，是境内外恐怖势力相互勾联、蓄意制造的暴力恐怖事件。长期以来，境内外"三股势力"勾结国际恐怖势力在新疆地区策划实施大量暴力恐怖活动，破坏新疆发展稳定。中方将继续与有关国家进一步加强合作，共同打击包括"东突"恐怖势力在内的恐怖组织。

(http://www.fmprc.gov.cn/ce/ceat/chn/wjbfyrth/t1055761.htm)

The recent violent terrorist attack in Xinjiang was maliciously launched by terrorist forces in and outside China. The "Three Forces" in and outside China has plotted and carried out a large number of violent terrorist activities in Xinjiang in collusion with international terrorist forces for a long time, undermining Xinjiang's stability and development. China will step up cooperation with relevant countries to jointly combat terrorist organizations, including the East Turkistan terrorist forces.

(http://www.fmprc.gov.cn/ce/ceuk/eng/HotTopics/fyrth/t1055812.htm)

今年"3·10"前后又出现了海外"藏独"分子试图冲闯中国驻某些国家外交机构的情况，这再次证明和暴露了"藏独"势力的分裂本质和暴力倾向。世界上没有任何国家承认所谓"西藏流亡政府"，没有任何国家承认西藏独立。很多国家都明确表示，反对"藏独"等分裂势力利用其领土从事反华分裂的政治活动，对此我们表示赞赏。

(http://edinburgh.china-consulate.org/chn/wjbfyrth/t663351.htm)

Around March 10 this year, Tibet-Independence forces tried to break into some Chinese overseas diplomatic missions, which once again testifies and exposes their nature of separatism and violence tendency. Not a single country in the world recognizes the so-called "Tibetan Government in Exile" and nor Tibet as independent. Many countries have explicitly expressed their opposition to the anti-China separatist and political activities by the Tibet-Independence separatist forces on their territory. We express our appreciation to that.

(http://www.fmprc.gov.cn/ce/ceuk/eng/zt/fyrth/t663634.htm)

学生译作讲评
Analysis of Students' Translation Practice

原文链接：http://www.gov.cn/gzdt/2014-01/01/content_2558276.htm

新闻原文：记者：日本安倍政府上台以来在对华政策上持续示强，前几天安倍还去参拜了靖国神社。与此同时，钓鱼岛问题仍陷僵局。您如何看待中日关系的走向？

学生译文：Reporter: Japan's Abe government, since its coming into power, has continued to hold tough policies toward China, and Shinzo Abe even visited the Yasukuni Shrine a few days ago. Meanwhile, the Diaoyu Island Issue still remains deadlocked. How do you interpret the future development of relations between China and Japan?

翻译评析：在英文中，尽量不要使用插入语，无谓地造成文本阅读上的困难。该句译文中，since its coming into power完全可以调到句首，而且coming into power的逻辑主语和句子主语一致，都是"日本安倍政府"，所以its可以省去。"参拜"的含义不是visit那么简单，应该改为paid homage to。remains本意就是"仍然保持"，所以它前面的still是多余的。interpret显然不是"看待"，而是"诠释""理解"的意思，应当改为view。"中日关系"可以使用更为简洁的表达方式China-Japan relations。

新闻原文：刘振民：去年以来，由于日方在钓鱼岛问题上制造"购岛"闹剧，中日关系持续面临严重困难。12月26日，日本首相安倍晋三逆历史潮流而动，公然挑战国际正义和人类良知，悍然参拜供奉有二战甲级战犯牌位的靖国神社，给本已陷入严峻局面的中日关系制造了新的重大政治障碍。

学生译文：Liu Zhenmin: Since last year, due to the farce of "Island Purchase" fabricated by Japan on Diaoyu Island Issue, China-Japan relations have continued to face serious difficulties. On December 26, Japan's Prime Minister Shinzo Abe, inversing the historical trend and openly challenging international justice and human conscience, brazenly visited the Yasukuni Shrine in which memorial tablets of Class A war criminals from World War II are consecrated. This has posed new and major political barriers to China-Japan relations which have already been in a severe situation.

翻译评析：从译文第一句可以看出，学生显然没有理清原句的逻辑关系。仔细分析就会发现，"中日关系持续面临严重困难"的时间起点并不是"去年"一整年，而恰恰是"购岛"闹剧事件，"去年"只是该闹剧事件的时间状语。调整后的译文为China-Japan relations have been beset by continuous, serious difficulties since the Japanese side created the farce of "purchasing" the Diaoyu Islands last year. 第二句中"逆历史潮流而动"并不表示要把整个历史潮流翻转过来，而只是其个人行为与历史潮流背道而驰，并且inverse也不能作为动词使用，可调整为going against the tide of history。"悍然"用brazenly感情色彩过于浓重，与原文不符，可调整为blatantly。"中日关系"本身表意就很清楚，所以其后的定语从句可以是非限定性的，即在which前面加上逗号。"本已陷入严峻局面"可调整为have already been beset by serious difficulties。

新闻原文：我们一贯主张本着"以史为鉴、面向未来"的精神，在中日四个政治文件的基础上发展长期健康稳定的中日关系。当务之急是日本必须纠正错误，停止挑衅言行，为两国关系改善作出切实努力。

学生译文：We always advocate developing long-term, healthy, and stable China-Japan relations on the basis of four political documents between China and Japan in the spirit of "taking history as a mirror and looking into the future". It is imperative that Japan must correct its mistakes, stop provocative words and deeds, and make practical efforts in improving the relations between the two countries.

翻译评析："我们一贯主张……"这一句中，"一贯"意即从过去的某个时间到现在一直是这种主张，属于完成时态，谓语可修改为have always advocated。"健康"在这里并不是指人的身体健康，不对应于healthy的概念，而应该是sound。"中日四个政治文件"是特定的文件，前面需要加上定冠词the。It is imperative后面的主语从句中应该使用should加动词原形构成的虚拟语气，should可以省略，所以学生译文中的must要去掉。最后的"作出切实努力"，其目的是"两国关系改善"，所以最好用不定式表达，即make practical efforts to improve。

新闻原文：记者：亚洲安全形势存在一些不确定因素。朝核等问题依然处于僵持状态，未来局势走向不确定性较大。中国将如何发挥作用，维护地区和平与稳定？

学生译文：Reporter: There exist some uncertain factors in the security situation in Asia. The Korean Peninsula nuclear issue and other issues are still in stalemate and the direction of future situation has considerable uncertainty. How will China play its role in maintaining regional peace and stability?

翻译评析：这里的there be句型显得语言很啰唆，完全可以使用更为简洁的主谓结构some uncertain factors exist。"朝核问题"可译为the Korean Peninsula nuclear issue或the Korean nuclear issue。"未来"实际修饰的是"走向"，而不是"局势"，所以正确的译文应该是the future direction of the situation。

新闻原文：刘振民：亚太地区形势总体稳定，但也存在一些热点敏感问题。中方高度关注朝鲜半岛局势发展，一直在为推动妥善解决朝鲜半岛核问题而积极劝和促谈，为维护半岛和平稳定作出不懈努力。实现朝鲜半岛无核化，维护半岛和平与稳定，通过对话协商以和平方式解决问题，这是中方坚定不移的立场。朝核问题由来已久、错综复杂，希望有关各方相向而行，多做增进信任、缓和局势的事，早日回归对话轨道。

学生译文：Liu Zhenmin: The overall situation in the Asia-Pacific region is stable, but there exist some hotspot and sensitive issues. China pays great attention to the development of the Korean Peninsula situation and always commits itself to actively promoting peace talks so as to promote proper solution to the Korean Peninsula nuclear issue, making unremitting efforts to maintain peace and stability on the Korean Peninsula. It is China's unswerving position to

立场表态类报道的翻译
Translation for Coverage of Positions and Attitudes

realize denuclearization of the Korean Peninsula, maintain peace and stability on the Korean Peninsula, and resolve the issues peacefully through dialogue and consultation. The Korean Peninsula nuclear issue is a long-standing and intricate issue. We hope that all relevant parties meet each other halfway, do more things to enhance trust and ease the situation, and return on the track of dialogue at an early date.

翻译评析：学生译文第一句中对"存在热点敏感问题"的翻译使用了there exist句型，不够简练，可改译为some hotspot and sensitive issues also exist。译文第二句中"一直在推动"应使用完成时态。commit一词的用法要注意，此处直接使用被动形式即可，也就是has always been committed to。问题的"解决"在正式场合下用resolution of，学生译文中的solution to表达的是"解决方案"，而非"解决"这一行为。原文段尾处"增进信任、缓和局势"旨在说明该做什么样的事，而不是做那些事的目的，可修改为do more things that can enhance trust and ease the situation。

新闻原文：记者：2013年，南海局势明显缓和，中国与周边国家海上合作进入新阶段。请您介绍中国在推动海上合作方面做了哪些工作，有哪些成果？

学生译文：Reporter: In 2013, the situation in South China Sea has been eased obviously, and the maritime cooperation between China and neighboring countries has stepped into a new stage. Please brief us on China's efforts to promote the maritime cooperation and the relevant achievements.

翻译评析：学生译文中主要是时态错误。In 2013确定了一个具体的过去的时间，后面紧跟的两个并列分句都应该使用一般过去时态，分别为was obviously eased和stepped into。

新闻原文：刘振民：我们的一贯立场是，中国对南沙群岛及其附近海域拥有无可争辩的主权，对于有关当事方围绕南沙群岛的岛礁争议及在南海部分海域的划界争议，应由直接当事方通过谈判妥善处理、和平解决，在争议解决前可以"搁置争议，共同开发"。我们为此作出了积极努力。2013年，我们同东盟国家积极落实《南海各方行为宣言》，并启动了在《宣言》框架下制订"南海行为准则"的磋商。中国分别同文莱、越南达成重要共识，在南海共同开发问题上向前迈出了一大步。

学生译文：Liu Zhenmin: Our position is consistent that China has indisputable sovereignty over the Nansha Islands and the adjacent waters. The relevant parties' disputes over some islands and reefs of the Nansha Islands and the demarcation disputes over some waters in South China Sea should be solved properly and peacefully by the parties directly related to the disputes through negotiations. All relevant parties may "shelve disputes and carry out joint development" before the disputes solved. To this end, we have made active efforts. In 2013, along with the ASEAN countries, we actively implemented the Declaration on the Conduct of Parties in the South China Sea (DOC), and launched the consultations on the formulation of the Code of Conduct in the South China Sea (COC) under the framework of the DOC. China has reached important consensuses with Brunei and Vietnam, taking a big step forward on the issue of jointly developing the South China Sea.

翻译评析："一贯立场"不能用一般现在时来表示，可调整为our position has always been that …。"划界争议"中的"争议"已由前面的disputes统领，此处只需说the demarcation of some waters即可。译文第二句末尾的Through negotiations最好前移，放在peacefully后面，使句子结构更为紧凑。原文中的"在争议解决前可以'搁置争议，共同开发'"一句，学生选择了添加主语All relevant parties的方式来组句，如果处理为Before the settlement of disputes, it is advisable to …的句式会更为妥贴。译文最后一句漏译了原文中的"分别"一词，可在Vietnam后面添加respectively。

实战练习
Translation Practice

一、请翻译下列有关立场与表态的语句（Translate the following sentences on declarations of positions and attitudes）

1. 中方对当前也门人道主义形势深表关切，欢迎有关方面作出人道主义停火的决定，希望这有助于推动也门当前局势尽快得到缓和。中方呼吁有关各方切实落实联合国安理会有关决议、海合会倡议等，通过政治对话化解分歧，早日恢复也门稳定和正常合法秩序。

    (http://news.xinhuanet.com/mil/2015-05/12/c_127790958.htm)

2. 我能够感觉到菲方一些人近来在南海问题上的躁动。中方已经多次明确阐述了有关立场。我想善意提醒菲方，中国不会欺负小国，但小国也不能无休止地无理取闹。希望菲方停止挑拨、挑衅，回到通过谈判协商解决问题的正确轨道上来。

    (http://xuan.news.cn/cloudnews/national/20150526/2385242_c.html)

3. 李登辉是顽固"台独"分子。日方不顾中方严正交涉，为李登辉赴日从事"台独"活动放行并提供便利。中方对此表示严重关切和强烈不满。台湾问题事关中国核心利益，中方一贯坚决反对任何人以任何形式在国际上从事"台独"分裂活动，坚决反对任何国家为"台独"分子提供政治平台。我们严肃敦促日方恪守《中日联合声明》等四个政治文件的原则和向中方作出的郑重承诺，坚持一个中国原则，慎重妥善处理涉台问题，避免给中日关系制造新的政治障碍。

    (http://www.fmprc.gov.cn/web/fyrbt_673021/dhdw_673027/t1283880.shtml)

4. 美军机对中方岛礁抵近侦察的举动，极易引发误判和海空意外事件，十分危险和不负责任。中方坚决反对美方这种挑衅行为，已就此向美方提出严正交涉。我要强调的是，中方维护国家主权和领土完整的意志坚如磐石。我们敦促美方纠正错误，保持理性，停止不负责任的言行。

    (http://www.fmprc.gov.cn/ce/cesg/chn/fyrth/t1266659.htm)

5. 以"东突厥斯坦伊斯兰运动"为首的"东突"暴力恐怖势力是中国国家安全面临的最严重恐怖威胁。中国政府将继续采取坚决措施,对暴力恐怖分子进行坚决打击,我们有决心、有信心、有能力打击暴恐分子的嚣张气焰。不论他们制造恐怖案件的目的是什么,都绝不会得逞。

(http://www.fmprc.gov.cn/ce/ceun/chn/zgylhg/jjalh/alhzh/fk/t1160549.htm)

二、请翻译下列一则有关外交表态的新闻(Translate the following news on declaration of attitudes)

2月21日晚,外交部副部长张业遂紧急召见美国驻华使馆临时代办康达,就美国总统奥巴马不顾中方强烈反对,执意会见达赖向美方提出严正交涉。

张业遂说,美方这一错误行为严重干涉中国内政,严重违反美方不支持"藏独"的承诺,严重违反国际关系基本准则,严重损害中美关系。中方对此表示强烈愤慨和坚决反对。

张业遂说,西藏是中国领土神圣不可分割的一部分,西藏事务纯属中国内政,美方无权干涉。中方同达赖的矛盾不是民族问题,不是宗教问题,也不是人权问题,而是维护祖国统一和反对分裂的重大原则问题。中方坚决反对任何外国允许达赖前往窜访,坚决反对任何国家政要以任何形式会见达赖。谁也不能动摇中国政府和人民反对外来干涉、捍卫国家主权和统一的意志和决心。

张业遂说,尊重彼此核心利益和重大关切,是确保中美关系健康稳定发展的关键。我们强烈敦促美方认真对待中方严正立场,恪守承认西藏是中国一部分、反对"西藏独立"的承诺,立即采取实际行动消除恶劣影响,停止利用涉藏问题干涉中国内政,停止纵容和支持达赖集团的反华分裂活动。美方必须以实际行动取信于中国政府和中国人民。

(http://news.xinhuanet.com/world/2014-02/22/c_119451066.htm)

参考译文
Versions for Reference

一、请翻译下列有关立场与表态的语句(Translate the following sentences on declarations of positions and attitudes)

1. The Chinese side expresses deep concerns about the current humanitarian situation in Yemen, welcomes the humanitarian cease-fire decision made by relevant parties and hopes this will help relax the situation in Yemen as soon as possible. The Chinese side calls on all parties concerned to implement relevant resolutions of the UN Security Council and initiatives of the Gulf Cooperation Council with concrete efforts, resolve

differences through political dialogues and restore stability and legal order to Yemen at an early date.

2. I can feel the restlessness and rashness of some people from the Philippines on issues of the South China Sea. China's relevant position has been made pretty clear on multiple occasions. Here is a gentle reminder to the Philippines: China will not bully small countries, but in the meanwhile, small countries shall not make trouble willfully and endlessly. We hope that the Philippine side would stop instigation and provocation and come back to the right track of resolving issues through negotiation and consultation.

3. Li Denghui is an obstinate propagandist of the "Taiwan independence". In disregard of China's solemn representations, the Japanese side allowed Li Denghui to visit Japan and provided convenience for his "Taiwan independence" activities in Japan. China hereby expresses deep concern and strong dissatisfaction about this. The Taiwan issue concerns the core interests of China. The Chinese side is constantly against any "Taiwan independence" separatist activity in the global arena done by anyone in any form, as well as providing political platform for such activity by any country. We solemnly urge the Japanese side to follow the principles of the four political documents such as the China-Japan Joint Declaration and its commitment to China, hold fast to the one-China policy, properly and prudently deal with Taiwan-related issues, and avoid installing new political barriers for the development of bilateral relations.

4. The close reconnaissance conducted by the US military aircraft of China's maritime features is highly likely to cause miscalculation and untoward incidents in the waters and airspace, and is utterly dangerous and irresponsible. China firmly opposes America's provocation, and has lodged solemn representations with the American side. I'd like to reiterate that China's determination to safeguard national sovereignty and territorial integrity is as firm as a rock. We urge the US side to correct its mistake, stay rational and cease irresponsible words and deeds.

5. The Eastern Turkestan terrorist forces, led by the Eastern Turkestan Islamic Movement, are the most serious terrorist threat to China's national security. The Chinese government will continue to take resolute action against those terrorists. We have the determination, confidence and capability to fight them. These terrorists will never succeed, regardless of the purpose of their attacks.

立场表态类报道的翻译
Translation for Coverage of Positions and Attitudes

二、请翻译下列一则有关外交表态的新闻（Translate the following news on declaration of attitudes）

On the evening of February 21, Executive Vice Foreign Minister Zhang Yesui urgently summoned Daniel J. Kritenbrink, Charge d'Affaires ad interim of the US Embassy in China and lodged solemn representations over US President Barack Obama's insisting on meeting with the Dalai Lama in disregard of China's strong opposition.

Zhang Yesui said that this erroneous act of the US side has grossly interfered in China's internal affairs, reneged on its commitment of not supporting "Tibet independence", severely violated the basic norms governing international relations and caused grave damages to China-US relations. China expresses strong indignation and firm opposition to that.

Zhang Yesui said that Tibet is a sacred and inalienable part of China. Tibet-related affairs fall entirely within the internal affairs of China, which allow no interference of the United States. The contradictions between the Chinese side and the Dalai Lama are neither an ethnic or religious issue nor a human rights issue, but a major principled issue of safeguarding China's national unity and opposing separation. China firmly opposes to the practice of any foreign country giving green light to the Dalai Lama's visit and resolutely opposes to any form of any national political heavyweights' meeting with the Dalai Lama. No one can shake the will and resolve of the Chinese government and people to combat outside interference and defend national sovereignty and unity.

Zhang Yesui said that respecting each other's core interests and major concerns is the key to ensure the healthy and stable development of China-US relations. We strongly urge the US side to take China's solemn position seriously, abide by the commitment of recognizing Tibet as a part of China and opposing "Tibet independence", take practical actions immediately to eliminate adverse effects, stop using Tibet-related issues to interfere in China's internal affairs, and stop conniving at and supporting the anti-China separatist activities of the Dalai clique. The US side must take concrete actions to win the trust of the Chinese government and the Chinese people.

单元小结
Summary

本单元主要介绍了立场与表态相关报道的翻译。立场表述最主要、最正式的形式是立场文件。通常外交表态有支持型、反对型和中立型三种。外交表态事关重大，要熟悉常用表达的真实涵义，翻译时仔细推敲、把握分寸。各种表态在英文中可以有多种表达方式，要根据上下文斟酌选用。我国涉及外交表态的话题除了在联合国常见的恐怖主义、网络安全、边境冲突、人权问题、核问题以外，还有涉疆问题、涉藏问题以及香港、澳门和台湾问题。要注意在这些地方，很多地名和人名并非按照汉语拼音的方式拼写，需要通过官方网站多多查证。译文中提到这些地方时，要格外谨慎，确保文字的准确性，避免引起误解的可能性，坚定地维护祖国统一和主权完整。对于反对势力的一些不正确的提法，引述时要加引号以示否定。总之，有关立场与表态的翻译需要非常谨慎，仔细斟酌，确保准确传达原文涵义。

参考文献：

丁立福：《中国南海岛礁定名维权百年风云之反思——写在第五次南海岛礁定名维权之前》，《海南大学学报》（人文社会科学版）2014年第3期。

高彬：《外交语言的特点及翻译策略探析》，《江苏科技大学学报》（社会科学版）2014年第3期。

胡健、范武邱：《"非典型"外交辞令及其翻译——以外交部例行记者会发言人答记者问为例》，《语言教育》2016年第1期。

李晓华：《网络时代"非典型"外交辞令的实效性》，《青年记者》2015年第24期。

杨烨：《外交理论与实务》，北京：外语教学与研究出版社，2008年。

UNIT 11

外交访谈报道的翻译
Translation for Coverage of Diplomatic Interviews

单元简介 Introduction

访谈是指两人或多人进行对话,由受访者回答采访者提出的问题,是新闻和媒体报道中经常采用的一种获取信息和阐明观点的重要方式。在外交访谈新闻中,外交界人士接受媒体采访或专访,就近期国内外热点话题、焦点问题等回答记者的提问,并阐明己方观点、立场或态度。

外交访谈的具体内容包括外交部有关人士回答记者有关地区形势或者我国外交政策的问题,我驻外使领馆工作人员就两国政治经贸关系和重大外事活动等接受采访,每年两会期间外交部部长回答记者提问等等。通过访谈,政府部门向外界阐述我国对外方针政策,对国内外重大事件发表见解,向世界传递中国的声音。读者不仅可以获取我国重要外交活动信息,还能了解我国政府的政策和立场。

C-E TRANSLATION OF DIPLOMATIC NEWS

外交访谈报道翻译范例分析
Sample of Translation for Coverage of Diplomatic Interviews

范例一（Sample I）

刘晓明大使接受英国天空新闻台《杰夫·兰德直播间》电视直播专访（节本）
2014/01/15
Ambassador Liu Xiaoming Talks to Jeff Randall on Sky News (Abbreviated Version)
2014/01/15

2014年1月14日晚，驻英国大使刘晓明在英国天空新闻台（SKY NEWS）演播室接受该台著名访谈节目《杰夫·兰德直播间》主持人杰夫·兰德直播电视专访。主持人就中共十八届三中全会、中国经济改革、中英经贸合作、媒体网络管理、东西方交流、中日关系等广泛问题向刘大使提问。访谈实录如下：

On the evening of January 14, 2014, H.E. Ambassador Liu Xiaoming had a live interview with Jeff Randall Live on Sky News. He answered questions from Jeff Randall on a wide range of issues, including the Third Plenum of the 18th Central Committee of the Communist Party of China, China's economic reform, China-UK economic and trade cooperation, media and internet management, exchanges between the East and the West and China-Japan relations. The transcript of the interview goes as follows:

***

兰德：显而易见，中国希望进入高端产业并成为全球商业领军者。当今世界，发展最为强劲的产业之一当属媒体。我们今天都看到了时代华纳有线电视公司招标的消息。然而，《纽约时报》、彭博社、脸谱、推特在华均被屏蔽。中国想要掩饰什么？

Jeff Randall: Clearly China wants to be in cutting-edge industries, wants to lead the way in global business. One of the world's booming businesses is media. We saw that bid today for Time Warner Cable. And yet, in China, the New York Times, Bloomberg, Facebook and Twitter are all blocked. What do you have to hide?

刘大使：中国依法管理媒体。重要的是，无论是中国媒体还是外国媒体都必须遵守中国法律，服务于人民的利益。我们关注的是信息健康以及是否有利于增进中外相互了解。

Ambassador Liu: We manage the media according to law. The important thing is the media, whether foreign or Chinese, they have to follow the law of China. And they have to serve the interests of the people. What we are concerned about is healthy content and whether it is in the interest of improving mutual understanding between China and the world.

外交访谈报道的翻译
Translation for Coverage of Diplomatic Interviews

兰德：你的意思是说，中国要的是"宣传"，而非"事实"？
Jeff Randall: Are you saying what you want is propaganda rather than the truth?

刘大使：这种说法是错误的，我们一直讲的就是事实。
Ambassador Liu: No. That's not true. We are looking for truth.

兰德：但是彭博社、脸谱和推特究竟会发表什么损害中国利益的信息？
Jeff Randall: But what will Bloomberg, Facebook and Twitter possibly publish that would damage your interests?

刘大使：这个问题你应该去问他们。我们希望他们在中国依法从业，遵守职业道德，而不是散布诋毁中国的谣言和偏见。这不利于促进中外相互了解。
Ambassador Liu: You should ask them. We would expect them to be a good citizen in China, rather than spreading rumours and bias against China. We don't think that serves the purpose of increasing mutual understanding between China and the outside world.

***

英国天空电视台是仅次于英国广播公司的英国第二大电视台，也是英最大的付费商业电视台。《杰夫·兰德直播间》是该台知名晚间财经和时事类访谈节目，每周一至周四19时至20时黄金时段播出，观众约100多万，主要是英政界、商界、金融界等精英人士。
BSKYB is the second largest broadcaster, next to BBC only, as well as the largest pay-TV broadcaster in the UK. Broadcast on the prime time of 19:00—20:00 from Monday to Thursday, Jeff Randall Live is a most-watched evening interview programme of BSKYB on financial and current affairs and reaches an audience of 1 million, mainly elites from the British political, business and financial circles.

新闻背景：由于历史原因以及文化价值观念等的不同，西方长期以来对中国存在各种误解，需要我们通过各种外交渠道予以纠正和澄清。驻英国大使刘晓明自2009年就任以来，多次接受英国电视台、报纸等各大媒体采访，并就中日关系、中国网络监管、"中国威胁论"等敏感问题列举事实，据理力争，驳斥西方的不当言论。范例一即是其中一例，在所节选的访谈对话中，刘大使针对西方媒体指责中国网络封锁的说法，给予了强有力的驳斥。译文在收录时略有调整。

原文链接：http://gb.cri.cn/42071/2014/01/16/5311s4392199.htm

译文链接：http://www.mfa.gov.cn/ce/ceuk/eng/ambassador/t1119274.htm

一、范例一文本结构分析（Text Structure Analysis of Sample I）

范例一是一则关于外交访谈的新闻报道，由标题、导语、正文和背景构成。外交访谈报道的标题通常信息含量较为全面，在有限的字符空间内尽可能全面表达访谈的主要信息点，包括采访者、受访者、访谈主题、访谈方式等。在范例一的标题中，主要信息就囊括了受访者（中国驻英国大使刘晓明）、采访者（英国天空新闻台的著名栏目《杰夫·兰德直播间》）、采访方式（电视直播专访）等。外交访谈报道的导语主要是为下文详细介绍访谈内容做铺垫，用简要的语言介绍访谈的参与人和主题等。外交访谈报道的正文是新闻报道的核心，具体到本例中是指访谈实录部分，它主要采用问答的形式呈现，即采访者提问，受访者回答。这种问与答的呈现形式在有关新闻发布会和媒体吹风会等的新闻报道中也会采用。在有些访谈报道的文末还会附有背景信息，即关于新闻采访者或采访机构的介绍，例如这则访谈报道中对英国天空新闻台及其栏目《杰夫·兰德直播间》的介绍。

二、范例一翻译解析（Translation Analysis of Sample I）

（一）外交访谈报道标题的翻译（Translation of Headlines of Coverage of Diplomatic Interviews）

外交访谈报道的标题中一般会明确访谈的具体形式（包括采访、专访、联合采访等）和访谈的主题，例如"驻尼日利亚大使顾小杰就李克强总理访尼接受驻尼中央媒体采访"。有时还会采用正副标题的形式，如"中国梦将惠及周边各国——驻哈萨克斯坦大使乐玉成接受《新一代报》采访"。有时，虽然新闻内容和形式均为访谈，但标题中却不直接出现"采访"等字样，例如"锐意进取，唱响亚洲合作主旋律——外交部副部长刘振民谈亚洲形势和周边外交"。还有的时候，整篇报道只有访谈问答部分，此时标题可能直接使用"采访实录"等字样。下面就通过一些实例，探讨外交访谈报道中标题的翻译。

王毅接受美国亚洲协会"了解中国"媒体团采访

(http://china.huanqiu.com/News/fmprc/2015-06/6701995.html)

Wang Yi Gives Interview to Press Corps "Understanding China" of Asia Society of US

(http://www.fmprc.gov.cn/mfa_eng/zxxx_662805/t1274348.shtml)

驻英国大使刘晓明就中英关系、安倍参拜靖国神社等问题接受中国驻英媒体联合采访

(http://world.people.com.cn/n/2014/0111/c1002-24088337.html)

Ambassador to the United Kingdom (UK) Liu Xiaoming Gives Joint Interview to Chinese Media in UK on China-UK Relations, Shinzo Abe's Visit to Yasukuni Shrine and

外交访谈报道的翻译
Translation for Coverage of Diplomatic Interviews **11 UNIT**

Other Issues

(http://wcm.fmprc.gov.cn/pub/eng/wjb/zwjg/zwbd/t1122490.shtml)

外交部副部长宋涛就第十六次中欧领导人会晤接受中央电视台采访实录

(http://www.fmprc.gov.cn/web/wjbxw_673019/t1101552.shtml)

Records of Vice Foreign Minister Song Tao's Interview to CCTV on the 16th China-EU Summit

(http://www.fmprc.gov.cn/ce/cenp/eng/zgwj/t1104200.htm)

白通社发表驻白俄罗斯大使崔启明接受专访实录

(http://wcm.fmprc.gov.cn/pub/chn/gxh/mtb/zwbd/dszlsjt/t1144496.htm)

Belarusian Telegraph Agency Publishes Record of Exclusive Interview with Ambassador to Belarus Cui Qiming

(http://www.fmprc.gov.cn/mfa_eng/wjb_663304/zwjg_665342/zwbd_665378/t1165237.shtml)

中国梦将惠及周边各国——驻哈萨克斯坦大使乐玉成接受《新一代报》采访

(http://www.fmprc.gov.cn/ce/ceka/chn/sgxx/t1095105.htm)

Chinese Dream Will Benefit Neighboring Countries——Chinese Ambassador to Kazakhstan Le Yucheng Interviewed by Novoye Pokoleniye

(http://wcm.fmprc.gov.cn/pub/eng/wjb/zwjg/zwbd/t1096025.shtml)

锐意进取，唱响亚洲合作主旋律——外交部副部长刘振民谈亚洲形势和周边外交

(http://www.fmprc.gov.cn/ce/cebe/chn/ssht/zgwj2014/t1115013.htm)

Forging Ahead with Determination and Sounding the Mainstream Melody of Asian Cooperation—— Vice Foreign Minister Liu Zhenmin's Comments on Asian Situation and Neighborhood Diplomacy

(http://www.fmprc.gov.cn/mfa_eng/wjdt_665385/zyjh_665391/t1114403.shtml)

驻瑞典大使陈育明接受人民网记者专访谈中国外交和中瑞关系——中国外交再创辉煌，中瑞关系更上层楼

(http://www.fmprc.gov.cn/ce/cese/chn/sgxx/dsjh/t1114843.htm)

Ambassador to Sweden Chen Yuming Gives Exclusive Interview to Journalist with People's Daily Online on China's Diplomacy and China-Sweden Relations——China's Diplomacy Achieves New Brilliance and China-Sweden Relations Reach New High

(http://www.fmprc.gov.cn/mfa_eng/wjb_663304/zwjg_665342/zwbd_665378/t1117954.shtml)

从以上实例可以看出，"接受采访"通常译为give interview to，或者有时也可译为be interviewed by，但要注意在新闻标题中通常省略被动语态的助动词be。"专访""联合采访"分别译为exclusive interview和joint interview，如果需要表明采访主题可以采用give interview on something 的句式来翻译。"采访实录"译为名词短语 record of the interview。原标题中未出现"采访""专访"等字样时可以采用名词短语 comments on 或动词短语 talk about 等方式来翻译。对于以主副标题形式表明访谈主题的，主题内容通常译为名词短语或动名词短语。确需翻译为完整的主谓句时务必注意，标题中应当采用现在时态，且句末不可添加任何标点符号。范例一中的标题比较特殊，因为采访者并不是常见的某个报社或某个电视台，而是具体到了一个栏目，并且恰巧是以主持人命名的谈话类节目，所以翻译成英语时做了变通，直接使用了"talk to + 主持人"的形式。

（二）外交访谈报道导语的翻译（Translation of News Leads in Coverage of Diplomatic Interviews）

外交访谈报道的开篇通常会有导语，介绍采访发生的时间、采访者、受访者、访谈主题以及访谈背景，如范例一以及下面的三个翻译实例所示：

2015年8月20日，中国驻尼日利亚大使顾小杰接受尼国家电视台国际频道专访，就中尼关系、中国人民抗日战争暨世界反法西斯战争胜利70周年、中非产能合作等问题回答记者提问。

(http://www.mfa.gov.cn/ce/ceng/chn/zngx/znwl/t1290368.htm)

On August 20, 2015, Chinese Ambassador Gu Xiaojie held an interview with Nigerian Television Authority (NTA) International Channel and answered questions concerning China-Nigeria relations, the 70th anniversary of the victory of the Chinese People's War of Resistance Against Japanese Aggression and World Anti-Fascist War, and industrial capacity cooperation between China and African countries.

(http://ng.chineseembassy.org/eng/zngx/cne/t1290370.htm)

2015年2月20日，阿联酋最大的英文报纸《海湾时报》出版了中国羊年春节专版，并刊登了对中国驻阿联酋大使常华的专访。主要内容如下：

(http://www.fmprc.gov.cn/ce/ceae/chn/xwdt/t1239570.htm)

On February 20, 2015, Gulf News, one of the best selling English newspapers in the UAE, published the interview with Ambassador Chang Hua and a special report on the Spring Festival of the Chinese year of sheep. The main content of the interview is as follows:

(http://ae.chineseembassy.org/eng/dshd/t1239574.htm)

中非合作论坛第八届高官会将于今年10月26日至27日在浙江省杭州市举行。中非合作论坛中方后续行动委员会秘书长、外交部非洲司司长卢沙野在会议前夕接受了新华社记者专访。

(http://www.fmprc.gov.cn/zflt/chn/zt/somAfrica2011/t869917.htm)

外交访谈报道的翻译
Translation for Coverage of Diplomatic Interviews

The 8th Senior Officials Meeting of Forum on China-Africa Cooperation (FOCAC) will be held in Hangzhou, Zhejiang Province, on October 26 and 27 this year. On the eve of this event, the Xinhua News Agency reporter interviewed Lu Shaye, Secretary-General of Chinese Follow-Up Committee of FOCAC and Director-General of Department of African Affairs at China's Ministry of Foreign Affairs.

(http://www.focac.org/eng/zt/som2011/t869918.htm)

上面的例句可以看出，访谈报道的导语基本就是标题的扩充版，增加了详细的日期、访谈发生的背景或事由以及更为详细的访谈主题。与标题翻译不同的是，标题翻译时常采用一般现在时态，而导语的翻译则要根据语句中的实际情况选用正确的时态。另外，世界各国的主流媒体有时汉语名称和英语名称未必完全对应，如上面第一个例句中的"尼日利亚国家电视台"，翻译时必须经过网络检索和查证。

（三）外交访谈问答的翻译（Translation of Questions and Answers in Diplomatic Interviews）

外交访谈实录部分通常按照现场实际问答的内容进行忠实的记录。此部分比较特殊的一点在于，原访谈很可能本身就是以英语展开，后来整理翻译为汉语，翻译方向与其他部分刚好相反。也有可能本身是以俄语、法语、德语等展开，然后翻译为汉语，再转译为英语，其译文可能会受到第一原语以及第一译文的影响。所以本部分我们将关注重点从如何翻译转移到访谈中的语言特点。西方记者或节目主持人在提问时，往往比较尖锐，且常常穷追不舍。请看以下两组记者提问实例，其中第一组摘自范例一：

你的意思是说，中国要的是"宣传"，而非"事实"？

中国与日本之间在一些无人居住的小岛问题上存在争端。许多人认为中国正在展示军事实力、清算旧账。不是这样吗？

Are you saying what you want is propaganda rather than the truth?

You have this dispute with Japan over uninhabited islands. Many see it as China flexing its military muscles and settling old scores. That is true, isn't it?

你知道日本对此有不同看法。

你是否认为日本仍是威胁？

你认为日本仍然对中国构成军事威胁？

我理解中国人民为何对安倍参拜如此愤怒。但这归根到底不是日本的内政吗？

(http://www.chinanews.com/gn/2014/01-07/5708717.shtml)

You know the Japanese would dispute that.

But do you still feel a military threat from Japan?

Do you still feel that military threat now is the question?

I can see why the Chinese would be angry about it, but ultimately is it not an internal Japanese matter?

(http://www.chinese-embassy.org.uk/eng/HotTopics/jpabe/t1115090.htm)

从以上例句可以看出非常明显的口语化风格，句子都比较短，语言也不像其他文本那么规范。在外交新闻报道中常用的"中方""英方"等说法被"你""我"这样的称谓所取代。而且you的指代并不相同，有时指代的是刘晓明大使本人，有时指代的是中国。提问方式上，第一组提问的译文中就用到了一般疑问句和反义疑问句两种形式。而第二组提问中的第一句则是通过陈述敏感事件引发受访者的否定、阐释或回应。如果采访者没有得到令他满意的答案，可能还会进一步追问，如第三句就是对第二句的追问。

针对国外媒体的某些敏感提问，我国的被采访者义正词严，坚决捍卫祖国的领土完整和国家尊严。如下面一组例句选自驻美国大使崔天凯接受CNN采访时的回答：

美方的立场是荒谬而且虚伪的。一方面要求别人不要使地区局势军事化，另一方面自己却如此频繁地派军舰前往这一地区。

美方的行为恰恰是罔顾国际法。美国至今未加入《联合国海洋法公约》。《公约》有关条款对正常的航行和飞越自由、安全和无害通过都有非常明确的规定，美方所作所为明显与之相违背。

事实很清楚。谁在向那里派军舰？谁在向那里派军机？并不是我们，而是美国。

(http://www.fmprc.gov.cn/web/dszlsjt_673036/ds_673038/t1309956.shtml)

Well, it is a very absurd and even hypocritical position to ask others not to militarize the region while oneself is sending military vessels there so frequently.

I think that this is done in total disregard of international law. If we look at the convention of the law of the sea — and, by the way, the United States is not yet a party to that Convention. But if we are looking at the provisions of the Convention, there are very, very clear provisions about safety of navigation, freedom of navigation or innocent transit. What the U.S. is doing is totally against the provisions, the letter and spirit of the Convention.

Well, I think that the fact is so clear. Who is sending military vessels there? Who is sending the military planes there? It's not us. It's the United States.

(http://wcm.fmprc.gov.cn/pub/ce/ceus/eng/dszl/dshd/t1310014.htm)

关注以上实例中的英文，就会发现大使在回答时用词非常到位，比如第一句中very

外交访谈报道的翻译
Translation for Coverage of Diplomatic Interviews

absurd and even hypocritical的递进关系；第二句total disregard中修饰成分total的使用；very, very clear provisions中两个very的连用，以及谈到美国违背《联合国海洋法公约》时的表达totally against the provisions, the letter and spirit of the Convention。最后一句中并没有使用it's not ... but ... that ...这样的句型，而是先使用短句进行强势发问，然后继续用短句铿锵有力地进行回答。这些语言点都值得从事外交翻译的译者学习，以便在外交翻译场合灵活运用语言手段，完整、准确、酣畅淋漓地表现出说话人的本意。

范例二（Sample II）

驻特立尼达和多巴哥大使夫人耿海凌接受特多国家电视台直播采访
2011/07/28
Ambassador's Wife Mrs. Geng Hailing on Dai Ailian Foundation
2011/07/29

2011年7月26日，中国驻特立尼达和多巴哥大使夫人耿海凌在特多国家电视台接受早间直播专题节目采访，表示为纪念在特多出生的杰出舞蹈家、有"中国现代舞蹈之母"美誉的戴爱莲先生，特多土生华人协会发起成立戴爱莲基金会，官方发布仪式即将举行。土生华人协会前主席坎布里奇女士和戴爱莲先生的侄子阿德里安·伊萨克一同参加了访谈。

On July 26, 2011, Mrs. Geng Hailing, wife of Chinese Ambassador to Trinidad and Tobago, talked about the Dai Ailian Foundation in an interview with "First Up", a live morning broadcasting program of C Television (CTV). Mrs. Geng said that Mme. Dai Ailian, born in Trinidad and Tobago, was a distinguished dancing artiste and known as "Mother of Chinese Modern Dance". The Chinese Association of Trinidad and Tobago (CATT) had recently set up a Foundation in her name, and its official launch was coming soon. Mrs. Christine Cambridge, the past CATT president and Mr. Adrian Isaac, Dai Ailian's nephew, also appeared in the interview.

耿海凌表示，戴爱莲是中国家喻户晓的舞蹈大师，在世界舞蹈艺术界有广泛影响力。在戴先生的出生地特多成立"戴爱莲基金会"具有特别的意义。耿海凌介绍说，戴先生亲自创办的北京舞蹈学院在了解到成立戴爱莲基金会的计划后，主动提出届时派团来特多参加官方发布仪式，并特意向特多提供一个全额奖学金名额作为"贺礼"。耿海凌指出，中特两国一直有密切的文化交流，戴爱莲基金会的成立一定会进一步促进这种交流深入向前发展。

Mrs. Geng Hailing said that Dai Ailian was an icon in China and enjoyed world fame as a dancing artiste. As she was born in Trinidad and Tobago, the setting up of the Dai Ailian Foundation there held a special meaning. Mrs. Geng told the audience that Beijing Dance Academy would send a delegation to attend the upcoming official launch of the Foundation and provide a full scholarship to dancers from Trinidad and Tobago. Beijing Dance Academy, established by Mme. Dai Ailian, made this special offer as soon as they learned about the Foundation. Mrs. Geng said that cultural exchanges had always been close between China and Trinidad and Tobago, and the establishment of the Foundation would surely further promote such exchanges.

坎布里奇和伊萨克也分别介绍了戴爱莲基金会的情况和戴爱莲的生平。坎布里奇表示，戴爱莲是特多华人的骄傲。土生华人协会在中国使馆的大力支持下发起创立戴爱莲基金会，是件令人激动的事情。协会将努力做好基金会有关工作，为推动中特两国人民的友好交往、促进两国文化交流做出贡献。

Mrs. Cambridge and Mr. Isaac respectively introduced the Dai Ailian Foundation and some life stories of Dai Ailian. Mrs. Cambridge said that the local Chinese people in Trinidad and Tobago were very proud of Dai Ailian, and it was a very exciting thing for CATT to set up the Dai Ailian Foundation. She also thanked the Chinese Embassy for the great support, and promised that CATT would do its best to promote the Foundation and make its own contribution to the promotion of cultural exchanges between the Republic of Trinidad and Tobago and the People's Republic of China as well as friendly exchanges between the two peoples.

新闻背景：驻外大使认真履行职责的同时，大使夫人往往也会积极参与各项外交活动，通常主要涉及文化、音乐、妇女、儿童、慈善等领域。戴爱莲是世界知名的华人舞蹈家、舞蹈教育家，亲自创建了北京舞蹈学院和中央芭蕾舞团，有"中国现代舞蹈之母"的美誉。1916年出生于特立尼达和多巴哥，1939年回国，曾获文化部授予的"造型表演艺术创作研究成就奖"，2006年在北京病逝。为纪念这位杰出的舞蹈艺术家，特多土生华人协会发起成立了戴爱莲基金会。中国驻特立尼达和多巴哥大使夫人耿海凌在特多国家电视台接受采访时谈到了基金会成立的消息。

原文链接：http://wcm.fmprc.gov.cn/pub/chn/gxh/wzb/zwbd/fnhd/t843435.htm

译文链接：http://tt.china-embassy.org/eng/zt/DAFTT2011/t843736.htm

外交访谈报道的翻译
Translation for Coverage of Diplomatic Interviews

一、范例二文本结构分析（Text Structure Analysis of Sample II）

范例二是外交访谈报道的另一种表现形式，它包括标题、导语、正文和结尾部分，结构上完全采用新闻报道的形式。导语部分与范例一相同，涵盖了访谈时间（2011年7月26日早上）、采访者（特多国家电视台早间直播专题节目）、受访者（中国驻特立尼达和多巴哥大使夫人耿海凌）以及访谈中涉及的主要信息（特多土生华人协会发起成立戴爱莲基金会）。范例二与范例一最大的区别在于正文部分，报道中并没有采用问答实录的形式将访谈过程原模原样地呈现给读者，而是经过归纳总结，以转述的形式将受访者的谈话要点集中展示出来。由于谈话内容已经过编辑总结提炼，所以访谈中的寒暄话语、过渡话语以及其他次要内容都已被删略。结尾部分是对访谈报道的信息补充，主要介绍了参加访谈的另外两人谈话的主要内容。范例二的另一显著差异是文化类访谈题材较为轻松，与范例一中针锋相对、立场严正的政治类访谈在语气措辞上明显不同。

二、范例二翻译解析（Translation Analysis of Sample II）

（一）外交访谈报道翻译中的信息重组（Restructuring of Information in Translation of Diplomatic Interviews）

外交新闻绝大多数都是政治性极强的报道，原文中的语言形式、信息推进顺序可能都传达着某种含义。翻译时译者需要谨慎小心、思虑周全，一般情况下应严格遵照原文，以异化的策略为主。但是访谈报道却略有不同，尤其是像范例二这种不涉及国家安全、领土争端等敏感话题，而旨在推动世界文化交流，促进各国友好关系发展的访谈，翻译时可以适当灵活一些，按照译语逻辑结构和语言特点对信息进行重组，以增强译文的可读性。例如：

> 耿海凌表示为纪念在特多出生的杰出舞蹈家、有"中国现代舞蹈之母"美誉的戴爱莲先生，特多土生华人协会发起成立戴爱莲基金会，官方发布仪式即将举行。
>
> Mrs. Geng said that Mme. Dai Ailian, born in Trinidad and Tobago, was a distinguished dancing artiste and known as "Mother of Chinese Modern Dance". The Chinese Association of Trinidad and Tobago (CATT) had recently set up a Foundation in her name, and its official launch was coming soon.
>
> 耿海凌介绍说，戴先生亲自创办的北京舞蹈学院在了解到成立戴爱莲基金会的计划后，主动提出届时派团来特多参加官方发布仪式，并特意向特多提供一个全额奖学金名额作为"贺礼"。
>
> Mrs. Geng told the audience that Beijing Dance Academy would send a delegation to attend the upcoming official launch of the Foundation and provide a full scholarship to dancers from Trinidad and Tobago. Beijing Dance Academy, established by Mme. Dai Ailian, has made this special offer as soon as they learned about the Foundation.

外交新闻汉英翻译
C-E TRANSLATION OF DIPLOMATIC NEWS

上面两个例句都选自范例二。原文都是典型的汉语构句方式,第一句中,前面首先是"为……"作为目的状语,然后再讲述"成立基金会"的事情,第二句同样是"了解到……之后"这样的时间信息先出现,重点内容"派团参加仪式和提供奖学金名额"处于句末,两句都体现了汉语"尾焦点"的信息呈现特点。而译文均对信息进行了重组,采用了拆译的方法,以更好地体现信息之间的逻辑关系。第二句更是对信息顺序做了调整,将"派团参加仪式和提供奖学金名额"提前,而把背景信息挪到下一句,通过"头焦点"的形式使得译文更加符合英语信息推进习惯,译文读起来更加地道。再比如下面的例子:

今天是中国春节,也就是中国农历新年,这是中国最重要的传统节日。我谨代表中国驻阿联酋大使馆,并以我个人的名义向旅阿中国公民致以节日的祝贺!

(http://www.fmprc.gov.cn/ce/ceaye/chn/xwdt/t1239570.htm)

Today is the Chinese Spring Festival, meaning a new year in the Chinese calendar. On the occasion of this most important traditional Chinese holiday, I would like to extend, on behalf of the Chinese Embassy in the UAE and also in my own name, our kind regards to all overseas Chinese in the UAE.

(http://ae.chineseembassy.org/eng/dshd/t1239574.htm)

这个翻译实例选自驻阿联酋大使常华接受阿联酋《海湾时报》春节专访时的谈话。汉语原文中"这是中国最重要的传统节日"与前面的语句共同构成对"春节"的介绍,属于同一个意群,因而放在同一句中。而英语译文该信息作为下一句中的时间状语,与后文的表达祝福成为一体,同时通过this most important traditional Chinese holiday的指代关系与上一句形成衔接,增强了译文的连贯性,更好地满足了英语"形合"的特点。

(二)报刊中书面访谈的翻译(Translation of Written Interviews on Newspapers)

无论是在电视台还是广播电台,访谈都是以口头形式展开的,而各大报刊中还存在一种书面访谈的形式。所谓书面访谈,是指在采访者与受访者不能面对面交谈的情况下,通过书面提问的形式进行采访并得到书面答复。相关报道一般都是以问答的形式原文刊登,语言风格可能偏书面化,也可能偏口语化。因为无法互动,每个提问和回答都会比较长,尤其是回答,力图将信息一次表达清楚。下面的翻译实例选自习近平主席2015年首次对美国进行国事访问前接受《华尔街日报》书面采访的双语文稿[①],限于篇幅,只展示了针对"反腐"这一个问题的回答部分。

反腐败是世界各国面临的共同任务,也是民心所向。中国共产党的根本宗旨

[①] http://language.chinadaily.com.cn/2015-09/23/content_21957085_11.htm

外交访谈报道的翻译
Translation for Coverage of Diplomatic Interviews

是全心全意为人民服务，中国共产党执政的基础是人民拥护，必须保持同人民群众的血肉联系。中国共产党不是生活在真空中，党内肯定会有这样那样的问题，腐败问题就是其中一个顽症。中国共产党敢于直面问题、纠正错误，善于自我净化、自我革新。人民群众最痛恨腐败，我们必须顺应民心。所以，要"老虎"、"苍蝇"一起打。中共十八大以来，我们加大了反腐败斗争力度，依法查处了一大批腐败分子，包括查处了曾经身居很高职位的一些人，赢得了中国人民的支持和赞扬。

Cracking down on corruption is what all countries must do and what their peoples wish to see. The ultimate purpose of the Chinese Communist Party is to serve the people wholeheartedly. Our Party owes its governing status to the support of the people, so we must maintain its flesh-and-blood ties with the people. The Party does not operate in a vacuum, so it has unavoidably found itself with problems of one kind or another. Corruption is just such a persistent one. The Party must be courageous enough to face up to the problem and go out to correct it through self-purification and self-rectification. Our people hate corruption more than anything else and we must act to allay their concerns. Therefore, we decided to go after both "tigers and flies," wrongdoers regardless of their ranks. Since the 18th CPC National congress, we have intensified anticorruption efforts, dealt with a large number of corrupt officials in accordance with law, including some who used to hold very high offices, and won extensive support and thumbs-up from the Chinese people.

关于反腐败制度建设，我有两句话，一句是"把权力关进制度的笼子里"，一句是"阳光是最好的防腐剂"。随着反腐败斗争向纵深推进，我们要着力形成不敢腐、不能腐、不想腐的体制机制。我们正在制定和完善相关法律法规，扎细扎密扎牢制度的笼子，真正把权力关进其中。关于官员财产公开，我们在2010年就通过有关规定，将领导干部收入等涉及财产性内容列入个人报告事项，每年定期抽查核实，现在核实的比例不断提高，任何人都不能例外。对不如实报告的人，我们有硬性的处理措施。

On institutional building in this respect, let me share with you two remarks I made. The first is that we must keep power in the cage of systemic checks. The other one is that transparency is the best precaution against corruption. As we go further in the anticorruption campaign, we will focus more on institutional building so that officials will not dare and cannot afford to be corrupt and, more importantly, have no desire to take that course. Right now, we are formulating and updating relevant laws and regulations to truly put power inside a more closely-knit cage of effective checks. With respect to asset disclosure by officials, we adopted relevant regulations back in 2010 to require such reporting which was subject to random check and verification every year. The proportion of verified reporting has increased steadily, and no one would take exception. Should anyone be found to be dishonest, they will be punished accordingly.

上面的实例虽然是书面形式，但是大量使用了生活化、口语化的表达，以体现"访谈"的特点。单句都比较短，而且多使用形象的比喻和借代。比如"'老虎''苍蝇'一起打"，这显然使用了借代的修辞手法，如果直译，英语读者无法形成预期联想，就会茫然不知所云。可是，意译后读者却又无法领略到原文当中借代之精妙，使其形象感顿失。译文最终采用了直译加解释的方法，译为"tigers and flies", wrongdoers regardless of their ranks，即保留了原文中的借体，又解释了他们所替代的本体，使得译语读者在准确理解文意的同时了解了原语中的文化信息。

"把权力关进制度的笼子里"和"阳光是最好的防腐剂"两句话同样用到了修辞手法，第一句相对好理解，显然是将"制度"比喻成了"笼子"，第二句就要难理解一些，"阳光"究竟指代什么？根据后文讲到的"官员财产公开"可以判断，"阳光"是说"反腐方面的信息要公开，要透明"。原文中的"防腐剂"显然不是平常意义上"用来防止食物腐烂的化学物质"，而是借用到政治领域表示"防止腐败的一剂良药"。经过这样的仔细分析后，译文第二句话中采用of结构in the cage of systemic checks，将本体"制度"和喻体"笼子"同时加以体现，第二句话则将"阳光"和"防腐剂"做了显化处理，直接译成transparency和precaution against corruption。

"不敢腐、不能腐、不想腐"是口语化的句子，采用的是排比修辞，表面上看似乎是并列关系，但仔细分析就会发现，前两点都是被动的"不腐败"，第三点是主动的"不腐败"，因而应当是"反腐"目标的重点，所以译文中添加了more importantly。总之，书面访谈的风格比较特殊，既是"访谈"，却又是"书面的"，翻译时需要仔细研读原文，注意把握话语风格和表意层次。

学生译作讲评
Analysis of Students' Translation Practice

原文链接：http://www.fmprc.gov.cn/mfa_chn//zwbd_602255/t1114168.shtml
新闻原文：新任驻克罗地亚大使邓英接受《晨报》专访
学生译文：The New Ambassador to Croatia Deng Ying Gives the Interview to *Jutarnji List*

翻译评析：译文中的interview是表达"采访"的最笼统的词，而原文已经说明了采访的具体形式，即"专访"，应当译为exclusive interview；"新任"的"任"在译文中没有体现出来，而且英语新闻标题当中一般应省略冠词，所以调整后的标题译文应当是Newly-appointed Ambassador to Croatia Deng Ying Gives Exclusive Interview to *Jutarnji List*。

新闻原文：2014年1月2日，克罗地亚发行量最大的日报《晨报》发表了对新任中国

外交访谈报道的翻译
Translation for Coverage of Diplomatic Interviews

驻克罗地亚大使邓英的专访文章。采访时逢2014年新年前夕，邓大使特别向克民众转达了中国人民的新年问候和良好祝愿，并就履新初步印象、中国—中东欧国家合作、中国未来发展等回答了提问。

学生译文：On January 2, 2014, *Jutarnji List*, the largest circulation of Croatian national daily published an article of the exclusive interview of Ambassador Deng Ying. Since the interview was on New Year's Eve of 2014, Ambassador Deng conveyed New Year greetings and good wishes of Chinese people to Croatian people and answered questions which include her initial impression on her assumption of the office, China-Central and East European countries cooperation and the future development of China.

翻译评析：译文中第一句话存在句法错误，同位语的核心词落在了circulation上，显然"发行量"不能作为该报纸名称的同位语并做出"发表文章"的动作。而且用Croatian来表示报纸的发行国家不妥，因为该词也可能表示"用这种语言出版的"。故同位语应修改为a daily newspaper with the largest circulation in Croatia。"对某人的采访"译文中interview后面的介词应该用with而不是of。"采访时逢"表示动作发生的时间与某个其他动作或事件重合，用was显得过于静态，可以调整为occurred。邓大使回答提问时所涉及的一系列话题用定语从句which include …无形中将句子结构复杂化，不符合语言的简练原则，直接用such as即可。另外，英语中需要使用缩写时，应当在第一次出现的地方给出全文，并在括号中以夹注的形式标注其缩写形式。这里的"中国—中东欧国家合作"译文可调整为cooperation between China and the Central and Eastern European Countries (CEEC)。

新闻原文：邓大使在采访中表示，克罗地亚风光秀美，人文底蕴深厚，人民热情善良。中克两国传统友谊深厚。建交二十一年来，两国关系取得了长足发展。双方政治互信加深，经贸、文化、旅游等领域的交流合作富有成效。克政府坚定奉行一个中国政策，支持中国统一大业，中方对此表示赞赏。随着克入盟，中克关系业已成为中欧关系的一部分。2013年中欧领导人共同发表了《中欧合作2020战略规划》，勾画了中国和欧洲合作的新蓝图，中欧相向而行，合作前景无限光明。希望加入欧盟能给克罗地亚带来新的发展机遇，也能为中克关系的发展创造更多有利条件。

学生译文：Ambassador Deng said in the interview that Croatia has beautiful scenery, profound cultural heritage and warm and kind people. China and Croatia enjoy profound traditional friendship. Since the establishment of diplomatic ties twenty-one years ago, the two countries have achieved considerable development in bilateral relations. Both sides have deepened mutual political trust and carried out fruitful exchanges and cooperation in the fields of economy and trade, culture and tourism. The Croatia government firmly upholds the One China policy and supports China's great course of reunification, which China highly appreciates. With Croatia's accession to the EU, China-Croatia relations have become a part of China-Europe relations. In 2013, China and Europe leaders jointly issued the China-EU 2020

Strategic Agenda for Cooperation, which draws up a new blueprint for cooperation between China and Europe. China and Europe move in the same direction and would enjoy more brilliant cooperation prospects. We hope that Croatia's accession to the EU would bring itself new development opportunities and would create better conditions for the development of China-Croatia relations.

翻译评析：汉语形式上比较松散，并不十分注重句子及各成分之间的逻辑关系。比如原文第一句"在采访中"实际上并非只作为这一句话的状语，而是统领接下来的几段话。也就是说，后面几段内容其实也都是邓大使在采访中说的。所以，in the interview 提到段首，并以逗号与句子主干隔开较好。"克罗地亚风光秀美，人文底蕴深厚，人民热情善良"一句的译文中用has搭配"风光"和"人文底蕴"没问题，搭配"善良人民"就不太符合表达习惯了。可以调整为is a nation with，即Croatia is a nation with beautiful scenery, profound cultural heritage and warm and kind people。原文第四句中的"政治互信加深"实际上是"两国关系长足发展"的结果和体现，而不是"双方做出了加深政治互信的动作"；"交流合作富有成效"也是对"合作结果"的描述，而不是在开展合作的时候就只选了"富有成效"的那些领域合作。另外，合作领域除了所列举的，还有个"等"字也被漏译了。该句可以修改为with deepened mutual political trust and fruitful achievements in exchanges and cooperation in such fields as economy, trade, culture and tourism，作为结果状语与前一句用逗号隔开。提到"中欧"时务必注意根据上下文仔细判断，这个词有可能是指"中部欧洲"central Europe，也有可能是指"中国与欧洲"China and Europe，还有可能是指"中国与欧盟"China and the EU。本段末句"加入欧盟"已经很清楚地点明这里的"欧"是指"欧盟"，而且学生已经通过网络检索找到了《中欧合作2020战略规划》的官方译文，其中"中欧"就用的是China-EU，可惜还是不够细心，未能推而广之，终将多个地方的"欧"错译成了Europe。最后两句译文中出现了三个would，这种虚拟情态的表达在外交翻译中比较少用，可以统一改为will。最后一句原文缺少主语，纵观全文，应该是邓大使表达了她本人的希望，所以不是We hope，而是She hopes。最后还有个小问题，原文是"创造有利条件"而不是"创造更好条件"，译文应当修改为create more favorable conditions。

新闻原文：邓大使强调，中国—中东欧国家合作为促进中国同中东欧国家的双边关系搭建了有效平台，已成为中欧关系新的增长点，也为中克关系的发展提供了更多新的可能。中方愿与克方一道，本着互利共赢的精神，不断提升合作水平，促进共同发展与繁荣。

学生译文：Ambassador Deng stressed that China-CEEC cooperation creates an effective platform for boosting bilateral relations among China and Central and Eastern European countries, which has become a new growth point for China-Europe relations and provided more new possibilities for the development of China-Croatia relations. In the spirit of mutual benefit and win-win result, China is willing to work together with Croatia to continuously upgrade

外交访谈报道的翻译
Translation for Coverage of Diplomatic Interviews

cooperation level and promote common development and prosperity.

翻译评析：原文中显然是把"中东欧国家"整体作为一方，探讨与"中国"之间的"双边"关系，而不是所有相关国家之间的"多边"关系，所以译文中的among China and Central and Eastern European countries不正确，应该修改为between China and the CEEC。"更多新的可能"中的修饰语"更多"和"新的"是并列关系，互相之间并不构成修饰关系，因而more和new之间应该加上and更合适一些。"可能"一词实际上指"机会""机遇"，而不能按照字面理解为possibilities，那意思就变成"中克关系发展前景未卜，存在多种可能性"了。所以此处译文应当修改为more and new opportunities。另外，译文最后一句中还有两处小的语法错误，一是win-win result应该加上-s，用复数形式，二是cooperation level前面需要加上定冠词the。

新闻原文：谈及中国未来发展，邓大使表示，中国新一届领导集体坚持改革开放，坚持走和平发展道路，坚持奉行互利共赢的开放战略，坚定维护国家利益。习近平主席将中国发展的目标升华为"中国梦"的战略思想，即实现国家富强、民族振兴和人民幸福。"中国梦"是和平、发展、合作、共赢的梦，与世界各国人民的美好梦想相通。中国在实现自身发展的同时将与各国更多分享发展机遇。中共十八届三中全会为中国未来发展指明了方向，为中国全面深化改革作出总体部署，涵盖政治、经济、文化、社会等15个领域，60项重大任务。中国高度重视发展与克罗地亚关系，愿将中国的机遇转变为两国共同的机遇。

学生译文：When it comes to China's future development, ambassador Deng said, the new leadership sticks to reform and opening-up, follows the path of peaceful development, remains committed to the opening strategy based on mutual benefit and win-win results, and firmly safeguards the national interests. President Xi Jinping expounds the Chinese development goal on the strategic conception of the Chinese Dream, which means to achieve prosperity of the country, rejuvenation of the nation and happiness of the people. The Chinese Dream is a dream of peace, development, cooperation, and win-win results, which is connected to the dreams of peoples of all countries. While achieving its own development, China will share more development opportunities with other countries. The third Plenary Session of the 18th Central Committee of the Communist Party of China (CPC) has pointed out the direction for China's future development and made the overall deployment for its comprehensive deepening of reform, covering 60 major tasks and 15 fields including politics, economy, culture, society, etc.. China attaches great importance to developing relations with Croatia and is willing to change its opportunity into the two countries' common opportunity.

翻译评析：译文第一句中，"大使"一词作为头衔使用时应当大写，而且"邓大使表示"是含有引述动词的主句，用来引导后面的宾语从句，而非插入语，所以此处应修改为Ambassador Deng said that …。宾语从句中的主语是"中国新一届领导集体"，译文中漏了"中国"一词。follows the path of peaceful development本身是正确的表达方法，但未能体现出原文中"坚持"的含义，如果为了避免与前一个"坚持"重复，可将后者译为adheres to。"互利共赢的开放战略"并非"基于互利共赢的开放战略"，译文中的based on缺乏根据。该句宾语从句部分的译文可调整为China's new leadership adheres to reform and opening-up, sticks to the path of peaceful development, remains committed to the opening strategy of mutual benefit and win-win results, and firmly safeguards the national interests. 译文第二句中主要动词选择错误，expounds显然无法表达"升华"的概念，正确的说法应当是sublimates China's development goal to the strategic concept of the "Chinese Dream"。原文第三句中的"与世界各国人民的美好梦想相通"用connected to不是很到位，可改为interconnected with。译文句末还应补上in the world（世界）。原文第四句中的"指明了方向"翻译时最好加上副词clearly，以区别于"指出了方向"。"15个领域，60项重大任务"是汉语中比较常见的表达方法，用逗号分开的两者之间绝对不是互相并列的关系，而是"60项重大任务"分布于"15个领域"内。简写形式如etc.一般不用于正式行文中，而且including本身只表示"包括"，并未穷尽列举，所以也不需要etc.。此处译文可以修改为covering 60 major tasks in 15 fields including politics, economy, culture and society。原文最后一句中的"转变机遇"用change太过生硬，可以改用turn一词。

新闻原文：文章还介绍邓英大使于2013年12月28日抵克，30日即向克总统约西波维奇递交国书。这是邓大使到任后首次接受克媒体采访。《晨报》评价邓大使温文优雅、热情谦和，刚刚履新即积极开展工作，并表示在任期内将努力推动中克双边关系发展。

学生译文：The article also mentioned that ambassador Deng Ying arrived in Croatia on December 28, 2013 and presented her credentials to Croatian President Ivo Josipović on December 30. This is her first interview with Croatian media after she took her office. *Jutarnji List* praised ambassador Deng as being gentle and elegant, warm and humble and appreciated her active work soon after assuming the office and her wish to positively promote the development of China-Croatia relations in her tenure.

翻译评析：原文中说"28日抵克，30日即向克总统递交国书"。"即"表示两个动作在时间上衔接得很紧，也就是后面所评价的"刚刚履新即积极开展工作"。译文将其处理为普通的两个并列谓语，使得这层意思完全丧失。可以考虑将译文调整为The article also mentioned that Ambassador Deng Ying presented her credentials to Croatian President Ivo Josipović on December 30, 2013, when she had only arrived in Croatia on December 28. 对于大使的评价"温文优雅、热情谦和"，译入英语后变成了四个词，并列写为gentle, elegant, warm and humble较恰当。"刚刚履新即积极开展工作"此处强调的是"一履新就投入工作"，而不是"工作很活跃"，译文改为her active involvement in her work更恰当一些。

外交访谈报道的翻译
Translation for Coverage of Diplomatic Interviews

实战练习
Translation Practice

一、请翻译下列外交访谈报道中的导语（Translate the following news leads in coverage of diplomatic interviews）

1. 2018年4月10日，驻加拿大大使卢沙野在使馆接受中加媒体集体采访。新华社、《人民日报》、加拿大通讯社、《环球邮报》《国家邮报》《渥太华生活》杂志、《赫芬顿邮报》加拿大版、华文媒体《七天》等媒体记者参加。以下为采访实录：

    (http://www.fmprc.gov.cn/web/dszlsjt_673036/t1550072.shtml)

2. 当地时间2月12日，外交部长王毅在德国慕尼黑出席叙利亚国际支持小组第四次外长会后接受路透社专访，就叙利亚局势、朝鲜半岛核问题、中美关系等回答了提问。

    (http://www.fmprc.gov.cn/web/zyxw/t1340286.shtml)

3. 2017年4月21日，中国驻莱索托大使孙祥华就使馆出版发布《我的中国故事2017》一书接受莱最大英文广播媒体顶点电台的直播专访。

    (http://www.fmprc.gov.cn/web/zwbd_673032/gzhd_673042/t1456204.shtml)

4. 2015年1月23日，驻赞比亚大使夫人耿海凌作为赞比亚中国妇女联合会名誉主席应约就联合会成立接受赞比亚《每日邮报》记者专访。

    (http://news.hexun.com/2015-01-27/172796948.html)

5. 2016年9月6日，国务委员杨洁篪在杭州接受媒体采访，介绍二十国集团领导人杭州峰会成果。全文如下：

    (http://www.fmprc.gov.cn/ce/ceph/chn/zgxw/t1397055.htm)

6. 2015年9月3日，驻英国大使刘晓明在英国BBC"新闻之夜"演播室接受该节目主持人罗伯特·佩斯顿直播专访，谈中国人民抗日战争暨世界反法西斯战争胜利70周年纪念活动的重要意义，并回答有关中国军费和经济形势等提问。专访实录如下：

    (http://sd.china.com.cn/a/2015/rdtj_0908/315311.html)

二、请翻译下面的外交访谈报道节录（Translate the following excerpt of a coverage of diplomatic interview）

乐玉成大使接受印度报业托拉斯采访

习主席此访是中国国家元首时隔8年再度访印，也是印度新政府成立后第一位到访的国家元首，这充分体现了中国政府对印度和中印关系的高度重视。

当前，中印两国都肩负着发展经济、改善民生、复兴民族的历史重任。两国发展理念和战略高度契合，应该加强政策沟通，实现优势互补，追求合作共赢。正是出于这一目的，习近平主席访印期间将同印方共同规划两国关系未来，对接两国发展战略，挖掘双方合作潜能，巩固和充实新时期中印战略合作伙伴关系。双方将签署有关在印建立工业园区、修建基础设施、扩大相互投资、加强地方合作以及人文交流等近20项合作协议，进一步深化中印利益融合。同时中印作为人口大国、亚洲大国、发展中大国和新兴大国，其双边关系内涵远远超过双边范畴，越来越具有全球性意义。正如习近平主席所指出，中印用一个声音说话，全世界都会倾听。中印携手合作，全世界都会关注。我相信，"中国能量"和"印度智慧"的结合定将释放出巨大潜能。中国龙和印度象强强联合，联袂共舞，不仅将造福中印，也必将惠及亚洲和世界。

(http://china.huanqiu.com/News/fmprc/2014-09/5144542.html)

参考译文
Versions for Reference

一、请翻译下列外交访谈报道中的导语（Translate the following news leads in coverage of diplomatic interviews）

1. On April 10, 2018, Ambassador Lu Shaye accepted an interview from the Chinese and Canadian media at the Chinese Embassy. Journalists from Xinhua News Agency, *People's Daily*, Canadian Press, *The Globe and Mail*, *National Post*, *Ottawa Life Magazine*, *The HuffPost* Canada, *Sept Days* attended the interview. The transcript of the interview is as follows:

2. On February 12 local time, after attending the fourth foreign ministers' meeting of the International Syria Support Group (ISSG) in Munich, Germany, Foreign Minister Wang Yi gave an exclusive interview to Reuters, answering questions on the situation of Syria, the Korean Peninsula nuclear issue, China-US relations and others.

3. On 21 April 2017, H.E. Dr. Sun Xianghua, Ambassador of China to Lesotho, received an interview broadcast live by Ultimate Radio on the booklet of *My China Stories 2017*, which was newly launched by the Chinese Embassy.

4. On January 23, 2015, Mme. Geng Hailing, wife of Chinese Ambassador to Zambia and Honorary President of the Chinese Ladies Union in Zambia (CLUZ), gave an exclusive interview upon request to the journalist of *Daily Mail of Zambia* on the founding of the CLUZ.

5. On September 6, 2016, State Councilor Yang Jiechi gave an interview in Hangzhou,

briefing the media on the results achieved in the G20 Hangzhou Summit. The transcript reads as follows:

6. On 3 September 2015, H.E. Ambassador Liu Xiaoming was invited to a live interview with BBC Newsnight hosted by Robert Peston. Ambassador Liu elaborated on the significance of the Commemoration of the 70th Anniversary of the Victory of the Chinese People's War of Resistance Against Japanese Aggression and the World Anti-Fascist War, and answered questions about China's military expenditure and China's economy. The full text is as follows:

二、请翻译下面的外交访谈报道节录（Translate the following excerpt of a coverage of diplomatic interview）

Chinese Ambassador Le Yucheng's Interview with PTI

The forthcoming visit of President Xi Jinping is another state visit by Chinese President to India in eight years. President Xi will also be the first head of state who pays a state visit to India after the new Indian government took office. It fully demonstrates the importance attached by the Chinese government to India and to China-India relations.

Currently, both China and India are shouldering the historical mission of developing economy, improving people's livelihood and thus rejuvenating their respective nation. With identical ideas and strategies of national development, both countries should enhance policy coordination and increase complementarity of each other's advantages so as to achieve win-win cooperation. It is for this purpose that President Xi Jinping will work together with the Indian side during his visit to draw the future plan of our bilateral relationship, including integrating each other's strategy of development and tapping potentials of bilateral collaboration so as to consolidate and enrich China-India partnership of strategic cooperation in the new era. The two sides will sign nearly 20 documents of cooperation regarding setting up industrial parks in India, infrastructure construction, expansion of mutual investment and strengthening local-level cooperation and cultural exchanges, which will further integrate our respective interests. Meanwhile, China and India are both countries with big populations, big countries in Asia, and major developing and emerging countries. The connotation of the bilateral relationship is far beyond bilateral scope and becomes more of global significance. As President Xi Jinping pointed out, as long as China and India speak with one voice, the world will listen; and as long as China and India cooperate hand in hand, the whole world will pay attention. I am confident that the combination of "China Energy" and "India Wisdom" will certainly release enormous potentials. A close and strong cooperation between Chinese Dragon with Indian Elephant will not only improve the welfare of both peoples, but also benefit Asia and the world at large.

单元小结
Summary

本单元主要介绍了外交访谈报道的翻译。外交访谈报道有时候会原文呈现访谈中的问答，有时候会采用转述报道的形式来呈现。通常，外交访谈报道主要由标题、导语、访谈实录或转述、结尾四部分组成。标题翻译时要注意区分采访、专访、联合采访等不同访谈形式。导语通常就是标题的扩展版，增加了更多的细节信息。其中采访机构的名称务必进行网络检索查证，保证其译文的准确性。访谈实录部分涉及一些常用套话，译者应当尽可能熟悉。由于访谈报道可能以口头直播形式展开，也可能以书面文稿形式进行，其语言可能偏书面化，也可能偏口语化，翻译时应当注意把握话语风格。对于口语化的语句，翻译时可以适当灵活一些，按照英语语言习惯对信息进行重组，使译文的逻辑结构更为顺畅。

延伸阅读

外交翻译是如何炼成的
张 璐

张璐，外交部翻译室英文处副处长，高级翻译，曾是胡锦涛主席、温家宝总理的首席翻译。在2010年上海世博会闭幕式、第十六届亚运会开幕式、十一届全国人大四次会议闭幕记者会上为温家宝总理担任翻译。在2013年3月杨洁篪外长答记者问时担任翻译。并在2014年3月国务院总理李克强与中外记者见面会上担任翻译。

给领导人当翻译，首先要有较高的政治敏感。翻译时要保持对原文的忠实，做到如实翻译。在一次记者会上，温总理澄清所谓中国在哥本哈根大会上"傲慢"的传言时提到，"……我从一位欧洲领导人那里知道，那天晚上有一个少数国家参加的会议……"因为我跟着总理去过哥本哈根，知道他指的"那位领导人"是谁，也知道这个人的性别。但当时总理并未提及这位领导人的名字，所以我在翻译时也不能直接说出这个人的名字，甚至不能表明性别。英文里有男"他"和女"她"的区别，所以在翻译时，我选择了用被动句式来表达。

外交访谈报道的翻译
Translation for Coverage of Diplomatic Interviews

当一个好翻译还要了解领导人说话的意图，可以结合当时的语境去"巧译"。大家对我在翻译总理古诗词时的表现给予了肯定。其实，古诗词翻译并不是我的强项，哪怕能再多给我一秒钟时间，我都能翻译得更加准确。我这次的表现，主要归功于平时的积累。我发现总理最喜欢引用刘禹锡、王安石和屈原的诗词。所以，给总理当翻译时，要结合他说话的语境，知道总理在这个时刻引用古诗词是想要传达怎样的一种精神。这一点很重要。

翻译中记好笔记非常重要。为了提高速度，部分内容可以用一些符号来代替。比如"四项基本原则"可以用"四"字来代替，"独立自主的和平外交政策"可以用"和"字外面加一个圈来代替。除此之外，领导人发言的时候，你不可能让他停下来，即使是连续10分钟的讲话，也得尽可能全部翻译出来。因此，记笔记是翻译的一个工作重点，这就需要不断地练习臂力。

要想成为一名合格的外交翻译，必须要经过"魔鬼训练"。经过非常严格的初试后，才能进入强化训练，由翻译室的几位前辈每天陪学员做大量的听力、口译和笔译练习。培训的强度很大，所用的教材时效性很强，基本上都是当天的新闻和评论，或近期的热点话题。经过层层遴选和千锤百炼，能够真正从事外交翻译的人如凤毛麟角。

（节录并编辑整理自网络资料，内容为张璐在2011年3月回到母校外交学院时为同学们所做的讲座）

UNIT 12

发表外交公报报道的翻译
Translation for Coverage of Issuing Diplomatic Communiqués

单元简介 Introduction

外交公报是国家、政府或政党之间就某些重大事项或问题经过会谈协商取得一致意见或达成谅解后，共同发布的正式文件。从产生方式上看，外交公报可以分为双方联合公报和会议公报。双方联合公报是在领导人会晤后签署，以明确双方对重大问题的看法和态度。会议公报是对国际会议进展情况和成果进行官方发布的公报。公报的名称可以体现为联合公报、联合新闻公报等多种字样。公报具有公开性、重要性、权威性等特点。从公报目的上看，外交公报可以分为新闻性公报、条约性公报和宣言性公报。新闻性公报一般是对领导人到访、国际会议召开以及其他重大事件的陈述，追求的是新闻的真实性和及时性。条约性公报则明确双方或多方对共同关心的事件各自承担的权利与义务，须经各自全权代表签署，对于当事国以后的外交活动具有一定的约束力。宣言性公报是在国际会议后各国元首或政府首脑共同发布，表明对某个全球问题的共同态度，承诺共同采取某项行动的公报。

发表外交公报类报道翻译范例分析
Sample of Translation for Coverage of Issuing Diplomatic Communiqués

范例一（Sample I）

上海合作组织成员国政府首脑（总理）理事会第十三次会议联合公报（全文）
（节本）
2014/12/16

Joint Communiqué on the Results of 13th Meeting of the Council of Heads of Government (Prime Ministers) of the Shanghai Cooperation Organization Member States (Full Text)
(Abbreviated Version)
2014/12/16

当地时间12月14日至15日，上海合作组织成员国政府首脑（总理）理事会第十三次会议在阿斯塔纳举行。会议发表联合公报，全文如下：

On December 14—15 local time, the 13th meeting of the Council of Heads of Government (Prime Ministers) of the Shanghai Cooperation Organization Member States was held in Astana. A joint communiqué was issued after the meeting. The full text is as follows:

上海合作组织成员国政府首脑（总理）理事会第十三次会议联合公报
Joint Communiqué on the Results of 13th Meeting of the Council of Heads of Government (Prime Ministers) of the Shanghai Cooperation Organization Member States

***

总理们在友好、建设性和务实的气氛中就国际和地区经济发展的广泛议题交换了意见。为落实上合组织成员国元首理事会2014年9月12日在杜尚别作出的决定，总理们研究了互利合作的优先方向。

The heads of government in a friendly, constructive and businesslike spirit exchanged views on a wide range of issues concerning the international and regional economic development, and in pursuance of the decisions of the Council of Heads of SCO Member States (Dushanbe, 12 September 2014) considered priority areas of mutually beneficial cooperation.

一、总理们指出，全球金融危机影响尚未完全消除，世界经济仍面临诸多挑战和负面影响。

1. The parties noted that the impact of the global financial economic crisis had yet to be fully overcome, and numerous challenges continued to affect the world economy.

因此，总理们重申，应采取共同措施，保障社会经济可持续发展，加强经贸和投资活动，发展经济和高技术领域合作，全面实现产业升级换代，完善交通物流、信息通信及其他领域基础设施，提升经济竞争力，提高上合组织成员国人民生活水平和质量。

In this regard, the parties confirmed the need to take joint measures with the aim of ensuring sustainable socioeconomic development of the SCO member states, boosting trade, economic and investment activities, developing cooperation in economic and high-tech sectors, modernizing various branches of industry, implementing projects aimed to develop transport logistics, information communications and other kinds of infrastructure, raising economic competitiveness and improving the living standards of citizens in SCO member countries.

***

五、总理们赞同加强上合组织成员国政府部门及商业机构之间的投资合作，建立实业界之间的直接联系。

5. The heads of government declared for boosting cooperation in investment between government bodies and business institutions and establishing direct contact among business communities of the SCO member states.

总理们强调，希望通过实施经济和人高科技领域、交通物流、信息通信及其他富有前景领域的具体项目，加强投资合作。总理们欢迎中方关于利用中华人民共和国组建的投资机制为上合组织区域内经济项目融资的建设。

The parties underlined their interest in invigorating investment cooperation by implementing concrete projects in economic and high-tech sectors, transport logistics, information communications and other promising areas. The heads of government welcomed the proposal of the Chinese side to finance economic projects in the SCO region through the investment mechanism established by the People's Republic of China.

总理们指出，上合组织成员国代表根据本组织活动计划并结合共同关切。参加了国际论坛、展览、圆桌会议等活动，取得丰硕成果。

The parties noted the fruitful work resulting from participation of SCO member states' representatives in international fora, exhibitions, roundtable seminars and the like in accordance with the SCO plan of activities and with due regard to the common interest.

***

二十一、总理们批准了本组织2015年预算，并就上合组织常设机构的财务和组织问题通过了决议。

21. The parties adopted the budget of the Organization for 2015, and took decisions on the issues concerning financial and organizational activities of the SCO permanent bodies.

***

上合组织成员国政府首脑（总理）理事会下次会议将于2015年在中华人民共和国举行。

The next meeting of the Council of Heads of Government (Prime Ministers) of the SCO

Member States is to take place in 2015 in the People's Republic of China.

> 新闻背景：上海合作组织是哈萨克斯坦、中国、吉尔吉斯、俄罗斯、塔吉克斯坦和乌兹别克斯坦于2001年6月15日在中国上海宣布成立的永久性政府间国际组织。宗旨在于：加强各成员国之间的相互信任与睦邻友好；鼓励成员国在政治、经贸、科技、文化、教育、能源、交通、旅游、环保及其他领域的有效合作；共同致力于维护和保障地区的和平、安全与稳定；推动建立民主、公正、合理的国际政治经济新秩序。其政府首脑理事会每年召开一次会议，并发表联合公报介绍会议成果。译文中的导语部分为笔者补译。
>
> 原文链接：http://news.xinhuanet.com/world/2014-12/16/c_1113652309.htm
>
> 译文链接：http://www.sectsco.org/EN123/show.asp?id=561

一、范例一文本结构分析（Text Structure Analysis of Sample I）

范例一是一则有关发表会议公报的新闻报道，主要内容为2014年12月14—15日上海合作组织成员国政府首脑理事会第十三次会议在阿斯塔纳举行并发表联合公报。新闻报道的第一部分为导语，首先介绍有关发表公报的几大新闻要素：时间（当地时间12月14日至15日）、地点（阿斯塔纳）、主题（上海合作组织成员国政府首脑理事会）以及事件（召开第十三次会议并发表联合公报）。导语中提供的是与该公报相关的周边信息。公报的主体内容则在新闻正文部分以全文的形式呈现。范例一中的公报属于新闻性公报，以第三人称的口吻写成，首先介绍了会议召开的时间、地点、与会方和主持方，然后总结阐述了会议过程和主要议题（总理们在友好、建设性和务实的气氛中就国际和地区经济发展的广泛议题交换了意见；研究了互利合作的优先方向）。公报的主要篇幅用来介绍会议成果（总理们重申……、强调……、批准了……），最后对会议承办方表示感谢并宣布下一次会议的召开时间和地点。

二、范例一翻译解析（Translation Analysis of Sample I）

（一）导语的翻译（Translation of the News Lead）

联合公报是指两个或两个以上国家、政府、政党、团体所共同发表的，关于国际重大问题、事件的会谈进展情况、经过、达成的协议的正式文件，用以表明双方或多方的共同看法；或作为对会议情况的正式报道；或作为经过谈判达成的约定权利与义务的协议文书。（覃良，2014：2）发表公报新闻报道的导语通常会介绍公报产生的背景，而发表公报最常见的背景有两种，一是召开大型国际会议，二是领导人出访和会晤，所以导语中通常会提供的信息包括时间、地点、事件以及参与国或其代表。范例一就是一则关

C-E TRANSLATION OF DIPLOMATIC NEWS

于大型会议发表公报的实例，下面再举一例：

二十国集团（G20）16日结束在此间举行的第九次领导人峰会并发表公报。公报指出，促进全球经济增长、改善民生和就业仍然是当前的首要任务。

(http://news.xinhuanet.com/world/2014-11/17/c_1113269291.htm)

On November 16 local time, the Group of Twenty (G20) concluded the 9th Leaders' Summit held during this period and issued a communiqué, which points out t at the current top priority is still to promote global economic growth, improve people's livelihood and increase employment.

(http://www.fmprc.gov.cn/mfa_eng/topics_665678/xjpzxcxesgjtldrdjcfhdadlyxxlfjjxgsfwbttpyjjdgldrhw/t1212255.shtml)

在上面的例句中，作为主语的the Group of Twenty能够做出"发表公报"的动作，因而直接采用issued a communiqué这样的表达。而范例一中的"政府首脑理事会第十三次会议"显然无法做出"发表公报"的动作，故英语译文调整为被动语态，采用a communiqué was released after the meeting这样的句型。另外，上面的例子中并没有像范例一那样以原文形式呈现公报，而是对公报内容进行总结概括，标志性语言包括"公报指出""公报称""公报还说"等等。下面再来看两个以外交访问为背景发表公报的例子：

应中国共产党中央委员会总书记、中华人民共和国主席的邀请，越南共产党中央委员会总书记阮富仲于2015年4月7日至10日对中华人民共和国进行正式访问。访问期间双方发表联合公报，全文如下：

(http://www.vccoo.com/v/316a2d?source=rss)

China and Vietnam have issued a joint communiqué pledging to manage maritime differences and protect peace and stability in the South China Sea, as the four-day visit of the General Secretary of the Communist Party of Vietnam Central Committee Nguyen Phu Trong to China came to an end.

(http://www.globaltimes.cn/content/1028977.shtml)

国务委员兼国防部长常万全16日结束对老挝的访问，中老双方当天发表联合新闻公报，公报全文如下：

(https://www.thepaper.cn/newsDetail_forward_1796834)

China and Laos have vowed to deepen bilateral high-level military exchanges and cooperation during a visit by Chinese State Councilor and Defense Minister Chang Wanquan to Laos which concluded on Saturday.

(http://english.sina.com/news/2017-09-16/detail-ifykynia7584367.shtml)

发表外交公报报道的翻译
Translation for Coverage of Issuing Diplomatic Communiqués

很明显，上面两个例子的中英文并非完全对应。这是因为，这些报道均来自新闻网站，分别遵循中英文各自对于新闻导语的写作要求。总体特点表现为，汉语为尾焦点句式，基本按照事件的进展顺序呈现（受到邀请、正式访问、发表公报）；而英语为头焦点句式，在句首即点明某国与某国发表公报或达成共识，只把访问作为背景信息补充在后面。中央人民政府网（www.gov.cn）和中国日报网（www.chinadaily.com.cn）多采用这种形式，以中英双语分别报道同一新闻事件。外交部官网则很少采用这种导语+公报原文或者公报概述的形式，而是倾向于直接发布公报全文。因此，翻译时不能仅仅着眼于文本，还要注意到委托人对于译文文体风格的要求。

（二）公报话题事件的翻译（Translation of the Topic Event of the Communiqué）

在新闻性公报中，正文的开篇通常会较为详细地介绍公报发表的背景，如果是出访会晤类，一般会介绍出访会晤的时间、地点、人物、会晤的具体活动等。如果是大型会议类，一般会介绍会议的时间、地点、宗旨、与会方、主持人、发言者等，如下面的例子所示：

应马尔代夫共和国总统阿卜杜拉·亚明·阿卜杜勒·加尧姆邀请，中华人民共和国主席习近平于2014年9月14日至16日对马尔代夫进行国事访问。

访问期间，习近平主席与亚明总统举行了会谈，会见了马斯赫议长。双方在亲切友好的氛围中就双边关系和共同关心的国际地区问题深入交换意见，达成了广泛共识。

(http://news.xinhuanet.com/world/2014-09/15/c_1112489669.htm)

At the invitation of His Excellency Abdulla Yameen Abdul Gayoom, President of the Republic of Maldives, His Excellency Xi Jinping, President of the People's Republic of China, paid a state visit to the Republic of Maldives from 14th to 16th September, 2014.

During the visit, President Xi Jinping held talks with President Abdulla Yameen Abdul Gayoom and met with Speaker of Parliament Honourable Abdulla Maseeh Mohamed. In a warm and friendly atmosphere, the leaders of the two countries had an in-depth exchange of views and reached broad consensus on China-Maldives relations as well as on international and regional issues of mutual interest.

(http://www.presidencymaldives.gov.mv/Documents/4380_17b69791-6_.pdf)

中华人民共和国与阿拉伯国家联盟成员国（以下简称"双方"）的外长们和阿盟秘书长，于2008年5月21日至22日在巴林王国首都麦纳麦召开"中国—阿拉伯国家合作论坛"（以下简称"论坛"）第三届部长级会议。

(http://www.cascf.org/chn/gylt/zywjyc/t540240.htm)

Foreign Ministers of the People's Republic of China and member states of the League of Arab States (hereinafter referred to as "the two sides") and Secretary General of the League of Arab States attended the third ministerial meeting of the China-Arab Cooperation Forum (hereinafter referred to as "the Forum") in Manama, the capital of the Kingdom of Bahrain, on 21—22 May 2008.

(http://www.chinaconsulatesf.org/eng/xw/t446472.htm)

从上面的第一个例子可见，公报属于非常正式的文体，领导人姓名和国家名称都应该使用全称，即使是多次出现也不例外。"对马尔代夫进行国事访问"的译文中依然使用the Republic of Maldives（马尔代夫共和国）的表述，而不简称为Maldives。对于领导人姓名，不但要使用全名，还在两国元首头衔前分别添加了His Excellency，在议长头衔前添加了Honourable以示尊贵。为了照顾到行文的简洁，可以参照法律文本的特点，用hereinafter referred to as来约定某些术语，如第二个例子所示，或者直接使用"hereinafter——简称"的形式来表达，如范例一中所示的hereinafter—the SCO or Organization。

接下来，公报会对领导人会晤进展情况或大型会议召开情况进行回顾和总结，如范例一中的下述段落所示：

总理们在友好、建设性和务实的气氛中就国际和地区经济发展的广泛议题交换了意见。为落实上合组织成员国元首理事会2014年9月12日在杜尚别作出的决定，总理们研究了互利合作的优先方向。

The heads of government in a friendly, constructive and businesslike spirit exchanged views on a wide range of issues concerning the international and regional economic development, and in pursuance of the decisions of the Council of Heads of SCO Member States (Dushanbe, 12 September 2014) considered priority areas of mutually beneficial cooperation.

再来看一则实例：

泰国政府2014年12月19日至20日在曼谷成功举办大湄公河次区域经济合作（GMS）第五次领导人会议，中方对此表示赞赏。泰方感谢中国政府予以支持，并为会议取得丰富成果发挥建设性作用。

(http://news.xinhuanet.com/2014-12/23/c_1113752385.htm)

The Chinese side expressed appreciation to the Royal Thai Government for hosting a successful meeting of the fifth Greater Mekong Sub-region Economic Cooperation Program (GMS) Summit on 19—20 December 2014 in Bangkok. The Thai side expressed appreciation to the Government of the People's Republic of China for the support and constructive role in ensuring the fruitful outcome of the meeting.

(http://news.xinhuanet.com/english/china/2014-12/24/c_133874594.htm)

公报属于正式文体，英语中习惯使用较长的复合句，汉语公报英译时要根据实际含义适当采用合译的方法。如上述选自范例一的例句，原文为完整的两句话，而译文将两句话中的状语前置，并分别翻译为in a friendly, constructive and businesslike spirit和in pursuance of the decisions of the Council of Heads of SCO Member States，两个短语均以in打头，然后用and并列连接，使得译文在形式上更为紧凑。另外，公报中提及以前的正式文件时，可以直接在括号内夹注时间和地点来加以明确，从而避免使用冗长的定语从句。例如上述选自范例一的例句中的…and in pursuance of the decisions of the Council of Heads of SCO Member States (Dushanbe, 12 September 2014) considered priority areas of mutually beneficial cooperation.第二个例句原文"中方对此表示赞赏"中的"此"是指前面所说的"泰国政府成功举办领导人会议"，因为该宾语成分太长，所以汉语的处理方法是将其前置。而英语句子习惯向右拓展，所以可将语序还原，翻译为The Chinese side expressed appreciation to the Royal Thai Government for…。紧接着的句子汉语原文中将"中国政府予以支持，并为会议取得丰富成果发挥建设性作用"作为"感谢"的宾语，而在英译时处理成"中国政府"作为宾语，以名词短语support and constructive role作为"感谢"的原因，同样起到了使行文变得紧凑的效果。

（三）公报事件成果的翻译（Translation of the Outcomes in the Communiqué）

新闻性公报的主要目的是向外界宣传会晤或会议所达成的成果，包括各方就某些问题发表的意见和达成的共识。基本格式为"两国政府同意"，"双方一致认为"，"与会各方承诺"，"元首们重申"等等。如下面的实例所示：

总理们指出，世界经济尽管出现一些复苏迹象，但国际金融经济危机的深层次影响尚未完全消除。许多发达国家已采取的危机应对措施仍未解决债务和财政赤字问题，并可能产生负面外溢效应。实体经济增长放缓或停滞，国际市场需求下降，部分国家社会紧张情绪加剧。

(http://news.xinhuanet.com/world/2013-11/29/c_118357891.htm)

The heads of government noted that despite certain signs of recovery in the global economy, the grave consequences of the international financial economic crisis have not been completely overcome. Current anti-crisis measures of many leading countries in the world leave unresolved the problems of state debt and deficits of national budgets, which may negatively affect the global economic environment. One is witnessing a slowing growth or stagnation in the real economy, decreasing demand in the global market, and escalating social tension in some countries.

(http://www.sectsco.org/EN123/show.asp?id=483)

双方主张应平衡处理好和平、安全、稳定与发展的关系，以解决冲突根源问题。对有关热点问题应综合施策，标本兼治。坚持对话协商解决地区争端。非洲是非洲人的非洲，国际社会应尊重非洲国家和非盟及非洲次区域组织在解决非洲问题上的主导地位，为非洲热点问题解决提供建设性帮助，反对外部势力出于自身利益干涉非洲内部事务。

(http://ru.china-embassy.org/chn/zgxw/t1080310.htm)

The two sides maintained that efforts should be made to strike a balance between peace, security, stability and development in order to deal with the root causes of conflicts. It is important to take a holistic approach to address both the symptoms and root causes of hotspot issues and to persevere with dialogue and negotiations in settling regional disputes. Africa belongs to the African people. The international community should respect the leading role of African countries, the AU, and Regional Economic Communities in settling Africa's problems, offer constructive assistance to Africa on hotspot issues, and oppose external forces interfering in Africa's internal affairs for their own interests.

(http://www.fmprc.gov.cn/mfa_eng/wjdt_665385/2649_665393/t1080313.shtml)

新闻性公报中的具体意见和共识一般是针对政治经济形势所发，汉语原文容易出现的问题是动词的施动者不明确，给译者造成困难。如上面的第一个例子，"世界经济出现一些复苏迹象"，显然不能理解为"世界经济"这个主语做出了"出现"这个谓语动作，译文将其处理为一个名词短语certain signs of recovery in the global economy，既解决了施动者不清的问题，又使得这一成分与后半句之间的联系更为紧密，句式更为简洁，符合英语的简洁性原则。第一例第二句话中的"并可能产生负面外溢效应"用到了"并"字，容易使译者误以为它和前一个动作并列做谓语，但稍加分析就会发现，产生"负面外溢效应"的并不是"危机应对措施"，而是"债务和财政赤字问题未能解决"这一事实，因而译者将"并可能产生负面外溢效应"处理为非限定性定语从句，以which来指代前面的事实，厘清了真正的主语。第一例最后一句话是几个并列的事实描述，如果逐个翻译为完整的句子，就会显得冗长和松散。译者在前面添加One is witnessing作为主干结构，而将并列事实全部名词化，使得动作过程被略去，只在问题层面进行探讨，加强了语义的凝重感和文体的正式程度，体现了外交文献的语言特点。（李战子、胡圣炜，2009：9）

第二个实例中首句说"双方主张应平衡处理好……关系"，原文并没有明确究竟是谁应该处理好这种关系。译者采用被动语态，以efforts作为主语，成功地绕开了这一难题。下一句"对有关热点问题应综合施策，标本兼治"依然存在相同的问题，究竟是谁去"标本兼治有关热点问题"？这一次，译者采用了It is important to的结构，只说明这件

发表外交公报报道的翻译
Translation for Coverage of Issuing Diplomatic Communiqués

事情很重要,应该做,而避免了盲目添加主语可能造成的译文失真问题。综上所述,遇到公报中句子主语并非谓语动词施动者的情况,译文中可以灵活运用名词化结构、被动语态、形式主语等多种语言手段,以保证语法和逻辑上的正确与规范。

除了上述形式外,公报中还可能直接表述各方的观点或共识,而不添加"双方强调"这样的转述引导成分。如下面的实例:

双方愿在世界贸易组织特别是发展中国家农业议题二十国协调组(G20)框架内加强协调与合作,共同反对各种形式的保护主义,努力推动多哈回合谈判在锁定已有成果的基础上,按照授权早日结束并取得全面、平衡的成果。

(http://paper.people.com.cn/rmrb/html/2009-05/20/content_256945.htm)

The two sides are ready to step up coordination and cooperation within the framework of the World Trade Organization, and in particular, that of G20, a group of developing countries with special interest in agriculture. They are ready to jointly oppose protectionism in any form and strive to achieve an early conclusion and a comprehensive and balanced outcome of the Doha round of negotiation by locking the already achieved outcomes and in accordance with the mandate.

(http://www.fmprc.gov.cn/mfa_eng/wjdt_665385/2649_665393/t566945.shtml)

此时译文发生的最明显的变化就是时态,转述引导成分"指出""重申"等是在会晤会议中已经发生的事件,所以统一采用一般过去时,而具体的观点或共识多为表态或承诺,应按照实际情况选用适当的时态,多为一般现在时或一般将来时。一个典型的现象是如果原文中出现"双方支持",尽管它与"双方强调"看起来非常相似,但从语义上分析,"双方支持"应该属于具体共识,而非转述引导成分,因而正确的翻译为The two sides support而非supported,或者将译文调整为The two sides expressed their support for …。

范例二(Sample II)

中华人民共和国和黑山共和国建立外交关系联合公报
Joint Communiqué on the Establishment of Diplomatic Relations Between the People's Republic of China and the Republic of Montenegro

一、中华人民共和国和黑山共和国根据两国人民的利益和愿望,决定自2006年7月6日起建立大使级外交关系。

I. The People's Republic of China and the Republic of Montenegro, in keeping with the interests and desire of the two peoples, have decided to establish diplomatic relations at the ambassadorial level as from 6 July 2006.

C-E TRANSLATION OF DIPLOMATIC NEWS

***

二、中华人民共和国和黑山共和国愿在相互尊重主权和领土完整、互不侵犯、互不干涉内政、平等互利、和平共处原则基础上，发展两国之间的友好合作关系。

II. The People's Republic of China and the Republic of Montenegro agree to develop friendship and cooperation on the basis of the principles of mutual respect for sovereignty and territorial integrity, mutual non-aggression, non-interference in each other's internal affairs, equality, mutual benefit and peaceful coexistence.

***

三、中华人民共和国尊重黑山共和国的独立、主权和领土完整。黑山共和国承认世界上只有一个中国，中华人民共和国政府是代表全中国的唯一合法政府，台湾是中国领土不可分割的一部分，反对任何形式的"台湾独立"，反对台湾加入任何必须由主权国家参加的国际和地区组织。黑山共和国承诺不与台湾建立任何形式的官方关系或进行官方往来。

III. The People's Republic of China respects the independence, sovereignty and territorial integrity of the Republic of Montenegro. The Republic of Montenegro recognizes that there is but one China in the world, that the Government of the People's Republic of China is the sole legal government representing the whole of China, and that Taiwan is an inalienable part of China's territory. It opposes "Taiwan independence" of any form and opposes Taiwan's accession to any international or regional organizations whose membership applies only to sovereign states. The Republic of Montenegro undertakes not to establish official relations of any form or have any official exchanges with Taiwan.

***

四、中华人民共和国和黑山共和国将根据平等互利的原则和国际惯例，互相为对方建立使馆和履行公务提供一切必要的协助。

IV. The People's Republic of China and the Republic of Montenegro agree to provide each other with all the necessary assistance for the establishment and performance of the functions of their respective embassies on the basis of equality and mutual benefit and in accordance with international practice.

***

中华人民共和国代表　李肇星
Representative of the People's Republic of China　Li Zhaoxing

黑山共和国代表　米奥德拉格·弗拉霍维奇
Representative of the Republic of Montenegro　Miodrag Vlahovic

二〇〇六年七月六日于北京
July 6, 2006　Beijing

发表外交公报报道的翻译
Translation for Coverage of Issuing Diplomatic Communiqués

> 新闻背景：黑山共和国位于巴尔干半岛西南部，是一个多山的小国。2003年，南斯拉夫社会主义联邦共和国解体，成立塞尔维亚和黑山联邦国家。2006年，黑山举行公民投票，正式宣布独立。同年6月，第60届联合国大会一致通过决议，接纳黑山共和国为第192个联合国成员国。我国于次月与黑山共和国发表联合公报，宣布正式建立外交关系。范例二即是该公报全文。
>
> 原文链接：http://www.fmprc.gov.cn/web/gjhdq_676201/gj_676203/oz_678770/1206_679258/1207_679270/t262904.shtml
>
> 译文链接：http://www.fmprc.gov.cn/mfa_eng/wjdt_665385/2649_665393/t263851.shtml

一、范例二文本结构分析（Text Structure Analysis of Sample II）

范例二是发表外交公报类报道的另一种形式，即直接呈现公报全文。范例二中的公报内容为中国与黑山共和国建立外交关系。此类公报属于条约性公报，通常第一条即开门见山，明确说出主题，即××国和××国基于××自××年××月××日起建立××级别的外交关系。如范例二中的"中国与黑山共和国根据两国人民的利益和愿望自2006年7月6日起建立大使级外交关系"。接下来的各条会阐述一些有关两国关系发展的原则性立场，相当于两国各自向对方所做的立场表态，要求两国在未来的发展中恪守公报中所做的承诺。如范例二中黑山共和国针对台湾问题所做的表态和承诺："黑山共和国承认世界上只有一个中国，中华人民共和国政府是代表全中国的唯一合法政府，台湾是中国领土不可分割的一部分，反对任何形式的'台湾独立'，反对台湾加入任何必须由主权国家参加的国际和地区组织。黑山共和国承诺不与台湾建立任何形式的官方关系或进行官方往来。"条约性公报最后一部分为双方代表签字以及签订时间和地点，表明双方认可公报内容并愿意遵照公报中的原则发展两国关系。可见，条约性公报比前面讲到的新闻性公报更为正式、庄重。

二、范例二翻译解析（Translation Analysis of Sample II）

条约性公报的文本具有法律文体的特点，行文上讲究正式规范、庄重严肃，很多表述都已形成固定表达，不可随意替换。

（一）公报中国名的翻译（Translation of the Names of Various Countries）

条约性公报反映双方或多方对共同关心的事件经过谈判达成的协议，规定各方承担的权利与义务等，须经各自全权代表签署，以昭信守。（周国宝，2012：243）可以说它是最为正式的文体之一，所以文本中无论是第几次提及国名都必须使用全称，不能使用缩略形式，如范例二中的"黑山共和国"the Republic of Montenegro。日常生活中，大家所熟知的通常都是国名简称，而由于政治体制的不同，世界上各个国家的全称格式并不相同。例如俄罗斯the Russian Federation，澳大利亚the Commonwealth of Australia，比利时the Kingdom of Belgium，波兰the Republic of Poland，卡塔尔the State of Qatar，阿富汗the Islamic State of Afghanistan，阿尔及利亚the Democratic People's Republic of Algeria，梵蒂冈the Vatican City State，阿联酋the United Arab Emirates，阿曼the Sultanate of Oman等等，种类繁多，难以穷举。翻译时务必使用词典、大百科或网络进行查证。另外，有几个经常用到的国名务必注意："美国"不翻译为America，因为它还有"美洲"的意思，正确的译法为the United States of America，简称为the US。"英国"不翻译为Britain或Great Britain，因为那样就排除了北爱尔兰，更不能翻译为England，这个词指"英格兰"，只是英国的四分之一，正确的译法为the United Kingdom of Great Britain and Northern Ireland，简称为the UK。"捷克"不翻译为Czech，无论原文是简称"捷克"还是全称"捷克共和国"，英文都要使用全称the Czech Republic。"朝鲜"和"韩国"不翻译为North Korea和South Korea，正确的译文分别为the Democratic People's Republic of Korea（简称DPRK）和the Republic of Korea（简称ROK）。

（二）公报中的固定句型（Fixed Expressions in the Communiqué）

作为一种外交文书，公报中常常使用一些长而复杂的句子，其中附加的大量从句和独立结构常居于显著地位，对主句进行补充、限制、修饰或解释，使句意的表达更加完整和严谨，避免出现歧义和误解，这对于政策性强、政治敏感度高的外事文体来说至关重要。翻译时要注意保持原句严谨、紧凑的特点，同时使译文句子通顺流畅。（李琴，2010：47）这一点在主要用于宣布建立或恢复外交关系的条约性公报中显得尤为突出，从下面列举的一些固定句式中可见一斑：

中华人民共和国政府和多米尼克国政府根据两国人民的利益和愿望，通过友好谈判，决定自二〇〇四年三月二十三日起相互承认并建立大使级外交关系。

(http://www.fmprc.gov.cn/web/gjhdq_676201/gj_676203/bmz_679954/1206_680204/1207_680216/t80939.shtml)

The Government of the People's Republic of China and the Government of the Commonwealth of Dominica, in conformity with the interests and desires of the two peoples, have decided, through friendly talks, to recognize each other and establish diplomatic relations at ambassadorial level as of 23 March 2004.

(http://www.fmprc.gov.cn/mfa_eng/wjb_663304/zzjg_663340/ldmzs_664952/gjlb_664956/Dominica_665058/DocumentsDominica_665060/t80957.shtml)

中华人民共和国政府和加拿大政府根据互相尊重主权和领土完整、互不干涉内政

Translation for Coverage of Issuing Diplomatic Communiqués

和平等互利的原则，决定自一九七○年十月十三日起，互相承认并建立外交关系。

(http://www.fmprc.gov.cn/web/gjhdq_676201/gj_676203/bmz_679954/1206_680426/1207_680438/t7481.shtml)

The Government of the People's Republic of China and the Government of Canada, in accordance with the principles of mutual respect for sovereignty and territorial integrity, non-interference in each other's internal affairs and equality and mutual benefit, have decided upon mutual recognition and the establishment of diplomatic relations, effective from October 13, 1970.

(http://ca.chineseembassy.org/eng/zjgx_1/jjls/t890224.htm)

中华人民共和国政府和南非共和国政府商定，在对等原则的基础上，根据《维也纳外交关系公约》的有关规定，为对方在各自首都建立大使馆和履行其职务提供一切必要的协助，并尽快互派大使。

(http://www.fmprc.gov.cn/ce/cgjb/chn/xwdt/lqgx/t179818.htm)

The Government of the People's Republic of China and the Government of the Republic of South Africa agree, on the basis of the principle of reciprocity and in accordance with the relevant provisions of the Vienna Convention on Diplomatic Relations, to provide each other with all the necessary assistance for the establishment and performances of the functions of diplomatic missions in their respective capitals and to exchange ambassadors as soon as possible.

(http://www.fmprc.gov.cn/mfa_eng/wjb_663304/zzjg_663340/fzs_663828/gjlb_663832/3094_664214/3095_664216/t16577.shtml)

库克群岛政府承认中华人民共和国为中国的唯一合法政府并重申其不与台湾发生任何形式的官方关系的一贯政策。

(http://www.fmprc.gov.cn/web/gjhdq_676201/gj_676203/dyz_681240/1206_681468/1207_681480/t4917.shtml)

The Cook Islands Government recognizes the Government of the People's Republic of China as the sole legal government of China. The Government of the Cook Islands reaffirms its long-standing policy not to enter into official relations with Taiwan in any form.

(http://www.chinaembassy.org.nz/eng/zxgxs/t39440.htm)

结合范例二以及上述实例可见，条约性公报为了保证逻辑的严密性而显得句子冗长、结构复杂、插入语明显增多。插入成份主要出现在两个位置，一是并列主语即两个国家名称之后，插入的多为"根据""基于"的内容。一是在谓语动词之后，不定式标识符号to之前，形成割裂的不定式，插入的多为"通过友好协商"等内容。最后一个例子反映了公报翻译中一个常用技巧，即拆译，通过对句子主语的重复恰恰起到了强调的作用。

（三）宣言式公报的翻译（Translation of the Declaration-type Communiqué）

除了前面两种公报外，还有一种宣言式公报，常见于会议公报中。宣言式公报的正文常常通篇使用第一人称复数，以宣言的形式表明与会方的观点和行动计划。如下面的实例所示：

> 我们，亚非国家领导人，于2015年4月22日至24日齐聚雅加达和万隆，举行亚非峰会，并围绕"加强南南合作，促进世界和平繁荣"主题，本着重振和加强我们的伙伴关系的精神，纪念1955年亚非会议召开60周年和亚非新型战略伙伴关系建立10周年。

(http://news.xinhuanet.com/world/2015-04/25/c_1115085420.htm)

> We, the Leaders of the Asian-African Countries, gathered in Jakarta and Bandung, Indonesia on 22—24 April 2015, at the Asian-African Summit, on the occasion of the 60th Anniversary of the 1955 Asian-African Conference and the 10th Anniversary of the New Asian-African Strategic Partnership under the theme "Strengthening South-South Cooperation to promote World Peace and Prosperity", in the spirit of revitalizing and enhancing our partnership.

(http://mirajnews.com/bandung-message-2015-strengthening-southsouth-cooperation-promote-world-peace-prosperity/60521/)

由于历史文化背景和语言习惯的不同，中西方受众在语篇信息的接收和逻辑思维习惯上存在差异，翻译时应当充分考虑这些差异，并根据目标语调整逻辑衔接和语篇结构。（庞宝坤、王丹，2014：23）上述例句就是一个典型的例子。汉语原文中谓语动词较多，包括"齐聚""举行"和"纪念"等。而英语译文只保留了gathered这一个谓语，将"举行亚非峰会"调整为"在亚非峰会上"，将"纪念"调整为"在……的日子"。这样调整的好处在于使译文成为只有一个主语和一个谓语的简单句，句子各个部分之间的逻辑关系更为紧密。

学生译作讲评
Analysis of Students' Translation Practice

原文链接：http://www.fmprc.gov.cn/web/gjhdq_676201/gj_676203/fz_677316/1206_678284/1207_678296/t1025317.shtml

公报原文：中华人民共和国和南非共和国联合公报

学生译文：Joint Communiqué between the People's Republic of China and the Republic of South Africa

翻译评析：如果标题中的介词超过5个字母，其首字母要和实词一样大写。故

between应为Between。

公报原文：一、应南非共和国总统雅各布·祖马阁下邀请，中华人民共和国主席习近平阁下于二〇一三年三月二十五日至二十六日对南非共和国进行国事访问。访问期间，习近平主席与祖马总统举行了会谈。

学生译文：At the invitation of President Jacob Zuma of the Republic of South Africa, President Xi Jinping of the People's Republic of China paid a state visit to South Africa from 25 to 26 March 2013. During his visit, President Xi Jinping held talks with President Jacob Zuma.

翻译评析：学生译文的主要问题是漏译。原文当中对两位元首均使用了"阁下"这样的敬称，在译文中必须有相应的体现，这也才符合公报使用正式语体的行文特点，因此两个President前面都要加上His Excellency，并注意首字母大写。"对南非共和国进行国事访问"中的国名应该使用全称the Republic of South Africa，一是由正式语体的特点决定，二是与原文保持一致。另外，译文中整体忘记了段落标号。原文使用的"一、二、三"为汉语特有的标号，译入英语后通常调整为罗马字符I, II, III等。

公报原文：二、双方高度评价建交十五年来中南关系从伙伴关系、到战略伙伴关系、再到全面战略伙伴关系的跨越式发展历程。双边关系的不断提升表明两国关系充满活力、重要性不断增强。双方还认为中南关系继续作为两国对外关系中最具活力、最重要的双边关系之一，越来越具有战略深度和全球意义。

学生译文：The two sides positively evaluated the great-leap-forward development of the bilateral relationship from a Partnership to a Strategic Partnership and then to a Comprehensive Strategic Partnership since 15 years ago. The continuous strengthening of bilateral relations shows that bilateral relations are full of vitality and the importance keeps growing. The two sides also noted that China-South Africa relationship is one of the most vibrant and the most important bilateral relationships between the two countries and is having more and more strategic depth and global significance.

翻译评析：第一句中的"高度评价"并不等同于"积极评价"，应该译为spoke highly of，而非positively evaluated，或者采取更灵活的方式，使用单一谓语动词applauded，该词的英文解释恰恰就是to commend highly。"跨越式发展"译为great-leap-forward development也没有错，但是在外交公报这样的正式文体中，连字符拼词形式未免显得过于口语化，应尽量避免使用。英文中有一个词phenomenal用在此处就非常合适，表示so good/great that it is unusual。另外，"建交十五年来"中的"建交"被漏译。第一句话的译文可以调整为The two sides applauded the phenomenal progress in the bilateral relationship from a Partnership to a Strategic Partnership and then to a Comprehensive Strategic Partnership since the establishment of bilateral diplomatic relations 15 years ago.第二句译文中bilateral relations连续出现了两次，读起来难免有啰唆之感。而且按照语言简洁性的原则，能用短语的地方就不鼓励使用句子，能用简单句的地方就应尽量避免使用复合句。做以下调整译文就会简洁许多:The continuous strengthening of the bilateral relationship is indicative of the vitality and growing importance of the relations between the two countries. 从第三句的译文看,学生显然没有读懂原文,两个国家如中国和南非之间并不存在多个双边关系,何来"之一"呢?原文的意思是说对于中国和南非而言,中南关系在各自的对外关系中都属于最重要的一个。"之一"也并不总是翻译为one of,介词among完全可以起到类似的作用。译文可以调整为The two sides also noted that China-South Africa relationship is among the most vibrant and important bilateral relationships each country has。

公报原文:三、双方同意,保持高层交流对话势头,充分发挥中南国家双边委员会、中国全国人大和南非国民议会定期交流、中南战略对话等机制作用。双方商定,2013年下半年在北京举行中南国家双边委员会第五次全体会议。

学生译文:The two sides agreed to maintain the momentum of high-level exchanges and dialogue and make such mechanisms as the bi-national commission, the regular exchange mechanism between the National Assembly of the Parliament of South Africa and the National People's Congress of China and the strategic dialogue play a bigger role. The two sides agreed to hold the 5th Plenary Session of the Bi-National Commission in Beijing in the second half of 2013.

翻译评析:"充分发挥"翻译为make … play a bigger role(发挥更大作用)意思并不完全对等,而且原文宾语(三个"机制")太长,使得相应译文中make后的宾语补足语太远,可读性比较差。如将make…play a bigger role改用bring … into full play会好很多,因为后者的宾语可以后置。另外,那三个"机制"是特指中南两国间的,应该理解为专有名词,首字母都要大写。相关部分调整后的译文为…and bring into full play such mechanisms as the Bi-National Commission, the Regular Exchange Mechanism between the National Assembly of the Parliament of South Africa and the National People's Congress of China and the Strategic Dialogue.

公报原文:四、两国领导人满意地看到,经贸合作已经成为推动两国关系发展的重要动力。《中南关于建立全面战略伙伴关系的北京宣言》为双方描绘出广阔的合作空间,应充分挖掘。双方将继续本着合作共赢的原则,切实加强两国经贸合作,以造福两国人民。[①]

学生译文:The leaders were glad to see that economic and trade cooperation has become an important driving force of the development of bilateral relations. The Beijing Declaration on the Establishment of a Comprehensive Strategic Partnership between the Republic of South Africa and the People's Republic of China offers the two sides a wide scope of cooperation, which should be fully utilized. The two sides will continue to follow the principle of win-win

---

① 为了节省篇幅,原文译文在收入本书时删去了下面的"五""六"两条,第二条也有部分删节。

cooperation and strengthen economic cooperation to benefit the peoples of both countries.

翻译评析：原文第一句中"满意地看到"核心词显然是"看到"，而译文were glad to see的核心词成了glad（满意），而且这个短语非常口语化，不宜出现在正式文体中，可修改为noted with satisfaction。原文第三句话中学生没有理顺句子各个部分之间的逻辑关系，"本着合作共赢的原则"只是"切实加强两国经贸合作"的状语，而非与其并列的谓语动作，另外，"经贸合作"中漏译了"贸"。相应的译文可调整为The two sides will continue to strengthen economic and trade cooperation based on the principle of win-win cooperation so as to benefit the peoples of both countries。

公报原文：七、两国领导人一致认为，在中非合作论坛带动下，中非关系取得全面发展，各领域务实合作不断深化，不仅使中非双方受益，也为世界的稳定和发展作出积极贡献。双方强调了支持非洲发展的优先领域。作为今后三年中非合作论坛共同主席国，双方将进一步加强在论坛事务中的合作，落实好中非合作论坛第五届部长级会议《北京宣言》和《北京行动计划（2013年至2015年）》，为中非关系发展注入新的动力，共同推动中非新型战略伙伴关系再上新台阶。

学生译文：Both leaders agreed that driven by the Forum on China-Africa Cooperation (FOCAC), China-Africa relations have gained comprehensive development and practical cooperation in various fields have been constantly deepened, which not only benefits the two sides, but also makes positive contributions to the stability and development of the world. They emphasized priority areas in support of African development. As Co-Chairs of FOCAC over the next three years, the two sides will further strengthen cooperation in FOCAC affairs, implement the Beijing Declaration and the Beijing Action Plan (2013–2015) of the Fifth Ministerial Conference of the FOCAC, inject new impetus to the development of China-Africa relations and elevate the new type of China-Africa Strategic Partnership to a higher level.

翻译评析：从译文第一句可以看出，学生没有把握住原文中的信息重点。领导人的观点主要在于"中非关系的相应发展使双方受益，为世界作出了贡献"。而译文却将该重点信息处理为非限定性定语从句，成了补充说明的次要信息。对比修改后的译文Both leaders agreed that the comprehensive development in China-Africa relations and continuous deepening of practical cooperation in various fields driven by the Forum on China-Africa Cooperation (FOCAC) not only benefits the two sides, but also contributes positively to the stability and development of the world，将"关系取得全面发展"和"合作不断深化"调整为名词短语后，句子信息重点立刻得以凸显。Not only … but also这个结构连接的并列成分最好在形式上能够一致，产生语言上的对称美。既然not only后为单一谓语动词benefits，but also后最好也使用单一谓语动词contributes，而不要使用makes contributions to。原文最后一句话中的动词"加强""落实""注入""推动"并非完全平级并列，后两个动作应该是前两个动作的结果。另外，相应译文中将"落实好"中的"好"字漏译，"共同推动"中的"共同"漏译。动词inject应该搭配介词into来使用。综上分析，译文可以调整为the two sides will further strengthen cooperation in FOCAC affairs, well implement the Beijing Declaration and the Beijing Action Plan (2013—2015) of the fifth Ministerial Conference of the FOCAC, thereby injecting new impetus into the development of China-Africa relations and jointly promoting the new type of China-Africa Strategic Partnership to a higher level。

公报原文：八、中方预祝南非成功举办金砖国家领导人第五次会晤，认为此次会晤将有力促进金砖国家内部合作、金砖国家对非合作以及金砖国家机制建设。双方将协同努力，共同落实好本次领导人会晤成果，推动金砖国家机制不断向前发展。

学生译文：China wished South Africa every success in hosting the Fifth BRICS Summit and is convinced that the meeting will promote cooperation within BRICS countries and between BRICS and African countries, as well as enhancing the BRICS mechanism. The two sides will make joint efforts to carry out the outcomes of the meeting and further advance the progress of the BRICS mechanism.

翻译评析：对于译文起首已经提到过的会晤the fifth BRICS Summit（"金砖国家领导人第五次会晤"），后文再次提到时应当继续沿用第一次使用的核心词，并大写首字母表示特指，即采用the Summit而非the meeting。"会晤"的作用首先是促进"合作"与"建设"两个并列项，译文中的enhancing the BRICS mechanism在语法上无法与前文形成并列关系。"合作"又进一步区分为"金砖国家内部合作"与"金砖国家对非合作"两类。这其中的逻辑关系一定要表述清楚。另外，"有力促进"中的"有力"被漏译。译文可调整为the Summit will powerfully promote cooperation among BRICS countries and between BRICS and African countries as well as the construction of the BRICS mechanism。译文最后一句仍然是语言逻辑没有理解正确，"推动"应该是"落实"的目的，而不是和它并列。译文可修改为The two sides will make joint efforts to well carry out the outcomes of the Summit so as to promote the BRICS mechanism for continuous progress。

公报原文：九、双方领导人还共同见证了旨在进一步加强和深化双边关系的多项政府间协议和谅解备忘录及企业间合同的签署。

学生译文：The two leaders witnessed the signing of a number of inter-governmental agreements, memorandums of understanding, and contracts between enterprises, aimed at strengthening and deepening bilateral relations.

翻译评析：学生译文中漏译了"还共同"的表述，在witnessed前面添加also jointly即可。"谅解备忘录"应当是和"协议"并列，都受"政府间"修饰。学生将"谅解备忘录"单独列出来，与"政府间协议"和"企业间合同"并列显然不合适。相关部分译文可以修改为the signing of a number of agreements and memorandums of understanding between governments as well as contracts between enterprises。

公报原文：十、两国领导人认为，此次访问取得圆满成功，标志着中南全面战略伙伴关系发展进入了新的历史阶段。

发表外交公报报道的翻译
Translation for Coverage of Issuing Diplomatic Communiqués

UNIT 12

学生译文： Both leaders shared the view that the visit was a great success and ushered in a new and historical phase of development for the Comprehensive Strategic Partnership between South Africa and China.

翻译评析： "此次访问取得圆满成功"中的"取得"是个动态动词，而相应译文中的was是个静态动词，可以考虑调整为achieved。

实战练习
Translation Practice

一、请翻译下列有关发表公报的语句（Translate the following sentences on issuing communiqués）。

1. 2011年5月2日，中国与海合会举行第二轮战略对话，会后双方发表新闻公报，全文如下：

    (http://www.fmprc.gov.cn/ce/cgjb/chn/xwdt/zgyw/t819920.htm)

2. 双方签署了涉及经济技术合作、司法、卫生和农业等领域的多项协议和法律文件。双方表示有必要就重大国际和地区问题加强磋商，以维护共同利益，促进和平、稳定与发展。中国政府同意安哥拉共和国在中华人民共和国澳门特别行政区设立总领事馆。

    (http://www.gov.cn/gongbao/content/2006/content_352482.htm)

3. 乌方重申坚持奉行一个中国政策，承认中华人民共和国政府是代表全中国的唯一合法政府，台湾是中国领土不可分割的一部分。乌方反对包括"法理台独"在内的任何形式的"台湾独立"，反对任何制造"两个中国"、"一中一台"的图谋，反对台湾加入任何必须由主权国家参加的国际和地区组织。

    (http://news.hexun.com/2007-11-03/101008187.html)

4. 中、加两国政府商定在六个月之内互派大使，并在平等互利的基础上，根据国际惯例，在各自首都为对方的建馆及其执行任务提供一切必要的协助。
    (http://www.fmprc.gov.cn/web/gjhdq_676201/gj_676203/bmz_679954/1206_680426/1207_680438/t7481.shtml)

5. 我们支持丝绸之路经济带和21世纪海上丝绸之路（"一带一路"）倡议。该倡议深受历史启迪又有鲜明时代特色，与亚洲互联互通建设相辅相成，将为沿线国家增进政治互信、深化经济合作和密切民间往来及文化交流注入强大动力，具有巨大合作潜力和广阔发展前景。我们欢迎并赞赏中国宣布成立丝路基金，为亚洲国家参与互联互通合作提供投融资支持。

    (http://paper.people.com.cn/rmrbhwb/html/2014-11/10/content_1497331.htm)

6. 为体现两国战略合作伙伴关系，双方决定建立两国国家元首/政府首脑定期互访机制。双方欢迎开通两国总理电话热线，两位领导人同意就共同关心的重要议题进行定期磋商。双方还同意建立中印外长年度互访机制。

(http://ru.china-embassy.org/chn/zgxw/t778838.htm)

二、请翻译下列一则发表外交公报的新闻片段（Translate the following news excerpt on issuing of a communiqué）。

2015年2月2日，中华人民共和国、俄罗斯联邦和印度共和国外长在中国（北京）举行第十三次会晤。

外长们认为，作为国际和地区有重要影响力的国家和新兴市场国家，中俄印需要本着开放、团结、相互理解与信任的精神，加强在国际事务中的协调，增进务实合作。外长们强调三国合作对维护国际和地区和平与稳定、推动全球经济增长与繁荣将发挥积极作用。

外长们重申坚定支持联合国作为最普遍的多边组织，协助国际社会维护国际和平与安全、促进共同发展、促进和保护人权。联合国具有普遍代表性，系全球治理和多边主义的核心。外长们回顾2005年世界首脑会议成果文件。外长们重申需要对联合国包括安理会进行全面改革，使其更有代表性和更有效率，以更好地应对全球挑战。中国、俄罗斯两国外长重申，两国重视印度在国际事务中的地位，理解并支持印度在联合国发挥更大作用的愿望。

外长们重申加强协调与合作，共同致力于维护亚太地区持久和平与稳定，欢迎亚洲相互协作与信任措施会议第四次峰会及其通过的《上海宣言》。外长们承诺共同致力于谋求共同、综合、合作、可持续安全。外长们呼吁在公认的国际法准则基础上建立开放、包容、不可分割和透明的地区安全与合作新架构。外长们欢迎继续在东亚峰会框架下讨论亚太地区安全架构。

(http://news.sina.com.cn/c/2015-02-02/233231473366.shtml)

参考译文
Versions for Reference

一、请翻译下列有关发表公报的语句（Translate the following sentences on issuing communiqués）。

1. On May 2, 2011, China and the Gulf Cooperation Council (GCC) held the second round of strategic dialogue and following the dialogue, the two sides issued a press communiqué. Following is the full text.
2. The two sides signed a number of agreements and legal documents on bilateral cooperation in the economic, technological, judicial, health and agricultural fields. They noted that it is imperative for the two countries to strengthen consultations on major international and regional issues in order to safeguard common interests and

发表外交公报报道的翻译
Translation for Coverage of Issuing Diplomatic Communiqués

promote peace, stability and development. Under an agreement, the Republic of Angola will set up a consulate general in the Macao Special Administrative Region of the People's Republic of China.

3. The Uzbek side reiterated its firm commitment to the One-China policy and recognition of the Government of the People's Republic of China as the sole legal government representing the whole China and Taiwan as an inalienable part of the Chinese territory. The Uzbek side is opposed to any form of "Taiwan independence", including "de jure Taiwan independence", or any attempt to create "two Chinas" or "one China, one Taiwan". It is opposed to Taiwan's membership in any international or regional organization where statehood is required.

4. The Chinese Government and the Canadian Government have agreed to exchange ambassadors within six months, and to provide all necessary assistance for the establishment and the performance of the functions of diplomatic missions in their respective capitals on the basis of equality and mutual benefit and in accordance with international practice.

5. We support the initiative of the "Silk Road Economic Belt" and the "21st Century Maritime Silk Road" (the Belt and Road Initiative), which draws inspiration from history and is closely related to our times, and is mutually reinforcing with connectivity development in Asia. There is enormous cooperation potential and development prospect for this initiative, which will inject strong impetus in enhancing political mutual trust, deepening economic cooperation, and promoting cultural and people-to-people exchanges among relevant countries. We welcome with appreciation China's announcement of creating the Silk Road Fund to provide investment and financing support for Asian countries' participation in connectivity cooperation.

6. Reflecting this partnership, the two sides decided to establish the mechanism of regular exchange of visits between Heads of State/Government. They welcomed the opening of the telephone hotline between the Prime Minister of India and Chinese Premier and agreed on regular consultations between the two leaders on issues of importance to both countries. They also agreed to establish the mechanism of annual exchange of visits between the two Foreign Ministers.

二、请翻译下列一则发表外交公报的新闻片段（**Translate the following news excerpt on issuing of a communiqué**）。

The Foreign Ministers of the Russians Federation, the Republic of India and the People's Republic of China held their 13th meeting in Beijing, China, on 2 February 2015.

The Ministers agreed that Russia, India and China (RIC), as countries with important influence at international and regional levels and emerging market economies, need to further strengthen coordination on global issues and practical cooperation, in the spirit of openness, solidarity, mutual understanding and trust. They emphasized that cooperation between their countries is conducive to maintaining international and regional peace and stability and promoting global economic growth and prosperity.

The Ministers reiterated their strong commitment to the United Nations as a universal multilateral organization entrusted with the mandate of helping the world community maintain international peace and security, advance common development and promote and protect human rights. The United Nations enjoys universal membership and is at the very center of global governance and multilateralism. The Ministers recalled the 2005 World Summit Outcome Document. They reaffirmed the need for a comprehensive reform of the United Nations, including its Security Council, with a view to making it more representative and efficient, so that it could better respond to global challenges. Foreign Ministers of China and Russia reiterated the importance they attached to the status of India in international affairs and supported its aspiration to play a greater role in the United Nations.

The Ministers reiterated their commitment to strengthening coordination and cooperation in a joint effort to maintain lasting peace and stability in the Asia-Pacific region, welcomed the 4th Summit of the Conference on Interaction and Confidence Building Measures in Asia (CICA) and the Shanghai Declaration adopted at the Summit. The Ministers pledged to work together to seek common, comprehensive, cooperative and sustainable security. They called for the development of an open, inclusive, indivisible and transparent security and cooperation architecture in the region on the basis of universally recognized principles of international law. In this regard, they welcomed the continued discussion on regional security architecture in the Asia-Pacific region under the framework of the East Asia Summit.

单元小结
Summary

本单元主要介绍了有关发表公报的新闻报道以及公报原文的翻译。由于公报政治性非常强，行文庄重严肃，总结起来需要非常严谨，所以大部分新闻报道都只用很短的导语加以介绍后即直接呈现公报原文。无论是新闻性公报、宣言性公报还是条约性公报，都属于正式文体，使用到的人名、国名、头衔、机构等专有名词都需要使用全称，即使多次出现也不例外。但是为了照顾行文的简洁性，也可参照法律文本，对某些术语约定相应的简称。汉语语言特点决定其结构较为松散，而公报作为正式文件，习惯使用较长的复合句，所以在汉译英时要注意理顺逻辑结构，适当合并分句。条约性公报基本使用固定句式，不容随意更改，应注意检索参考以往类似公报的译文。如果发表公报的报道是以转述的形式展开，译文中要注意根据转述动词的具体词义及语境区分使用正确的时态。语句较长时，要特别注意把握和凸显句子的信息重点。

参考文献：

李琴:《英语外交文书的文体特征及其翻译》,《中国ESP研究》2010年第1期。

李战子、胡圣炜:《汉英外交文献语言特点的功能语言学阐释》,《外国语文》2009年第6期。

庞宝坤、王丹:《目的论视角下的外事文本英译——以王毅在第68届联大一般性辩论上的发言稿为例》,《长春教育学院学报》2014年第14期。

覃良:《从应用翻译视角下看中国外交部声明公告》,西安:陕西师范大学,2014年。

周国宝:《现代国际礼仪》,北京:北京师范大学出版社,2012年。

13 UNIT

发表外交声明报道的翻译
Translation for Coverage of Issuing Diplomatic Statements

单元简介 Introduction

外交声明是指国家、政府及有关部门、政党或其领导人对某些有国际影响的事件、问题公开表明态度或看法的正式文件。从声明事由上看，大型会议结束后通常会发表主席声明或会议声明，表达与会各国对某些问题的共同意愿、态度、主张或应共同遵守的原则等。两国、两党、两个政府间也常常会发表联合声明，就某些问题表明各自的权利与义务。国家或其外交部还可能针对某一重大事件单方面发表声明，相当于书面地、正式地对该事件做出表态。从表现形式上，外交声明可以分为新闻式和宣言式，新闻式声明是以第三人称的口吻对相关事件和表态做出客观报道，而宣言式声明则是以第一人称的口吻表明立场、发表观点、宣布行动计划等。

发表外交声明报道的翻译
Translation for Coverage of Issuing Diplomatic Statements

发表外交声明报道翻译范例分析
Sample of Translation for Coverage of Issuing Diplomatic Statements

范例一（Sample I）

第十七次中国—东盟领导人会议主席声明（节本）
2014/12/01

CHAIRMAN'S STATEMENT OF THE 17th ASEAN–CHINA SUMMIT
(Abbreviated Version)
2014/12/01

2014年11月13日，第十七次中国—东盟（10+1）领导人会议在缅甸内比都举行。会议发表《主席声明》，积极评价中国—东盟关系取得的进展，并对进一步推进各领域务实合作做出规划。全文如下：

On November 13, 2014, the 17th ASEAN-China (10+1) Summit was held in Nay Pyi Taw, Myanmar. A Chairman's Statement was issued at the Summit, speaking positively of the progress gained in ASEAN-China relations and making plans for further promotion of practical cooperation in various fields. The following is the full text:

一、第十七次中国—东盟领导人会议于2014年11月13日在缅甸内比都举行。会议由缅甸联邦共和国总统吴登盛阁下主持。中华人民共和国国务院总理李克强和东盟各成员国国家元首或政府首脑出席会议。

1. The 17th ASEAN-China Summit chaired by President of the Republic of the Union of Myanmar, H.E. U Thein Sein, was held in Nay Pyi Taw, Myanmar, on 13 November 2014. The Summit was attended by all Heads of State/Government of the Member States of the Association of Southeast Asian Nations (ASEAN) and H.E. Li Keqiang, Premier of the State Council of the People's Republic of China.

二、我们认识到中国是东盟最活跃的对话伙伴之一，为促进地区发展、和平、稳定与繁荣做出贡献。鉴此，东盟国家领导人赞赏中方在东盟共同体建设过程中积极参与东盟与中日韩、东亚峰会、东盟防长扩大会、东盟地区论坛等东盟主导的机制，并以此支持东盟在不断演变的地区架构中的中心地位。

2. We acknowledge that China is one of ASEAN's most active Dialogue Partners contributing to the development and promotion of peace, stability and prosperity in the region. In this context, the ASEAN Leaders appreciate China's support for ASEAN Centrality in the evolving regional architecture, including through ASEAN-led processes, such as the ASEAN

Plus Three (APT), the East Asia Summit (EAS), the ASEAN Defense Ministers' Meeting-Plus (ADMM-Plus) and the ASEAN Regional Forum (ARF) in the ASEAN Community building process.

***

七、我们致力于促进战略关系，保持高层交往和密切接触，继续深化政治互信。为此，我们期待进一步探讨中方提出的签署"中国—东盟国家睦邻友好合作条约"的可行性。

7. We are committed to promoting strategic relations, maintaining high-level exchanges and close contact, and continuing to deepen mutual trust and confidence in the political sphere. In this connection, we look forward to further exploring China's proposal for a Treaty on Good-Neighborliness, Friendship and Cooperation.

八、我们同意将2015年确定为"中国—东盟海洋合作年"。我们欢迎中方提出的使用中国—东盟海上合作基金的全面规划，为海上互联互通、海洋科技、海洋科考、海上搜救、灾害管理、航行安全等合作提供资金支持。我们满意地注意到各方承诺充分用好中国—东盟合作基金。

8. We agreed to designate the year 2015 as the "ASEAN-China Year of Maritime Cooperation". We welcome China's comprehensive plan for utilizing the ASEAN-China Maritime Cooperation Fund to provide financial support for ASEAN-China cooperation in the areas of maritime connectivity, marine science and technology as well as maritime scientific research, search and rescue, disaster management, and navigation safety. We noted with satisfaction the commitment of all sides to fully utilize the ASEAN-China Cooperation Fund.

***

我们对2014年7月3日在北京举行中国—东盟思想库网络首次国家协调员会议表示欢迎，期待双方进一步加强学术交流。

We welcome the first Country Coordinator's Meeting of the Network of ASEAN-China Think-Tanks (NACT CCM) which was held in Beijing, China, on July 3, 2014, and look forward to increased academic exchanges between ASEAN and China.

新闻背景：东盟是东南亚国家联盟的简称，于1967年8月在泰国曼谷宣告成立。成员国包括印度尼西亚、马来西亚、菲律宾、新加坡、泰国、文莱、越南、老挝、缅甸和柬埔寨，秘书处设在雅加达。中国于1991年开始正式与东盟对话，并于2010年正式建成中国—东盟自由贸易区。2012年8月，中国驻东盟使团成立。中国—东盟（10+1）领导人会议为中国—东盟关系的发展做出战略规划和指导，目前已经举行到第17次。2014年是中国—东盟文化交流年，也是中国—东盟关系"钻

发表外交声明报道的翻译
Translation for Coverage of Issuing Diplomatic Statements

石十年"的开局之年。中国—东盟关系步入起点更高、内涵更广、合作更深的新阶段。译文中的第一自然段为笔者补译。

原文链接：http://www.fmprc.gov.cn/web/ziliao_674904/1179_674909/t1215662.shtml

译文链接：http://www.fmprc.gov.cn/mfa_eng/zxxx_662805/t1215668.shtml

一、范例一文本结构分析（Text Structure Analysis of Sample I）

范例一是一则发表主席声明的相关报道。主席声明是外交声明中比较常见的一种类型，通常发表于大型国际会议后，具体到范例一中是指2014年11月13日在缅甸内比都举行的第十七次中国—东盟（10+1）领导人会议。该报道的第一自然段为导语，介绍有关该主席声明的几大新闻要素：时间（2014年11月13日）、地点（缅甸内比都）、事由（第十七次中国—东盟领导人会议）和主要内容（积极评价中国—东盟关系取得的进展，并对进一步推进各领域务实合作做出规划）。导语部分向公众传达了新闻事件的基本脉络，但不做细节展开。报道的正文部分则直接将主席声明全文呈现，以便更为全面、更为准确地向公众传达与会领导人的主要观点。范例一中的声明属于宣言式声明，以第一人称的口吻写成，通篇使用了"我们注意到……"，"我们同意……"，"我们欢迎……"这样的语句结构。主要涉及的观点包括促进中国—东盟战略伙伴关系，维护地区和平稳定与海上安全，支持次区域合作等。

二、范例一翻译解析（Translation Analysis of Sample I）

（一）领导人头衔的翻译（Translation of Leaders' Titles）

外交声明是国家、政府、政党、团体或其领导人、发言人对重大事件或问题表明立场或主张时所发表的文件，具有一定的权威性。（姜秋霞，2009：37）在外交新闻报道中，尤其是涉及较为正式的文书时，各国领导人的头衔务必准确翻译，因为不同的头衔代表着不同的级别，体现着相关国家的政治制度，翻译时需要严格遵循原文，注意区分不同称谓之间的细小差别。

在外交新闻中，提及各国领导人时，常见的说法有"元首""政府首脑""国家领导人"等。"元首"是一个国家在实际上或形式上对内对外的最高代表，翻译为head of state，复数只体现在核心词head上，即heads of state。"政府首脑"是管理国家事务的行政机关的领导人，翻译为head of government，复数同样只体现在核心词head上。这两个表达在范例一中都有用到。"领导人"是一个比较笼统的说法，指的是具有特定职务或级别的、具有领导地位的人物。"国家领导人"一般翻译为state leader，复数体现在leader上。在正式文本中，对于上述领导人，除了基本的官衔称呼外，英文中常常还要添加His Excellency或其简称H.E.，以示对领导人的尊重。这一称谓也经常用于各国大使姓名前。对于君主制国家的皇室成员，根据其级别高低一般要在姓名前添加His Majesty或者His (Royal) Highness，若为女性则相应地将His替换为Her。

由于政治体制不同，各国领导人在各自国家机关中的地位和权利并不相同，其英语名称中会有所体现。比如同是"总理"，中国称为Premier，印度称为Prime Minister，而德国称为Chancellor。汉语新闻稿中有时候会有"两国总理"这样的说法，如果两国总理的英语称谓并不相同，最好不要用其中一国的称谓统一指代，如the two Prime Ministers，建议将其还原为各自的头衔加姓名，如Chancellor Angela Merkel and Prime Minister Narendra Modi。即使称谓相同，实际权力和地位也未必相同，比如美国的"总统"和德国的"总统"英文都是President，但是在各自国家机关中的地位明显不同。所以，涉及领导人头衔的翻译时，一般应该避免使用××and his counterpart这样的表述。以下是外交声明新闻报道中一则涉及领导人称谓的翻译实例，请注意其中文莱元首"苏丹"的英文表达法：

应中华人民共和国主席习近平阁下的邀请，文莱达鲁萨兰国苏丹和国家元首苏丹·哈吉·哈桑纳尔·博尔基亚·穆伊扎丁·瓦达乌拉陛下于2013年4月4日至7日对中国进行国事访问。访问期间，习近平主席同哈桑纳尔苏丹举行了双边会谈，国务院总理李克强、全国人大常委会委员长张德江分别会见了哈桑纳尔苏丹一行。

(http://news.xinhuanet.com/2013-04/05/c_124543197.htm)

At the invitation of His Excellency Xi Jinping, President of the People's Republic of China, His Majesty Sultan Haji Hassanal Bolkiah Mu'izzaddin Waddaulah, the Sultan and Yang Di-Pertuan of Brunei Darussalam, made a state visit to the People's Republic of China from 4 to 7 April 2013. During the visit, His Majesty held bilateral talks with His Excellency Xi Jinping, and met with His Excellency Li Keqiang, Premier of China's State Council as well as His Excellency Zhang Dejiang, Chairman of the Standing Committee of China's National People's Congress.

(http://www.fmprc.gov.cn/mfa_eng/wjdt_665385/2649_665393/t1029400.shtml)

上面实例中的"文莱达鲁萨兰国苏丹和国家元首苏丹·哈吉·哈桑纳尔·博尔基亚·穆伊扎丁·瓦达乌拉陛下"可以说是相当长的"头衔+人名"了，乍一看会让很多人不明所以，不知所措。实际上，通过网络查询可知，文莱达鲁萨兰国（Brunei Darussalam）是位于亚洲东南部的一个国家，通常简称为文莱。文莱的国家元首称为苏丹（Sultan of Brunei），完整的头衔为His Majesty The Sultan and Yang Di-Pertuan of Brunei Darussalam，其中His Majesty是尊称，"陛下"的意思，Yang Di-Pertuan是由马来语转写而来，意为(he) who is Lord，因而完整头衔在汉语中称为"文莱达鲁萨兰国苏丹和国家元首陛下"。"哈吉·哈桑纳尔·博尔基亚·穆伊扎丁·瓦达乌拉"是完整的姓名。文莱居民大部分是马来人，其姓名结构与信奉伊斯兰教的马来人相同，一般都由多节组成，每节分别表示不同的意思，如"哈吉"就是"去伊斯兰教圣地麦加朝圣过"的标记。

"哈吉"前面又另外缀了一个"苏丹",则是姓名前面所冠的称号,表示"最高统治者"的意思。

(二)外交声明中长句的翻译(Translation of Long Sentences in Diplomatic Statements)

外交声明属于书面性的正式文本,为了表意完整和严密,语句中的信息含量会比较大。而汉语是一种意合的语言,呈竹型结构,在单一维度上向前后扩展,其各个部分之间的逻辑关系比较模糊,这就为翻译造成了一定的困难。英译时,需要先对整句话认真解读,理清逻辑层次和修饰关系,将各个部分按照树型结构重建,才能产出正确的、表达到位的译文来。例如:

鉴此,东盟国家领导人赞赏中方在东盟共同体建设过程中积极参与东盟与中日韩、东亚峰会、东盟防长扩大会、东盟地区论坛等东盟主导的机制,并以此支持东盟在不断演变的地区架构中的中心地位。

In this context, the ASEAN Leaders appreciate China's support for ASEAN Centrality in the evolving regional architecture through active participation in ASEAN-led mechanisms such as the ASEAN Plus Three (APT), the East Asia Summit (EAS), the ASEAN Defense Ministers' Meeting-Plus (ADMM-Plus) and the ASEAN Regional Forum (ARF) in the ASEAN Community building process.

上面的例句来自范例一。由于原文中提到了多个并列的"机制",使得句子主干成分之间相隔比较远,读起来略显拗口。经过仔细研读,大体可以抽出该句的主干成分为主语"东盟国家领导人"+谓语"赞赏"+宾语"中方参与机制并以此支持东盟地位"。但继续分析不难看出,"赞赏"的主要是对其地位的"支持",而"参与机制"只是"支持"的具体方式。因而译文中进行了大胆的合理化调整,直接以名词support作为宾语,既简化了句子结构,又突出了重点。可见,核心词的认真甄别对于长句翻译是非常重要的。下面再看一例:

双方强调将充分发挥由中国国务院国务委员分别与印尼政治、法律和安全统筹部长、经济统筹部长牵头的中印尼副总理级对话和高层经济对话、两国外交部长牵头的政府间双边合作联委会等各领域、各层级交流合作机制作用,统筹协调两国各领域合作,为中印尼全面战略伙伴关系向纵深发展做好科学设计和总体规划。

(http://news.xinhuanet.com/2015-03/26/c_127625705.htm)

The two sides agreed to fully leverage the role of cooperation mechanisms in various areas and at various levels, such as the Bilateral Dialogue between China's State Councilor and Indonesia's Coordinating Minister for Political, Legal and Security Affairs and the High-Level Economic Dialogue between China's State Councilor and Indonesia's

Coordinating Minister for Economic Affairs, as well as Joint Commission for Bilateral Cooperation between the Ministers of Foreign Affairs of the two countries, so as to better coordinate bilateral cooperation in various fields and make scientific design and overall plan for deepening China-Indonesia comprehensive strategic partnership.

(http://www.fmprc.gov.cn/mfa_eng/zxxx_662805/t1249201.shtml)

这个例句的原文读起来也是颇为费解，原因是使用了修饰语过长的偏正结构。这种情况英译时一般建议将修饰语调整为介词短语、分词短语、后置定语等，以符合目标语中修饰成分后置的特点。（冯伟年，2012：72）该例原文中第一个逗号之前的部分经过仔细分析，可以抽出其主干成分为"发挥合作机制的作用"leverage the role of cooperation mechanisms，然后再把各个修饰成分如"各领域、各层级"以及两个"由……牵头的……（机制）"分别添加在合适的位置即可。该句的其余部分"统筹协调合作，做好规划"表面上看似乎是和前面并列的，但是仔细思考不难发现，"发挥合作机制的作用"正是为了"统筹协调合作"，因而译文将这里的逻辑关系处理为so as to是比较合适的。另一种可选的译法是以"统筹协调合作"作为"双方强调"的核心宾语，而将"发挥合作机制的作用"处理为"统筹协调合作"时所采取的手段或方式，用介词by或through来连接，即译为The two sides agreed to better coordinate bilateral cooperation in various fields by fully leveraging the role of cooperation mechanisms …, and make scientific design and overall plan for…也是符合原文逻辑的。再看最后一个实例：

双方认为需加强气候变化合作，以准备《联合国气候变化框架公约》之下适用于所有缔约方的一项议定书、另一法律文书或具有法律效力的议定成果，在2015年巴黎举行的《公约》第21次缔约方会议通过。

(http://ru.china-embassy.org/chn/zgxw/t1142797.htm)

Both sides recognized the need to strengthen cooperation on climate change in preparing a protocol, another legal instrument or an agreed outcome with legal force under the United Nations Framework Convention on Climate Change applicable to all Parties to be adopted in 2015 at the Conference of Parties to the Convention (COP21) in Paris.

(http://www.eeas.europa.eu/statements/docs/2014/140331_02_en.pdf)

这个例句的原文读起来有些琐碎，译文没有把"需要加强气候变化合作"翻译为一个小句，而是调整为以need作为核心词，凸显了"加强气候变化合作"的必要性。与后文的连接处译文使用了一个小小的介词in，将后文处理为"加强气候变化合作"的大背景，是比较巧妙的。"议定成果……在会议上通过"显然不能作为"双方认为"的宾语，前文中已经明确表示"议定成果"还在"准备"当中，译文将其处理为to be adopted结构，以不定式表将来，准确传递了原文的真实涵义。

（三）声明中小标题的翻译（Translation of Subheadings in Diplomatic Statements）

当声明全文比较长时，可能会使用小标题将全文分节，以便清晰地区分各节的主要内容。翻译时最常用的方法是将小标题全部名词化，采用名词或动名词形式。如下面的例子所示：

加强政治对话和战略沟通
Strengthening Political Dialogue and Strategic Communication
构建更加紧密发展伙伴关系的下步规划
Next Steps in Closer Developmental Partnership
人文交流
Cultural and People-to-people Exchanges
新的合作领域
New Avenues for Cooperation
跨境合作
Trans-border Cooperation
塑造国际地区议程
Shaping the Regional and Global Agenda

原文链接：(http://www.fmprc.gov.cn/web/ziliao_674904/1179_674909/t1264174.shtml)

译文链接：(http://www.fmprc.gov.cn/mfa_eng/wjdt_665385/2649_665393/t1265496.shtml)

上面的小标题实例选自2015年中印联合声明。从实例中可以看出，小标题通常会用到两种结构，一是名词结构，如"人文交流"，翻译时译为名词结构即可；一是动宾结构，如"加强政治对话和战略沟通"，翻译时可调整为动名词结构。上面的最后一个小标题"塑造国际地区议程"需要仔细解读，根据小标题下面的正文可以做出正确理解，该短语为动宾结构，而非定语+核心名词的结构。再看下面一个实例：

共同愿景与全球治理	Common Vision and Global Governance
国际经济金融事务	International Economic and Financial Issues
国际贸易	International Trade
消除贫困	Fight Against Poverty
气候变化	Climate Change
不同文明联盟	Alliance of Civilizations
"金砖四国"领导人第三次正式会晤	III BRIC Summit

原文链接：(http://www.fmprc.gov.cn/web/ziliao_674904/1179_674909/t688360.shtml)

译文链接：(http://www.fmprc.gov.cn/mfa_eng/wjdt_665385/2649_665393/t688366.shtml)

该例选自"金砖四国"领导人于2010年4月在巴西利亚举行第二次正式会晤时发表的联合声明，领导人在如上各个方面取得共识。注意汉语小标题中的"消除贫困"也属于动宾结构，但此处翻译时并未采用动名词结构，而是做了调整，以名词fight作为核心词，后接补充修饰成分against poverty。另外，"不同文明联盟"属于主谓结构，英译时同样调整成了"核心名词+修饰成分"的结构。

当然，根据具体表达需要的不同，也会出现其他形式的小标题，如下面的实例所示，此时译文与原文一致，也采用了完整的句子作为小标题：

论坛各成员方重申在地区海空搜救协调与合作中应遵循以下原则：
论坛各成员应努力采取以下措施加强地区搜救合作：
ARF participants reiterate the importance of the following statements, among others, in regional coordination and cooperation on maritime and aeronautical SAR:
ARF participants should endeavor to take the following measures to strengthen regional cooperation on maritime and aeronautical SAR:

原文链接：(http://www.fmprc.gov.cn/web/ziliao_674904/1179_674909/t1181699.shtml)

译文链接：(http://www.fmprc.gov.cn/mfa_eng/wjdt_665385/2649_665393/t1181700.shtml)

范例二（Sample II）

中欧气候变化联合声明（节本）
2015年6月29日

China–EU Joint Statement on Climate Change (Abbreviated Version)
29 June 2015

一、中国和欧盟（以下称"双方"）认识到他们在应对全球气候变化这一人类面临的重大挑战方面具有重要作用。该挑战的严重性需要双方为了共同利益、在可持续的经济社会发展框架下建设性地一起努力。

1. China and the EU (hereinafter referred to as "the Two Sides") recognize their critical roles in combating global climate change, one of the greatest threats facing humanity. The seriousness of the challenge calls upon the two sides to work constructively together for the common good, in the context of sustainable economic and social development.

Translation for Coverage of Issuing Diplomatic Statements

二、双方将为了人类长远福祉，有效地推动可持续的资源集约、绿色低碳、气候适应型发展，同时双方认识到，有力度的应对气候变化行动将在本国、本区域和全球层面带来保障能源安全、促进增长、增加就业、保障健康、推动创新、实现可持续发展等一系列协同效应。

2. The Two Sides underline that China and the EU are effectively embarking on sustainable, resource efficient, green, low-carbon and climate resilient development for the well-being of people in the long term, recognizing the co-benefits of ambitious climate actions, domestically, regionally and globally, in terms of energy security, productivity, employment, health, innovation and sustainable development.

***

九、双方同意：

（一）开展合作，在保持强劲经济增长的同时发展低成本高效益的低碳经济；

（二）提升气候变化合作在中欧双边关系中的地位；

（三）进一步加强双方向资源集约、绿色低碳、气候适应型经济和社会转型的政策对话与务实合作；

（四）在上述背景下进一步加强各自分析能力，以探索高效管用的路径和政策工具；

（五）以现有中欧碳排放交易能力建设合作项目为基础并加以拓展，进一步加强碳市场方面的已有双边合作，并在今后几年共同研究碳排放交易相关问题；

9. The Two Sides agree to:

• cooperate on developing a cost-effective low-carbon economy while maintaining robust economic growth;

• elevate the cooperation on climate change in the EU and China bilateral relations;

• further enhance their policy dialogue and practical cooperation on the transformation to a resource efficient, green, low-carbon and climate resilient economy and society;

• in this context to further strengthen the respective analytical capacities in exploring efficient and effective pathways and policy instruments;

• further enhance existing bilateral cooperation on carbon markets, building upon and expanding on the on-going EU-China emission trading capacity building project and work together in the years ahead on the issues related to carbon emissions trading;

外交新闻汉英翻译
C-E TRANSLATION OF DIPLOMATIC NEWS

> 新闻背景：气候变化是指气候平均状态统计学意义上的巨大改变或者持续较长一段时间（典型的为10年或更长）的气候变动。全球气候变化会导致海平面上升，影响农业和生态，加剧其他灾害，给人类带来难以估量的损失。为了应对气候变化，世界上各个国家都在积极出台相应的措施。联合国政府间谈判委员会于1992年达成的《联合国气候变化框架公约》是国际社会就该问题进行国际合作的一个基本框架。范例二是中国与欧盟于2015年发布的联合声明。双方重申了发达国家所承诺的目标，强调了到2020年加速落实应对气候变化行动的重要性。
>
> 原文链接：http://www.fmprc.gov.cn/web/ziliao_674904/1179_674909/t1277066.shtml
>
> 译文链接：http://en.ccchina.gov.cn/archiver/ccchinaen/UpFile/Files/Default/20150630160147006208.pdf

一、范例二文本结构分析（Text Structure Analysis of Sample II）

范例二是发表声明类报道的另一种形式，即直接呈现声明全文，具体为中国与欧盟就应对气候变化发布的联合声明。全文共分为九条，从第一条开始即直接进入主题，提纲挈领地阐述了声明的主要参与者（中国与欧盟）、大背景（面临全球气候变化这一严重挑战）和主要内容（双方将在可持续的经济社会发展框架下建设性地一起努力）。第二条到第八条为声明的第二部分，主要表明了双方对于应对全球气候变化的观点和态度，包括"立即加强全球应对气候变化行动"，"有效地推动可持续的资源集约、绿色低碳、气候适应型发展"等。第九条为第三部分，主要宣布了双方已经议定的一些具体措施，共包括十三个细目，如"开展合作，在保持强劲经济增长的同时发展低成本高效益的低碳经济"，"建立中欧低碳城市伙伴关系，促进关于低碳和气候适应型城市政策、规划和最佳实践的相互交流"，"加强气候相关科学研究合作和技术创新合作"以及"探索在双边及国际层面开展低碳和气候适应型投资及能力建设合作的机会"等等。

二、范例二翻译解析（Translation Analysis of Sample II）

外交声明的种类比较多，最常见的是两国之间关于领导人会晤取得共识的联合声明，例如《中华人民共和国政府和秘鲁共和国政府联合声明》[①]，和国际组织或会议发布的主席声明，例如范例一，主题多集中在双/多边关系、务实合作、未来发展等方面，其结构与联合公报基本类似，翻译时可以参看本书中有关发表外交公报的章节。第二类是国家或组织针对某专题发表的外交声明，内容主要涉及气候变化、能源安全、灾害管理、打击跨国犯罪等方面。上面的范例二即是此类。第三类是针对某国际事件做出表态

---

① http://wcm.fmprc.gov.cn/pub/chn/pds/ziliao/1179/t1266314.htm

的外交声明，如我国外交部2012年针对日本宣布"购岛"所发表的声明①。

（一）外交声明中无主句的翻译（Translation of Sentences with No Subjects in Diplomatic Statements）

汉语中存在大量的无主句，常常采用"话题—评说"的句子构架，而非主谓结构。我国发表的外交声明，常常表现出这种主题突出的特点，英译时应当分析句意、梳理关系，将其转为英语的主语突出结构。（姜秋霞，2009：43）外交声明中无主语的句子大致有三种，第一种如范例二第九条所示，前文中有一个主语作为统领，即"双方"，后面并列多项决策时不再重复出现主语。这种情况相对来说比较容易处理，只要将分项所列的祈使句全部译为动词不定式即可，如范例二第九条对应译文中由agree to引领了数个并列的动词不定式，因为统领句中已经有了to，所以并列项直接以动词原形开始。或者也可以如下例所示，保留所有的动词不定式标志符号to：

为此，双方商定：

一、加强经贸、货币、财政政策交流。为对重振世界经济做出贡献，两国政府均出台了稳定金融和非金融领域经济形势内容广泛的一揽子方案。双方愿在可能的范围内，支持对方根据自身情况为促进增长所采取的举措。

二、将在现有基础上寻求新的合作领域，为经济增长注入新的活力。尤其是扩大在气候变化、能源、环境技术和循环经济、医药和生物技术、基础设施、交通和物流、金融服务、信息和通信技术领域的合作。

(http://www.fmprc.gov.cn/web/ziliao_674904/1179_674909/t534496.shtml)

Therefore, the two sides have agreed on the following:

First, to strengthen exchanges on economic, trade, monetary and fiscal policies. To contribute to revitalizing the world economy, the two governments both introduced extensive package plans to stabilize the financial and non-financial sectors. The two sides will support, to the extent possible, measures taken by the other side in light of its conditions to promote economic growth.

Second, to explore new cooperation areas on the existing basis and inject new vitality into economic growth. In particular, cooperation will be expanded in such areas as climate change, energy, environmental technology and circular economy, medicine and bio-technology, infrastructure, transportation and logistics, financial services and ICT.

(http://www.fmprc.gov.cn/mfa_eng/wjdt_665385/2649_665393/t536227.shtml)

第二种是原文中没有主语，但是经过仔细分析，可以在不超出原文表意的前提下将

---

① 《中国外交部就日本宣布"购岛"发表声明（全文）》，http://news.xinhuanet.com/world/2012-09/10/c_113026288.htm

其调整为完整的句子，即主语谓语齐备的句子，如下面的实例所示：

部长们坚信，在中东地区发生剧变的情况下，绝不能让中东和平进程沦为不确定性的牺牲品。必须加倍努力推进和平进程，并继续致力于解决以巴冲突，恢复巴人民的合法权利。需要根据1967年边界及相关领土交换推动两国方案取得实质性进展，这是满足以巴两国人民愿望的唯一途径，最终实现建立一个安全的以色列国和一个拥有主权、独立、民主、生存能力、能与以色列比邻而居并与本地区其他邻国和平共处的巴勒斯坦国。必须找到一条出路以打破当前僵局，并在各方之间展开有意义的谈判。

(http://www.fmprc.gov.cn/web/gjhdq_676201/gjhdqzz_681964/lhg_682206/zywj_682242/t1270499.shtml)

Ministers are convinced that the Middle East Peace Process must not become a casualty of uncertainty in the context of dramatic changes in the region. Efforts must be redoubled to move the Peace Process forward and to continue to work for a solution to the Israeli-Palestinian conflict and restoration of the legal rights of Palestinian people. Meaningful progress is needed towards a two state solution along 1967 borders with agreed land swaps, as the only way to meet the national aspirations of Israelis and Palestinians, leading to a safe and secure State of Israel and a sovereign, independent, democratic, viable and contiguous State of Palestine living in peace and security alongside each other and with their other neighbours in the region. A way must be found to overcome the current stalemate and establish substantial negotiations between the parties.

(http://www.mofa.go.jp/policy/economy/asem/asem10/chair1106.html)

上面的段落汉语原文中，从第二句起，包含了三个祈使句，分别以"必须""需要"和"必须"起句。为了更清楚地观察该段话的语境，前一句"部长们相信……"也一并摘录在此。如果按照承前省略的原则，三个祈使句的主语就都成了"部长们"，显然这不是原文想要表达的含义。译文中通过被动语态的形式，分别以efforts, meaningful progress和a way作为句子主语，既忠实地表达了原文的含义，又成功地解决了句子结构中缺少主语的问题。

第三种如下面的实例所示，声明全文以逐条表态的形式来呈现，此处摘取的前三条分别以"对……表示赞赏""认识到"和"忆及"起首。这些句子都没有明确的主语，前文中也找不到任何成分进行统领。该声明的官方译文对于三条表态全部采用了动词-ing形式，从而解决了句子缺少主语的问题。

2014年8月10日，东盟地区论坛发表《关于加强海空搜救协调与合作声明》，全文如下：

发表外交声明报道的翻译

Translation for Coverage of Issuing Diplomatic Statements

对2014年3月马来西亚失联航班MH370上的失踪人员以及2014年4月韩国"世越号"客轮遇难者家属表示同情；对参与上述两起事件搜救合作的国家所做出的努力表示赞赏；

认识到海空事故给地区人民生命和财产安全带来风险；

忆及论坛在推动各成员加强搜救协调与合作方面所做出的努力；

(http://www.fmprc.gov.cn/web/ziliao_674904/1179_674909/t1181699.shtml)

The chairman of ASEAN Regional Forum (ARF), on behalf of its participants, issued the following statement:

Expressing sympathies to the families of those on the missing Malaysia Airlines flight MH370 in March 2014 and the victims on the car ferry Sewol of the Republic of Korea in April 2014, and extending appreciation for the search and rescue (SAR) efforts by the participating nations in the above-mentioned incidents,

Realizing that incidents at sea and in the air pose a risk to human lives and property in the region,

Recalling the efforts ARF has made in promoting maritime and aeronautical SAR coordination and cooperation among its participants,

(http://www.fmprc.gov.cn/mfa_eng/wjdt_665385/2649_665393/t1181700.shtml)

（二）外交声明中主题知识的翻译（Translation of Subject Knowledge in Diplomatic Statements）

对于专题类外交声明，译者面对的一个主要难点就是相关背景知识的欠缺。比如范例二中出现了这样一个表述："平衡处理减缓、适应、资金、技术开发和转让、能力建设、行动和支持的透明度"。译者如果不了解有关气候变化公约的主要内容，就可能对这个片段做出多种猜测性解读，无法正确翻译。其实，经过查询相关网站和书籍，就会发现这个片段的基本结构非常简单，那就是"平衡地处理"+多个并列宾语。"减缓"是指相关国家自主减少和控制温室气体排放。"适应"是指制定适应气候变化的计划和措施。"行动和支持的透明度"是指各个国家所采取的减排行动以及在该方面给予他国的支持应当透明化，做到信息公开。所有这些并列宾语都是关于各方进行气候变化谈判的主要内容，基本上已经形成固定表达，正所谓"难者不会，会者不难"。

除了气候变化外，能源安全、灾害管理、反恐等也是当今全球热点议题。中国与美国、欧盟都签订了能源安全联合声明，其中也会经常涉及各个领域的专业术语和表达，需要译者有所了解。如下面的翻译实例所示：

支持东盟努力加强人道主义协调并增强应对重大灾害的领导作用，尤其是与地区备灾安排、特别是与东盟地区备灾安排建立联系及/或为其自愿划拨适当的专用物资和设备，以及/或就需求评估等制定最佳的共同程序和机制，以有效及时地调集划拨物资和设备。

(http://www.fmprc.gov.cn/web/ziliao_674904/1179_674909/t814509.shtml)

Support the effort of ASEAN at enhancing humanitarian coordination and strengthening leadership to respond to major disasters, in particular, by developing linkages to, and/or voluntarily earmarking assets and capacities as appropriate for regional standby arrangements, in particular, the ASEAN Standby Arrangements for Disaster Relief and Emergency Response, and/or developing optimal common procedures and mechanisms, including those for needs assessment, to mobilize assets and capacities as appropriate in an effective and timely manner.

(http://www.asean.org/?static_post=cha-am-hua-hin-statement-on-east-asia-summit-eas-disaster-management-cha-am-hua-hin-thailand-25-october-2009)

我们重申，愿一如既往地积极参加金融行动特别工作组及欧亚反洗钱与反恐融资小组，以切断毒品及其前体非法贸易融资，并争取使欧亚反洗钱与反恐融资小组和金融行动特别工作组将其作为单独的工作方向。

(http://wcm.fmprc.gov.cn/pub/chn/gxh/zlb/smgg/t554795.htm)

We reaffirm our intention to continue participating in the activities of the Financial Action Task Force (FATF) and the Eurasian Group on combating Money-Laundering and Financing of Terrorism (EAG), in particular with a view to stop the financial flows related to illicit trafficking in drugs and their precursors, and to make it a separate area in the EAG and FATF activities.

(http://archive.mid.ru//Brp_4.nsf/arh/E3D58AFDD2019131C3257586005C652C?OpenDocument)

上面的两个例子分别来自于《东亚峰会灾害管理帕塔亚声明》以及《上海合作组织成员国和阿富汗伊斯兰共和国关于打击恐怖主义、毒品走私和有组织犯罪的声明》。第一个例子既有"地区备灾安排"这样的专业术语，又存在多个"尤其是/特别是"和多个"及/或"而使得原文非常费解。只有经过仔细研读，并查询相关的专业背景知识，才能理清句子的层级关系。句子的最高层是"在两方面对于东盟给予支持"，即"加强协调"和"增强领导作用"，然后着重强调了其中的三点"与地区备灾安排建立联系"，"为其划拨物资和设备"以及"制定最佳程序和机制"。而所谓的"地区备灾安排"主要是指"东盟地区备灾安排"，"制定最佳程序和机制"是针对"需求评估等方面"。只有完全理解了各种专业表述，翻译问题才能迎刃而解。第二个例子涉及金融领域和禁毒领域的专业表达，如"反洗钱""反恐融资小组""毒品前体"等，其中尤其要注意"欧亚反洗钱与反恐融资小组"的英文缩写为EAG，只取了全称的前两个单词Eurasian Group。还要注意末句并不是"使……小组和……工作组成为单独的工作方向"，而是"促使小组和工作组将其（切断毒品及其前体非法贸易融资）作为单独的工作方向"。

发表外交声明报道的翻译
Translation for Coverage of Issuing Diplomatic Statements

对于不熟悉的领域务必仔细研读原文，才不会发生理解上的偏差。

（三）声明中表态的翻译（Translation of Attitude Announcement in Diplomatic Statements）

声明中还有一种表态型的，通常为单方面发布，专门针对重大国际事件表明己方的立场和态度。字里行间都有不少政治含义，选字用词必须照顾到政治考虑。（过家鼎，2005：20—22）请看以下两则实例：

日本发生特大地震和大规模海啸，造成大量人员伤亡和严重财产损失。上海合作组织对死难者表示沉痛哀悼。

上海合作组织成员国向日本政府和人民深表同情，将继续协助日方克服困难，消除此次自然灾害后果。

(http://www.fmprc.gov.cn/web/ziliao_674904/1179_674909/t806971.shtml)

Regarding the devastating earthquake and tsunami in Japan which have caused catastrophic consequences, numerous human casualties and considerable property damage, the Shanghai Cooperation Organization is conveying sincere condolences and deepest sympathy to the families of the dead and injured.

Expressing solidarity with the people and government of Japan, the Shanghai Cooperation Organization member states will continue to assist the Japanese side in overcoming difficulties and dealing with the aftermath of natural disasters.

(http://www.sectsco.org/EN123/Yolder.asp)

今天，朝鲜民主主义人民共和国不顾国际社会普遍反对，再次进行核试验，中国政府对此表示<u>坚决反对</u>。

实现半岛无核化、防止核扩散、维护东北亚和平稳定，是中方的坚定立场。我们强烈敦促朝方信守无核化承诺，停止采取任何恶化局势的行动。

(http://www.fmprc.gov.cn/web/zyxw/t1329851.shtml)

Today, the Democratic People's Republic of Korea (DPRK) conducted once again a nuclear test in disregard of widespread opposition from the international community. The Chinese government <u>is firmly opposed to</u> that.

To realize denuclearization on the Korean Peninsula, prevent nuclear proliferation and safeguard peace and stability of Northeast Asia is China's firm position. We strongly urge the DPRK side to honor its commitment to denuclearization and stop taking actions that worsen the situation.

(http://www.fmprc.gov.cn/mfa_eng/zxxx_662805/t1329861.shtml)

此类声明的基本结构是首先陈述基本事实，如"朝鲜再次进行了核试验"，然后立即表明态度，即"中国表示坚决反对"。表态用语应当明确、坚定，如译文中的画线部分。为了凸显正式性，句子主语多为国家或政府机构，如the Chinese government或the Shanghai Cooperation Organization等。

学生译作讲评
Analysis of Students' Translation Practice

原文链接：http://news.xinhuanet.com/politics/2015-08/31/c_1116430408.htm

声明原文：一　双方将继续遵循发展全面战略伙伴关系的方针，赋予两国关系新的内涵。

学生译文：First, the Two Sides will continue to follow the policy of developing the all-round strategic partnership and give new meaning to the bilateral relations.

翻译评析：汉语中使用的"一、二、三"属于层级较高的标号，译入英语时通常调整为罗马字符I, II, III。而把first, second, third留给层级稍低的标号，如"（一）、（二）、（三）"使用。"全面战略伙伴关系"在外交部的官方译文中一般译为comprehensive strategic partnership，而all-round通常对应"全方位"。"赋予两国关系新的内涵"的译文用词不够正式和庄重，可以调整为endow the bilateral relations with new connotations。

声明原文：中国支持哈萨克斯坦提出的旨在建立欧亚大陆平衡与建设性关系、巩固地区及世界和平与稳定的国际倡议，包括继续举办世界和传统宗教领袖大会。

学生译文：China supports the international initiatives proposed by Kazakhstan that aim to build balanced and constructive relations between the Eurasia and consolidate regional and world peace and stability and that include continuing to hold the Congress of Leaders of World and Traditional Religions.

翻译评析：欧亚大陆是欧洲大陆和亚洲大陆的合称，是看作一体的，自然不存在between the Eurasia一说，修改为in Eurasia即可。第一个定语从句that aim to和第二个定语从句and that include并不是并列关系。"旨在"是明确的修饰限定关系，而"包括"只是对前述"国际倡议"的补充说明，因此应当在stability后面使用逗号断句，后接including…加以解释。译文可调整为… that aim to build balanced and constructive relations in Eurasia and consolidate regional and world peace and stability, including continuing to hold the Congress of Leaders of World and Traditional Religions.

声明原文：双方重申，不从事任何违反《联合国宪章》宗旨和原则，有损双方主权、领土完整和破坏边界的活动。

学生译文：The Two Sides reiterated that they are not engaged in any activities that violate the purposes and principles of the UN Charter, impair the sovereignty and territorial integrity of both sides and disrupt the borders.

翻译评析：学生译文中使用的是reiterate加一般现在时态的宾语从句，其意为"双方再次强调他们当前没有从事某些活动"，是一种自我辩护。而原文中的"重申"实际上是一种承诺，是"保证永远不从事某些活动"，所以译文表意出现了严重差错。译文中"有损双方主权"和前面的"违反《联合国宪章》"之间漏了连词，注意此处应该用or而不是and，表示"不从事这些活动中的任何一种"。译文可以修改为The Two Sides reiterated their commitments to not being engaged in any activities that violate the purposes and principles of the UN Charter or impair the sovereignty and territorial integrity or disrupt the borders of the Two Sides.注意其中的commitments一词后面的to是介词，不是不定式，因而后接动名词。

声明原文：二 双方强调，中国"丝绸之路经济带"倡议和哈萨克斯坦"光明之路"新经济政策相辅相成，有利于深化两国全面合作。双方将以此为契机进一步加强产能与投资合作。

学生译文：Second, the Two Sides stressed that China's "Silk Road Economic Belt" initiative and Kazakhstan "Shining Path" new economic policies complement each other, which is conducive to deepen bilateral cooperation in an all-round way. The Two Sides will take this opportunity to further strengthen cooperation on capacity and investment.

翻译评析：为了表意清晰，一般应该尽量避免名词短语的直线堆积，如学生译文中的China's "Silk Road Economic Belt" initiative and Kazakhstan "Shining Path" new economic policies，可以调整为China's initiative of the "Silk Road Economic Belt" and Kazakhstan's new economic policies of the "Bright Road"。"光明之路"从语言本身来讲，翻译为Shining Path并没有错，但是这个短语在英语中已经有了别的含义，它是指秘鲁的两大主要反叛组织之一，成立于1970年，采用游击战术并从事暴力恐怖活动。哈萨克斯坦的新经济政策显然不能继续沿用此名来翻译，因此翻译为Bright Road。be conducive to中的to是介词，后面应该跟动名词形式deepening。cooperation后面的介词应该用in而非on。"产能"最好使用全称production capacity，如果仅仅使用capacity，可能会被理解为"容量"等别的含义。

声明原文：双方将本着开放精神和协商、协作、互利原则，共同就"丝绸之路经济带"倡议和"光明之路"新经济政策进行对接开展合作。

学生译文：The Two Sides will be in line with the spirit of opening-up and the principles of negotiation, collaboration and mutual benefit to make connections with China's "Silk Road Economic Belt" initiative and Kazakhstan "Shining Path" new economic policies.

翻译评析：学生译文显然没有抓住句子的核心思想。原文的主要谓语应该是"开展合作"，只不过前面添加了"本着……原则"，"就……"两个状语而已。所以译文的整体结构需要重新调整。另外，collaboration一词有"勾结""串谋"的消极暗示，应当避免在这里使用。"对接"一词通常翻译为integration。本句译文可以修改为The Two Sides will conduct cooperation together in the integration of the initiative of the "Silk Road

Economic Belt" and the new economic policies of the "Bright Road" in line with the spirit of opening-up and the principles of consultation, coordination and mutual benefit.

声明原文：双方同意在上述倡议框架内加强区域间互联互通，基础设施建设、贸易、旅游和投资领域合作。

学生译文：The Two Sides agreed to strengthen the regional interconnection and inter-working and cooperation in infrastructure construction, trade, tourism and investment areas within the framework of the initiatives.

翻译评析：原文是"区域间"，而非"区域的"，学生译文中采用了regional一词，彻底改变了原文想要表达的含义，应该改为inter-regional。"互联互通"的英文表达在外交部官网也经过数次调整，最终确定为connectivity。"互联互通"与"各领域合作"是上一级并列关系，"基础设施建设、贸易、旅游、投资"是下一级并列关系，为了能够加以区分，可在上一级使用as well as连接，而在下一级使用and连接。另外，"上述倡议"中的"上述"被漏译。修正后的译文为The Two Sides agreed to strengthen inter-regional connectivity as well as cooperation in areas such as infrastructure construction, trade, tourism and investment within the framework of the above initiatives.

声明原文：双方强调，2017年在阿斯塔纳举办专项世博会具有重要意义。中方已正式确认出席2017年世博会，并将在世博会上展示中国有效利用能源方面的理念和主张。

学生译文：The Two Sides stressed that hosting the Specialized World Exposition in Astana in 2017 is of great significance. China has officially confirmed its attendance in the World Exposition 2017 and will exhibit the ideals and propositions with which China effectively use the energy.

翻译评析："2017年世博会"习惯上简写为Expo 2017。Attendance后面搭配的介词应该是at而不是in。译文末句的定语从句with which…用得非常累赘，不符合语言的简练原则。ideals一词可能是学生用词错误，也可能是拼写错误。该句的译文可以重新调整为China has officially confirmed its attendance at the Expo 2017 and will exhibit its ideas and propositions on effectively utilizing energy at the Expo.

声明原文：双方认为，在实施产能与投资领域的合作项目过程中，应当注意环境保护，鼓励企业采用高新技术，创造节能型、高附加值产能，生产具有竞争力的产品。

学生译文：The Two Sides thought that during the projects process of implementing the cooperation in the areas of capacity and investment, we should pay attention to environment protection, encourage enterprises to adopt the high technology, create the energy-saving and high value-added capacity and produce the competitive products.

翻译评析："认为"是表明观点的常用词，正式的译法是hold。学生译文中使用的thought是"原以为"的意思，表意完全错误。"在实施产能与投资领域的合作项目过程中"这个成分学生完全没有读懂，所以译文中用错了核心词。其实这里的主干成分是"在实施过程中"，而不是像学生理解的"在项目过程中"。紧接着的译文中学生添加了主语we是不可取的译法，因为we的指代不明。汉语中缺少主语的情况翻译时可以转为被动句式。另外，译文中存在多个误用的定冠词the。此句调整后的译文为The Two Sides hold that during the implementation of cooperative projects in the areas of production capacity and investment, attention should be paid to environmental protection, and enterprises should be encouraged to adopt high and new technology, create energy-saving and high value-added production capacity and produce competitive products.

声明原文：双方将提出并支持产能和投资领域的大型合作项目，并将协助和支持本国金融机构向落实合作项目的两国企业提供融资。

学生译文：The Two Sides will propose and support major cooperation projects in capacity and investment areas and will assist and support the domestic financial institution to provide the finance to the businesses of the two countries which have implemented their cooperative projects.

翻译评析："产能和投资领域"应当翻译为in the areas of production capacity and investment。译文后半段的翻译问题比较多。support没有后接不定式作宾语补足语的用法，即不用于support sb. to do sth.的结构。"融资"是一种行为，英文为financing而不是finance。"落实合作项目的企业"并不是说"已经落实了"，而是"在落实过程当中"就会需要"融资服务"。因此本句后半段译文可修改为and will assist and support domestic financial institutions in providing financing service to enterprises of the two countries which implement the cooperative projects.

声明原文：双方将根据本国法律，在主管部门协助下，在实施合作项目所需的签证办理问题上相互提供必要协助。

学生译文：The Two Sides will mutually provide necessary assistance on the visa processing problems needed for implementing the cooperative projects in accordance with its national laws and with the assistance of competent departments.

翻译评析：此处的"签证办理问题"显然只是个"事项"而不是个"难题"，而且needed一词是多余的，去掉后表意依然完整。译文可修改为The Two Sides will mutually provide necessary assistance on the issue of visa processing for implementing cooperative projects in accordance with its national laws and with the assistance of competent departments.

实战练习
Translation Practice

一、请翻译下列有关发表声明的语句（Translate the following sentences on issuing statements）。

1. 双方同意进一步加强司法、执法领域合作，加强在打击跨国犯罪、禁毒、反贪、追逃追赃、网络安全、出入境管理以及执法能力建设领域务实合作，承诺在情报信息交流、案件协查、缉捕和遣返犯罪嫌疑人等方面相互支持。

(http://world.people.com.cn/n/2015/0327/c1002-26757586.html)

2. 双方欢迎"亚洲基础设施投资银行（亚投行）协定"谈判结束，认可欧盟及其成员国的支持。双方强调，亚投行与现有多边开发银行相互补充，以可持续方式解决亚洲基础设施投资的大量需求，期待亚投行早日投入运行。欧盟期待未来与亚投行进行合作。

(http://news.xinhuanet.com/2015-06/30/c_1115774915.htm)

3. 双方回顾了2015年12月4日至5日在南非举行的中非合作论坛约翰内斯堡峰会，以及峰会后在论坛框架下开展多边、双边落实峰会成果合作的进展情况，就加强协调配合，深入推进论坛峰会成果落实工作，促进中非合作共赢、共同发展等议题进行了广泛、深入的讨论，达成以下共识：

(http://www.fmprc.gov.cn/web/ziliao_674904/1179_674909/t1385940.shtml)

4. 作为国际新秩序中的两个主要国家，中印之间的互动超越双边范畴，对地区、多边和国际事务具有重要影响。双方同意，不仅要就影响国际和平、安全和发展的动向加强协商，还将协调立场，并共同塑造地区和全球事务议程和结果。双方同意继续加强在中俄印、金砖国家、二十国集团等多边机制中的协调配合，促进发展中国家的利益，推动建设美好世界。

(http://www.fmprc.gov.cn/ce/cemx/chn/xw/t1264174.htm)

5. 关于减少温室气体和其他空气污染物排放的务实合作行动，双方已就工作组下启动的五个合作领域实施计划达成一致，包括载重汽车和其他汽车减排、智能电网、碳捕集利用和封存、温室气体数据的收集和管理、建筑和工业能效，并承诺投入相当精力和资源以确保在第六轮中美战略与经济对话前取得实质性成果。

(http://news.cntv.cn/2014/02/15/ARTI1392443479891990.shtml)

6. 为落实习近平主席和杜特尔特总统的共识，两国建立了中菲南海问题磋商机制，双方对此表示欢迎。这有助于双方管控和防止海上事件、加强海上对话合作、促进双边关系稳定发展。双方同意在包括海洋环保、减灾等领域加强合作，包括进一步探讨可能的海洋科考合作。

(http://www.fmprc.gov.cn/web/ziliao_674904/1179_674909/t1511205.shtml)

二、请翻译下面一则外交声明（Translate the following diplomatic statement）。

第三轮中日韩北极事务高级别对话联合声明

一、2018年6月8日，第三轮中日韩北极事务高级别对话在中国上海举行。中华人民共和国外交部北极事务特别代表高风、大韩民国外交部北极事务大使康祯植、

发表外交声明报道的翻译
Translation for Coverage of Issuing Diplomatic Statements

日本国外务省北极事务大使山本荣二率团出席对话。

二、三方团长确认了中日韩北极事务高级别对话作为2015年第六次中日韩领导人会议成果之一所发挥的积极作用。三方团长重申三国在北极事务,尤其是科学研究方面开展合作的重要性。2018年5月9日第七次中日韩领导人会议联合宣言对此予以认可。

三、三方团长认为变化中的北极带来的机遇和挑战具有全球意义和国际影响,重申以规则为基础维护北极和平、稳定和建设性合作对国际社会的重要性。通过本次对话,中华人民共和国、日本国和大韩民国从东亚国家视角提出在北极问题上面临的共同挑战,并再次强调三国愿为促进北极和平、稳定和可持续发展作出贡献的意愿。

四、注意到三国各自在北极政策方面的最新进展,三方团长欢迎今年1月发布的第一份《中国的北极政策》白皮书,以及日本国为进一步巩固其北极政策之目的而通过的第三份《海洋政策基本计划》。他们期待大韩民国计划在未来几个月公布的第二份《北极政策总体规划》。三方团长强调了政策对话对三国加强相互理解和促进北极合作的重要意义。

五、三方团长继续将促进科学研究作为三国合作的优先领域。三方团长支持就北极考察情况加强信息交流,并鼓励数据共享和进一步实施联合考察。他们亦探讨了在其他领域开展北极合作的可能性。

(http://www.fmprc.gov.cn/ce/cein/chn/zgbd/t705967.htm)

参考译文
Versions for Reference

一、请翻译下列有关发表声明的语句(**Translate the following sentences on issuing statements**)。

1. The two sides agreed to further enhance cooperation in judicature and law enforcement, especially practical cooperation in combating transnational crimes, anti-drug trafficking, anti-corruption, extradition of corrupt officials who have fled abroad and asset recovery, cyber-security, border entry and exit management, and law enforcement capacity building, and promised to render support to each other in intelligence sharing, case investigation, arrest and repatriation of suspects, and other aspects.

2. Both sides welcomed the conclusion of negotiations on the Articles of Agreement for the Asian Infrastructure Investment Bank (AIIB) and recognized the support rendered by the EU and its Member States. They stressed that the AIIB should complement the existing multilateral development banks in addressing Asia's extensive needs for infrastructure investment in a sustainable manner, and anticipated that it will begin

operating at an early date. The EU looked forward to cooperating with the AIIB in the future.

3. Both sides recalled the Johannesburg Summit of the FOCAC convened in South Africa from 4 to 5 December 2015, as well as post-Summit progress made in bilateral and multilateral cooperation to implement the Summit outcomes under the framework of the FOCAC. Both sides went through intense and comprehensive discussions on topics of strengthening coordination, intensifying efforts on further implementation of follow-up actions of the Johannesburg Summit, and promoting China-Africa win-win cooperation for common development, and reached the following consensus:

4. As two major powers in the emerging world order, engagement between India and China transcends the bilateral dimension and has a significant bearing on regional, multilateral and global issues. Both Sides agreed to not only step up their consultations on developments affecting international peace, security and development but also coordinate their positions and work together to shape the regional and global agenda and outcomes. They agreed to further strengthen coordination and cooperation in multilateral mechanisms including RIC, BRICS and G20, and promote the interests of developing countries and the building of a better world.

5. Regarding practical cooperative actions to reduce greenhouse gas emissions and other air pollutants, the two sides have reached agreement on the implementation plans for the five initiatives launched under the working group, including emission reductions from heavy duty and other vehicles, smart grids, carbon capture utilization and storage, collecting and managing greenhouse gas emissions data, and energy efficiency in buildings and industry, and commit to devote significant effort and resources to secure concrete results by the Sixth China-U.S. Strategic and Economic Dialogue in 2014.

6. Both sides welcome the implementation of the consensus between President Xi Jinping and President Rodrigo Roa Duterte to establish a Bilateral Consultation Mechanism on the South China Sea as a way to manage and prevent incidents at sea, enhance maritime dialogue and cooperation, and pursue a stable growth of bilateral relations. Both sides agree to strengthen maritime cooperation in areas such as marine environmental protection, disaster risk reduction, including possible cooperation in marine scientific research, subject to further consultations.

发表外交声明报道的翻译
Translation for Coverage of Issuing Diplomatic Statements
UNIT 13

二、请翻译下面一则外交声明（Translate the following diplomatic statement）。

Joint Statement of the Third Trilateral High-Level Dialogue on the Arctic

1. The Third Trilateral High-Level Dialogue on the Arctic was held on June 8, 2018 in Shanghai, China. Mr. Gao Feng, Special Representative for Arctic Affairs of the Ministry of Foreign Affairs of the People's Republic of China, Mr. Kang Jeong-sik, Ambassador for Arctic Affairs of the Ministry of Foreign Affairs of the Republic of Korea, and Mr. Eiji Yamamoto, Ambassador in charge of Arctic Affairs of the Ministry of Foreign Affairs of Japan attended this Dialogue as the Heads of Delegations (HoDs).

2. The three HoDs recognized the positive role of the Trilateral High-Level Dialogue on the Arctic as one of the outcomes of the Sixth Trilateral Summit in 2015. The HoDs also reaffirmed the importance to promote trilateral cooperation on the Arctic, especially in the area of scientific research, as endorsed in the Joint Declaration of the Seventh Trilateral Summit on May 9, 2018.

3. The three HoDs recognized that the changing Arctic brings about opportunities and challenges with global implications and international impacts, and reaffirmed the importance for the international community to maintain peace, stability and constructive cooperation in a rule-based manner. Through this Dialogue, the People's Republic of China, Japan and the Republic of Korea addressed common challenges over the Arctic, from the perspective of East Asian countries, and reiterated their intention to make contributions to promoting peace, stability and sustainable development in the Arctic.

4. Noting the latest progress on their respective Arctic policies, the three HoDs welcomed the first white paper on China's Arctic Policy publicized this January, and the third Basic Plan on Ocean Policy adopted by Japan to further strengthen its policy in the Arctic. They also noted with expectation that ROK is planning to announce its 2nd Arctic Policy Master Plan in the coming months. The HoDs stressed the importance of policy dialogue in enhancing mutual understanding and facilitating cooperation in the Arctic among the three countries.

5. The three HoDs continued to promote scientific research as priority for cooperation among the three countries. The HoDs supported the enhancement of the exchange of information on Arctic expeditions, and encouraged the sharing of scientific data and further development of collaborative surveys. They also discussed the possibility of exploring other areas for cooperation in the Arctic.

单元小结
Summary

　　本单元主要介绍了发表外交声明报道及外交声明文本的翻译。领导人出访或会谈后常常会发表两国间或两国政府间联合声明,其中要注意领导人头衔的细微差异,做到精准翻译。大型会议后也常常发表主席声明,内容较多时可能分成若干小标题,翻译时一般应处理为名词化结构,保证各个小标题形式上的统一。对于针对气候变化、能源安全等专业问题发表的声明,翻译时需要广泛检索查证,保证准确理解其中涉及的主题知识,以确保翻译的忠实性和准确性。对于外交声明中的长句和复杂句,应当仔细研读,逐个剥离修饰成分,找准句子的主干结构,确定译文语句的总体框架结构。对于无明确主语的、通篇以动词直接起句的声明,在翻译时一般处理为动词-ing形式。针对某些重大国际事件,有些国家或组织也可能单方面发表声明,表明己方立场,翻译时要做到态度鲜明、表意清楚。

参考文献:

冯伟年:《汉英笔译》,西安:西安交通大学出版社,2012年。

过家鼎:《〈中英关于香港问题的联合声明〉翻译中的政治考虑》,《上海翻译》2005年第2期。

姜秋霞:《外事笔译》,北京:外语教学与研究出版社,2009年。

14 UNIT

签署外交备忘录报道的翻译
Translation for Coverage of Signing Diplomatic Memorandum

单元简介 Introduction

外交备忘录是国家间或外交代表机关之间使用的一种外交文书，用来说明就某一事件、问题进行交涉时在事实上、立场上、法律方面的细节，或用来重申外交会谈中的谈话内容。

外交备忘录递送方式分为当场面交、会谈后送交、作照会的附件三种：在外交会谈或交涉中，为对方便于记忆谈话内容或避免误解，可预先写成备忘录面交对方，也可在会谈后将要点用备忘录的方式送交对方，或作为照会、公报、声明等文件的补充附件。

外交备忘录文本具有措辞严谨、语言庄重、复杂程度较高，篇章结构严密等特点。签署外交备忘录的新闻报道中通常涉及签署双方、签署时间和场合、备忘录名称、签署意义等内容，报道语言精练、语体正式、内容客观。

外交新闻汉英翻译
C-E TRANSLATION OF DIPLOMATIC NEWS

签署外交备忘录报道翻译范例分析
Sample of Translation for Coverage of Signing Diplomatic Memorandum

> 范例一（Sample I）

中美签署发展合作谅解备忘录
2015-09-26
China, US Sign MOU on Development Cooperation
2015-09-26

美国当地时间9月25日，在习近平主席对美进行国事访问期间，中国商务部高虎城部长与美国国际发展署负责人伦哈特在华盛顿签署了《中华人民共和国商务部和美国国际发展署关于中美发展合作及建立交流沟通机制谅解备忘录》。这提升了两国在国际发展领域的交流与合作水平，丰富了中美双边关系的内涵。

On September 25 the US local time, and during President Xi Jinping's state visit to the US, Minister of Commerce Gao Hucheng and the head of United States Agency for International Development (USAID) Alfonso Lenhardt signed "the Memorandum of Understanding (MOU) between Chinese Ministry of Commerce and the United States Agency for International Development (USAID) on Development Cooperation and Establishing Communication Mechanism", which enhanced the level of communication and cooperation between the two countries on international development and enriched the connotation of China-US bilateral relations.

近两年来，中美两国在尊重各自国情和受援国意愿的前提下，在东帝汶、阿富汗等国开展了农业和培训领域的发展合作试点，在共同抗击西非埃博拉疫情过程中进行了配合，初步建立了合作关系，使中美发展合作有了一定基础。中国商务部与美国国际发展署作为两国发展业务的主管部门，通过签署备忘录建立了交流沟通机制。双方一致同意将在"受援国提出、受援国同意、受援国主导"的前提下，发挥各自优势，在农业、卫生、人力资源培训等领域开展项目合作，循序渐进地拓展中美发展合作领域，为推动国际发展合作注入新的能量，为消灭全球贫困和饥饿作出新的贡献。

In the past two years, on the basis of respecting each other's national conditions and the will of the recipient countries, China and the US carried out pilot projects for developing cooperation in agriculture and training in East Timor and Afghanistan, cooperated with each other in combating Ebola in West Africa, and established the cooperation relation initially, providing foundation to China and the US for development cooperation. As the competent departments of development of the two countries, Chinese Ministry of Commerce and the

签署外交备忘录报道的翻译
Translation for Coverage of Signing Diplomatic Memorandum

UNIT 14

USAID established the communication mechanism through the signing of MOU. The two sides agreed that, on the basis of "put forward by the recipient countries, agreed by the recipient countries and led by the recipient countries", the two countries should give full play of each other's advantages, and carry out cooperation in agriculture, sanitation and human resources training, to gradually broaden the fields of China-US development cooperation, to inject new power for international development and to make new contributions to eliminating poverty and hunger of the world.

> 新闻背景：中国商务部与美国国际开发署2015年12月25日在华盛顿签署发展合作谅解备忘录。根据这份备忘录，中美双方一致同意遵循"受援国提出、受援国同意、受援国主导"的前提推动和实施中美发展合作项目。在受援国发挥主导作用的前提下，共同决定合作领域、内容和方式。备忘录明确中美双方的发展合作领域将与受援国的需求相一致，特别强调支持和改善民生。双方已确定在粮食安全、公共卫生、人道主义援助等领域重点开展合作，今后将循序渐进地拓展其他发展合作领域。
>
> 原文链接：http://www.mofcom.gov.cn/article/ae/ai/201509/20150901123031.shtml
>
> 译文链接：http://english.mofcom.gov.cn/article/newsrelease/significantnews/201510/20151001131878.shtml

一、范例一文本结构分析（Text Structure Analysis of Sample I）

范例一是一则关于签署外交备忘录的新闻报道，标题简明扼要，并未具体说明备忘录全称。第一段为新闻导语，其中包括签署双方（中国商务部高虎城部长与美国国际发展署负责人伦哈特）、签署时间（美国当地时间9月25日）、签署地点（华盛顿）、备忘录名称（《中华人民共和国商务部和美国国际发展署关于中美发展合作及建立交流沟通机制谅解备忘录》）、签署意义（提升两国交流与合作水平，丰富中美双边关系的内涵）等内容。第二段主要回顾以往中美发展合作基础，签署备忘录的目的（通过签署备忘录建立交流沟通机制），以及两国未来发展合作使命和蓝图。

二、范例一翻译解析（Translation Analysis of Sample I）

签署外交备忘录的新闻报道中通常会介绍备忘录全称，以及签署备忘录的缔约方政府或政府部门、机构名称等，下面就着重对谅解备忘录名称的翻译以及缔约方名称的翻译进行归纳和整理。

（一）谅解备忘录名称的翻译（Translation of MOU Titles）

在签署备忘录的新闻报道中，标题一般都会简要概括备忘录名称，少数新闻会在标题中使用全称。备忘录全称往往出现在新闻导语中。

谅解备忘录是国际协议一种通常的叫法，指双方经过协商、谈判达成共识后，用文本的方式记录下来，"谅解"旨在表明"协议双方要互相体谅，妥善处理彼此的分歧和争议"。"谅解备忘录"相应的英文表达为memorandum of understanding，有时也可写成memo of understanding或MOU。①

谅解备忘录的名称常见形式为"××机构和××机构关于……谅解备忘录"，如《中华人民共和国商务部和俄罗斯联邦经济发展部关于电子商务合作的谅解备忘录》。在相关新闻报道中，有时也会先说明双方机构，再给出备忘录名称，如"商务部与英国国际发展部签署《关于加强发展合作，有效落实可持续发展目标的伙伴关系谅解备忘录》"。"××和××关于……方面的谅解备忘录"一般英译为Memorandum of Understanding between ×× and ×× on ...。汉语备忘录名称需加书名号，英文备忘录名称需要实词首字母大写。请看下面具体实例：

《中华人民共和国商务部和俄罗斯联邦经济发展部关于电子商务合作的谅解备忘录》

(http://www.gov.cn/xinwen/2018-06/10/content_5297587.htm)

The Memorandum of Understanding on E-commerce Cooperation between the Ministry of Commerce of China and the Ministry of Economic Development of Russia

(http://english.mofcom.gov.cn/article/newsrelease/significantnews/201806/20180602754949.shtml)

《中华人民共和国政府与阿曼苏丹国政府关于共同推进丝绸之路经济带与21世纪海上丝绸之路建设的谅解备忘录》

(http://om.mofcom.gov.cn/article/jmxw/201805/20180502744408.shtml)

Memorandum of Understanding on Jointly Promoting the Construction of the Silk Road Economic Belt and the 21st Century Maritime Silk Road Between the Government of the People's Republic of China and the Government of the Sultanate of Oman.

(http://www.fmprc.gov.cn/ce/cegr/eng/zgyw/t1560128.htm)

《关于加强中英两国地方贸易投资合作的谅解备忘录》

(http://news.xinhuanet.com/mrdx/2015-10/23/c_134742620.htm)

Memorandum of Understanding on Strengthening Local Trade and Investment

---

① 谅解备忘录, http://baike.baidu.com/link?url=Aqs32ZKadvlBokfYkfaMSKtciiq5phEzuCzP79NSs5ZusnC5zKoLs4Gx2dqNFVMgej6c-eAAAqdO_dAAVR_Xya

Cooperation Between China and the UK

(http://www.china-embassy.org/eng/zgyw/t1309374.htm)

《中英清洁能源伙伴关系谅解备忘录》

(http://news.xinhuanet.com/mrdx/2015-10/23/c_134742620.htm)

Memorandum of Understanding on Partnership Between China and the UK in Clean Energy

(http://www.china-embassy.org/eng/zgyw/t1309374.htm)

（二）谅解备忘录缔约方的翻译 (Translation of MOU Parties)

谅解备忘录多数情况下具有条约性质，是两个或两个以上国家的政府或政府部门签订的条约性文件，记载缔约各方在谈判中各自所持立场，以及缔约各方已达成的在某一具体问题上彼此间的权利和义务，并由缔约各方代表签字。

在签署谅解备忘录的新闻报道中，缔约方可以是国家政府，如1990年5月24日缔结的《中华人民共和国政府和乌拉圭东岸共和国政府关于植物检疫合作的谅解备忘录》，也可以是政府部门，如1999年4月9日签订的《中华人民共和国外交部和卡塔尔国外交部谅解备忘录》。一般情况下，缔约双方享有对等的外交地位。对谅解备忘录缔约方进行英译时，需要通过网络或工具书等检索、查找并确认相关专有名词的专有译法。请看下面具体实例：

海关总署与英国皇家税务与海关署签署《关于海关事务的合作与行政互助的谅解备忘录》

(http://news.xinhuanet.com/mrdx/2015-10/23/c_134742620.htm)

General Administration of Customs and Her Majesty's Revenue and Customs of the UK signed the "Memorandum of Understanding on Cooperation and Mutual Administrative Assistance in Customs Service."

(http://www.china-embassy.org/eng/zgyw/t1309374.htm)

商务部与英国国际发展部签署《关于加强发展合作，有效落实可持续发展目标的伙伴关系谅解备忘录》

(http://news.xinhuanet.com/mrdx/2015-10/23/c_134742620.htm)

Ministry of Commerce and UK's Department for International Development signed the "Memorandum of Understanding on Strengthening Partnership in Development Cooperation and Effectively Implementing Goals of Sustainable Development".

(http://www.china-embassy.org/eng/zgyw/t1309374.htm)

国务院发展研究中心与英国国际发展部签署《关于中英发展知识合作伙伴的谅解备忘录》

(http://news.xinhuanet.com/mrdx/2015-10/23/c_134742620.htm)

Development Research Center of the State Council and UK's Department for International Development signed the "Memorandum of Understanding on Developing Knowledge Partnership Between China and the UK".

(http://www.china-embassy.org/eng/zgyw/t1309374.htm)

银监会与英国审慎监管局签署《双边监管合作谅解备忘录》

(http://news.xinhuanet.com/mrdx/2015-10/23/c_134742620.htm)

China Banking Regulatory Commission and UK's Prudential Regulation Authority signed the "Memorandum of Understanding on Bilateral Regulatory Cooperation."

(http://www.china-embassy.org/eng/zgyw/t1309374.htm)

（三）签署外交备忘录报道中常见表达的翻译 (Translation of Frequently Used Expressions in Coverage of Signing Diplomatic Memorandum)

1. "在……的见证下"的翻译

一般情况下，如果谅解备忘录的签署发生在会议、会谈或会见结束后，那么签署备忘录的新闻中往往会提及见证人，最为常见的表述是"在……的见证下"，"……共同见证了……的签署"，可分别翻译为under the witness of ...或witnessed by ...，和... jointly witnessed the signing of ...。请参看下面具体实例。此外，下面实例中涉及我国近年来个别重要备忘录的签署，其名称和缔约方的翻译方法也需格外留意，如《北京市人民政府与亚洲基础设施投资银行谅解备忘录》以及《中、匈、塞三国合作建设匈塞铁路谅解备忘录》。

10月21日，在习近平主席和英国首相卡梅伦的见证下，中国商务部部长高虎城分别与英国商业、创新与技能大臣贾维德、英国国际发展大臣格里宁签署了《中华人民共和国商务部和大不列颠及北爱尔兰联合王国商业、创新与技能部关于加强中英两国地方贸易投资合作的谅解备忘录》和《中华人民共和国商务部和大不列颠及北爱尔兰联合王国国际发展部关于加强发展合作，有效落实可持续发展目标的伙伴关系谅解备忘录》。

(http://world.people.com.cn/n/2015/1022/c1002-27729533.html)

On October 21, witnessed by President Xi Jinping and British Prime Minister David Cameron, Minister of Commerce Gao Hucheng signed with British Secretary of State for Business, Innovation and Skills Sajid Javid and British Secretary of State for International Development Justine Greening respectively the "Memorandum of Understanding Between Chinese Ministry of Commerce and the Department of Business, Innovation and Skills of the United Kingdom of Great Britain and Northern Ireland on Strengthening Bilateral Local Trade and Investment Cooperation" and the "Memorandum of Understanding Between Chinese Ministry of Commerce and the Department of

签署外交备忘录报道的翻译
Translation for Coverage of Signing Diplomatic Memorandum
UNIT 14

International Development of the United Kingdom of Great Britain and Northern Ireland on Strengthening Development Cooperation and the Partnership, Implementing the Goals of Sustainable Development".

(http://english.mofcom.gov.cn/)

会前,李克强同出席亚投行理事会成立大会的57个创始成员国代表团团长合影,并见证中国外交部、北京市政府分别与亚投行签署《中华人民共和国政府与亚洲基础设施投资银行总部协定》和《北京市人民政府与亚洲基础设施投资银行谅解备忘录》。

(http://news.xinhuanet.com/mrdx/2016-01/17/c_135016667.htm)

Prior to the meeting, Li Keqiang took a group photo with the heads of delegation from 57 founding member states, and witnessed the signing of the "Agreement Between the Government of the People's Republic of China and the Asian Infrastructure Investment Bank Headquarters" and the "Memorandum of Understanding Between the People's Government of Beijing Municipality and the Asian Infrastructure Investment Bank" by the Ministry of Foreign Affairs and the Beijing Municipal Government respectively with the AIIB.

(http://www.fmprc.gov.cn/ce/cgmb/eng/zgyw/t1333119.htm)

会见后,李克强与三国总理共同见证了《中、匈、塞三国合作建设匈塞铁路的谅解备忘录》和中、匈、塞、马四国通关便利化等合作文件的签署。

(http://paper.people.com.cn/rmrbhwb/html/2014-12/18/content_1511578.htm)

After the meeting, Li Keqiang and the three Prime Ministers jointly witnessed the signing of the Memorandum of Understanding on Jointly Building the Hungary-Serbia Railway among China, Hungary and Serbia, and cooperation documents on customs clearance facilitation among China, Hungary, Serbia and Macedonia.

(http://news.xinhuanet.com/english/2015-12/24/c_134948122.htm)

2. 签署备忘录意义和成果的翻译

备忘录是国家间或外交代表机关之间在外交活动与事务交涉中,用于叙述事实或陈述与补充本方的观点、意见,为便于对方记忆,避免发生误解而制定的外交文书。因此,备忘录是两国在外交事务中共同采取行动、方针或政策的成文或不成文的共识。签署谅解备忘录表明达成协议的双方要互相体谅,妥善处理彼此的分歧和争议。因此,备忘录的签署往往是外交活动的重要成果,对双方合作交流、友好往来具有标志性意义。有关签署外交备忘录的新闻报道中会利用相应的篇幅来描述备忘录的签署意义及成果,如"通过签署备忘录为双方建立交流沟通机制"(establish the communication mechanism through the signing of MOU)、"……具有划时代意义"(... is of epoch-making significance)、"备忘录是……访问的成果"(the Memorandum is the important achievement of …'s visit）等；通过备忘录的签署，合作双方可以"为……注入新的能量"（inject new power for）、"为……注入活力"（inject vitality into）、"为……做出新的贡献"（make new contributions to）等。请看下面具体实例：

中国商务部与美国国际发展署作为两国发展业务的主管部门，通过签署备忘录建立了交流沟通机制。双方一致同意将在"受援国提出、受援国同意、受援国主导"的前提下，发挥各自优势，在农业、卫生、人力资源培训等领域开展项目合作，循序渐进地拓展中美发展合作领域，为推动国际发展合作注入新的能量，为消灭全球贫困和饥饿作出新的贡献。

(http://www.mofcom.gov.cn/article/ae/ai/201509/20150901123031.shtml)

As the competent departments of development of the two countries, Chinese Ministry of Commerce and the USAID established the communication mechanism through the signing of MOU. The two sides agreed that, on the basis of "put forward by the recipient countries, agreed by the recipient countries and led by the recipient countries", the two countries should give full play of each other's advantages, and carry out cooperation in agriculture, sanitation and human resources training, to gradually broaden the fields of China-US development cooperation, to inject new power for international development and to make new contributions to eliminating poverty and hunger of the world.

(http://english.mofcom.gov.cn/article/newsrelease/significantnews/201510/20151001131878.shtml)

会见结束后，张明与祖马共同出席中国与非盟关于促进中国与非洲开展铁路、公路和区域航空网络和工业化领域合作的谅解备忘录换文仪式，并共同会见记者。张明表示，备忘录是划时代协议，是李总理访问非盟总部重要成果，中方愿与非盟方共同努力，推动有关项目取得积极进展。

(http://www.fmprc.gov.cn/zflt/chn/zxxx/t1232842.htm)

After the meeting, Zhang Ming and Zuma jointly attended the China-AU ceremony of exchanging the Memorandums of Understanding (MOU) on promoting the cooperation between China and Africa in such fields as railway, road and regional aviation network and industrialization, and they also jointly met the press. Zhang Ming said that the Memorandum is a landmark agreement and also the important achievement of Premier Li Keqiang's visit to headquarters of the AU. China is willing to make joint efforts with the AU to promote positive progress of relevant projects.

(http://www.fmprc.gov.cn/mfa_eng/wjbxw/t1233843.shtml)

Translation for Coverage of Signing Diplomatic Memorandum

范例二（Sample II）

中华人民共和国国防部和美利坚合众国国防部
关于建立重大军事行动相互通报
信任措施机制的谅解备忘录
（节本）

Memorandum of Understanding Between the United States of America Department of Defense and the People's Republic of China Ministry of National Defense on Notification of Major Military Activities Confidence-building Measures Mechanism (Abbreviated Version)

一、前言

中华人民共和国国防部和美利坚合众国国防部（下称双方）：

PREAMBLE

The United States Department of Defense and the People's Republic of China Ministry of National Defense (hereinafter referred to as the "sides"):

重申双方致力于发展中美新型军事关系，这是双边关系中不可或缺的组成部分；

申明双方致力于改善关系、加深相互理解，减少风险，减少误解误判的可能性；

Reaffirm the commitment to the development of a new model of US-China military-to-military relations, which is an integral part of the bilateral relationship;

Affirm that both sides are committed to improve relations, deepen mutual understanding, reduce risk, and reduce the potential for misunderstanding and miscalculation;

认可双方本着公平和开放的精神，通过建立军事信任措施，寻求推进双边关系；

Recognize that both sides seek to advance the bilateral relationship through military confidence-building measures, undertaken in a spirit of equality and openness;

落实习近平主席和奥巴马总统的共识，建立重大军事行动相互通报信任措施机制；

Realize the consensus between President Barack Obama and President Xi Jinping, and to establish a notification of major military activities confidence-building measures initiative;

确定以重大军事行动相互通报机制为基础，双方交流重大军事行动信息，通过相互通报和信息共享增进互信；

申明通报的目标是减少误解、防止误判、有效管理风险和危机；

建立一个双方可交流重大军事行动信息的机制，遵循建设性合作、互利、互信、互惠、对等的原则，并与国际公认的行为准则相符。

Determine that this mechanism for notification of major military activities forms the basis from which both sides exchange notifications of military activities and strengthen confidence and mutual trust through reciprocal notifications and information sharing;

Affirm that notifications should aim to reduce misunderstanding, prevent miscalculation, and manage risk and crisis effectively; and

Establish a mechanism to inform when both sides would exchange notifications of major military activities on the basis of the principles of constructive cooperation, mutual interest, mutual trust, mutual benefit, and reciprocity, consistent with accepted international norms of behavior.

***

本谅解备忘录包括：

附件一：通报重大安全政策和战略的发展变化；

附件二：观摩军事演习和行动。

经双方协商一致，可增加新的附件。

本谅解备忘录于［时间］在［地点］签署，一式两份，每份均用中文和英文写成。

This MOU contains:

Annex I: Notification of Major Security Policy and Strategy Developments

Annex II: Observation of Military Exercises and Activities

Additional annexes may be added upon the consent of both sides.

This MOU is signed at Beijing and Washington, on October 31 and November 4, 2014 in both Chinese and English.

***

中华人民共和国国防部	The Ministry of National Defense of the People's Republic of China
常万全	*常万全*
美利坚合众国国防部	The Department of Defense of the United States of America
Chuck Hagel	*Chuck Hagel*

新闻背景：2013年6月，中美两国元首在安纳伯格庄园会晤期间，习近平主席提出建立两个互信机制的倡议，得到奥巴马总统的积极回应。此后，两国防务部门和军队通过多种渠道，进行了10余轮深入磋商和沟通。在双方共同努力下，双方就签署关于"两个互信机制"的谅解备忘录达成共识，即《关于建立重大军事行动相互通报信任措施机制谅解备忘录》和《关于海空相遇安全行为准则谅解备忘录》。

原文链接：http://www.mod.gov.cn/affair/2014-12/05/content_4555795.htm

译文链接：http://www.defense.gov/Portals/1/Documents/pubs/141112_Memorandum Of UnderstandingOn Notification.pdf

签署外交备忘录报道的翻译
Translation for Coverage of Signing Diplomatic Memorandum

一、范例二文本结构分析（Text Structure Analysis of Sample II）

2014年11月12日，中美两国国防部长签署《关于建立重大军事行动相互通报信任措施机制谅解备忘录》。该备忘录一式两份，每份均用中文和英文写成，包括标题、正文、落款、附件四部分。正文部分包括前言和四条内容，附件一、二分别包括与通报重大安全政策和战略的发展变化，以及观摩军事演习和行动相关各四条内容。

正文部分说明中美建立一个双方可交流重大军事行动信息的机制，以及在此机制下，双方授权机构的义务和遵守原则。

正文最后备忘录签署的地点分别是北京和华盛顿，日期分别是2014年10月31日和11月4日。日期和地点均为手写。

落款处由中华人民共和国国防部部长常万全和美利坚合众国国防部部长查克·哈格尔（Chuck Hagel）分别手写签名。

附件一有关通报重大安全政策和战略的发展变化的目的、内容和双方职责。附件二有关观摩军事演习和行动的意义、目标、活动规则，以及观摩方和主办方各自的职责和应遵守的原则。因篇幅所限，原文有所删节。

二、范例二翻译解析（Translation Analysis of Sample II）

谅解备忘录是国际协议的一种，行文特点与法律合同文本类似，具有逻辑严谨、句法结构复杂和措辞正式等特点。英文备忘录中，常见名词化结构、介词结构、被动语态，以及主从复合结构以突显语体的正式和严谨。下面针对范例二中的翻译问题进行分析。

（一）句法结构复杂(Complicated Syntactical Structure)

为体现备忘录逻辑严密这一特点，无论是汉语文本还是英语文本，复杂结构都是最佳的句法选择之一。汉译英时，需要结合英汉语言各自的句法特征，在确保忠实于汉语逻辑关系的基础上，增加必要的衔接手段，或者进行语序调整，以符合英语语言的表达习惯。

1. 增加衔接手段

汉语是一种意合语言，词句之间大多由意义结合，没有明确的衔接成分，而英语作为一种形合语言，常用衔接手段形成主句和从句之间相互嵌套的主从结构。在英语复合结构的句子中，如果一个句子包含两个或更多的主谓结构，其中一个为主句，其他为从属句，主要信息由主句来表达，背景细节等次要信息则由从句来描述。从句可以包含更次一级的从句，而下一级的从句又可以再包含下一级的从句，从而形成层次复杂、主次交错的立体结构。从句往往由从属连词或关系代词引导。请看范例二中的具体实例：

中华人民共和国国防部和美利坚合众国国防部（下称双方）：

确定以重大军事行动相互通报机制为基础，双方交流重大军事行动信息，通过相互通报和信息共享增进互信；

The United States Department of Defense and the People's Republic of China Ministry of National Defense (hereinafter referred to as the "sides"):

Determine <u>that</u> this mechanism for notification of major military activities forms the basis <u>from which</u> both sides exchange notifications of military activities and strengthen confidence and mutual trust <u>through</u> reciprocal notifications and information sharing;

本例中，英文通过两个从句相互嵌套形成复合句，即that从句（宾语从句）和which从句（定语从句）。在that引导的宾语从句中，以this mechanism作为主语，forms the basis作为谓语和宾语，再嵌套一个从句from which,修饰basis。在which引导的定语从句中，以both sides做主语，谓语动词分别是exchange和strengthen。中文"通过相互通报和信息共享"这一方式状语，在英文中通过介词短语through reciprocal notifications and information sharing后置实现。这样，英文句子结构紧凑，逻辑严密，最大限度地实现了"意"到"形"的转换。

中华人民共和国国防部和美利坚合众国国防部（下称双方）：

建立一个双方可交流重大军事行动信息的机制，遵循建设性合作、互利、互信、互惠、对等的原则，并与国际公认的行为准则相符。

The United States Department of Defense and the People's Republic of China Ministry of National Defense:

Establish a mechanism to inform <u>when both sides</u> would exchange notifications of major military activities <u>on the basis of</u> the principles of constructive cooperation, mutual interest, mutual trust, mutual benefit, and reciprocity, <u>consistent with</u> accepted international norms of behavior.

本例中，汉语各分句都是以谓语动词起首，"建立……""遵循……""并与……相符"，各分句之间没有明显的连接词。英文中，首先确定"建立一个机制"是这一句的主干结构和核心内容，其他都是围绕这一主干结构的修饰成分，因此，"一个双方可交流重大军事行动信息的"在英文中可以处理为不定式to inform，置于mechanism之后表目的，其中又包含when引导的状语从句 when both sides would exchange notifications of major military activities。"遵循……的原则"在中文中是指建立机制要遵循原则，因此，在英文中以on the basis of这一介词结构来和主句动词establish搭配，形成establish a mechanism ... on the basis of ...的主干结构。"并与……相符"在中文中是指建立与国际公认的行为准则相符的机制，在英文中，形容词+介词结构consistent with做后置定语，进一步修饰中心词mechanism。这样主从结构相嵌，英文逻辑非常清晰。

签署外交备忘录报道的翻译
Translation for Coverage of Signing Diplomatic Memorandum

中华人民共和国国防部外事办公室和美利坚合众国国防部长办公室是执行本机制与实施通报的授权机构，通报的实施通过外交和军事渠道进行。

The United States Department of Defense, Office of the Secretary of Defense, and the People's Republic of China, Ministry of National DefenseForeign Affairs Office, are the authorized agencies for executing this mechanism and accomplishing notifications, which are to be effected through diplomatic andmilitary channels.

本例中，中文由两个分句组成，两分句之间从形式上看并没有连接词。英文中，先确定句子主干为主系表结构The United States Department of Defense, Office of the Secretary of Defense, and the People's Republic of China, Ministry of National Defense Foreign Affairs Office are the authorized agencies。将定语"执行本机制与实施通报的"在英文中转换为介词结构做状语for executing this mechanism and accomplishing notifications。原文第二个分句，在英文中采取which引导非限定性定语从句，用which指代上文的notifications，从而形成具有从句结构的英文复合句。

2. 调整语序

汉语和英语句子结构的主要差异在于定语和状语的位置。汉语的定语通常是在其所修饰的中心词前面，而英语的定语则有前置和后置两种情况。汉语的状语通常位于主语之后、谓语之前，而英语的状语位置则灵活多变，可以出现在句首、句末，也可以放在被修饰语的前面或者后面。汉语转换为英语时大多数情况需要根据汉语的语意，按照英语语序规范对原文语序进行必要的调整。请看范例二中的具体实例：

年度评估工作组会议在中美国防部工作会晤框架下在中美两国轮流举行。年度评估工作组会议应在国防部工作会晤前及时举行。

The annual assessment working group meetings should be hosted on a rotating basis by the U.S. and Chinese sides, taking place under the framework of the Defense Policy Coordination Talks. The annual assessment working group meeting should take place immediately prior to the Defense Policy Coordination Talks.

本例中的第一句，汉语的状语"在中美国防部工作会晤框架下"在主语和谓语之间，而英语中，将状语以分词的形式taking place under the framework of …置于句末；第二句，汉语的状语"在国防部工作会晤前"依然出现在主语和谓语之间，转换为英语时仍然进行了语序调整，将其处理为介词结构prior to …放在句末。

鉴于官方出版物、公告和发言在增加透明度和增进相互了解方面的重要性，双方寻求通过定期交换主要官方出版物和官方声明的相关信息，以增进对彼此安全政策、战略及意图的理解。

Recognizing the importance of speeches, pronouncements, and official publications in increasing transparency and improving mutual understanding, both sides seek to foster greater comprehension of each other's security policy, strategy, and intent through regular exchanges of information related to major official publications and statements.

本例汉语文本中定语"官方出版物、公告和发言在增加透明度和增进相互了解方面的"修饰"重要性",位于该名词之前,英文中在中心词前一般不出现冗长的定语,因此,英文文本将其处理为of介词结构,位于importance之后,做后置定语。汉语文本中的方式状语"通过定期交换主要官方出版物和官方声明的相关信息",在英语中依然调整了语序,置于句末。

双方授权机构应至少提前两周建议并设置年度评估工作组会议日程,同时交换上次年度会议以来开展通报的清单。

No less than two weeks prior to the annual assessment working group meeting, both authorized agencies should propose and set a meeting agenda and exchange papers listing notifications that took place after the previous annual assessment working group meeting.

本例中,汉语文本中的时间状语"至少提前两周"出现在主语之后、谓语之前,英文中将时间状语放置在句首No less than two weeks prior to …。汉语中,定语"上次年度会议以来开展通报的"修饰名词"清单","上次年度会议以来开展"又作为定语修饰"通报"。因此,在转换为英语时,首先确定中心词papers,将现在分词listing notifications后置,以修饰papers;再利用that引导定语从句,置于notifications这一中心词之后对其进行修饰,从而使得句式结构平衡,信息焦点突显。

(二)措辞正式 (Formality in Diction)

作为一种正式的外交文书,谅解备忘录具有法律文本色彩,措辞严谨、语体正式。转换为英语时,常通过采用名词化结构、介词结构,以及被动语态等方式,体现原语文本正式、严肃的语体特征。

1. 名词化结构

汉语句子中动词的使用非常频繁,一句话里可以出现多个动词,而在英文中,名词化结构使用频率越高,语体的正式程度则越高。请看范例二中的具体实例:

中华人民共和国国防部和美利坚合众国国防部(下称双方):
重申双方致力于发展中美新型军事关系,这是双边关系中不可或缺的组成部分;

签署外交备忘录报道的翻译
Translation for Coverage of Signing Diplomatic Memorandum UNIT 14

The United States Department of Defense and the People's Republic of China Ministry of National Defense (hereinafter referred to as the "sides"):

Reaffirm the commitment to the development of a new model of U.S.-China military-to-military relations, which is an integral part of the bilateral relationship;

除年度评估工作组会议外，经协商一致，双方授权机构可决定举行定期和不定期磋商，以交换信息，进行通报，研究框架内活动相关问题，或讨论附件增加事宜。

In addition to the annual assessment working group meeting, both authorized agencies intend to hold periodic and ad hoc consultations as mutually determined for the purpose of exchanging information and notifications, and to consider questions related to activities within this mechanism or to discuss the inclusion of future annexes.

年度评估工作组会议回顾上次年度会议以来的情况，向国防部工作会晤提交联合评估意见。

At the annual assessment working group meeting, both sides should review activities that took place during the period after the previous annual meeting and produce a joint assessment report for submission to the Defense Policy Coordination Talks.

上面第1例中，"致力于发展……"译成英文时转换为名词结构the commitment to the development of；第2例中"以交换信息，进行通报"这一目的状语，对应的英文中使用了for the purpose of的介词结构来表达，"附件增加"在英文中同样采取了名词结构the inclusion of；第3例中，"向……提交"在英文中采用了名词结构for submission to。

2. 介词结构

外交备忘录在汉译英的过程中，常常采用介词结构，以体现句子信息分布均匀、语言正式、结构紧凑的特点。请看范例二中的具体实例：

本谅解备忘录长期有效，双方自愿支持，一方可通过向对方提交书面通知予以终止。

Both sides voluntarily support this MOU, which is of unlimited duration and may be discontinued by either side upon written notice to the other side.

本谅解备忘录不影响任何一方签署的相关协议之义务，同样，在本谅解备忘录下进行的活动不损害第三方利益。

This MOU should not affect the obligations of either side under relevant agreements. Likewise, activities under this MOU should not occur at the expense of the interests of third parties.

本谅解备忘录是公开的，但任何一方未经另一方书面同意，不得向第三方披露

345

在本机制下获取的通报内容。

Although this MOU is in the public domain, neither side should disclose to third parties the content of notifications received under this mechanism without the written approval of the other side.

以上第1例中,"长期有效"转换为英文时,采用了"be+of+名词"结构,译为is of unlimited duration;"通过向对方提交书面通知"这一方式状语,在英文文本中转换为介词结构upon written notice to the other side,措辞简练且语义清晰。第2例中,"相关协议之义务"的意思是相关协议规约下的义务,英文介词under巧妙体现了"之"这一所属关系;"损害……利益"这一动宾结构,在英文中直接采用介词短语at the expense of the interests of …,使得语言既地道又自然。第3例中,形容词"公开的"在英文中采用了介词结构in the public domain,用于表达"公开"这一状态和性质;"未经另一方书面同意"转换为介词结构without the approval of …放置于句末,突出信息重点,使得句式结构紧凑而有序。

3. 被动语态

许多汉语句子中并没有明显的被动"标记",如"被""受""由""为"等表被动意义的助词。翻译时,可以根据其表达的被动意义译成英语的被动语态。还有一些形式上是主动句的汉语句子,根据上下文衔接和凸显句子重心的需要,也可以处理为英文的被动句。请看范例二中的具体实例:

经协商一致,双方可对外发布联合声明。
A joint statement may be released to the public once concurred in by both sides.
年度评估工作组会议在中美国防部工作会晤框架下在中美两国轮流举行。
The annual assessment working group meetings should be hosted on a rotating basis by the U.S. and Chinese sides, taking place under the framework of the Defense Policy Coordination Talks.

以上第1例中,汉语是主动句,英语则使用被动语态,既突出了句子的重心a joint statement,又使得英文简洁流畅;第2例中,汉语也是主动句,但英语中并未将"在中美两国轮流举行"处理为地点状语,而是转换为被动语态,也符合英语的表达方式和行文规范。

汉语有别于英语的一大特点,就是无主句大量存在,且形式多样。在英语里,除祈使句及其他一些特殊情况外,句子必须有主语。在汉英翻译时,必须根据两种语言的特点做相应的转换,采用被动语态就是最常用的转换方法之一。再来看范例二中的几则实例:

经双方协商一致，可增加新的附件。

Additional annexes <u>may be added</u> upon the consent of both sides.

在合适情况下，可于重要声明公开发布之前或同时向对方通报。

When appropriate, notification briefings <u>could be provided</u> prior to or simultaneous with the public release of major announcements.

对于本谅解备忘录的解释或所规定的行动如有不同意见，应由双方协商解决。

Any disagreement concerning the interpretation of or activities under this MOU <u>should be resolved by</u> consultation between both sides.

以上三个例句都属于汉语的无主句。第1例将汉语的宾语"附件"转换为英语的主语，第2例将汉语的宾语"通报"转换为英语的主语，均采取了被动语态。第3例中，汉语虽没有明显的主语，但是不难看出这句话的意思是说双方不同意见应当由双方协商解决，实际上汉语文本中也出现了被动标记词"由"，因此，转换为英语时将disagreement作为主语，采取了被动语态。

学生译作讲评
Analysis of Students' Translation Practice

原文链接：http://english.mofcom.gov.cn/article/zt_cv/lanmua/201512/20151201224251.shtml

新闻原文：中俄达成促进双边贸易的多项举措

学生译文：China and Russia Reach Several Measures on Promoting Bilateral Trade

翻译评析："达成……举措"学生译为reach measures，这样的动宾搭配是中式英语，可以改为agree on measures。

新闻原文：12月17日下午，中俄总理第二十次定期会晤期间，在国务院总理李克强和俄罗斯总理梅德韦杰夫共同见证下，商务部高虎城部长与俄经济发展部第一副部长利哈乔夫签署《关于促进双边贸易的谅解备忘录》，商务部、黑龙江省人民政府与俄工业贸易部、经济发展部共同签署了《关于筹备和举办中俄博览会的谅解备忘录》。

学生译文：In the afternoon of December 17, during the 20th China-Russia Premiers Regular Meeting, witnessed by the Chinese Premier Li Keqiang and the Russian Prime Minister Medvedev, the Chinese Minister of Commerce Gao Hucheng and the Russian First Vice Minister of Economic Development Likhachev signed the Memorandum of Understanding on Promoting Bilateral Trade. Chinese Ministry of Commerce, the People's Government of Heilongjiang and the Russian Ministry of Industry and the Russian Ministry of Economic Development signed the Memorandum of Understanding on Preparing and Holding the China-Russia Expo.

翻译评析：关于时间的表述，"12月17日下午"这一具体时间，介词应该使用on the afternoon of ...。中文原文中虽没出现具体的年份2015年，但基于新闻文本客观性、时效性的特点和需要，最好补充完整，改为On the afternoon of December 17, 2015。

关于会议名称的表述，"中俄总理第二十次定期会晤"在官方新闻媒体中常翻译为the 20th Regular Meeting between Chinese Premier and Russian Prime Minister。

关于外国官员姓名的表述，在新闻中第一次出现官员姓名的时候，要用"姓+名"的全称形式，之后再次出现时，可以姓称呼。俄罗斯总理"梅德韦杰夫"和俄经济发展部第一副部长"利哈乔夫"的姓名在第一次出现时，应该翻译为Dmitry Medvedev和Alexey Likhachev，学生译文中没有使用全名。

关于官员头衔的表述，在官衔前面不需要加定冠词the，因此"国务院总理李克强和俄罗斯总理梅德韦杰夫"应该改为Premier Li Keqiang and Prime Minister Dmitry Medvedev of Russia；"商务部高虎城部长与俄经济发展部第一副部长利哈乔夫"可以改为Chinese Minister of Commerce Gao Hucheng and Russian First Deputy Minister of Economic Development Alexey Likhachev。

"黑龙江省人民政府"，应当补充Heilongjiang Province，改为the People's Government of Heilongjiang Province，而"俄工业贸易部"这一部门机构名称属于专有名词，学生漏译"贸易"，应补充为the Russian Ministry of Industry and Trade。

最后一句，学生译文按照原文顺序将"商务部、黑龙江省人民政府与俄工业贸易部、经济发展部"依次译出，主语过长，信息布局不均匀，略显头重脚轻，可以改为The Ministry of Commerce and the People's Government of Heilongjiang Province signed the "Memorandum of Understanding on Preparing and Holding the China-Russia Expo with the Russian Ministry of Industry and Trade and the Russian Ministry of Economic Development".

新闻原文：在《关于促进双边贸易的谅解备忘录》中，双方达成了促进双边贸易的15项举措，内容包括扩大相互市场准入、支持俄在华设立俄罗斯贸易中心、开展俄进口替代政策框架下的贸易和投资合作、推动两国跨境电子商务、扩大服务贸易、打造中俄博览会、加大金融支持、提升便利化水平等。

学生译文：In the Memorandum of Understanding on Promoting Bilateral Trade, the two parties agreed on 15 measures to promote the bilateral trade, such as lifting restrictions for market access mutually, supporting Russia to set up Russian Trade Center in China, carrying out trade and investment cooperation under the framework of Russian policy of import substitution, promoting the cross-border e-commerce of the two countries, expanding service trade, forging China-Russia Expo, strengthening financial support and enhancing facilitation.

翻译评析："双方"在这则新闻中指中俄两国，学生译文中的two parties指代不明。"双方"常译为the two sides，或both sides。在外交新闻中，例如"中方"，"美方"，"俄方"等表述，可以译为the Chinese side, the American side, the Russian side, 或直接译为China, the US, Russia。

签署外交备忘录报道的翻译
Translation for Coverage of Signing Diplomatic Memorandum

"扩大相互市场准入"学生翻译为market access mutually是逐字翻译的中式英语，也没有表明相应的意思，可以改为expanding each other's market access更加简明易懂。"俄罗斯贸易中心"并不是专有名词，这里的贸易中心并不特指，因此不应大写首字母。"俄进口替代政策"为避免产生歧义，不建议翻译为Russian policy of …，可以改为Russia's policy of import substitution或者Russia's import substitution policy，从而明确"进口替代政策"与"俄罗斯"之间的从属关系。"两国跨境电子商务"指两国之间的电子商务，介词使用应当明确，建议将of the two countries改为between the two countries。

新闻原文：今年以来，受全球大宗商品价格下跌等外部因素影响，中俄贸易额有所下降，但双方合作仍有不少积极因素。中国继续保持俄第一大贸易伙伴地位，在俄外贸中的比重不降反升，达到12%，自俄进口主要大宗商品规模保持两位数增长，投资合作有增无减，能源、核能、航天、航空、高铁、基础设施建设等领域的战略性大项目全面推进，金融合作显著加强，均显示出两国经贸合作的基础牢固，势头良好。

学生译文：Since the beginning of this year, affected by the price dropping of world bulk commodities, China-Russia trade witnessed a certain decrease, but there were still many positive factors in the bilateral cooperation. China was still the largest trade partner of Russia, and its proportion in Russian foreign trade has increased to 12%. The import of bulk commodities from Russia kept a growth of double digit rate. The investment cooperation also increased. Major strategic projects in energy, nuclear energy, aviation, aerospace, high-speed rail and infrastructure construction are comprehensively promoted. Financial cooperation was strengthened obviously. All of these showed that the bilateral economic and trade cooperation enjoyed a solid foundation and sound trend.

翻译评析：译文第一句中，"今年以来"学生翻译为since the beginning of this year，这个时间状语就意味着其后的主句时态应该为现在完成时，所以学生译文中谓语witnessed应改为has witnessed；"但双方合作仍有不少积极因素"应该是就目前而言，所以时态不应该是过去时，可以改为一般现在时but there are still many positive factors。"全球大宗商品"可以改为global bulk commodities，"中俄贸易额"应补充为China-Russia trade volume。

"在能源、核能、航天、航空、高铁、基础设施建设等领域的……"一句，学生译文没有把"等"这个模糊概念译出来，建议改为major strategic projects in fields such as …。此外，"航天、航空、高铁"这几个名词的翻译建议修改为aerospace, aviation, high-speed rails。关于"金融合作显著加强"，副词"显著"的选用，remarkably比obviously语气更肯定。最后，"两国经贸合作的基础牢固，势头良好"这句中，trend表达的是趋势和方向，然而"势头"常选用momentum，意为动力和力量，比trend更加贴近原文语义。

整个这一段译文的时态都采用了过去式，事实上，原文描述的都是目前的情况。综合上述讲评，可将该段译文调整为：Since the beginning of this year, affected by the price dropping of global bulk commodities, China-Russia trade volume has witnessed a certain decrease, but there are still many positive factors in the bilateral cooperation. China is still the largest trade partner of Russia, and its proportion in Russian foreign trade has increased to 12%. The import of bulk commodities from Russia has kept a growth of double digit rate. The investment cooperation is also increased. Major strategic projects in fields such as energy, nuclear energy, aerospace, aviation, high-speed rails and infrastructure construction are comprehensively promoted. Financial cooperation is remarkably strengthened. All of these show that the economic and trade cooperation between the two countries enjoy a solid foundation and sound momentum.

实战练习
Translation Practice

一、请翻译下列一则签署外交备忘录的新闻报道，注意备忘录标题、缔约方以及常见表达的翻译。(Translate the following coverage of signing MOU and pay attention to the translation of MOU titles, MOU parties as well as some frequently used expressions.)

积极落实习近平主席关于南南合作重要举措
商务部与联合国相关机构签署合作谅解备忘录

9月27日，商务部部长高虎城在纽约会见了联合国副秘书长、联合国最不发达国家、内陆发展中国家和小岛屿发展中国家事务高级代表阿查亚，就习近平主席在南南合作圆桌会上宣布举措的落实工作交换了意见。

高虎城表示，习近平主席在访问联合国总部时，提出了新时期扩大深化南南合作的重要建议和重大举措。中方愿加强与联合国最不发达国家、内陆发展中国家和小岛屿发展中国家办公室的合作，积极落实习近平主席出席联合国成立70周年系列峰会成果。阿查亚赞赏中方为支持最不发达国家、内陆发展中国家和小岛屿发展中国家发展所做的贡献。阿查亚表示将与中方一道努力，帮助最不发达国家、内陆发展中国家和小岛屿发展中国家实现联合国2030年可持续发展目标。

会见结束后，高虎城与阿查亚签署了《支持最不发达国家、内陆发展中国家和小岛屿发展中国家落实2030年可持续发展议程的谅解备忘录》，明确双方将在南南合作框架下，在农业、卫生、减贫、贸易促进和生态保护等领域，对最不发达国家、内陆发展中国家和小岛屿发展中国家开展能力建设培训合作，帮助他们早日实现联合国2030年可持续发展目标。

(http://english.mofcom.gov.cn/article/zt_cv/lanmua/201510/20151001137013.shtml)

签署外交备忘录报道的翻译

Translation for Coverage of Signing Diplomatic Memorandum

二、请翻译下列外交备忘录，注意备忘录文本的结构和语言特点。(**Translate the following MOU and pay attention to its text structure and language features.**)

关于反垄断和反托拉斯合作的谅解备忘录
中华人民共和国国家发展和改革委员会
中华人民共和国商务部
中华人民共和国国家工商行政管理总局
（一方）
美利坚合众国司法部
美利坚合众国联邦贸易委员会
（另一方）

合作宗旨

中华人民共和国国家发展和改革委员会、商务部、国家工商行政管理总局（合称中国反垄断执法机构）；美利坚合众国联邦贸易委员会、司法部（合称美国反托拉斯机构）。

希望通过在中国反垄断执法机构与美国反托拉斯机构之间创设一个长期的合作框架，更有效地执行其竞争法律和政策，认识到，中国反垄断执法机构与美国反托拉斯机构之间开展技术合作有利于营造使双方的竞争法律和政策得以合理、有效实施的环境，从而促进市场有效运行，增进本国公民经济福利，认识到，为竞争法律和政策的有效实施建立运行良好的制度，不仅涉及各自反垄断执法机构或反托拉斯机构，而且也涉及政府机构和司法机关，以及法律、商业和学术界，并认识到，中美两国负责竞争法律和政策的政府机构之间建立良好的沟通渠道，包括中国反垄断执法机构与美国反托拉斯机构之间创设该长期合作框架，有助于改善和加强中美两国之间的关系。

希望就以下事项进行合作：

合作方式

中国反垄断执法机构与美国反托拉斯机构为本谅解备忘录（备忘录）合作参与方，本备忘录规定了合作的框架。

中国反垄断执法机构与美国反托拉斯机构的合作框架包括两部分：第一部分是备忘录各方共同参加的竞争政策高层对话（共同对话）；第二部分是备忘录各方之间就竞争执法和政策开展进行交流与合作。

关于第一部分，除非另有约定，共同对话应在中国和美国轮流举行，并由相关反垄断执法机构或反托拉斯机构轮流主办。中国反垄断执法机构和美国反托拉斯机构定期举行共同对话，原则上每年举行一次。任何一方均可提议在共同对话框架下成立专题工作组，就相关竞争政策和法律的具体问题进行讨论。专题工作组会议可以与共同对话同期召开，也可以由各反垄断执法机构或反托拉斯机构根据需要达成一致意见后单独召开，以满足其具体需要。

关于第二部分，中国反垄断执法机构和美国反托拉斯机构可以在共同对话之外单独开展高层或工作层面的沟通与合作。

中美双方不设牵头部门。各家机构将各自指定一位联络官员，以便促进为推动本备忘录的实施而进行的接触。

各家机构之间的沟通可通过电话、电子邮件、视频会议、会晤或其他适当的方式进行。

如一方负责竞争政策、法律执行的部门发生重大变化，中国反垄断执法机构和美国反托拉斯机构将及时通知另一方。

合作内容

中国反垄断执法机构和美国反托拉斯机构一致同意，在有可合理获得的资源的前提下，在如下方面开展合作符合双方的共同利益：1、相互及时通报各自司法辖区内竞争政策及执法方面的重要动态；2、通过开展竞争政策和法律方面的活动（如培训、研讨、考察、实习等方式），加强双方的能力建设；3、在适当的时候，双方进行反垄断执法经验交流；4、就竞争执法和政策事项相互寻求信息或建议；5、就竞争法律、法规、规章和指南的修改提出评论；6、就多边竞争法律和政策交换意见；7、在提高企业、其他政府机构以及社会公众竞争政策和法律意识方面交流经验。

双方一致认为，当中国反垄断执法机构和美国反托拉斯机构正在调查相关事项时，在机构执法利益、法律限制和可获得资源允许范围内，在案件调查中适当开展合作符合双方共同利益。中国反垄断执法机构和美国反托拉斯机构将在本备忘录项下定期对上述活动的效果进行评估，以确保合作各方的预期和需求能够得到满足。

工作计划

每家中国反垄断执法机构和美国反托拉斯机构将在本备忘录项下就合作事项分别制定详细的工作计划，包括执法能力建设及其他活动，并在必要时对其修改和更新。

保密要求

双方理解，如果有关信息被拥有该信息的机构所属国家的法律所禁止或与该机构的利益相冲突，中国反垄断执法机构和美国反托拉斯机构将不与对方交流该等信息。就被交流信息而言，信息获得方应在本国法律许可的范围内对保密信息承担保密义务。

生效日期

在本备忘录项下的合作自签字之日起生效。本备忘录旨在建立一种建议性框架。本备忘录无意创设任何具有法律约束力的权利或义务，不改变现有法律、合同或条约，不限制各方根据其他双边或多边协议或安排向对方寻求或提供协助，也不排斥其他技术合作项目。

本备忘录的理解或实施出现的任何问题将由本备忘录各方协商解决。

2011年7月27日签署于北京，一式五份。每份文本均用中文和英文写成，两种文本均为同等正式的文本。

中华人民共和国 国家发展和改革委员会	中华人民共和国 商务部	中华人民共和国 国家工商行政管理总局

美利坚合众国联邦贸易委员会	美利坚合众国司法部

(https://www.ftc.gov/policy/cooperation-agreements/us-china-memorandum-understanding-antitrust-antimonopoly-cooperation)

参考译文
Versions for Reference

一、请翻译下列一则签署外交备忘录的新闻报道，注意备忘录标题、缔约方以及常见表达的翻译。(Translate the following coverage of signing MOU and pay attention to the translation of MOU titles, MOU parties as well as some frequently used expressions.)

Actively Implement the Important Measures on South–South Cooperation by President Xi Jinping MOFCOM and the Relevant Organizations of the UN Sign the Memorandum of Understanding on Cooperation

On September 27, Minister of Commerce Gao Hucheng met with Deputy Secretary General of the United Nations, High Representative for the UN Office of the High Representative for the Least Development Countries, Landlocked Developing Countries and Small Island Developing States (UN-OHRLLS) Gyan Chandra Acharya in New York, and exchanged views on the implementation work announced at the South-South Cooperation Round Table Meeting by President Xi Jinping.

Gao Hucheng said that when visiting the headquarters of the UN, President Xi Jinping proposed the significant suggestions and measures on expanding and deepening the South-

South Cooperation in the new period. China is willing to strengthen the cooperation with the UN-OHRLLS, actively implement the achievements of the series of summits marking the 70th anniversary of the founding of the UN attended by President Xi Jinping. Acharya praised the contributions made by China to supporting the least development countries, landlocked countries and small island developing states. He said that the UN will work with China to help these countries to realize the 2030 UN Sustainable Development Goals (SDGs).

After the meeting, Gao Hucheng and Acharya signed the "MOU on Supporting the Least Developed Countries, Landlocked Countries and Small Island Developing States to Achieve the 2030 UN Sustainable Development Goals", making it clear that both sides will carry out the cooperation in training of the capacity building with the least developed countries, landlocked countries and small island developing states in the fields of agriculture, health, poverty reduction, trade promotion and ecological protection under the framework of the South-South cooperation, so as to help them to achieve the 2030 UN Sustainable Development Goals at an early date.

二、请翻译下列外交备忘录，注意备忘录文本的结构和语言特点。(**Translate the following MOU and pay attention to its text structure and language features.**)

**MEMORANDUM OF UNDERSTANDING ON ANTITRUST AND ANTIMONOPOLY COOPERATION BETWEEN
THE UNITED STATES DEPARTMENT OF JUSTICE AND FEDERAL TRADE COMMISSION, ON THE ONE HAND,
AND
THE PEOPLE'S REPUBLIC OF CHINA NATIONAL DEVELOPMENT AND REFORM COMMISSION,
MINISTRY OF COMMERCE, AND STATE ADMINISTRATION FOR INDUSTRY AND COMMERCE, ON THE OTHER HAND**

OBJECTIVES

The United States Federal Trade Commission, the United States Department of Justice (together the "U.S. antitrust agencies"); and the People's Republic of China National Development and Reform Commission, Ministry of Commerce, and State Administration for Industry and Commerce (together the "PRC antimonopoly agencies").

Desiring to enhance the effective enforcement of their competition laws and policies by creating a framework for long-term cooperation between the U.S. antitrust agencies and the PRC antimonopoly agencies,

Recognizing the benefit of technical cooperation between the U.S. antitrust agencies and the PRC antimonopoly agencies in order to enhance an environment in which the sound and effective enforcement of competition law and policy supports the efficient operation of markets and economic welfare of the citizens of their respective nations,

Recognizing that the development of a well-functioning system for effectively implementing competition law and policy involves the respective antitrust or antimonopoly agencies, and also other government agencies, the judiciary, and the legal, business, and academic sectors, and

Recognizing that establishing good communications between U.S. and PRC government agencies on competition law and policy, including establishing this framework for cooperation between the U.S. antitrust agencies and the PRC antimonopoly agencies, will contribute to improving and strengthening the relationship between the United States and China, intend to cooperate as follows:

STRUCTURE

The U.S. antitrust agencies and the PRC antimonopoly agencies are the counterparts of this Memorandum of Understanding ("Memorandum"), which sets out a framework for cooperation.

The framework for cooperation between the U.S. antitrust agencies and the PRC antimonopoly agencies is composed of two parts: the first is the joint dialogue among all parties to this Memorandum on competition policy at the senior official level (the "joint dialogue") and the second is communication and cooperation on competition law enforcement and policy between individual U.S. antitrust agencies and PRC antimonopoly agencies.

With regard to the first part, unless otherwise agreed, the location of the joint dialogue should alternate between China and the United States, and the host should alternate among the relevant antitrust or antimonopoly agencies. The U.S. antitrust agencies and the PRC antimonopoly agencies intend to convene the joint dialogue periodically, in principle once a year. Based upon the initiative of either side, the parties to this Memorandum may establish ad hoc working groups under the joint dialogue to facilitate discussions on particular issues regarding competition policy and laws. The ad hoc working groups could be conducted in tandem with the joint dialogue or separately as agreed by the individual antitrust or antimonopoly agencies to satisfy their particular needs.

With regard to the second part, the U.S. antitrust agencies and each of the PRC antimonopoly agencies, individually, may also engage in communication and cooperation, separate from the joint dialogue, at the senior or working level.

No agency leads the cooperation under this Memorandum on behalf of each side. Each agency plans to appoint a liaison for the purpose of facilitating contact in furtherance of this Memorandum.

Communications between the agencies may be carried out by telephone, electronic mail, videoconference, meeting, or other means, as appropriate.

The U.S. antitrust agencies and the PRC antimonopoly agencies intend to notify the other promptly of significant changes regarding their authorities responsible for competition policy and law enforcement.

CONTENT

The U.S. antitrust agencies and the PRC antimonopoly agencies recognize that it is in their common interest to work together, including in the following areas, subject to reasonably available resources: (a) keeping each other informed of significant competition policy and enforcement developments in their respective jurisdictions; (b) enhancing each agency's capabilities with appropriate activities related to competition policy and law such as training programs, workshops, study missions and internships; (c) exchanging experiences on competition law enforcement, when appropriate; (d) seeking information or advice from one another regarding matters of competition law enforcement and policy; (e) providing comments on proposed changes to competition laws, regulations, rules and guidelines; (f) exchanging views with respect to multilateral competition law and policy; and (g) exchanging experiences in raising companies', other government agencies' and the public's awareness of competition policy and law.

Each agency recognizes that, when a U.S. antitrust and a PRC antimonopoly agency are investigating related matters, it may be in those agencies' common interest to cooperate in appropriate cases, consistent with those agencies' enforcement interests, legal constraints, and available resources. The U.S. antitrust agencies and the PRC antimonopoly agencies plan to evaluate the effectiveness of the above-mentioned activities under this Memorandum on a regular basis to ensure that their expectations and needs are being met.

WORK PLANS

The U.S. antitrust agencies and each individual PRC antimonopoly agency intend to develop detailed work plans of cooperative activities under this Memorandum, which may include law enforcement capacity building and other activities, and to revise and update such work plans as necessary.

Translation for Coverage of Signing Diplomatic Memorandum

CONFIDENTIALITY

It is understood that the U.S. antitrust agencies and the PRC antimonopoly agencies do not intend to communicate information to the other if such communication is prohibited by the laws governing the agency possessing the information or would be incompatible with that agency's interests. Insofar as information is communicated, the recipient should, to the extent consistent with its laws, maintain the confidentiality of any such information communicated to it in confidence.

EFFECTIVE DATE

Cooperation under this Memorandum is effective as of the date of signature. This Memorandum is intended to set forth an advisory framework. Nothing in this Memorandum is intended to create legally binding rights or obligations, to change existing law, contracts or treaties, to prevent the parties to this Memorandum from seeking or providing assistance to one another pursuant to other bilateral or multilateral agreements or arrangements, or to exclude other technical cooperation projects.

The parties to this Memorandum intend to consult regarding any questions concerning the understanding or implementation of this Memorandum.

Signed in Beijing on July 27, 2011, in five copies, in the Chinese and English languages, with both versions being equally official.

/s/ Jon Leibowitz		/s/ Christine A. Varney
United States Federal Trade Commission		United States Department of Justice
/s/ Peng Sen	/s/ Gao Hucheng	/s/ Zhong Youping
PRC National Development and Reform Commission	PRC Ministry of Commerce	PRC State Administration for Industry and Commerce

单元小结
Summary

本单元主要探讨签署外交备忘录新闻报道的翻译，总结了备忘录标题、签署缔约方、见证人以及签署意义和成果等常见表达的翻译方法；对谅解备忘录中英文文本的结构和语言特点进行了对比和分析，探讨相应的转换规律和技巧。范例一介绍了备忘录名称的常见表达及其翻译，总结了签署备忘录新闻中的常见表述并探讨相关翻译方法；范例二总结了谅解备忘录的主要文本结构、模式以及写作规范，并就备忘录中英文文本进行语言分析，总结出备忘录文本句法结构复杂、措辞严谨正式等语体风格。针对复杂句式结构，在汉英转换时，可以调整语序以及增加相应的衔接手段；针对措辞正式的语言风格，结合汉英两种语言特征的异同，着重介绍了以名词结构、介词结构以及被动态的使用为主的翻译方法。通过本单元的学习，能够帮助译者掌握签署备忘录新闻以及备忘录文本的写作规则、文本特点以及语言规范，在翻译时准确、地道地传达原文信息和风格。

延伸阅读

对外文书的应用

对外文书是对外交往的书信形式，是进行对外交涉和礼仪往来的一种重要手段。各种文书均体现国家的对外方针政策和有关法规，所以起草和发送对外文书是政策性很强的工作。即使是一件纯属礼节性的函件，如果格式与行文不合常规，也可能引起收件人的误解和不愉快，如果文内有其他错误，则会造成更为严重的后果。因此，书写对外文书要求文字严谨、精练、准确，客套用语合乎惯例，格式要美观大方，打印要整洁。

收到各类文书要尽快处理，切勿拖压，尤其是外交上的文书往来，收下回复或不予置理以至拒收退回，都反映一种政治态度。因此对外文书处理要十分慎重。一般情况下，除某些纯属通知性的文电外，应以相应的文书进行答复或复谢。

一、几种对外文书

（一）照会

照会分正式照会和普通照会两种。

正式照会由国家元首、政府首脑、外交部长、大使、代办、临时代办等人签名发出，并用第一人称写成。一般不盖机关印章。普通照会由外交机关（外交部）或外交代表机关发出，行文用第三人称，加盖机关印章，一般不签字。但有的国家要求加盖印章后再由使节或授权的外交官签名。正式照会和普通照会的区别还在于它们使用范围不同。

正式照会用于：1. 重大事情的通知。如国家领导人的变更，大使、领事的更换，承认、断交、复交等事项的正式通知。2. 重要问题的交涉。如建议缔结或修改条约，建议召开双边、多边国际会议，互设领事馆，委托代管本国财产，国家元首、政府首脑的访问以及其他有关政治、军事、经济等重要问题的交涉。3. 隆重的礼仪表示。如表示庆贺、吊唁等等。4. 为了表示对某一件事的特别重视，也有使用正式照会的。

普通照会用于进行一般交涉、行政性通知、办理日常事务、交际往来。由于外交文书日趋简化，普通照会的使用范围也越来越广，政府之间关于重要国际问题的来往，现在也多使用普通照会。

普通照会以同样内容普遍分发给当地各外交代表机关的，亦称通告照会。例如，外交部用以向外交团发送各种事务性通知、规定、条例等照会，以及各外交代表机关用以通知大使、临时代办离任、返任，外交官到离任、例假日等。这类通告照会可复印，受文机关可写"各国驻××国外交代表机关"。

（二）对外函件

对外函件（包括外交函件）形式简便，使用范围较广。国家领导人、外交人员以及各部门各机构写给外国相应人员与机构的书信都可采用这种形式。根据内容情况，凡属重要者，视为正式函件，凡属事务性者，视为便函。一般说来，领导人和外交代表之间的亲笔签名信即属外交函件。

（三）备忘录

备忘录是外交代表机关之间使用的一种外交文书，用来说明就某一事件、问题进行交涉时在事实上、立场上、法律方面的细节，或用来重申外交会谈中的谈话内容。可面交或送交对方，无客套语、致敬语，开头就叙述事实。在会谈或交涉中为了对方便于记忆谈话的内容或避免误解，可预先写成备忘录面交对方，也可在谈话后将要点用备忘录送交对方。为了叙述事实或陈述、补充自己的观点、意见或驳复对方的观点、意见，如果用照会过于郑重时，可使用备忘录。有时为了提醒某一件事，作为一种客气的催询，也可送交备忘录。

备忘录也可以作为正式照会或普通照会的附件。

面交的备忘录，不编号、不写抬头、不盖章；送交的则要编号、写抬头、要盖章。有的标上"备忘录"三字。

（四）电报

国家领导人、外交代表，各部门和机构亦常用电报同外国相应人员及单位进行文书往来。电报多用于祝贺、慰问、吊唁及各种事务性联系。抬头应写清受电人国名、地名、职衔、姓名，发电人亦应具职衔和全名或机构名称。

电报可直发收电人，亦可发有关国家外交部转或通过驻外使馆转交。

二、对外文书使用的要求

格式：使用对外文书首先要注意格式，不要用错。如外长和外交代表使用正式照会，不要用普通照会的格式，非外交代表机构使用对外函件，不要用照会格式等等。

人称：人称要与文书格式相适应。正式照会、外交函件、电报均是以签署人的口气用第一人称写成。在正式照会中，一般不用"我们"一词，普通照会一般以单位名义用第三人称写成，称对方亦用第三人称，不可用"贵方"或"贵馆"等措辞，而是重提受照机关的名称。以机构名义书写的对外函件亦用第三人称。

另外，签署者与受文者要相适应，即人对人、单位对单位。如：正式照会是人对人，普通照会是单位对单位。在个人对个人的外交文书中讲究身份对等，如元首对元首,总理对总理,外长对外长。但也有特殊情况,如大使作为国家的全权代表可对外长、总理、元首,而代办一般只对外长。其他的对外函件可根据实际情况书写。

客套用语:客套用语要与格式相适应。如普通照会开头的"××向××致意"这一客套用语不能用作个人函件中的开头语,非外交机关发的对外文书也不用这一套语,照会结尾的致敬语使用时要注意与双方的身份、关系和场合相适应。如,致代办处的文书一般用"顺致敬意"或"顺致崇高的敬意";给外交部和大使馆的文书则一般用"顺致崇高的敬意"。事务性的文书,亦用"顺致崇高的敬意"。

致敬语不能自成一页,应紧跟正文后另起一段。

称呼:文书抬头即受文人的职衔、姓名等要全称,文中第一出现职衔、姓名也要全称。第二次出现则可用简称。

国名:文书信封和文中的抬头的国名等均用全称。文中第一次出现时用全称,以后可用简称。但有些国家由于情况特殊,如朝鲜民主主义共和国国名则须用全称。

有些国家由于发生革命、政变或其他原因,国名可能改变,须随时注意,不要写错。

译文:对外文书一般以本国文字为正本。但为了使收件人能够确切理解文件的实质内容,往往附有收件国文字或通用的第三国文字的译文。在本国向外国常驻代表机关发送事务性函件,也可仅用本国文字,不附译文。较为重要的文书则附以译文为好(有的国家译文本上注有"非正式译文"字样)。各国套语用法以及行文格式与中文不同,翻译时应注意,要符合各种文字的用法。一般函电也可用接受国文字或通用文字书写。

三、备忘录格式范例

备忘录例一:对外表态

××总理致××国总理××的备忘录

一、 中国政府欢迎并且支持一九××年×月×日至×日在××举行的××会议为促进中×两国解决××问题所作的努力。

二、××××××××××××××××××××××××××××。

以上两点只在中×双方官员会晤以前和会晤期间有效,不影响双方官员会晤中提出的其他建议和作出的最后决定。

××年×月×日于××

注:此件是作为照会附件发出的备忘录。

备忘录例二：陈述意见
备忘录

根据××国政府关于××关于协定的建议，中国政府表示同意进行签订该协定的谈判。

中国政府的意见，在××协定中应包括下列各款：

……

……

当然上述各款可按双方愿望补充或变更。

请将上述事宜转达贵国政府。

××年×月×日于××

注：此件为面交备忘录。

来源：外交部网站
(http://www.fmprc.gov.cn/web/ziliao_674904/lbzs_674975/t9025.shtml)

UNIT 15

外交函电报道的翻译
Translation for Coverage of Diplomatic Correspondence

单元简介
Introduction

外交函电可分为外交函件和外交电报。

外交函件是国家领导人、外交代表之间进行外事交涉的来往信函，用于交流双方的观点、意见，协商与联系解决问题，有时也用于国家机关、团体、企事业单位和地方政府领导人致他国相应机构和人士交涉事务。根据通信双方的身份及通信内容的重要程度，分为正式函件和便函。正式函件用于国家领导人、外交部长、大使、代办等有全权代表身份者交涉重要事项，如邀请、应邀、致谢、建议、表态、吊唁、慰问等，是庄重的外交信件。便函用于事务性内容，如一般的祝贺、吊唁、馈赠、邀请进餐或观看演出、借还物品等。

外交电报是一国的领导人、外交机关及其派出机构或代表发给他国或国际组织和代表的公务电报，是一种常用的快速通讯的外交文书，其内容与用法同外交函件相似，有邀请电、贺电、唁电、慰问电、感谢电等。电文简短，文字精练。

外交函电报道翻译范例分析
Sample of Translation for Coverage of Diplomatic Correspondence

范例一（Sample I）

习近平致信祝贺"2015·北京人权论坛"开幕（节本）
2015/09/16

Xi Jinping Sends Letter Congratulating on the Opening of Beijing Forum on Human Rights 2015 (Abbreviated Version)
2015/09/16

"2015·北京人权论坛"16日在京开幕。国家主席习近平发来贺信，强调实现人民充分享有人权是人类社会的共同奋斗目标。要加强不同文明交流互鉴、促进各国人权交流合作，推动各国人权事业更好发展。

On September 16, 2015, the Beijing Forum on Human Rights 2015 opened in Beijing. President Xi Jinping sent a congratulatory letter, stressing that making people fully enjoy human rights is a common objective of the human society. We should enhance exchanges and mutual learning among different civilizations and push exchanges and cooperation among all countries, thus ensure a better development of human rights cause in all countries.

习近平在贺信中指出，在中国人民抗日战争暨世界反法西斯战争胜利70周年之际，本届"北京人权论坛"以"和平与发展：世界反法西斯战争的胜利与人权进步"为主题，有利于推动各方对保障人类和平权、发展权的深入思考。

Xi Jinping pointed out in his congratulatory letter that on the occasion of the 70th anniversary of the victory of the Chinese People's War of Resistance against Japanese Aggression as well as the World Anti-Fascist War, the Beijing Forum on Human Rights this year, which is themed with "Peace and Development: The Victory of the World Anti-Fascist War and Human Rights Advancement", will help prompt all parties involved to deeply reflect on the guarantee of peace and development rights of mankind.

习近平强调，近代以后，中国人民历经苦难，深知人的价值、基本人权、人格尊严对社会发展进步的重大意义，倍加珍惜来之不易的和平发展环境，将坚定不移走和平发展道路、坚定不移推进中国人权事业和世界人权事业。

Xi Jinping stressed that the Chinese people, having gone through much suffering in modern times, are fully aware of the great significance of human value, basic human rights and human dignity to social development and progress, deeply cherish the hard-won peaceful development environment, and will unswervingly pursue a peaceful development path and steadfastly advance human rights cause both in China and the rest of the world.

习近平指出，中国共产党和中国政府始终尊重和保障人权。长期以来，中国坚持把人权的普遍性原则同中国实际相结合，不断推动经济社会发展，增进人民福祉，促进社会公平正义，加强人权法治保障，努力促进经济、社会、文化权利和公民、政治权利全面协调发展，显著提高了人民生存权、发展权的保障水平，走出了一条适合中国国情的人权发展道路。

Xi Jinping pointed out that the Communist Party of China (CPC) and the Chinese government always respect and protect human rights. For a long time, China, by connecting the universality principle of human rights with China's reality, constantly advances social and economic development, improves people's welfare, promotes social fairness and justice, strengthens legal guarantee of human rights and strives for a comprehensive and coordinated development of economic, social and cultural rights as well as civil and political rights. This has significantly elevated the guarantee level of people's existence and development rights and paved a development path for human rights suitable to China's national conditions.

习近平强调，人权保障没有最好，只有更好。国际社会应该积极推进世界人权事业，尤其是要关注广大发展中国家民众的生存权和发展权。中国人民正在为实现中华民族伟大复兴的中国梦而奋斗，这将在更高水平上保障中国人民的人权，促进人的全面发展。

Xi Jinping emphasized that there is no best but better human rights guarantee. The international community should actively push forward global human rights cause and, particularly, pay attention to existence and development rights of people in developing countries. The Chinese people are striving for the realization of the Chinese Dream of great rejuvenation of the Chinese nation, which will guarantee Chinese people's human rights at a higher level and promote their comprehensive development.

***

"北京人权论坛"创立于2008年，已成功举办7届，成为各国开展人权交流、探讨人权合作的重要平台。来自30多个国家和地区的官员、学者等出席本届论坛。

Established in 2008, the Beijing Forum on Human Rights has successfully held seven sessions and become an important platform for all countries to carry out human rights exchanges and discuss human rights cooperation. Officials and scholars from over 30 countries and regions attended this year's Forum.

外交函电报道的翻译
Translation for Coverage of Diplomatic Correspondence

> 新闻背景：由中国人权研究会和中国人权发展基金会联合举办的"2015·北京人权论坛"于2015年9月16日至17日在北京举行。本届论坛的主题为"和平与发展：世界反法西斯战争的胜利与人权进步"。来自世界30余个国家和地区的100多位人权高级官员、专家学者和相关机构负责人出席论坛。自2008年以来，北京人权论坛已成功举办7届。每届论坛均有上百名来自世界多个国家、地区及国际组织的政府官员和专家学者参加，就国际人权领域的重大问题进行坦诚交流和深入讨论。范例一选自外交部官方网站对于此次论坛发布的双语报道，原文和译文均略有删节和修改。
>
> 原文链接：http://www.fmprc.gov.cn/web/wjdt_674879/gjldrhd_674881/t1297090.shtml
>
> 译文链接：http://www.fmprc.gov.cn/mfa_eng/wjdt_665385/wshd_665389/t1297895.shtml

一、范例一文本结构分析（Text Structure Analysis of Sample I）

范例一是一则典型的有关贺信的报道，主要内容为习近平主席向2015年9月16日至17日召开的"2015·北京人权论坛"表示祝贺。全文可分为三个部分。第一部分（第一段）为导语，介绍了习主席贺信的主要精神。第二部分是新闻的主体部分，包括第二、三、四、五段，具体展示了贺信的内容，包括本届论坛的意义、中国方面对人权问题的重视、对国际社会的期待等。这一部分通常是此类新闻报道的重点。第三部分，即结尾段，交代了论坛的成立时间、举办届数、重要意义，以及本届论坛的参会规模与人员构成等背景信息。

二、范例一翻译解析（Translation Analysis of Sample I）

（一）外交函电新闻标题的翻译 (Translation of Headlines of Coverage of Diplomatic Correspondence)

贺电/贺信是非常常见的一类外交函电，涉及的事由多种多样，包括某国家或国际组织领导人当选或就职、重大国际会议召开、国际合作项目开工、建交周年纪念等。贺信的题目多采用"某领导人致信/致函/致电（另一领导人）祝贺某某事由"的格式。祝贺事由一般以名词性短语形式出现在标题的末尾，以on/for/upon等介词引导。

请看下列贺信报道的标题及翻译，注意斜体标注的部分：

习近平致函祝贺老挝建国40周年

(http://www.gxnews.com.cn/staticpages/20151202/newgx565eef14-14027246.shtml)

Xi Jinping *Sends Letter Congratulating on* 40th Anniversary of Lao People's

Democratic Republic

(http://ph.china-embassy.org/eng/chinew/t1321197.htm)

2018年7月1日，国家主席习近平致电在毛里塔尼亚首都努瓦克肖特举行的非洲联盟第31届首脑会议，向非洲国家和人民热烈祝贺会议的召开。

(http://www.fmprc.gov.cn/web/wjdt_674879/gjldrhd_674881/t1573119.shtml)

On July 1, 2018, Chinese President Xi Jinping on Sunday warmly congratulated African countries and their people on the opening of the African Union (AU) summit in Nouakchott, the capital of Mauritania.

(http://www.fmprc.gov.cn/mfa_eng/wjdt_665385/wshd_665389/t1573155.shtml)

习近平就土库曼斯坦获得永久中立国地位20周年向土库曼斯坦总统致贺信

(http://cpc.people.com.cn/n/2015/1211/c64094-27917998.html)

Xi Jinping *Sends Message of Congratulations to* President of Turkmenistan *on* 20th Anniversary of Turkmenistan's Obtainment of Status of Permanent Neutrality

(http://gr.china-embassy.org/eng/zgyw/t1324340.htm)

李克强致电祝贺奥利就任尼泊尔新总理

(http://news.xinhuanet.com/politics/2015-10/12/c_1116800129.htm)

Li Keqiang *Sends Congratulatory Message to* Khadga Prasad Oli *for* Assuming Office as Prime Minister of Nepal

(http://www.fmprc.gov.cn/mfa_eng/wjb_663304/zzjg_663340/yzs_663350/xwlb_663352/t1305732.shtml)

2018年7月9日，国家主席习近平同卡塔尔国埃米尔塔米姆互致贺电，热烈庆祝两国建交30周年。

(http://www.fmprc.gov.cn/web/wjdt_674879/gjldrhd_674881/t1575313.shtml)

On July 9, Chinese President Xi Jinping on Monday exchanged congratulations with Qatari Emir Sheikh Tamim bin Hamad Al Thani on the 30th anniversary of the establishment of diplomatic relations.

(http://www.fmprc.gov.cn/mfa_eng/wjdt_665385/wshd_665389/t1575560.shtml)

以上可见，"致函/致信/致电祝贺""致贺信"等的常见英文表达有以下两类：send letter/message to congratulate/congratulating/of congratulations或send congratulatory letter/message。两类表达的主要区别在于"贺信"之"贺"作为修饰语出现的形式（形容词、分词、不定式还是介词短语）和位置（前置还是后置）。若是与对方"互致贺信"，则常用表达为exchange congratulatory letters/messages (with)。

（二）逻辑与断句（Logical Relationship and Sentence Segmentation）

范例一第一段第三句中，"要①加强不同文明交流互鉴、②促进各国人权交流合作，③推动各国人权事业更好发展"这三点信息看似并列，实则有着更深层次的逻辑联系，即采取措施"加强不同文明交流互鉴、促进各国人权交流合作"，是为了实现"推动各国人权事业更好发展"的目标。出于这一考虑，译文用thus连接了③和①②，使逻辑关系更清晰（We should enhance exchanges and mutual learning among different civilizations and push exchanges and cooperation among all countries, thus ensure a better development of human rights cause in all countries.）。

第二段中，习近平对本届论坛作出了高度评价，称它"以'和平与发展：世界反法西斯战争的胜利与人权进步'为主题，有利于推动各方对保障人类和平权、发展权的深入思考"。其中，"有利于……"是评价的主要内容，为关键信息，而论坛主题则相对次要。因此，译文将前者翻译为句子的主干部分，而把后者放在了非限定性定语从句中（… the Beijing Forum on Human Rights this year, which is themed with "Peace and Development: The Victory of the World Anti-Fascist War and Human Rights Advancement", will help prompt all parties involved to deeply reflect on the guarantee of peace and development rights of mankind.）。

第三段强调了中国对人权问题的重视："中国人民历经苦难，深知人的价值、基本人权、人格尊严对社会发展进步的重大意义，倍加珍惜来之不易的和平发展环境，将坚定不移走和平发展道路、坚定不移推进中国人权事业和世界人权事业"。其中，"历经苦难"是前提条件，即正因为中国人民经受了苦难才更懂得珍惜。翻译时应作相应处理，将这层因果关系表达出来（… the Chinese people, *having gone through/who have gone through* much suffering in modern times …）。

第四段的难点是并列结构的理解。经过分析，"坚持把人权的普遍性原则同中国实际相结合……走出了一条适合中国国情的人权发展道路"可作如下理解：中国（通过）"坚持把人权的普遍性原则同中国实际相结合"的做法，"不断推动经济社会发展，增进人民福祉，促进社会公平正义，加强人权法治保障，努力促进经济、社会、文化权利和公民、政治权利全面协调发展"，（从而）"显著提高了人民生存权、发展权的保障水平，走出了一条适合中国国情的人权发展道路"。括号中增补的文字梳理了原文的逻辑关系，在译文中体现为连接词的使用和适当的断句，从而使译文的逻辑关系更加明晰（For a long time, China, by connecting the universality principle of human rights with China's reality, constantly advances social and economic development, improves people's welfare, promotes social fairness and justice, strengthens legal guarantee of human rights and strives for a comprehensive and coordinated development of economic, social and cultural rights as well as civil and political rights. This has significantly elevated the guarantee level of people's existence and development rights and paved a development path for human rights suitable to China's national conditions.）

（三）重复表达的翻译（Translation of Repetition）

外交新闻中词语的重复往往是出于加强语气、表示强调等目的，不可随意合并或删减。但是，为了避免字面的重复和用词的单调，翻译时可选用英文中的同义词和近义词。第三段中，修饰词"坚定不移"出现了两次："将坚定不移走和平发展道路、坚定不移推进中国人权事业和世界人权事业"。译文用unswervingly和steadfastly分别将其译出，保证了用词的丰富和原句语气的传达（… will unswervingly pursue a peaceful development path and steadfastly advance human rights cause both in China and the rest of the world … ）。

三、外交贺电报道常用表达及翻译（Translation of Frequently Used Expressions in Coverage of Congratulatory Letters）

上文提到，外交贺电的事由包括领导人当选或就职、重大国际活动、建交周年纪念等。相关报道的导语和正文会简要介绍贺电事由并表达祝贺之情。如果涉及两国关系，还会对双方关系的历史进行回顾，对未来发展提出期待等。请观察下列例句中的斜体部分：

国务院总理李克强8日致电英国首相卡梅伦，祝贺他领导英国保守党在大选中获胜。

(http://cpc.people.com.cn/n/2015/0509/c64094-26973513.html)

On May 8, 2015, Premier Li Keqiang *sent a message to* Prime Minister David Cameron of the United Kingdom (UK) *to congratulate him on leading* the Conservative Party to *win the general election* in the UK.

(http://losangeles.china-consulate.org/eng/topnews/t1263250.htm)

习近平在贺电中表示，在瑟利夫总统坚强领导下，利比里亚政府和人民全力以赴抗击埃博拉疫情并终结疫情，中国政府和人民对此表示热烈祝贺和高度赞赏。中方愿积极参与"后埃博拉时期"经济社会重建。中方将加强两国各领域友好互利合作，更好地惠及两国人民。

(http://politics.people.com.cn/n/2015/0525/c70731-27054010.html)

Xi Jinping *said in his congratulatory message that* the Chinese government and people *warmly congratulate on and highly appreciate* the fact that the Liberian government and people, under the staunch leadership of President Ellen Johnson Sirleaf, spared no efforts to fight against the Ebola epidemic and terminated the epidemic. China *is ready to actively participate in* economic and social reconstruction of the "post-Ebola" period. China will *strengthen friendly and mutually beneficial cooperation* in various areas between the two countries so as to better benefit the two peoples.

(http://www.fmprc.gov.cn/mfa_eng/wjb_663304/zzjg_663340/fzs_663828/xwlb_663830/t1267289.shtml)

习近平指出,共同举办2016"中美旅游年"是我去年9月对美国进行国事访问期间双方达成的一项重要成果。值此2016"中美旅游年"开幕之际,我谨代表中国政府和人民,并以我个人的名义,对旅游年的开幕表示热烈的祝贺,对远道而来的美国朋友表示热烈的欢迎。

(http://www.fmprc.gov.cn/web/wjdt_674879/gjldrhd_674881/t1344280.shtml)

Xi Jinping *pointed out that* the 2016 China-US Tourism Year co-organized by China and the US is an important achievement reached by both sides during my state visit to the US last September. *On the occasion of* this opening ceremony of the 2016 China-US Tourism Year, *on behalf of the Chinese government and the Chinese people*, and *in my own name*, I would like to *extend my warm congratulations to* the launching of the China-US Tourism Year and my warm welcome to American friends coming from afar.

(http://www.fmprc.gov.cn/mfa_eng/zxxx_662805/t1344847.shtml)

范例二(Sample II)

李克强总理就李光耀逝世向新加坡总理李显龙致唁电
2015/03/23

Premier Li Keqiang Sends Message of Condolences to Prime Minister Lee Hsien Loong of Singapore over the Death of Lee Kuan Yew
2015/03/23

2015年3月23日,国务院总理李克强就新加坡前总理李光耀不幸逝世向新加坡总理李显龙致唁电。李克强代表中国政府和人民并以个人的名义,向新加坡政府和人民表示沉痛哀悼,向李显龙及家人致以深切慰问。

On March 23, 2015, Premier Li Keqiang sent message of condolences to Prime Minister Lee Hsien Loong of Singapore over the sad news of the death of Lee Kuan Yew, former Prime Minister of Singapore. On behalf of the Chinese government and people and in his own name, Li Keqiang expressed deep condolences to the Singaporean government and people and profound sympathy to Lee Hsien Loong and his family.

李克强在唁电中表示,李光耀先生和中国老一辈领导人共同推开了中新友好合作大门,他为中新关系和中国改革开放作出的贡献必将载入史册。李光耀先生是世界公认的战略家和政治家,是新加坡的开国之父和发展之父,也是东盟的创建者之一,他为本地

外交新闻汉英翻译
C-E TRANSLATION OF DIPLOMATIC NEWS

区的和平与发展作出了重要贡献。

In his message of condolences, Li Keqiang said that Mr. Lee Kuan Yew, together with older generations of Chinese leadership, opened a door to China-Singapore friendly cooperation. His contributions to China-Singapore relations and China's reform and opening-up will surely be written into the annals of history. Mr. Lee Kuan Yew, as a worldly recognized strategist and statesman, the founding father and developer of Singapore as well as one of the founders of the Association of Southeast Asian Nations (ASEAN), had made significant contributions to peace and development in the region.

李克强表示，新加坡是中国重要的友好邻邦。中方愿同新方共同努力，弘扬两国几代领导人共同开创和精心培育的友好传统，推动中新友好合作关系不断向前发展。

Li Keqiang said that Singapore is one of the key friendly neighboring countries of China. China stands ready to work together with Singapore to carry forward the friendly tradition co-initiated and carefully nurtured by several generations of leaderships of the two countries and to continuously advance the China-Singapore friendly cooperative relations.

新闻背景：2015年3月24日，新加坡开国元首李光耀因病逝世，享年91岁。国务院总理李克强向新加坡总理李显龙发出唁电，表示哀悼。范例二选自外交部网站就此所作的双语报道，译文略有修改。

原文链接：http://www.fmprc.gov.cn/web/wjdt_674879/gjldrhd_674881/t1247570.shtml

译文链接：http://www.fmprc.gov.cn/mfa_eng/wjdt_665385/wshd_665389/t1248427.shtml

---

一、范例二文本结构分析（Text Structure Analysis of Sample II）

唁电/慰问电也是常见的一类外交函电，多为一国领导人就他国前任或现任领导人去世、他国发生地震、洪水、重大疫情、恐怖袭击等自然或人为灾害表示哀悼或慰问。有关唁电/慰问电的新闻报道多由导语和主体两部分构成。导语简要说明事由，表达哀悼或慰问之情。主体部分涉及函电的核心内容，如灾害发生的时间、波及范围、造成的损失等信息，有时还会向对方表达中方提供必要援助的意愿。范例二为非常典型的有关唁电的报道。导语部分写明唁电事由，即新加坡前总理李光耀病逝，主体部分介绍唁电的主要内容，包括对李光耀生前主要成就的回顾和对中新关系所作贡献的高度评价。

二、范例二翻译解析（Translation Analysis of Sample II）

唁电/慰问电相关中文报道的标题通常采用"××（人或机构）就××（事由）向××（人或机构）致唁电/慰问电"的格式。英文翻译时常用 ... sends/extends message/letter of condolences to ... on/over ... 结构来表达。请看下列唁电/慰问电相关报道的标题及翻译，注意斜体标注的部分：

习近平就亚洲航空公司客机失事向印尼总统致慰问电
(http://news.xinhuanet.com/politics/2014-12/30/c_127348316.htm)
Xi Jinping *Sends Letter of Condolences* to Indonesian President *over* the Crash of the Indonesian Passenger Plane
(http://in.china-embassy.org/eng/zgxw/t1290655.htm)

习近平就沙特国王阿卜杜拉逝世向沙特新任国王萨勒曼致唁电
(http://news.xinhuanet.com/politics/2015-01/23/c_1114112767.htm)
Xi Jinping *Sends Message of Condolences* to New King Salman bin Abdulaziz Al Saud of Saudi Arabia *over* the Death of King Abdullah bin Abdulaziz Al Saud of Saudi Arabia
(http://www.fmprc.gov.cn/mfa_eng/zxxx_662805/t1231748.shtml)

习近平就巴基斯坦发生重大恐怖袭击事件向巴总统侯赛因致慰问电
(http://news.xinhuanet.com/politics/2016-03/29/c_1118474696.htm)
Xi Jinping *Sends Message of Condolences* to Pakistani President Mamnoon Hussain *on* the Severe Terrorist Attack in Pakistan
(http://www.fmprc.gov.cn/mfa_eng/zxxx_662805/t1352069.shtml)

习近平就比利时首都布鲁塞尔系列恐怖袭击事件向比利时国王菲利普致慰问电
(http://news.xinhuanet.com/politics/2016-03/23/c_1118417185.htm)
Xi Jinping *Sends Message of Condolences* to King Philippe of Belgium *on* a Series of Terrorist Attacks in Belgian Capital Brussels
(http://www.fmprc.gov.cn/mfa_eng/zxxx_662805/t1350710.shtml)

中文提到某位领导人时，一般使用"头衔+名字"的语序，例如"加拿大总理特鲁多"，"俄罗斯总统普京"。英译时，头衔和名字哪个在前，哪个在后，需依情况而定。范例二第一段中出现的"新加坡总理李显龙"和"新加坡前总理李光耀"这两个头衔在译文中的语序就有所不同。为了体现与李克强身份的对等，李显龙作为新加坡总理的头衔先出现。而李光耀作为一个政治伟人，他的名字所承载的意义要大于他曾经是新加坡总理这一身份。出于这一考虑，也为了使句子表达更流畅，译文中先出现名字，头衔紧随其后。

第二段中，李克强对李光耀为中新关系和地区和平与发展所作的贡献做出了高度评价，称"李光耀先生和中国老一辈领导人共同推开了中新友好合作大门"。本段第一句中"李光耀先生和中国老一辈领导人"为两个主语并列，但鉴于本范例是就李光耀逝世所发的唁电，应突出李光耀的重要地位和作用，因而译文以李光耀为主语，而将原句的另一个主语处理为相对次要的附属成分（together with …）。另外，第一句后半部分（"他……载入史册"）与前半部分是相对独立的两层意思，故而译文中重新起句。本段第二句，"李光耀先生是世界公认的战略家和政治家，是新加坡的开国之父和发展之父，也是东盟的创建者之一，他为本地区的和平与发展作出了重要贡献"可以有两种处理方法。一种是认为本句中的代词"他"前后讲了两层意思，因而在此处断句，可以译为：Mr. Lee Kuan Yew is a worldly recognized strategist and statesman, the founding father and developer of Singapore as well as one of the founders of the Association of Southeast Asian Nations (ASEAN). He had made significant contributions to peace and development in the region。另一种可以将其理解为"作为世界公认的战略家和政治家，新加坡的开国之父和发展之父，东盟的创建者之一，李光耀先生为本地区的和平与发展作出了重要贡献"，即译文的处理方法。

第三段第二句中，李克强表达了与新方共同努力的愿望（"中方愿同新方共同努力，弘扬两国几代领导人共同开创和精心培育的友好传统，推动中新友好合作关系不断向前发展"），句中用到了"愿""弘扬""推动"等动词。其中，"愿与新方共同努力"是谓语的主体部分，而"弘扬"和"推动"所引导的内容则是希望通过共同努力所实现的目标。故此在译文中将前者翻译为主句谓语，后两者处理为表示目的的动词不定式短语（China stands ready to work together with Singapore to carry forward the friendly tradition co-initiated and carefully nurtured by several generations of leaderships of the two countries and to continuously advance the China-Singapore friendly cooperative relations）。

三、外交唁电报道常见表达与翻译（Translation of Frequently Used Expressions in Coverage of Condolence Messages）

外交唁电/慰问电涉及的事由较为单一，主要包括自然灾害、重大事故、恐怖袭击和他国或国际组织（前）领导人逝世等。相关新闻报道多对事件进行概述，传达我国领导人的哀悼、慰问以及谴责等感情。有时，当其他国家遭遇重大灾害或事故时，我方还会表达提供必要援助的意愿。请注意观察下列例句中斜体标注的常用表达：

国家主席习近平22日就比利时首都布鲁塞尔系列恐怖袭击事件向比利时国王菲利普致慰问电，对袭击行径予以强烈谴责，向不幸遇难者表示深切的哀悼，向伤者和遇难者家属表示诚挚的慰问。

(http://news.xinhuanet.com/politics/2016-03/23/c_1118417185.htm)

On March 22, 2016, President Xi Jinping *sent a message of condolences to* King

Translation for Coverage of Diplomatic Correspondence

Philippe of Belgium on *a series of terrorist attacks* in Brussels, the capital of Belgium, *expressing strong condemnation* to the attack and *extending deep condolences* to the victims, and *sincere sympathies* to *the bereaved families and the injured.*

(http://www.fmprc.gov.cn/mfa_eng/zxxx_662805/t1350710.shtml)

2015年11月11日，国务院总理李克强就德国前总理施密特不幸逝世向德国总理默克尔致唁电，代表中国政府和人民并以个人的名义，向德方表示深切哀悼，向施密特家人表示诚挚慰问。

(http://www.fmprc.gov.cn/web/wjdt_674879/gjldrhd_674881/t1314035.shtml)

On November 11, 2015, Premier Li Keqiang *sent a message of condolences to* German Chancellor, Angela Merkel, over the death of Helmut Schmidt, a former chancellor of the Federal Republic of Germany. In the message, Li, *on behalf of the Chinese government and people and in his own name, mourned the death* of Schmidt and *extended sympathies to* Schmidt's family.

(http://news.xinhuanet.com/english/2015-11/11/c_134806888.htm)

国家主席习近平25日就德国之翼航空公司客机失事造成包括德国、西班牙籍乘客在内的大量人员遇难，分别向德国总统高克、西班牙国王费利佩六世致慰问电。习近平代表中国政府和人民并以个人的名义，对遇难者表示深切的哀悼，向遇难者的亲属表示诚挚的慰问。

(http://news.xinhuanet.com/politics/2015-03/25/c_1114764055.htm)

On March 25, 2015, President Xi Jinping *sent separate messages of condolences to* President Joachim Gauck of Germany and King Felipe VI of Spain over the death of a considerable number of people including passengers from Germany and Spain caused by the crash of a Germanwings flight. *On behalf of the Chinese government and people and in his own name*, President Xi Jinping *conveyed deep condolences to the victims and expressed sincere sympathies to their families.*

(http://www.fmprc.gov.cn/mfa_eng/zxxx_662805/t1249212.shtml)

习近平表示，中方愿为莫方开展救灾工作提供帮助，相信在莫桑比克政府领导下，莫桑比克人民一定能够战胜灾害、重建家园。

(http://news.xinhuanet.com/politics/2015-01/28/c_1114157931.htm)

Xi Jinping said that *China is willing to assist* Mozambique in *disaster relief*, and believes that the Mozambican people will be bound to *overcome the natural disasters* and *rebuild their homeland* under the leadership of the Mozambican government.

(http://www.fmprc.gov.cn/mfa_eng/wjdt_665385/wshd_665389/t1233451.shtml)

C-E TRANSLATION OF DIPLOMATIC NEWS

范例三(Sample III)

习近平同法国总统奥朗德通电话
2015/12/15

Xi Jinping Holds Telephone Talks with President Francois Hollande of France
2015/12/15

2015年12月14日晚,国家主席习近平应约同法国总统奥朗德通电话。

On the evening of December 14, 2015, President Xi Jinping held telephone talks at request with President Francois Hollande of France.

习近平首先对联合国气候变化巴黎大会取得成功表示祝贺。习近平指出,巴黎大会成功通过《巴黎协定》,为2020年后全球合作应对气候变化指明了方向,具有历史性意义。中方一直坚定支持法方办好大会,与法方及有关各方密切沟通,赞赏法方作为东道主付出的巨大努力。中方为大会成功作出了自己的贡献。中法双方应该同各方一道,推动《巴黎协定》有效实施,推动国际应对气候变化向前发展。巴黎大会的成功表明,国际社会完全可以通过合作对话解决重大国际问题。

Xi Jinping firstly congratulated on the success of the UN Climate Change Conference in Paris. Xi Jinping pointed out that the Paris Agreement, successfully adopted by the Paris conference, charted the course for the post-2020 global cooperation in tackling climate change and is of historic significance. The Chinese side always firmly supports the French side in earnestly hosting the conference by maintaining close communication with France and other relevant sides and appreciates the great efforts of the French side as the host. China also made its contribution to the success of the conference. The two countries should, together with other sides, promote the effective implementation of the Paris Agreement and push forward the development of global solution to climate change. The success of the Paris conference indicates that the international community is fully capable of solving major international issues through cooperation and dialogues.

习近平强调,2015年中法全面战略伙伴关系取得新进展。希望明年双方继续努力,保持高水平政治交往和战略互信,深化核能、航空、金融、人文等交流合作,提高绿色、低碳、可持续发展领域合作水平,推动改善全球治理,并就重大国际和地区问题密切沟通和协调。中方愿同法方加强在二十国集团框架内合作,共同促进全球经济增长。

Xi Jinping stressed that the China-France comprehensive strategic partnership has made new progress in 2015. He hopes that both sides will continue their efforts to maintain high-level political exchanges and strategic mutual trust, deepen exchanges and cooperation in nuclear power, aviation, finance, people-to-people and cultural exchanges and other fields, elevate the cooperation level in areas of green, low-carbon and sustainable development, advance the improvement of global governance and keep close communication and coordination in major international and regional issues. The Chinese side stands ready to intensify cooperation with the French side under the G20 framework so as to jointly boost global economic growth.

奥朗德表示，赞同习主席对法中关系的评价。再次感谢习主席出席联合国气候变化巴黎大会开幕活动，感谢中方为大会成功达成《巴黎协定》作出突出贡献。《巴黎协定》是有力度、有雄心的，符合国际社会共同利益。各方应该共同努力，有效落实协定，努力实现巴黎大会确定的目标。《巴黎协定》也为法中两国在绿色增长、民用核能等领域深化合作开辟了新前景。法方赞同加强两国在国际事务中合作，将全力支持中方办好2016年二十国集团杭州峰会。

Francois Hollande noted that he agrees with President Xi Jinping's comment on France-China relations. He thanked President Xi Jinping again for attending the opening events of the UN Climate Change Conference in Paris, and thanked the Chinese side for its outstanding contribution to the successful reaching of the Paris Agreement. The strong and ambitious Paris Agreement conforms to the common interests of the international community. All sides should join forces to effectively carry out the agreement and make efforts to achieve the goals set by the Paris conference. The Paris Agreement also opened up new prospects for France and China in deepening cooperation in such areas as green growth and civil nuclear energy. The French side agrees to strengthen bilateral cooperation in international affairs and will fully support the Chinese side in hosting the 2016 G20 Summit in Hangzhou.

新闻背景：2015年12月14日晚，国家主席习近平应约同法国总统奥朗德通电话。双方就巴黎气候大会的成功召开和中法两国加强各方面合作交换了意见。范例三选自外交部网站对此所作的双语报道，译文略有修改。

原文链接：http://www.fmprc.gov.cn/web/wjdt_674879/gjldrhd_674881/t1324320.shtml

译文链接：http://www.fmprc.gov.cn/mfa_eng/wjdt_665385/wshd_665389/t1324810.shtml

一、范例三文本结构分析（Text Structure Analysis of Sample III）

国家元首之间的通话要经过事先通报、提前约定。领导人表达通话意愿后，两国的外交部门认真协调、商定时间，双方达成一致后，两国领导人才能按照约定的时间与对方进行通话。通常，两国领导人遇到一些事务需要直接商谈，或需要了解对方对某些问题的看法，但又不能马上会面时就会采用打电话的方式进行沟通。近年来，特别是习近平就任国家主席以来，我国领导人与外国领导人的交流更加频繁，这一方面表明我国在国际事务中的影响力越来越大，其他国家越来越重视中国对国际问题的看法，更需要及时与中国沟通；另一方面也反映出我国领导人越来越主动地参与国际事务，通过电话与其他国家的领导人保持交流，展现我国积极沟通、积极解决问题的"积极外交"姿态。

范例三是典型的有关国家领导人之间通电话的报道。导语部分交代通话的时间和通话双方，主体部分介绍通话的主要内容。中方所作的报道一般先介绍中方领导人的谈话内容，再给出对方领导人所作的回应。

二、范例三翻译解析（Translation Analysis of Sample III）

对于外国领导人的名字，中文通常不出现全名，而是约定俗成地保留名和姓其中之一，再加上头衔，如"德国总理默克尔"，"前美国国务卿希拉里"，"英国首相卡梅伦"等。而在英文中，尤其是人名首次在文中出现时，一般写全名，如"German Chancellor Angela Merkel"，"Former Secretary of State Hillary Rodham Clinton"，"British Prime Minister David Cameron"。再次出现时，可按照中文译名习惯保留姓或名，也可使用全名。范例三中的"奥朗德"一律用了全名Francois Hollande。

第二段第二句按字面理解是主语"巴黎大会"加三个谓语："巴黎大会①成功通过《巴黎协定》；②为2020年后全球合作应对气候变化指明了方向；③具有历史性意义"。但结合上下文与新闻背景，真正实现②和③的是《巴黎协定》而非巴黎大会，因而该句译为英文时，可将主语调整为"巴黎大会上通过的《巴黎协定》。"第二段第三句中，中方"支持法方办好大会"的具体表现形式或者方式为"与法方及有关各方密切沟通"。鉴于这一层逻辑关系，这两个短语不可简单地处理成并列关系，而应将"与法方及有关各方密切沟通"处理为方式状语，修饰谓语动词support。第四句主语为"中法双方"，在本篇报道的上下文语境中，"双方"所指代的对象非常明确，后续翻译中可以不再出现"中法"两国国名字样,而是改用the two countries等表述方式。

第三段继续介绍习近平主席在通电话过程中所做作的表态。因为习主席在电话中所表达的希望是一般事实，不是过去一次性发生的动作，故而谓语动词用一般现在时。本段最后一句中，"中方愿同法方加强在二十国集团框架内合作"是前提，"共同促进全球经济增长"是希望达成的效果，因此使用连接词so as to表明句子的逻辑关系。

第四段第三句，奥朗德对《巴黎协定》做出了高度评价，称它"有力度、有雄心"，并且"符合国际社会共同利益"。如果按照原句语序处理，会出现谓语动词从be动词到实义动词的切换：The Paris Agreement is strong and ambitious, and conforms to the common interests of the international community。译文将原句中作表语的两个形容词改为主语的前置定语，译为The strong and ambitious Paris Agreement conforms to the common interests of the international community，可以使表达更加简洁有力。

外交函电报道的翻译

Translation for Coverage of Diplomatic Correspondence

三、外交通话报道常用表达及翻译（Translation of Frequently Used Expressions in Coverage of Telephone Talks Between Political Leaders）

外交部公布的两国领导人或国际组织领导人之间通电话的信息多使用"××（应约）与××（头衔加人名）通电话"的表达方式，即×× holds telephone talks with ×× (at/upon request)。通话事由一般不在标题中体现。参见下列标题及翻译：

王毅应约同美国国务卿克里通电话
                  (http://world.people.com.cn/n1/2016/0108/c157278-28027041.html)
Wang Yi *Holds Telephone Talks at Request* with Secretary of State John Kerry of US
         (http://www.fmprc.gov.cn/mfa_eng/wjdt_665385/wshd_665389/t1326773.shtml)

习近平同越共中央总书记阮富仲通电话
                  (http://politics.people.com.cn/n/2015/0211/c1024-26550053.html)
Xi Jinping *Holds Telephone Talks* with General Secretary Nguyen Phu Trong of the Central Committee of the Communist Party of Viet Nam
                (http://www.fmprc.gov.cn/mfa_eng/zxxx_662805/t1237502.shtml)

国家主席习近平应约同美国总统特朗普通电话
          (http://www.fmprc.gov.cn/web/wjdt_674879/gjldrhd_674881/t1557718.shtml)
President Xi Jinping held telephone talks at request with President Donald Trump of the United States (US).
          (http://www.fmprc.gov.cn/mfa_eng/wjdt_665385/wshd_665389/t1558195.shtml)

李克强应约同国际货币基金组织总裁拉加德通电话
          (http://www.fmprc.gov.cn/web/wjdt_674879/gjldrhd_674881/t1336045.shtml)
Li Keqiang *Holds Telephone Talks* with IMF Managing Director Christine Lagarde *at Request*
              (http://www.fmprc.gov.cn/mfa_eng/zxxx_662805/t1336812.shtml)

领导人通电话内容多为就近期两国关系、地区及国际重大事务发表看法、交换意见。下列例句中的斜体部分标注出了外交通话报道中常见的一些表达：

2018年5月4日，国家主席习近平应约同韩国总统文在寅通电话。

习近平指出，当前，中韩关系保持良好发展态势，我同总统先生达成的各项共识正在逐步得到落实。中方高度重视中韩关系，愿同韩方加强沟通，深化务实合作，推进人文交流，使中韩关系朝着符合双方共同利益的方向稳步前进。
                  (http://www.fmprc.gov.cn/web/zyxw/t1556767.shtml)

On May 4, 2018, President Xi Jinping held telephone talks *at request* with President Moon Jae-in of the Republic of Korea (ROK).

Xi Jinping *pointed out* that at present, the relations between China and the ROK have *maintained a sound momentum* of development. The various consensus reached by Mr. President and me is being gradually implemented. China attaches great importance to bilateral relations and is willing to, together with the ROK, strengthen communication, deepen practical cooperation, and promote people-to-people and cultural exchanges so that China-ROK relations could steadily move forward in the direction that is in line with *the common interests of both sides.*

(http://www.fmprc.gov.cn/mfa_eng/wjdt_665385/wshd_665389/t1557482.shtml)

2016年1月28日上午，国务院总理李克强应约同国际货币基金组织总裁拉加德通电话，就世界和中国经济金融形势等问题深入交换意见。

(http://www.fmprc.gov.cn/web/wjdt_674879/gjldrhd_674881/t1336045.shtml)

On the morning of January 28, 2016, Premier Li Keqiang held telephone talks with Managing Director of the International Monetary Fund (IMF) Christine Lagarde at request, *exchanging in-depth views on* economic and financial situation in China and the world at large.

(http://www.fmprc.gov.cn/mfa_eng/zxxx_662805/t1336812.shtml)

2016年1月21日下午，国务院总理李克强应约同德国总理默克尔通电话，就中德关系以及双方共同关心的国际和地区问题交换意见。

(http://www.fmprc.gov.cn/web/wjdt_674879/gjldrhd_674881/t1333745.shtml)

On the afternoon of January 21, 2016, Premier Li Keqiang held telephone talks with Chancellor Angela Merkel of Germany at request, *exchanging views on* China-Germany relations and *international and regional issues of common concern.*

(http://gr.china-embassy.org/eng/zgyw/t1334588.htm)

2015年11月24日，国务委员杨洁篪应约同美国国务卿克里通电话。双方均表示，中美两国将同法国及其他各方一道，为即将举行的气候变化巴黎大会取得成功作出贡献。

(http://www.fmprc.gov.cn/web/wjdt_674879/gjldrhd_674881/t1317811.shtml)

On November 24, 2015, State Councilor Yang Jiechi held telephone talks with Secretary of State John Kerry of the US at request. *Both sides said that* China and the US will work with France and other sides to contribute to the success of the forthcoming UN Climate Change Conference in Paris.

(http://www.fmprc.gov.cn/mfa_eng/zxxx_662805/t1318566.shtml)

此外，这类报道中还有如下动词经常出现："指出"（note/point out）、"表示"（express）、"强调"（stress/emphasize）和"表示赞赏"（appreciate）等。

外交函电报道的翻译
Translation for Coverage of Diplomatic Correspondence

15 UNIT

学生译作讲评
Analysis of Students' Translation Practice

原文链接：http://news.xinhuanet.com/world/2014-12/03/c_1113508952.htm

新闻原文：习近平同欧洲理事会主席图斯克通电话

学生译文：Xi Jinping Talks over Phone with President Donald Tusk of European Council

翻译评析：学生译文表达不够规范。国家或国际组织领导人之间"通电话"不是一般意义上的talk over phone，而是"进行电话会谈"（hold telephone talks/conversation）。可改译为：Xi Jinping Holds Telephone Talks with President Donald Tusk of European Council。

新闻原文：2014年12月3日，国家主席习近平应约同新一届欧洲理事会主席图斯克通电话。

学生译文：On December 3, 2014, President Xi Jinping, at request, talked over phone with the new President of the European Council, Donald Tusk.

翻译评析：与标题类似，学生译文首先是选词正式程度不够。"talked over the phone"是指非正式的通电话，用于一般的个人之间。而一国领导人与其他国家或国际组织领导人"通电话"，其实指的是"电话会谈/对话"，是一个比较正式的外交概念，规范的表达应为hold a telephone talk/conversation。其次，at request取"应约"之意时，多用于at sb.'s request或at the request of sb.结构。既然原文没有具体提到应谁之约，译文最好选择可以单独使用的upon request。最后是头衔翻译的问题。鉴于图斯克的头衔较长（"新一届欧洲理事会主席"），可将"the new President of the European Council, Donald Tusk"改为人名在前、头衔在后的顺序，即Donald Tusk, the new President of the European Council，阅读起来更加流畅。如果通话对方头衔较短，则不受此限制，如U.S. President Barack Obama。

新闻原文：图斯克表示，我感谢习近平主席在我就任之际发来贺电并应约同我通话，这体现了习近平主席对欧中关系的高度重视。我愿意同习近平主席保持良好工作关系，期待着早日同习近平主席会面。

学生译文：Tusk said that he thanked President Xi Jinping for sending a message of congratulation on the occasion of his new appointment and holding a telephone conversation with him at request, which reflect that President Xi Jinping pays high attention to Europe-China relations. He was willing to maintain a good working relationship with President Xi Jinping and was looking forward to meeting with him soon.

翻译评析："在……之际"表明贺电事由，"on the occasion of"表达略显啰唆，介词"upon"即可体现这一层意思，即upon his new appointment。文中指明图斯克已经"就任"，而不仅仅是得到任命（"appointment"），可选用assume office的名词形式office assumption。此次通电话是由图斯克方发出的邀请，因此本段中的"应约"不同于

379

外交新闻汉英翻译
C-E TRANSLATION OF DIPLOMATIC NEWS

第一段的"应约",指习近平主席接受他的邀约(accept his request)。"体现"一词的宾语中心词是"高度重视",在译文中应突出这一点。可将reflect之后的宾语从句改为名词短语,即reflect the great importance that President Xi Jinping attaches to…。在冠词的选择上,a good working relationship与the good working relationship虽然仅是一个冠词之差,但表达的意思却有较大区别:前者泛指"(一种)良好的工作关系",并不能说明目前双方关系的现状;而后者则包含了"(现有的这种)良好的工作关系"的意思,更能拉近双方的距离。"欧中关系"中的"欧",不是地理概念上的欧洲,而是欧盟这一国家共同体,因此不可用Europe,而要用European Union (EU)。学生译文中所有的"欧"均指向欧洲,类似错误以下不再赘述。语法方面,which的先行词是"习近平主席向图斯克发贺电并应约与他通电话"一事,是单数概念,因而后面的谓语动词应用单数第三人称形式(reflects)。此外,习主席应约与图斯克通电话一事是过去发生的,应选用一般过去时,但双方在电话会谈中所做出的致谢和表达的期望却不以时间为转移。因此,"感谢""愿意""期望"等三个动词均应选用一般现在时。

新闻原文:习近平指出,中欧都是世界格局中的重要力量,中欧关系非常重要。今年春天我访问欧盟总部,同时任欧盟领导人确定共同打造和平、增长、改革、文明四大伙伴关系,为中欧关系发展作出了规划,这一共识正得到有效落实。

学生译文:Xi Jinping pointed out that since both China and Europe are important power in the world pattern, China-Europe relations are of great significance. When visiting the headquarters of the European Union (EU) this spring, I have confirmed with then leaders of the EU to jointly develop four major partnerships for peace, growth, reform and civilization, charting the course for the development of the China-Europe relations. This consensus is being effectively put into practice.

翻译评析:首先,第一句中的"中欧都是世界格局中的重要力量,中欧关系非常重要"两层意思之间是并列关系。学生译文用since一词连接,意思变成了"因为中欧是世界格局中的重要力量,所以中欧关系非常重要",但原句并没有这样的因果关系。可改译为:China and the EU are both vital forces in the world pattern and the China-EU relationship is very important。

新闻原文:明年是中欧建交40周年,中欧关系正进入承前启后、成熟稳定、蓬勃发展的新时期。我愿同你一道努力,保持中欧高层交往和各领域密切交流势头,继续推进中欧合作2020战略规划,实现互利共赢,加强在重大国际地区问题上的沟通和协调,在全球层面体现中欧关系的战略性,推动中欧全面战略伙伴关系持续健康稳定发展。

学生译文:Next year will be the 40th anniversary of the establishment of diplomatic relationship between China and the EU, and China-Europe relations are entering into a new period featured by transitional, mature, stable, and booming nature. I am willing to work together with you to promote sustained, healthy and stable development of China-Europe comprehensive strategic partnership by maintaining the momentum of high-level interactions between China and the EU and close exchanges in all fields, keeping carrying forward the China-EU 2020 Strategic Agenda for Cooperation to achieve win-win results, and strengthening communication and coordination on major international and regional issues to embody a strategic China-Europe relations at a global level.

翻译评析：看到"中欧关系正进入承前启后、成熟稳定、蓬勃发展的新时期"一句中的三个四字词，译员首先会考虑将其翻译成结构相同、字数接近的英文并列词或短语。但仔细分析这三个四字词的结构，可以看到："承前启后"表示"连接过去与未来"（link the past and the future），"成熟稳定"是两个独立的概念（maturity, stability），而"蓬勃发展"则是一个"形容词+名词"的偏正短语（vigorous development）。因此，要将这三个四字词译为形式上对仗工整的并列结构并不容易。出于上述考虑，在翻译时应优先保证原词意思的准确传达，而不应执着于形式的对仗。可将其译为：The China-EU relationship is now stepping into a new era linking the past and the future and featuring maturity, stability and vigorous development。本段翻译的一大重点和难点是"保持中欧高层交往和各领域密切交流势头，继续推进中欧合作2020战略规划，实现互利共赢，加强在重大国际地区问题上的沟通和协调，在全球层面体现中欧关系的战略性，推动中欧全面战略伙伴关系持续健康稳定发展"这一长句的处理。经过深入的分析和梳理，可以将这句话分为如下四个层次：①保持中欧高层交往和各领域密切交流势头；②继续推进中欧合作2020战略规划，以实现互利共赢；③加强在重大国际地区问题上的沟通和协调，从而在全球层面体现中欧关系的战略性；④推动中欧全面战略伙伴关系持续健康稳定发展。这四个层次之间是并列关系，学生译文将第四点作为最终目的，其他三点作为手段，这样的理解是不准确的。可将其改译为：I am willing to make joint efforts with you to keep the momentum of China-EU high-level exchanges and close communication in various fields, continue to promote the China-EU 2020 Strategic Agenda for Cooperation for mutual benefits and win-win results, enhance communication and coordination on major international and regional issues to reflect the strategic importance of the China-EU relationship at the global level, and promote the China-EU comprehensive strategic partnership for continuous, sound and stable development。注意，本句中的"互利"（mutual benefits）与"共赢"(win-win results)是两个独立的概念，不可省略任何一个。用词方面，"Next year will be …"选词不够庄重，可将be改为mark，译为Next year marks the 40th anniversary of the establishment of the diplomatic relationship between China and the EU。语法方面，"then leader"之前要加上定冠词the。

新闻原文：图斯克表示，习近平主席对欧盟总部的访问取得成功，为欧中关系发展奠定了基础。加强欧中四大伙伴关系，对双方、对世界都具有重大意义。欧方愿以明年欧中建交40周年为契机，同中方加强政治交往，扩大各领域务实合作，共同推动欧中全面战略伙伴关系发展。

学生译文：Tusk said that President Xi Jinping's successful visit to the headquarters of the EU has laid a foundation for the development of Europe-China relations. It is of great significance for China and the EU as well as the world to strengthen the four major partnerships between China and the EU. The EU is willing to take the opportunity of the 40th anniversary of the establishment of the diplomatic relationship between the EU and China to strengthen political exchanges with China and expand practical cooperation in all fields so as to promote the development of Europe-China comprehensive strategic partnership.

翻译评析：学生译文第二句选用it作为形式主语，将实际主语"加强欧中四大伙伴关系"翻译为动词不定式短语to strengthen the four major partnerships between China and the EU，语义和语法上并无错误。但出于使表达简洁清楚、不引起歧义的考虑，保留原句的结构、将上述短语直接用作英文句子的主语更好。可改译为：Enhancing the four major partnerships between the EU and China is of great significance to both sides and to the world at large。在上文已经多次提到中国与欧盟的情况下，第二句中的"双方"用both sides表示即可，不需要将China和EU再次重复。另外，时间概念一定要明确。第三句"以明年欧中建交40周年为契机"中的"明年"切不可漏掉，即补充为：The EU is willing to take the opportunity of the 40th anniversary of the establishment of the EU-China diplomatic relationship next year to … 。最后，标点使用要规范。应在译文第三句中表示目的的连接词"so as to …"之前加上逗号。

实战练习
Translation Practice

一、请翻译下列外交函电报道的标题（Translate the following headlines of reports on diplomatic correspondences）

1. 习近平致电祝贺班达里就任尼泊尔新总统
   (http://news.xinhuanet.com/2015-11/02/c_1117017114.htm)
2. 习近平致信祝贺2015中非媒体领袖峰会召开
   (http://cpc.people.com.cn/n/2015/1202/c64094-27878818.html)
3. 习近平就贝宁前总统克雷库逝世向贝宁总统亚伊致唁电
   (http://news.xinhuanet.com/world/2015-10/21/c_1116891278.htm)
4. 习近平致申办冬奥会代表团的贺信
   (http://politics.people.com.cn/n/2015/0801/c1024-27394803.html)
5. 李克强就哥伦比亚山体滑坡向桑托斯总统致慰问电
   (http://news.xinhuanet.com/2015-05/20/c_1115353726.htm)
6. 国家主席习近平应约同英国首相特雷莎·梅通电话。
   (http://www.fmprc.gov.cn/web/zyxw/t1552545.shtml)

外交函电报道的翻译

Translation for Coverage of Diplomatic Correspondence

7. 李克强总理和萨摩亚总理图伊拉埃帕互致贺电 庆祝中萨建交40周年
   (http://politics.people.com.cn/n/2015/1106/c1024-27787471.html)
8. 李克强总理就尼泊尔地震向尼泊尔总理柯伊拉腊致慰问电
   (http://news.xinhuanet.com/world/2015-04-25/c_127733244.htm)
9. 李克强应约同希腊总理齐普拉斯通电话
   (http://news.xinhuanet.com/world/2015-02-12/c_1114351548.htm)
10. 习近平主席和印尼总统佐科分别向中印尼副总理级人文交流机制首次会议致贺信
    (http://politics.people.com.cn/n/2015/0528/c1024-27066780.html)

二、请翻译下列外交函电报道中的句子（Translate the following sentences in reports on diplomatic correspondences）

1. 陈庆炎在贺电中表示，新中建交25年来，双边关系不断发展，两国人民友谊日益紧密。我期待着同阁下携手努力，以牢固的双边关系为基础，进一步深化拓展双边合作，更好地造福两国人民。
   (http://www.fmprc.gov.cn/web/wjdt_674879/gjldrhd_674881/t1303434.shtml)
2. 习近平表示，惊悉贵国发生强烈地震，造成人员和财产严重损失。我谨代表中国政府和人民，并以我个人的名义，对不幸遇难者表示沉痛的哀悼，对遇难者家属和受伤人员表示诚挚的慰问。我相信，在总统女士和智利政府坚强领导下，智利人民一定能够战胜灾害，重建家园。
   (http://www.fmprc.gov.cn/web/wjdt_674879/gjldrhd_674881/t1298357.shtml)
3. 习近平在贺电中说，瑞士是最早同新中国建交的西方国家之一。建交65年来，中瑞友谊历久弥新，各领域务实合作成果丰硕。中方高度重视中瑞友好合作关系，相信在双方共同努力下，中瑞关系将取得更大发展，更好造福两国和两国人民。
   (http://www.fmprc.gov.cn/web/wjdt_674879/gjldrhd_674881/t1296479.shtml)
4. 2015年11月11日，国务院总理李克强就德国前总理施密特不幸逝世向德国总理默克尔致唁电，代表中国政府和人民并以个人的名义，向德方表示深切哀悼，向施密特家人表示诚挚慰问。
   (http://www.fmprc.gov.cn/web/wjdt_674879/gjldrhd_674881/t1314035.shtml)
5. 国务院总理李克强20日同阿富汗首席执行官阿卜杜拉互致贺电，热烈庆祝两国建交60周年暨"中阿友好合作年"。
   (http://news.xinhuanet.com/politics/2015-01-20/c_1114065154.htm)
6. 特鲁多在致辞中感谢李克强总理专门发来贺信。特鲁多说，大熊猫幼仔出生适逢加中建交45周年，这是两国人民友谊与合作的象征。加拿大政府高度重视发展对华关系。加方愿同中方一道努力，加强两国高级别交往，深化经贸、人文等广泛领域合作，推动加中关系不断取得新进展。
   (http://www.fmprc.gov.cn/web/wjdt_674879/gjldrhd_674881/t1346065.shtml)

三、请翻译下列一则外交函电报道（Translate the following report on diplomatic correspondence）

李克强致信祝贺匈塞铁路项目塞尔维亚段正式启动

2015年12月23日，国务院总理李克强致信祝贺匈塞铁路项目塞尔维亚段正式启动。塞尔维亚总理武契奇出席启动仪式并致辞。

李克强在贺信中表示，匈塞铁路作为中国同塞尔维亚、匈牙利三方合作的旗舰项目，它的启动标志着中、匈、塞合作迈出新的重要步伐，也表明中国同中东欧国家务实合作站在了新的历史起点上。

李克强指出，中方愿同塞方以及匈方携手努力，按照业已达成的共识和协定，扎实高效推进匈塞铁路项目建设，确保高质量按期完工，力争早日通车。相信这不仅将有力推动地区基础设施建设和互联互通，增进当地人们福祉，促进欧洲一体化进程，也有利于更好对接中欧发展战略，深化中欧国际产能与投资等重点领域合作，实现互利共赢。

武契奇在致辞中表示，感谢塞中双方工作团队为匈塞铁路项目推进付出的辛勤努力，并表示，匈塞铁路项目的启动，是塞中务实合作的又一个重大突破，也是两国战略伙伴关系水平进一步提升的充分体现，对"16+1合作"深入发展具有重要意义。匈塞铁路大大拉近了塞与欧洲中心地带的距离，有助于将塞打造成为地区交通、物流枢纽。塞尔维亚愿与中国伙伴继续共同努力，确保实现匈塞铁路2018年通车的目标。

(http://www.fmprc.gov.cn/web/wjdt_674879/gjldrhd_674881/t1327564.shtml)

参考译文
Versions for Reference

一、请翻译下列外交函电报道的标题（Translate the following headlines of reports on diplomatic correspondences）

1. Xi Jinping Sends Message Congratulating Bidhya Devi Bhandari on Assuming Office as New President of Nepal
2. Xi Jinping Sends Message to Congratulate on Opening of 2015 China-Africa Media Summit
3. Xi Jinping Sends Message of Condolences to Benin President Thomas Yayi Boni over the death of Former President Mathieu Kérékou of Benin
4. Xi Jinping's Congratulatory Message to the Delegation of Winter Olympics Bidding

外交函电报道的翻译
Translation for Coverage of Diplomatic Correspondence 15 UNIT

5. Li Keqiang Sends Message of Condolences to President Juan Manuel Santos over Landslide in Colombia
6. President Xi Jinping held telephone talks at request with Prime Minister Theresa May of the United Kingdom (UK).
7. Premier Li Keqiang and Prime Minister Tuilaepa Sailele Malielegaoi of Samoa Exchange Congratulatory Messages on 40th Anniversary of the Establishment of China-Samoa Diplomatic Relations
8. Premier Li Keqiang Sends Message of Condolences to Prime Minister Sushil Koirala over the Earthquake in Nepal
9. Li Keqiang Holds Telephone Talks with Prime Minister Alexis Tsipras of Greece at Request
10. President Xi Jinping and President Joko Widodo of Indonesia Send Congratulatory Letters to the First Meeting of the Cultural and People-to-people Exchanges Mechanism (PEM) Between China and Indonesia at the Vice Premier's Level

二、请翻译下列外交函电报道中的句子（Translate the following sentences in reports on diplomatic correspondences）

1. Tony Tan Keng Yam noted in the message that Singapore-China relations are developing continuously since the establishment of bilateral diplomatic relationship 25 years ago, and the friendship between the two peoples is becoming increasingly close. He looks forward to, together with President Xi Jinping, further deepening and expanding bilateral cooperation on the basis of solid bilateral relations to better benefit the two peoples.
2. Xi Jinping said that I was shocked to learn that your country was hit by the violent earthquake which caused heavy causalities and loss of property. On behalf of the Chinese government and people and in my own name, I would like to extend profound condolences to the victims and sincere sympathies to the bereaved families and the injured. I believe that under the strong leadership of Mme. President and the Chilean government, the Chilean people will surely overcome the disaster and rebuild their homes.
3. Xi noted that Switzerland was among the first Western countries to forge diplomatic relations with the People's Republic of China. The vigorous bilateral relations have been constantly enhanced over the past 65 years and remarkable achievements have been scored in pragmatic cooperation in various areas, Xi said. China attaches great importance to the development of its friendly relations with Switzerland, said Xi, who expressed the belief that greater progress will be made with joint efforts for the benefits of the two countries and two peoples.

4. On November 11, 2015, Chinese Premier Li Keqiang sent a message of condolences to his German counterpart, Angela Merkel, over the death of Helmut Schmidt, a former chancellor of the Federal Republic of Germany. In the message, Li, on behalf of the Chinese government and people and in his own name, mourned the death of Schmidt and extended sympathies to Schmidt's family.

5. On January 20, 2015, Premier Li Keqiang and Chief Executive Officer Abdullah Abdullah of Afghanistan exchanged congratulatory messages, warmly celebrating the 60th anniversary of the establishment of the bilateral diplomatic relationship as well as the Year for China-Afghanistan Friendly Cooperation.

6. In his speech, Canadian Prime Minister Justin Trudeau expressed his gratitude to Premier Li for the latter's letter of congratulation. The birth of the twin panda cubs, which coincided with the 45th anniversary of the establishment of full diplomatic relations between Canada and China, is a symbol of the friendship and cooperation between the Canadian and Chinese peoples, said Trudeau. The Canadian government attaches great importance to the development of its relations with China and is willing to work together with China to enhance trade and economic cooperation and exchange more high-level visits between the two nations, said the Canadian leader.

三、请翻译下列一则外交函电报道（Translate the following report on diplomatic correspondence）

Li Keqiang Sends Message to Congratulate on Official Launch of the Serbian Section of the Hungary–Serbia Railway Project

On December 23, 2015, Premier Li Keqiang sent a message to congratulate on the official launch of the Serbian section of the Hungary-Serbia railway project. Prime Minister Aleksandar Vucic of Serbia attended and addressed the launch ceremony.

Li Keqiang noted in the congratulatory message that the launch of the Hungary-Serbia railway, which is a flagship project of trilateral cooperation among China, Serbia and Hungary, represents that cooperation among the three countries has taken a new and important step forward and indicates that China's practical cooperation with the Central and Eastern European countries has stood at a new historical starting point.

Li Keqiang pointed out that the Chinese side stands ready to make joint efforts with the Serbian side and the Hungarian side to earnestly and efficiently advance the construction of the Hungary-Serbia railway project according to consensus and agreements concluded, in a bid to ensure high-quality completion as scheduled and opening of the railway as early as possible. It is believed that this will not only vigorously boost infrastructure construction and connectivity in the region, increase the local people's benefits and facilitate the European integration process, but also help better dovetail the development strategies of China and Europe as well as deepen China-EU cooperation in international production capacity, investment and other key areas for mutual benefits and win-win results.

Aleksandar Vucic expressed in his address appreciation for the arduous efforts made by both Chinese and Serbian work teams to push ahead the Hungary-Serbia railway project, noting that the launch of the project is another major breakthrough in Serbia-China practical cooperation. It is also full manifestation of the further enhancement of the strategic partnership between the two countries and bears great significance to the in-depth development of the "16+1" cooperation. The Hungary-Serbia railway significantly brings Serbia closer to the heartland of Europe, and will help build Serbia into a regional pivot of transportation and logistics. Serbia stands ready to continuously work together with its partner China to ensure the goal of opening the Hungary-Serbia railway by 2018.

单元小结
Summary

本单元主要介绍了外交函电报道的翻译。目前最常见的外交函电形式为国家领导人就他国领导人当选就职、重大国际活动的举办、他国（前）领导人逝世、地震洪水、恐怖袭击等事由向其他国家领导人、国际组织、国际会议主办方等发出贺信、贺电、唁电、慰问电等，以及不同国家领导人之间就两国关系及国际与地区事务通电话等。有关外交函电的新闻报道一般结构相对简单，多在导语部分简要说明发函时间及函电事由，主体部分具体介绍函电内容。此类报道的标题格式相对固定，常用表达也较多，但在翻译涉及具体事由的部分时仍须注意人名和地名的拼写、头衔的表达等。总之，有关外交函电的报道形式单一但内容多样，翻译时虽有一定的套路可以遵循，但仍需要译者认真谨慎，仔细查证。

世界主要国家外交机构及外交职衔
Diplomatic Organs and Diplomatic Titles in Major Countries

（一）中华人民共和国外交机关

国家对外进行外交交往的机关分为：国内的外交机关与派往国外的外交机关。

国内的中央外交机关包括：国家元首、政府首脑和外交部。

派遣到国外的外交机关分为：常驻的外交机关与临时的外交机关。

常驻的外交机关依其馆长的级别分为三级：大使馆、公使馆和代办处。

大使馆是最高级的外交代表机关，由大使领导；公使馆是第二级的代表机关，由公使领导；代办处是最低级的外交代表机关，由代办领导。

广义的常驻外交代表机关还有向国际组织派遣的代表团办事处。

临时的外交机关指派往国外执行临时性任务的外交代表团（或称使团）。临时的外交机关又分为参加外国庆典的礼节性使团，与出席国际会议、进行谈判、签订条约等的政治性使团。它们一般由大使、特使或代表团团长领导。

（二）中华人民共和国驻外外交机构

中华人民共和国驻外外交机构包括中华人民共和国驻外国的使馆、领馆以及常驻联合国等政府间国际组织的代表团等代表机构。

1. 使馆 Embassy

大使馆是一国在建交国首都派驻的常设外交代表机关。大使馆代表整个国家的利益，全面负责两国关系，馆长一般是大使，也可以是公使或者其他等级的由派遣国委派的外交人员，由国家元首任命并作为国家元首的代表履行职责。大使馆的首要职责是代表派遣国，促进两国的政治关系，其次是促进经济、文化、教育、科技、军事等方面的关系，使馆同时具有领事职能。大使馆的职责范围遍及驻在国各个地区，领事馆则负责所辖地区。大使馆通常受政府和外交部门的直接领导，而领事馆通常接受外交部门和所在国大使馆的双重领导。

亚洲：

驻阿富汗大使馆

EMBASSY OF THE PEOPLE'S REPUBLIC OF CHINA IN THE ISLAMIC REPUBLIC OF AFGHANISTAN

驻大韩民国大使馆

EMBASSY OF THE PEOPLE'S REPUBLIC OF CHINA IN THE REPUBLIC OF KOREA

世界主要国家外交机构及外交职衔
Diplomatic Organs and Diplomatic Titles in Major Countries

驻日本国大使馆
EMBASSY OF THE PEOPLE'S REPUBLIC OF CHINA IN JAPAN

驻印度尼西亚共和国大使馆
EMBASSY OF THE PEOPLE'S REPUBLIC OF CHINA IN THE REPUBLIC OF INDONESIA

驻朝鲜民主主义人民共和国大使馆
EMBASSY OF THE PEOPLE'S REPUBLIC OF CHINA IN THE DEMOCRATIC PEOPLE'S REPUBLIC OF KOREA

非洲：

驻南非共和国大使馆
EMBASSY OF THE PEOPLE'S REPUBLIC OF CHINA IN THE REPUBLIC OF SOUTH AFRICA

驻刚果民主共和国大使馆
EMBASSY OF THE PEOPLE'S REPUBLIC OF CHINA IN THE DEMOCRATIC REPUBLIC OF CONGO

驻刚果共和国大使馆
EMBASSY OF THE PEOPLE'S REPUBLIC OF CHINA IN THE REPUBLIC OF CONGO

驻苏丹共和国大使馆
EMBASSY OF THE PEOPLE'S REPUBLIC OF CHINA IN THE REPUBLIC OF THE SUDAN

驻津巴布韦共和国大使馆
EMBASSY OF THE PEOPLE'S REPUBLIC OF CHINA IN THE REPUBLIC OF ZIMBABWE

欧洲：

驻比利时王国大使馆
EMBASSY OF THE PEOPLE'S REPUBLIC OF CHINA IN THE KINGDOM OF BELGIUM

驻德意志联邦共和国大使馆
EMBASSY OF THE PEOPLE'S REPUBLIC OF CHINA IN THE FEDERAL REPUBLIC OF GERMANY

驻意大利共和国大使馆
EMBASSY OF THE PEOPLE'S REPUBLIC OF CHINA IN THE REPUBLIC OF ITALY

驻大不列颠及北爱尔兰联合王国大使馆
EMBASSY OF THE PEOPLE'S REPUBLIC OF CHINA IN THE UNITED KINGDOM OF THE GREAT BRITAIN AND NORTHERN IRELAND

驻法兰西共和国大使馆
EMBASSY OF THE PEOPLE'S REPUBLIC OF CHINA IN THE REPUBLIC OF FRANCE

北美洲：

驻古巴共和国大使馆
EMBASSY OF THE PEOPLE'S REPUBLIC OF CHINA IN THE REPUBLIC OF CUBA

外交新闻汉英翻译
C-E TRANSLATION OF DIPLOMATIC NEWS

驻墨西哥合众国大使馆
EMBASSY OF THE PEOPLE'S REPUBLIC OF CHINA IN THE UNITED MEXICAN STATES
驻加拿大大使馆
EMBASSY OF THE PEOPLE'S REPUBLIC OF CHINA IN CANADA
驻美利坚合众国大使馆
EMBASSY OF THE PEOPLE'S REPUBLIC OF CHINA IN THE UNITED STATES OF AMERICA
驻特立尼达和多巴哥共和国大使馆
EMBASSY OF THE PEOPLE'S REPUBLIC OF CHINA IN THE REPUBLIC OF TRINIDAD AND TOBAGO

南美洲：
驻阿根廷共和国大使馆
EMBASSY OF THE PEOPLE'S REPUBLIC OF CHINA IN ARGENTINA
驻巴西联邦共和国大使馆
EMBASSY OF THE PEOPLE'S REPUBLIC OF CHINA IN THE FEDERATIVE REPUBLIC OF BRAZIL
驻厄瓜多尔共和国大使馆
EMBASSY OF THE PEOPLE'S REPUBLIC OF CHINA IN THE REPUBLIC OF ECUADOR
驻秘鲁共和国大使馆
EMBASSY OF THE PEOPLE'S REPUBLIC OF CHINA IN THE REPUBLIC OF PERU
驻哥伦比亚共和国大使馆
EMBASSY OF THE PEOPLE'S REPUBLIC OF CHINA IN THE REPUBLIC OF COLOMBIA

大洋洲：
驻澳大利亚大使馆
EMBASSY OF THE PEOPLE'S REPUBLIC OF CHINA IN AUSTRALIA
驻巴布亚新几内亚独立国大使馆
EMBASSY OF THE PEOPLE'S REPUBLIC OF CHINA IN PAPUA NEW GUINEA
驻新西兰大使馆
EMBASSY OF THE PEOPLE'S REPUBLIC OF CHINA IN NEW ZEALAND
驻汤加大使馆
EMBASSY OF THE PEOPLE'S REPUBLIC OF CHINA IN KINGDOM OF TONGA
驻斐济共和国大使馆
EMBASSY OF THE PEOPLE'S REPUBLIC OF CHINA IN THE REPUBLIC OF FIJI

2. 领事馆 Consulate
领事馆是一国驻在他国某个城市的领事代表机关的总称，有总领事馆（consulates general）、领事

世界主要国家外交机构及外交职衔
Diplomatic Organs and Diplomatic Titles in Major Countries

馆（consulate）、副领事馆（vice-consulate or consular agency）等，负责管理当地本国侨民和其他领事事务。许多国家在多数国家只设大使馆，不设领事馆。是否设领事馆以及设立领事馆的级别，主要看侨民和领事业务的多少以及所在地区的重要性，并依照对等原则进行。如中国在美国设有大使馆和5个总领事馆，负责各自辖区内的领事业务。在个别小国，外国只设领事馆和派驻领事官员。现今，中国在172个建交国设有165个大使馆、81个总领事馆。

亚洲：

驻迪拜总领事馆（阿联酋）
CONSULATE-GENERAL OF THE PEOPLE'S REPUBLIC OF CHINA IN DUBAI

驻大阪总领事馆（日本）
CONSULATE-GENERAL OF THE PEOPLE'S REPUBLIC OF CHINA IN OSAKA

驻古晋总领事馆（马来西亚）
CONSULATE-GENERAL OF THE PEOPLE'S REPUBLIC OF CHINA IN KUCHING

驻孟买总领事馆（印度）
CONSULATE-GENERAL OF THE PEOPLE'S REPUBLIC OF CHINA IN MUMBAI

驻清迈总领事馆（泰国）
CONSULATE-GENERAL OF THE PEOPLE'S REPUBLIC OF CHINA IN CHIANGMAI

非洲：

驻亚历山大总领事馆（埃及）
CONSULATE-GENERAL OF THE PEOPLE'S REPUBLIC OF CHINA IN ALEXANDRIA

驻约翰内斯堡总领事馆（南非）
CONSULATE-GENERAL OF THE PEOPLE'S REPUBLIC OF CHINA IN JOHANNESBURG

驻德班总领事馆（南非）
CONSULATE-GENERAL OF THE PEOPLE'S REPUBLIC OF CHINA IN DURBAN

驻拉各斯总领事馆（尼日利亚）
CONSULATE-GENERAL OF THE PEOPLE'S REPUBLIC OF CHINA IN LAGOS

驻桑给巴尔总领事馆（坦桑尼亚）
CONSULATE-GENERAL OF THE PEOPLE'S REPUBLIC OF CHINA IN ZANZIBAR

欧洲：

驻汉堡总领事馆（德国）
CONSULATE-GENERAL OF THE PEOPLE'S REPUBLIC OF CHINA IN HAMBURG

驻圣彼得堡总领事馆（俄罗斯）
CONSULATE-GENERAL OF THE PEOPLE'S REPUBLIC OF CHINA IN ST. PETERSBURG

驻里昂总领事馆（法国）
CONSULATE-GENERAL OF THE PEOPLE'S REPUBLIC OF CHINA IN LYON

C-E TRANSLATION OF DIPLOMATIC NEWS

驻米兰总领事馆（意大利）
CONSULATE-GENERAL OF THE PEOPLE'S REPUBLIC OF CHINA IN MILANO
驻曼彻斯特总领事馆（英国）
CONSULATE-GENERAL OF THE PEOPLE'S REPUBLIC OF CHINA IN MANCHESTER

北美洲：
驻多伦多总领事馆（加拿大）
CONSULATE-GENERAL OF THE PEOPLE'S REPUBLIC OF CHINA IN TORONTO
驻蒙特利尔总领事馆（加拿大）
CONSULATE-GENERAL OF THE PEOPLE'S REPUBLIC OF CHINA IN MONTREAL
驻纽约总领事馆（美国）
CONSULATE-GENERAL OF THE PEOPLE'S REPUBLIC OF CHINA IN NEW YORK
驻旧金山总领事馆（美国）
CONSULATE-GENERAL OF THE PEOPLE'S REPUBLIC OF CHINA IN SAN FRANCISCO
驻蒂华纳总领事馆（墨西哥）
CONSULATE-GENERAL OF THE PEOPLE'S REPUBLIC OF CHINA IN TIJUANA

南美洲：
驻里约热内卢总领事馆（巴西）
CONSULATE-GENERAL OF THE PEOPLE'S REPUBLIC OF CHINA IN RIO DE JANEIRO
驻圣保罗总领事馆（巴西）
CONSULATE-GENERAL OF THE PEOPLE'S REPUBLIC OF CHINA IN SAO PAULO
驻伊基克总领事馆（智利）
CONSULATE-GENERAL OF THE PEOPLE'S REPUBLIC OF CHINA IN IQUIQUE
驻巴兰基亚领事馆（哥伦比亚）
CONSULATE OF THE PEOPLE'S REPUBLIC OF CHINA IN BARRANQUILLA
驻瓜亚基尔总领事馆（厄瓜多尔）
CONSULATE-GENERAL OF THE PEOPLE'S REPUBLIC OF CHINA IN GUAYAQUIL

大洋洲：
驻阿德莱德总领事馆（澳大利亚）
CONSULATE-GENERAL OF THE PEOPLE'S REPUBLIC OF CHINA IN ADELAIDE
驻悉尼总领事馆（澳大利亚）
CONSULATE-GENERAL OF THE PEOPLE'S REPUBLIC OF CHINA IN SYDNEY
驻布里斯班总领事馆（澳大利亚）
CONSULATE-GENERAL OF THE PEOPLE'S REPUBLIC OF CHINA IN BRISBANE

世界主要国家外交机构及外交职衔
Diplomatic Organs and Diplomatic Titles in Major Countries

驻奥克兰总领事馆（新西兰）
CONSULATE-GENERAL OF THE PEOPLE'S REPUBLIC OF CHINA IN AUCKLAND
驻克赖斯特彻奇总领事馆（新西兰）
CONSULATE-GENERAL OF THE PEOPLE'S REPUBLIC OF CHINA IN CHRISTCHURCH

3. 驻外团、处 Chinese Missions to International Organizations and Representative Offices Abroad

中国常驻联合国日内瓦办事处和瑞士其他国际组织代表团（Permanent Mission of the People's Republic of China to the United Nations Office at Geneva and Other International Organizations in Switzerland），非正式简称"驻日内瓦代表团"或者"常驻联合国日内瓦办事处"，是中国外交部的一个常设驻外机构，其职责之一就是制订国际规则和国际标准。

中华人民共和国常驻联合国代表团（Permanent Mission of the People's Republic of China to the United Nations）是中华人民共和国政府派驻于美国纽约的常驻联合国总部的外交代表机构，隶属于中华人民共和国外交部。现任领导：常驻联合国代表刘结一（Permanent Representative to the UN: Ambassador Liu Jieyi）。

中国常驻维也纳联合国和其他国际组织代表团（Permanent Mission of the People's Republic of China to the United Nations and Other International Organizations in Vienna）是中国外交部常驻奥地利维也纳的外交机构。非正式简称"维也纳代表团"。由于联合国在维也纳设有办事处，维也纳有众多联合国机构和其他国际组织。中国常驻维也纳代表团主要履行与各国常驻联合国（维也纳）代表团、联合国办事处以及设在维也纳的政府间组织和非政府组织进行联络和处理各项日常事务的职能，特别是与各国在军控与防扩散及外空活动等议题展开磋商。

中国驻欧盟使团（Mission of the People's Republic of China to the European Union）是中国外交部常驻欧盟总部所在地比利时布鲁塞尔的外交机构。驻欧盟使团的前身是"驻欧共体使团"，自1975年正式成立以来，促进和推动了中欧关系的发展。1975年中欧正式建交，双方都迫切地希望推动双方的正常交往，所以驻欧共体使团应运而生。1993年欧洲联盟（欧盟）正式成立，驻欧共体使团随后改名为驻欧盟使团。中国驻欧盟使团的主要职责就是成为沟通中欧双方的桥梁，促进双方进一步增进相互了解和信任，为中欧关系的未来发展奠定更加坚实的基础。

中国驻东盟使团（Mission of the People's Republic of China to ASEAN）是中国常驻东南亚国家联盟（东盟）的外交机构。于2012年在雅加达设常驻团。中国设立驻东盟使团和派常驻大使，是加强与东盟机制化联系的重要举措，体现了中方对中国—东盟关系的重视，以推动中国—东盟战略伙伴关系不断取得新进展。

中国驻非盟使团（Mission of the People's Republic of China to the African Union），总部所在地埃塞俄比亚首都亚的斯亚贝巴。加强同非洲国家的团结合作是中国对外政策的重要基础。非盟是引领非洲国家团结进步的一面旗帜，在非洲经济社会发展、和平与安全和一体化进程中发挥日益重要的作用。

中华人民共和国常驻联合国亚洲及太平洋经济社会委员会代表处（Permanent Mission to the United Nations Economic and Social Commission for Asia and the Pacific（ESCAP））代表中国政府负责与ESCAP（联合国亚洲及太平洋经济社会委员会）交往、联系，协助中国国内有关单位出席ESCAP届会和各专题委员会会议，负责安排中国与 ESCAP 合作基金项目和中国参与 ESCAP 举办的各类培训、研讨活动等。1978年7月，中国向 ESCAP 派出常驻代表。

中华人民共和国常驻世界贸易组织代表团（Permanent Mission to the World Trade Organization (WTO) in Switzerland）是代表中国政府在世界贸易组织（WTO）行使权利和履行义务的常设机构。主要职责是代表中国政府处理与WTO秘书处及WTO成员常驻日内瓦代表机构之间的日常事务；参加WTO各机构在日内瓦总部举行的各类会议和磋商；根据授权，负责与WTO其他成员及其常驻日内瓦代表机构进行多、双边谈判、交涉和磋商；跟踪和审议其他成员贸易政策及其对WTO各个协定的执行情况；跟踪WTO法律框架发展动向；配合国内主管部门处理中国同其他成员的贸易争端；从事与多边贸易体制有关重要问题的调研，向国内提供有关信息、综合分析及建议，供主管部门决策时参考；承担中国政府交办的与WTO其他事务相关的各项任务。中国常驻世界贸易组织代表团于2002年1月28日在瑞士日内瓦正式挂牌，并开始代表中国政府行使职能。

中华人民共和国常驻禁止化学武器组织代表团（Permanent Missions to the Organization For the Prohibition of Chemical Weapons）是中华人民共和国常驻禁止化学武器组织的代表。《禁止化学武器公约》生效后，为更好地维护国家利益，中国政府于1997年5月正式设立常驻禁止化学武器代表团，常驻代表由驻荷兰大使兼任，就公约相关事务代表中国政府与禁止化学武器组织及其他缔约国代表团进行联系及交涉。现任常驻代表为张军大使，常驻副代表为陈凯参赞。

中华人民共和国常驻国际海底管理局代表处（Permanent Mission to the International Sea Bed Authority）是中华人民共和国常驻国际海底管理局的代表。国际海底管理局是《联合国海洋法公约》缔约国按照《公约》第十一部分和《关于执行〈公约〉第十一部分的协定》所确立的国际海底区域制度，组织和控制成员国在国家管辖范围外的深海底进行的活动，特别是管理该区域矿物资源的组织。管理局是一个独立的政府间组织。

中国海地贸易发展办事处（Office of Commercial Development of China in Haiti）于1997年1月在海地太子港正式挂牌成立，是中海两国高层领导共同努力的结果。1991年海地政变以来，中国在联合国一直支持和平解决海地问题，支持阿里斯蒂德总统回国恢复民主秩序。1996年2月普雷瓦尔总统致函江泽民主席，感谢中国政府始终不渝地支持海地恢复宪政秩序的进程，并希望加强两国之间的对话。7月，常驻联合国代表秦华孙应海地政府邀请访海，会见了海总统、总理、外长、议长等，并转交了江主席致海总统的复函。9月，两国政府签署互设商务办事处协议，钱其琛副总理兼外长出席签字仪式并与海方举行了会谈。中国海地贸易发展办事处成立以来，双边关系得到了进一步发展，双方往来有所增强。

（三）驻外外交人员的职务（外交职务和领事职务）

1. 外交职务分为

特命全权大使、代表、副代表、公使、公使衔参赞、参赞、一等秘书、二等秘书、三等秘书、随员。

2. 领事职务分为

总领事、副总领事、领事、副领事、领事随员。

世界主要国家外交机构及外交职衔
Diplomatic Organs and Diplomatic Titles in Major Countries

3. 驻外外交人员实行外交衔级

外交衔级设七级：大使衔、公使衔、参赞衔、一等秘书衔、二等秘书衔、三等秘书衔、随员衔。

4. 外交职务与外交衔级的基本对应关系

特命全权大使：大使衔；

代表、副代表：大使衔、公使衔、参赞衔；

公使、公使衔参赞：公使衔；

参赞：参赞衔；

一等秘书：一等秘书衔；

二等秘书：二等秘书衔；

三等秘书：三等秘书衔；

随员：随员衔。

5. 领事职务与外交衔级的基本对应关系

总领事：大使衔、公使衔、参赞衔；

副总领事：参赞衔；

领事：参赞衔、一等秘书衔、二等秘书衔；

副领事：三等秘书衔、随员衔；

领事随员：随员衔。

6. 馆长

馆长是驻外外交机构的行政首长，驻外外交机构实行馆长负责制。馆长统一领导驻外外交机构的各项工作。

特命全权大使为大使馆的馆长；

代表为常驻联合国等政府间国际组织的代表机构的馆长；

总领事为总领事馆的馆长；

领事为领事馆的馆长。

7. 外交官衔

特命全权大使　Ambassador Extraordinary and Plenipotentiary

公使　Minister

常驻代表　Permanent Representative

公使衔参赞　Minister-Counselor

参赞　Counselor

一等秘书　First Secretary

二等秘书　Second Secretary

三等秘书　Third Secretary

专员/随员　Attaché

代办　Charge d'Affaires

临时代办　Charge d'Affaires ad Interim

外交新闻汉英翻译
C-E TRANSLATION OF DIPLOMATIC NEWS

政务参赞　Political Counselor

商务参赞　Commercial Counselor

经济参赞　Economic Counselor

新闻文化参赞　Press and Cultural Counselor

商务代表　Trade Representative

武官　Military Attaché

档案秘书　Secretary-Archivist

总领事　Consul General

领事　Consul

（四）世界主要国家外交部及外交部长

外交部是主管国家对外事务的机关，在大多数国家称为外交部，但美国称为国务院，英国称为外交和联邦事务部，瑞士称为联邦外交事务部。

1. 美国国务院

美国国务院（United States Department of State，有时亦用State Department），美国联邦政府主管外交并兼管部分内政事务的行政部门，直属美国政府管理的外事机构，相当于外交部，其行政负责人为国务卿。美国国务院为美国最庞大的政府机构之一，位于美国首都华盛顿特区。美国国务院于1789年9月由美国外交部改组而成，在政府各部中居首席地位。

国务卿（Secretary of States）是美国国务院的行政首长，由总统任命（经参议院同意）并对总统负责，是仅次于正、副总统的高级行政官员，是总统外交事务的主要顾问，内阁会议和国家安全委员会的首席委员。国务卿对总统发布的某些文告有副署之责。现任的国务卿是约翰·克里（John Forbes Kerry）。

2. 英国外交和联邦事务部：

外交和联邦事务部（Foreign and Commonwealth Office，通常叫作Foreign Office或FCO）是英国负责推广海外利益的政府部门，由外交部及联邦事务部于1968年合并而被创设。外交和联邦事务部的首长是外交及联邦事务大臣，通常被简称为"外交大臣"。这个职位与财政大臣和内政大臣一起被看作内阁的三个最有威望的职位。这些职位与首相一起构成重大国务官位。

外交及联邦事务大臣简称外交大臣或外相（Foreign Secretary），是英国政府的成员，负责主理英国的对外事务，并且是外交及联邦事务部的长官。该职在1968年设立，由外交大臣（Secretary of State for Foreign Affairs）及联邦事务大臣（Secretary of State for Commonwealth Affairs）两职合并而成，两职所统领的部门也合二为一。现任外交大臣是菲利普·哈蒙德（Philip Hammond），他于2014年7月就任。

3. 日本外务省

日本外务省（Ministry of Foreign Affairs of Japan）是负责日本国对外关系的行政机关，包括对外政策、派驻使节、通商航海及缔结条约的事项，并且作为驻外单位与国内政府沟通的桥梁，负责情报收集分析、旅外侨民照顾及保护和文化宣传等事务。

世界主要国家外交机构及外交职衔
Diplomatic Organs and Diplomatic Titles in Major Countries
Appendix I

日本外务大臣（Minister for Foreign Affairs），简称日本外相或外务相，是处理国家外交任务的，是日本内阁中最重要的职位之一，一般由执政党内的实力派议员担任。日本内阁总理大臣（也称首相）如有事、出访或者生病时，在没有副总理大臣的情况下，外务大臣往往会被指定代行总理大臣职务。现任日本外务大臣为岸田文雄（Fumio Kishida）。

4. 瑞士联邦外交事务部

瑞士联邦委员会是瑞士的国家行政机关，其中的七名委员各自掌管一个联邦政府部门，并且在惯例上轮流担任瑞士联邦主席（总统）。根据惯例，主席与副主席是以每年轮流方式由每一位成员轮替。瑞士主席并非瑞士的国家元首，一般来说，官方的外交访问实际上是由联邦外交事务部所执行，访问代表人是经由全体委员会成员认可产生。

瑞士联邦外交事务部（Federal Department of Foreign Affairs FDFA）是瑞士联邦处理外交关系事务的政治部门，1978年前名为瑞士政治部。

瑞士联邦外交事务部长（Head of the Federal Department of Foreign Affairs）是瑞士联邦委员之一，现任部长为迪迪埃·布尔克哈尔特（Didier Burkhalter）。

5. 韩国外交部

韩国外交部（Ministry of Foreign Affairs of the Republic of Korea）是韩国政府负责外交及其他对外事务的最高机关。1948年7月17日大韩民国临时政府依据政府组织法成立外交部，其职掌外交、对外经济、国际情势分析及海外侨胞等事务。1948年8月15日大韩民国政府正式运作开始，其后在一些友好国家如美国、英国和法国设立大使馆及公使馆，在日本和联合国也设有代表机构。1998年韩国实行政府再造计划，外交部改组为外交通商部并增设通商交涉本部长一职，其职责为研拟与对外关系牵涉的法律事务、对外贸易协商和对外经贸事务。2013年3月25日韩国外交通商部正式更名为韩国外交部，剥离贸易谈判职能。现任韩国外交部长官（Minister of Foreign Affairs）为尹炳世（Yun Byung-se）。

6. 俄罗斯联邦外交部

俄罗斯联邦外交部（Ministry of Foreign Affairs of the Russia Federation），为俄罗斯联邦政府组成部门之一，负责俄罗斯的外交事务。俄罗斯联邦外交部的前身为苏联对外关系部。现任外交部长（Foreign Minister）为谢尔盖·维克托罗维奇·拉夫罗夫（Sergey Viktorovich Lavrov），2004年上任至今。

（五）中美外交部主要组织机构及官员

中国外交部主要组织机构：

办公厅　　The General Office

政策规划司　　Policy Planning Department

亚洲司　　The Department of Asian Affairs

西亚北非司　　The Department of West Asian and North African Affairs

非洲司　　The Department of African Affairs

欧亚司　　The Department of European-Central Asian Affairs

欧洲司　　The Department of European Affairs

北美大洋洲司　The Department of North American and Oceanian Affairs

拉丁美洲和加勒比司　The Department of Latin American and Caribbean Affairs

国际司　The Department of International Organizations and Conferences

国际经济司　The Department of International Economic Affairs

军控司　The Department of Arms Control

条约法律司　The Department of Treaty and Law

边界与海洋事务司　The Department of Boundary and Ocean Affairs

新闻司　The Information Department

礼宾司　The Protocol Department

领事司　The Department of Consular Affairs (Centre for Consular Assistance and Protection)

香港澳门台湾事务司　The Department of Hong Kong, Macao and Taiwan Affairs

翻译司　The Department of Translation and Interpretation

外事管理局　The Department of Foreign Affairs Management

涉外安全事务司　The Department of External Security Affairs

干部司　The Department of Personnel

离退休干部局　The Bureau for Retired Personnel

行政司　The Administrative Department

财务司　The Department of Finance

机关党委（党部委国外工作局）　Department for Party-related Affairs/ Department for Diplomatic Missions Abroad

档案馆　The Bureau of Archives

服务中心　Department of Services for Foreign Ministry Home and Overseas Offices

主要官员：

司长　Director-General

副司长　Deputy Director-General

办公厅主任　Director-General

外事管理局（The Department of Foreign Affairs Management）局长　Director-General

离退休干部局（The Bureau for Retired Personnel）局长　Director-General

机关党委（党部委国外工作局）（Department for Party-related Affairs/ Department for Diplomatic Missions Abroad）常务副书记（局长）　Executive Deputy Secretary（Director-General）；副书记（副局长）　Deputy Secretaries（Deputy Directors-General）

档案馆（The Bureau of Archives）馆长　Chief Archivist；副馆长　Deputy Chief Archivist

服务中心（Department of Services for Foreign Ministry Home and Overseas Offices）主任　Director-General；纪委书记　Secretary of the Commission for Discipline Inspection

世界主要国家外交机构及外交职衔
Diplomatic Organs and Diplomatic Titles in Major Countries

美国外交部主要组织机构：

Bureau of International Information Programs　国际情资计划局

Bureau of African Affairs　非洲事务局

Bureau of East Asian and Pacific Affairs　东亚暨太平洋事务局

Bureau of European and Eurasian Affairs　欧洲暨欧亚事务局

Bureau of Near Eastern Affairs　近东事务局

Bureau of South and Central Asian Affairs　南亚暨中亚事务局

Bureau of Western Hemisphere Affairs　西半球事务局

Bureau of Administration　行政局

Bureau of Consular Affairs　领务局

Bureau of Diplomatic Security　外交安全局

Bureau of Human Resources　人力资源局

Bureau of Economic and Business Affairs　经济暨商业局

Educational and Cultural Affairs　教育暨文化局

Bureau of Public Affairs　公共事务局

Bureau of Political-Military Affairs　外交军事事务局

Bureau of Oceans and International Environmental and Scientific Affairs　海洋及国际环境暨科学事务局

Bureau of Population, Refugees, and Migration　人口、难民及移民局

Bureau of Legislative Affairs　立法事务局

Bureau of Intelligence and Research　情报研究局

Bureau of International Narcotics and Law Enforcement Affairs　国际毒品暨强制法事务局

Bureau of Information Resource Management　资讯管理局

Bureau of International Security and Nonproliferation　国际安全暨防核武扩散局

Bureau of Democracy, Human Rights, and Labor　民主人权暨劳工局

Office to Monitor and Combat Trafficking in Persons　人际冲突与监督办公室

Office of the Coordinator for Counterterrorism　反恐协调办公室

Office of Foreign Missions　外交机关办公室

Office of Inspector General　督察长办公室

Office of Civil Rights　民权办公室

Office of the Legal Adviser　法务顾问办公室

Office of Allowances　预算处

Office of Authentications　验证处

Office of Policy, Planning and Resources for Public Diplomacy and Public Affairs　公共外交及公共事务暨政策及计划资讯处

Office of Inspector General　检察处

Office of Civil Rights　民权处

外交新闻汉英翻译
C-E TRANSLATION OF DIPLOMATIC NEWS

Overseas Buildings Operations　外馆运作机构

Executive Secretariat　执行秘书处

主要官员：

国务卿　Secretary

副国务卿　Deputy Secretary

次卿　Under Secretary

助卿　Assistant Secretary

副助卿　Deputy Assistant Secretary

幕僚长　Chief of Staff

国务顾问　Counselor

Appendix

国内外主要外交新闻网站
Major Diplomatic News Websites Home and Abroad

中华人民共和国外交部官网

http://www.fmprc.gov.cn/mfa_eng/

中华人民共和国外交部是中华人民共和国国务院内主管外交事务的组成部门，负责处理中华人民共和国政府与世界其他国家政府及政府间国际组织的外交事务。其官网以中、英、法、西、俄、阿等六种文字向国内外发布中国的外交政策、外交动态、外交知识以及领事服务等方面的信息。外交动态信息每日更新，涵盖领导人活动、外事日程、部领导活动、司局新闻、发言人表态、吹风会、大使任免、驻外报道等方面。因定位为官方消息发布而非新闻媒体，故文体风格并不完全遵照新闻报道的写作模式。英文稿件由中文全文直译得来。

中华人民共和国常驻联合国代表团官网

http://www.china-un.org/eng/

中华人民共和国常驻联合国代表团是中华人民共和国政府派驻于美国纽约的常驻联合国总部的外交代表机构。官网以中、英两种语言发布代表团在联合国参加活动的消息、在联合国各种会议上的发言以及外交部记者招待会相关报道。文体风格与外交部官网保持一致，中英文稿件基本做到完全对应。

中华人民共和国常驻联合国日内瓦办事处和瑞士其他国际组织代表团官网

http://www.china-un.ch/eng/

中华人民共和国常驻联合国日内瓦办事处和瑞士其他国际组织代表团是中国外交部的一个常设驻外机构。官网以中、英两种语言发布代表团在瑞士日内瓦参加各种国际组织活动的消息、在各种国际组织会议上的发言、中国外交要闻、外交相关重要讲话与文件以及外交部记者招待会相关报道。文体风格与外交部官网保持一致，中英文稿件基本做到完全对应。

中华人民共和国驻维也纳联合国和其他国际组织代表团官网

http://www.chinesemission-vienna.at/eng/

中华人民共和国驻维也纳联合国和其他国际组织代表团是中国外交部的又一个常设驻外机构，主要履行与各国常驻联合国（维也纳）代表团、联合国办事处以及设在维也纳的政府间组织和非政府组织进行联络和处理各项日常事务的职能。官网以中、英两种语言报道代表团在奥地利维也纳的各项活动、会议与发言以及中国外交要闻和外交部记者招待会等内容。文体风格与外交部官网保持一致，中英文稿件

外交新闻汉英翻译
C-E TRANSLATION OF DIPLOMATIC NEWS

基本做到完全对应。

中华人民共和国驻欧盟使团官网

http://www.chinamission.be/eng/

中华人民共和国驻欧盟使团是中国外交部常驻欧盟总部所在地比利时布鲁塞尔的外交机构，旨在促进中欧关系的发展。官网以中、英两种语言发布，新闻内容主要包括中国与欧盟之间政治经济合作方面的报道，大使的重要讲话，外交部记者招待会，以及中国国内的重要外交新闻报道。

中华人民共和国驻东盟使团官网

http://asean.chinamission.org.cn/eng/

中华人民共和国驻东盟使团是中国外交部常驻东南亚国家联盟的外交机构，办公地点位于印度尼西亚的雅加达。官网以中、英两种语言发布，主要报道大使的重要讲话，中国与东盟之间的政治交往，外交部记者招待会，一带一路专题，人民日报针对外交领域的评论文章以及学术界关于外交事件的观点讨论等，内容较为丰富。

中华人民共和国驻非盟使团官网

http://au.fmprc.gov.cn/eng/

中华人民共和国驻非盟使团是中国外交部常驻非洲联盟的外交机构，总部设在埃塞俄比亚首都亚的斯亚贝巴。官网以中、英两种语言发布，主要报道大使的重要会晤，中国与非盟之间的政治交往，外交部记者招待会以及中国国内的重要外交新闻。

上海合作组织官网

http://www.sectsco.org/EN123/

上海合作组织是哈萨克斯坦共和国、中华人民共和国、吉尔吉斯斯坦共和国、俄罗斯联邦、塔吉克斯坦共和国和乌兹别克斯坦共和国于2001年6月15日在中国上海宣布成立的永久性政府间国际组织。官网以中、英、俄三种语言报道上合组织的各项会议、领导人讲话以及各成员国的相关新闻。同时提供上合组织往年发布的联合声明、联合公报、行动计划等。

亚太经济合作组织官网

http://www.apec.org/

亚太经济合作组织是亚太地区最具影响的经济合作官方论坛，中国是其成员之一。官网只提供英语网页。发布的内容涵盖多个方面，包括高官活动、重要会议、领导人讲话、会议成果文件等。

博鳌亚洲论坛官网

http://english.boaoforum.org/

博鳌亚洲论坛是一个旨在促进和深化本地区内和本地区与世界其他地区间的经济交流、协调与合作

国内外主要外交新闻网站
Major Diplomatic News Websites Home and Abroad

的非政府、非营利性的国际组织，于2001年2月27日正式宣告成立，中国海南博鳌为论坛总部的永久地所在。官网以中、英两种语言发布消息，介绍论坛历年来召开的各次会议并刊登领导人讲话全文。

中日韩三国合作秘书处官网

http://tcs-asia.org/dnb/main/

中日韩三国合作秘书处是经中华人民共和国、日本国和大韩民国三国政府批准建立的，旨在促进三国之间和平与共同繁荣的国际组织，于2011年9月成立。官网以中、英、日、韩四中语言发布，新闻内容主要涉及秘书处领导人的出访、三方合作事务、秘书处工作等。

中非合作论坛官网

http://www.focac.org/eng/

中非合作论坛正式成立于2000年10月，旨在加强和促进中国与非洲国家之间的友谊与合作。官网以中、英、法三种语言发布，主要介绍有关中非关系的政治交往、经贸合作、人文交流，以及论坛部长级会议的文件、讲话、评论等内容。

中国—东盟中心官网

http://www.asean-china-center.org/english/

东南亚国家联盟（简称东盟）于1967年8月在曼谷成立，宗旨和目标是本着平等与合作精神，共同促进本地区的经济增长、社会进步和文化发展。中国是其对话伙伴国。中国—东盟对话关系已经走过了二十多年的历程。官网以中、英两种语言介绍中国与东盟之间的各种合作。Documents（文件讲话）版块可查阅到中国与东盟或其某个成员国之间有关政治交往、经贸投资、文化教育等方面的联合声明、新闻公报、谅解备忘录等文件以及各次会议上的领导人致辞等内容。

中国—拉共体论坛官网

http://www.chinacelacforum.org/eng/

中国—拉共体论坛于2014年7月成立，旨在促进中国与拉美和加勒比共同体及其成员国之间的合作。官网以中、英、西三种语言发布，主要介绍中拉论坛的合作机制，发布论坛相关的新闻报道，刊登论坛的主要成果文件等。

中华人民共和国驻美利坚合众国大使馆官网

http://us.chineseembassy.org/eng/

中华人民共和国驻大不列颠及北爱尔兰联合王国大使馆官网

http://www.chinese-embassy.org.uk/eng/

中华人民共和国驻澳大利亚大使馆官网

http://au.chineseembassy.org/eng/

中华人民共和国驻外大使馆是中国在建交国首都派驻的常设外交代表机关，旨在促进中国与建交国

外交新闻汉英翻译
C-E TRANSLATION OF DIPLOMATIC NEWS

的政治关系。官网通常以中文和建交国官方语言两种文字发布消息,以上仅为示例性地列举了几个建交国官方语言为英语的网站。官网内容涵盖领导人出访、两国关系往来、外交部发言人表态、大使馆新闻等。外文稿件基本由中文稿件直译得来,整体风格遵照外交部官网风格。

中国政府网

http://english.gov.cn/

中华人民共和国中央人民政府门户网站(简称"中国政府网")是中国电子政务建设的重要组成部分,以中、英两种语言面向社会提供政务信息和与政府业务相关的服务。State Council版块下按照国务院领导人分别报道其相关活动,其中涉及大量外交方面的内容。News版块下设有International Exchanges栏目,报道中国与其他国家之间的各种外交活动。Premier版块专门发布有关总理的各项消息,其中News栏目报道总理的重要活动及相关消息。以上报道文稿主要转自新华网、中国日报网等媒体。另外,Premier版块下还设有Speeches栏目,发布总理在各个国际会议上的讲话译文,均为全文直译。

新华网

http://www.xinhuanet.com/english/

新华通讯社是中国的国家通讯社,在世界各地有一百多个分社。新华网是其主办的中国重点新闻网站,被称为"中国最有影响力网站",每天24小时不间断地通过中、英、西、法、俄、日、阿、德等十三种文字向全球发布新闻信息。外交新闻涉及领导人出访、会晤、讲话以及对国际事件的表态等相关报道。新华网的中英文网页各自按照新闻采编的模式独立撰写,互相之间并不严格对应。

人民网

http://en.people.cn/

人民网是世界十大报纸之一《人民日报》建设的以新闻为主的大型网上信息交互平台,以"多语种、全媒体、全球化、全覆盖"为目标,以"报道全球、传播中国"为己任。共有中、英、日、法、西、俄、阿、韩、德、葡等十个语种的版本。其Opinions版块和Special Coverage版块对领导人出访、会晤、国际会议、外交表态等消息以及各方观点与评论均有报道。中文网页以原创稿件为主,英文网页中的相关报道主要转自新华网、中国日报网等其他媒体。

中国网

http://www.china.org.cn/

中国网是中华人民共和国国务院新闻办公室和国家互联网信息办公室领导,中国外文出版发行事业局管理的国家重点新闻网站。通过中、英、法、西、德、日、俄、阿、韩、世界语等十个语种发布报道。其World版块开设有"Diplomatic Exchanges" "FM Press Releases"报道中国的各项外交活动以及外交部发言人对各种外交事件的表态等。另有"Full Coverage"栏目以专题的形式全面报道国家领导人出访、国际会议、重要国际事件等。稿件部分原创,部分转自新华网、央视网等。总体特点符合新闻文体,中英文网页不追求对应。

中国日报网

http://www.chinadaily.com.cn/

中国日报网是中国最大的英文资讯门户，是国务院新闻办（中共中央外宣办）主管的中国日报旗下网站，拥有中、英、法共三种文字的版面。其World版块下设有China-Japan, China-US, China-Europe, China-Africa四个栏目分别报道中国与相关国家的外交关系与事件。另有Highlights栏目以专题的形式讲述重大外交活动、外交理念等。大量稿件转自新华网、央视网等。总体遵循新闻编译的风格。中文网页外交方面的新闻报道相对较少。

央视网

http://english.cntv.cn/

央视网是由中央电视台主办的国家网络广播电视播出机构，除了中文页面外，还推出了英、西、法、阿、俄、韩等六个外语频道。外交方面的新闻涉及领导人出访、外交部长活动、国际会议等。特点是大多数新闻页面在提供新闻文稿的基础上还配有剪辑自CCTVNews的新闻视频，可以观看到新闻现场的实际情景，听到发言人的讲话原声，因而在稿件的撰写方面与纯文字稿件有所不同。

国际在线

http://english.cri.cn/

国际在线是中国国际广播电台主办的政府重点新闻网站，通过中、英、西、德、葡、法、俄、日、阿等61种语言发布，主要提供新闻、文化和经济类信息，并以丰富的音频节目为特色。News版块报道国内外重大事件，很多原创稿件都配有音频。其中的In Depth栏目以专题的形式报道领导人出访及国际会议等内容。另有Opinions版块涉及对上述活动进行评论的报道，稿件主要转自新华网和中国日报网。

环球网

http://www.globaltimes.cn/

环球网是由人民网和环球时报共同投资设立的大型中英文双语新闻门户网站。外交新闻主要包括领导人活动、中国与其他国家双边关系、重大国际事件等。在China版块下设有Diplomacy栏目，专门报道外交相关的消息，除部分原创稿件外，其他稿件主要转自新华网。

中国公共外交协会官网

http://www.chinapda.org.cn/eng/

中国公共外交协会是由中国公共外交领域专家学者、知名人士、相关机构和企业等自愿参加组成的全国性、非营利性社会组织。网站汉语内容较为丰富，"时事资讯"栏目提供大量有关国家领导人、外交部、国际会议等方面的新闻报道。英语网页还在建设当中，News版块只有寥寥数条报道，且较为陈旧。

外交新闻汉英翻译
C-E TRANSLATION OF DIPLOMATIC NEWS

美国国务院官网

http://www.state.gov/

美国国务院是美国联邦政府主管外交并兼管部分内政事务的行政部门，相当于外交部，其行政负责人为国务卿。官网只提供英文网页。Policy Issues版块中有针对中国的专栏，内容包括中美关系相关政策、会晤、通话等。Public Diplomacy & Public Affairs版块下的Daily Press Briefings和Press Releases栏目发布记者招待会和答记者问的文字转写稿。

英国外交和联邦事务部官网

https://www.gov.uk/government/organisations/foreign-commonwealth-office/

英国外交和联邦事务部是英国负责推广海外利益的政府部门，由外交部及联邦事务部合并而来。部门负责人是外交及联邦事务大臣，通常简称为"外交大臣"。官网首页只提供英文，在Worldwide版块下按照不同国家链接至不同网页。UK and China网页提供中、英两种文字，介绍两国关系中的外交活动、文件等。

加拿大外交、贸易和发展部官网

http://www.international.gc.ca/international/index.aspx?lang=eng/

加拿大外交、贸易和发展部主要负责管理外交和领事关系，鼓励加拿大的国际贸易并支持人文主义活动。官网提供英、法两种语言，内容多以服务公民为主，有少量针对部长活动、讲话、会谈等内容的报道。与中国相关的报道目前集中在《中加投资促进及保护协议》（FIPA）方面。

澳大利亚外交事务和贸易部官网

http://www.dfat.gov.au/

澳大利亚外交事务和贸易部是负责澳大利亚外交关系和贸易政策的政府部门。主要目标包括提升澳大利亚安全，为澳大利亚经济、就业和生活水平增长做出贡献等。官网只提供英文网页。内容以服务公民为主，仅在News, speeches and media版块对几位部长的外交活动进行报道，并全文刊登几位部长发表过的文章或讲话。

俄罗斯联邦外交部官网

http://www.mid.ru/en/main_en/

俄罗斯联邦外交部是负责俄罗斯外交事务的政府部门，其基本目标是在周边地区创造有助于俄罗斯经济和政治发展的环境。官网以俄、英、德、法、西等五种语言发布消息。新闻报道内容涵盖外交部领导的出访、会见、通话，发言人表态，俄罗斯与其他国家的双边关系等等。部分新闻页面还提供有视频或音频资料。

德意志联邦外交部官网

http://www.auswaertiges-amt.de/EN/

德意志联邦外交部是德意志联邦共和国的政府部门之一，掌管德国外交政策以及欧盟关系。官网提供德、英、俄、法、西、葡等多个语种的界面。在Foreign & European Policy版块中发布了德意志联邦对区域热点、和平与安全、人权等问题的外交政策，其中的Bilateral relations栏目中可按国别搜索，中德之间的外交活动记录并不多，主要涉及外交部长讲话、中德联合公报等。

法国外交部官网

http://www.france.diplomatie.fr/en/

法国外交部是法国专门负责管理与外国之间关系的政府部门。官网具有法、德、英、西、阿、中等六个语种的网页。在French foreign policy版块中有对各种国际事件的报道及法国的表态。Country files版块中登载有法国对中国发生的新闻事件的表态以及中法之间合作的相关报道。

日本外务省官网

http://www.mofa.go.jp/

日本外务省是日本政府负责对外关系事务的最高机关，职责范围包括对外政策、派驻使节、通商航海及缔结条约等事项。官网提供日、英两种语言的网页。News版块专门发布首相、外务大臣等人在各种场合的讲话英译稿以及所召开过的新闻发布会的文字转写稿。Policy版块发布外交政策方面的各种消息。Countries & Regions版块中按国别分类，登载了有关中日关系的文件和对双边会谈的报道。

美国驻华大使馆官网

http://beijing.usembassy-china.org.cn/

美国驻华大使馆为美国在中国的官方办事机构，官网以英、中两种语言发布。News版块内容丰富，报道范围涵盖中美战略与经济对话、高层互访、重要讲话、气候变化、区域安全、知识产权等话题。还提供有少量关于中美关系发展的视频资料。

欧洲联盟驻华代表团官网

http://eeas.europa.eu/delegations/china/eu_china/political_relations/index_en.htm

欧洲联盟驻华代表团是欧洲委员会常设在中国的代表机构，职责是处理中国与欧洲联盟之间的官方关系。主页上发布大量有关中欧关系的报道，内容包括欧盟外交政策、中欧合作、中欧会谈、发言人表态等方面。

（以上链接均为相应网站英文版）

中国外交术语英译
English for Chinese Diplomatic Terms

"十三五"规划	Thirteenth Five-Year Plan
"一带一路"倡议	Belt and Road Initiative
《联合国气候变化框架公约》	United Nations Framework Convention on Climate Change
《南海各方行为宣言》	Declaration on the Conduct of Parties in the South China Sea
《中欧合作2020战略规划》	China-EU 2020 Strategic Agenda for Cooperation
2015年后发展议程	Post-2015 Development Agenda
2030年可持续发展议程	2030 Agenda for Sustainable Development
21世纪海上丝绸之路	21st Century Maritime Silk Road
包容性增长	inclusive growth
暴力恐怖活动	violent and terrorist activity
本币互换	currency swap
产能合作	production capacity cooperation
持续、健康、稳定发展	sustained, sound and stable development
传统友好	traditional friendship
创新、协调、绿色、开放、共享的发展理念	development philosophy of innovation, coordination, environment protection, openness and sharing
创新驱动发展	innovation-driven development
大国	major country
大众创业、万众创新	mass entrepreneurship and innovation
德国工业4.0	German Industry 4.0
低碳智慧型城市	low-carbon smart city
第三方合作	third-party cooperation
第三方市场	third-party market
东盟共同体	ASEAN Community
独立自主的和平外交政策	independent foreign policy of peace
多边机制	multilateral mechanism
多边外交	multilateral diplomacy

中国外交术语英译
English for Chinese Diplomatic Terms

二轨	Track Two
共同、综合、合作、可持续安全	common, comprehensive, cooperative and sustainable security
共同但有区别的责任	common but differentiated responsibilities
共同发展	common development
共同关心的问题	issues of common concern/topics of common interest
共同利益	common interests
国际关系民主化	democratization of international relations
国际和地区事务	international and regional affairs
国际货币基金组织特别提款权货币篮子	special drawing rights currency basket of the International Monetary Fund
国际治理体系	international governance system
国家自主贡献	Intended Nationally Determined Contributions
国事访问	state visit
航行自由	freedom of navigation
合法权益	legitimate rights and interests
合作共赢	win-win cooperation
和而不同	harmony in diversity
核心利益	core interests
互利共赢	mutual benefits and win-win results
互利合作	mutually beneficial cooperation
互联互通	connectivity
互致贺信	exchange congratulatory letters
结构调整	structural adjustment
经济社会发展	economic and social development
开放战略	open strategy
冷战思维	Cold War mentality
良性互动	sound interaction
两廊一圈	Two Corridors and One Circle
零和博弈	zero sum game
绿色发展	green development
轮值主席国	rotating presidency
贸易伙伴	trading partner
孟中印缅经济走廊	Bangladesh-China-India-Myanmar Economic Corridor
睦邻友好政策	good-neighborly and friendly policy

C-E TRANSLATION OF DIPLOMATIC NEWS

南海行为准则	codes of conduct in the South China Sea
南南合作援助基金	South-South Cooperation Assistance Fund
凝聚共识	pool consensus
欧亚经济联盟	Eurasian Economic Union
气候变化大会	Climate Change Conference
气候变化南南合作基金	South-South Cooperation Fund on Climate Change
亲、诚、惠、容	amity, sincerity, mutual benefits and inclusiveness
求同存异	seek common ground while reserving differences
区域经济一体化	regional economic integration
区域全面经济伙伴关系协定	Regional Comprehensive Economic Partnership
全方位合作伙伴关系	all-round cooperative partnership
全面战略合作伙伴关系	comprehensive strategic cooperative partnership
全面战略伙伴关系	comprehensive strategic partnership
全面战略协作伙伴关系	comprehensive strategic partnership of coordination
全天候战略合作伙伴关系	all-weather strategic partnership of cooperation
热点问题	hot-spot issues
人类命运共同体	community with a shared future for mankind
人文交流	people-to-people and cultural exchanges
沙特阿拉伯王储继承人	Deputy Crown Prince of Saudi Arabia
深入交换意见	have in-depth exchanges of views
十八届五中全会	fifth plenary session of 18th CPC Central Committee
世界反法西斯战争	World Anti-Fascist War
世界经济复苏	world economic recovery
双边投资协定	bilateral investment agreement
丝绸之路经济带	Silk Road Economic Belt
苏伊士经贸合作区	Suez Economic and Trade Cooperation Zone
特殊的战略伙伴关系	special strategic partnership
务实合作	practical cooperation
相向而行	meet each other half way
小康社会	moderately prosperous society
亚太经合组织领导人非正式会议	Economic Leaders' Meeting of the Asia-Pacific Economic Cooperation
亚洲基础设施投资银行	Asian Infrastructure Investment Bank
伊朗核问题全面协议	Joint Comprehensive Plan of Action on the Iranian nuclear issue

以合作共赢为核心的新型国际关系	new type of international relations featuring win-win cooperation
元首	head of state
战略对话	strategic dialogue
战略沟通	strategic communication
战略合作关系	strategic cooperative relations
战略伙伴关系	strategic partnership
战略友好关系	strategic friendly relations
正确义利观	correct viewpoint on righteousness and benefit
正式访问	official visit
政府间无息贷款	inter-governmental interest-free loan
政治互信	political mutual trust
中巴经济走廊	China-Pakistan Economic Corridor
中国—东盟关系协调国	coordinator of China-ASEAN relations
中国—联合国和平与发展基金	China-UN Peace and Development Fund
中国梦	Chinese dream
中国人民抗日战争	Chinese People's War of Resistance Against Japanese Aggression
中国特色大国外交	major-country diplomacy with Chinese characteristics
中国制造2025	Made in China 2025
中美新型大国关系	new model of major-country relationship between China and the US
中欧和平、增长、改革、文明四大伙伴关系	China-EU four major partnerships for peace, growth, reform and civilization
重大关切	major concerns
周边外交	neighborhood diplomacy
最不发达国家	least developed countries